Chapter 12   Section 12.2
    Red: Identifies dollar and percentage changes in dividends.
    Blue: Identifies dividends.

Chapter 13   Section 13.2
    Red: Identifies the proposed capital structure.
    Blue: Identifies the current capital structure.
    Sections 13.4 and 13.6
    Red: Identifies Firm L.
    Blue: Identifies Firm U.

Chapter 16   Throughout the chapter
    Red: Identifies income statement data.
    Blue: Identifies balance sheet data.
    Section 16.4
    Red: Identifies total cash collections.
    Blue: Identifies total cash disbursements.
    Gold: Identifies net cash inflows.

Chapter 17   Throughout the chapter
    Red: Identifies numbers exceeding the cost-minimizing restock
                    quantity.
    Blue: Identifies numbers falling below the cost-minimizing restock
                    quantity.
    Gold: Identifies cost-minimizing quantity.

THIRD EDITION

Essentials *of* Corporate Finance

Franco Modigliani Professor of Finance and Economics
Sloan School of Management, Massachusetts Institute of Technology

Benninga and Sarig
Corporate Finance: A Valuation Approach

Block and Hirt
Foundations of Financial Management
Ninth Edition

Brealey and Myers
Principles of Corporate Finance
Sixth Edition

Brealey, Myers and Marcus
Fundamentals of Corporate Finance
Third Edition

Brooks
FinGame Online 3.0

Bruner
Case Studies in Finance: Managing for Corporate Value Creation
Third Edition

Chew
The New Corporate Finance: Where Theory Meets Practice
Third Edition

Graduate Management Admissions Council, Robert F. Bruner, Kenneth Eades and Robert Harris
Essentials of Finance: With an Accounting Review
Fully Interactive CD-ROM Derived from Finance Interactive 1997 Pre-MBA Edition
Finance Interactive: Pre-MBA Series 2000
Second Edition

Grinblatt and Titman
Financial Markets and Corporate Strategy

Helfert
Techniques of Financial Analysis: A Guide to Value Creation
Tenth Edition

Higgins
Analysis for Financial Management
Sixth Edition

Hite
A Programmed Learning Guide to Finance

Kester, Fruhan, Piper and Ruback
Case Problems in Finance
Eleventh Edition

Nunnally and Plath
Cases in Finance
Second Edition

Ross, Westerfield and Jaffe
Corporate Finance
Fifth Edition

Ross, Westerfield and Jordan
Essentials of Corporate Finance
Third Edition

Ross, Westerfield and Jordan
Fundamentals of Corporate Finance
Fifth Edition

Smith
The Modern Theory of Corporate Finance
Second Edition

White
Financial Analysis with an Electronic Calculator
Fourth Edition

Bodie, Kane and Marcus
Essentials of Investments
Fourth Edition

Bodie, Kane and Marcus
Investments
Fourth Edition

Cohen, Zinbarg and Zeikel
Investment Analysis and Portfolio Management
Fifth Edition

Corrado and Jordan
Fundamentals of Investments: Valuation and Management

Farrell
Portfolio Management: Theory and Applications
Second Edition

Hirt and Block
Fundamentals of Investment Management
Sixth Edition

Jarrow
Modelling Fixed Income Securities and Interest Rate Options

Shimko
The Innovative Investor
Excel Version

Cornett and Saunders
Fundamentals of Financial Institutions Management

Rose
Commercial Bank Management
Fourth Edition

Rose
Money and Capital Markets: Financial Institutions and Instruments in a Global Marketplace
Seventh Edition

Rose and Kolari
Financial Institutions: Understanding and Managing Financial Services
Fifth Edition

Santomero and Babbel
Financial Markets, Instruments, and Institutions
Second Edition

Saunders
Financial Institutions Management:
A Modern Perspective
Third Edition

Eun and Resnick
International Financial Management
Second Edition

Kester and Luehrman
Case Problems in International Finance
Second Edition

Levi
International Finance
Third Edition

Levich
International Financial Markets:
Prices and Policies
Second Edition

Brueggeman and Fisher
Real Estate Finance and Investments
Tenth Edition

Corgel, Ling and Smith
Real Estate Perspectives: An Introduction to Real Estate
Fourth Edition

Lusht
Real Estate Valuation: Principles and Applications

Allen, Melone, Rosenbloom and VanDerhei
Pension Planning: Pension, Profit-Sharing, and Other Deferred Compensation Plans
Eighth Edition

Crawford
Life and Health Insurance Law
Eighth Edition (LOMA)

Harrington and Niehaus
Risk Management and Insurance

Hirsch
Casualty Claim Practice
Sixth Edition

Kapoor, Dlabay and Hughes
Personal Finance
Fifth Edition

Skipper
International Risk and Insurance:
An Environmental-Managerial Approach

Williams, Smith and Young
Risk Management and Insurance
Eighth Edition

THIRD EDITION

Essentials

_of_ Corporate

Finance

Stephen A. Ross
Massachusetts Institute of Technology

Randolph W. Westerfield
University of Southern California

Bradford D. Jordan
University of Kentucky

McGraw-Hill
Irwin

Boston   Burr Ridge, IL   Dubuque, IA   Madison, WI   New York   San Francisco   St. Louis
Bangkok   Bogotá   Caracas   Kuala Lumpur   Lisbon   London   Madrid   Mexico City
Milan   Montreal   New Delhi   Santiago   Seoul   Singapore   Sydney   Taipei   Toronto

To our families and friends with love and gratitude
—S.A.R.   R.W.W.   B.D.J.

McGraw-Hill Higher Education
*A Division of The **McGraw-Hill** Companies*

Published by McGraw-Hill/Irwin, an imprint of The McGraw-Hill Companies, Inc. 1221 Avenue of the Americas, New York, NY, 10020. Copyright © 2001, 1999, 1996, by The McGraw-Hill Companies, Inc. All rights reserved. No part of this publication may be reproduced or distributed in any form or by any means, or stored in a data base or retrieval system, without the prior written consent of The McGraw-Hill Companies, Inc., including, but not limited to, in any network or other electronic storage or transmission, or broadcast for distance learning.

Some ancillaries, including electronic and print components, may not be available to customers outside the United States.

This book is printed on acid-free paper.

4 5 6 7 8 9 0 DOW/DOW 0 9 8 7 6 5 4 3 2

ISBN 0-07-234052-5 (student edition)
ISBN 0-07-234063-0 (annotated instructor's edition)

Vice president and editor-in-chief: *Rob Zwettler*
Publisher: *John Biernat*
Associate editor: *Michele Janicek*
Development editor: *Erin Riley*
Executive marketing manager: *Rhonda Seelinger*
Senior project manager: *Jean Lou Hess*
Production supervisor: *Rose Hepburn*
Coordinator freelance design: *Pam Verros*
Supplement coordinator: *Betty Hadala*
New media: *Ann Rogula, Mark Molsky*
Cover illustrator: *Paul D. Turnbaugh*
Cover design: *Michael Warrell*
Interior design: *Michael Warrell*
Compositor: *Carlisle Communications, Ltd.*
Typeface: *10/12 Times Roman*
Printer: *R. R. Donnelley & Sons Company*

Library of Congress Cataloging-in-Publication Data

Ross, Stephen A.
    Essentials of corporate finance / Stephen A. Ross, Randolph W. Westerfield, Bradford D. Jordan.—3rd ed.
       p. cm.—(The McGraw-Hill/Irwin series in finance, insurance, and real estate)
      Includes bibliographical references and indexes.
      ISBN 0-07-234052-5 (alk. paper)—ISBN 0-07-234063-0 (alk. paper)
      1. Corporations—Finance, I. Westerfield, Randolph. II. Jordan, Bradford D. III. Title. IV. Series.

HG4026.R676 2001
658.15—dc21   00-048680

www.mhhe.com

ABOUT THE AUTHORS

Stephen A. Ross
Sloan School of Management
Massachusetts Institute of Technology

Stephen Ross is presently the Franco Modigliani Professor of Financial Economics at the Sloan School of Management, Massachusetts Institute of Technology. One of the most widely published authors in finance and economics, Professor Ross is recognized for his work in developing the Arbitrage Pricing Theory, as well as for having made substantial contributions to the discipline through his research in signaling, agency theory, option pricing, and the theory of the term structure of interest rates, among other topics. A past president of the American Finance Association, he currently serves as an associate editor of several academic and practitioner journals. He is a trustee of CalTech, and a director of the College Retirement Equity Fund (CREF), Freddie Mac, and Algorithmics, Inc. He is also the cochairman of Roll and Ross Asset Management Corporation.

Randolph W. Westerfield
Marshall School of Business
University of Southern California

Randolph W. Westerfield is Dean of the University of Southern California's Marshall School of Business and holder of the Robert R. Dockson Dean's Chair of Business Administration.

From 1988 to 1993, Professor Westerfield served as the chairman of the School's finance and business economics department and the Charles B. Thornton Professor of Finance. He came to USC from the Wharton School, University of Pennsylvania, where he was the chairman of the finance department and member of the finance faculty for 20 years. He is a member of the board of directors of the AACSB—the international association for management education, as well as Health Management Associates (HMA), and William Lyon Homes (WLH). His areas of expertise include corporate financial policy, investment management and analysis, mergers and acquisitions, and stock market price behavior.

Professor Westerfield has been consultant to a number of corporations, including AT&T, Mobil Oil and Pacific Enterprises, as well as to the United Nations, the U.S. Departments of Justice and Labor, and the State of California.

Bradford D. Jordan
Gatton College of Business and Economics
University of Kentucky

Bradford D. Jordan is Professor of Finance and Gatton Research Professor at the Gatton College of Business and Economics, University of Kentucky. He has a long-standing interest in both applied and theoretical issues in corporate finance, and he has extensive experience teaching all levels of corporate finance and financial management policy. Professor Jordan has published numerous articles in leading journals on issues such as cost of capital, capital structure, and the behavior of security prices. He is a past president of the Southern Finance Association, and he is coauthor (with Charles J. Corrado) of *Fundamentals of Investments: Valuation and Management,* a leading investments text, also published by McGraw-Hill/Irwin.

FROM THE AUTHORS

WITH THE THIRD EDITION OF *Essentials of Corporate Finance,* we have continued to refine our focus on our target audience, which is the undergraduate student taking a core course in business or corporate finance. This can be a tough course to teach. One reason is that the class is usually required of all business students, so it is not uncommon for a majority of the students to be non-finance majors. In fact, this may be the only finance course many of them will ever have. With this in mind, our goal in *Essentials* is to convey the most important concepts and principles at a level that is approachable for the widest possible audience.

To achieve our goal, we have worked to distill the subject down to its bare essentials (hence, the name of this book), while retaining a decidedly modern approach to finance. We have always maintained that the subject of corporate finance can be viewed as the working of a few very powerful intuitions. We also think that understanding the "why" is just as important, if not more so, than understanding the "how," especially in an introductory course. Based on the gratifying market feedback we have received from our first two editions, as well as from our other text, *Fundamentals of Corporate Finance* (now in its 5th edition), many of you agree.

By design, this book is not encyclopedic. As the table of contents indicates, we have a total of 18 chapters. Chapter length is about 30 pages, so the text is aimed squarely at a single-term course, and most of the book can be realistically covered in a typical semester or quarter. Writing a book for a one-term course necessarily means some picking and choosing, both with regard to topics and depth of coverage. Throughout, we strike a balance by introducing and covering the essentials (there's that word again!) while leaving some more specialized topics to follow-up courses.

The other things we have always stressed, and have continued to improve with this edition, are readability and pedagogy. *Essentials* is written in a relaxed, conversational style that invites the students to join in the learning process rather than being a passive information absorber. We have found that this approach dramatically increases students' willingness to read and learn on their own. Between larger and larger class sizes and the ever-growing demands on faculty time, we think this is an essential (!) feature for a text in an introductory course.

Throughout the development of this book, we have continued to take a hard look at what is truly relevant and useful. In doing so, we have worked to downplay purely theoretical issues and minimize the use of extensive and elaborate calculations to illustrate points that are either intuitively obvious or of limited practical use.

As a result of this process, three basic themes emerge as our central focus in writing *Essentials of Corporate Finance:*

An Emphasis on Intuition We always try to separate and explain the principles at work on a common sense, intuitive level before launching into any specifics. The underlying ideas are discussed first in very general terms and then by way of examples that illustrate in more concrete terms how a financial manager might proceed in a given situation.

A Unified Valuation Approach We treat net present value (NPV) as the basic concept underlying corporate finance. Many texts stop well short of consistently integrating this important principle. The most basic and important notion, that NPV represents the excess of market value over cost, often is lost in an overly mechanical approach that emphasizes computation at the expense of comprehension. In contrast, every subject we cover is firmly rooted in valuation, and care is taken throughout to explain how particular decisions have valuation effects.

A Managerial Focus Students shouldn't lose sight of the fact that financial management concerns management. We emphasize the role of the financial manager as decision maker, and we stress the need for managerial input and judgment. We consciously avoid "black box" approaches to finance, and, where appropriate, the approximate, pragmatic nature of financial analysis is made explicit, possible pitfalls are described, and limitations are discussed.

Today, as we prepare to once again enter the market, our goal is to stick with and build on the principles that have brought us this far. However, based on an enormous amount of feedback we have received from you and your colleagues, we have made this edition and its package even more flexible than previous editions. We offer flexibility in coverage and pedagogy by providing a wide variety of features in the book to help students to learn about corporate finance. We also provide flexibility in package options by offering the most extensive collection of teaching, learning, and technology aids of any corporate finance text. Whether you use just the textbook, or the book in conjunction with other products, we believe you will find a combination with this edition that will meet your current as well as your changing needs.

Stephen A. Ross
Randolph W. Westerfield
Bradford D. Jordan

We designed *Essentials of Corporate Finance* to be as flexible and modular as possible. There are a total of nine parts, and, in broad terms, the instructor is free to decide the particular sequence. Further, within each part, the first chapter generally contains an overview and survey. Thus, when time is limited, subsequent chapters can be omitted. Finally, the sections placed early in each chapter are generally the most important, and later sections frequently can be omitted without loss of continuity. For these reasons, the instructor has great control over the topics covered, the sequence in which they are covered, and the depth of coverage.

Considers the goal of the corporation, the corporate form of organization, and the role of the financial manager. Also covers the various functional areas within finance and relates finance to other business areas.

Briefly reviews key accounting concepts and succinctly discusses cash flow versus accounting income, market value versus book value, and taxes.

Discusses key ratios and also covers sustainable growth. If desired, this chapter can be omitted without affecting the flow of subsequent chapters.

First of two chapters covering time value of money, allowing for a building block approach to this difficult subject.

Contains detailed coverage on use of financial calculators and spreadsheets.

Covers bond valuation and yields, bond types and market operations, the yield curve, and the Fisher effect.

In addition to the dividend growth model, stock market operations and the interpretation of prices in the financial press are explained, including the new decimal format.

Contains new, up-to-date survey results on corporate capital budgeting practices.

Extensive coverage on NPV estimates.

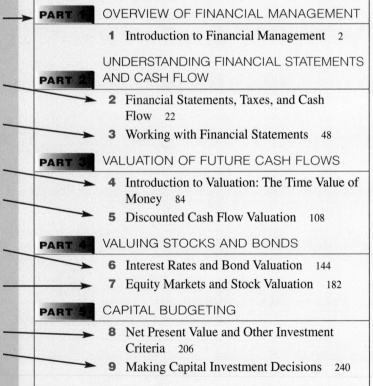

Gives students a feel for typical rates of return on financial assets and also an historical perspective on risk.

Discusses the expected return/risk trade-off and develops the security market line in a highly intuitive way that bypasses much of the usual portfolio theory and statistics.

Presents various approaches for determining cost of capital and suitable discount rates for risky projects.

Contains an intuitive discussion of optimal capital structure and also briefly considers the bankruptcy process.

Succinctly covers dividends and corporate payout policies.

Covers venture capital and contains new, up-to-date coverage of IPOs, including the 1999 experience.

Presents a general survey of short-term financial management, which is useful when time does not permit a more in-depth treatment.

Contains greater detail on cash, credit, and inventory management.

Introduces key aspects of international finance; includes up-to-date coverage on the euro.

Real Financial Decisions

We have included two key features that help students connect chapter concepts to how decision makers use this material in the real world.

In addition to illustrating relevant concepts and presenting up-to-date coverage, *Essentials of Corporate Finance* strives to present the material in a way that makes it coherent and easy to understand. To meet the varied needs of the intended audience, *Essentials of Corporate Finance* is rich in valuable learning tools and support.

Each feature can be categorized by the benefit to the student:

- Real Financial Decisions
- Application Tools
- Study Aids

APPLE COMPUTER began as a two-man partnership in a garage. It grew rapidly and, by 1985, became a large publicly traded corporation with 60 million shares of stock and a total market value in excess of $1 billion. At that time, the firm's more visible cofounder, 30-year-old Steven Jobs, owned seven million shares of Apple stock worth about $120 million.

Despite his stake in the company and his role in its founding and success, Jobs was forced to relinquish operating responsibilities in 1985 when Apple's financial performance turned sour, and he subsequently resigned altogether.

Of course, you can't keep a good entrepreneur down. Jobs formed Pixar Animation Studios, the company that is responsible for the animation in the hit movies *Toy Story*, *A Bug's Life*, and *Toy Story 2*. Pixar went public in 1995, and, following an enthusiastic reception by the stock market, Jobs's 80 percent stake was valued at about $1.1 billion.

Chapter-Opening Vignettes with Functional Integration Links

Each chapter begins with a recent real-world event to introduce students to chapter concepts. Since many non-finance majors will use this text, a brief paragraph linking the vignette and chapter concepts to majors in marketing, management, and accounting is included.

Reality Bytes Boxes

Most chapters include at least one *Reality Bytes* box, which takes a chapter issue and shows how it is being used right now in everyday financial decision making.

reality BYTES

SHE'S MADE OF PLASTIC, AND SHE'S FANTASTIC!

It used to be that trading in collectibles such as baseball cards, art, and old toys occurred mostly at auctions, swap meets, and collectible shops, all of which were limited to regional traffic. However, with the growing popularity of online auctions such as eBay, trading in collectibles has expanded to an international arena. The most visible form of collectible is probably the baseball trading card, but Furbies, Beanie Babies, and Pokémon cards have been extremely hot collectibles in the recent past. However, it's not just fad items that spark collectors' interest; virtually anything of sentimental value from days gone by is considered collectible, and, more and more, these things are being viewed as investments.

Collectibles typically provide no cash flows, except when sold, and condition and buyer sentiment are the major determinants of value. The rates of return on such investments have been staggering at times, but care is needed in interpreting them. For example, a Schwinn B6 boy's bicycle cost about $45 when it was new in 1949, and it was a beauty. Assuming it was still in like-new condition in 2000, it would have been worth $675, about 15 times its original cost. While this looks to the untrained eye like a huge gain, the actual return on investment is only about 5.5 percent per year for the 51-year life of the investment. In contrast, a typical share of common stock earned, on average, a return of about 11.5 percent over that same period. Then there's the problem of storing the bike and keeping it in like-new condition, hardly a small detail.

Barbie dolls are a lot easier to store. An original Barbie sold for about $3 when it was introduced in March 1959. An original in mint condition (and never removed from its package) might have been worth about $7,000 in 2000, which represents a whopping return of 20.8 percent per year.

The world of collectibles is, of course, a global phenomenon. Christie's, the well-known auction house, holds an annual auction of model railway toys around Christmas. In 1998, a Marklin (the manufacturer) three-piece station house set would have been worth about £6,000. It originally sold for about £3 in 1913. Again, to the untrained eye, that appears to be an enormous gain, but the return actually works out to be about 9.4 percent a year.

Looking back, of these investments, the Barbie doll did the best. The problem is that to earn this return, you had to purchase the toy when it was new and store it (without opening it) for all those years. Looking ahead, the corresponding problem is predicting what the future value of a toy will be. You can earn a positive return on investment only if the market value of your asset rises above the purchase price at some point. That, of course, is rarely assured. For example, most collectors say that the Barbies that are mass-marketed in discount stores today will probably have little or no value as collectibles at any time in the future, so we don't recommend them for your retirement investing.

Application Tools

Realizing that there is more than one way to solve problems in corporate finance, we include two sections that will not only encourage students to learn different problem-solving methods, but that will also help them learn or brush up on their financial calculator and Excel spreadsheet skills.

Calculator Hints

Calculator Hints is a self-contained section in various chapters that first introduces students to calculator basics, and then illustrates how to solve problems with the calculator. Appendix D goes into more detailed instructions by solving problems with two specific calculators.

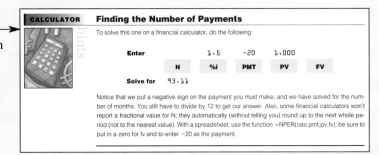

CALCULATOR

Finding the Number of Payments

To solve this one on a financial calculator, do the following:

Enter		1.5	−20	1,000	
	N	**%i**	**PMT**	**PV**	**FV**
Solve for	93.11				

Notice that we put a negative sign on the payment you must make, and we have solved for the number of months. You still have to divide by 12 to get our answer. Also, some financial calculators won't report a fractional value for N; they automatically (without telling you) round up to the next whole period (not to the nearest value). With a spreadsheet, use the function =NPER(rate,pmt,pv,fv); be sure to put in a zero for fv and to enter −20 as the payment.

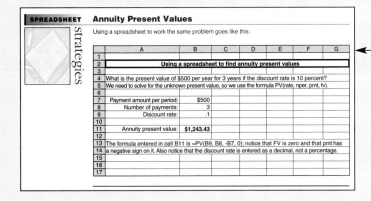

SPREADSHEET strategies

Annuity Present Values

Using a spreadsheet to work the same problem goes like this:

	A	B	C	D	E	F	G
1							
2		*Using a spreadsheet to find annuity present values*					
3							
4	What is the present value of $500 per year for 3 years if the discount rate is 10 percent?						
5	We need to solve for the unknown present value, so we use the formula PV(rate, nper, pmt, fv).						
6							
7	Payment amount per period:	$500					
8	Number of payments:	3					
9	Discount rate:	.1					
10							
11	Annuity present value:	$1,243.43					
12							
13	The formula entered in cell B11 is =PV(B9, B8, -B7, 0); notice that FV is zero and that pmt has						
14	a negative sign on it. Also notice that the discount rate is entered as a decimal, not a percentage.						
15							
16							
17							

Spreadsheet Strategies

The unique Spreadsheet Strategies feature is also in a self-contained section, and shows students how to set up spreadsheets to solve problems—a vital part of every business student's education.

Spreadsheet Templates

Almost every chapter ends with a list of problems that are linked to spreadsheet software available in the Student Center of the Web site at www.mhhe.com/rwj. These Excel templates are a valuable extension of the Spreadsheet Strategies feature.

www.mhhe.com/rwj

Spreadsheet Templates 6, 10, 19

Study Aids

We want students to get the most from this book and their course, and we realize that students have different learning styles and study needs. We therefore present a number of study features to appeal to a wide range of students.

Learning Objectives

Each chapter begins with a number of learning objectives that are key to the student's understanding of the chapter.

TO GET THE MOST OUT OF THE CHAPTER,
WHEN YOU ARE FINISHED STUDYING IT, MAKE
SURE YOU HAVE A GOOD UNDERSTANDING OF:

- The basic types of financial management decisions and the role of the financial manager

- The goal of financial management

- The financial implications of the different forms of business organization

- The conflicts of interest that can arise between managers and owners

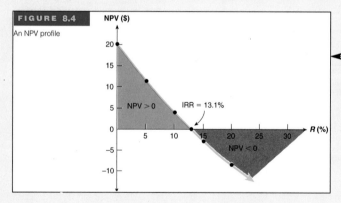

FIGURE 8.4 An NPV profile

Pedagogical Use of Color

We use a full color palette in *Essentials* to not only make the text more inviting, but, more importantly, as a functional element to help students follow the discussion. In almost every chapter, color plays an important, largely self-evident role. A guide to the use of color is found on the endsheets.

Critical Thinking Questions

Every chapter ends with a set of Critical Thinking Questions that challenge the student to apply the concepts they have learned from the real-world examples in the chapter to new situations.

CRITICAL THINKING AND CONCEPTS REVIEW

1. **The Financial Management Decision Process.** What are the three types of financial management decisions? For each type of decision, give an example of a business transaction that would be relevant.

2. **Sole Proprietorships and Partnerships.** What are the four primary disadvantages to the sole proprietorship and partnership forms of business organization? What benefits are there to these types of business organization as opposed to the corporate form?

3. **Corporations.** What is the primary disadvantage of the corporate form of organization? Name at least two of the advantages of corporate organization.

4. **Corporate Finance Organization.** In a large corporation, what are the two distinct groups that report to the chief financial officer? Which group is the focus of corporate finance?

5. **Goal of Financial Management.** What goal should always motivate the actions of the firm's financial manager?

Concept Questions

Chapter sections are intentionally kept short to promote a step-by-step, building-block approach to learning. Each section is then followed by a series of short concept questions that highlight the key ideas just presented. Students use these questions to make sure they can identify and understand the most important concepts as they read.

CONCEPT QUESTIONS

1.6a What is a dealer market? How do dealer and auction markets differ?
1.6b What is the largest auction market in the United States?
1.6c What does *OTC* stand for? What is the large OTC market for stocks called?

Summary Tables

These tables succinctly restate key principles, results, and equations. They appear whenever it is useful to emphasize and summarize a group of related concepts.

I. The cash flow identity

Cash flow from assets = Cash flow to creditors (bondholders)
                       + Cash flow to stockholders (owners)

II. Cash flow from assets

Cash flow from assets = Operating cash flow
                       − Net capital spending
                       − Change in net working capital (NWC)

where

Operating cash flow = Earnings before interest and taxes (EBIT)
                     + Depreciation − Taxes
Net capital spending = Ending net fixed assets − Beginning net fixed assets
                     + Depreciation
Change in NWC = Ending NWC − Beginning NWC

III. Cash flow to creditors (bondholders)

Cash flow to creditors = Interest paid − Net new borrowing

IV. Cash flow to stockholders (owners)

Cash flow to stockholders = Dividends paid − Net new equity raised

TABLE 2.5

Cash flow summary

Numbered Examples

Separate numbered and titled examples are extensively integrated into the chapters. These examples provide detailed applications and illustrations of the text material in a step-by-step format. Each example is completely self-contained so that students don't have to search for additional information. Based on our classroom testing, these examples are among the most useful learning aids because they provide both detail and explanation.

EXAMPLE 3.2 | **Payables Turnover**

Here is a variation on the receivables collection period. How long, on average, does it take for Prufrock Corporation to *pay* its bills? To answer, we need to calculate the accounts payable turnover rate using cost of goods sold. We will assume that Prufrock purchases everything on credit.

The cost of goods sold is $1,344, and accounts payable are $344. The turnover is therefore $1,344/$344 = 3.9 times. So payables turned over about every 365/3.9 = 94 days. On average, then, Prufrock takes 94 days to pay. As a potential creditor, we might take note of this fact.

Key Terms

These are printed in blue the first time they appear, and are defined within the text and in the margin.

As shown in Figure 2.1, the difference between a firm's current assets and its current liabilities is called **net working capital**. Net working capital is positive when current assets exceed current liabilities. Based on the definitions of current assets and current liabilities, this means that the cash that will become available over the next 12 months exceeds the cash that must be paid over that same period. For this reason, net working capital is usually positive in a healthy firm.

net working capital
Current assets less current liabilities.

Key Equations

These are called out in the text and identified by equation numbers. Appendix B shows the key equations by chapter.

Profit Margin   Companies pay a great deal of attention to their *profit margin:*

$$\text{Profit margin} = \frac{\text{Net income}}{\text{Sales}} \qquad [3.14]$$

$$= \frac{\$363}{\$2,311} = 15.7\%$$

Highlighted Phrases

Throughout the text, important ideas are presented separately and printed in a blue box to indicate their importance the students.

Given that the goal of financial management is to increase share value, our discussion in this section leads us to the *net present value rule:*

An investment should be accepted if the net present value is positive and rejected if it is negative.

Chapter Summary and Conclusions

These paragraphs review the chapter's key points and provide closure to the chapter.

SUMMARY AND CONCLUSIONS

This chapter has introduced you to the basic principles of present value and discounted cash flow valuation. In it, we explained a number of things about the time value of money, including:

1. For a given rate of return, the value at some point in the future of an investment made today can be determined by calculating the future value of that investment.
2. The current worth of a future cash flow can be determined for a given rate of return by calculating the present value of the cash flow involved.
3. The relationship between present value and future value for a given rate r and time t is given by the basic present value equation:

$$PV = FV_t/(1 + r)^t$$

As we have shown, it is possible to find any one of the four components (PV, FV_t, r, or t) given the other three.

Chapter Review and Self-Test Problems

Review and self-test problems appear after the chapter summaries. Detailed answers to the self-test problems immediately follow. These questions and answers allow students to test their abilities in solving key problems related to the content of the chapter.

CHAPTER REVIEW AND SELF-TEST PROBLEMS

5.1 Present Values with Multiple Cash Flows. A first-round draft choice quarterback has been signed to a three-year, $10 million contract. The details provide for an immediate cash bonus of $1 million. The player is to receive $2 million in salary at the end of the first year, $3 million the next, and $4 million at the end of the last year. Assuming a 10 percent discount rate, is this package worth $10 million? How much is it worth?

5.2 Future Value with Multiple Cash Flows. You plan to make a series of deposits in an interest-bearing account. You will deposit $1,000 today, $2,000 in two years, and $8,000 in five years. If you withdraw $3,000 in three years and $5,000 in seven years, how much will you have after eight years if the interest rate is 9 percent? What is the present value of these cash flows?

5.3 Annuity Present Value. You are looking into an investment that will pay you $12,000 per year for the next 10 years. If you require a 15 percent return, what is the most you would pay for this investment?

5.4 APR versus EAR. The going rate on student loans is quoted as 9 percent APR. The terms of the loan call for monthly payments. What is the effective annual rate, or EAR, on such a student loan?

End-of-Chapter Questions and Problems

We have found that many students learn better when they have plenty of opportunity to practice. We therefore provide extensive end-of-chapter questions and problems—many more than in the previous edition. The questions and problems are generally segregated into two levels—Basic and Intermediate. All problems are fully annotated so that students and instructors can readily identify particular types. Throughout the text, we have worked to supply interesting problems that illustrate real-world applications of chapter material. Answers to selected end-of-chapter questions appear in Appendix C.

QUESTIONS AND PROBLEMS

Basic
(Questions 1–15)

1. **Simple Interest versus Compound Interest.** First Rajan Bank pays 5 percent simple interest on its savings account balances, whereas First Mullineaux Bank pays 5 percent interest compounded annually. If you made a $5,000 deposit in each bank, how much more money would you earn from your First Mullineaux Bank account at the end of 10 years?

2. **Calculating Future Values.** For each of the following, compute the future value:

Present Value Value	Years	Interest Rate	Future Value
$ 2,250	4	18%	
9,310	9	6	
76,355	15	12	

We have made every effort to include the support material that is most critical for you and your students. Each product has been significantly revised and refreshed for the Third Edition.

Instructor Supplements

Annotated Instructor's Edition (AIE)
ISBN 0072340630

All your teaching resources are tied together here!

This handy resource contains extensive references to the Instructor's Manual regarding Lecture Tips, Ethics Notes, International Notes, and the availability of PowerPoint slides. The Lecture Tips vary in content and purpose—providing an alternative perspective on a subject, suggesting important points to be stressed, giving further examples, or recommending other readings. The Ethics Notes present background on topics that can be used to motivate classroom discussion of finance-related ethical issues. Other annotations include: notes for the Real-World Tips; Concept Questions; Self-Test Problems; End-of-Chapter Problems; Videos; and answers to the end-of-chapter problems.

Instructor's Manual, prepared by Cheri Etling, University of Tampa
ISBN 0072340568

A great place to find new lecture ideas!

This thoroughly updated IM contains two sections. The first section contains a chapter outline and other lecture materials designed for use with the Annotated Instructor's Edition. There is an annotated outline for each chapter, and included in the outlines are Lecture Tips, Real-World Tips, Ethics Notes, suggested PowerPoint slides, and, when appropriate, a video synopsis. Detailed solutions for all end-of-chapter problems appear in the second section.

Test Bank, prepared by David Kuipers, Texas Tech University
ISBN 0072340592

New format for a better testing process!

The Third Edition Test Bank has been thoroughly reorganized to more closely link with the text. Each chapter is divided into four parts: Part I contains questions that test the understanding of key terms in the book. Part II includes questions patterned after the learning objectives, concept questions, chapter-opening vignettes, boxes, and high-lighted phrases. Part III contains multiple-choice and true/false problems patterned after the end-of-chapter questions, in basic and intermediate levels. Part IV provides essay questions to test problem-solving skills and more advanced understanding of concepts.

Instructor's Presentation Manager CD-ROM
0072423439

Keep all the supplements in one place!

This CD contains all the necessary supplements—Instructor's Manual, Solutions, Test Bank, and PowerPoint slides—all in one useful product in an electronic format.

Computerized Testing Software
ISBN 0072340614 (Windows)
Create your own test in a snap!

This software includes an easy-to-use menu system that allows quick access to all the powerful features available. The Keyword Search option lets you browse through the test bank for problems containing a specific word or phrase. Password protection is available for saved tests or for the entire database. Questions can be added, modified, or deleted.

TeleTest
McGraw-Hill/Irwin's free customized exam preparation service!

Simply choose your desired questions from the Test Bank and call McGraw-Hill/Irwin at 1-800-338-3987. Test and answer keys are printed on a laser printer according to the specifications provided and mailed to you.

PowerPoint Presentation System, prepared by Cheri Etling, University of Tampa
ISBN 0072340576
Now with more lecture outlines!

This presentation has been thoroughly revised to include more lecture-oriented slides. The presentation also includes exhibits and examples both from the book and from outside sources. Applicable slides have Web links that take you directly to specific Internet sites, or a spreadsheet link to show an example in Excel. You can also go to the Notes Pages function for more tips in presenting the slides. There is also a separate section that contains selected worked-out solutions. If you have PowerPoint installed on your PC, you have the ability to edit, print, or rearrange the complete transparency presentation to meet your specific needs.

Transparency Acetates
ISBN 0072340606
Add visuals to your course!

All of the chapter presentations in PowerPoint are produced in an acetate package for use with an overhead projector.

Videos
ISBN 0072423420
New set of videos on hot topics!

McGraw-Hill/Irwin produced a new series of finance videos that are 10-minute case studies on topics such as Financial Markets, Careers, Rightsizing, Capital Budgeting, EVA, and International Finance. Discussion questions for these videos are available in the Instructor's Center at www.mhhe.com/rwj.

Student Supplements

The Wall Street Journal **Edition**
ISBN 0072340649
Great way to bring in more current events!
Through a unique arrangement with Dow Jones, the price of this version of the student text includes a 10-week subscription to *The Wall Street Journal.* This business daily newspaper's coverage of financial topics, both domestic and global, is unparalleled by any other business periodical. Please contact your McGraw-Hill/Irwin representative for ordering information.

Student Problem Manual, prepared by Thomas Eyssell, University of Missouri—St. Louis
ISBN 007234055X
Need additional help solving problems?
This valuable resource provides students with additional problems for practice. Each chapter begins with Concepts for Review, followed by Chapter Highlights. These re-emphasize the key terms and concepts in the chapter. A short Concept Test, averaging 10 questions and answers, appears next. Each chapter concludes with additional problems for the student to review. Answers to these problems appear at the end of the Student Problem Manual.

Ready Notes
ISBN 0072340541
Improved listening and attention = improved retention!
This innovative student supplement provides students with an inexpensive note-taking system that contains a reduced copy of every slide in the PowerPoint Presentation System. With a copy of each slide in front of them, students can listen and record your comments about each point instead of hurriedly copying the slide into their notebooks. Ask your McGraw-Hill/Irwin representative about packaging options.

Financial Analysis with an Electronic Calculator, Fourth Edition, by Mark A. White, University of Virginia, McIntire School of Commerce
ISBN 0072299738
Need help with your financial calculator?
The information and procedures in this supplementary text enable students to master the use of financial calculators and develop a working knowledge of financial mathe-matics and problem solving. Complete instructions are included for solving all major problem types on three popular models: HP 10-B, TI BA II Plus, and Sharp EL733A. Hands-on problems with detailed solutions allow students to practice the skills outlined in the text and obtain instant reinforcement. *Financial Analysis with an Electronic Calculator* is a self-contained supplement to the introductory financial management course.

Digital Solutions

Online Learning Center (OLC)
www.mhhe.com/rwj

Check out this site for additional teaching and learning support!

- The Instructor Center provides all of the supplements in an on-line format and is an excellent resource for additional teaching tools. *This Week in Finance,* coordinated by Thomas H. Eyssell, University of Missouri—St. Louis, is continually updated to provide current events and teaching tips. The site is password-protected—you can obtain the password either by registering at the site or contacting your McGraw-Hill representative.

- The Student Center includes McGraw-Hill/Irwin's eLearning Sessions—an on-line study guide by chapter, with interactive study aids and quizzes. The spreadsheet software that is tied to end-of-chapter problems is found here, as well as a career corner, and other relevant links. Students who purchase a new book will receive a passcode card that gives them access to these assets.

- The Information Center provides information about the book, authors, and other McGraw-Hill/Irwin products.

Finance Resources Access Network (FRAN)
www.mhhe.com/fran
Make us your resource for all of your courses!
Looking for additional support for corporate finance or one of your other courses?
Check out the McGraw-Hill/Irwin finance supersite. Coordinated by faculty members around the country, this continuously updated site provides you with current events, teaching tips, and lots of other resources for teaching support.

PageOut
The Course Web Site Development Center
www.pageout.net
This Web page generation software, free to adopters, is designed to help professors just beginning to explore Web site options. In just a few minutes, even the most novice computer user can have a course Web site. Complete the PageOut templates with your course information, and you will have an interactive syllabus online. This feature lets you post content to coincide with your lectures. When students visit your PageOut Web site, your syllabus will direct them to components of McGraw-Hill Web content germane to your text or specific material of your own. Other features include:

- Specific question selection for quizzes.
- Ability to copy your course and share it with colleagues or as a foundation for a new semester.

- Enhanced grade book with reporting features.
- Ability to use the PageOut discussion area or add your own third party discussion tool.
- Password-protected courses.

Short on time? Let us do the work. Send your course materials to our McGraw-Hill service team. They will call you by phone for a 30-minute consultation. A team member will then create your PageOut Web site and provide training to get you up and running. Contact your local McGraw-Hill publisher's representative for details.

ACKNOWLEDGMENTS

Clearly, our greatest debt is to our many colleagues (and their students) around the world who, like us, wanted to try an alternative to what they were using and made the switch to our first and second editions. Our plan for developing and improving *Essentials* revolved around the detailed feedback we received from many of our colleagues who had an interest in the book and regularly teach the introductory course. These dedicated scholars and teachers to whom we are very grateful are:

Karan Bhanot, University of Texas—San Antonio
Rick Borgman, University of Maine
Ray Brooks, Oregon State University
Susan Crain, Southern Illinois University—Edwardsville
Raymond Cox, Central Michigan University
William H. Dare, Southwest Texas State University
Wallace Davidson, Southern Illinois University
Philip DeMoss, West Chester University
Anand Desai, Kansas State University
Jeanette Diamond, University of Nebraska at Omaha
Gregg Dimkoff, Grand Valley State University
Tom Downs, University of Alabama
Bill Francis, University of North Carolina—Charlotte
E. Bruce Frederickson, Syracuse University
Robert Hartl, University of Southern Indiana
Eric Higgins, Drexel University
Donald G. Hyde, Chattanooga State Tech
Alan Robert Jung, San Francisco State University
Stephen Kapplin, University of South Florida
Kashi Khazeh, Salisbury State University
Yong-Cheol Kim, Clemson University
Ladd Kochman, Kennesaw State University
Reinhold Lamb, University of North Carolina—Charlotte
Lee McClain, Western Washington University
Melissa Melancon, Grambling State University
Lalatendu Misra, University of Texas at San Antonio
John Mitchell, Central Michigan University
Karlyn Mitchell, North Carolina State University
Jonathan S. Moulton, Oregon State University
Therese Pactwa, Florida International University
Glenn Pettengill, Emporia State University
Thomas Rietz, University of Iowa
Sandeep Singh, SUNY—Brockport
Sudhir Singh, Frostburg State University
Madeline S. Thimmes, Utah State University
Guatam Vora, University of New Mexico
Edward R. Wolfe, Western Kentucky University
Matthew Wong, St. John's University

We owe a special debt to our colleagues for their dedicated work on the many supplements that accompany this text: Cheri Etling, University of Tampa, for her extensive revision and improvement of the Instructor's Manual, PowerPoint slides, and Annotated Instructor's Edition; David Kuipers, Texas Tech University, for completely revamping the Test Bank; Thomas H. Eyssell, University of Missouri—St. Louis, for his revision of the Student Problem Manual, creation of the eLearning Sessions, and updating of the *This Week in Finance* feature on the Online Learning Center; Randy D. Jorgensen, Creighton University, for working closely with us to develop the *Reality Bytes* feature in the text; and Joe Smolira, Belmont University, for his help with the PowerPoint slides and Instructor's Manual.

The following University of Kentucky graduate students did outstanding work on this edition of *Essentials*: Steve Allen, John Gonas, and Mike Highfield. To them fell the unenviable task of technical proofreading, and, in particular, careful checking of each and every calculation throughtout the text.

Finally, in every phase of this project, we have been privileged to have the complete and unwavering support of a great organization, McGraw-Hill/Irwin. We especially thank the McGraw-Hill/Irwin sales organization. The suggestions they provided, their professionalism in assisting potential adopters, and their service to current adopters have been a major factor in our success.

We are deeply grateful to the select group of professionals who served as our development team on this edition: Michele Janicek, Associate Editor; Erin Riley, Development Editor; Rhonda Seelinger, Executive Marketing Manager; John Biernat, Publisher; Jean Lou Hess, Senior Project Manager; Pam Verros, Designer; and Lori Koetters, Senior Production Supervisor. Others at McGraw-Hill/Irwin, too numerous to list here, have improved the book in countless ways.

Throughout the development of this edition, we have taken great care to discover and eliminate errors. Our goal is to provide the best textbook available on the subject. To ensure that future editions are error free, we will gladly offer $10 per arithmetic error to the first individual reporting it as a modest token of our appreciation. More than this, we would like to hear from instructors and students alike. Please send us your comments by using the feedback form on the Essentials of Corporate Finance Online Learning Center at www.mhhe.com/rwj.

Stephen A. Ross
Randolph W. Westerfield
Bradford D. Jordan

BRIEF CONTENTS

CONTENTS

PART 7   LONG-TERM FINANCING

CHAPTER 12
Cost of Capital

CHAPTER 13
Leverage and Capital Structure

CHAPTER 14
Dividends and Dividend Policy

PART 8   SHORT-TERM FINANCIAL MANAGEMENT

CHAPTER 16
Short-Term Financial Planning

CHAPTER 17
Working Capital Management

PART 9   TOPICS IN BUSINESS FINANCE

CHAPTER 18

International Aspects of Financial Management

LIST OF BOXES

REALITY BYTES

THIRD EDITION

Essentials *of* Corporate Finance

CHAPTER | 1

Introduction to Financial Management

TO GET THE MOST OUT OF THE CHAPTER, WHEN YOU ARE FINISHED STUDYING IT, MAKE SURE YOU HAVE A GOOD UNDERSTANDING OF:

- The basic types of financial management decisions and the role of the financial manager

- The goal of financial management

- The financial implications of the different forms of business organization

- The conflicts of interest that can arise between managers and owners

APPLE COMPUTER began as a two-man partnership in a garage. It grew rapidly and, by 1985, became a large publicly traded corporation with 60 million shares of stock and a total market value in excess of $1 billion. At that time, the firm's more visible cofounder, 30-year-old Steven Jobs, owned seven million shares of Apple stock worth about $120 million.

Despite his stake in the company and his role in its founding and success, Jobs was forced to relinquish operating responsibilities in 1985 when Apple's financial performance turned sour, and he subsequently resigned altogether.

Of course, you can't keep a good entrepreneur down. Jobs formed Pixar Animation Studios, the company that is responsible for the animation in the hit movies *Toy Story, A Bug's Life,* and *Toy Story 2.* Pixar went public in 1995, and, following an enthusiastic reception by the stock market, Jobs's 80 percent stake was valued at about $1.1 billion. Finally, just to show that what goes around comes around, in 1997, Apple's future was still in doubt, and the company, struggling for relevance in a "Wintel" world, decided to go the sequel route when it hired a new interim chief executive officer (CEO): Steven Jobs! By introducing such innovative products as the iMac, Jobs led a successful turnaround at Apple, and, in January 2000, Apple officially dropped the interim tag from the CEO title.

Understanding Jobs's journey from garage-based entrepreneur to corporate executive to ex-employee and, finally, to CEO takes us into issues involving the corporate form of organization, corporate goals, and corporate control, all of which we discuss in this chapter.

In fact, whether your primary interest is accounting, finance, management, marketing, or some other area, this chapter brings you face-to-face with the most central of all questions for a business: Why are we here? Put more precisely: What is the goal of our business? Although this chapter focuses on the goal of business from a financial manager's perspective, we hope you will recognize that the issues we raise and the conclusions we draw are actually much broader and apply to all participants in the decision-making process. Also, for those of you interested in starting a small business of any type, this chapter provides some important information (and warnings) regarding the different types of business organization you might choose.

To begin our study of financial management, we address two central issues. First: What is corporate, or business, finance and what is the role of the financial manager? Second: What is the goal of financial management?

1.1 | FINANCE: A QUICK LOOK

Before we plunge into our study of "corp. fin.," we think a quick overview of the finance field might be a good idea. Our goal is to clue you in on some of the most important areas in finance and some of the career opportunities available in each. We also want to illustrate some of the ways finance fits in with other areas such as marketing, management, and accounting.

The Four Basic Areas

Traditionally, financial topics are grouped into four main areas:

1. Corporate finance
2. Investments
3. Financial institutions
4. International finance

We discuss each of these next.

Corporate Finance   The first of these four areas, corporate finance, is the main subject of this book. We begin covering this subject with our next section, so we will wait until then to get into any details. One thing we should note is that the term *corporate finance* seems to imply that what we cover is only relevant to corporations, but the truth is that almost all of the topics we consider are much broader than that. Maybe *business finance* would be a little more descriptive, but even this is too narrow because at least half of the subjects we discuss in the pages ahead are really basic financial ideas and principles applicable across all the various areas of finance and beyond.

Investments   Broadly speaking, the investments area deals with financial assets such as stocks and bonds. Some of the more important questions include:

1. What determines the price of a financial asset such as a share of stock?
2. What are the potential risks and rewards associated with investing in financial assets?
3. What is the best mixture of the different types of financial assets to hold?

Students who specialize in the investments area have various career opportunities. Being a stockbroker is one of the most common. Stockbrokers often work for large companies such as Merrill Lynch, advising customers on what types of investments to consider and helping them make buy and sell decisions. Financial advisers play a similar role, but are not necessarily brokers.

Portfolio management is a second investments-related career path. Portfolio managers, as the name suggests, manage money for investors. For example, individual investors frequently buy into mutual funds. Such funds are simply a means of pooling money that is then invested by a portfolio manager. Portfolio managers also invest and manage money for pension funds, insurance companies, and many other types of institutions.

Security analysis is a third area. A security analyst researches individual investments, such as stock in a particular company, and makes a determination as to whether the price is right. To do so, an analyst delves deeply into company and industry reports, along with a variety of other information sources. Frequently, brokers and portfolio managers rely on security analysts for information and recommendations.

These investments-related areas, like many areas in finance, share an interesting feature. If they are done well, they can be very rewarding financially (translation: You can make a lot of money). The bad news, of course, is that they can be very demanding and very competitive, so they are definitely not for everybody.

Financial Institutions Financial institutions are basically businesses that deal primarily in financial matters. Banks and insurance companies would probably be the most familiar to you. Institutions such as these employ people to perform a wide variety of finance-related tasks. For example, a commercial loan officer at a bank would evaluate whether a particular business has a strong enough financial position to warrant extending a loan. At an insurance company, an analyst would decide whether a particular risk was suitable for insuring and what the premium should be.

International Finance International finance isn't so much an area as it is a specialization within one of the main areas we described above. In other words, careers in international finance generally involve international aspects of either corporate finance, investments, or financial institutions. For example, some portfolio managers and security analysts specialize in non-U.S. companies. Similarly, many U.S. businesses have extensive overseas operations and need employees familiar with such international topics as exchange rates and political risk. Banks frequently are asked to make loans across country lines, so international specialists are needed there as well.

Why Study Finance?

Who needs to know finance? In a word, you. In fact, there are many reasons you need a working knowledge of finance even if you are not planning a finance career. We explore some of these next.

Marketing and Finance If you are interested in marketing, you need to know finance because, for example, marketers constantly work with budgets, and they need to understand how to get the greatest payoff from marketing expenditures and programs. Analyzing costs and benefits of projects of all types is one of the most important aspects of finance, so the tools you learn in finance are vital in marketing research, the design of marketing and distribution channels, and product pricing, just to name a few areas.

Financial analysts rely heavily on marketing analysts, and the two frequently work together to evaluate the profitability of proposed projects and products. As we will see in a later chapter, sales projections are a key input in almost every type of new product analysis, and such projections are often developed jointly between marketing and finance.

Beyond this, the finance industry employs marketers to help sell financial products such as bank accounts, insurance policies, and mutual funds. Financial services marketing is one of the most rapidly growing types of marketing, and successful financial services marketers are very well compensated. To work in this area, you obviously need to understand financial products.

Accounting and Finance For accountants, finance is required reading. In smaller businesses in particular, accountants are often required to make financial decisions as well as perform traditional accounting duties. Further, as the financial world continues to grow more complex, accountants have to know finance to understand the implications of many of the newer types of financial contracts and the impact they have on financial statements. Beyond this, cost accounting and business finance are particularly closely related, sharing many of the same subjects and concerns.

Financial analysts make extensive use of accounting information; they are some of the most important end users. Understanding finance helps accountants recognize what types of information are particularly valuable and, more generally, how accounting information is actually used (and abused) in practice.

Management and Finance   One of the most important areas in management is strategy. Thinking about business strategy without simultaneously thinking about financial strategy is an excellent recipe for disaster, and, as a result, management strategists must have a very clear understanding of the financial implications of business plans.

In broader terms, management employees of all types are expected to have a strong understanding of how their jobs impact profitability, and they are also expected to be able to work within their areas to improve profitability. This is precisely what studying finance teaches you: What are the characteristics of activities that create value?

You and Finance   Perhaps the most important reason to know finance is that you will have to make financial decisions that will be very important to you personally. Today, for example, when you go to work for almost any type of company, you will be asked to decide how you want to invest your retirement funds. We'll see in a later chapter that what you choose to do can make an enormous difference in your future financial well-being. On a different note, is it your dream to start your own business? Good luck if you don't understand basic finance before you start; you'll end up learning it the hard way. Want to know how big your student loan payments are going to be before you take out that next loan? Maybe not, but we'll show you how to calculate them anyway.

These are just a few of the ways that finance will affect your personal and business lives. Whether you want to or not, you are going to have to examine and understand financial issues, and you are going to have to make financial decisions. We want you to do so wisely, so keep reading.

CONCEPT QUESTIONS

1.1a   What are the major areas in finance?

1.1b   Besides wanting to pass this class, why do you need to understand finance?

1.2 | BUSINESS FINANCE AND THE FINANCIAL MANAGER

Now we proceed to define business finance and the financial manager's job.

What Is Business Finance?

Imagine you were to start your own business. No matter what type you started, you would have to answer the following three questions in some form or another:

1.   What long-term investments should you take on? That is, what lines of business will you be in and what sorts of buildings, machinery, and equipment will you need?

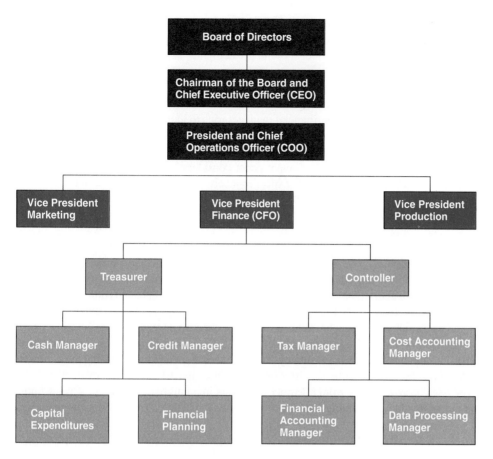

FIGURE 1.1

A simplified organizational chart. The exact titles and organization differ from company to company.

2. Where will you get the long-term financing to pay for your investment? Will you bring in other owners or will you borrow the money?
3. How will you manage your everyday financial activities such as collecting from customers and paying suppliers?

These are not the only questions, but they are among the most important. Business finance, broadly speaking, is the study of ways to answer these three questions. We'll be looking at each of them in the chapters ahead.

The Financial Manager

The financial management function is usually associated with a top officer of the firm, often called the chief financial officer (CFO) or vice president of finance. Figure 1.1 is a simplified organizational chart that highlights the finance activity in a large firm. As shown, the vice president of finance coordinates the activities of the treasurer and the controller. The controller's office handles cost and financial accounting, tax payments, and management information systems. The treasurer's office is responsible for managing the firm's cash and credit, its financial planning, and its capital expenditures. These treasury activities are all related to the three general questions raised above, and the chapters ahead deal primarily with these issues. Our study thus bears mostly on activities usually associated with the treasurer's office. In a smaller firm, the treasurer and controller might be the same person, and there would be only one office.

Financial Management Decisions

As our discussion above suggests, the financial manager must be concerned with three basic types of questions. We consider these in greater detail next.

Capital Budgeting   The first question concerns the firm's long-term investments. The process of planning and managing a firm's long-term investments is called **capital budgeting.** In capital budgeting, the financial manager tries to identify investment opportunities that are worth more to the firm than they cost to acquire. Loosely speaking, this means that the value of the cash flow generated by an asset exceeds the cost of that asset.

Regardless of the specific investment under consideration, financial managers must be concerned with how much cash they expect to receive, when they expect to receive it, and how likely they are to receive it. Evaluating the *size, timing,* and *risk* of future cash flows is the essence of capital budgeting. In fact, whenever we evaluate a business decision, the size, timing, and risk of the cash flows will be, by far, the most important things we will consider.

capital budgeting

The process of planning and managing a firm's long-term investments.

Capital Structure   The second question for the financial manager concerns how the firm obtains the financing it needs to support its long-term investments. A firm's **capital structure** (or financial structure) refers to the specific mixture of long-term debt and equity the firm uses to finance its operations. The financial manager has two concerns in this area. First: How much should the firm borrow? Second: What are the least expensive sources of funds for the firm?

In addition to deciding on the financing mix, the financial manager has to decide exactly how and where to raise the money. The expenses associated with raising long-term financing can be considerable, so different possibilities must be carefully evaluated. Also, businesses borrow money from a variety of lenders in a number of different ways. Choosing among lenders and among loan types is another job handled by the financial manager.

capital structure

The mixture of debt and equity maintained by a firm.

Working Capital Management   The third question concerns **working capital** management. The term *working capital* refers to a firm's short-term assets, such as inventory, and its short-term liabilities, such as money owed to suppliers. Managing the firm's working capital is a day-to-day activity that ensures the firm has sufficient resources to continue its operations and avoid costly interruptions. This involves a number of activities related to the firm's receipt and disbursement of cash.

Some questions about working capital that must be answered are the following: (1) How much cash and inventory should we keep on hand? (2) Should we sell on credit to our customers? (3) How will we obtain any needed short-term financing? If we borrow in the short term, how and where should we do it? This is just a small sample of the issues that arise in managing a firm's working capital.

working capital

A firm's short-term assets and liabilities.

Conclusion   The three areas of corporate financial management we have described—capital budgeting, capital structure, and working capital management—are very broad categories. Each includes a rich variety of topics, and we have indicated only a few of the questions that arise in the different areas. The chapters ahead contain greater detail.

CONCEPT QUESTIONS

1.2a   What is the capital budgeting decision?

1.2b   What do you call the specific mixture of long-term debt and equity that a firm chooses to use?

1.2c   Into what category of financial management does cash management fall?

FORMS OF BUSINESS ORGANIZATION `1.3`

Large firms in the United States, such as IBM and Exxon, are almost all organized as corporations. We examine the three different legal forms of business organization—sole proprietorship, partnership, and corporation—to see why this is so.

Sole Proprietorship

A **sole proprietorship** is a business owned by one person. This is the simplest type of business to start and is the least regulated form of organization. For this reason, there are more proprietorships than any other type of business, and many businesses that later become large corporations start out as small proprietorships.

The owner of a sole proprietorship keeps all the profits. That's the good news. The bad news is that the owner has *unlimited liability* for business debts. This means that creditors can look to the proprietor's personal assets for payment. Similarly, there is no distinction between personal and business income, so all business income is taxed as personal income.

The life of a sole proprietorship is limited to the owner's life span, and, importantly, the amount of equity that can be raised is limited to the proprietor's personal wealth. This limitation often means that the business is unable to exploit new opportunities because of insufficient capital. Ownership of a sole proprietorship may be difficult to transfer since this requires the sale of the entire business to a new owner.

sole proprietorship
A business owned by a single individual.

Partnership

A **partnership** is similar to a proprietorship, except that there are two or more owners (partners). In a *general partnership,* all the partners share in gains or losses, and all have unlimited liability for *all* partnership debts, not just some particular share. The way partnership gains (and losses) are divided is described in the *partnership agreement.* This agreement can be an informal oral agreement, such as "let's start a lawn mowing business," or a lengthy, formal written document.

In a *limited partnership,* one or more *general partners* will run the business and have unlimited liability, but there will be one or more *limited partners* who do not actively participate in the business. A limited partner's liability for business debts is limited to the amount that partner contributes to the partnership. This form of organization is common in real estate ventures, for example.

partnership
A business formed by two or more individuals or entities.

The advantages and disadvantages of a partnership are basically the same as those for a proprietorship. Partnerships based on a relatively informal agreement are easy and inexpensive to form. General partners have unlimited liability for partnership debts, and the partnership terminates when a general partner wishes to sell out or dies. All income is taxed as personal income to the partners, and the amount of equity that can be raised is limited to the partners' combined wealth. Ownership by a general partner is not easily transferred because a new partnership must be formed. A limited partner's interest can be sold without dissolving the partnership, but finding a buyer may be difficult.

Because a partner in a general partnership can be held responsible for all partnership debts, having a written agreement is very important. Failure to spell out the rights and duties of the partners frequently leads to misunderstandings later on. Also, if you are a limited partner, you must not become deeply involved in business decisions unless you are willing to assume the obligations of a general partner. The reason is that if things go badly, you may be deemed to be a general partner even though you say you are a limited partner.

Based on our discussion, the primary disadvantages of sole proprietorships and partnerships as forms of business organization are (1) unlimited liability for business debts on the part of the owners, (2) limited life of the business, and (3) difficulty of transferring ownership. These three disadvantages add up to a single, central problem: The ability of such businesses to grow can be seriously limited by an inability to raise cash for investment.

Corporation

corporation

A business created as a distinct legal entity owned by one or more individuals or entities.

The **corporation** is the most important form (in terms of size) of business organization in the United States. A corporation is a legal "person" separate and distinct from its owners, and it has many of the rights, duties, and privileges of an actual person. Corporations can borrow money and own property, can sue and be sued, and can enter into contracts. A corporation can even be a general partner or a limited partner in a partnership, and a corporation can own stock in another corporation.

Not surprisingly, starting a corporation is somewhat more complicated than starting the other forms of business organization. Forming a corporation involves preparing *articles of incorporation* (or a charter) and a set of *bylaws.* The articles of incorporation must contain a number of things, including the corporation's name, its intended life (which can be forever), its business purpose, and the number of shares that can be issued. This information must normally be supplied to the state in which the firm will be incorporated. For most legal purposes, the corporation is a "resident" of that state.

The bylaws are rules describing how the corporation regulates its own existence. For example, the bylaws describe how directors are elected. The bylaws may be amended or extended from time to time by the stockholders.

In a large corporation, the stockholders and the managers are usually separate groups. The stockholders elect the board of directors, who then select the managers. Management is charged with running the corporation's affairs in the stockholders' interests. In principle, stockholders control the corporation because they elect the directors.

As a result of the separation of ownership and management, the corporate form has several advantages. Ownership (represented by shares of stock) can be readily transferred, and the life of the corporation is therefore not limited. The corporation borrows money in its own name. As a result, the stockholders in a corporation have limited liability for corporate debts. The most they can lose is what they have invested.

The relative ease of transferring ownership, the limited liability for business debts, and the unlimited life of the business are the reasons why the corporate form is superior when it comes to raising cash. If a corporation needs new equity, it can sell new shares of stock and attract new investors. The number of owners can be huge; larger corporations have many thousands or even millions of stockholders. For example, AT&T has about 3.7 million stockholders and General Motors has about a million.

The corporate form has a significant disadvantage. Since a corporation is a legal person, it must pay taxes. Moreover, money paid out to stockholders in the form of dividends is taxed again as income to those stockholders. This is *double taxation,* meaning that corporate profits are taxed twice: at the corporate level when they are earned and again at the personal level when they are paid out.

A Corporation by Another Name . . .

The corporate form has many variations around the world. Exact laws and regulations differ, of course, but the essential features of public ownership and limited liability remain. These firms are often called *joint stock companies, public limited companies,* or *limited liability companies.*

Table 1.1 gives the names of a few well-known international corporations, their country of origin, and a translation of the abbreviation that follows the company name.

Company	Country of Origin	Type of Company	Translation	**TABLE 1.1**
Porsche AG	Germany	Aktiengesellschaft	Corporation	International
Bayerische Motoren Werke (BMW) AG	Germany	Aktiengesellschaft	Corporation	corporations
Dornier GmBH	Germany	Gesellshaft mit Beschraenkter Haftung	Cooperative with limited liability	
Rolls-Royce PLC	United Kingdom	Public limited company	Public limited company	
Shell UK Ltd.	United Kingdom	Limited	Corporation	
Unilever NV	Netherlands	Naamloze Vennootschap	Limited liability company	
Fiat SpA	Italy	Societa per Azioni	Public limited company	
Volvo AB	Sweden	Aktiebolag	Joint stock company	
Peugeot SA	France	Sociétét Anonyme	Joint stock company	

CONCEPT QUESTIONS

1.3a What are the three forms of business organization?

1.3b What are the primary advantages and disadvantages of sole proprietorships and partnerships?

1.3c What is the difference between a general and a limited partnership?

1.3d Why is the corporate form superior when it comes to raising cash?

THE GOAL OF FINANCIAL MANAGMENT 1.4

To study financial decision making, we first need to understand the goal of financial management. Such an understanding is important because it leads to an objective basis for making and evaluating financial decisions.

Profit Maximization

Profit maximization would probably be the most commonly cited business goal, but this is not a very precise objective. Do we mean profits this year? If so, then actions such as deferring maintenance, letting inventories run down, and other short-run, cost-cutting measures will tend to increase profits now, but these activities aren't necessarily desirable.

The goal of maximizing profits may refer to some sort of "long-run" or "average" profits, but it's unclear exactly what this means. First, do we mean something like accounting net income or earnings per share? As we will see, these numbers may have little to do with what is good or bad for the firm. Second, what do we mean by the long run? As a famous economist once remarked, in the long run, we're all dead! More to the point, this goal doesn't tell us the appropriate trade-off between current and future profits.

The Goal of Financial Management in a Corporation

The financial manager in a corporation makes decisions for the stockholders of the firm. Given this, instead of listing possible goals for the financial manager, we really need to answer a more fundamental question: From the stockholders' point of view, what is a good financial management decision?

If we assume stockholders buy stock because they seek to gain financially, then the answer is obvious: Good decisions increase the value of the stock, and poor decisions decrease it.

Given our observations, it follows that the financial manager acts in the shareholders' best interests by making decisions that increase the value of the stock. The appropriate goal for the financial manager in a corporation can thus be stated quite easily:

> The goal of financial management is to maximize the current value per share of the existing stock.

The goal of maximizing the value of the stock avoids the problems associated with the different goals we discussed above. There is no ambiguity in the criterion, and there is no short-run versus long-run issue. We explicitly mean that our goal is to maximize the *current* stock value. Of course, maximizing stock value is the same thing as maximizing the market price per share.

A More General Financial Management Goal

Given our goal as stated above (maximize the value of the stock), an obvious question comes up: What is the appropriate goal when the firm has no traded stock? Corporations are certainly not the only type of business, and the stock in many corporations rarely changes hands, so it's difficult to say what the value per share is at any given time.

As long as we are dealing with for-profit businesses, only a slight modification is needed. The total value of the stock in a corporation is simply equal to the value of the owners' equity. Therefore, a more general way of stating our goal is:

> Maximize the market value of the existing owners' equity.

With this goal in mind, it doesn't matter whether the business is a proprietorship, a partnership, or a corporation. For each of these, good financial decisions increase the market value of the owners' equity and poor financial decisions decrease it.

Finally, our goal does not imply that the financial manager should take illegal or unethical actions in the hope of increasing the value of the equity in the firm. What we mean is that the financial manager best serves the owners of the business by identifying goods and services that add value to the firm because they are desired and valued in the free marketplace.

CONCEPT QUESTIONS

1.4a　What is the goal of financial management?

1.4b　What are some shortcomings of the goal of profit maximization?

THE AGENCY PROBLEM AND CONTROL OF THE CORPORATION | 1.5

We've seen that the financial manager in a corporation acts in the best interests of the stockholders by taking actions that increase the value of the firm's stock. However, we've also seen that in large corporations ownership can be spread over a huge number of stockholders. This dispersion of ownership arguably means that management effectively controls the firm. In this case, will management necessarily act in the best interests of the stockholders? Put another way, might not management pursue its own goals at the stockholders' expense? We briefly consider some of the arguments below.

Agency Relationships

The relationship between stockholders and management is called an *agency relationship*. Such a relationship exists whenever someone (the principal) hires another (the agent) to represent his or her interest. For example, you might hire someone (an agent) to sell a car that you own while you are away at school. In all such relationships, there is a possibility of conflict of interest between the principal and the agent. Such a conflict is called an **agency problem.**

Suppose you hire someone to sell your car and you agree to pay her a flat fee when she sells the car. The agent's incentive in this case is to make the sale, not necessarily to get you the best price. If you paid a commission of, say, 10 percent of the sales price instead of a flat fee, then this problem might not exist. This example illustrates that the way an agent is compensated is one factor that affects agency problems.

agency problem
The possibility of conflict of interest between the owners and management of a firm.

Management Goals

To see how management and stockholder interests might differ, imagine that a corporation is considering a new investment. The new investment is expected to favorably impact the stock price, but it is also a relatively risky venture. The owners of the firm will wish to take the investment (because the share value will rise), but management may not because there is the possibility that things will turn out badly and management jobs will be lost. If management does not take the investment, then the stockholders may lose a valuable opportunity. This is one example of an *agency cost*.

It is sometimes argued that, left to themselves, managers would tend to maximize the amount of resources over which they have control, or, more generally, business power or wealth. This goal could lead to an overemphasis on business size or growth. For example, cases where management is accused of overpaying to buy another company just to increase the size of the business or to demonstrate corporate power are not uncommon. Obviously, if overpayment does take place, such a purchase does not benefit the owners of the purchasing company.

Our discussion indicates that management may tend to overemphasize organizational survival to protect job security. Also, management may dislike outside interference, so independence and corporate self-sufficiency may be important goals.

Do Managers Act in the Stockholders' Interests?

Whether managers will, in fact, act in the best interests of stockholders depends on two factors. First, how closely are management goals aligned with stockholder goals? This question relates to the way managers are compensated. Second, can management be replaced if

CLIFFORD W. SMITH JR. ON MARKET INCENTIVES FOR ETHICAL BEHAVIOR

Ethics is a topic that has been receiving increased interest in the business community. Much of this discussion has been led by philosophers and has focused on moral principles. Rather than review these issues, I want to discuss a complementary (but often ignored) set of issues from an economist's viewpoint. Markets impose potentially substantial costs on individuals and institutions that engage in unethical behavior. These market forces thus provide important incentives that foster ethical behavior in the business community.

At its core, economics is the study of making choices. I thus want to examine ethical behavior simply as one choice facing an individual. Economic analysis suggests that in considering an action, you identify its expected costs and benefits. If the estimated benefits exceed the estimated costs, you take the action; if not, you don't. To focus this discussion, let's consider the following specific choice: Suppose you have a contract to deliver a product of a specified quality. Would you cheat by reducing quality to lower costs in an attempt to increase profits?

Economics implies that the higher the expected costs of cheating, the more likely ethical actions will be chosen. This simple principle has several implications.

First, the higher the probability of detection, the less likely an individual is to cheat. This implication helps us understand numerous institutional arrangements for monitoring in the marketplace. For example, a company agrees to have its financial statements audited by an external public accounting firm. This periodic professional monitoring increases the probability of detection, thereby reducing any incentive to misstate the firm's financial condition.

Second, the higher the sanctions imposed if cheating is detected, the less likely an individual is to cheat. Hence, a business transaction that is expected to be repeated between the same parties faces a lower probability of cheating because the lost profits from the forgone stream of future sales provide powerful incentives for contract compliance. However, if continued corporate existence is more uncertain, so are the expected costs of forgone future sales. Therefore, firms in financial difficulty are more likely to cheat than financially healthy firms. Firms thus have incentives to adopt financial policies that help credibly bond against cheating. For example, if product quality is difficult to assess prior to purchase, customers doubt a firm's claims about product quality. Where quality is more uncertain, customers are only willing to pay lower prices. Such firms thus have particularly strong incentives to adopt financial policies that imply a lower probability of insolvency. Therefore, such firms should have lower leverage, have fewer leases, and engage in more hedging.

Third, the expected costs are higher if information about cheating is rapidly and widely distributed to potential future customers. Thus, information services like Consumer Reports, which monitor and report on product quality, help deter cheating. By lowering the costs for potential customers to monitor quality, such services raise the expected costs of cheating.

Finally, the costs imposed on a firm that is caught cheating depend on the market's assessment of the ethical breach. Some actions viewed as clear transgressions by some might be viewed as justifiable behavior by others. Ethical standards also vary across markets. For example, a payment that, if disclosed in the U.S., would be labeled a bribe might be viewed as a standard business practice in another place. The costs imposed will be higher the greater the consensus that the behavior was unethical.

Establishing and maintaining a reputation for ethical behavior is a valuable corporate asset in the business community. This analysis suggests that a firm concerned about the ethical conduct of its employees should pay careful attention to potential conflicts among the firm's management, employees, customers, creditors, and shareholders. Consider Sears, the department store giant that was found to be charging customers for auto repairs of questionable necessity. In an effort to make the company more service oriented (in the way that competitors like Nordstrom are), Sears initiated an across-the-board policy of commission sales. But what works in clothing and housewares does not always work the same way in the auto repair shop. A customer for a man's suit knows as much as the salesperson about the product. But many auto repair customers know little about the inner workings of their cars and thus are more likely to rely on employee recommendations in deciding on purchases. Sears's compensation policy resulted in recommendations of unnecessary repairs to customers. Sears would not have had to deal with its repair shop problems and the consequent erosion of its reputation had it anticipated that its commission sales policy would encourage auto shop employees to cheat its customers.

Clifford W. Smith Jr. is the Clarey Professor of Finance at the University of Rochester's Simon School of Business Administration. He is an editor of the *Journal of Financial Economics*. His research focuses on corporate financial policy and the structure of financial institutions.

they do not pursue stockholder goals? This issue relates to control of the firm. As we will discuss, there are a number of reasons to think that, even in the largest firms, management has a significant incentive to act in the interests of stockholders.

Managerial Compensation   Management will frequently have a significant economic incentive to increase share value for two reasons. First, managerial compensation, particularly at the top, is usually tied to financial performance in general and oftentimes to share value in particular. For example, managers are frequently given the option to buy stock at a fixed price. The more the stock is worth, the more valuable is this option. The second incentive managers have relates to job prospects. Better performers within the firm will tend to get promoted. More generally, those managers who are successful in pursuing stockholder goals will be in greater demand in the labor market and thus command higher salaries.

In fact, managers who are successful in pursuing stockholder goals can reap enormous rewards. For example, Stephen Case, CEO of America Online, received about $120 million in 1999 alone, which is less than Oprah Winfrey ($150 million), but way more than Britney Spears ($15 million). For the five-year period ending in 1999, Michael D. Eisner of Walt Disney received well over $300 million. However, these numbers pale in comparison to what recently hired execs at Web-related companies have received. For example, including the value of stock options and other items, Margaret Whitman of on-line auctioneer eBay received a total pay package valued (as of March 2000) right at $1 billion!

Control of the Firm   Control of the firm ultimately rests with stockholders. They elect the board of directors, who, in turn, hires and fires management. The mechanism by which unhappy stockholders can act to replace existing management is called a *proxy fight*. A proxy is the authority to vote someone else's stock. A proxy fight develops when a group solicits proxies in order to replace the existing board, and thereby replace existing management.

Another way that management can be replaced is by takeover. Those firms that are poorly managed are more attractive as acquisitions than well-managed firms because a greater profit potential exists. Thus, avoiding a takeover by another firm gives management another incentive to act in the stockholders' interests.

Conclusion   The available theory and evidence are consistent with the view that stockholders control the firm and that stockholder wealth maximization is the relevant goal of the corporation. Even so, there will undoubtedly be times when management goals are pursued at the expense of the stockholders, at least temporarily.

Agency problems are not unique to corporations; they exist whenever there is a separation of ownership and management. This separation is most pronounced in corporations, but it certainly exists in partnerships and proprietorships as well.

Stakeholders

Our discussion thus far implies that management and stockholders are the only parties with an interest in the firm's decisions. This is an oversimplification, of course. Employees, customers, suppliers, and even the government all have a financial interest in the firm.

These various groups are called **stakeholders** in the firm. In general, a stakeholder is someone other than a stockholder or creditor who potentially has a claim on the cash flows of the firm. Such groups will also attempt to exert control over the firm, perhaps to the detriment of the owners.

stakeholder

Someone other than a stockholder or creditor who potentially has a claim on the cash flows of the firm.

1.6 | FINANCIAL MARKETS AND THE CORPORATION

We've seen that the primary advantages of the corporate form of organization are that ownership can be transferred more quickly and easily than with other forms and that money can be raised more readily. Both of these advantages are significantly enhanced by the existence of financial markets, and financial markets play an extremely important role in corporate finance.

Cash Flows to and from the Firm

The interplay between the corporation and the financial markets is illustrated in Figure 1.2. The arrows in Figure 1.2 trace the passage of cash from the financial markets to the firm and from the firm back to the financial markets.

Suppose we start with the firm selling shares of stock and borrowing money to raise cash. Cash flows to the firm from the financial markets (A). The firm invests the cash in current and fixed (or long-term) assets (B). These assets generate some cash (C), some of which goes to pay corporate taxes (D). After taxes are paid, some of this cash flow is reinvested in the firm (E). The rest goes back to the financial markets as cash paid to creditors and shareholders (F).

FIGURE 1.2

Cash flows between the firm and the financial markets

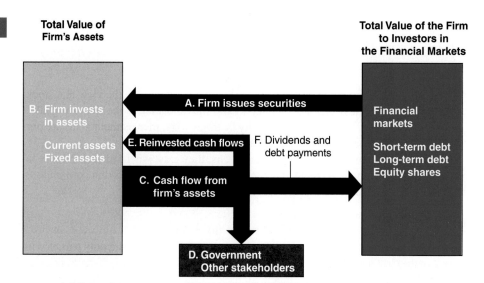

A. Firm issues securities to raise cash.
B. Firm invests in assets.
C. Firm's operations generate cash flow.
D. Cash is paid to government as taxes. Other stakeholders may receive cash.
E. Reinvested cash flows are plowed back into firm.
F. Cash is paid out to investors in the form of interest and dividends.

A financial market, like any market, is just a way of bringing buyers and sellers together. In financial markets, it is debt and equity securities that are bought and sold. Financial markets differ in detail, however. The most important differences concern the types of securities that are traded, how trading is conducted, and who the buyers and sellers are. Some of these differences are discussed next.

Primary versus Secondary Markets

Financial markets function as both primary and secondary markets for debt and equity securities. The term *primary market* refers to the original sale of securities by governments and corporations. The *secondary markets* are those in which these securities are bought and sold after the original sale. Equities are, of course, issued solely by corporations. Debt securities are issued by both governments and corporations. In the discussion that follows, we focus on corporate securities only.

Primary Markets   In a primary-market transaction, the corporation is the seller, and the transaction raises money for the corporation. Corporations engage in two types of primary-market transactions: public offerings and private placements. A public offering, as the name suggests, involves selling securities to the general public, whereas a private placement is a negotiated sale involving a specific buyer.

By law, public offerings of debt and equity must be registered with the Securities and Exchange Commission (SEC). Registration requires the firm to disclose a great deal of information before selling any securities. The accounting, legal, and selling costs of public offerings can be considerable.

Partly to avoid the various regulatory requirements and the expense of public offerings, debt and equity are often sold privately to large financial institutions such as life insurance companies or mutual funds. Such private placements do not have to be registered with the SEC and do not require the involvement of underwriters (investment banks that specialize in selling securities to the public).

Secondary Markets   A secondary-market transaction involves one owner or creditor selling to another. It is therefore the secondary markets that provide the means for transferring ownership of corporate securities. Although a corporation is only directly involved in a primary-market transaction (when it sells securities to raise cash), the secondary markets are still critical to large corporations. The reason is that investors are much more willing to purchase securities in a primary-market transaction when they know that those securities can later be resold if desired.

Dealer versus auction markets   There are two kinds of secondary markets: *auction* markets and *dealer* markets. Generally speaking, dealers buy and sell for themselves, at their own risk. A car dealer, for example, buys and sells automobiles. In contrast, brokers and agents match buyers and sellers, but they do not actually own the commodity that is bought or sold. A real estate agent, for example, does not normally buy and sell houses.

Dealer markets in stocks and long-term debt are called *over-the-counter* (OTC) markets. Most trading in debt securities takes place over the counter. The expression *over the counter* refers to days of old when securities were literally bought and sold at counters in offices around the country. Today, a significant fraction of the market for stocks and almost all of the market for long-term debt have no central location; the many dealers are connected electronically.

Auction markets differ from dealer markets in two ways. First, an auction market, or exchange, has a physical location (like Wall Street). Second, in a dealer market, most of the buying and selling is done by the dealer. The primary purpose of an auction market, on the other hand, is to match those who wish to sell with those who wish to buy. Dealers play a limited role.

Trading in corporate securities The equity shares of most of the large firms in the United States trade in organized auction markets. The largest such market is the New York Stock Exchange (NYSE), which accounts for more than 85 percent of all the shares traded in auction markets. Other auction exchanges include the American Stock Exchange (AMEX) and regional exchanges such as the Pacific Stock Exchange.

In addition to the stock exchanges, there is a large OTC market for stocks. In 1971, the National Association of Securities Dealers (NASD) made available to dealers and brokers an electronic quotation system called NASDAQ (NASD Automated Quotations system, pronounced "naz-dak" and now spelled "Nasdaq"). There are roughly three times as many companies on Nasdaq as there are on NYSE, but they tend to be much smaller in size and trade less actively. There are exceptions, of course. Both Microsoft and Intel trade OTC, for example. Nonetheless, the total value of Nasdaq stocks is significantly less than the total value of NYSE stocks.

There are many large and important financial markets outside the United States, of course, and U.S. corporations are increasingly looking to these markets to raise cash. The Tokyo Stock Exchange and the London Stock Exchange (TSE and LSE, respectively) are two well-known examples. The fact that OTC markets have no physical location means that national borders do not present a great barrier, and there is now a huge international OTC debt market. Because of globalization, financial markets have reached the point where trading in many instruments never stops; it just travels around the world.

Listing Stocks that trade on an organized exchange are said to be *listed* on that exchange. In order to be listed, firms must meet certain minimum criteria concerning, for example, asset size and number of shareholders. These criteria differ for different exchanges.

NYSE has the most stringent requirements of the exchanges in the United States. For example, to be listed on NYSE, a company is expected to have a market value for its publicly held shares of at least $60 million and a total of at least 2,000 shareholders with at least 100 shares each. There are additional minimums on earnings, assets, and number of shares outstanding.

CONCEPT QUESTIONS

1.6a What is a dealer market? How do dealer and auction markets differ?

1.6b What is the largest auction market in the United States?

1.6c What does *OTC* stand for? What is the large OTC market for stocks called?

SUMMARY AND CONCLUSIONS

This chapter has introduced you to some of the basic ideas in business finance. In it, we saw that:

1. Business finance has three main areas of concern:
   a. Capital budgeting. What long-term investments should the firm take?
   b. Capital structure. Where will the firm get the long-term financing to pay for its investments? In other words, what mixture of debt and equity should we use to fund our operations?

    c. Working capital management. How should the firm manage its everyday financial activities?

2. The goal of financial management in a for-profit business is to make decisions that increase the value of the stock, or, more generally, increase the market value of the equity.

3. The corporate form of organization is superior to other forms when it comes to raising money and transferring ownership interests, but it has the significant disadvantage of double taxation.

4. There is the possibility of conflicts between stockholders and management in a large corporation. We called these conflicts agency problems and discussed how they might be controlled and reduced.

Of the topics we've discussed thus far, the most important is the goal of financial management. Throughout the text, we will be analyzing many different financial decisions, but we always ask the same question: How does the decision under consideration affect the value of the equity in the firm?

CRITICAL THINKING AND CONCEPTS REVIEW

1. **The Financial Management Decision Process.** What are the three types of financial management decisions? For each type of decision, give an example of a business transaction that would be relevant.

2. **Sole Proprietorships and Partnerships.** What are the four primary disadvantages to the sole proprietorship and partnership forms of business organization? What benefits are there to these types of business organization as opposed to the corporate form?

3. **Corporations.** What is the primary disadvantage of the corporate form of organization? Name at least two of the advantages of corporate organization.

4. **Corporate Finance Organization.** In a large corporation, what are the two distinct groups that report to the chief financial officer? Which group is the focus of corporate finance?

5. **Goal of Financial Management.** What goal should always motivate the actions of the firm's financial manager?

6. **Agency Problems.** Who owns a corporation? Describe the process whereby the owners control the firm's management. What is the main reason that an agency relationship exists in the corporate form of organization? In this context, what kinds of problems can arise?

7. **Primary versus Secondary Markets.** You've probably noticed coverage in the financial press of an initial public offering (IPO) of a company's securities. Is an IPO a primary-market transaction or a secondary-market transaction?

8. **Auction versus Dealer Markets.** What does it mean when we say the New York Stock Exchange is an auction market? How are auction markets different from dealer markets? What kind of market is Nasdaq?

9. **Not-for-Profit Firm Goals.** Suppose you were the financial manager of a not-for-profit business (a not-for-profit hospital, perhaps). What kinds of goals do you think would be appropriate?

10. **Ethics and Firm Goals.** Can our goal of maximizing the value of the stock conflict with other goals, such as avoiding unethical or illegal behavior? In particular, do you think subjects like customer and employee safety, the environment, and the general good of society fit in this framework, or are they essentially ignored? Try to think of some specific scenarios to illustrate your answer.

11. **International Firm Goal.**   Would our goal of maximizing the value of the stock be different if we were thinking about financial management in a foreign country? Why or why not?

12. **Agency Problems.**   Suppose you own stock in a company. The current price per share is $25. Another company has just announced that it wants to buy your company and will pay $35 per share to acquire all the outstanding stock. Your company's management immediately begins fighting off this hostile bid. Is management acting in the shareholders' best interests? Why or why not?

13. **Agency Problems and Corporate Ownership.**   Corporate ownership varies around the world. Historically, individuals have owned the majority of shares in public corporations in the United States. In Germany and Japan, however, banks, other large financial institutions, and other companies own most of the stock in public corporations. Do you think agency problems are likely to be more or less severe in Germany and Japan than in the United States? Why? In recent years, large financial institutions such as mutual funds and pension funds have been becoming the dominant owners of stock in the United States, and these institutions are becoming more active in corporate affairs. What are the implications of this trend for agency problems and corporate control?

14. **Executive Compensation.**   Critics have charged that compensation to top management in the United States is simply too high and should be cut back. For example, focusing on large corporations, Jack F. Welch Jr. of GE (also known as "Neutron Jack") has been one of the best-compensated CEOs in the United States, earning about $40 million in 1997 alone and $100 million over the 1993–97 period. Are such amounts excessive? In answering, it might be helpful to recognize that superstar athletes such as Tiger Woods, top entertainers such as Tim Allen and Oprah Winfrey, and many others at the top of their respective fields earn at least as much, if not a great deal more.

CHAPTER 2

Financial Statements, Taxes, and Cash Flow

THERE ARE BASICALLY FOUR THINGS THAT YOU SHOULD BE CLEAR ON WHEN YOU HAVE FINISHED STUDYING THIS CHAPTER:

- The difference between accounting value (or "book" value) and market value

- The difference between accounting income and cash flow

- The difference between average and marginal tax rates

- How to determine a firm's cash flow from its financial statements.

WHEN EXACTLY is revenue revenue? It used to be easy to tell, but lately it's become downright dot-complicated! Consider, for example, priceline.com, the on-line service that lets consumers bid their own price for airline tickets, car rentals, hotel rooms, and the like. Priceline takes on-line bids from consumers and, if a bid fits the seller's requirements, fills the order by buying the good or service and immediately reselling it to the bidder. Here is where it gets interesting: Although priceline.com might own the item for no more than a nanosecond, it records the entire price paid by the customer as revenue. Of course, it also records the cost of the item sold as a cost of the sale, but in the world of Internet stocks, where revenue growth seems to matter a great deal, the practice certainly should give investors pause.

Priceline is not alone, however, in employing what some view as questionable accounting practices. Healtheon/WebMD, the Internet health company, provides content for "health channels" in return for a portion of the advertising revenues generated by the sites. But, by prearranged agreement, Healtheon then turns right around and pays a sizable chunk of the advertising money it receives back to its partner in the form of commissions. Healtheon books all of the money coming in as revenue even though part of it has been previously committed for return to the site owner. VerticalNet, another Internet-based company, routinely books revenue from barter transactions even though the transactions are essentially swaps of goods or services and no cash actually changes hands.

These examples are troublesome because they seem to suggest that a company's financial performance depends on accounting decisions; but, as we will see, this is not true. Instead, this chapter shows that underneath all the accounting numbers lurks the financial truth. Our job is to uncover that truth by examining the all-important substance known as *cash flow*.

I n this chapter, we examine financial statements, taxes, and cash flow. Our emphasis is not on preparing financial statements. Instead, we recognize that financial statements are frequently a key source of information for financial decisions, so our goal is to briefly examine such statements and point out some of their more relevant features. We pay special attention to some of the practical details of cash flow.

As you read, pay particular attention to two important differences: (1) the difference between accounting value and market value, and (2) the difference between accounting income and cash flow. These distinctions will be important throughout the book.

2.1 | THE BALANCE SHEET

The **balance sheet** is a snapshot of the firm. It is a convenient means of organizing and summarizing what a firm owns (its *assets*), what a firm owes (its *liabilities*), and the difference between the two (the firm's *equity*) at a given point in time. Figure 2.1 illustrates how the balance sheet is constructed. As shown, the left-hand side lists the assets of the firm, and the right-hand side lists the liabilities and equity.

Assets: The Left-Hand Side

Assets are classified as either *current* or *fixed*. A fixed asset is one that has a relatively long life. Fixed assets can either be *tangible,* such as a truck or a computer, or *intangible,* such as a trademark or patent. A current asset has a life of less than one year. This means that the asset will normally convert to cash within 12 months. For example, inventory would normally be purchased and sold within a year and is thus classified as a current asset. Obviously, cash itself is a current asset. Accounts receivable (money owed to the firm by its customers) is also a current asset.

Liabilities and Owners' Equity: The Right-Hand Side

balance sheet
Financial statement showing a firm's accounting value on a particular date.

The firm's liabilities are the first thing listed on the right-hand side of the balance sheet. These are classified as either *current* or *long-term.* Current liabilities, like current assets, have a life of less than one year (meaning they must be paid within the year), and they are listed before long-term liabilities. Accounts payable (money the firm owes to its suppliers) is one example of a current liability.

FIGURE 2.1

The balance sheet. Left side: Total value of assets. Right side: Total value of liabilities and shareholders' equity.

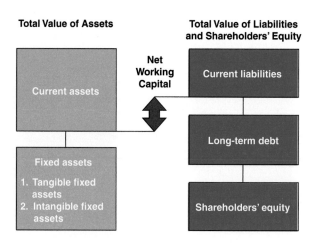

A debt that is not due in the coming year is classified as a long-term liability. A loan that the firm will pay off in five years is one such long-term debt. Firms borrow over the long term from a variety of sources. We will tend to use the terms *bonds* and *bondholders* generically to refer to long-term debt and long-term creditors, respectively.

Finally, by definition, the difference between the total value of the assets (current and fixed) and the total value of the liabilities (current and long-term) is the *shareholders' equity,* also called *common equity* or *owners' equity.* This feature of the balance sheet is intended to reflect the fact that, if the firm were to sell all of its assets and use the money to pay off its debts, then whatever residual value remained would belong to the shareholders. So, the balance sheet "balances" because the value of the left-hand side always equals the value of the right-hand side. That is, the value of the firm's assets is equal to the sum of its liabilities and shareholders' equity:[1]

$$\text{Assets} = \text{Liabilities} + \text{Shareholders' equity} \qquad [2.1]$$

This is the balance sheet identity, or equation, and it always holds because shareholders' equity is defined as the difference between assets and liabilities.

Net Working Capital

As shown in Figure 2.1, the difference between a firm's current assets and its current liabilities is called **net working capital**. Net working capital is positive when current assets exceed current liabilities. Based on the definitions of current assets and current liabilities, this means that the cash that will become available over the next 12 months exceeds the cash that must be paid over that same period. For this reason, net working capital is usually positive in a healthy firm.

net working capital
Current assets less current liabilities.

Building the Balance Sheet | EXAMPLE 2.1

A firm has current assets of $100, net fixed assets of $500, short-term debt of $70, and long-term debt of $200. What does the balance sheet look like? What is shareholders' equity? What is net working capital?

In this case, total assets are $100 + 500 = $600 and total liabilities are $70 + 200 = $270, so shareholders' equity is the difference: $600 − 270 = $330. The balance sheet would thus look like:

Assets		Liabilities and Shareholders' Equity	
Current assets	$100	Current liabilities	$ 70
Net fixed assets	500	Long-term debt	200
		Shareholders' equity	330
		Total liabilities and	
Total assets	$600	shareholders' equity	$600

Net working capital is the difference between current assets and current liabilities, or $100 − 70 = $30.

Table 2.1 shows a simplified balance sheet for the fictitious U.S. Corporation. There are three particularly important things to keep in mind when examining a balance sheet: liquidity, debt versus equity, and market value versus book value.

---

[1]The terms *owners' equity, shareholders' equity,* and *stockholders' equity* are used interchangeably to refer to the equity in a corporation. The term *net worth* is also used. Variations exist in addition to these.

U.S. CORPORATION Balance Sheets as of December 31, 1999 and 2000 ($ In Millions)					
	1999	2000		1999	2000
Assets			**Liabilities and Owners' Equity**		
Current assets			Current liabilities		
Cash	$ 104	$ 160	Accounts payable	$ 232	$ 266
Accounts receivable	455	688	Notes payable	196	123
Inventory	553	555	Total	$ 428	$ 389
Total	$1,112	$1,403			
Fixed assets					
Net fixed assets	$1,644	$1,709	Long-term debt	$ 408	$ 454
			Owners' equity		
			Common stock and paid-in surplus	600	640
			Retained earnings	1,320	1,629
			Total	$1,920	$2,269
			Total liabilities and		
Total assets	$2,756	$3,112	owners' equity	$2,756	$3,112

Liquidity

Liquidity refers to the speed and ease with which an asset can be converted to cash. Gold is a relatively liquid asset; a custom manufacturing facility is not. Liquidity really has two dimensions: ease of conversion versus loss of value. Any asset can be converted to cash quickly if we cut the price enough. A highly liquid asset is therefore one that can be quickly sold without significant loss of value. An illiquid asset is one that cannot be quickly converted to cash without a substantial price reduction.

Assets are normally listed on the balance sheet in order of decreasing liquidity, meaning that the most liquid assets are listed first. Current assets are relatively liquid and include cash and those assets that we expect to convert to cash over the next 12 months. Accounts receivable, for example, represent amounts not yet collected from customers on sales already made. Naturally, we hope these will convert to cash in the near future. Inventory is probably the least liquid of the current assets, at least for many businesses.

Fixed assets are, for the most part, relatively illiquid. These consist of tangible things such as buildings and equipment that don't convert to cash at all in normal business activity (they are, of course, used in the business to generate cash). Intangible assets, such as a trademark, have no physical existence but can be very valuable. Like tangible fixed assets, they won't ordinarily convert to cash and are generally considered illiquid.

Liquidity is valuable. The more liquid a business is, the less likely it is to experience financial distress (that is, difficulty in paying debts or buying needed assets). Unfortunately, liquid assets are generally less profitable to hold. For example, cash holdings are the most liquid of all investments, but they sometimes earn no return at all—they just sit there. There is therefore a trade-off between the advantages of liquidity and forgone potential profits.

Debt versus Equity

To the extent that a firm borrows money, it usually gives first claim to the firm's cash flow to creditors. Equity holders are only entitled to the residual value, the portion left after creditors are paid. The value of this residual portion is the shareholders' equity in the firm, which is just the value of the firm's assets less the value of the firm's liabilities:

Shareholders' equity = Assets − Liabilities

This is true in an accounting sense because shareholders' equity is defined as this residual portion. More importantly, it is true in an economic sense: If the firm sells its assets and pays its debts, whatever cash is left belongs to the shareholders.

The use of debt in a firm's capital structure is called *financial leverage.* The more debt a firm has (as a percentage of assets), the greater is its degree of financial leverage. As we discuss in later chapters, debt acts like a lever in the sense that using it can greatly magnify both gains and losses. So financial leverage increases the potential reward to shareholders, but it also increases the potential for financial distress and business failure.

Market Value versus Book Value

The true value of any asset is its *market* value, which is simply the amount of cash we would get if we actually sold it. In contrast, the values shown on the balance sheet for the firm's assets are *book values* and generally are not what the assets are actually worth. Under **Generally Accepted Accounting Principles (GAAP),** audited financial statements in the United States generally show assets at *historical cost.* In other words, assets are "carried on the books" at what the firm paid for them, no matter how long ago they were purchased or how much they are worth today.

Generally Accepted Accounting Principles (GAAP)
The common set of standards and procedures by which audited financial statements are prepared.

For current assets, market value and book value might be somewhat similar since current assets are bought and converted into cash over a relatively short span of time. In other circumstances, they might differ quite a bit. Moreover, for fixed assets, it would be purely a coincidence if the actual market value of an asset (what the asset could be sold for) were equal to its book value. For example, a railroad might own enormous tracts of land purchased a century or more ago. What the railroad paid for that land could be hundreds or thousands of times less than what it is worth today. The balance sheet would nonetheless show the historical cost.

Managers and investors will frequently be interested in knowing the market value of the firm. This information is not on the balance sheet. The fact that balance sheet assets are listed at cost means that there is no necessary connection between the total assets shown and the market value of the firm. Indeed, many of the most valuable assets that a firm might have—good management, a good reputation, talented employees—don't appear on the balance sheet at all.

Similarly, the owners' equity figure on the balance sheet and the true market value of the equity need not be related. For financial managers, then, the accounting value of the equity is not an especially important concern; it is the market value that matters. Henceforth, whenever we speak of the value of an asset or the value of the firm, we will normally mean its *market value.* So, for example, when we say the goal of the financial manager is to increase the value of the stock, we mean the market value of the stock.

Market versus Book Values | **EXAMPLE 2.2**

The Klingon Corporation has fixed assets with a book value of $700 and an appraised market value of about $1,000. Net working capital is $400 on the books, but approximately $600 would be realized if all the current accounts were liquidated. Klingon has $500 in long-term debt, both book value and market value. What is the book value of the equity? What is the market value?

We can construct two simplified balance sheets, one in accounting (book value) terms and one in economic (market value) terms:

			KLINGON CORPORATION Balance Sheets Market Value versus Book Value			
	Book	**Market**		**Book**	**Market**
Assets			**Liabilities and Shareholders' Equity**		
Net working capital	$ 400	$ 600	Long-term debt	$ 500	$ 500
Net fixed assets	700	1,000	Shareholders' equity	600	1,100
	$1,100	$1,600		$1,100	$1,600

In this example, shareholders' equity is actually worth almost twice as much as what is shown on the books. The distinction between book and market values is important precisely because book values can be so different from true economic value.

CONCEPT QUESTIONS

2.1a What is the balance sheet identity?

2.1b What is liquidity? Why is it important?

2.1c What do we mean by financial leverage?

2.1d Explain the difference between accounting value and market value. Which is more important to the financial manager? Why?

2.2 | THE INCOME STATEMENT

The **income statement** measures performance over some period of time, usually a quarter or a year. The income statement equation is:

$$\text{Revenues} - \text{Expenses} = \text{Income} \qquad [2.2]$$

income statement
Financial statement summarizing a firm's performance over a period of time.

If you think of the balance sheet as a snapshot, then you can think of the income statement as a video recording covering the period between a before and an after picture. Table 2.2 gives a simplified income statement for U.S. Corporation.

The first thing reported on an income statement would usually be revenue and expenses from the firm's principal operations. Subsequent parts include, among other things, financing expenses such as interest paid. Taxes paid are reported separately. The last item is *net income* (the so-called bottom line). Net income is often expressed on a per-share basis and called *earnings per share (EPS)*.

As indicated, U.S. paid cash dividends of $103. The difference between net income and cash dividends, $309, is the addition to retained earnings for the year. This amount is added to the cumulative retained earnings account on the balance sheet. If you'll look back at the two balance sheets for U.S. Corporation, you'll see that retained earnings did go up by this amount, $1,320 + 309 = $1,629.

EXAMPLE 2.3 | Earnings and Dividends per Share

Suppose U.S. had 200 million shares outstanding at the end of 1998. Based on the income statement above, what was EPS? What were dividends per share?

TABLE 2.2

Income statement for
U.S. Corporation

U.S. CORPORATION 1998 Income Statement ($ in Millions)		
Net sales		$1,509
Cost of goods sold		750
Depreciation		65
Earnings before interest and taxes		$ 694
Interest paid		70
Taxable income		$ 624
Taxes		212
Net income		$ 412
Dividends	$103	
Addition to retained earnings	309	

From the income statement, U.S. had a net income of $412 million for the year. Total dividends were $103 million. Since 200 million shares were outstanding, we can calculate earnings per share and dividends per share as follows:

$$\text{Earnings per share} = \text{Net income/Total shares outstanding}$$
$$= \$412/200 = \$2.06 \text{ per share}$$
$$\text{Dividends per share} = \text{Total dividends/Total shares outstanding}$$
$$= \$103/200 = \$.515 \text{ per share}$$

When looking at an income statement, the financial manager needs to keep three things in mind: GAAP, cash versus noncash items, and time and costs.

GAAP and the Income Statement

An income statement prepared using GAAP will show revenue when it accrues. This is not necessarily when the cash comes in. The general rule (the realization principle) is to recognize revenue when the earnings process is virtually complete and the value of an exchange of goods or services is known or can be reliably determined. In practice, this principle usually means that revenue is recognized at the time of sale, which need not be the same as the time of collection.

Expenses shown on the income statement are based on the matching principle. The basic idea here is to first determine revenues as described above and then match those revenues with the costs associated with producing them. So, if we manufacture a product and then sell it on credit, the revenue is realized at the time of sale. The production and other costs associated with the sale of that product would likewise be recognized at that time. Once again, the actual cash outflows may have occurred at some very different times.

As a result of the way revenues and expenses are reported, the figures shown on the income statement may not be at all representative of the actual cash inflows and outflows that occurred during a particular period. The accompanying **Reality Bytes** box illustrates just how important the difference can be.

Noncash Items

A primary reason that accounting income differs from cash flow is that an income statement contains **noncash items.** The most important of these is *depreciation.* Suppose a

noncash items
Expenses charged against revenues that do not directly affect cash flow, such as depreciation.

A BITTER PILL FOR MCKESSON'S STOCKHOLDERS

Want to know a quick way to eliminate $9 billion worth of the market value of your company's stock? It's easy; just write off about $42 million in sales as being of questionable quality. While no company aspires to doing such a thing, that's exactly what happened at McKesson HBOC Inc., the big health care supply management and information technology company, at the end of April 1999.

McKesson's tale of woe dates back to its acquisition three months earlier of HBO & Co., a health care information management business, for $12 billion in stock. While many investors panned the acquisition, citing the lack of available synergies between the two companies, none anticipated the bad news that was to come. A major consideration in the acquisition price was the rapid growth in sales at HBO. Sales growth had recently been very strong, with what one analyst called "a string of remarkable quarters."

All of that came crashing down in April, however. At issue were sales contracts for software HBO provided to hospitals and doctors for tracking finances, clinical outcomes, and similar items. The sales were apparently booked in full at the time they were contracted despite the fact that the contracts contained contingencies that hadn't yet been met. Although McKesson believed the contingencies would eventually be removed, it conceded that, until they were, the sales should not have been recorded as revenue. In fact, the restatement of these sales effectively cut in half the sales growth from these types of contracts for HBO for the previous year.

The ultimate disposition of these sales is instructive because it emphasizes the differences between accounting income and cash flow and what investors think of the two. The contracts were booked as sales even though the company might never receive a bit of the cash it expected from the contracts. Investors did not take the news well. When the company restated its earnings for the previous quarter and then slashed its profit projection for the coming fiscal year from $3 a share to $2.50 per share, stockholders voted with their feet, ultimately trimming the stock price by 48 percent, from $65.75 down to $34.50. That's fully 75 percent of the value of the acquisition cost of HBO in the first place. However, investors weren't done yet, as the value of the company's stock further declined to below $19 a share in early 2000. As this example makes clear, not all sales are cash inflows and investors know the difference when confronted with the discrepancies between the two.

firm purchases a fixed asset for $5,000 and pays in cash. Obviously, the firm has a $5,000 cash outflow at the time of purchase. However, instead of deducting the $5,000 as an expense, an accountant might depreciate the asset over a five-year period.

If the depreciation is straight-line and the asset is written down to zero over that period, then $5,000/5 = $1,000 would be deducted each year as an expense.[2] The important thing to recognize is that this $1,000 deduction isn't cash—it's an accounting number. The actual cash outflow occurred when the asset was purchased.

The depreciation deduction is simply another application of the matching principle in accounting. The revenues associated with an asset would generally occur over some length of time. So the accountant seeks to match the expense of purchasing the asset with the benefits produced from owning it.

As we will see, for the financial manager, the actual timing of cash inflows and outflows is critical in coming up with a reasonable estimate of market value, so we need to learn how to separate the cash flows from the noncash accounting entries.

---

[2]By "straight-line," we mean that the depreciation deduction is the same every year. By "written down to zero," we mean that the asset is assumed to have no value at the end of five years.

Time and Costs

It is often useful to think of the future as having two distinct parts: the short run and the long run. These are not precise time periods. The distinction has to do with whether costs are fixed or variable. In the long run, all business costs are variable. Given sufficient time, assets can be sold, debts can be paid, and so on.

If our time horizon is relatively short, however, some costs are effectively fixed—they must be paid no matter what (property taxes, for example). Other costs such as wages to laborers and payments to suppliers are still variable. As a result, even in the short run, the firm can vary its output level by varying expenditures in these areas.

The distinction between fixed and variable costs is important, at times, to the financial manager, but the way costs are reported on the income statement is not a good guide as to which costs are which. The reason is that, in practice, accountants tend to classify costs as either product costs or period costs.

Product costs include such things as raw materials, direct labor expense, and manufacturing overhead. These are reported on the income statement as costs of goods sold, but they include both fixed and variable costs. Similarly, period costs are incurred during a particular time period and might be reported as selling, general, and administrative expenses. Once again, some of these period costs may be fixed and others may be variable. The company president's salary, for example, is a period cost and is probably fixed, at least in the short run.

CONCEPT QUESTIONS

2.2a What is the income statement equation?

2.2b What are the three things to keep in mind when looking at an income statement?

2.2c Why is accounting income not the same as cash flow?

TAXES | 2.3

Taxes can be one of the largest cash outflows that a firm experiences. The size of the tax bill is determined through the tax code, an often amended set of rules. In this section, we examine corporate tax rates and how taxes are calculated. Taxes for partnerships and proprietorships are computed using the personal income tax schedules; we don't discuss these here, but the general procedures are the same as for corporate taxes.

If the various rules of taxation seem a little bizarre or convoluted to you, keep in mind that the tax code is the result of political, not economic, forces. As a result, there is no reason why it has to make economic sense.

Corporate Tax Rates

Corporate tax rates in effect for 2000 are shown in Table 2.3. A peculiar feature is that corporate tax rates are not strictly increasing. As shown, corporate tax rates rise from 15 percent to 39 percent, but they drop back to 34 percent on income over $335,000. They then rise to 38 percent and subsequently fall to 35 percent.

According to the originators of the current tax rules, there are only four corporate rates: 15 percent, 25 percent, 34 percent, and 35 percent. The 38 and 39 percent brackets arise because of "surcharges" applied on top of the 34 and 35 percent rates. A tax is a tax is a tax, however, so there are really six corporate tax brackets, as we have shown.

TABLE 2.3

Corporate tax rates

Taxable Income	Tax Rate
$ 0– 50,000	15%
50,001– 75,000	25
75,001– 100,000	34
100,001– 335,000	39
335,001–10,000,000	34
10,000,001–15,000,000	35
15,000,001–18,333,333	38
18,333,334+	35

Average versus Marginal Tax Rates

average tax rate
Total taxes paid divided by total taxable income.

In making financial decisions, it is frequently important to distinguish between average and marginal tax rates. Your **average tax rate** is your tax bill divided by your taxable income, in other words, the percentage of your income that goes to pay taxes. Your **marginal tax rate** is the extra tax you would pay if you earned one more dollar. The percentage tax rates shown in Table 2.3 are all marginal rates. Put another way, the tax rates in Table 2.3 apply to the part of income in the indicated range only, not all income.

marginal tax rate
Amount of tax payable on the next dollar earned.

The difference between average and marginal tax rates can best be illustrated with a simple example. Suppose our corporation has a taxable income of $200,000. What is the tax bill? From Table 2.3, we can figure our tax bill as:

$$.15(\$\ 50,000) \qquad\quad = \$\ 7,500$$
$$.25(\$\ 75,000 - 50,000) \ = \quad 6,250$$
$$.34(\$100,000 - 75,000) \ = \quad 8,500$$
$$.39(\$200,000 - 100,000) = \underline{\quad 39,000}$$
$$\underline{\$61,250}$$

Our total tax is thus $61,250.

In our example, what is the average tax rate? We had a taxable income of $200,000 and a tax bill of $61,250, so the average tax rate is $61,250/200,000 = 30.625%. What is the marginal tax rate? If we made one more dollar, the tax on that dollar would be 39 cents, so our marginal rate is 39 percent.

EXAMPLE 2.4 | **Deep in the Heart of Taxes**

Algernon, Inc., has a taxable income of $85,000. What is its tax bill? What is its average tax rate? Its marginal tax rate?

From Table 2.3, the tax rate applied to the first $50,000 is 15 percent; the rate applied to the next $25,000 is 25 percent; and the rate applied after that up to $100,000 is 34 percent. So Algernon must pay .15 × $50,000 + .25 × 25,000 + .34 × (85,000 − 75,000) = $17,150. The average tax rate is thus $17,150/85,000 = 20.18%. The marginal rate is 34 percent since Algernon's taxes would rise by 34 cents if it had another dollar in taxable income.

Table 2.4 summarizes some different taxable incomes, marginal tax rates, and average tax rates for corporations. Notice how the average and marginal tax rates come together at 35 percent.

(1) **Taxable Income**	(2) **Tax Rate**	(3) **Total Tax**	(3)/(1) **Average Tax Rate**
$ 45,000	15%	$ 6,750	15.00%
70,000	25	12,500	17.86
95,000	34	20,550	21.63
250,000	39	80,750	32.30
1,000,000	34	340,000	34.00
17,500,000	38	6,100,000	34.86
50,000,000	35	17,500,000	35.00
100,000,000	35	35,000,000	35.00

TABLE 2.4

Corporate taxes and tax rates

With a *flat-rate* tax, there is only one tax rate, and this rate is the same for all income levels. With such a tax, the marginal tax rate is always the same as the average tax rate. As it stands now, corporate taxation in the United States is based on a modified flat-rate tax, which becomes a true flat rate for the highest incomes.

In looking at Table 2.4, notice that the more a corporation makes, the greater is the percentage of taxable income paid in taxes. Put another way, under current tax law, the average tax rate never goes down, even though the marginal tax rate does. As illustrated, for corporations, average tax rates begin at 15 percent and rise to a maximum of 35 percent.

It will normally be the marginal tax rate that is relevant for financial decision making. The reason is that any new cash flows will be taxed at that marginal rate. Since financial decisions usually involve new cash flows or changes in existing ones, this rate will tell us the marginal effect on our tax bill.

There is one last thing to notice about the tax code as it affects corporations. It's easy to verify that the corporate tax bill is just a flat 35 percent of taxable income if our taxable income is more than $18.33 million. Also, for the many midsize corporations with taxable incomes in the $335,000 to $10,000,000 range, the tax rate is a flat 34 percent. Since we will usually be talking about large corporations, you can assume that the average and marginal tax rates are 35 percent unless we explicitly say otherwise.

CONCEPT QUESTIONS

2.3a What is the difference between a marginal and an average tax rate?

2.3b Do the wealthiest corporations receive a tax break in terms of a lower tax rate?
Explain.

CASH FLOW | 2.4

At this point, we are ready to discuss perhaps one of the most important pieces of financial information that can be gleaned from financial statements: *cash flow*. By cash flow, we simply mean the difference between the number of dollars that came in and the number that went out. For example, if you were the owner of a business, you might be very interested in how much cash you actually took out of your business in a given year. How to determine this amount is one of the things we discuss next.

There is no standard financial statement that presents this information in the way that we wish. We will therefore discuss how to calculate cash flow for U.S. Corporation and point out how the result differs from that of standard financial statement calculations. Important note: there is a standard financial accounting statement called the *statement of cash flows,* but it is concerned with a somewhat different issue that should not be confused with what is discussed in this section.

From the balance sheet identity, we know that the value of a firm's assets is equal to the value of its liabilities plus the value of its equity. Similarly, the cash flow from the firm's assets must equal the sum of the cash flow to creditors and the cash flow to stockholders (or owners, if the business is not a corporation):

$$\text{Cash flow from assets} = \text{Cash flow to creditors}$$
$$+ \text{Cash flow to stockholders} \qquad [2.3]$$

This is the cash flow identity. What it reflects is the fact that a firm generates cash through its various activities, and that cash is either used to pay creditors or else is paid out to the owners of the firm. We discuss the various things that make up these cash flows next.

Cash Flow from Assets

cash flow from assets

The total of cash flow to creditors and cash flow to stockholders, consisting of the following: operating cash flow, capital spending, and changes in net working capital.

Cash flow from assets involves three components: operating cash flow, capital spending, and change in net working capital. **Operating cash flow** refers to the cash flow that results from the firm's day-to-day activities of producing and selling. Expenses associated with the firm's financing of its assets are not included since they are not operating expenses.

In the normal course of events, some portion of the firm's cash flow is reinvested in the firm. *Capital spending* refers to the net spending on fixed assets (purchases of fixed assets less sales of fixed assets). Finally, *the change in net working capital* is the amount spent on net working capital. It is measured as the change in net working capital over the period being examined and represents the net increase in current assets over current liabilities. The three components of cash flow are examined in more detail below. In all our examples, all amounts are in millions of dollars.

operating cash flow

Cash generated from a firm's normal business activities.

Operating Cash Flow   To calculate operating cash flow (OCF), we want to calculate revenues minus costs, but we don't want to include depreciation since it's not a cash outflow, and we don't want to include interest because it's a financing expense. We do want to include taxes, because taxes are, unfortunately, paid in cash.

If we look at U.S. Corporation's income statement (Table 2.2), we see that earnings before interest and taxes (EBIT) are $694. This is almost what we want since it doesn't include interest paid. We need to make two adjustments. First, recall that depreciation is a noncash expense. To get cash flow, we first add back the $65 in depreciation since it wasn't a cash deduction. The other adjustment is to subtract the $212 in taxes since these were paid in cash. The result is operating cash flow:

U.S. CORPORATION
2000 Operating Cash Flow

Earnings before interest and taxes	$ 694
+ Depreciation	65
− Taxes	212
Operating cash flow	$ 547

U.S. Corporation thus had a 2000 operating cash flow of $547.

Operating cash flow is an important number because it tells us, on a very basic level, whether or not a firm's cash inflows from its business operations are sufficient to cover its everyday cash outflows. For this reason, a negative operating cash flow is often a sign of trouble.

There is an unpleasant possibility for confusion when we speak of operating cash flow. In accounting practice, operating cash flow is often defined as net income plus depreciation. For U.S. Corporation, this would amount to $412 + 65 = $477. The accounting definition of operating cash flow differs from ours in one important way: Interest is deducted when net income is computed. Notice that the difference between the $547 operating cash flow we calculated and this $477 is $70, the amount of interest paid for the year. This definition of cash flow thus considers interest paid to be an operating expense. Our definition treats it properly as a financing expense. If there were no interest expense, the two definitions would be the same.

To finish our calculation of cash flow from assets for U.S. Corporation, we need to consider how much of the $547 operating cash flow was reinvested in the firm. We consider spending on fixed assets first.

Capital Spending Net capital spending is just money spent on fixed assets less money received from the sale of fixed assets. At the end of 1999, net fixed assets for U.S. Corporation (Table 2.1) were $1,644. During the year, we wrote off (depreciated) $65 worth of fixed assets on the income statement. So, if we didn't purchase any new fixed assets, net fixed assets would have been $1,644 − 65 = $1,579 at year's end. The 2000 balance sheet shows $1,709 in net fixed assets, so we must have spent a total of $1,709 − 1,579 = $130 on fixed assets during the year:

Ending net fixed assets	$1,709
− Beginning net fixed assets	1,644
+ Depreciation	65
Net investment in fixed assets	$ 130

This $130 is our net capital spending for 2000.

Could net capital spending be negative? The answer is yes. This would happen if the firm sold off more assets than it purchased. The *net* here refers to purchases of fixed assets net of any sales of fixed assets.

Change in Net Working Capital In addition to investing in fixed assets, a firm will also invest in current assets. For example, going back to the balance sheet in Table 2.1, we see that at the end of 2000, U.S. had current assets of $1,403. At the end of 1999, current assets were $1,112, so, during the year, U.S. invested $1,403 − 1,112 = $291 in current assets.

As the firm changes its investment in current assets, its current liabilities will usually change as well. To determine the change in net working capital, the easiest approach is just to take the difference between the beginning and ending net working capital (NWC) figures. Net working capital at the end of 2000 was $1,403 − 389 = $1,014. Similarly, at the end of 1999, net working capital was $1,112 − 428 = $684. So, given these figures, we have:

Ending NWC	$1,014
− Beginning NWC	684
Change in NWC	$ 330

Net working capital thus increased by $330. Put another way, U.S. Corporation had a net investment of $330 in NWC for the year.

Conclusion   Given the figures we've come up with, we're ready to calculate cash flow from assets. The total cash flow from assets is given by operating cash flow less the amounts invested in fixed assets and net working capital. So, for U.S., we have:

U.S. CORPORATION
2000 Cash Flow from Assets

Operating cash flow	$ 547
− Net capital spending	130
− Change in NWC	330
Cash flow from assets	$ 87

From the cash flow identity above, this $87 cash flow from assets equals the sum of the firm's cash flow to creditors and its cash flow to stockholders. We consider these next.

It wouldn't be at all unusual for a growing corporation to have a negative cash flow. As we shall see below, a negative cash flow means that the firm raised more money by borrowing and selling stock than it paid out to creditors and stockholders that year.

Cash Flow to Creditors and Stockholders

cash flow to creditors

A firm's interest payments to creditors less net new borrowings.

cash flow to stockholders

Dividends paid out by a firm less net new equity raised.

The cash flows to creditors and stockholders represent the net payments to creditors and owners during the year. They are calculated in a similar way. **Cash flow to creditors** is interest paid less net new borrowing; **cash flow to stockholders** is dividends paid less net new equity raised.

Cash Flow to Creditors   Looking at the income statement in Table 2.2, we see that U.S. paid $70 in interest to creditors. From the balance sheets in Table 2.1, long-term debt rose by $454 − 408 = $46. So, U.S. Corporation paid out $70 in interest, but it borrowed an additional $46. Net cash flow to creditors is thus:

U.S. CORPORATION
2000 Cash Flow to Creditors

Interest paid	$70
− Net new borrowing	46
Cash flow to creditors	$24

Cash flow to creditors is sometimes called *cash flow to bondholders;* we will use these terms interchangeably.

Cash Flow to Stockholders   From the income statement, dividends paid to stockholders amount to $103. To get net new equity raised, we need to look at the common stock and paid-in surplus account. This account tells us how much stock the company has sold. During the year, this account rose by $40, so $40 in net new equity was raised. Given this, we have:

U.S. CORPORATION
2000 Cash Flow to Stockholders

Dividends paid	$103
− Net new equity raised	40
Cash flow to stockholders	$ 63

The cash flow to stockholders for 2000 was thus $63.

I. The cash flow identity

Cash flow from assets = Cash flow to creditors (bondholders)
+ Cash flow to stockholders (owners)

II. Cash flow from assets

Cash flow from assets = Operating cash flow
− Net capital spending
− Change in net working capital (NWC)

where

Operating cash flow = Earnings before interest and taxes (EBIT)
+ Depreciation − Taxes

Net capital spending = Ending net fixed assets − Beginning net fixed assets
+ Depreciation

Change in NWC = Ending NWC − Beginning NWC

III. Cash flow to creditors (bondholders)

Cash flow to creditors = Interest paid − Net new borrowing

IV. Cash flow to stockholders (owners)

Cash flow to stockholders = Dividends paid − Net new equity raised

TABLE 2.5

Cash flow summary

Conclusion

The last thing that we need to do is to verify that the cash flow identity holds to be sure that we didn't make any mistakes. From above, cash flow from assets is $87. Cash flow to creditors and stockholders is $24 + 63 = $87, so everything checks out. Table 2.5 contains a summary of the various cash flow calculations for future reference.

As our discussion indicates, it is essential that a firm keep an eye on its cash flow. The following serves as an excellent reminder of why doing so is a good idea, unless the firm's owners wish to end up in the "Po'" house.

Quoth the Banker, "Watch Cash Flow"

Once upon a midnight dreary as I pondered weak and weary
Over many a quaint and curious volume of accounting lore,
Seeking gimmicks (without scruple) to squeeze through
some new tax loophole,
Suddenly I heard a knock upon my door,
Only this, and nothing more.

Then I felt a queasy tingling and I heard the cash a-jingling
As a fearsome banker entered whom I'd often seen before.
His face was money-green and in his eyes there could be seen
Dollar-signs that seemed to glitter as he reckoned up the score.
"Cash flow," the banker said, and nothing more.

I had always thought it fine to show a jet black bottom line.
But the banker sounded a resounding, "No.
Your receivables are high, mounting upward toward the sky;
Write-offs loom. What matters is cash flow."
He repeated, "Watch cash flow."

Then I tried to tell the story of our lovely inventory
Which, though large, is full of most delightful stuff.
But the banker saw its growth, and with a mighty oath
He waved his arms and shouted, "Stop! Enough!
Pay the interest, and don't give me any guff!"

Next I looked for noncash items which could add ad infinitum
To replace the ever-outward flow of cash,

But to keep my statement black I'd held depreciation back,
And my banker said that I'd done something rash.
　　　He quivered, and his teeth began to gnash.

When I asked him for a loan, he responded, with a groan,
That the interest rate would be just prime plus eight,
And to guarantee my purity he'd insist on some security—
All my assets plus the scalp upon my pate.
　　　Only this, a standard rate.

Though my bottom line is black, I am flat upon my back,
My cash flows out and customers pay slow.
The growth of my receivables is almost unbelievable:
The result is certain—unremitting woe!
And I hear the banker utter an ominous low mutter,
　　　"Watch cash flow."

　　　　　　　　　　　　　　　　　　Herbert S. Bailey Jr.

Source: Reprinted from the January 13, 1975, issue of *Publishers Weekly,* published by R. R. Bowker, a Xerox company. Copyright © 1975 by the Xerox Corporation.

To which we can only add: "Amen."

An Example: Cash Flows for Dole Cola

This extended example covers the various cash flow calculations discussed in the chapter. It also illustrates a few variations that may arise.

Operating Cash Flow   During the year, Dole Cola, Inc., had sales and cost of goods sold of $600 and $300, respectively. Depreciation was $150 and interest paid was $30. Taxes were calculated at a straight 34 percent. Dividends were $30. (All figures are in millions of dollars.) What was operating cash flow for Dole? Why is this different from net income?

　　　The easiest thing to do here is to go ahead and create an income statement. We can then pick up the numbers we need. Dole Cola's income statement is given below.

DOLE COLA
2000 Income Statement

Net sales		$600
Cost of goods sold		300
Depreciation		150
Earnings before interest and taxes		$150
Interest paid		30
Taxable income		$120
Taxes		41
Net income		$ 79
Dividends	$30	
Addition to retained earnings	49	

　　　Net income for Dole was thus $79. We now have all the numbers we need. Referring back to the U.S. Corporation example and Table 2.5, we have:

DOLE COLA
2000 Operating Cash Flow

Earnings before interest and taxes	$150
+ Depreciation	150
− Taxes	41
Operating cash flow	$259

As this example illustrates, operating cash flow is not the same as net income, because depreciation and interest are subtracted out when net income is calculated. If you recall our earlier discussion, we don't subtract these out in computing operating cash flow because depreciation is not a cash expense and interest paid is a financing expense, not an operating expense.

Net Capital Spending   Suppose beginning net fixed assets were $500 and ending net fixed assets were $750. What was the net capital spending for the year?

From the income statement for Dole, depreciation for the year was $150. Net fixed assets rose by $250. Dole thus spent $250 along with an additional $150, for a total of $400.

Change in NWC and Cash Flow from Assets   Suppose Dole Cola started the year with $2,130 in current assets and $1,620 in current liabilities. The corresponding ending figures were $2,260 and $1,710. What was the change in NWC during the year? What was cash flow from assets? How does this compare to net income?

Net working capital started out as $2,130 − 1,620 = $510 and ended up at $2,260 − 1,710 = $550. The change in NWC was thus $550 − 510 = $40. Putting together all the information for Dole Cola, we have:

DOLE COLA
2000 Cash Flow from Assets

Operating cash flow	$259
− Net capital spending	400
− Change in NWC	40
Cash flow from assets	−$181

Dole had a cash flow from assets of −$181. Net income was positive at $79. Is the fact that cash flow from assets was negative a cause for alarm? Not necessarily. The cash flow here is negative primarily because of a large investment in fixed assets. If these are good investments, then the resulting negative cash flow is not a worry.

Cash Flow to Creditors and Stockholders   We saw that Dole Cola had cash flow from assets of −$181. The fact that this is negative means that Dole raised more money in the form of new debt and equity than it paid out for the year. For example, suppose we know that Dole didn't sell any new equity for the year. What was cash flow to stockholders? To creditors?

Since it didn't raise any new equity, Dole's cash flow to stockholders is just equal to the cash dividend paid:

DOLE COLA
2000 Cash Flow to Stockholders

Dividends paid	$30
− Net new equity	0
Cash flow to stockholders	$30

Now, from the cash flow identity, the total cash paid to creditors and stockholders was −$181. Cash flow to stockholders is $30, so cash flow to creditors must be equal to −$181 − 30 = −$211:

Cash flow to creditors + Cash flow to stockholders = −$181

Cash flow to creditors + $30   = −$181

Cash flow to creditors   = −$211

Since we know that cash flow to creditors is −$211 and interest paid is $30 (from the income statement), we can now determine net new borrowing. Dole must have borrowed $241 during the year to help finance the fixed asset expansion:

DOLE COLA
2000 Cash Flow to Creditors

Interest paid	$ 30
− Net new borrowing	241
Cash flow to creditors	−$211

CONCEPT QUESTIONS

2.4a What is the cash flow identity? Explain what it says.

2.4b What are the components of operating cash flow?

2.4c Why is interest paid not a component of operating cash flow?

SUMMARY AND CONCLUSIONS

This chapter has introduced you to some of the basics of financial statements, taxes, and cash flow. In it we saw that:

1. The book values on an accounting balance sheet can be very different from market values. The goal of financial management is to maximize the market value of the stock, not its book value.

2. Net income as it is computed on the income statement is not cash flow. A primary reason is that depreciation, a noncash expense, is deducted when net income is computed.

3. Marginal and average tax rates can be different, and it is the marginal tax rate that is relevant for most financial decisions.

4. The marginal tax rate paid by the corporations with the largest incomes is 35 percent.

5. There is a cash flow identity much like the balance sheet identity. It says that cash flow from assets equals cash flow to creditors and stockholders.

The calculation of cash flow from financial statements isn't difficult. Care must be taken in handling noncash expenses, such as depreciation, and in not confusing operating costs with financing costs. Most of all, it is important not to confuse book values with market values and accounting income with cash flow.

CHAPTER REVIEW AND SELF-TEST PROBLEM

2.1 **Cash Flow for Rasputin Corporation.** This problem will give you some practice working with financial statements and figuring cash flow. Based on the following information for Rasputin Corporation, prepare an income statement for 2000 and balance sheets for 1999 and 2000. Next, following our U.S. Corporation examples in the chapter, calculate cash flow from assets for Rasputin, cash flow to creditors, and cash flow to stockholders for 2000. Use a 34 percent tax rate throughout. You can check your answers below.

	1999	2000
Sales	$3,790	$3,990
Cost of goods sold	2,043	2,137
Depreciation	975	1,018
Interest	225	267
Dividends	200	225
Current assets	2,140	2,346
Net fixed assets	6,770	7,087
Current liabilities	994	1,126
Long-term debt	2,869	2,956

Answer to Chapter Review and Self-Test Problem

2.1 In preparing the balance sheets, remember that shareholders' equity is the residual. With this in mind, Rasputin's balance sheets are as follows:

RASPUTIN CORPORATION
Balance Sheets as of December 31, 1999 and 2000

	1999	2000		1999	2000
Current assets	$2,140	$2,346	Current liabilities	$ 994	$1,126
Net fixed assets	6,770	7,087	Long-term debt	2,869	2,956
			Equity	5,047	5,351
			Total liabilities and and shareholders' equity		
Total assets	$8,910	$9,433	and shareholders' equity	$8,910	$9,433

The income statement is straightforward:

RASPUTIN CORPORATION
2000 Income Statement

Sales	$3,990
Cost of goods sold	2,137
Depreciation	1,018
Earnings before interest and taxes	$ 835
Interest paid	267
Taxable income	$ 568
Taxes (34%)	193
Net income	$ 375
Dividends	$225
Addition to retained earnings	150

Notice that we've used a flat 34 percent tax rate. Also notice that the addition to retained earnings is just net income less cash dividends.

We can now pick up the figures we need to get operating cash flow:

RASPUTIN CORPORATION
2000 Operating Cash Flow

Earnings before interest and taxes	$ 835
+ Depreciation	1,018
− Current taxes	74
Operating cash flow	$1,660

Next, we get the capital spending for the year by looking at the change in fixed assets, remembering to account for the depreciation:

Ending fixed assets	$7,087
− Beginning fixed assets	6,770
+ Depreciation	1,018
Net investment in fixed assets	$1,335

After calculating beginning and ending NWC, we take the difference to get the change in NWC:

Ending NWC	$1,220
− Beginning NWC	1,146
Change in NWC	$ 74

We now combine operating cash flow, net capital spending, and the change in net working capital to get the total cash flow from assets:

RASPUTIN CORPORATION
2000 Cash Flow from Assets

Operating cash flow	$1,660
− Net capital spending	1,335
− Change in NWC	74
Cash flow from assets	$ 251

To get cash flow to creditors, notice that long-term borrowing increased by $87 during the year and that interest paid was $267, so:

RASPUTIN CORPORATION
2000 Cash Flow to Creditors

Interest paid	$267
− Net new borrowing	87
Cash flow to creditors	$180

Finally, dividends paid were $225. To get net new equity, we have to do some extra calculating. Total equity was up by $5,351 − 5,047 = $304. Of this increase, $150 was from additions to retained earnings, so $154 in new equity was raised during the year. Cash flow to stockholders was thus:

RASPUTIN CORPORATION
2000 Cash Flow to Stockholders

Dividends paid	$225
− Net new equity	154
Cash flow to stockholders	$ 71

As a check, notice that cash flow from assets ($251) does equal cash flow to creditors plus cash flow to stockholders ($180 + 71 = $251).

CRITICAL THINKING AND CONCEPTS REVIEW

1. **Liquidity.** What does liquidity measure? Explain the trade-off a firm faces between high liquidity and low liquidity levels.

2. **Accounting and Cash Flows.** Why is it that the revenue and cost figures shown on a standard income statement may not be representative of the actual cash inflows and outflows that occurred during a period?

3. **Book Values versus Market Values.** In preparing a balance sheet, why do you think standard accounting practice focuses on historical cost rather than market value?

4. **Operating Cash Flow.** In comparing accounting net income and operating cash flow, what two items do you find in net income that are not in operating cash flow? Explain what each is and why it is excluded in operating cash flow.

5. **Book Values versus Market Values.** Under standard accounting rules, it is possible for a company's liabilities to exceed its assets. When this occurs, the owners' equity is negative. Can this happen with market values? Why or why not?

6. **Cash Flow from Assets.** Suppose a company's cash flow from assets was negative for a particular period. Is this necessarily a good sign or a bad sign?

7. **Operating Cash Flow.** Suppose a company's operating cash flow was negative for several years running. Is this necessarily a good sign or a bad sign?

8. **Net Working Capital and Capital Spending.** Could a company's change in NWC be negative in a given year? (Hint: Yes.) Explain how this might come about. What about net capital spending?

9. **Cash Flow to Stockholders and Creditors.** Could a company's cash flow to stockholders be negative in a given year? (Hint: Yes.) Explain how this might come about. What about cash flow to creditors?

10.   **Firm Values.**   In December 1995, Texaco announced it would take a fourth-quarter charge of $640 million against earnings, changing its quarterly results from a profit to a loss. Texaco was not alone. Other oil companies, such as Phillips Petroleum, Mobil, and Chevron, all planned to take significant charges as well. Poor performance wasn't the issue. Instead, oil companies were forced by accounting rule changes to recalculate the value of oil fields shown on their financial statements. The new values were substantially smaller, and, as a result, the reported assets of these companies fell in value by hundreds of millions of dollars.

So, did stockholders in Texaco lose $640 million as a result of accounting rule changes? The answer: Probably not. What do you think is the basis for this conclusion?

QUESTIONS AND PROBLEMS

Basic
(Questions 1–13)

1.   **Building a Balance Sheet.**   McGwire Bat Factory, Inc., has current assets of $3,000, net fixed assets of $8,000, current liabilities of $1,300, and long-term debt of $5,000. What is the value of the shareholders' equity account for this firm? How much is net working capital?

2.   **Building an Income Statement.**   Taco Swell, Inc., has sales of $375,000, costs of $195,000, depreciation expense of $25,000, interest expense of $16,000, and a tax rate of 35 percent. What is the net income for this firm?

3.   **Dividends and Retained Earnings.**   Suppose the firm in Problem 2 paid out $35,000 in cash dividends. What is the addition to retained earnings?

4.   **Per-Share Earnings and Dividends.**   Suppose the firm in Problem 3 had 20,000 shares of common stock outstanding. What is the earnings per share, or EPS, figure? What is the dividends per share figure?

5.   **Market Values and Book Values.**   Klingon Widgets, Inc., purchased new cloaking machinery three years ago for $4 million. The machinery can be sold to the Romulans today for $3 million. Klingon's current balance sheet shows net fixed assets of $850,000, current liabilities of $750,000, and net working capital of $600,000. If all the current accounts were liquidated today, the company would receive $1.25 million cash. What is the book value of Klingon's assets today? What is the market value?

6.   **Calculating Taxes.**   The Gonas Co. had $245,000 in 2000 taxable income. Using the rates from Table 2.3 in the chapter, calculate the company's 2000 income taxes.

7.   **Tax Rates.**   In Problem 6, what is the average tax rate? What is the marginal tax rate?

8.   **Calculating OCF.**   Lutz, Inc., has sales of $8,750, costs of $4,250, depreciation expense of $1,200, and interest expense of $980. If the tax rate is 35 percent, what is the operating cash flow, or OCF?

9.   **Calculating Net Capital Spending.**   Tyson Obedience School's December 31, 1999, balance sheet showed net fixed assets of $3.8 million, and the December 31, 2000, balance sheet showed net fixed assets of $3.9 million. The company's 2000 income statement showed a depreciation expense of $750,000. What was Tyson's net capital spending for 2000?

10.   **Calculating Additions to NWC.**   The December 31, 1999, balance sheet of Serena's Tennis Shop, Inc., showed current assets of $900 and current liabilities of $325. The December 31, 2000, balance sheet showed current assets of $925 and current liabilities of $475. What was the company's 2000 change in net working capital, or NWC?

— 11. **Cash Flow to Creditors.** The December 31, 1999, balance sheet of Pearl Jelly, Inc., showed long-term debt of $1.5 million, and the December 31, 2000, balance sheet showed long-term debt of $1.8 million. The 2000 income statement showed an interest expense of $210,000. What was the firm's cash flow to creditors during 2000?

— 12. **Cash Flow to Stockholders.** The December 31, 1999, balance sheet of Pearl Jelly, Inc., showed $300,000 in the common stock account and $4.6 million in the additional paid-in surplus account. The December 31, 2000, balance sheet showed $350,000 and $5.0 million in the same two accounts, respectively. If the company paid out $100,000 in cash dividends during 2000, what was the cash flow to stockholders for the year?

13. **Calculating Total Cash Flows.** Given the information for Pearl Jelly, Inc., in Problems 11 and 12, suppose you also know that the firm's net capital spending for 2000 was $850,000, and that the firm reduced its net working capital investment by $235,000. What was the firm's 2000 operating cash flow, or OCF?

14. **Calculating Total Cash Flows.** Faulk Co. shows the following information on its 2000 income statement: sales = $95,000; costs = $51,000; other expenses = $2,750; depreciation expense = $8,000; interest expense = $7,000; taxes = $8,925; dividends = $3,200. In addition, you're told that the firm issued $1,415 in new equity during 2000, and redeemed $3,000 in outstanding long-term debt.

   a. What is the 2000 operating cash flow?

   b. What is the 2000 cash flow to creditors?

   c. What is the 2000 cash flow to stockholders?

   d. If net fixed assets increased by $9,500 during the year, what was the addition to NWC?

Intermediate
(Questions 14–22)

—ᐟ 15. **Using Income Statements.** Given the following information for Pitino Pizza Co., calculate the depreciation expense: sales = $25,000; costs = $18,000; addition to retained earnings = $2,000; dividends paid = $800; interest expense = $1,050; tax rate = 35 percent.

16. **Preparing a Balance Sheet.** Prepare a balance sheet for Tim's Couch Corp. as of December 31, 2000, based on the following information: cash = $185,000; patents and copyrights = $725,000; accounts payable = $550,000; accounts receivable = $205,000; tangible net fixed assets = $4,000,000; inventory = $430,000; notes payable = $175,000; accumulated retained earnings = $3,550,000; long-term debt = $825,000.

17. **Residual Claims.** Evander Ear Repair, Inc., is obligated to pay its creditors $2,200 during the year.

   a. What is the value of the shareholders' equity if assets equal $2,400?

   b. What if assets equal $1,800?

18. **Marginal versus Average Tax Rates.** (Refer to Table 2.3) Corporation Growth has $90,000 in taxable income, and Corporation Income has $9,000,000 in taxable income.

   a. What is the tax bill for each firm?

   b. Suppose both firms have identified a new project that will increase taxable income by $10,000. How much in additional taxes will each firm pay? Why is this amount the same?

19. **Net Income and OCF.** During 2000, Belyk Paving Co. had sales of $2,000,000. Cost of goods sold, administrative and selling expenses, and depreciation expenses were $1,200,000, $300,000, and $400,000, respectively. In addition, the company

had an interest expense of $150,000 and a tax rate of 35 percent. (Ignore any tax loss carry-back or carry-forward provisions.)

    a. What is Belyk's net income for 2000?

    b. What is its operating cash flow?

    c. Explain your results in (a) and (b).

20.   **Accounting Values versus Cash Flows.** In Problem 19, suppose Belyk Paving Co. paid out $400,000 in cash dividends. Is this possible? If no new investments were made in net fixed assets or net working capital, and if no new stock was issued during the year, what do you know about the firm's long-term debt account?

21.   **Calculating Cash Flows.** Titan Football Manufacturing had the following operating results for 2000: sales = $12,200; cost of goods sold = $9,000; depreciation expense = $1,600; interest expense = $200; dividends paid = $300. At the beginning of the year, net fixed assets were $8,000, current assets were $2,000, and current liabilities were $1,500. At the end of the year, net fixed assets were $8,400, current assets were $3,100, and current liabilities were $1,800. The tax rate for 2000 was 34 percent.

    a. What is net income for 2000?

    b. What is the operating cash flow for 2000?

    c. What is the cash flow from assets for 2000? Is this possible? Explain.

    d. If no new debt was issued during the year, what is the cash flow to creditors? What is the cash flow to stockholders? Explain and interpret the positive and negative signs of your answers in (a) through (d).

22.   **Calculating Cash Flows.** Consider the following abbreviated financial statements for Cabo Wabo, Inc.:

CABO WABO, INC. Partial Balance Sheets as of December 31, 1999 and 2000							**CABO WABO, INC.** 2000 Income Statement	
	1999	**2000**			**1999**	**2000**	Sales	$14,200
Assets			*Liabilities and Owners' Equity*				Costs	7,120
							Depreciation	1,200
Current assets	$ 950	$1,006	Current liabilities		$ 410	$ 602	Interest paid	216
Net fixed assets	4,400	4,600	Long-term debt		2,400	2,800		

    a. What is owners' equity for 1999 and 2000?

    b. What is the change in net working capital for 2000?

    c. In 2000, Cabo Wabo purchased $2,000 in new fixed assets. How much in fixed assets did Cabo Wabo sell? What is the cash flow from assets for the year? (The tax rate is 35 percent.)

    d. During 2000, Cabo Wabo raised $600 in new long-term debt. How much long-term debt must Cabo Wabo have paid off during the year? What is the cash flow to creditors?

www.mhhe.com/rwj

Spreadsheet Templates 6, 10, 19

3

Working with Financial Statements

THE MOST IMPORTANT THING TO CARRY AWAY FROM THIS CHAPTER IS A GOOD UNDERSTANDING OF:

- How to standardize financial statements for comparison purposes

- How to compute and, more importantly, interpret some common ratios

- The determinants of a firm's profitability and growth

- Some of the problems and pitfalls in financial statement analysis

AT THE BEGINNING of 2000, shares of stock in Johnson and Johnson were trading for about $93.25. At that price, Johnson and Johnson had a price-to-earnings (PE) ratio of 37, meaning that investors were willing to pay $37 for every dollar in income earned by Johnson and Johnson. At the same time, investors were willing to pay a stunning $735 for each dollar earned by Yahoo! and a meager $9 and $8 for each dollar earned by General Motors and Kmart, respectively. And then there were stocks like Red Hat, Inc., which, despite having no earnings (a loss, actually), had a stock price of about $211 a share. Meanwhile, the average stock in the Standard and Poor's (S&P) 500 index, which contains 500 of the largest publicly traded companies in the U.S. had a PE ratio of about 31, so Johnson and Johnson was about average in this regard.

As we look at these numbers, an obvious question arises: Why were investors willing to pay so much for a dollar of Yahoo!'s earnings and so much less for a dollar earned by General Motors? To understand the answer, we need to delve into subjects such as relative profitability and growth potential, and we also need to know how to compare financial and operating information across companies. By a remarkable coincidence, that is precisely what this chapter is about.

The PE ratio is just one example of a financial ratio. As we will see in this chapter, there is a wide variety of such ratios, all designed to summarize specific aspects of a firm's financial position. In addition to discussing financial ratios and what they mean, we will have quite a bit to say about who uses this information and why.

Everybody needs to understand ratios. Managers will find that almost every business characteristic, from profitability to employee productivity, is summarized in some kind of ratio. Marketers examine ratios dealing with costs, markups, and margins. Production personnel focus on ratios dealing with issues such as operating efficiency. Accountants need to understand ratios because, among other things, ratios are one of the most common and important forms of financial statement information.

In fact, regardless of your field, you may very well find that your compensation is tied to some ratio or group of ratios. Perhaps that is the best reason to study up!

n Chapter 2, we discussed some of the essential concepts of financial statements and cash flows. This chapter continues where our earlier discussion left off. Our goal here is to expand your understanding of the uses (and abuses) of financial statement information.

A good working knowledge of financial statements is desirable simply because such statements, and numbers derived from those statements, are the primary means of communicating financial information both within the firm and outside the firm. In short, much of the language of business finance is rooted in the ideas we discuss in this chapter.

In the best of all worlds, the financial manager has full market value information about all of the firm's assets. This will rarely (if ever) happen. So the reason we rely on accounting figures for much of our financial information is that we are almost always unable to obtain all (or even part) of the market information that we want. The only meaningful yardstick for evaluating business decisions is whether or not they create economic value (see Chapter 1). However, in many important situations, it will not be possible to make this judgment directly because we can't see the market value effects.

We recognize that accounting numbers are often just pale reflections of economic reality, but they frequently are the best available information. For privately held corporations, not-for-profit businesses, and smaller firms, for example, very little direct market value information exists at all. The accountant's reporting function is crucial in these circumstances.

Clearly, one important goal of the accountant is to report financial information to the user in a form useful for decision making. Ironically, the information frequently does not come to the user in such a form. In other words, financial statements don't come with a user's guide. This chapter is a first step in filling this gap.

TABLE 3.1

	PRUFROCK CORPORATION Balance Sheets as of December 31, 1999 and 2000 ($ in millions)	
	1999	**2000**
Assets		
Current assets		
Cash	$ 84	$ 98
Accounts receivable	165	188
Inventory	393	422
Total	$ 642	$ 708
Fixed assets		
Net plant and equipment	$2,731	$2,880
Total assets	$3,373	$3,588
Liabilities and Owners' Equity		
Current liabilities		
Accounts payable	$ 312	$ 344
Notes payable	231	196
Total	$ 543	$ 540
Long-term debt	$ 531	$ 457
Owners' equity		
Common stock and paid-in surplus	$ 500	$ 550
Retained earnings	1,799	2,041
Total	$2,299	$2,591
Total liabilities and owners' equity	$3,373	$3,588

STANDARDIZED FINANCIAL STATEMENTS | 3.1

One obvious thing we might want to do with a company's financial statements is to compare them to those of other, similar companies. We would immediately have a problem, however. It's almost impossible to directly compare the financial statements for two companies because of differences in size.

For example, Ford and GM are obviously serious rivals in the auto market, but GM is much larger (in terms of assets), so it is difficult to compare them directly. For that matter, it's difficult to even compare financial statements from different points in time for the same company if the company's size has changed. The size problem is compounded if we try to compare GM and, say, Toyota. If Toyota's financial statements are denominated in yen, then we have a size *and* a currency difference.

To start making comparisons, one obvious thing we might try to do is to somehow standardize the financial statements. One very common and useful way of doing this is to work with percentages instead of total dollars. The resulting financial statements are called **common-size statements.** We consider these next.

Common-Size Balance Sheets

For easy reference, Prufrock Corporation's 1999 and 2000 balance sheets are provided in Table 3.1. Using these, we construct common-size balance sheets by expressing each item as a percentage of total assets. Prufrock's 1999 and 2000 common-size balance sheets are shown in Table 3.2.

common-size statement

A standardized financial statement presenting all items in percentage terms. Balance sheet items are shown as a percentage of assets and income statement items as a percentage of sales.

TABLE 3.2

PRUFROCK CORPORATION
Common-Size Balance Sheets
December 31, 1999 and 2000

	1999	2000	Change
Assets			
Current assets			
Cash	2.5%	2.7%	+ .2%
Accounts receivable	4.9	5.2	+ .3
Inventory	11.7	11.8	+ .1
Total	19.1	19.7	+ .6
Fixed assets			
Net plant and equipment	80.9	80.3	− .6
Total assets	100.0%	100.0%	.0%
Liabilities and Owners' Equity			
Current liabilities			
Accounts payable	9.2%	9.6%	+ .4%
Notes payable	6.8	5.5	− 1.3
Total	16.0	15.1	− .9
Long-term debt	15.7	12.7	− 3.0
Owners' equity			
Common stock and paid-in surplus	14.8	15.3	+ .5
Retained earnings	53.3	56.9	+ 3.6
Total	68.1	72.2	+ 4.1
Total liabilities and owners' equity	100.0%	100.0%	.0%

Notice that some of the totals don't check exactly because of rounding errors. Also notice that the total change has to be zero since the beginning and ending numbers must add up to 100 percent.

In this form, financial statements are relatively easy to read and compare. For example, just looking at the two balance sheets for Prufrock, we see that current assets were 19.7 percent of total assets in 2000, up from 19.1 percent in 1999. Current liabilities declined from 16.0 percent to 15.1 percent of total liabilities and equity over that same time. Similarly, total equity rose from 68.1 percent of total liabilities and equity to 72.2 percent.

Overall, Prufrock's liquidity, as measured by current assets compared to current liabilities, increased over the year. Simultaneously, Prufrock's indebtedness diminished as a percentage of total assets. We might be tempted to conclude that the balance sheet has grown "stronger."

Common-Size Income Statements

A useful way of standardizing the income statement shown in Table 3.3 is to express each item as a percentage of total sales, as illustrated for Prufrock in Table 3.4.

TABLE 3.3

PRUFROCK CORPORATION 2000 Income Statement ($ in millions)		
Sales		$2,311
Cost of goods sold		1,344
Depreciation		276
Earnings before interest and taxes		$ 691
Interest paid		141
Taxable income		$ 550
Taxes (34%)		187
Net income		$ 363
Dividends	$121	
Addition to retained earnings	242	

TABLE 3.4

PRUFROCK CORPORATION Common-Size Income Statement 2000		
Sales		100.0%
Cost of goods sold		58.2
Depreciation		11.9
Earnings before interest and taxes		29.9
Interest paid		6.1
Taxable income		23.8
Taxes (34%)		8.1
Net income		15.7%
Dividends	5.2%	
Addition to retained earnings	10.5	

This income statement tells us what happens to each dollar in sales. For Prufrock, interest expense eats up $.061 out of every sales dollar and taxes take another $.081. When all is said and done, $.157 of each dollar flows through to the bottom line (net income), and that amount is split into $.105 retained in the business and $.052 paid out in dividends.

These percentages are very useful in comparisons. For example, a very relevant figure is the cost percentage. For Prufrock, $.582 of each $1.00 in sales goes to pay for goods sold. It would be interesting to compute the same percentage for Prufrock's main competitors to see how Prufrock stacks up in terms of cost control.

CONCEPT QUESTIONS

3.1a Why is it often necessary to standardize financial statements?

3.1b Describe how common-size balance sheets and income statements are formed.

RATIO ANALYSIS | 3.2

Another way of avoiding the problems involved in comparing companies of different sizes is to calculate and compare **financial ratios**. Such ratios are ways of comparing and investigating the relationships between different pieces of financial information. We cover some of the more common ratios next, but there are many others that we don't touch on.

financial ratios
Relationships determined from a firm's financial information and used for comparison purposes.

One problem with ratios is that different people and different sources frequently don't compute them in exactly the same way, and this leads to much confusion. The specific definitions we use here may or may not be the same as ones you have seen or will see elsewhere. If you are ever using ratios as a tool for analysis, you should be careful to document how you calculate each one, and, if you are comparing your numbers to those of another source, be sure you know how their numbers are computed.

We will defer much of our discussion of how ratios are used and some problems that come up with using them until a bit later in the chapter. For now, for each of the ratios we discuss, several questions come to mind:

1. How is it computed?
2. What is it intended to measure, and why might we be interested?
3. What is the unit of measurement?
4. What might a high or low value be telling us? How might such values be misleading?
5. How could this measure be improved?

Financial ratios are traditionally grouped into the following categories:

1. Short-term solvency, or liquidity, ratios
2. Long-term solvency, or financial leverage, ratios
3. Asset management, or turnover, ratios
4. Profitability ratios
5. Market value ratios

We will consider each of these in turn. In calculating these numbers for Prufrock, we will use the ending balance sheet (2000) figures unless we explicitly say otherwise. Also notice that the various ratios are color keyed to indicate which numbers come from the **income statement** and which come from the balance sheet

Short-Term Solvency, or Liquidity, Measures

As the name suggests, short-term solvency ratios as a group are intended to provide information about a firm's liquidity, and these ratios are sometimes called *liquidity measures*. The primary concern is the firm's ability to pay its bills over the short run without undue stress. Consequently, these ratios focus on current assets and current liabilities.

For obvious reasons, liquidity ratios are particularly interesting to short-term creditors. Since financial managers are constantly working with banks and other short-term lenders, an understanding of these ratios is essential.

One advantage of looking at current assets and liabilities is that their book values and market values are likely to be similar. Often (though not always), these assets and liabilities just don't live long enough for the two to get seriously out of step. On the other hand, like any type of near-cash, current assets and liabilities can and do change fairly rapidly, so today's amounts may not be a reliable guide to the future.

Current Ratio   One of the best-known and most widely used ratios is the *current ratio*. As you might guess, the current ratio is defined as:

$$\text{Current ratio} = \frac{\text{Current assets}}{\text{Current liabilities}} \tag{3.1}$$

For Prufrock, the 2000 current ratio is:

$$\text{Current ratio} = \frac{\$708}{\$540} = 1.31 \text{ times}$$

Because current assets and liabilities are, in principle, converted to cash over the following 12 months, the current ratio is a measure of short-term liquidity. The unit of measurement is either dollars or times. So, we could say Prufrock has $1.31 in current assets for every $1 in current liabilities, or we could say Prufrock has its current liabilities covered 1.31 times over.

To a creditor, particularly a short-term creditor such as a supplier, the higher the current ratio, the better. To the firm, a high current ratio indicates liquidity, but it also may indicate an inefficient use of cash and other short-term assets. Absent some extraordinary circumstances, we would expect to see a current ratio of at least 1, because a current ratio of less than 1 would mean that net working capital (current assets less current liabilities) is negative. This would be unusual in a healthy firm, at least for most types of businesses.

The current ratio, like any ratio, is affected by various types of transactions. For example, suppose the firm borrows over the long term to raise money. The short-run effect would be an increase in cash from the issue proceeds and an increase in long-term debt. Current liabilities would not be affected, so the current ratio would rise.

Finally, note that an apparently low current ratio may not be a bad sign for a company with a large reserve of untapped borrowing power.

EXAMPLE 3.1 | **Current Events**

Suppose a firm were to pay off some of its suppliers and short-term creditors. What would happen to the current ratio? Suppose a firm buys some inventory. What happens in this case? What happens if a firm sells some merchandise?

The first case is a trick question. What happens is that the current ratio moves away from 1. If it is greater than 1 (the usual case), it will get bigger, but if it is less than 1, it will get smaller. To see this, suppose the firm has $4 in current assets and $2 in current liabilities for a current ratio of 2. If we use $1 in cash to reduce current liabilities, then the new current ratio is ($4 − 1)/($2 − 1) = 3. If we reverse the original situation to $2 in current assets and $4 in current liabilities, then the change will cause the current ratio to fall to 1/3 from 1/2.

The second case is not quite as tricky. Nothing happens to the current ratio because cash goes down while inventory goes up—total current assets are unaffected.

In the third case, the current ratio would usually rise because inventory is normally shown at cost and the sale would normally be at something greater than cost (the difference is the markup). The increase in either cash or receivables is therefore greater than the decrease in inventory. This increases current assets, and the current ratio rises.

Quick (or Acid-Test) Ratio   Inventory is often the least liquid current asset. It's also the one for which the book values are least reliable as measures of market value since the quality of the inventory isn't considered. Some of the inventory may later turn out to be damaged, obsolete, or lost.

More to the point, relatively large inventories are often a sign of short-term trouble. The firm may have overestimated sales and overbought or overproduced as a result. In this case, the firm may have a substantial portion of its liquidity tied up in slow-moving inventory.

To further evaluate liquidity, the *quick,* or *acid-test, ratio* is computed just like the current ratio, except inventory is omitted:

$$\text{Quick ratio} = \frac{\text{Current assets} - \text{Inventory}}{\text{Current liabilities}} \qquad [3.2]$$

Notice that using cash to buy inventory does not affect the current ratio, but it reduces the quick ratio. Again, the idea is that inventory is relatively illiquid compared to cash.

For Prufrock, this ratio in 2000 was:

$$\text{Quick ratio} = \frac{\$708 - 422}{\$540} = .53 \text{ times}$$

The quick ratio here tells a somewhat different story than the current ratio, because inventory accounts for more than half of Prufrock's current assets. To exaggerate the point, if this inventory consisted of, say, unsold nuclear power plants, then this would be a cause for concern.

Cash Ratio   A very short-term creditor might be interested in the *cash ratio:*

$$\text{Cash ratio} = \frac{\text{Cash}}{\text{Current liabilities}} \qquad [3.3]$$

You can verify that this works out to be .18 times for Prufrock.

Long-Term Solvency Measures

Long-term solvency ratios are intended to address the firm's long-run ability to meet its obligations, or, more generally, its financial leverage. These ratios are sometimes called *financial leverage ratios* or just *leverage ratios*. We consider three commonly used measures and some variations.

Total Debt Ratio   The *total debt ratio* takes into account all debts of all maturities to all creditors. It can be defined in several ways, the easiest of which is:

$$\text{Total debt ratio} = \frac{\text{Total assets} - \text{Total equity}}{\text{Total assets}} \qquad [3.4]$$

$$= \frac{\$3,588 - 2,591}{\$3,588} = .28 \text{ times}$$

In this case, an analyst might say that Prufrock uses 28 percent debt.[1] Whether this is high or low or whether it even makes any difference depends on whether or not capital structure matters, a subject we discuss in a later chapter.

Prufrock has $.28 in debt for every $1 in assets. Therefore, there is $.72 in equity ($1 − .28) for every $.28 in debt. With this in mind, we can define two useful variations on the total debt ratio, the *debt-equity ratio* and the *equity multiplier:*

$$\text{Debt-equity ratio} = \text{Total debt/Total equity} \qquad [3.5]$$
$$= \$.28/\$.72 = .39 \text{ times}$$
$$\text{Equity multiplier} = \text{Total assets/Total equity} \qquad [3.6]$$
$$= \$1/\$.72 = 1.39 \text{ times}$$

The fact that the equity multiplier is 1 plus the debt-equity ratio is not a coincidence:

$$\text{Equity multiplier} = \text{Total assets/Total equity} = \$1/\$.72 = 1.39$$
$$= (\text{Total equity} + \text{Total debt})/\text{Total equity}$$
$$= 1 + \text{Debt-equity ratio} = 1.39 \text{ times}$$

The thing to notice here is that given any one of these three ratios, you can immediately calculate the other two, so they all say exactly the same thing.

Times Interest Earned Another common measure of long-term solvency is the *times interest earned* (TIE) *ratio.* Once again, there are several possible (and common) definitions, but we'll stick with the most traditional:

$$\text{Times interest earned ratio} = \frac{\text{EBIT}}{\text{Interest}} \qquad [3.7]$$
$$= \frac{\$691}{\$141} = 4.9 \text{ times}$$

As the name suggests, this ratio measures how well a company has its interest obligations covered, and it is often called the interest coverage ratio. For Prufrock, the interest bill is covered 4.9 times over.

Cash Coverage A problem with the TIE ratio is that it is based on EBIT, which is not really a measure of cash available to pay interest. The reason is that depreciation, a non-cash expense, has been deducted out. Since interest is most definitely a cash outflow (to creditors), one way to define the *cash coverage ratio* is:

$$\text{Cash coverage ratio} = \frac{\text{EBIT} + \text{Depreciation}}{\text{Interest}} \qquad [3.8]$$
$$= \frac{\$691 + 276}{\$141} = \frac{\$967}{\$141} = 6.9 \text{ times}$$

The numerator here, EBIT plus depreciation, is often abbreviated EBDIT (earnings before depreciation, interest, and taxes). It is a basic measure of the firm's ability to generate cash from operations, and it is frequently used as a measure of cash flow available to meet financial obligations.

---

[1]Total equity here includes preferred stock (discussed in Chapter 7), if there is any. An equivalent numerator in this ratio would be (Current liabilities + Long-term debt).

Asset Management, or Turnover, Measures

We next turn our attention to the efficiency with which Prufrock uses its assets. The measures in this section are sometimes called *asset utilization ratios*. The specific ratios we discuss can all be interpreted as measures of turnover. What they are intended to describe is how efficiently, or intensively, a firm uses its assets to generate sales. We first look at two important current assets, inventory and receivables.

Inventory Turnover and Days' Sales in Inventory   During the year, Prufrock had a cost of goods sold of $1,344. Inventory at the end of the year was $422. With these numbers, *inventory turnover* can be calculated as:

$$\text{Inventory} = \frac{\text{Cost of goods sold}}{\text{Inventory}} \qquad [3.9]$$

$$= \frac{\$1,344}{\$422} = 3.2 \text{ times}$$

In a sense, we sold off, or turned over, the entire inventory 3.2 times. As long as we are not running out of stock and thereby forgoing sales, the higher this ratio is, the more efficiently we are managing inventory.

If we know that we turned our inventory over 3.2 times during the year, then we can immediately figure out how long it took us to turn it over on average. The result is the average *days' sales in inventory:*

$$\text{Days' sales in inventory} = \frac{365 \text{ days}}{\text{Inventory turnover}} \qquad [3.10]$$

$$= \frac{365}{3.2} = 114 \text{ days}$$

This tells us that, roughly speaking, inventory sits 114 days on average before it is sold. Alternatively, assuming we used the most recent inventory and cost figures, it will take about 114 days to work off our current inventory.

For example, we frequently hear things like "Majestic Motors has a 60 days' supply of cars." This means that, at current daily sales, it would take 60 days to deplete the available inventory. We could also say that Majestic has 60 days of sales in inventory.

Receivables Turnover and Days' Sales in Receivables   Our inventory measures give some indication of how fast we can sell products. We now look at how fast we collect on those sales. The *receivables turnover* is defined in the same way as inventory turnover:

$$\text{Receivables turnover} = \frac{\text{Sales}}{\text{Accounts receivable}} \qquad [3.11]$$

$$= \frac{\$2,311}{\$188} = 12.3 \text{ times}$$

Loosely speaking, we collected our outstanding credit accounts and reloaned the money 12.3 times during the year.[2]

---

[2]Here we have implicitly assumed that all sales are credit sales. If they were not, then we would simply use total credit sales in these calculations, not total sales.

This ratio makes more sense if we convert it to days, so the *days' sales in receivables* is:

$$\text{Days' sales in receivables} = \frac{365 \text{ days}}{\text{Receivables turnovers}} \qquad [3.12]$$

$$= \frac{365}{12.3} = 30 \text{ days}$$

Therefore, on average, we collect on our credit sales in 30 days. For obvious reasons, this ratio is very frequently called the *average collection period* (ACP).

Also note that if we are using the most recent figures, we can also say that we have 30 days' worth of sales currently uncollected. We will learn more about this subject when we study credit policy in a later chapter.

EXAMPLE 3.2 | Payables Turnover

Here is a variation on the receivables collection period. How long, on average, does it take for Prufrock Corporation to *pay* its bills? To answer, we need to calculate the accounts payable turnover rate using cost of goods sold. We will assume that Prufrock purchases everything on credit.

The cost of goods sold is $1,344, and accounts payable are $344. The turnover is therefore $1,344/$344 = 3.9 times. So payables turned over about every 365/3.9 = 94 days. On average, then, Prufrock takes 94 days to pay. As a potential creditor, we might take note of this fact.

Total Asset Turnover Moving away from specific accounts like inventory or receivables, we can consider an important "big picture" ratio, the *total asset turnover* ratio. As the name suggests, total asset turnover is:

$$\text{Total asset turnover} = \frac{\text{Sales}}{\text{Total assets}} \qquad [3.13]$$

$$= \frac{\$2,311}{\$3,588} = .64 \text{ times}$$

In other words, for every dollar in assets, we generated $.64 in sales.

A closely related ratio, the *capital intensity ratio,* is simply the reciprocal of (that is, 1 divided by) total asset turnover. It can be interpreted as the dollar investment in assets needed to generate $1 in sales. High values correspond to capital intensive industries (such as public utilities). For Prufrock, total asset turnover is .64, so, if we flip this over, we get that capital intensity is $1/.64 = $1.56. That is, it takes Prufrock $1.56 in assets to create $1 in sales.

EXAMPLE 3.3 | More Turnover

Suppose you find that a particular company generates $.40 in sales for every dollar in total assets. How often does this company turn over its total assets?

The total asset turnover here is .40 times per year. It takes 1/.40 = 2.5 years to turn assets over completely.

Profitability Measures

The three measures we discuss in this section are probably the best known and most widely used of all financial ratios. In one form or another, they are intended to measure how efficiently the firm uses its assets and how efficiently the firm manages its operations. The focus in this group is on the bottom line, net income.

Profit Margin   Companies pay a great deal of attention to their *profit margin:*

$$\text{Profit margin} = \frac{\text{Net income}}{\text{Sales}}$$ [3.14]

$$= \frac{\$363}{\$2,311} = 15.7\%$$

This tells us that Prufrock, in an accounting sense, generates a little less than 16 cents in profit for every dollar in sales.

All other things being equal, a relatively high profit margin is obviously desirable. This situation corresponds to low expense ratios relative to sales. However, we hasten to add that other things are often not equal.

For example, lowering our sales price will usually increase unit volume, but will normally cause profit margins to shrink. Total profit (or, more importantly, operating cash flow) may go up or down; so the fact that margins are smaller isn't necessarily bad. After all, isn't it possible that, as the saying goes, "Our prices are so low that we lose money on everything we sell, but we make it up in volume!"?[3]

Return on Assets   *Return on assets* (ROA) is a measure of profit per dollar of assets. It can be defined several ways, but the most common is:

$$\text{Return on assets} = \frac{\text{Net income}}{\text{Total assets}}$$ [3.15]

$$= \frac{\$363}{\$3,588} = 10.12\%$$

Return on Equity   *Return on equity* (ROE) is a measure of how the stockholders fared during the year. Since benefiting shareholders is our goal, ROE is, in an accounting sense, the true bottom-line measure of performance. ROE is usually measured as:

$$\text{Return on equity} = \frac{\text{Net income}}{\text{Total equity}}$$ [3.16]

$$= \frac{\$363}{\$2,591} = 14\%$$

For every dollar in equity, therefore, Prufrock generated 14 cents in profit, but, again, this is only correct in accounting terms.

Because ROA and ROE are such commonly cited numbers, we stress that it is important to remember they are accounting rates of return. For this reason, these measures should properly be called *return on book assets* and *return on book equity*. In addition, ROE is sometimes called *return on net worth*. Whatever it's called, it would be inappropriate to compare the result to, for example, an interest rate observed in the financial markets.

The fact that ROE exceeds ROA reflects Prufrock's use of financial leverage. We will examine the relationship between these two measures in more detail below.

---

[3]No, it's not; margins can be small, but they do need to be positive!

Market Value Measures

Our final group of measures is based, in part, on information not necessarily contained in financial statements—the market price per share of the stock. Obviously, these measures can only be calculated directly for publicly traded companies.

We assume that Prufrock has 33 million shares outstanding and the stock sold for $88 per share at the end of the year. If we recall that Prufrock's net income was $363 million, then we can calculate that its earnings per share were:

$$\text{EPS} = \frac{\text{Net income}}{\text{Shares outstanding}} = \frac{\$363}{\cdot 33} = \$11 \qquad [3.17]$$

Price-Earnings Ratio   The first of our market value measures, the *price-earnings,* or PE, *ratio* (or multiple), is defined as:

$$\text{PE ratio} = \frac{\text{Price per share}}{\text{Earnings per share}} \qquad [3.18]$$

$$= \frac{\$88}{\$11} = 8 \text{ times}$$

In the vernacular, we would say that Prufrock shares sell for eight times earnings, or we might say that Prufrock shares have, or "carry," a PE multiple of 8.

Since the PE ratio measures how much investors are willing to pay per dollar of current earnings, higher PEs are often taken to mean that the firm has significant prospects for future growth. Of course, if a firm had no or almost no earnings, its PE would probably be quite large; so, as always, care is needed in interpreting this ratio.

Market-to-Book Ratio   A second commonly quoted measure is the *market-to-book ratio:*

$$\text{Market-to-book ratio} = \frac{\text{Market value per share}}{\text{Book value per share}} \qquad [3.19]$$

$$= \frac{\$88}{\$2,591/33} = \frac{\$88}{\$78.5} = 1.12 \text{ times}$$

Notice that book value per share is total equity (not just common stock) divided by the number of shares outstanding.

Since book value per share is an accounting number, it reflects historical costs. In a loose sense, the market-to-book ratio therefore compares the market value of the firm's investments to their cost. A value less than 1 could mean that the firm has not been successful overall in creating value for its stockholders.

This completes our definition of some common ratios. We could tell you about more of them, but these are enough for now. We'll leave it here and go on to discuss some ways of using these ratios instead of just how to calculate them. Table 3.5 summarizes the ratios we've discussed.

TABLE 3.5	Common financial ratios

I. Short-term solvency, or liquidity, ratios

$$\text{Current ratio} = \frac{\text{Current assets}}{\text{Current liabilities}}$$

$$\text{Quick ratio} = \frac{\text{Current assets} - \text{Inventory}}{\text{Current liabilities}}$$

$$\text{Cash ratio} = \frac{\text{Cash}}{\text{Current liabilities}}$$

II. Long-term solvency, or financial leverage, ratios

$$\text{Total debt ratio} = \frac{\text{Total assets} - \text{Total equity}}{\text{Total assets}}$$

$$\text{Debt-equity ratio} = \text{Total debt/Total equity}$$

$$\text{Equity multiplier} = \text{Total assets/Total equity}$$

$$\text{Times interest earned ratio} = \frac{\text{EBIT}}{\text{Interest}}$$

$$\text{Cash coverage ratio} = \frac{\text{EBIT} + \text{Depreciation}}{\text{Interest}}$$

III. Asset utilization, or turnover, ratios

$$\text{Inventory} = \frac{\text{Cost of goods sold}}{\text{Inventory}}$$

$$\text{Days' sales in inventory} = \frac{365 \text{ days}}{\text{Inventory turnover}}$$

$$\text{Receivables turnover} = \frac{\text{Sales}}{\text{Accounts receivable}}$$

$$\text{Days' sales in receivables} = \frac{365 \text{ days}}{\text{Receivables turnover}}$$

$$\text{Total asset turnover} = \frac{\text{Sales}}{\text{Total assets}}$$

$$\text{Capital intensity} = \frac{\text{Total assets}}{\text{Sales}}$$

IV. Profitability ratios

$$\text{Profit margin} = \frac{\text{Net income}}{\text{Sales}}$$

$$\text{Return on assets (ROA)} = \frac{\text{Net income}}{\text{Total assets}}$$

$$\text{Return on equity (ROE)} + \frac{\text{Net income}}{\text{Total equity}}$$

$$\text{ROE} = \frac{\text{Net income}}{\text{Sales}} \times \frac{\text{Sales}}{\text{Assets}} \times \frac{\text{Assets}}{\text{Equity}}$$

V. Market value ratios

$$\text{Price} = \text{earnings ratio} = \frac{\text{Price per share}}{\text{Earnings per share}}$$

$$\text{Market-to-book ratio} = \frac{\text{Market value per share}}{\text{Book value per share}}$$

QONCEPT QUESTIONS

3.2a What are the five groups of ratios? Give two or three examples of each kind.

3.2b Turnover ratios all have one of two figures as numerators. What are these two figures? What do these ratios measure? How do you interpret the results?

3.2c Profitability ratios all have the same figure in the numerator. What is it? What do these ratios measure? How do you interpret the results?

3.2d Given the total debt ratio, what other two ratios can be computed? Explain how.

THE DU PONT IDENTITY   3.3

As we mentioned in discussing ROA and ROE, the difference between these two profitability measures is a reflection of the use of debt financing, or financial leverage. We illustrate the relationship between these measures in this section by investigating a famous way of decomposing ROE into its component parts

To begin, let's recall the definition of ROE:

$$\text{Return on equity} = \frac{\text{Net income}}{\text{Total equity}}$$

If we were so inclined, we could multiply this ratio by Assets/Assets without changing anything:

$$\text{Return on equity} = \frac{\text{Net income}}{\text{Total equity}} = \frac{\text{Net income}}{\text{Total equity}} \times \frac{\text{Assets}}{\text{Assets}}$$

$$= \frac{\text{Net income}}{\text{Assets}} \times \frac{\text{Assets}}{\text{Total equity}}$$

Notice that we have expressed the ROE as the product of two other ratios—ROA and the equity multiplier:

$$\text{ROE} = \text{ROA} \times \text{Equity multiplier} = \text{ROA} \times (1 + \text{Debt-equity ratio})$$

Looking back at Prufrock, for example, we see that the debt-equity ratio was .39 and ROA was 10.12 percent. Our work here implies that Prufrock's ROE, as we previously calculated, is:

$$\text{ROE} = 10.12\% \times 1.39 = 14\%$$

We can further decompose ROE by multiplying the top and bottom by total sales:

$$\text{ROE} = \frac{\text{Sales}}{\text{Sales}} \times \frac{\text{Net income}}{\text{Assets}} \times \frac{\text{Assets}}{\text{Total equity}} \qquad [3.20]$$

If we rearrange things a bit, ROE is:

$$\text{ROE} = \underbrace{\frac{\text{Net income}}{\text{Sales}} \times \frac{\text{Sales}}{\text{Assets}}}_{\text{Return on assets}} \times \frac{\text{Assets}}{\text{Total equity}}$$

$$= \text{Profit margin} \times \text{Total asset turnover} \times \text{Equity multiplier}$$

What we have now done is to partition ROA into its two component parts, profit margin and total asset turnover. This last expression is called the **Du Pont identity,** after the Du Pont Corporation, which popularized its use.

We can check this relationship for Prufrock by noting that the profit margin was 15.7 percent and the total asset turnover was .64. ROE should thus be:

$$\text{ROE} = \text{Profit margin} \times \text{Total asset turnover} \times \text{Equity multiplier}$$

$$= \quad 15.7\% \quad \times \quad .64 \quad \times \quad 1.39$$

$$= \quad 14\%$$

This 14 percent ROE is exactly what we had before.

The Du Pont identity tells us that ROE is affected by three things:

1. Operating efficiency (as measured by profit margin)
2. Asset use efficiency (as measured by total asset turnover)
3. Financial leverage (as measured by the equity multiplier)

Weakness in either operating or asset use efficiency (or both) will show up in a diminished return on assets, which will translate into a lower ROE.

Considering the Du Pont identity, it appears that a firm could leverage up its ROE by increasing its amount of debt. It turns out this will only happen if the firm's ROA exceeds the interest rate on the debt. More importantly, the use of debt financing has a number of other effects, and, as we discuss at some length in later chapters, the amount of leverage a firm uses is governed by its capital structure policy.

The decomposition of ROE we've discussed in this section is a convenient way of systematically approaching financial statement analysis. If ROE is unsatisfactory by some measure, then the Du Pont identity tells you where to start looking for the reasons.

CONCEPT QUESTIONS

3.3a Return on assets, or ROA, can be expressed as the product of two ratios. Which two?

3.3b Return on equity, or ROE, can be expressed as the product of three ratios. Which three?

INTERNAL AND SUSTAINABLE GROWTH | 3.4

A firm's return on assets and return on equity are frequently used to calculate two additional numbers, both of which have to do with the firm's ability to grow. We examine these next, but first we introduce two basic ratios.

Dividend Payout and Earnings Retention

As we have seen in various places, a firm's net income gets divided into two pieces. The first piece is cash dividends paid to stockholders. Whatever is left over is the addition to retained earnings. For example, from Table 3.3, Prufrock's net income was $363, of which $121 was paid out in dividends. If we express dividends paid as a percentage of net income, the result is the *dividend payout ratio:*

$$\text{Dividend payout ratio} = \text{Cash dividends/Net income} \qquad [3.21]$$
$$= \$121/\$363$$
$$= 33 \ 1/3\%$$

What this tells us is that Prufrock pays out one-third of its net income in dividends.

Anything Prufrock does not pay out in the form of dividends must be retained in the firm, so we can define the *retention ratio* as:

$$\text{Retention ratio} = \text{Addition to retained earnings/Net income} \qquad [3.22]$$
$$= \$242/\$363$$
$$= 66 \ 2/3\%$$

So, Prufrock retains two-thirds of its net income. The retention ratio is also known as the *plowback ratio* because it is, in effect, the portion of net income that is plowed back into the business.

Notice that net income must either be paid out or plowed back, so the dividend payout and plowback ratios have to add up to 1. Put differently, if you know one of these figures, you can figure the other one immediately.

Payout and Retention | EXAMPLE 3.4

The Manson-Marilyn Corporation routinely pays out 40 percent of net income in the form of dividends. What is its plowback ratio? If net income was $800, how much did stockholders actually receive?

If the payout ratio is 40 percent, then the retention, or plowback, ratio must be 60 percent since the two have to add up to 100 percent. Dividends were 40 percent of $800, or $320.

---

reality | BYTES

GROWING BROKE: A BY-THE-BOOK CASE?

Suppose you start your own Web-based business, a bookstore perhaps. You might assume that after a short period of lingering in relative obscurity, a column in the *New York Times* praising your business would be just the ticket to launch you on your way. You would probably be right . . . but, you might also find it's just what it would take to sink your business. That is precisely what happened to www.Positively-You.com, a Web-based bookstore operating out of Cedar Falls, Iowa.

Lyle Bowlin launched Positively-You, an on-line bookstore, in 1998 with the help of his wife. They were able to earn a small profit for four months by keeping expenses to a minimum, operating the business mostly out of their living room. Then, on February 26, 1999, a glowing review of the business appeared in an op-ed column in the *New York Times*. Virtually overnight, orders grew from an average of $2,000 a month to $50,000 a month. The Bowlins, overwhelmed by the growth, enlisted the aid of their book club group to help pack and ship the orders. Meanwhile, there were more op-ed pieces, an article in *Time* magazine, appearances on television, and even collaboration on a book designed to help others start a Web-based business. It appeared to be just the kind of favorable attention a young, growing business needs.

The brisk pace of business and the positive media attention led several of the book club members to invest a total of $50,000 in the young company. An additional $30,000 in capital was raised from another local business. The bookstore operations were moved into rented office space, and soon there was a small staff of people on the payroll. But that was just the beginning of the firm's growing pains. Positively-You's profit margins were thin, about 16 cents per dollar of merchandise sold. This compared to an estimated 20 cents per dollar profit

that was being earned by Barnes&Noble.com, the fast-growing, high-volume competitor. To make matters worse, Positively-You allowed its customers to designate that 10 percent of the profit on their purchases go to the nonprofit organization of their choice. This further pared the bookstore's already thin margins. The founders hoped this would lead nonprofit organizations to steer business their way and that what the firm lacked in margins could be made up in volume. Alas, the referrals never materialized.

There were other problems as well. The company was losing money on shipping because it was matching Amazon.com's flat $2.95 shipping fee. In addition, since there wasn't enough capital for Positively-You to build its own database of books, it was forced to rent a database, which, while a cheap alternative, provided the firm little control over content or pricing. By August, sales were down to $12,000 a month and the firm was woefully short on cash. The local business investor contributed another $10,000 to the firm, hoping to get it through the upcoming Christmas season. Meanwhile, Positively-You raised its prices even though that meant charging more than its large competitor Amazon.com in many cases.

The firm never made it to Christmas. By December 14, Positively-You was out of cash and the Web site was shut down. In the end, the firm's own success was its undoing in the ultracompetitive business of being an on-line bookstore. It just didn't have the capital and cash flow to compete, and its investors eventually ended up losing everything they had put into the business. All of this might make you wonder how Amazon.com and Barnes&Noble.com can survive on such thin margins. Well, we're still waiting for them to turn a profit as well, aren't we?

ROA, ROE, and Growth

Investors and others are frequently interested in knowing how rapidly a firm's sales can grow. The important thing to recognize is that if sales are to grow, assets have to grow as well, at least over the long run. Further, if assets are to grow, then the firm must somehow obtain the money to pay for the needed acquisitions. In other words, growth has to be financed, and as a direct corollary, a firm's ability to grow depends on its financing policies. As the accompanying *Reality Bytes* box illustrates, properly managing growth is vital.

A firm has two broad sources of financing, *internal* and *external.* Internal financing simply refers to what the firm earns and subsequently plows back into the business. External financing refers to funds raised by either borrowing money or selling stock.

The Internal Growth Rate Suppose a firm has a policy of financing growth using only internal financing. This means that the firm won't borrow any funds and won't sell any new stock. How rapidly can the firm grow? The answer is given by the **internal growth rate:**

$$\text{Internal growth rate} = \frac{\text{ROA} \times b}{1 - \text{ROA} \times b} \qquad [3.23]$$

internal growth rate
The maximum possible growth rate for a firm that relies only on internal financing.

where ROA is, as usual, return on assets, and b is the retention, or plowback, ratio we just discussed.

For example, for the Prufrock Corporation, we earlier calculated ROA as 10.12 percent. We also saw that the retention ratio is 66 2/3 percent, or 2/3, so the internal growth rate is:

$$\begin{aligned}
\text{Internal growth rate} &= \frac{\text{ROA} \times b}{1 - \text{ROA} \times b} \\
&= \frac{.1012 \times (2/3)}{1 - .1012 \times (2/3)} \\
&= 7.23\%
\end{aligned}$$

Thus, if Prufrock relies solely on internally generated financing, it can grow at a maximum rate of 7.23 percent per year.

The Sustainable Growth Rate If a firm only relies on internal financing, then, through time, its total debt ratio will decline. The reason is that assets will grow, but total debt will remain the same (or even fall if some is paid off). Frequently, firms have a particular total debt ratio or equity multiplier that they view as optimal (why this is so is the subject of Chapter 13).

With this in mind, we now consider how rapidly a firm can grow if (1) it wishes to maintain a particular total debt ratio and (2) it is unwilling to sell new stock. There are various reasons why a firm might wish to avoid selling stock, and equity sales by established firms are actually a relatively rare occurrence. Given these two assumptions, the maximum growth rate that can be achieved, called the **sustainable growth rate,** is:

$$\text{Sustainable growth rate} = \frac{\text{ROE} \times b}{1 - \text{ROE} \times b} \qquad [3.24]$$

sustainable growth rate
The maximum possible growth rate for a firm that maintains a constant debt ratio and doesn't sell new stock.

Notice that this is the same as the internal growth rate, except that ROE is used instead of ROA.

Looking at Prufrock, we earlier calculated ROE as 14 percent, and we know that the retention ratio is 2/3, so we can easily calculate sustainable growth as:

$$\begin{aligned}
\text{Sustainable growth rate} &= \frac{\text{ROE} \times b}{1 - \text{ROE} \times b} \\
&= \frac{.14 \times (2/3)}{1 - .14 \times (2/3)} \\
&= 10.29\%
\end{aligned}$$

If you compare this sustainable growth rate of 10.29 percent to the internal growth rate of 7.23 percent, you might wonder why it is larger. The reason is that, as the firm grows, it will have to borrow additional funds if it is to maintain a constant debt ratio. This new borrowing is an extra source of financing in addition to internally generated funds, so Prufrock can expand more rapidly.

Determinants of Growth In our previous section, we saw that the return on equity, or ROE, could be decomposed into its various components using the Du Pont identity. Since

ROE appears so prominently in the determination of the sustainable growth rate, the factors important in determining ROE are also important determinants of growth.

As we saw, ROE can be written as the product of three factors:

ROE = Profit margin × Total asset turnover × Equity multiplier

If we examine our expression for the sustainable growth rate, we see that anything that increases ROE will increase the sustainable growth rate by making the top bigger and the bottom smaller. Increasing the plowback ratio will have the same effect.

Putting it all together, what we have is that a firm's ability to sustain growth depends explicitly on the following four factors:

1. Profit margin. An increase in profit margin will increase the firm's ability to generate funds internally and thereby increase its sustainable growth.

2. Total asset turnover. An increase in the firm's total asset turnover increases the sales generated for each dollar in assets. This decreases the firm's need for new assets as sales grow and thereby increases the sustainable growth rate. Notice that increasing total asset turnover is the same thing as decreasing capital intensity.

3. Financial policy. An increase in the debt-equity ratio increases the firm's financial leverage. Since this makes additional debt financing available, it increases the sustainable growth rate.

4. Dividend policy. A decrease in the percentage of net income paid out as dividends will increase the retention ratio. This increases internally generated equity and thus increases internal and sustainable growth.

The sustainable growth rate is a very useful number. What it illustrates is the explicit relationship between the firm's four major areas of concern: its operating efficiency as measured by profit margin, its asset use efficiency as measured by total asset turnover, its financial policy as measured by the debt-equity ratio, and its dividend policy as measured by the retention ratio. If sales are to grow at a rate higher than the sustainable growth rate, the firm must increase profit margins, increase total asset turnover, increase financial leverage, increase earnings retention, or sell new shares.

The two growth rates, internal and sustainable, are summarized in Table 3.6.

TABLE 3.6	
Summary of internal and sustainable growth rates	**I. Internal growth rate**
	$$\text{Internal growth rate} = \frac{\text{ROA} \times b}{1 - \text{ROA} \times b}$$
	where
	ROA = Return on assets = Net income/Total assets
	b = Plowback (retention) ratio
	= Addition to retained earnings/Net income
	The internal growth rate is the maximum growth rate that can be achieved with no external financing of any kind.
	II. Sustainable growth rate
	$$\text{Sustainable growth rate} = \frac{\text{ROE} \times b}{1 - \text{ROE} \times b}$$
	where
	ROE = Return on equity = Net income/Total equity
	b = Plowback (retention) ratio
	= Addition to retained earnings/Net income
	The sustainable growth rate is the maximum growth rate that can be achieved with no external equity financing while maintaining a constant debt-equity ratio.

USING FINANCIAL STATEMENT INFORMATION | 3.5

Our last task in this chapter is to discuss in more detail some practical aspects of financial statement analysis. In particular, we will look at reasons for doing financial statement analysis, how to go about getting benchmark information, and some of the problems that come up in the process.

Why Evaluate Financial Statements?

As we have discussed, the primary reason for looking at accounting information is that we don't have, and can't reasonably expect to get, market value information. It is important to emphasize that, whenever we have market information, we will use it instead of accounting data. Also, if there is a conflict between accounting and market data, market data should be given precedence.

Financial statement analysis is essentially an application of "management by exception." In many cases, such analysis will boil down to comparing ratios for one business with some kind of average or representative ratios. Those ratios that seem to differ the most from the averages are tagged for further study.

Internal Uses   Financial statement information has a variety of uses within a firm. Among the most important of these is performance evaluation. For example, managers are frequently evaluated and compensated on the basis of accounting measures of performance such as profit margin and return on equity. Also, firms with multiple divisions frequently compare the performance of those divisions using financial statement information.

Another important internal use of financial statement information involves planning for the future. Historical financial statement information is very useful for generating projections about the future and for checking the realism of assumptions made in those projections.

External Uses   Financial statements are useful to parties outside the firm, including short-term and long-term creditors and potential investors. For example, we would find such information quite useful in deciding whether or not to grant credit to a new customer.

We would also use this information to evaluate suppliers, and suppliers would use our statements before deciding to extend credit to us. Large customers use this information to decide if we are likely to be around in the future. Credit-rating agencies rely on financial statements in assessing a firm's overall creditworthiness. The common theme here is that financial statements are a prime source of information about a firm's financial health.

We would also find such information useful in evaluating our main competitors. We might be thinking of launching a new product. A prime concern would be whether the competition would jump in shortly thereafter. In this case, we would be interested in our competitors' financial strength to see if they could afford the necessary development.

Finally, we might be thinking of acquiring another firm. Financial statement information would be essential in identifying potential targets and deciding what to offer.

Choosing a Benchmark

Given that we want to evaluate a division or a firm based on its financial statements, a basic problem immediately comes up. How do we choose a benchmark, or a standard of comparison? We describe some ways of getting started in this section.

Time-Trend Analysis   One standard we could use is history. Suppose we found that the current ratio for a particular firm is 2.4 based on the most recent financial statement information. Looking back over the last 10 years, we might find that this ratio has declined fairly steadily over that period.

Based on this, we might wonder if the liquidity position of the firm has deteriorated. It could be, of course, that the firm has made changes that allow it to more efficiently use its current assets, that the nature of the firm's business has changed, or that business practices have changed. If we investigate, we might find any of these possible explanations. This is an example of what we mean by management by exception—a deteriorating time trend may not be bad, but it does merit investigation.

Peer Group Analysis   The second means of establishing a benchmark is to identify firms similar in the sense that they compete in the same markets, have similar assets, and operate in similar ways. In other words, we need to identify a *peer group*. There are obvious problems with doing this since no two companies are identical. Ultimately, the choice of which companies to use as a basis for comparison is subjective.

One common way of identifying potential peers is based on **Standard Industrial Classification (SIC) codes.** These are four-digit codes established by the U.S. government for statistical reporting purposes. Firms with the same SIC code are frequently assumed to be similar.

The first digit in an SIC code establishes the general type of business. For example, firms engaged in finance, insurance, and real estate have SIC codes beginning with 6. Each additional digit narrows down the industry. So, companies with SIC codes beginning with 60 are mostly banks and banklike businesses, those with codes beginning with 602 are mostly commercial banks, and SIC code 6025 is assigned to national banks that are members of the Federal Reserve system. Table 3.7 is a list of selected two-digit codes (the first two digits of the four-digit SIC codes) and the industries they represent.

Standard Industrial Classification (SIC) code

U.S. government code used to classify a firm by its type of business operations.

TABLE 3.7		
Selected two-digit SIC codes	Agriculture, Forestry, and Fishing	Transportation, Communication, Electric, Gas, and Sanitary Service
	01 Agriculture production—crops	45 Transportation by air
	02 Forestry	49 Electric, gas, and sanitary services
	Mining	Retail Trade
	10 Metal mining	54 Food stores
	13 Oil and gas extraction	55 Auto dealers and gas stations
	Construction	58 Eating and drinking places
	15 Building construction	Finance, Insurance, and Real Estate
	16 Construction other than building	60 Banking
	Manufacturing	63 Insurance
	28 Chemicals and allied products	65 Real Estate
	29 Petroleum refining	Services
	35 Machinery, except electrical	78 Motion pictures
	37 Transportation equipment	80 Health services
		82 Educational services

Beginning in 1997, a new industry classification system was instituted. Specifically, the North American Industry Classification System (NAICS, pronounced "nakes") is intended to replace the older SIC codes, and it probably will eventually. Currently, however, SIC codes are widely used.

SIC codes are far from perfect. For example, suppose you were examining financial statements for Wal-Mart, the largest retailer in the United States. The relevant SIC code is 5310, Department Stores. In a quick scan of the nearest financial database, you would find about 20 large, publicly owned corporations with this same SIC code, but you might not be too comfortable with some of them. Kmart would seem to be a reasonable peer, but Neiman-Marcus also carries the same industry code. Are Wal-Mart and Neiman-Marcus really comparable?

As this example illustrates, it is probably not appropriate to blindly use SIC code–based averages. Instead, analysts often identify a set of primary competitors and then compute a set of averages based on just this group. Also, we may be more concerned with a group of the top firms in an industry, not the average firm. Such a group is called an *aspirant group,* because we aspire to be like them. In this case, a financial statement analysis reveals how far we have to go.

With these caveats about SIC codes in mind, we can now take a look at a specific industry. Suppose we are in the retail furniture business. Table 3.8 contains some condensed common-size financial statements for this industry from RMA, one of many sources of such information. Table 3.9 contains selected ratios from the same source.

There is a large amount of information here. On the right in Table 3.8 we have current information reported for different groups based on sales. Within each sales group, common-size information is reported. For example, firms with sales in the $10 million to $25 million range have Cash & Equivalents equal to 7.2 percent of total assets. There are 73 companies in this group out of 681 in all.

On the left we have three years' worth of summary historical information for the entire group. For example, Profit Before Taxes fell from 2.5 percent of sales to 2.1 percent over that time.

Table 3.9 contains some selected ratios, again reported by sales groups on the right and time period on the left. To see how we might use this information, suppose our firm has a current ratio of 2. Based on the ratios in the table, is this value unusual?

Looking at the current ratio for the overall group for the most recent year (third column from the left), we see that three numbers are reported. The one in the middle, 1.7, is the median, meaning that half of the 681 firms had current ratios that were lower and half had higher current ratios. The other two numbers are the upper and lower quartiles. So, 25 percent of the firms had a current ratio larger than 2.6 and 25 percent had a current ratio smaller than 1.2. Our value of 2 falls comfortably within these bounds, so it doesn't appear too unusual. This comparison illustrates how knowledge of the range of ratios is important in addition to knowledge of the average. Notice how stable the current ratio has been for the last three years.

More Ratios | EXAMPLE 3.5

Take a look at the numbers reported for Sales/Receivables and EBIT/Interest in Table 3.9. What are the overall median values? What are these ratios?

If you look back at our discussion, you will see that these are the receivables turnover and times interest earned, TIE, ratios. The median value for receivables turnover for the entire group is 31.3 times. So, the days in receivables would be 365/31.3 = 12, which is the bold-faced number reported. The median for the TIE is 2.3 times. The number in parentheses indicates that the calculation is meaningful for, and therefore based on, only 605 of the 681 companies. In this case, the reason is probably that only 605 companies paid any significant amount of interest.

Selected financial statement information

			RETAILERS—FURNITURE			SIC# 5712			
Comparative Historical Data						**Current Data Sorted by Sales**			
31	53		# Postretirement Benefits						
			Type of Statement						
69	75	76	Unqualified	3	5	5	5	12	46
119	145	133	Reviewed	4	34	19	39	30	7
241	255	240	Compiled	49	106	39	31	13	2
42	54	62	Tax Returns	21	24	11	4		2
122	169	170	Other	26	57	19	27	18	23
4/1/94– 3/31/95	**4/1/95– 3/31/96**	**4/1/96– 3/31/97**		224 (4/1–9/30/96)				457 (10/1/96–3/31/97)	
ALL	**ALL**	**ALL**		**0–1MM**	**1–3MM**	**3–5MM**	**5–10MM**	**10–25MM**	**25MM & OVER**
593	698	681	**NUMBER OF STATEMENTS**	103	226	93	106	73	80
%	%	%	**ASSETS**	%	%	%	%	%	%
7.2	6.7	6.7	Cash & Equivalents	6.1	7.3	6.7	6.0	7.2	6.0
16.1	18.6	17.9	Trade Receivables - (net)	17.2	15.2	16.9	18.6	18.2	26.0
52.0	49.7	48.9	Inventory	46.1	53.3	52.9	50.0	48.0	35.2
1.4	1.6	1.4	All Other Current	1.7	1.2	.6	1.4	1.7	2.3
76.7	76.6	74.9	Total Current	71.0	77.1	77.1	75.9	75.1	69.6
17.4	16.9	17.5	Fixed Assets (net)	21.2	15.4	16.2	16.4	17.1	22.4
1.0	1.2	1.7	Intangibles (net)	2.9	1.4	1.6	1.1	1.0	2.3
4.9	5.2	5.9	All Other Non-Current	4.9	6.1	5.1	6.6	6.9	5.8
100.0	100.0	100.0	Total	100.0	100.0	100.0	100.0	100.0	100.0
			LIABILITIES						
9.2	10.7	11.0	Notes Payable-Short Term	13.1	10.5	10.8	9.8	11.6	11.0
2.9	3.2	3.0	Cur. Mat.-L/T/D	4.4	3.1	3.4	2.8	2.2	1.4
18.7	18.5	17.9	Trade Payables	13.8	16.1	20.5	20.5	21.7	18.3
.4	.3	.3	Income Taxes Payable	.2	.3	.1	.3	.3	.6
14.9	13.5	13.8	All Other Current	11.1	12.4	15.7	15.1	18.1	13.3
46.1	46.2	46.0	Total Current	42.6	42.4	50.6	48.4	53.9	44.6
13.4	12.4	13.2	Long Term Debt	22.0	12.1	11.6	10.5	9.1	14.1
.2	.2	.1	Deferred Taxes	.1	.0	.1	.3	.1	.3
3.4	3.4	3.6	All Other Non-Current	3.3	3.0	3.9	3.9	4.7	3.7
36.9	37.9	37.1	Net Worth	31.9	42.4	33.8	36.9	32.2	37.3
100.0	100.0	100.0	Total Liablilities & Net Worth	100.0	100.0	100.0	100.0	100.0	100.0
			INCOME DATA						
100.0	100.0	100.0	Net Sales	100.0	100.0	100.0	100.0	100.0	100.0
39.4	38.9	39.3	Gross Profit	41.3	39.3	37.6	39.2	38.9	39.1
36.6	36.5	36.6	Operating Expenses	38.1	36.4	36.2	37.0	36.4	35.2
2.8	2.4	2.7	Operating Profit	3.3	2.9	1.4	2.2	2.6	3.9
.3	.3	.6	All Other Expenses (net)	1.3	.4	.3	.4	.6	.8
2.5	2.1	2.1	Profit Before Taxes	2.0	2.5	1.1	1.8	2.0	3.1

M = $ thousand   MM = $ million

Interpretation of Statement Studies Figures: RMA cautions that the studies be regarded only as a general guideline and not as an absolute industry norm. This is due to limited samples within categories, the categorization of companies by their primary Standard Industrial Classification (SIC) number only, and different methods of operations by companies within the same industry. For these reasons, RMA recommends that the figures be used only as general guidelines in addition to other methods of financial analysis.

Problems with Financial Statement Analysis

We close out our chapter on working with financial statements by discussing some additional problems that can arise in using financial statements. In one way or another, the basic problem with financial statement analysis is that there is no underlying theory to help us identify which items or ratios to look at and to guide us in establishing benchmarks.

As we discuss in other chapters, there are many cases where financial theory and economic logic provide guidance in making judgments about value and risk. Very little such help exists with financial statements. This is why we can't say which ratios matter the most and what a high or low value might be.

Selected ratios

	RETAILERS—FURNITURE		SIC# 5712		

| Comparative Historical Data | | | | Current Data Sorted by Sales | | | | | |

				# Postretirement Benefits								
31	53			**Type of Statement**								
69	75	76		Unqualified	3	5	5	5	12	46
119	145	133		Reviewed	4	34	19	39	30	7
241	255	240		Compiled	49	106	39	31	13	2
42	54	62		Tax Returns	21	24	11	4		2
122	169	170		Other	26	57	19	27	18	23
4/1/94–3/31/95	4/1/95–3/31/96	4/1/96–3/31/97			224 (4/1–9/30/96)			457 (10/1/96–3/31/97)		
ALL	ALL	ALL			0–1MM	1–3MM	3–5MM	5–10MM	10–25MM	25MM & OVER
593	698	681		**NUMBER OF STATEMENTS**	103	226	93	106	73	80
				RATIOS						
2.7	2.5	2.6		Current	2.9	3.1	2.6	2.4	2.1	2.4
1.7	1.7	1.7			1.8	1.9	1.5	1.5	1.4	1.4
1.2	1.3	1.2			1.2	1.3	1.1	1.2	1.1	1.2
1.0	1.0	1.0		Quick	1.3	.9	.9	1.0	.8	1.2
(592) .4	.5	(678) .4			(102) .6	(224) .4	.3	.4	.4	.6
.2	.2	.2			.2	.2	.1	.2	.1	.2
2 181.1	3 137.9	2 182.5		Sales Receivables	2 177.0	1 298.5	2 212.3	3 110.1	2 188.6	4 93.4
10 36.5	13 27.6	12 31.3			14 25.7	11 34.6	11 31.9	14 26.2	9 41.3	21 17.7
36 10.2	43 8.5	41 9.0			49 7.5	31 11.7	33 11.2	41 8.9	39 9.3	74 4.9
79 4.6	76 4.8	76 4.8		Cost of Sales/Inventory	76 4.8	94 3.9	74 4.9	70 5.2	64 5.7	54 6.7
118 3.1	118 3.1	122 3.0			135 2.7	135 2.7	122 3.0	111 3.3	107 3.4	101 3.6
166 2.2	166 2.2	174 2.1			203 1.8	192 1.9	174 2.1	152 2.4	146 2.5	130 2.8
22 16.8	22 16.8	20 17.9		Cost of Sales/Payable	11 33.0	18 20.3	21 17.7	22 16.7	25 14.6	25 14.8
38 9.6	37 9.9	37 9.8			30 12.0	35 10.4	30 12.1	38 9.6	45 8.2	41 8.9
55 6.6	61 6.0	59 6.2			58 6.3	54 6.7	64 5.7	59 6.2	62 5.9	61 6.0
4.5	4.4	4.4		Sales/Working Capital	3.4	4.0	5.1	5.6	6.6	4.9
8.9	8.7	9.0			7.0	7.0	11.0	11.8	14.2	12.6
23.0	21.4	24.4			26.9	16.0	50.1	22.5	52.7	33.5
7.9	6.2	6.0		EBIT/Interest	5.6	6.3	6.0	4.2	6.0	8.3
(522) 3.1	(621) 2.5	(605) 2.3			(90) 1.9	(191) 2.2	(83) 2.1	(100) 2.4	(67) 2.8	(74) 3.4
1.4	1.3	1.1			.1	1.1	.7	1.2	1.2	1.4
5.1	4.8	4.2		Net Profit + Depr., Dep.,		3.8	2.9	3.7	10.4	7.9
(199) 2.0	(193) 1.9	(163) 1.9		Amort./Cur. Mat. L/T/D	(40) 1.8	(29) 1.1	(27) 1.6	(24) 3.1	(36) 4.2
.8	.8	.8				.5	.4	1.1	1.2	1.9
.2	.2	.1		Fixed/Worth	.1	.1	.2	.2	.2	.3
.4	.4	.4			.6	.3	.4	.4	.5	.6
1.0	.8	1.0			2.1	.7	.9	.9	1.1	1.4
.9	.8	.9		Debt/Worth	1.0	.7	.9	.9	1.2	1.0
1.8	1.7	1.8			2.2	1.4	2.1	2.0	1.9	1.9
3.7	3.7	4.2			6.5	3.4	5.1	3.9	6.5	4.1
34.3	28.1	29.7		% Profit Before Taxes/Tangible	41.8	27.8	24.3	23.2	41.3	30.9
(547) 14.9	(647) 12.8	(621) 12.1		Net Worth	(86) 19.9	(206) 9.0	(85) 8.4	(99) 10.7	(67) 14.3	(78) 17.6
4.3	2.7	1.9			.7	.7	.6	2.3	4.4	6.4
11.8	9.6	10.3		% Profit Before Taxes/Total	14.4	11.2	6.8	7.6	11.7	11.2
5.4	4.3	4.2		Assets	5.7	4.3	2.9	3.4	4.7	5.8
1.0	.8	.3			–3.8	.2	–1.1	.7	1.0	1.8
45.3	55.6	53.2		Sales/Net Fixed Assets	45.7	69.6	64.2	53.8	42.3	25.3
22.0	24.3	21.9			15.2	26.5	30.5	28.3	19.9	12.1
10.1	10.9	9.0			5.7	12.5	11.3	11.1	10.8	6.8
3.5	3.5	3.5		Sales/Total Assets	3.0	3.4	3.6	3.8	3.5	3.7
2.7	2.6	2.6			1.9	2.6	2.6	2.8	3.0	2.2
1.8	1.7	1.7			1.2	1.7	2.0	2.0	2.2	1.3
.5	.5	.5		% Depr., Dep., Amort./Sales	.8	.4	.5	.5	.5	.7
(525) .9	(627) .8	(590) .9			(78) 1.4	(194) .8	(84) .9	(97) .8	(64) .8	(73) 1.1
1.4	1.3	1.4			2.6	1.4	1.2	1.1	1.3	1.9
2.3	2.1	2.2		% Officers', Directors',	3.4	2.7	2.1	1.7	1.1	1.3
(295) 4.0	(342) 3.9	(306) 3.8		Owners' Comp./Sales	(48) 5.4	(122) 4.3	(46) 3.6	(49) 2.6	(29) 1.9	(12) 2.4
6.4	6.5	6.3			8.6	6.5	5.2	4.7	3.6	6.3
7184284M	8937358M	9896243M		Net Sales ($)	63634M	421255M	350655M	732743M	1052882M	7275074M
3751132M	4494242M	5171917M		Total Assets ($)	43170M	209025M	153939M	304881M	428781M	4032121M

M = $ thousand   MM = $ million

One particularly severe problem is that many firms are conglomerates, owning more or less unrelated lines of business. The consolidated financial statements for such firms don't really fit any neat industry category. Going back to department stores, for example, Sears has an SIC code of 6710 (Holding Offices) because of its diverse financial and retailing operations. More generally, the kind of peer group analysis we have been describing is going to work best when the firms are strictly in the same line of business, the industry is competitive, and there is only one way of operating.

Another problem that is becoming increasingly common is that major competitors and natural peer group members in an industry may be scattered around the globe. The automobile industry is an obvious example. The problem here is that financial statements from outside the United States do not necessarily conform at all to GAAP (more precisely, different countries can have different GAAPs). The existence of different standards and procedures makes it very difficult to compare financial statements across national borders.

Even companies that are clearly in the same line of business may not be comparable. For example, electric utilities engaged primarily in power generation are all classified in the same group (SIC 4911). This group is often thought to be relatively homogeneous. However, utilities generally operate as regulated monopolies, so they don't compete with each other. Many have stockholders, and many are organized as cooperatives with no stockholders. There are several different ways of generating power, ranging from hydroelectric to nuclear, so the operating activities can differ quite a bit. Finally, profitability is strongly affected by regulatory environment, so utilities in different locations can be very similar but show very different profits.

Several other general problems frequently crop up. First, different firms use different accounting procedures—for inventory, for example. This makes it difficult to compare statements. Second, different firms end their fiscal years at different times. For firms in seasonal businesses (such as a retailer with a large Christmas season), this can lead to difficulties in comparing balance sheets because of fluctuations in accounts during the year. Finally, for any particular firm, unusual or transient events, such as a one-time profit from an asset sale, may affect financial performance. In comparing firms, such events can give misleading signals.

CONCEPT QUESTIONS

3.5a What are some uses for financial statement analysis?

3.5b What are SIC codes and how might they be useful?

3.5c Why do we say that financial statement analysis is management by exception?

3.5d What are some of the problems that can come up with financial statement analysis?

SUMMARY AND CONCLUSIONS

This chapter has discussed aspects of financial statement analysis including:

1. Standardized financial statements. We explained that differences in firm size make it difficult to compare financial statements, and we discussed how to form common-size statements to make comparisons easier.

2. Ratio analysis. Evaluating ratios of accounting numbers is another way of comparing financial statement information. We therefore defined and discussed a number of the most commonly reported and used financial ratios. We also discussed the famous

Du Pont identity as a way of analyzing financial performance, and we examined the connection between profitability, financial policy, and growth.

3. Using financial statements. We described how to establish benchmarks for comparison purposes and discussed some of the types of information that are available. We then examined some of the potential problems that can arise.

After you have studied this chapter, we hope that you will have some perspective on the uses and abuses of financial statements. You should also find that your vocabulary of business and financial terms has grown substantially.

CHAPTER REVIEW AND SELF-TEST PROBLEMS

3.1 **Common-Size Statements.** Below are the most recent financial statements for Wildhack. Prepare a common-size income statement based on this information. How do you interpret the standardized net income? What percentage of sales goes to cost of goods sold?

WILDHACK CORPORATION
2000 Income Statement
($ in millions)

Sales		$3,756
Cost of goods sold		2,453
Depreciation		490
Earnings before interest and taxes		$ 813
Interest paid		613
Taxable income		$ 200
Taxes (34%)		68
Net income		$ 132
Dividends	$46	
Addition to retained earnings	86	

WILDHACK CORPORATION
Balance Sheets as of December 31, 1999 and 2000
($ in millions)

Assets	1999	2000	Liabilities and Owners' Equity	1999	2000
Current assets			Current liabilities		
Cash	$ 120	$ 88	Accounts payable	$ 124	$ 144
Accounts receivable	224	192	Notes payable	1,412	1,039
Inventory	424	368	Total	$1,536	$1,183
Total	$ 768	$ 648	Long-term debt	$1,804	$2,077
Fixed assets			Owners' equity		
Net plant			Common stock		
and equipment	$5,228	$5,354	and paid-in surplus	300	300
			Retained earnings	2,356	2,442
Total assets	$5,996	$6,002	Total	$2,656	$2,742
			Total liabilities and owner's equity	$5,996	$6,002

3.2   **Financial Ratios.**   Based on the balance sheets and income statement in the previous problem, calculate the following ratios for 2000:

Current ratio   _____
Quick ratio   _____
Cash ratio   _____
Inventory turnover   _____
Receivables turnover   _____
Days' sales in inventory   _____
Days' sales in receivables   _____
Total debt ratio   _____
Times interest earned ratio   _____
Cash coverage ratio   _____

3.3   **ROE and the Du Pont Identity.**   Calculate the 2000 ROE for the Wildhack Corporation and then break down your answer into its component parts using the Du Pont identity.

3.4   **Sustainable Growth.**   Based on the following information, what growth rate can Corwin maintain if no external financing is used? What is the sustainable growth rate?

CORWIN COMPANY
Financial Statements

Income Statement		Balance Sheet			
Sales	$2,750	Current assets	$ 600	Long-term debt	$ 200
Cost of sales	2,400	Net fixed assets	800	Equity	1,200
Tax (34%)	119	Total	$1,400	Total	$1,400
Net income	$ 231				
Dividends	$ 77				

■ Answers to Chapter Review and Self-Test Problems

3.1   We've calculated the common-size income statement below. Remember that we simply divide each item by total sales.

WILDHACK CORPORATION
2000 Common-Size Income Statement

Sales		100.0%
Cost of goods sold		65.3
Depreciation		13.0
Earnings before interest and taxes		21.6
Interest paid		16.3
Taxable income		5.3
Taxes (34%)		1.8
Net income		3.5%
Dividends	1.2%	
Addition to retained earnings	2.3	

Net income is 3.5 percent of sales. Since this is the percentage of each sales dollar that makes its way to the bottom line, the standardized net income is the firm's profit margin. Cost of goods sold is 65.3 percent of sales.

3.2   We've calculated the ratios below based on the ending figures. If you don't remember a definition, refer back to Table 3.5.

Current ratio	$648/$1,183	= .55 times
Quick ratio	$280/$1,183	= .24 times
Cash ratio	$88/$1,183	= .07 times
Inventory turnover	$2,453/$368	= 6.7 times
Receivables turnover	$3,756/$192	= 19.6 times
Days' sales in inventory	365/6.7	= 54.5 days
Days' sales in receivables	365/19.6	= 18.6 days
Total debt ratio	$3,260/$6,002	= 54.3%
Times interest earned ratio	$813/$613	= 1.33 times
Cash coverage ratio	$1,303/$613	= 2.13 times

3.3 The return on equity is the ratio of net income to total equity. For Wildhack, this is $132/$2,742 = 4.8%, which is not outstanding. Given the Du Pont identity, ROE can be written as:

$$\text{ROE} = \text{Profit margin} \times \text{Total asset turnover} \times \text{Equity multiplier}$$
$$= \$132/\$3,756 \ \times \ \$3,756/\$6,002 \quad \times \quad \$6,002/\$2,742$$
$$= \quad 3.5\% \quad \times \quad\quad .626 \quad\quad \times \quad\quad 2.19$$
$$= \quad 4.8\%$$

Notice that return on assets, ROA, is 3.5% × .626 = 2.2%.

3.4 Corwin retains $b = (1 - .33) = .67$ of net income. Return on assets is $231/$1,400 = 16.5%. The internal growth rate is:

$$\frac{\text{ROA} \times b}{1 - \text{ROA} \times b} = \frac{.165 \times .67}{1 - .165 \times .67}$$
$$= 12.36\%$$

Return on equity for Corwin is $231/$1,200 = 19.25%, so we can calculate the sustainable growth rate as:

$$\frac{\text{ROE} \times b}{1 - \text{ROE} \times b} = \frac{.1925 \times .67}{1 - .1925 \times .67}$$
$$= 14.81\%$$

CRITICAL THINKING AND CONCEPTS REVIEW

1. **Current Ratio.** What effect would the following actions have on a firm's current ratio? Assume that net working capital is positive.
   a. Inventory is purchased.
   b. A supplier is paid.
   c. A short-term bank loan is repaid.
   d. A long-term debt is paid off early.
   e. A customer pays off a credit account.
   f. Inventory is sold at cost.
   g. Inventory is sold for a profit.

2. **Current Ratio and Quick Ratio.** In recent years, Dixie Co. has greatly increased its current ratio. At the same time, the quick ratio has fallen. What has happened? Has the liquidity of the company improved?

3. **Current Ratio.** Explain what it means for a firm to have a current ratio equal to .50. Would the firm be better off if the current ratio were 1.50? What if it were 15.0? Explain your answers.

4. **Financial Ratios.** Fully explain the kind of information the following financial ratios provide about a firm:
    a. Quick ratio
    b. Cash ratio
    c. Capital intensity ratio
    d. Total asset turnover
    e. Equity multiplier
    f. Long-term debt ratio
    g. Times interest earned ratio
    h. Profit margin
    i. Return on assets
    j. Return on equity
    k. Price-earnings ratio

5. **Standardized Financial Statements.** What types of information do common-size financial statements reveal about the firm? What is the best use for these common-size statements?

6. **Peer Group Analysis.** Explain what peer group analysis means. As a financial manager, how could you use the results of peer group analysis to evaluate the performance of your firm? How is a peer group different from an aspirant group?

7. **Du Pont Identity.** Why is the Du Pont identity a valuable tool for analyzing the performance of a firm? Discuss the types of information it reveals as compared to ROE considered by itself.

8. **Industry-Specific Ratios.** Specialized ratios are sometimes used in specific industries. For example, the so-called book-to-bill ratio is closely watched for semiconductor manufacturers. A ratio of .93 indicates that for every $100 worth of chips shipped over some period, only $93 worth of new orders were received. In August 1998, the North American semiconductor equipment industry's book-to-bill ratio declined to .60, the lowest level since 1995, when analysts first began following it. Three-month average shipments in August were down 5 percent from July figures, while three-month average bookings were down 14.7 percent. What is this ratio intended to measure? Why do you think it is so closely followed?

9. **Industry-Specific Ratios.** So-called "same-store sales" are a very important measure for companies as diverse as McDonald's and Sears. As the name suggests, examining same-store sales means comparing revenues from the same stores or restaurants at two different points in time. Why might companies focus on same-store sales rather than total sales?

10. **Industry-Specific Ratios.** There are many ways of using standardized financial information beyond those discussed in this chapter. The usual goal is to put firms on an equal footing for comparison purposes. For example, for auto manufacturers, it is common to express sales, costs, and profits on a per-car basis. For each of the following industries, give an example of an actual company and discuss one or more potentially useful means of standardizing financial information:
    a. Public utilities
    b. Large retailers
    c. Airlines
    d. On-line services
    e. Hospitals
    f. College textbook publishers

QUESTIONS AND PROBLEMS

1. **Calculating Liquidity Ratios.** SDJ, Inc., has net working capital of $950, current liabilities of $3,100, and inventory of $1,500. What is the current ratio? What is the quick ratio?

2. **Calculating Profitability Ratios.** Emmitt's Excavating has sales of $46 million, total assets of $30 million, and total debt of $12 million. If the profit margin is 14 percent, what is net income? What is ROA? What is ROE?

3. **Calculating the Average Collection Period.** Pirate Lumber Yard has a current accounts receivable balance of $357,682. Credit sales for the year just ended were $2,621,508. What is the receivables turnover? The days' sales in receivables? How long did it take on average for credit customers to pay off their accounts during the past year?

4. **Calculating Inventory Turnover.** McCain Corporation has ending inventory of $852,621, and cost of goods sold for the year just ended was $2,143,812. What is the inventory turnover? The days' sales in inventory? How long on average did a unit of inventory sit on the shelf before it was sold?

5. **Calculating Leverage Ratios.** Walker's Cay Charters, Inc., has a total debt ratio of .28. What is its debt-equity ratio? What is its equity multiplier?

6. **Calculating Market Value Ratios.** Sandy's Baby-sitting, Inc., had additions to retained earnings for the year just ended of $250,000. The firm paid out $200,000 in cash dividends, and it has ending total equity of $5 million. If Sandy's currently has 400,000 shares of common stock outstanding, what are earnings per share? Dividends per share? What is book value per share? If the stock currently sells for $25 per share, what is the market-to-book ratio? The price-earnings ratio?

7. **Du Pont Identity.** If Roten Rooters, Inc., has an equity multiplier of 1.90, total asset turnover of 1.30, and a profit margin of 14 percent, what is its ROE?

8. **Du Pont Identity.** Corrado Cricket Removal has a profit margin of 11 percent, total asset turnover of 1.55, and ROE of 18.50 percent. What is this firm's debt-equity ratio?

9. **Calculating Average Payables Period.** For the past year, BDJ, Inc., had a cost of goods sold of $9,541. At the end of the year, the accounts payable balance was $1,800. How long on average did it take the company to pay off its suppliers during the year? What might a large value for this ratio imply?

10. **Equity Multiplier and Return on Equity.** Zurek Fried Chicken Company has a debt-equity ratio of 1.40. Return on assets is 6.5 percent, and total equity is $310,000. What is the equity multiplier? Return on equity? Net income?

11. **Internal Growth.** If Highfield Hobby Shop has a 22 percent ROA and a 25 percent payout ratio, what is its internal growth rate?

12. **Sustainable Growth.** If the Daly Driving School has a 21 percent ROE and an 80 percent payout ratio, what is its sustainable growth rate?

13. **Sustainable Growth.** Based on the following information, calculate the sustainable growth rate for Pete's Pies:

   Profit margin = 9.5%
   Capital intensity ratio = .60
   Debt-equity ratio = .50
   Net income = $20,000
   Dividends = $5,000

   What is the ROE here?

__ 14.   **Sustainable Growth.**   Assuming the following ratios are constant, what is the sustainable growth rate?

Total asset turnover = 2.30
Profit margin   = 8.0%
Equity multiplier   = 2.25
Payout ratio   = 40%

Bethesda Mining Company reports the following balance sheet information for 1999 and 2000. Use this information to work Problems 15 through 17.

BETHESDA MINING COMPANY
Balance Sheets as of December 31, 1999 and 2000

	1999	2000		1999	2000
Assets			**Liabilities and Owners' Equity**		
Current assets					
Cash	$ 14,682	$ 17,950	Current liabilities		
Accounts receivable	44,306	47,626	Accounts payable	$147,024	$125,300
Inventory	91,636	120,580	Notes payable	68,382	90,928
Total	$150,624	$186,156	Total	$215,406	$216,228
Fixed Assets			Long-term debt	$100,000	$ 50,000
Net plant and equipment	$518,864	$547,016	Owners' equity		
			Common stock and paid-in surplus	$150,000	$150,000
			Retained earnings	204,082	316,944
			Total	$354,082	$466,944
Total assets	$669,488	$733,172	Total liabilities and owners' equity	$669,488	$733,172

15.   **Preparing Standardized Financial Statements.**   Prepare the 1999 and 2000 common-size balance sheets for Bethesda Mining.

16.   **Calculating Financial Ratios.**   Based on the balance sheets given for Bethesda Mining, calculate the following financial ratios for each year:
    a. Current ratio
    b. Quick ratio
    c. Cash ratio
    d. Debt-equity ratio and equity multiplier
    e. Total debt ratio

17.   **Du Pont Identity.**   Suppose that the Bethesda Mining Company had sales of $1,743,281 and net income of $159,550 for the year ending December 31, 2000. Calculate the Du Pont identity.

18.   **Du Pont Identity.**   The Polish Exotic Pet Company has an ROA of 12 percent, an 8 percent profit margin, and an ROE of 23 percent. What is the company's total asset turnover? What is the equity multiplier?

__ 19.   **Return on Assets.**   Wade's Water Witching Service has a profit margin of 15 percent on sales of $20,000,000. If the firm has debt of $7,500,000 and total assets of $22,500,000, what is the firm's ROA?

→ 20. **Calculating Internal Growth.** The most recent financial statements for Filer Manufacturing Co. are shown below:

Income Statement			Balance Sheet			
Sales	$20,158		Current assets	$15,000	Debt	$42,000
Costs	7,254		Fixed assets	49,000	Equity	22,000
Taxable income	$12,904		Total	$64,000	Total	$64,000
Tax (34%)	4,387					
Net Income	$ 8,517					

Assets and costs are proportional to sales. Debt and equity are not. Filer Manufacturing maintains a constant 40 percent dividend payout ratio. No external financing is possible. What is the internal growth rate?

→ 21. **Calculating Sustainable Growth.** For Filer Manufacturing in Problem 20, what is the sustainable growth rate?

22. **Total Asset Turnover.** Kaleb's Karate Supply had a profit margin of 7 percent, sales of $10 million, and total assets of $6 million. What was total asset turnover? If management set a goal of increasing total asset turnover to 2.25 times, what would the new sales figure need to be, assuming no increase in total assets?

23. **Return on Equity.** Taylor's Cleaning Service has a total debt ratio of .75, total debt of $150,000, and net income of $20,000. What is Taylor's return on equity?

24. **Market Value Ratios.** Joe's Jalopies has a current stock price of $80. For the past year the company had net income of $4,500,000, total equity of $20,000,000, and 3.2 million shares of stock outstanding. What is the earnings per share (EPS)? Price-earnings ratio? Book value per share? Market-to-book ratio?

25. **Profit Margin.** Bob's Billiards has total assets of $10,000,000 and a total asset turnover of 3.2 times. If the return on assets is 10 percent, what is Bob's profit margin?

→ 26. **Using the Du Pont Identity.** Y3K, Inc., has sales of $2,250, total assets of $900, and a debt-equity ratio of 1.00. If its return on equity is 11 percent, what is its net income?

27. **Ratios and Fixed Assets.** The Hooya Company has a long-term debt ratio (i.e., the ratio of long-term debt to total assets) of 0.55 and a current ratio of 1.35. Current liabilities are $750, sales are $3,650, profit margin is 8.5 percent, and ROE is 24.5 percent. What is the amount of the firm's net fixed assets?

28. **Profit Margin.** In response to complaints about high prices, a grocery chain is the following advertising campaign: "If you pay your child 50 cents to go buy $25 worth of groceries, then your child makes twice as much on the trip as we do." You've collected the following information from the grocery chain's financial statements:

(millions)	
Sales	$300.0
Net income	3.0
Total assets	70.0
Total debt	45.0

Evaluate the grocery chain's claim. What is the basis for the statement this claim misleading? Why or why not?

Intermediate (Questions 6–42)

29. **Using the Du Pont Identity.** The Jordan Company has net income of $125,300. There are currently 18.20 days' sales in receivables. Total assets are $725,000, total receivables are $106,400, and the debt-equity ratio is 0.85. What is Jordan's profit margin? Its total asset turnover? Its ROE?

30. **Calculating the Cash Coverage Ratio.** Tommy Wooten Inc.'s net income for the most recent year was $5,250. The tax rate was 34 percent. The firm paid $1,784 in total interest expense and deducted $1,250 in depreciation expense. What was Tommy Wooten's cash coverage ratio for the year?

31. **Calculating the Times Interest Earned Ratio.** For the most recent year, Nugent's Nougats, Inc., had sales of $450,000, cost of goods sold of $110,000, depreciation expense of $58,000, and additions to retained earnings of $65,320. The firm currently has 20,000 shares of common stock outstanding, and the previous year's dividends per share were $1.80. Assuming a 34 percent income tax rate, what was the times interest earned ratio?

32. **Return on Assets.** A fire has destroyed a large percentage of the financial records of the Carter Company. You have the task of piecing together information in order to release a financial report. You have found the return on equity to be 16 percent. Sales were $1,200,000, the total debt ratio was .40, and total debt was $200,000. What is the return on assets (ROA)?

33. **Ratios and Foreign Companies.** King Albert Carpet PLC had a 2000 net loss of £8,254 on sales of £154,392 (both in thousands of pounds). What was the company's profit margin? Does the fact that these figures are quoted in a foreign currency make any difference? Why? In dollars, sales were $324,223. What was the net loss in dollars?

Some recent financial statements for Smolira Golf, Inc., follow. Use this information to work Problems 34 through 36.

SMOLIRA GOLF, INC.
Balance Sheets as of December 31, 1999 and 2000

Assets	1999	2000	Liabilities and Owners' Equity	1999	2000
Current assets			Current liabilities		
Cash	$ 1,040	$ 644	Accounts payable	$ 1,704	$ 1,872
Accounts receivable	2,904	$ 3,812	Notes payable	826	858
Inventory	6,218	5,910	Other	60	418
	$10,162	$10,366	Total	$ 2,590	$ 3,148
Fixed			Long-term debt	$ 6,234	$ 5,000
Net p equip d	$19,088	$20,066	Owners' equity		
			Common stock and paid-in surplus	$20,000	$20,000
			Retained earnings	426	2,284
Total asset			Total	$20,426	$22,284
	$29,250	$30,432	Total	$29,250	$30,432

SMOLIRA GOLF, INC.
2000 Income Statement

Sales	$22,400
Cost of goods sold	7,800
Depreciation	1,300
Earnings before interest and taxes	$13,300
Interest paid	1,170
Taxable income	$12,130
Taxes (34%)	4,124
Net income	$8,006

Dividends	$6,148	
Addition to retained earnings	1,858	

34. **Calculating Financial Ratios.** Find the following financial ratios for Smolira Golf (use year-end figures rather than average values where appropriate):

   Short-term solvency ratios

   a. Current ratio   _____

   b. Quick ratio   _____

   c. Cash ratio   _____

   Asset utilization ratios

   d. Total asset turnover   _____

   e. Inventory turnover   _____

   f. Receivables turnover   _____

   Long-term solvency ratios

   g. Total debt ratio   _____

   h. Debt-equity ratio   _____

   i. Equity multiplier   _____

   j. Times interest earned ratio _____

   k. Cash coverage ratio   _____

   Profitability ratios

   l. Profit margin   _____

   m. Return on assets   _____

   n. Return on equity   _____

35. **Du Pont Identity.** Construct the Du Pont identity for Smolira Golf.

36. **Market Value Ratios.** Smolira Golf has 1,000 shares of common stock outstanding, and the market price for a share of stock at the end of 2000 was $63. What is the price-earnings ratio? What are the dividends per share? What is the market-to-book ratio at the end of 2000?

37. **Growth and Profit Margin.** The Bradley Brake Co. wishes to maintain a growth rate of 7 percent a year, a debt-equity ratio of .45, and a dividend payout ratio of 60 percent. The ratio of total assets to sales is constant at 1.40. What profit margin must the firm achieve?

38. Growth and Debt-Equity Ratio. A firm wishes to maintain a growth rate of 10 percent and a dividend payout ratio of 40 percent. The ratio of total assets to sales is constant at 1.1, and profit margin is 9 percent. If the firm also wishes to maintain a constant debt-equity ratio, what must it be?

39. Growth and Assets. A firm wishes to maintain a growth rate of 7 percent and a dividend payout ratio of 60 percent. The current profit margin is 12 percent and the firm uses no external financing sources. What must total asset turnover be?

40. Sustainable Growth. Based on the following information, calculate the sustainable growth rate for Candlebox, Inc.:

Profit margin	= 9.5%
Total asset turnover	= 1.20
Total debt ratio	= .60
Payout ratio	= 75%

What is the ROA here?

41. Sustainable Growth and Outside Financing. You've collected the following information about Yi's Yams, Inc.:

Sales	= $90,000
Net income	= $6,000
Dividends	= $1,800
Total debt	= $45,000
Total equity	= $22,000

What is the sustainable growth rate for Yi's Yams, Inc.? If it does grow at this rate, how much new borrowing will take place in the coming year, assuming a constant debt-equity ratio? What growth rate could be supported with no outside financing at all?

42. Constraints on Growth. Paglia's Pasta, Inc., wishes to maintain a growth rate of 12 percent per year and a debt-equity ratio of .20. Profit margin is 6 percent, and total asset turnover is constant at 1.05. Is this growth rate possible? To answer, determine what the dividend payout ratio must be. How do you interpret the result?

www.mhhe.com/rwj

Spreadsheet Templates 2, 14, 15

CHAPTER | 4

Introduction to Valuation: The Time Value of Money

THERE ARE THREE ESSENTIAL THINGS YOU SHOULD LEARN FROM THIS CHAPTER:

■ How to determine the future value of an investment made today

■ How to determine the present value of cash to be received at a future date

■ How to find the return on investment

ON DECEMBER 2, 1982, General Motors Acceptance Corporation (GMAC), a subsidiary of General Motors, offered some securities for sale to the public. Under the terms of the deal, GMAC promised to repay the owner of one of these securities $10,000 on December 1, 2012, but investors would receive nothing until then. Investors paid GMAC $500 for each of these securities, so they gave up $500 on December 2, 1982, for the promise of a $10,000 payment 30 years later. Such a security, for which you pay some amount today in exchange for a promised lump sum to be received at a future date, is about the simplest possible type.

Is giving up $500 in exchange for $10,000 in 30 years a good deal? On the plus side, you get back $20 for every $1 you put up. That probably sounds good, but, on the downside, you have to wait 30 years to get it. What you need to know is how to analyze this trade-off; this chapter gives you the tools you need.

Specifically, our goal here is to introduce you to one of the most important principles in finance, the time value of money. What you will learn is how to determine the value today of some cash flow to be received later. This is a very basic business skill, and it underlies the analysis of many different types of investments and financing arrangements. In fact, almost all business activities, whether they originate in marketing, management, operations, or strategy, involve comparing outlays made today to benefits projected for the future. How to do this comparison is something everyone needs to understand; this chapter gets you started.

O ne of the basic problems faced by the financial manager is how to determine the value today of cash flows expected in the future. For example, the jackpot in a PowerBall™ lottery drawing was $110 million. Does this mean the winning ticket was worth $110 million? The answer is no because the jackpot was actually going to pay out over a 20-year period at a rate of $5.5 million per year. How much was the ticket worth then? The answer depends on the time value of money, the subject of this chapter.

In the most general sense, the phrase *time value of money* refers to the fact that a dollar in hand today is worth more than a dollar promised at some time in the future. On a practical level, one reason for this is that you could earn interest while you waited; so a dollar today would grow to more than a dollar later. The trade-off between money now and money later thus depends on, among other things, the rate you can earn by investing. Our goal in this chapter is to explicitly evaluate this trade-off between dollars today and dollars at some future time.

A thorough understanding of the material in this chapter is critical to understanding material in subsequent chapters, so you should study it with particular care. We will present a number of examples in this chapter. In many problems, your answer may differ from ours slightly. This can happen because of rounding and is not a cause for concern.

4.1 | FUTURE VALUE AND COMPOUNDING

future value (FV)

The amount an investment is worth after one or more periods.

The first thing we will study is future value. **Future value (FV)** refers to the amount of money an investment will grow to over some period of time at some given interest rate. Put another way, future value is the cash value of an investment at some time in the future. We start out by considering the simplest case, a single-period investment.

Investing for a Single Period

Suppose you were to invest $100 in a savings account that pays 10 percent interest per year. How much would you have in one year? You would have $110. This $110 is equal to your original *principal* of $100 plus $10 in interest that you earn. We say that $110 is the future value of $100 invested for one year at 10 percent, and we simply mean that $100 today is worth $110 in one year, given that 10 percent is the interest rate.

In general, if you invest for one period at an interest rate of r, your investment will grow to $(1 + r)$ per dollar invested. In our example, r is 10 percent, so your investment grows to $1 + .10 = 1.1$ dollars per dollar invested. You invested $100 in this case, so you ended up with $100 \times 1.10 = $110.

Investing for More Than One Period

Going back to our $100 investment, what will you have after two years, assuming the interest rate doesn't change? If you leave the entire $110 in the bank, you will earn $110 \times .10 = $11 in interest during the second year, so you will have a total of $110 + 11 = $121. This $121 is the future value of $100 in two years at 10 percent. Another way of looking at it is that one year from now you are effectively investing $110 at 10 percent for a year. This is a single-period problem, so you'll end up with $1.1 for every dollar invested, or $110 \times 1.1 = $121 total.

This $121 has four parts. The first part is the $100 original principal. The second part is the $10 in interest you earn in the first year, and the third part is another $10 you earn in the second year, for a total of $120. The last $1 you end up with (the fourth part) is interest you earn in the second year on the interest paid in the first year: $10 \times .10 = $1.

This process of leaving your money and any accumulated interest in an investment for more than one period, thereby reinvesting the interest, is called **compounding.** Compounding the interest means earning **interest on interest,** so we call the result **compound interest.** With **simple interest,** the interest is not reinvested, so interest is earned each period only on the original principal.

Interest on Interest | EXAMPLE 4.1

Suppose you locate a two-year investment that pays 14 percent per year. If you invest $325, how much will you have at the end of the two years? How much of this is simple interest? How much is compound interest?

At the end of the first year, you will have $325 × (1 + .14) = $370.50. If you reinvest this entire amount, and thereby compound the interest, you will have $370.50 × 1.14 = $422.37 at the end of the second year. The total interest you earn is thus $422.37 – 325 = $97.37. Your $325 original principal earns $325 × .14 = $45.50 in interest each year, for a two-year total of $91 in simple interest. The remaining $97.37 – 91 = $6.37 results from compounding. You can check this by noting that the interest earned in the first year is $45.50. The interest on interest earned in the second year thus amounts to $45.50 × .14 = $6.37, as we calculated.

compounding

The process of accumulating interest in an investment over time to earn more interest.

interest on interest

Interest earned on the reinvestment of previous interest payments.

compound interest

Interest earned on both the initial principal and the interest reinvested from prior periods.

simple interest

Interest earned only on the original principal amount invested.

We now take a closer look at how we calculated the $121 future value. We multiplied $110 by 1.1 to get $121. The $110, however, was $100 also multiplied by 1.1. In other words:

$121 = $110 × 1.1

       = ($100 × 1.1) × 1.1

       = $100 × (1.1 × 1.1)

       = $100 × 1.1^2

       = $100 × 1.21

At the risk of belaboring the obvious, let's ask: How much would our $100 grow to after three years? Once again, in two years, we'll be investing $121 for one period at 10 percent. We'll end up with $1.1 for every dollar we invest, or $121 × 1.1 = $133.1 total. This $133.1 is thus:

$133.1 = $121 × 1.1

        = ($110 × 1.1) × 1.1

        = ($100 × 1.1) × 1.1 × 1.1

        = $100 × (1.1 × 1.1 × 1.1)

        = $100 × 1.1^3

        = $100 × 1.331

You're probably noticing a pattern to these calculations, so we can now go ahead and state the general result. As our examples suggest, the future value of $1 invested for t periods at a rate of r per period is:

Future value = $1 × (1 + r)^t [4.1]

The expression $(1 + r)^t$ is sometimes called the *future value interest factor* (or just *future value factor*) for $1 invested at r percent for t periods and can be abbreviated as FVIF(r, t).

TABLE 4.1	Year	Beginning Amount	Interest Earned	Ending Amount
Future value of $100 at 10 percent	1	$100.00	$10.00	$110.00
	2	110.00	11.00	121.00
	3	121.00	12.10	133.10
	4	133.10	13.31	146.41
	5	146.41	14.64	161.05
			Total interest $61.05	

In our example, what would your $100 be worth after five years? We can first compute the relevant future value factor as:

$$(1 + r)^t = (1 + .10)^5 = 1.1^5 = 1.6105$$

Your $100 will thus grow to:

$$\$100 \times 1.6105 = \$161.05$$

The growth of your $100 each year is illustrated in Table 4.1. As shown, the interest earned in each year is equal to the beginning amount multiplied by the interest rate of 10 percent.

In Table 4.1, notice that the total interest you earn is $61.05. Over the five-year span of this investment, the simple interest is $100 × .10 = $10 per year, so you accumulate $50 this way. The other $11.05 is from compounding.

Figure 4.1 illustrates the growth of the compound interest in Table 4.1. Notice how the simple interest is constant each year, but the compound interest you earn gets bigger every year. The size of the compound interest keeps increasing because more and more interest builds up and there is thus more to compound.

Future values depend critically on the assumed interest rate, particularly for long-lived investments. Figure 4.2 illustrates this relationship by plotting the growth of $1 for different rates and lengths of time. Notice that the future value of $1 after 10 years is about $6.20 at a 20 percent rate, but it is only about $2.60 at 10 percent. In this case, doubling the interest rate more than doubles the future value.

To solve future value problems, we need to come up with the relevant future value factors. There are several different ways of doing this. In our example, we could have multiplied 1.1 by itself five times. This would work just fine, but it would get to be very tedious for, say, a 30-year investment.

Fortunately, there are several easier ways to get future value factors. Most calculators have a key labeled "y^x." You can usually just enter 1.1, press this key, enter 5, and press the "=" key to get the answer. This is an easy way to calculate future value factors because it's quick and accurate.

Alternatively, you can use a table that contains future value factors for some common interest rates and time periods. Table 4.2 contains some of these factors. Table A.1 in Appendix A at the end of the book contains a much larger set. To use the table, find the column that corresponds to 10 percent. Then look down the rows until you come to five periods. You should find the factor that we calculated, 1.6105.

Tables such as Table 4.2 are not as common as they once were because they predate inexpensive calculators and are only available for a relatively small number of rates. Interest rates are often quoted to three or four decimal places, so the tables needed to deal with these accurately would be quite large. As a result, the "real world" has moved away from using them. We will emphasize the use of a calculator in this chapter.

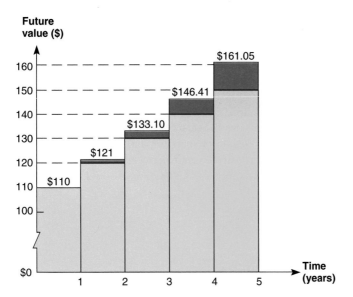

Future value ($)

$161.05

160

150          $146.41

140

130          $133.10

120          $121

110    $110

100

$0

         1   2   3   4   5   **Time (years)**

Growth of $100 original amount at 10% per year. Blue
shaded area represents the portion of the total that results
from compounding of interest.

FIGURE 4.1

Future value, simple
interest, and
compound interest

Future value of $1 ($)

7

6   20%

5

4   15%

3   10%

2   5%

1   0%

    1   2   3   4   5   6   7   8   9   10   **Time (years)**

FIGURE 4.2

Future value of $1 for
different periods and
rates

Number of Periods	Interest Rates			
	5%	**10%**	**15%**	**20%**
1	1.0500	1.1000	1.1500	1.2000
2	1.1025	1.2100	1.3225	1.4400
3	1.1576	1.3310	1.5209	1.7280
4	1.2155	1.4641	1.7490	2.0736
5	1.2763	1.6105	2.0114	2.4883

TABLE 4.2

Future value interest
factors

These tables still serve a useful purpose. To make sure you are doing the calculations correctly, pick a factor from the table and then calculate it yourself to see that you get the same answer. There are plenty of numbers to choose from.

EXAMPLE 4.2 | Compound Interest

You've located an investment that pays 12 percent. That rate sounds good to you, so you invest $400. How much will you have in three years? How much will you have in seven years? At the end of seven years, how much interest have you earned? How much of that interest results from compounding?

Based on our discussion, we can calculate the future value factor for 12 percent and three years as:

$$(1 + r)^t = 1.12^3 = 1.4049$$

Your $400 thus grows to:

$$\$400 \times 1.4049 = \$561.97$$

After seven years, you will have:

$$\$400 \times 1.12^7 = \$400 \times 2.2107 = \$884.27$$

Thus, you will more than double your money over seven years.

Since you invested $400, the interest in the $884.27 future value is $884.27 − 400 = $484.27. At 12 percent, your $400 investment earns $400 × .12 = $48 in simple interest every year. Over seven years, the simple interest thus totals 7 × $48 = $336. The other $484.27 − 336 = $148.27 is from compounding.

The effect of compounding is not great over short time periods, but it really starts to add up as the horizon grows. To take an extreme case, suppose one of your more frugal ancestors had invested $5 for you at a 6 percent interest rate 200 years ago. How much would you have today? The future value factor is a substantial $1.06^{200} = 115{,}125.90$ (you won't find this one in a table), so you would have $5 × 115,125.90 = $575,629.50 today. Notice that the simple interest is just $5 × .06 = $.30 per year. After 200 years, this amounts to $60. The rest is from reinvesting. Such is the power of compound interest!

EXAMPLE 4.3 | How Much for That Island?

To further illustrate the effect of compounding for long horizons, consider the case of Peter Minuit and the Indians. In 1626, Minuit bought all of Manhattan Island for about $24 in goods and trinkets. This sounds cheap, but the Indians may have gotten the better end of the deal. To see why, suppose the Indians had sold the goods and invested the $24 at 10 percent. How much would it be worth today?

Roughly 370 years have passed since the transaction. At 10 percent, $24 will grow by quite a bit over that time. How much? The future value factor is approximately:

$$(1 + r)^t = 1.1^{370} \approx 2{,}000{,}000{,}000{,}000{,}000$$

That is, 2 followed by 15 zeroes. The future value is thus on the order of $24 × 2 quadrillion, or about $48 *quadrillion* (give or take a few hundreds of trillions).

Well, $48 quadrillion is a lot of money. How much? If you had it, you could buy the United States. All of it. Cash. With money left over to buy Canada, Mexico, and the rest of the world, for that matter.

This example is something of an exaggeration, of course. In 1626, it would not have been easy to locate an investment that would pay 10 percent every year without fail for the next 370 years.

Using a Financial Calculator

CALCULATOR

hints

Although there are the various ways of calculating future values we have described so far, many of you will decide that a financial calculator is the way to go. If you are planning on using one, you should read this extended hint; otherwise, skip it.

A financial calculator is simply an ordinary calculator with a few extra features. In particular, it knows some of the most commonly used financial formulas, so it can directly compute things like future values.

Financial calculators have the advantage that they handle a lot of the computation, but that is really all. In other words, you still have to understand the problem; the calculator just does some of the arithmetic. In fact, there is an old joke (somewhat modified) that goes like this: Anyone can make a mistake on a time value of money problem, but to really screw one up takes a financial calculator! We therefore have two goals for this section. First, we'll discuss how to compute future values. After that, we'll show you how to avoid the most common mistakes people make when they start using financial calculators.

How to Calculate Future Values with a Financial Calculator Examining a typical financial calculator, you will find five keys of particular interest. They usually look like this:

For now, we need to focus on four of these. The keys labeled **PV** and **FV** are just what you would guess, present value and future value. The key labeled **N** refers to the *n*umber of periods, which is what we have been calling *t*. Finally, **%i** stands for the *i*nterest rate, which we have called *r*.[1]

If we have the financial calculator set up right (see our next section), then calculating a future value is very simple. Take a look back at our question involving the future value of $100 at 10 percent for five years. We have seen that the answer is $161.05. The exact keystrokes will differ depending on what type of calculator you use, but here is basically all you do:

1. Enter −100. Press the **PV** key. (The negative sign is explained below.)
2. Enter 10. Press the **%i** key. (Notice that we entered 10, not .10; see below.)
3. Enter 5. Press the **N** key.

Now we have entered all of the relevant information. To solve for the future value, we need to ask the calculator what the FV is. Depending on your calculator, you either press the button labeled "CPT" (for compute) and then press **FV**, or else you just press **FV**. Either way, you should get 161.05. If you don't (and you probably won't if this is the first time you have used a financial calculator!), we will offer some help in our next section.

Before we explain the kinds of problems that you are likely to run into, we want to establish a standard format for showing you how to use a financial calculator. Using the example we just looked at, in the future, we will illustrate such problems like this:

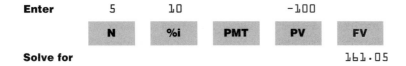

Enter	5	10		−100	
	N	**%i**	**PMT**	**PV**	**FV**
Solve for					161.05

---

[1]The reason financial calculators use N and %i is that the most common use for these calculators is determining loan payments. In this context, N is the number of payments and %i is the interest rate on the loan. But, as we will see, there are many other uses of financial calculators that don't involve loan payments and interest rates.

Here is an important tip: Appendix D in the back of the book contains some more detailed instructions for the most common types of financial calculators. See if yours is included, and, if it is, follow the instructions there if you need help. Of course, if all else fails, you can read the manual that came with the calculator.

How to Get the Wrong Answer Using a Financial Calculator   There are a couple of common (and frustrating) problems that cause a lot of trouble with financial calculators. In this section, we provide some important *dos* and *don'ts*. If you just can't seem to get a problem to work out, you should refer back to this section.

There are two categories we examine, three things you need to do only once and three things you need to do every time you work a problem. The things you need to do just once deal with the following calculator settings:

1. *Make sure your calculator is set to display a large number of decimal places.* Most financial calculators only display two decimal places; this causes problems because we frequently work with numbers—like interest rates—that are very small.

2. *Make sure your calculator is set to assume only one payment per period or per year.* Most financial calculators assume monthly payments (12 per year) unless you say otherwise.

3. *Make sure your calculator is in "end" mode.* This is usually the default, but you can accidently change to "begin" mode.

If you don't know how to set these three things, see Appendix D or your calculator's operating manual. There are also three things you need to do *every time you work a problem:*

1. *Before you start, completely clear out the calculator.* This is very important. Failure to do this is the number one reason for wrong answers; you simply must get in the habit of clearing the calculator every time you start a problem. How you do this depends on the calculator (see Appendix D), but you must do more than just clear the display. For example, on a Texas Instruments BA II Plus you must press **2nd** then **CLR TVM** for *clear time value of money.* There is a similar command on your calculator. Learn it!

    Note that turning the calculator off and back on won't do it. Most financial calculators remember everything you enter, even after you turn them off. In other words, they remember all your mistakes unless you explicitly clear them out. Also, if you are in the middle of a problem and make a mistake, *clear it out and start over.* Better to be safe than sorry.

2. *Put a negative sign on cash outflows.* Most financial calculators require you to put a negative sign on cash outflows and a positive sign on cash inflows.[2] As a practical matter, this usually just means that you should enter the present value amount with a negative sign (because normally the present value represents the amount you give up today in exchange for cash inflows later). By the same token, when you solve for a present value, you shouldn't be surprised to see a negative sign.

3. *Enter the rate correctly.* Financial calculators assume that rates are quoted in percent, so if the rate is .08 (or 8 percent), you should enter 8, not .08.

If you follow these guidelines (especially the one about clearing out the calculator), you should have no problem using a financial calculator to work almost all of the problems in this and the next few chapters. We'll provide some additional examples and guidance where appropriate.

---

[2]The Texas Instruments BA-35 is an exception; it doesn't require negative signs to be entered.

CONCEPT QUESTIONS

4.1a What do we mean by the future value of an investment?

4.1b What does it mean to compound interest? How does compound interest differ from simple interest?

4.1c In general, what is the future value of $1 invested at r per period for t periods?

PRESENT VALUE AND DISCOUNTING | 4.2

When we discuss future value, we are thinking of questions like the following: What will my $2,000 investment grow to if it earns a 6.5 percent return every year for the next six years? The answer to this question is what we call the future value of $2,000 invested at 6.5 percent for six years (verify that the answer is about $2,918).

There is another type of question that comes up even more often in financial management that is obviously related to future value. Suppose you need to have $10,000 in 10 years, and you can earn 6.5 percent on your money. How much do you have to invest today to reach your goal? You can verify that the answer is $5,327.26. How do we know this? Read on.

The Single-Period Case

We've seen that the future value of $1 invested for one year at 10 percent is $1.10. We now ask a slightly different question: How much do we have to invest today at 10 percent to get $1 in one year? In other words, we know the future value here is $1, but what is the **present value (PV)?** The answer isn't too hard to figure out. Whatever we invest today will be 1.1 times bigger at the end of the year. Since we need $1 at the end of the year:

Present value $\times$ 1.1 = $1

Or, solving for the present value:

Present value = $1/1.1 = $.909

In this case, the present value is the answer to the following question: What amount, invested today, will grow to $1 in one year if the interest rate is 10 percent? Present value is thus just the reverse of future value. Instead of compounding the money forward into the future, we **discount** it back to the present.

present value (PV)
The current value of future cash flows discounted at the appropriate discount rate.

discount
Calculate the present value of some future amount.

Single-Period PV | EXAMPLE 4.4

Suppose you need $400 to buy textbooks next year. You can earn 7 percent on your money. How much do you have to put up today?

We need to know the PV of $400 in one year at 7 percent. Proceeding as above:

Present value $\times$ 1.07 = $400

We can now solve for the present value:

Present value = $400 $\times$ (1/1.07) = $373.83

Thus, $373.83 is the present value. Again, this just means that investing this amount for one year at 7 percent will result in your having a future value of $400.

From our examples, the present value of $1 to be received in one period is generally given as:

$$PV = \$1 \times [1/(1 + r)] = \$1/(1 + r)$$

We next examine how to get the present value of an amount to be paid in two or more periods into the future.

Present Values for Multiple Periods

Suppose you need to have $1,000 in two years. If you can earn 7 percent, how much do you have to invest to make sure that you have the $1,000 when you need it? In other words, what is the present value of $1,000 in two years if the relevant rate is 7 percent?

Based on your knowledge of future values, you know that the amount invested must grow to $1,000 over the two years. In other words, it must be the case that:

$$
\begin{aligned}
\$1,000 &= PV \times 1.07 \times 1.07 \\
&= PV \times 1.07^2 \\
&= PV \times 1.1449
\end{aligned}
$$

Given this, we can solve for the present value:

Present value = $1,000/1.1449 = $873.44

Therefore, $873.44 is the amount you must invest in order to achieve your goal.

EXAMPLE 4.5 | **Saving Up**

You would like to buy a new automobile. You have $50,000, but the car costs $68,500. If you can earn 9 percent, how much do you have to invest today to buy the car in two years? Do you have enough? Assume the price will stay the same.

What we need to know is the present value of $68,500 to be paid in two years, assuming a 9 percent rate. Based on our discussion, this is:

$$PV = \$68,500/1.09^2 = \$68,500/1.1881 = \$57,655.08$$

You're still about $7,655 short, even if you're willing to wait two years.

---

discount rate
The rate used to calculate the present value of future cash flows.

discounted cash flow (DCF) valuation
Valuation calculating the present value of a future cash flow to determine its value today.

As you have probably recognized by now, calculating present values is quite similar to calculating future values, and the general result looks much the same. The present value of $1 to be received t periods into the future at a discount rate of r is:

$$PV = \$1 \times [1/(1 + r)^t] = \$1/(1 + r)^t \qquad [4.2]$$

The quantity in brackets, $1/(1 + r)^t$, goes by several different names. Since it's used to discount a future cash flow, it is often called a *discount factor*. With this name, it is not surprising that the rate used in the calculation is often called the **discount rate**. We will tend to call it this in talking about present values. The quantity in brackets is also called the *present value interest factor* (or just *present value factor*) for $1 at r percent for t periods and is sometimes abbreviated as PVIF(r,t). Finally, calculating the present value of a future cash flow to determine its worth today is commonly called **discounted cash flow (DCF) valuation.**

To illustrate, suppose you need $1,000 in three years. You can earn 15 percent on your money. How much do you have to invest today? To find out, we have to determine the pres-

Number of Periods	Interest Rates			
	5%	**10%**	**15%**	**20%**
1	.9524	.9091	.8696	.8333
2	.9070	.8264	.7561	.6944
3	.8638	.7513	.6575	.5787
4	.8227	.6830	.5718	.4823
5	.7835	.6209	.4972	.4019

TABLE 4.3

Present value interest factors

ent value of $1,000 in three years at 15 percent. We do this by discounting $1,000 back three periods at 15 percent. With these numbers, the discount factor is:

$$1/(1 + .15)^3 = 1/1.5209 = .6575$$

The amount you must invest is thus:

$$\$1,000 \times .6575 = \$657.50$$

We say that $657.50 is the present, or discounted, value of $1,000 to be received in three years at 15 percent.

There are tables for present value factors just as there are tables for future value factors, and you use them in the same way (if you use them at all). Table 4.3 contains a small set of these factors. A much larger set can be found in Table A.2 in Appendix A.

In Table 4.3, the discount factor we just calculated, .6575, can be found by looking down the column labeled "15%" until you come to the third row. Of course, you could use a financial calculator, as we illustrate next.

CALCULATOR hints

You solve present value problems on a financial calculator just like you do future value problems. For the example we just examined (the present value of $1,000 to be received in three years at 15 percent), you would do the following:

Enter	3	15			1,000
	N	%i	PMT	PV	FV
Solve for				−657.50	

Notice that the answer has a negative sign; as we discussed above, that's because it represents an outflow today in exchange for the $1,000 inflow later.

Deceptive Advertising | EXAMPLE 4.6

Recently, some businesses have been saying things like "Come try our product. If you do, we'll give you $100 just for coming by!" If you read the fine print, what you find out is that they will give you a savings certificate that will pay you $100 in 25 years or so. If the going interest rate on such certificates is 10 percent per year, how much are they really giving you today?

What you're actually getting is the present value of $100 to be paid in 25 years. If the discount rate is 10 percent per year, then the discount factor is:

$$1/1.1^{25} = 1/10.8347 = .0923$$

This tells you that a dollar in 25 years is worth a little more than nine cents today, assuming a 10 percent discount rate. Given this, the promotion is actually paying you about .0923 × $100 = $9.23. Maybe this is enough to draw customers, but it's not $100.

As the length of time until payment grows, present values decline. As Example 4.6 illustrates, present values tend to become small as the time horizon grows. If you look out far enough, they will always get close to zero. Also, for a given length of time, the higher the discount rate is, the lower is the present value. Put another way, present values and discount rates are inversely related. Increasing the discount rate decreases the PV and vice versa.

The relationship between time, discount rates, and present values is illustrated in Figure 4.3. Notice that by the time we get to 10 years, the present values are all substantially smaller than the future amounts.

CONCEPT QUESTIONS

4.2a What do we mean by the present value of an investment?

4.2b The process of discounting a future amount back to the present is the opposite of doing what?

4.2c What do we mean by discounted cash flow, or DCF, valuation?

4.2d In general, what is the present value of $1 to be received in t periods, assuming a discount rate of r per period?

FIGURE 4.3

Present value of $1 for different periods and rates

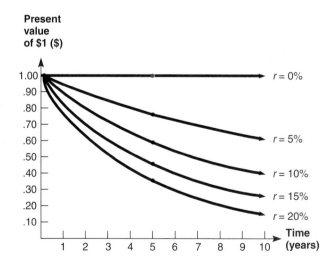

MORE ON PRESENT AND FUTURE VALUES | 4.3

If you look back at the expressions we came up with for present and future values, you will see there is a very simple relationship between the two. We explore this relationship and some related issues in this section.

Present versus Future Value

What we called the present value factor is just the reciprocal of (that is, 1 divided by) the future value factor:

Future value factor $= (1 + r)^t$

Present value factor $= 1/(1 + r)^t$

In fact, the easy way to calculate a present value factor on many calculators is to first calculate the future value factor and then press the **1/x** key to flip it over.

If we let FV_t stand for the future value after t periods, then the relationship between future value and present value can be written very simply as one of the following:

$$PV \times (1 + r)^t = FV_t$$
$$PV = FV_t/(1 + r)^t = FV_t \times [1/(1 + r)^t] \qquad [4.3]$$

This last result we will call the *basic present value equation*. We will use it throughout the text. There are a number of variations that come up, but this simple equation underlies many of the most important ideas in finance.

Evaluating Investments | EXAMPLE 4.7

To give you an idea of how we will be using present and future values, consider the following simple investment. Your company proposes to buy an asset for $335. This investment is very safe. You will sell off the asset in three years for $400. You know you could invest the $335 elsewhere at 10 percent with very little risk. What do you think of the proposed investment?

This is not a good investment. Why not? Because you can invest the $335 elsewhere at 10 percent. If you do, after three years it will grow to:

$$\$335 \times (1 + r)^t = \$335 \times 1.1^3$$
$$= \$335 \times 1.331$$
$$= \$445.89$$

Since the proposed investment only pays out $400, it is not as good as other alternatives we have. Another way of saying the same thing is to notice that the present value of $400 in three years at 10 percent is:

$$\$400 \times [1/(1 + r)^t] = \$400/1.1^3 = \$400/1.331 = \$300.53$$

This tells us that we only have to invest about $300 to get $400 in three years, not $335. We will return to this type of analysis later on.

Determining the Discount Rate

It will turn out that we will frequently need to determine what discount rate is implicit in an investment. We can do this by looking at the basic present value equation:

$$PV = FV_t/(1 + r)^t$$

There are only four parts to this equation: the present value (PV), the future value (FV$_t$), the discount rate (r), and the life of the investment (t). Given any three of these, we can always find the fourth.

EXAMPLE 4.8 | Finding *r* for a Single-Period Investment

You are considering a one-year investment. If you put up $1,250, you will get back $1,350. What rate is this investment paying?

First, in this single-period case, the answer is fairly obvious. You are getting a total of $100 in addition to your $1,250. The implicit rate on this investment is thus $100/1,250 = 8 percent.

More formally, from the basic present value equation, the present value (the amount you must put up today) is $1,250. The future value (what the present value grows to) is $1,350. The time involved is one period, so we have:

$$\$1,250 = \$1,350/(1 + r)^1$$
$$1 + r = \$1,350/1,250 = 1.08$$
$$r = 8\%$$

In this simple case, of course, there was no need to go through this calculation, but, as we describe below, it gets a little harder when there is more than one period.

To illustrate what happens with multiple periods, let's say that we are offered an investment that costs us $100 and will double our money in eight years. To compare this to other investments, we would like to know what discount rate is implicit in these numbers. This discount rate is called the *rate of return*, or sometimes just *return*, on the investment. In this case, we have a present value of $100, a future value of $200 (double our money), and an eight-year life. To calculate the return, we can write the basic present value equation as:

$$PV = FV_t/(1 + r)^t$$
$$\$100 = \$200/(1 + r)^8$$

It could also be written as:

$$(1 + r)^8 = \$200/100 = 2$$

We now need to solve for *r*. There are three ways we could do it:

1. Use a financial calculator. (See below.)
2. Solve the equation for $1 + r$ by taking the eighth root of both sides. Since this is the same thing as raising both sides to the power of ⅛, or .125, this is actually easy to do with the **y^x** key on a calculator. Just enter 2, then press **y^x**, enter .125, and press the **=** key. The eighth root should be about 1.09, which implies that *r* is 9 percent.
3. Use a future value table. The future value factor for eight years is equal to 2. If you look across the row corresponding to eight periods in Table A.1, you will see that a future value factor of 2 corresponds to the 9 percent column, again implying that the return here is 9 percent.

Actually, in this particular example, there is a useful "back of the envelope" means of solving for *r*—the Rule of 72. For reasonable rates of return, the time it takes to double your money is given approximately by $72/r\%$. In our example, this means that $72/r\% = 8$ years, implying that *r* is 9 percent as we calculated. This rule is fairly accurate for discount rates in the 5 percent to 20 percent range.

The nearby **Reality Bytes** box provides some examples of rates of return on collectibles. See if you can verify the numbers reported there.

Double Your Fun | EXAMPLE 4.9

You have been offered an investment that promises to double your money every 10 years. What is the approximate rate of return on the investment?

From the Rule of 72, the rate of return is given approximately by $72/r\% = 10$, so the rate is approximately $72/10 = 7.2\%$. Verify that the exact answer is 7.177 percent.

A slightly more extreme example involves money bequeathed by Benjamin Franklin, who died on April 17, 1790. In his will, he gave 1,000 pounds sterling to Massachusetts and the city of Boston. He gave a like amount to Pennsylvania and the city of Philadelphia. The money was paid to Franklin when he held political office, but he believed that politicians should not be paid for their service (it appears that this view is not widely shared by modern-day politicians).

Franklin originally specified that the money should be paid out 100 years after his death and used to train young people. Later, however, after some legal wrangling, it was agreed that the money would be paid out in 1990, 200 years after Franklin's death. By that time, the Pennsylvania bequest had grown to about $2 million; the Massachusetts bequest had grown to $4.5 million. The money was used to fund the Franklin Institutes in Boston and Philadelphia. Assuming that 1,000 pounds sterling was equivalent to 1,000 dollars, what rate of return did the two states earn (the dollar did not become the official U.S. currency until 1792)?

For Pennsylvania, the future value is $2 million and the present value is $1,000. There are 200 years involved, so we need to solve for r in the following:

$$\$1,000 = \$2 \text{ million}/(1 + r)^{200}$$
$$(1 + r)^{200} = 2,000$$

Solving for r, we see that the Pennsylvania money grew at about 3.87 percent per year. The Massachusetts money did better; verify that the rate of return in this case was 4.3 percent. Small differences can add up!

│ CALCULATOR

We can illustrate how to calculate unknown rates using a financial calculator using these numbers. For Pennsylvania, you would do the following:

As in our previous examples, notice the minus sign on the present value, representing Franklin's outlay made many years ago. What do you change to work the problem for Massachusetts?

reality BYTES

SHE'S MADE OF PLASTIC, AND SHE'S FANTASTIC!

It used to be that trading in collectibles such as baseball cards, art, and old toys occurred mostly at auctions, swap meets, and collectible shops, all of which were limited to regional traffic. However, with the growing popularity of on-line auctions such as eBay, trading in collectibles has expanded to an international arena. The most visible form of collectible is probably the baseball trading card, but Furbies, Beanie Babies, and Pokémon cards have been extremely hot collectibles in the recent past. However, it's not just fad items that spark collectors' interest; virtually anything of sentimental value from days gone by is considered collectible, and, more and more, these things are being viewed as investments.

Collectibles typically provide no cash flows, except when sold, and condition and buyer sentiment are the major determinants of value. The rates of return on such investments have been staggering at times, but care is needed in interpreting them. For example, a Schwinn B6 boy's bicycle cost about $45 when it was new in 1949, and it was a beauty. Assuming it was still in like-new condition in 2000, it would have been worth $675, about 15 times its original cost. While this looks to the untrained eye like a huge gain, the actual return on investment is only about 5.5 percent per year for the 51-year life of the investment. In contrast, a typical share of common stock earned, on average, a return of about 11.5 percent over that same period. Then there's the problem of storing the bike and keeping it in like-new condition, hardly a small detail.

Barbie dolls are a lot easier to store. An original Barbie sold for about $3 when it was introduced in March 1959. An original in mint condition (and never removed from its package) might have been worth about $7,000 in 2000, which represents a whopping return of 20.8 percent per year.

The world of collectibles is, of course, a global phenomenon. Christie's, the well-known auction house, holds an annual auction of model railway toys around Christmas. In 1998, a Marklin (the manufacturer) three-piece station house set would have been worth about £6,000. It originally sold for about £3 in 1913. Again, to the untrained eye, that appears to be an enormous gain, but the return actually works out to be about 9.4 percent a year.

Looking back, of these investments, the Barbie doll did the best. The problem is that to earn this return, you had to purchase the toy when it was new and store it (without opening it) for all those years. Looking ahead, the corresponding problem is predicting what the future value of a toy will be. You can earn a positive return on investment only if the market value of your asset rises above the purchase price at some point. That, of course, is rarely assured. For example, most collectors say that the Barbies that are mass-marketed in discount stores today will probably have little or no value as collectibles at any time in the future, so we don't recommend them for your retirement investing.

EXAMPLE 4.10 | Saving for College

You estimate that you will need about $80,000 to send your child to college in eight years. You have about $35,000 now. If you can earn 20 percent per year, will you make it? At what rate will you just reach your goal?

If you can earn 20 percent, the future value of your $35,000 in eight years will be:

$$FV = \$35,000 \times 1.20^8 = \$35,000 \times 4.2998 = \$150,493.59$$

So you will make it easily. The minimum rate is the unknown r in the following:

$$FV = \$35,000 \times (1 + r)^8 = \$80,000$$

$$(1 + r)^8 = \$80,000/35,000 = 2.2857$$

Therefore, the future value factor is 2.2857. Looking at the row in Table A.1 that corresponds to eight periods, we see that our future value factor is roughly halfway between the ones shown for 10 percent

(2.1436) and 12 percent (2.4760), so you will just reach your goal if you earn approximately 11 percent. To get the exact answer, we could use a financial calculator or we could solve for r:

$(1 + r)^8 = \$80{,}000/35{,}000 = 2.2857$

$1 + r = 2.2857^{(1/8)} = 2.2857^{.125} = 1.1089$

$r = 10.89\%$

Only 18,262.5 Days to Retirement | **EXAMPLE 4.11**

You would like to retire in 50 years as a millionaire. If you have \$10,000 today, what rate of return do you need to earn to achieve your goal?

The future value is \$1,000,000. The present value is \$10,000, and there are 50 years until retirement. We need to calculate the unknown discount rate in the following:

$\$10{,}000 = \$1{,}000{,}000/(1 + r)^{50}$

$(1 + r)^{50} = 100$

The future value factor is thus 100. You can verify that the implicit rate is about 9.65 percent.

Finding the Number of Periods

Suppose we were interested in purchasing an asset that costs \$50,000. We currently have \$25,000. If we can earn 12 percent on this \$25,000, how long until we have the \$50,000? Finding the answer involves solving for the last variable in the basic present value equation, the number of periods. You already know how to get an approximate answer to this particular problem. Notice that we need to double our money. From the Rule of 72, this will take about $72/12 = 6$ years at 12 percent.

To come up with the exact answer, we can again manipulate the basic present value equation. The present value is \$25,000, and the future value is \$50,000. With a 12 percent discount rate, the basic equation takes one of the following forms:

$\$25{,}000 = \$50{,}000/1.12^t$

$\$50{,}000/25{,}000 = 1.12^t = 2$

We thus have a future value factor of 2 for a 12 percent rate. We now need to solve for t. If you look down the column in Table A.1 that corresponds to 12 percent, you will see that a future value factor of 1.9738 occurs at six periods. It will thus take about six years, as we calculated. To get the exact answer, we have to explicitly solve for t (or use a financial calculator). If you do this, you will find that the answer is 6.1163 years, so our approximation was quite close in this case.

CALCULATOR

If you do use a financial calculator, here are the relevant entries:

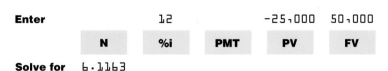

Enter	12		−25,000	50,000
	N	**%i**	**PMT**	**PV**	**FV**
Solve for	6.1163				

Summary of time value of money calculations

I. Symbols

PV = Present value, what future cash flows are worth today

FV_t = Future value, what cash flows are worth in the future

r = Interest rate, rate of return, or discount rate per period—typically, but not always, one year

t = Number of periods—typically, but not always, the number of years

C = Cash amount

II. Future value of C invested at r percent per period for t periods

$FV_t = C \times (1 + r)^t$

The term $(1 + r)^t$ is called the *future value factor*.

III. Present value of C to be received in t periods at r percent per period

$PV = C /(1 + r)^t$

The term $1/(1 + r)^t$ is called the *present value factor*.

IV. The basic present value equation giving the relationship between present and future value is

$PV = FV_t /(1 + r)^t$

EXAMPLE 4.12 | **Waiting for Godot**

You've been saving up to buy the Godot Company. The total cost will be $10 million. You currently have about $2.3 million. If you can earn 5 percent on your money, how long will you have to wait? At 16 percent, how long must you wait?

At 5 percent, you'll have to wait a long time. From the basic present value equation:

$2.3 = $10/1.05^t$

$1.05^t = 4.35$

$t = 30$ years

At 16 percent, things are a little better. Verify for yourself that it will take about 10 years.

This example finishes our introduction to basic time value of money concepts. Table 4.4 summarizes present value and future value calculations for future reference.

SPREADSHEET strategies

Using a Spreadsheet for Time Value of Money Calculations

More and more, businesspeople from many different areas (and not just finance and accounting) rely on spreadsheets to do all the different types of calculations that come up in the real world. As a result, in this section, we will show you how to use a spreadsheet to handle the various time value of money problems we presented in this chapter. We will use Microsoft Excel™, but the commands are similar for other types of software. We assume you are already familiar with basic spreadsheet operations.

As we have seen, you can solve for any one of the following four potential unknowns: future value, present value, the discount rate, or the number of periods. With a spreadsheet, there is a separate formula for each. In Excel, these are as follows:

To Find	Enter This Formula
Future value	= FV (rate,nper,pmt,pv)
Present value	= PV (rate,nper,pmt,fv)
Discount rate	= RATE (nper,pmt,pv,fv)
Number of periods	= NPER (rate,pmt,pv,fv)

In these formulas, pv and fv are present and future value, nper is the number of periods, and rate is the discount, or interest, rate.

There are two things that are a little tricky here. First, unlike a financial calculator, the spreadsheet requires that the rate be entered as a decimal. Second, as with most financial calculators, you have to put a negative sign on either the present value or the future value to solve for the rate or the number of periods. For the same reason, if you solve for a present value, the answer will have a negative sign unless you input a negative future value. The same is true when you compute a future value.

To illustrate how you might use these formulas, we will go back to an example in the chapter. If you invest $25,000 at 12 percent per year, how long until you have $50,000? You might set up a spreadsheet like this:

	A	B	C	D	E	F	G	H
1								
2		Using a spreadsheet for time value of money calculations						
3								
4	If we invest $25,000 at 12 percent, how long until we have $50,000? We need to solve							
5	for the unknown number of periods, so we use the formula NPER (rate, pmt, pv, fv).							
6								
7	Present value (pv):	$25,000						
8	Future value (fv):	$50,000						
9	Rate (rate):	.12						
10								
11	Periods:	**6.116255**						
12								
13	The formula entered in cell B11 is =NPER(B9,0,-B7,B8); notice that pmt is zero and that pv							
14	has a negative sign on it. Also notice that the rate is entered as a decimal, not a percentage.							

CONCEPT QUESTIONS

4.3a What is the basic present value equation?

4.3b What is the Rule of 72?

SUMMARY AND CONCLUSIONS

This chapter has introduced you to the basic principles of present value and discounted cash flow valuation. In it, we explained a number of things about the time value of money, including:

1. For a given rate of return, the value at some point in the future of an investment made today can be determined by calculating the future value of that investment.

2. The current worth of a future cash flow can be determined for a given rate of return by calculating the present value of the cash flow involved.

3. The relationship between present value and future value for a given rate r and time t is given by the basic present value equation:

$$PV = FV_t/(1 + r)^t$$

As we have shown, it is possible to find any one of the four components (PV, FV_t, r, or t) given the other three.

The principles developed in this chapter will figure prominently in the chapters to come. The reason for this is that most investments, whether they involve real assets or financial assets, can be analyzed using the discounted cash flow, or DCF, approach. As a result, the DCF approach is broadly applicable and widely used in practice. Before going on, therefore, you might want to do some of the problems below.

CHAPTER REVIEW AND SELF-TEST PROBLEMS

4.1   **Calculating Future Values.**   Assume you deposit $1,000 today in an account that pays 8 percent interest. How much will you have in four years?

4.2   **Calculating Present Values.**   Suppose you have just celebrated your 19th birthday. A rich uncle set up a trust fund for you that will pay you $100,000 when you turn 25. If the relevant discount rate is 11 percent, how much is this fund worth today?

4.3   **Calculating Rates of Return.**   You've been offered an investment that will double your money in 12 years. What rate of return are you being offered? Check your answer using the Rule of 72.

4.4   **Calculating the Number of Periods.**   You've been offered an investment that will pay you 7 percent per year. If you invest $10,000, how long until you have $20,000? How long until you have $30,000?

Answers to Chapter Review and Self-Test Problems

4.1   We need to calculate the future value of $1,000 at 8 percent for four years. The future value factor is:

$$1.08^4 = 1.3605$$

The future value is thus $1,000 \times 1.3605 = \$1,360.50$.

4.2   We need the present value of $100,000 to be paid in six years at 11 percent. The discount factor is:

$$1/1.11^6 = 1/1.8704 = .5346$$

The present value is thus about $53,460.

4.3   Suppose you invest, say, $100. You will have $200 in 12 years with this investment. So, $100 is the amount you have today, the present value, and $200 is the amount you will have in 12 years, or the future value. From the basic present value equation, we have:

$$\$200 = \$100 \times (1 \times r)^{12}$$
$$2 = (1 \times r)^{12}$$

From here, we need to solve for r, the unknown rate. As shown in the chapter, there are several different ways to do this. We will take the 12th root of 2 (by raising 2 to the power of 1/12):

$$2^{(1/12)} = 1 + r$$
$$1.0595 = 1 + r$$
$$r = 5.95\%$$

Using the Rule of 72, we have $72/t = r\%$, or $72/12 = 6\%$, so our answer looks good (remember that the Rule of 72 is only an approximation).

CRITICAL THINKING AND CONCEPTS REVIEW

1. **Present Value.** The basic present value equation has four parts. What are they?

2. **Compounding.** What is compounding? What is discounting?

3. **Compounding and Periods.** As you increase the length of time involved, what happens to future values? What happens to present values?

4. **Compounding and Interest Rates.** What happens to a future value if you increase the rate r? What happens to a present value?

5. **Ethical Considerations.** Take a look back at Example 4.6. Is it deceptive advertising? Is it unethical to advertise a future value like this without a disclaimer?

    To answer the next five questions, refer to the GMAC security we discussed to open the chapter.

6. **Time Value of Money.** Why would GMAC be willing to accept such a small amount today ($500) in exchange for a promise to repay 20 times that amount ($10,000) in the future?

7. **Call Provisions.** GMAC has the right to buy back the securities anytime it wishes by paying $10,000 (this is a term of this particular deal). What impact does this feature have on the desirability of this security as an investment?

8. **Time Value of Money.** Would you be willing to pay $500 today in exchange for $10,000 in 30 years? What would be the key considerations in answering yes or no? Would your answer depend on who is making the promise to repay?

9. **Investment Comparison.** Suppose that when GMAC offered the security for $500, the U.S. Treasury had offered an essentially identical security. Do you think it would have had a higher or lower price? Why?

10. **Length of Investment.** The GMAC security is actively bought and sold on the New York Stock Exchange. If you looked in *The Wall Street Journal* today, do you think the price would exceed the $500 original price? Why? If you looked in the year 2006, do you think the price would be higher or lower than today's price? Why?

QUESTIONS AND PROBLEMS

1. **Simple Interest versus Compound Interest.** First Rajan Bank pays 5 percent simple interest on its savings account balances, whereas First Mullineaux Bank pays 5 percent interest compounded annually. If you made a $5,000 deposit in each bank, how much more money would you earn from your First Mullineaux Bank account at the end of 10 years?

Basic
(Questions 1–15)

2. **Calculating Future Values.** For each of the following, compute the future value:

Present Value	Years	Interest Rate	Future Value
$ 2,250	4	18%	
9,310	9	6	
76,355	15	12	
183,796	21	8	

3. **Calculating Present Values.** For each of the following, compute the present value:

Present Value	Years	Interest Rate	Future Value
	6	4%	$ 15,451
	8	12	51,557
	16	22	886,073
	25	20	550,164

4. **Calculating Interest Rates.**   Solve for the unknown interest rate in each of the following:

Present Value	Years	Interest Rate	Future Value
$ 221	3		$ 307
425	9		761
25,000	15		136,771
40,200	30		255,810

5. **Calculating the Number of Periods.**   Solve for the unknown number of years in each of the following:

Present Value	Years	Interest Rate	Future Value
$ 250		4%	$ 1,284
1,941		9	4,341
21,320		23	402,662
32,500		34	173,439

6. **Calculating Interest Rates.**   Assume the total cost of a college education will be $250,000 when your child enters college in 18 years. You presently have $25,000 to invest. What annual rate of interest must you earn on your investment to cover the cost of your child's college education?

7. **Calculating the Number of Periods.**   At 10 percent interest, how long does it take to double your money? To quadruple it?

8. **Calculating Interest Rates.**   You are offered an investment that requires you to put up $10,000 today in exchange for $50,000 15 years from now. What is the annual rate of return on this investment?

9. **Calculating the Number of Periods.**   You're trying to save to buy a new $120,000 Ferrari. You have $30,000 today that can be invested at your bank. The bank pays 4 percent annual interest on its accounts. How long will it be before you have enough to buy the car?

10. **Calculating Present Values.**   Imprudential, Inc., has an unfunded pension liability of $825 million that must be paid in 20 years. To assess the value of the firm's stock, financial analysts want to discount this liability back to the present. If the relevant discount rate is 8 percent, what is the present value of this liability?

11. **Calculating Present Values.**   You have just received notification that you have won the $2 million first prize in the Millennium Lottery. However, the prize will be awarded on your 100th birthday (assuming you're around to collect), 80 years from now. What is the present value of your windfall if the appropriate discount rate is 14 percent?

12. **Calculating Future Values.**   Your coin collection contains 50 1952 silver dollars. If your parents purchased them for their face value when they were new, how much will your collection be worth when you retire in 2050, assuming they appreciate at a 3.5 percent annual rate?

13. **Calculating Interest Rates and Future Values.**   A 1949 Vincent Black Shadow Series B vintage motorcycle (of which only 80 were made) sold for about $45,000 in 1996. If you were fortunate enough to have purchased one new for $630 in 1949, what return did you earn on your investment? If the value of a $20,000 1998 Bimota Supermono appreciates at the same rate, what will it be worth in another 47 years?

14. **Calculating Present Values.**   Hot Wheels cars were sold at auction in 1995 by Christie's International PLC for $100 each. At the time, it was estimated that this represented a 27.7 percent annual rate of return. For this to be true, what must the cars have sold for new in 1975?

15. **Calculating Rates of Return.** Although appealing to more refined tastes, art as a collectible has not always performed so profitably. During 1995, Christie's auctioned the William de Kooning painting *Untitled.* The highest bid of $1.95 million was rejected by the owner, who had purchased the painting at the height of the art market in 1989 for $3.52 million. Had the seller accepted the bid, what would his annual rate of return have been?

16. **Calculating Rates of Return.** Referring to the GMAC security we discussed at the very beginning of the chapter:

    a. Based upon the $500 price, what rate was GMAC paying to borrow money?

    b. Suppose that on December 1, 2000, this security's price was $4,490.22. If an investor had purchased it for $500 at the offering and sold it on this day, what annual rate of return would she have earned?

    c. If an investor had purchased the security at market on December 1, 2000, and held it until it matured, what annual rate of return would she have earned?

Intermediate
(Questions 16–25)

17. **Calculating Present Values.** Suppose you are still committed to owning a $120,000 Ferrari (see Question 9). If you believe your mutual fund can achieve a 10.5 percent annual rate of return and you want to buy the car in 10 years on the day you turn 30, how much must you invest today?

18. **Calculating Future Values.** You have just made your first $2,000 contribution to your individual retirement account. Assuming you earn an 11 percent rate of return and make no additional contributions, what will your account be worth when you retire in 45 years? What if you wait 10 years before contributing? (Does this suggest an investment strategy?)

19. **Calculating Future Values.** You are scheduled to receive $24,000 in two years. When you receive it, you will invest it for six more years at 6 percent per year. How much will you have in eight years?

20. **Calculating the Number of Periods.** You expect to receive $60,000 at graduation in two years. You plan on investing it at 7 percent until you have $120,000. How long will you wait from now? (Better than the situation in Question 9, but still no Ferrari.)

21. **Calculating Future Values.** You have $10,000 to deposit. Roten Bank offers 12 percent per year compounded monthly (1 percent per month), while Brook Bank offers 12 percent but will only compound annually. How much will your investment be worth in 10 years at each bank?

22. **Calculating Interest Rates.** An investment offers to quadruple your money in 30 months (don't believe it). What rate per six months are you being offered?

23. **Calculating the Number of Periods.** You can earn .4 percent per month at your bank. If you deposit $1,200, how long must you wait until your account has grown to $2,500?

24. **Calculating Present Values.** You need $60,000 in eight years. If you can earn .75 percent per month, how much will you have to deposit today?

25. **Calculating Present Values.** You have decided that you want to be a millionaire when you retire in 40 years. If you can earn an 11 percent return, how much do you have to invest today? What if you can earn 7 percent?

www.mhhe.com/rwj

Spreadsheet Templates 3, 4, 15, 18

5

Discounted Cash Flow Valuation

AFTER STUDYING THIS CHAPTER, YOU SHOULD HAVE A GOOD UNDERSTANDING OF:

- How to determine the future and present value of investments with multiple cash flows

- How loan payments are calculated and how to find the interest rate on a loan

- How loans are amortized or paid off

- How interest rates are quoted (and misquoted)

THE SIGNING OF big-name athletes is often accompanied by great fanfare, but the numbers are sometimes misleading. For example, in October 1998, the New York Mets signed catcher Mike Piazza to a $91 million contract, the richest deal in baseball history. Not bad, especially for someone who makes a living using the "tools of ignorance" (jock jargon for a catcher's equipment).

However, while Piazza's contract value was reported to be $91 million, the total was actually payable over several years. It consisted of a signing bonus of $7.5 million ($4 million payable in 1999, $3.5 million in 2002) plus a salary of $83.5 million. The salary was to be distributed as $6 million in 1999, $11 million in 2000, $12.5 million in 2001, $9.5 million in 2002, $14.5 million in 2003, and $15 million in both 2004 and 2005. Of course, we recognize that once the time value of money is considered, Piazza didn't really get $91 million. So, how much did he get? This chapter gives you the "tools of knowledge" to answer this question.

In our previous chapter, we learned how to examine single, lump-sum future payments to determine their current, or present, value. This is a useful skill, but we need to go further and figure out how to handle multiple future payments because that is the much more common situation. For example, most loans (including student loans) involve receiving a lump sum today and making future payments.

More generally, most types of business decisions, including decisions concerning marketing, operations, and strategy, involve the comparison of costs incurred today with cash inflows hoped for later. Evaluating the cost-benefit trade-off requires the tools that we develop in this chapter.

Because discounted cash flow valuation is so important, students who learn this material well will find that life is much easier down the road. Getting it straight now will save you a lot of headaches later.

I n our previous chapter, we covered the basics of discounted cash flow valuation. However, so far, we have only dealt with single cash flows. In reality, most investments have multiple cash flows. For example, if Sears is thinking of opening a new department store, there will be a large cash outlay in the beginning and then cash inflows for many years. In this chapter, we begin to explore how to value such investments.

When you finish this chapter, you should have some very practical skills. For example, you will know how to calculate your own car payments or student loan payments. You will also be able to determine how long it will take to pay off a credit card if you make the minimum payment each month (a practice we do not recommend). We will show you how to compare interest rates to determine which are the highest and which are the lowest, and we will also show you how interest rates can be quoted in different, and at times deceptive, ways.

5.1 FUTURE AND PRESENT VALUES OF MULTIPLE CASH FLOWS

Thus far, we have restricted our attention to either the future value of a lump-sum present amount or the present value of some single future cash flow. In this section, we begin to study ways to value multiple cash flows. We start with future value.

Future Value with Multiple Cash Flows

Suppose you deposit $100 today in an account paying 8 percent. In one year, you will deposit another $100. How much will you have in two years? This particular problem is relatively easy. At the end of the first year, you will have $108 plus the second $100 you deposit, for a total of $208. You leave this $208 on deposit at 8 percent for another year. At the end of this second year, the account is worth:

$208 × 1.08 = $224.64

Figure 5.1 is a *time line* that illustrates the process of calculating the future value of these two $100 deposits. Figures such as this one are very useful for solving complicated problems. Anytime you are having trouble with a present or future value problem, drawing a time line will usually help you to see what is happening.

In the first part of Figure 5.1, we show the cash flows on the time line. The most important thing is that we write them down where they actually occur. Here, the first cash flow occurs today, which we label as Time 0. We therefore put $100 at Time 0 on the time line. The second $100 cash flow occurs one year from today, so we write it down at the point labeled as Time 1. In the second part of Figure 5.1, we calculate the future values one period at a time to come up with the final $224.64.

EXAMPLE 5.1 | **Saving Up Revisited**

You think you will be able to deposit $4,000 at the end of each of the next three years in a bank account paying 8 percent interest. You currently have $7,000 in the account. How much will you have in three years? In four years?

At the end of the first year, you will have:

$7,000 × 1.08 + 4,000 = $11,560

At the end of the second year, you will have:

$11,560 × 1.08 + 4,000 = $16,484.80

Repeating this for the third year gives:

$16,484.80 × 1.08 + 4,000 = $21,803.58

Therefore, you will have $21,803.58 in three years. If you leave this on deposit for one more year (and don't add to it), at the end of the fourth year you'll have:

$21,803.58 × 1.08 = $23,547.87

When we calculated the future value of the two $100 deposits, we simply calculated the balance as of the beginning of each year and then rolled that amount forward to the next year. We could have done it another, quicker way. The first $100 is on deposit for two years at 8 percent, so its future value is:

$$\$100 \times 1.08^2 = \$100 \times 1.1664 = \$116.64$$

The second $100 is on deposit for one year at 8 percent, and its future value is thus:

$$\$100 \times 1.08 = \$108.00$$

The total future value, as we previously calculated, is equal to the sum of these two future values:

$$\$116.64 + 108 = \$224.64$$

Based on this example, there are two ways to calculate future values for multiple cash flows: (1) compound the accumulated balance forward one year at a time or (2) calculate the future value of each cash flow first and then add these up. Both give the same answer, so you can do it either way.

To illustrate the two different ways of calculating future values, consider the future value of $2,000 invested at the end of each of the next five years. The current balance is zero, and the rate is 10 percent. We first draw a time line as shown in Figure 5.2.

On the time line, notice that nothing happens until the end of the first year when we make the first $2,000 investment. This first $2,000 earns interest for the next four (not five) years. Also notice that the last $2,000 is invested at the end of the fifth year, so it earns no interest at all.

Figure 5.3 illustrates the calculations involved if we compound the investment one period at a time. As illustrated, the future value is $12,210.20.

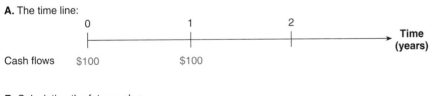

A. The time line:

	0	1	2	Time (years)
Cash flows	$100	$100		

B. Calculating the future value:

	0	1	2	Time (years)
Cash flows	$100	$100		
	×1.08	+108	×1.08	
Future values		$208	$224.64	

FIGURE 5.1

Drawing and using a time line

FIGURE 5.2

Time line for $2,000 per year for five years

FIGURE 5.3

Future value calculated by compounding forward one period at a time

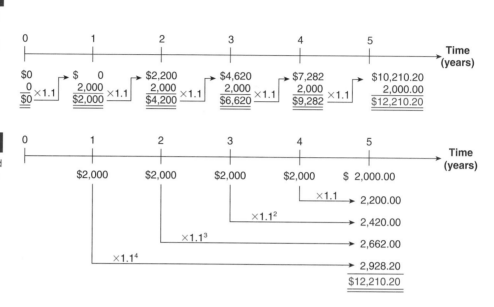

FIGURE 5.4

Future value calculated by compounding each cash flow separately

Figure 5.4 goes through the same calculations, but it uses the second technique. Naturally, the answer is the same.

EXAMPLE 5.2 | Saving Up Once Again

If you deposit $100 in one year, $200 in two years, and $300 in three years, how much will you have in three years? How much of this is interest? How much will you have in five years if you don't add additional amounts? Assume a 7 percent interest rate throughout.

We will calculate the future value of each amount in three years. Notice that the $100 earns interest for two years, and the $200 earns interest for one year. The final $300 earns no interest. The future values are thus:

$$
\begin{array}{ll}
\$100 \times 1.07^2 & = \$114.49 \\
\$200 \times 1.07 & = 214.00 \\
+\$300 & = \underline{\$300.00} \\
\text{Total future value} & = \underline{\underline{\$628.49}}
\end{array}
$$

The future value is thus $628.49. The total interest is:

$$\$628.49 - (100 + 200 + 300) = \$28.49$$

How much will you have in five years? We know that you will have $628.49 in three years. If you leave that in for two more years, it will grow to:

$$\$628.49 \times 1.07^2 = \$628.49 \times 1.1449 = \$719.56$$

Notice that we could have calculated the future value of each amount separately. Once again, be careful about the lengths of time. As we previously calculated, the first $100 earns interest for only four years, the second deposit earns three years' interest, and the last earns two years' interest:

$$\$100 \times 1.07^4 = \$100 \times 1.3108 = \$131.08$$
$$\$200 \times 1.07^3 = \$200 \times 1.2250 = 245.01$$
$$+\$300 \times 1.07^2 = \$300 \times 1.1449 = \underline{343.47}$$
$$\text{Total future value} = \underline{\underline{\$719.56}}$$

Present Value with Multiple Cash Flows

It will turn out that we will very often need to determine the present value of a series of future cash flows. As with future values, there are two ways we can do it. We can either discount back one period at a time, or we can just calculate the present values individually and add them up.

Suppose you need $1,000 in one year and $2,000 more in two years. If you can earn 9 percent on your money, how much do you have to put up today to exactly cover these amounts in the future? In other words, what is the present value of the two cash flows at 9 percent?

The present value of $2,000 in two years at 9 percent is:

$$\$2,000/1.09^2 = \$1,683.36$$

The present value of $1,000 in one year is:

$$\$1,000/1.09 = \$917.43$$

Therefore, the total present value is:

$$\$1,683.36 + 917.43 = \$2,600.79$$

To see why $2,600.79 is the right answer, we can check to see that after the $2,000 is paid out in two years, there is no money left. If we invest $2,600.79 for one year at 9 percent, we will have:

$$\$2,600.79 \times 1.09 = \$2,834.86$$

We take out $1,000, leaving $1,834.86. This amount earns 9 percent for another year, leaving us with:

$$\$1,834.86 \times 1.09 = \$2,000$$

This is just as we planned. As this example illustrates, the present value of a series of future cash flows is simply the amount that you would need today in order to exactly duplicate those future cash flows (for a given discount rate).

An alternative way of calculating present values for multiple future cash flows is to discount back to the present one period at a time. To illustrate, suppose we had an investment that was going to pay $1,000 at the end of every year for the next five years. To find the present value, we could discount each $1,000 back to the present separately and then add the results up. Figure 5.5 illustrates this approach for a 6 percent discount rate. As shown, the answer is $4,212.37 (ignoring a small rounding error).

Alternatively, we could discount the last cash flow back one period and add it to the next-to-the-last cash flow:

$$\$1,000/1.06 + 1,000 = \$943.40 + 1,000 = \$1,943.40$$

FIGURE 5.5

Present value calculated by discounting each cash flow separately

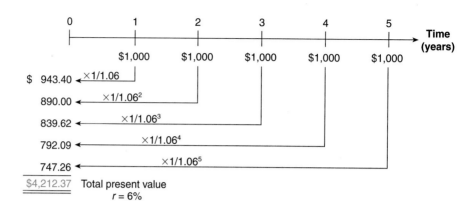

FIGURE 5.6

Present value calculated by discounting back one period at a time

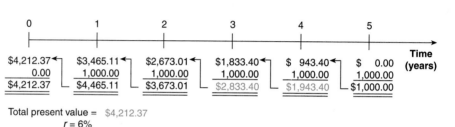

We could then discount this amount back one period and add it to the Year 3 cash flow:

$$\$1,943.40/1.06 + 1,000 = \$1,833.40 + 1,000 = \$2,833.40$$

This process could be repeated as necessary. Figure 5.6 illustrates this approach and the remaining calculations.

As the accompanying *Reality Bytes* box shows, calculating present values is a vital step in comparing alternative cash flows. We will have much more to say on this subject in subsequent chapters.

EXAMPLE 5.3 **How Much Is It Worth?**

You are offered an investment that will pay you $200 in one year, $400 the next year, $600 the next year, and $800 at the end of the next year. You can earn 12 percent on very similar investments. What is the most you should pay for this one?

We need to calculate the present value of these cash flows at 12 percent. Taking them one at a time gives:

$$\$200 \times 1/1.12^1 = \$200/1.1200 = \$178.57$$
$$\$400 \times 1/1.12^2 = \$400/1.2544 = 318.88$$
$$\$600 \times 1/1.12^3 = \$600/1.4049 = 427.07$$
$$+\$800 \times 1/1.12^4 = \$800/1.5735 = \underline{508.41}$$
$$\text{Total present value} = \underline{\$1,432.93}$$

If you can earn 12 percent on your money, then you can duplicate this investment's cash flows for $1,432.93, so this is the most you should be willing to pay.

JACKPOT!

I f you or someone you know is a regular lottery player, you probably already understand that winning a big lottery jackpot is about as likely as getting struck by lightning. However, you may also know that if you are a lucky winner, you will usually get to choose to take all of your money immediately or else receive a series of payments over some number of periods. Perhaps nowhere else is the blurring of the lines between the value of a lump sum and the value of a stream of payments more frequent.

For example, in April 1999, a baby-sitter from Massachusetts struck it rich by winning the $197 million jackpot in the Massachusetts Big Game lottery. As with most jackpots, however, the prize money was not actually all it appeared to be. To collect the full $197 million, the baby-sitter would have to accept equal annual payments over 26 years, amounting to about $7,576,923 per year. As you can determine, using what you have already learned, the present value of this annuity is quite a bit less than the advertised jackpot. Assuming a discount rate of 10 percent, the present value of the payments is about $69.4 million, a tidy sum, but not quite $197 million.

Instead of taking the annuity payments, the baby-sitter chose to receive a lump-sum payment of $104 million immediately. Did she make the right choice? Well, see if you agree that at a discount rate of 5.45 percent she would be indifferent between the two options. At rates greater than that, she would be better off with the lump-sum payment. By the way, her odds of winning the lottery were a staggering 76 million to 1. Lucky, indeed!

The story was similar in the June drawing of the California Lottery, when a machine company supervisor won the $87 million jackpot. He was faced with a similar choice of receiving equal annual installments over a 26-year period or $40.6 million up front. He, too, chose the lump sum. His break-even interest rate was a little higher at 6.72 percent, but taking the one sum still would appear to have been a good choice on his part.

Some lotteries make your decision a little tougher. The Ontario Lottery will pay you either $1,000 a week for the rest of your life or $675,000 right away. (That's in Canadian dollars, by the way.) Of course, there is the chance that you might die in the near future, so the lottery guarantees that your heirs will collect the $1,000 weekly payments until the 20th anniversary of the first payment or until you would have turned 91, whichever comes first. This payout scheme complicates your decision quite a bit. If you live for only the 20-year minimum, the break-even interest rate between the two options is about 4.8 percent per year, compounded weekly. If you expect to live a lot longer than the 20-year minimum, you might be better off accepting the $1,000 per week for life. Of course, if you manage to invest the $675,000 lump sum at a rate of return of about 8 percent per year (compounded weekly), you can have your cake and eat it too since the investment will return payments of $1,000 at the end of each week forever! Taxes complicate the decision in this case because the lottery payments are all on an aftertax basis. Thus, the rates of return in this example would be aftertax as well.

The choice between a lump sum and an annuity is often even more complicated. Taxes matter, as does the current financial condition of the winner. Furthermore, one hindrance to taking the lump sum might be the amount of money that has to be invested. For example, in the case of the baby-sitter, she had $104 million to invest. Most of us have never had an investment portfolio of that size to manage before, and that alone would probably be enough to make anyone uneasy. And, in the Ontario lottery, taking the annuity payment is essentially a bet that you will live long enough to make your decision the correct one. In any case, most studies show that lottery winners generally don't make wise choices with their winnings regardless of how they take their payments, so, if you win, it's not always that first decision that is the most crucial.

How Much Is It Worth? Part 2 | EXAMPLE 5.4

You are offered an investment that will make three $5,000 payments. The first payment will occur four years from today. The second will occur in five years, and the third will follow in six years. If you can earn 11 percent, what is the most this investment is worth today? What is the future value of the cash flows?

We will answer the questions in reverse order to illustrate a point. The future value of the cash flows in six years is:

$$\$5,000 \times 1.11^2 + 5,000 \times 1.11 + 5,000 = \$6,160.50 + 5,550 + 5,000$$
$$= \$16,710.50$$

The present value must be:

$$\$16,710.50/1.11^6 = \$8,934.12$$

Let's check this. Taking them one at a time, the PVs of the cash flows are:

$$\$5,000 \times 1/1.11^6 = \$5,000/1.8704 = \$2,673.20$$
$$\$5,000 \times 1/1.11^5 = \$5,000/1.6851 = 2,967.26$$
$$+\$5,000 \times 1/1.11^4 = \$5,000/1.5181 = \underline{3,293.65}$$
$$\text{Total present value} = \underline{\underline{\$8,934.12}}$$

This is as we previously calculated. The point we want to make is that we can calculate present and future values in any order and convert between them using whatever way seems most convenient. The answers will always be the same as long as we stick with the same discount rate and are careful to keep track of the right number of periods.

How to Calculate Present Values with Multiple Future Cash Flows Using a Financial Calculator

To calculate the present value of multiple cash flows with a financial calculator, we will simply discount the individual cash flows one at a time using the same technique we used in our previous chapter, so this is not really new. There is a shortcut, however, that we can show you. We will use the numbers in Example 5.3 to illustrate.

To begin, of course we first remember to clear out the calculator! Next, from Example 5.3, the first cash flow is $200 to be received in one year and the discount rate is 12 percent, so we do the following:

Now you can write down this answer to save it, but that's inefficient. All calculators have a memory where you can store numbers. Why not just save it there? Doing so cuts way down on mistakes because you don't have to write down and/or rekey numbers, and it's much faster.

Next we value the second cash flow. We need to change N to 2 and FV to 400. As long as we haven't changed anything else, we don't have to reenter %i or clear out the calculator, so we have:

You save this number by adding it to the one you saved in our first calculation, and so on for the remaining two calculations.

As we will see in a later chapter, some financial calculators will let you enter all of the future cash flows at once, but we'll discuss that subject when we get to it.

How to Calculate Present Values with Multiple Future Cash Flows Using a Spreadsheet

SPREADSHEET

strategies

Just as we did in our previous chapter, we can set up a basic spreadsheet to calculate the present values of the individual cash flows as follows. Notice that we have simply calculated the present values one at a time and added them up:

	A	B	C	D	E	F
1						
2			Using a spreadsheet to value multiple future cash flows			
3						
4	What is the present value of $200 in one year, $400 the next year, $600 the next year, and					
5	$800 the last year if the discount rate is 12 percent?					
6						
7	Rate:	.12				
8						
9	Year	Cash flows	Present values	Formula used		
10	1	$200	$178.57	=PV($B$7,A10,0,-B10)		
11	2	$400	$318.88	=PV($B$7,A11,0,-B11)		
12	3	$600	$427.07	=PV($B$7,A12,0,-B12)		
13	4	$800	$508.41	=PV($B$7,A13,0,-B13)		
14						
15		Total PV:	$1,432.93	=SUM(C10:C13)		
16						
17	Notice the negative signs inserted in the PV formulas. These just make the present values have					
18	positive signs. Also, the discount rate in cell B7 is entered as $B$7 (an "absolute" reference) because					
19	it is used over and over. We could have just entered ".12" instead, but our approach is more flexible.					
20						
21						
22						

A Note on Cash Flow Timing

In working present and future value problems, cash flow timing is critically important. In almost all such calculations, it is implicitly assumed that the cash flows occur at the *end* of each period. In fact, all the formulas we have discussed, all the numbers in a standard present value or future value table, and, very importantly, all the preset (or default) settings on a financial calculator or spreadsheet assume that cash flows occur at the end of each period. Unless you are very explicitly told otherwise, you should always assume that this is what is meant.

As a quick illustration of this point, suppose you are told that a three-year investment has a first-year cash flow of $100, a second-year cash flow of $200, and a third-year cash flow of $300. You are asked to draw a time line. Without further information, you should always assume that the time line looks like this:

On our time line, notice how the first cash flow occurs at the end of the first period, the second at the end of the second period, and the third at the end of the third period.

5.2 | VALUING LEVEL CASH FLOWS: ANNUITIES AND PERPETUITIES

We will frequently encounter situations where we have multiple cash flows that are all the same amount. For example, a very common type of loan repayment plan calls for the borrower to repay the loan by making a series of equal payments for some length of time. Almost all consumer loans (such as car loans) and home mortgages feature equal payments, usually made each month.

More generally, a series of constant, or level, cash flows that occur at the end of each period for some fixed number of periods is called an ordinary **annuity;** or, more correctly, the cash flows are said to be in ordinary annuity form. Annuities appear very frequently in financial arrangements, and there are some useful shortcuts for determining their values. We consider these next.

annuity
A level stream of cash flows for a fixed period of time.

Present Value for Annuity Cash Flows

Suppose we were examining an asset that promised to pay $500 at the end of each of the next three years. The cash flows from this asset are in the form of a three-year, $500 ordinary annuity. If we wanted to earn 10 percent on our money, how much would we offer for this annuity?

From the previous section, we know that we can discount each of these $500 payments back to the present at 10 percent to determine the total present value:

$$\text{Present value} = \$500/1.1^1 + 500/1.1^2 + 500/1.1^3$$
$$= \$500/1.10 + 500/1.21 + 500/1.331$$
$$= \$454.55 + 413.22 + 375.66$$
$$= \$1,243.43$$

This approach works just fine. However, we will often encounter situations where the number of cash flows is quite large. For example, a typical home mortgage calls for monthly payments over 30 years, for a total of 360 payments. If we were trying to determine the present value of those payments, it would be useful to have a shortcut.

Since the cash flows on an annuity are all the same, we can come up with a very useful variation on the basic present value equation. It turns out that the present value of an annuity of C dollars per period for t periods when the rate of return, or interest rate, is r is given by:

$$\text{Annuity present value} = C \times \left(\frac{1 - \text{Present value factor}}{r} \right)$$
$$= C \times \left\{ \frac{1 - [1/(1 + r)^t]}{r} \right\} \qquad [5.1]$$

The term in parentheses on the first line is sometimes called the present value interest factor for annuities and abbreviated PVIFA(r,t).

The expression for the annuity present value may look a little complicated, but it isn't difficult to use. Notice that the term in square brackets on the second line, $1/(1 + r)^t$, is the same present value factor we've been calculating. In our example just above, the interest rate is 10 percent and there are three years involved. The usual present value factor is thus:

$$\text{Present value factor} = 1/1.1^3 = 1/1.331 = .75131$$

To calculate the annuity present value factor, we just plug this in:

$$
\begin{aligned}
\text{Annuity present value factor} &= (1 - \text{Present value factor})/r \\
&= (1 - .75131)/.10 \\
&= .248685/.10 = 2.48685
\end{aligned}
$$

Just as we calculated before, the present value of our $500 annuity is then:

$$\text{Annuity present value} = \$500 \times 2.48685 = \$1,243.43$$

How Much Can You Afford? | **EXAMPLE 5.5**

After carefully going over your budget, you have determined you can afford to pay $632 per month towards a new sports car. You call up your local bank and find out that the going rate is 1 percent per month for 48 months. How much can you borrow?

To determine how much you can borrow, we need to calculate the present value of $632 per month for 48 months at 1 percent per month. The loan payments are in ordinary annuity form, so the annuity present value factor is:

$$
\begin{aligned}
\text{Annuity PV factor} &= (1 - \text{Present value factor})/r \\
&= [1 - (1/1.01^{48})]/.01 \\
&= (1 - .6203)/.01 = 37.9740
\end{aligned}
$$

With this factor, we can calculate the present value of the 48 payments of $632 each as:

$$\text{Present value} = \$632 \times 37.9740 = \$24,000$$

Therefore, $24,000 is what you can afford to borrow and repay.

Annuity Tables Just as there are tables for ordinary present value factors, there are tables for annuity factors as well. Table 5.1 contains a few such factors; Table A.3 in Appendix A contains a larger set. To find the annuity present value factor we just calculated, look for the row corresponding to three periods and then find the column for 10 percent. The

Number of Periods	Interest Rates			
	5%	**10%**	**15%**	**20%**
1	.9524	.9091	.8696	.8333
2	1.8594	1.7355	1.6257	1.5278
3	2.7232	2.4869	2.2832	2.1065
4	3.5460	3.1699	2.8550	2.5887
5	4.3295	3.7908	3.3522	2.9906

TABLE 5.1

Annuity present value interest factors

number you see at that intersection should be 2.4869 (rounded to four decimal places), as we calculated. Once again, try calculating a few of these factors yourself and compare your answers to the ones in the table to make sure you know how to do it. If you are using a financial calculator, just enter $1 as the payment and calculate the present value; the result should be the annuity present value factor.

CALCULATOR hints

Annuity Present Values

To find annuity present values with a financial calculator, we need to use the **PMT** key (you were probably wondering what it was for). Compared to finding the present value of a single amount, there are two important differences. First, we enter the annuity cash flow using the **PMT** key, and, second, we don't enter anything for the future value, **FV**. So, for example, the problem we have been examining is a three-year, $500 annuity. If the discount rate is 10 percent, we need to do the following (after clearing out the calculator!):

Enter	3	10	500		
	N	**%i**	**PMT**	**PV**	**FV**
Solve for				−1,243.43	

As usual, we get a negative sign on the PV.

SPREADSHEET strategies

Annuity Present Values

Using a spreadsheet to work the same problem goes like this:

	A	B	C	D	E	F	G
1							
2	Using a spreadsheet to find annuity present values						
3							
4	What is the present value of $500 per year for 3 years if the discount rate is 10 percent?						
5	We need to solve for the unknown present value, so we use the formula PV(rate, nper, pmt, fv).						
6							
7	Payment amount per period:	$500					
8	Number of payments:	3					
9	Discount rate:	.1					
10							
11	Annuity present value:	**$1,243.43**					
12							
13	The formula entered in cell B11 is =PV(B9, B8, -B7, 0); notice that FV is zero and that pmt has						
14	a negative sign on it. Also notice that the discount rate is entered as a decimal, not a percentage.						
15							
16							
17							

Finding the Payment Suppose you wish to start up a new business that specializes in the latest of health food trends, frozen yak milk. To produce and market your product, the Yakee Doodle Dandy, you need to borrow $100,000. Because it strikes you as unlikely that this particular fad will be long-lived, you propose to pay off the loan quickly by making five equal annual payments. If the interest rate is 18 percent, what will the payments be?

In this case, we know that the present value is $100,000. The interest rate is 18 percent, and there are five years. The payments are all equal, so we need to find the relevant annuity factor and solve for the unknown cash flow:

$$\text{Annuity present value} = \$100,000 = C \times (1 - \text{Present value factor})/r$$
$$\$100,000 = C \times (1 - 1/1.18^5)/.18$$
$$= C \times (1 - .4371)/.18$$
$$= C \times 3.1272$$
$$C = \$100,000/3.1272 = \$31,978$$

Therefore, you'll make five payments of just under $32,000 each.

Annuity Payments — CALCULATOR hints

Finding annuity payments is easy with a financial calculator. In our example just above, the PV is $100,000, the interest rate is 18 percent, and there are five years. We find the payment as follows:

Enter	5	18		100,000	
	N	%i	PMT	PV	FV
Solve for			-31,978		

Here we get a negative sign on the payment because the payment is an outflow for us.

Annuity Payments — SPREADSHEET strategies

Using a spreadsheet to work the same problem goes like this:

	A	B	C	D	E	F	G
1							
2	Using a spreadsheet to find annuity payments						
3							
4	What is the annuity payment if the present value is $100,000, the interest rate is 18 percent, and						
5	there are 5 periods? We need to solve for the unknown payment in an annuity, so we use the						
6	formula PMT(rate, nper, pv, fv)						
7							
8	Annuity present value:	$100,000					
9	Number of payments:	5					
10	Discount rate:	.18					
11							
12	Annuity payment:	($31,977.78)					
13							
14	The formula entered in cell B12 is =PMT(B10, B9, -B8, 0); notice that fv is zero and that the payment has						
15	a negative sign because it is an outflow to us.						

Finding the Number of Payments | EXAMPLE 5.6

You ran a little short on your spring break vacation, so you put $1,000 on your credit card. You can only afford to make the minimum payment of $20 per month. The interest rate on the credit card is 1.5 percent per month. How long will you need to pay off the $1,000?

What we have here is an annuity of $20 per month at 1.5 percent per month for some unknown length of time. The present value is $1,000 (the amount you owe today). We need to do a little algebra (or else use a financial calculator):

$$\$1,000 = \$20 \times (1 - \text{Present value factor})/.015$$

$$(\$1,000/20) \times .015 = 1 - \text{Present value factor}$$

$$\text{Present value factor} = .25 = 1/(1 + r)^t$$

$$1.015^t = 1/.25 = 4$$

At this point, the problem boils down to asking the following question: How long does it take for your money to quadruple at 1.5 percent per month? Based on our previous chapter, the answer is about 93 months:

$$1.015^{93} = 3.99 \approx 4$$

It will take you about 93/12 = 7.75 years at this rate.

CALCULATOR hints

Finding the Number of Payments

To solve this one on a financial calculator, do the following:

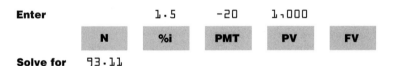

Enter		1.5	-20	1,000	
	N	**%i**	**PMT**	**PV**	**FV**
Solve for	93.11				

Notice that we put a negative sign on the payment you must make, and we have solved for the number of months. You still have to divide by 12 to get our answer. Also, some financial calculators won't report a fractional value for N; they automatically (without telling you) round up to the next whole period (not to the nearest value). With a spreadsheet, use the function =NPER(rate,pmt,pv,fv); be sure to put in a zero for fv and to enter −20 as the payment.

Finding the Rate   The last question we might want to ask concerns the interest rate implicit in an annuity. For example, an insurance company offers to pay you $1,000 per year for 10 years if you will pay $6,710 up front. What rate is implicit in this 10-year annuity?

In this case, we know the present value ($6,710), we know the cash flows ($1,000 per year), and we know the life of the investment (10 years). What we don't know is the discount rate:

$$\$6,710 = \$1,000 \times (1 - \text{Present value factor})/r$$

$$\$6,710/1,000 = 6.71 = \{1 - [1/(1 + r)^{10}]\}/r$$

So, the annuity factor for 10 periods is equal to 6.71, and we need to solve this equation for the unknown value of r. Unfortunately, this is mathematically impossible to do directly. The only way to do it is to use a table or trial and error to find a value for r.

If you look across the row corresponding to 10 periods in Table A.3, you will see a factor of 6.7101 for 8 percent, so we see right away that the insurance company is offering just about 8 percent. Alternatively, we could just start trying different values until we got very

close to the answer. Using this trial-and-error approach can be a little tedious, but, fortunately, machines are good at that sort of thing.[1]

To illustrate how to find the answer by trial and error, suppose a relative of yours wants
to borrow $3,000. She offers to repay you $1,000 every year for four years. What interest
rate are you being offered?

The cash flows here have the form of a four-year, $1,000 annuity. The present value is
$3,000. We need to find the discount rate, r. Our goal in doing so is primarily to give you a
feel for the relationship between annuity values and discount rates.

We need to start somewhere, and 10 percent is probably as good a place as any to begin. At 10 percent, the annuity factor is:

Annuity present value factor = $(1 - 1/1.10^4)/.10 = 3.1699$

The present value of the cash flows at 10 percent is thus:

Present value = $1,000 × 3.1699 = $3,169.90

You can see that we're already in the right ballpark.

Is 10 percent too high or too low? Recall that present values and discount rates move
in opposite directions: Increasing the discount rate lowers the PV and vice versa. Our present value here is too high, so the discount rate is too low. If we try 12 percent:

Present value = $1,000 × $(1 - 1/1.12^4)/.12 = $3,037.35

Now we're almost there. We are still a little low on the discount rate (because the PV is a
little high), so we'll try 13 percent:

Present value = $1,000 × $(1 - 1/1.13^4)/.13 = $2,974.47

This is less than $3,000, so we now know that the answer is between 12 percent and 13 per-
cent, and it looks to be about 12.5 percent. For practice, work at it for a while longer and
see if you find that the answer is about 12.59 percent.

Finding the Rate

CALCULATOR hints

Alternatively, you could use a financial calculator to do the following:

Enter	4		1,000	−3,000	
	N	**%i**	**PMT**	**PV**	**FV**
Solve for		12.59			

Notice that we put a negative sign on the present value (why?). With a spreadsheet, use the function
=RATE(nper,pmt,pv,fv); be sure to put in a zero for fv and to enter 1,000 as the payment and −3,000
as the pv.

---

[1]Financial calculators rely on trial and error to find the answer. That's why they sometimes appear to be "thinking" before coming up with the answer. Actually, it is possible to directly solve for r if there are fewer than five
periods, but it's usually not worth the trouble.

Future Value for Annuities

On occasion, it's also handy to know a shortcut for calculating the future value of an annuity. As you might guess, there are future value factors for annuities as well as present value factors. In general, the future value factor for an annuity is given by:

$$\text{Annuity FV factor} = (\text{Future value factor} - 1)/r$$
$$= [(1 + r)^t - 1]/r \qquad \text{[5.2]}$$

To see how we use annuity future value factors, suppose you plan to contribute $2,000 every year into a retirement account paying 8 percent. If you retire in 30 years, how much will you have?

The number of years here, t, is 30, and the interest rate, r, is 8 percent, so we can calculate the annuity future value factor as:

$$\text{Annuity FV factor} = (\text{Future value factor} - 1)/r$$
$$= (1.08^{30} - 1)/.08$$
$$= (10.0627 - 1)/.08$$
$$= 113.2832$$

The future value of this 30-year, $2,000 annuity is thus:

$$\text{Annuity future value} = \$2,000 \times 113.2832$$
$$= \$226,566.4$$

CALCULATOR hints

Future Values of Annuities

Of course, you could solve this problem using a financial calculator by doing the following:

Enter	30	8	−2,000		
	N	**%i**	**PMT**	**PV**	**FV**
Solve for					226,566.42

Notice that we put a negative sign on the payment (why?). With a spreadsheet, use the function =FV(rate,nper,pmt,pv); be sure to put in a zero for pv and to enter −2,000 as the payment.

A Note on Annuities Due

So far, we have only discussed ordinary annuities. These are the most important, but there is a variation that is fairly common. Remember that with an ordinary annuity, the cash flows occur at the end of each period. When you take out a loan with monthly payments, for example, the first loan payment normally occurs one month after you get the loan. However, when you lease an apartment, the first lease payment is usually due immediately. The second payment is due at the beginning of the second month, and so on. A lease is an example of an **annuity due**. An annuity due is an annuity for which the cash flows occur at the beginning of each period. Almost any type of arrangement in which we have to prepay the same amount each period is an annuity due.

There are several different ways to calculate the value of an annuity due. With a financial calculator, you simply switch it into "due" or "beginning" mode. It is very important to re-

annuity due

An annuity for which the cash flows occur at the beginning of the period.

member to switch it back when you are finished! Another way to calculate the present value of an annuity due can be illustrated with a time line. Suppose an annuity due has five payments of $400 each, and the relevant discount rate is 10 percent. The time line looks like this:

Notice how the cash flows here are the same as those for a *four*-year ordinary annuity, except that there is an extra $400 at Time 0. For practice, verify that the present value of a four-year $400 ordinary annuity at 10 percent is $1,267.95. If we add on the extra $400, we get $1,667.95, which is the present value of this annuity due.

There is an even easier way to calculate the present or future value of an annuity due. If we assume that cash flows occur at the end of each period when they really occur at the beginning, then we discount each one by one period too many. We could fix this by simply multiplying our answer by $(1 + r)$, where r is the discount rate. In fact, the relationship between the value of an annuity due and an ordinary annuity with the same number of payments is just:

$$\text{Annuity due value} = \text{Ordinary annuity value} \times (1 + r) \qquad [5.3]$$

This works for both present and future values, so calculating the value of an annuity due involves two steps: (1) calculate the present or future value as though it were an ordinary annuity, and (2) multiply your answer by $(1 + r)$.

Perpetuities

We've seen that a series of level cash flows can be valued by treating those cash flows as an annuity. An important special case of an annuity arises when the level stream of cash flows continues forever. Such an asset is called a **perpetuity** since the cash flows are perpetual. Perpetuities are also called **consols,** particularly in Canada and the United Kingdom. See Example 5.7 for an important example of a perpetuity.

Since a perpetuity has an infinite number of cash flows, we obviously can't compute its value by discounting each one. Fortunately, valuing a perpetuity turns out to be the easiest possible case. The present value of a perpetuity is simply:

$$\text{PV for a perpetuity} = C/r \qquad [5.4]$$

For example, an investment offers a perpetual cash flow of $500 every year. The return you require on such an investment is 8 percent. What is the value of this investment? The value of this perpetuity is:

$$\text{Perpetuity PV} = C/r = \$500/.08 = \$6,250$$

This concludes our discussion of valuing investments with multiple cash flows. For future reference, Table 5.2 contains a summary of the annuity and perpetuity basic calculations we described.

perpetuity
An annuity in which the cash flows continue forever.

consol
A type of perpetuity.

Preferred Stock | **EXAMPLE 5.7**

Preferred stock (or preference stock) is an important example of a perpetuity. When a corporation sells preferred stock, the buyer is promised a fixed cash dividend every period (usually every quarter) forever. This dividend must be paid before any dividend can be paid to regular stockholders, hence the term *preferred.*

TABLE 5.2

Summary of annuity
and perpetuity
calculations

I. **Symbols**
   PV = Present value, what future cash flows are worth today
   FV_t = Future value, what cash flows are worth in the future
   r = Interest rate, rate of return, or discount rate per period—typically, but not always, one year
   t = Number of periods—typically, but not always, the number of years
   C = Cash amount

II. **Future value of C invested per period for t periods at r percent per period**
   $$FV_t = C \times [(1 + r)^t - 1]/r$$
   A series of identical cash flows is called an annuity, and the term $[(1 + r)^t - 1]/r$ is called the *annuity future value factor*.

III. **Present value of C per period for t periods at r percent per period**
   $$PV = C \times \{1 - [1/(1 + r)^t]\}/r$$
   The term $\{1 - [1/(1 + r)^t]\}/r$ is called the *annuity present value factor*.

IV. **Present value of a perpetuity of C per period**
   $$PV = C/r$$
   A perpetuity has the same cach flow every year forever.

Suppose the Fellini Co. wants to sell preferred stock at $100 per share. A very similar issue of preferred stock already outstanding has a price of $40 per share and offers a dividend of $1 every quarter. What dividend will Fellini have to offer if the preferred stock is going to sell?

The issue that is already out has a present value of $40 and a cash flow of $1 every quarter forever. Since this is a perpetuity:

   Present value = $40 = $1 \times (1/r)

   $r = 2.5\%$

To be competitive, the new Fellini issue will also have to offer 2.5 percent *per quarter;* so, if the present value is to be $100, the dividend must be such that:

   Present value = $100 = C \times (1/.025)

   $C = \$2.5$ (per quarter)

CONCEPT QUESTIONS

5.2a In general, what is the present value of an annuity of C dollars per period at a discount rate of r per period? The future value?

5.2b In general, what is the present value of a perpetuity?

5.3 | COMPARING RATES: THE EFFECT OF COMPOUNDING PERIODS

The last issue we need to discuss has to do with the way interest rates are quoted. This subject causes a fair amount of confusion because rates are quoted in many different ways. Sometimes the way a rate is quoted is the result of tradition, and sometimes it's the result of legislation. Unfortunately, at times, rates are quoted in deliberately deceptive ways to mislead borrowers and investors. We will discuss these topics in this section.

Effective Annual Rates and Compounding

If a rate is quoted as 10 percent compounded semiannually, then what this means is that the investment actually pays 5 percent every six months. A natural question then arises: Is 5 percent every six months the same thing as 10 percent per year? It's easy to see that it is not. If you invest $1 at 10 percent per year, you will have $1.10 at the end of the year. If you invest at 5 percent every six months, then you'll have the future value of $1 at 5 percent for two periods, or:

$$\$1 \times 1.05^2 = \$1.1025$$

This is $.0025 more. The reason is very simple. What has occurred is that your account was credited with $1 × .05 = 5 cents in interest after six months. In the following six months, you earned 5 percent on that nickel, for an extra 5 × .05 = .25 cents.

As our example illustrates, 10 percent compounded semiannually is actually equivalent to 10.25 percent per year. Put another way, we would be indifferent between 10 percent compounded semiannually and 10.25 percent compounded annually. Anytime we have compounding during the year, we need to be concerned about what the rate really is.

In our example, the 10 percent is called a stated, or quoted, interest rate. Other names are used as well. The 10.25 percent, which is actually the rate that you will earn, is called the effective annual rate (EAR). To compare different investments or interest rates, we will always need to convert to effective rates. Some general procedures for doing this are discussed next.

stated interest rate
The interest rate expressed in terms of the interest payment made each period. Also, quoted interest rate.

Calculating and Comparing Effective Annual Rates

To see why it is important to work only with effective rates, suppose you've shopped around and come up with the following three rates:

Bank A: 15 percent, compounded daily
Bank B: 15.5 percent, compounded quarterly
Bank C: 16 percent, compounded annually

effective annual rate (EAR)
The interest rate expressed as if it were compounded once per year.

Which of these is the best if you are thinking of opening a savings account? Which of these is best if they represent loan rates?

To begin, Bank C is offering 16 percent per year. Since there is no compounding during the year, this is the effective rate. Bank B is actually paying .155/4 = .03875, or 3.875 percent, per quarter. At this rate, an investment of $1 for four quarters would grow to:

$$\$1 \times 1.03875^4 = \$1.1642$$

The EAR, therefore, is 16.42 percent. For a saver, this is much better than the 16 percent rate Bank C is offering; for a borrower, it's worse.

Bank A is compounding every day. This may seem a little extreme, but it is very common to calculate interest daily. In this case, the daily interest rate is actually:

$$.15/365 = .000411$$

This is .0411 percent per day. At this rate, an investment of $1 for 365 periods would grow to:

$$\$1 \times 1.000411^{365} = \$1.1618$$

The EAR is 16.18 percent. This is not as good as Bank B's 16.42 percent for a saver, and not as good as Bank C's 16 percent for a borrower.

This example illustrates two things. First, the highest quoted rate is not necessarily the best. Second, the compounding during the year can lead to a significant difference between the quoted rate and the effective rate. Remember that the effective rate is what you get or what you pay.

If you look at our examples, you see that we computed the EARs in three steps. We first divided the quoted rate by the number of times that the interest is compounded. We then added 1 to the result and raised it to the power of the number of times the interest is compounded. Finally, we subtracted the 1. If we let m be the number of times the interest is compounded during the year, these steps can be summarized simply as:

$$\text{EAR} = (1 + \text{Quoted rate}/m)^m - 1 \qquad \qquad [5.5]$$

For example, suppose you were offered 12 percent compounded monthly. In this case, the interest is compounded 12 times a year; so m is 12. You can calculate the effective rate as:

$$
\begin{aligned}
\text{EAR} &= (1 + \text{Quoted rate}/m)^m - 1 \\
&= (1 + .12/12)^{12} - 1 \\
&= 1.01^{12} - 1 \\
&= 1.126825 - 1 \\
&= 12.6825\%
\end{aligned}
$$

EXAMPLE 5.8 | What's the EAR?

A bank is offering 12 percent compounded quarterly. If you put $100 in an account, how much will you have at the end of one year? What's the EAR? How much will you have at the end of two years?

The bank is effectively offering 12%/4 = 3% every quarter. If you invest $100 for four periods at 3 percent per period, the future value is:

$$
\begin{aligned}
\text{Future value} &= \$100 \times 1.03^4 \\
&= \$100 \times 1.1255 \\
&= \$112.55
\end{aligned}
$$

The EAR is 12.55 percent: $100 × (1 + .1255) = $112.55.

We can determine what you would have at the end of two years in two different ways. One way is to recognize that two years is the same as eight quarters. At 3 percent per quarter, after eight quarters, you would have:

$$\$100 \times 1.03^8 = \$100 \times 1.2668 = \$126.68$$

Alternatively, we could determine the value after two years by using an EAR of 12.55 percent; so after two years you would have:

$$\$100 \times 1.1255^2 = \$100 \times 1.2688 = \$126.68$$

Thus, the two calculations produce the same answer. This illustrates an important point. Anytime we do a present or future value calculation, the rate we use must be an actual or effective rate. In this case, the actual rate is 3 percent per quarter. The effective annual rate is 12.55 percent. It doesn't matter which one we use once we know the EAR.

EXAMPLE 5.9 | Quoting a Rate

Now that you know how to convert a quoted rate to an EAR, consider going the other way. As a lender, you know you want to actually earn 18 percent on a particular loan. You want to quote a rate that features monthly compounding. What rate do you quote?

In this case, we know that the EAR is 18 percent, and we know that this is the result of monthly compounding. Let q stand for the quoted rate. We thus have:

$$EAR = (1 + \text{Quoted rate}/m)^m - 1$$
$$.18 = (1 + q/12)^{12} - 1$$
$$1.18 = (1 + q/12)^{12}$$

We need to solve this equation for the quoted rate. This calculation is the same as the ones we did to find an unknown interest rate in Chapter 4:

$$1.18^{(1/12)} = 1 + q/12$$
$$1.18^{.08333} = 1 + q/12$$
$$1.0139 = 1 + q/12$$
$$q = .0139 \times 12$$
$$= 16.68\%$$

Therefore, the rate you would quote is 16.68 percent, compounded monthly.

EARs and APRs

Sometimes it's not altogether clear whether a rate is an effective annual rate or not. A case in point concerns what is called the **annual percentage rate (APR)** on a loan. Truth-in-lending laws in the United States require that lenders disclose an APR on virtually all consumer loans. This rate must be displayed on a loan document in a prominent and unambiguous way.

Given that an APR must be calculated and displayed, an obvious question arises: Is an APR an effective annual rate? Put another way: If a bank quotes a car loan at 12 percent APR, is the consumer actually paying 12 percent interest? Surprisingly, the answer is no. There is some confusion over this point, which we discuss next.

The confusion over APRs arises because lenders are required by law to compute the APR in a particular way. By law, the APR is simply equal to the interest rate per period multiplied by the number of periods in a year. For example, if a bank is charging 1.2 percent per month on car loans, then the APR that must be reported is $1.2\% \times 12 = 14.4\%$. So, an APR is in fact a quoted, or stated, rate in the sense we've been discussing. For example, an APR of 12 percent on a loan calling for monthly payments is really 1 percent per month. The EAR on such a loan is thus:

$$EAR = (1 + APR/12)^{12} - 1$$
$$= 1.01^{12} - 1 = 12.6825\%$$

annual percentage rate (APR)

The interest rate charged per period multiplied by the number of periods per year.

What Rate Are You Paying? | **EXAMPLE 5.10**

A typical credit card agreement quotes an interest rate of 18 percent APR. Monthly payments are required. What is the actual interest rate you pay on such a credit card?

Based on our discussion, an APR of 18 percent with monthly payments is really $.18/12 = .015$, or 1.5 percent, per month. The EAR is thus:

$$EAR = (1 + .18/12)^{12} - 1$$
$$= 1.015^{12} - 1$$
$$= 1.1956 - 1$$
$$= 19.56\%$$

This is the rate you actually pay.

The difference between an APR and an EAR probably won't be all that great, but it is somewhat ironic that truth-in-lending laws sometimes require lenders to be *un*truthful about the actual rate on a loan.

EARs, APRs, Financial Calculators, and Spreadsheets

A financial calculator will convert a quoted rate (or an APR) to an EAR and back. Unfortunately, the specific procedures are too different from calculator to calculator for us to illustrate in general terms; you'll have to consult Appendix D or your calculator's operating manual. Typically, however, what we have called EAR is labeled "EFF" (for *effective*) on a calculator. More troublesome is the fact that what we have called a quoted rate (or an APR) is labeled "NOM" (for *nominal*). Unfortunately, the term *nominal rate* has come to have a different meaning that we will see in our next chapter. So, just remember that *nominal* in this context means quoted or APR.

With a spreadsheet, we can easily do these conversions. To convert a quoted rate (or an APR) to an effective rate in Excel, for example, use the formula EFFECT(nominal_rate,npery), where nominal_rate is the quoted rate or APR and npery is the number of compounding periods per year. Similarly, to convert an EAR to a quoted rate, use NOMINAL(effect_rate,npery), where effect_rate is the EAR.

CONCEPT QUESTIONS

5.3a If an interest rate is given as 12 percent, compounded daily, what do we call this rate?

5.3b What is an APR? What is an EAR? Are they the same thing?

5.3c In general, what is the relationship between a stated interest rate and an effective interest rate? Which is more relevant for financial decisions?

5.4 | LOAN TYPES AND LOAN AMORTIZATION

Whenever a lender extends a loan, some provision will be made for repayment of the principal (the original loan amount). A loan might be repaid in equal installments, for example, or it might be repaid in a single lump sum. Because the way that the principal and interest are paid is up to the parties involved, there is actually an unlimited number of possibilities.

In this section, we describe a few forms of repayment that come up quite often; more complicated forms can usually be built up from these. The three basic types of loans are pure discount loans, interest-only loans, and amortized loans. Working with these loans is a very straightforward application of the present value principles that we have already developed.

Pure Discount Loans

The pure discount loan is the simplest form of loan. With such a loan, the borrower receives money today and repays a single lump sum at some time in the future. A one-year, 10 percent pure discount loan, for example, would require the borrower to repay $1.1 in one year for every dollar borrowed today.

Because a pure discount loan is so simple, we already know how to value one. Suppose a borrower was able to repay $25,000 in five years. If we, acting as the lender, wanted a 12 percent interest rate on the loan, how much would we be willing to lend? Put another way, what value would we assign today to that $25,000 to be repaid in five years? Based on our work in Chapter 4, we know that the answer is just the present value of $25,000 at 12 percent for five years:

Present value = $25,000/1.12^5

$\qquad$ = $25,000/1.7623

$\qquad$ = $14,186

Pure discount loans are very common when the loan term is short, say, a year or less. In recent years, they have become increasingly common for much longer periods.

Treasury Bills | **EXAMPLE 5.11**

When the U.S. government borrows money on a short-term basis (a year or less), it does so by selling what are called *Treasury bills,* or *T-bills* for short. A T-bill is a promise by the government to repay a fixed amount at some time in the future, for example, 3 months or 12 months.

Treasury bills are pure discount loans. If a T-bill promises to repay $10,000 in 12 months, and the market interest rate is 7 percent, how much will the bill sell for in the market?

Since the going rate is 7 percent, the T-bill will sell for the present value of $10,000 to be paid in one year at 7 percent, or:

Present value = $10,000/1.07 = $9,345.79

Interest-Only Loans

A second type of loan has a repayment plan that calls for the borrower to pay interest each period and to repay the entire principal (the original loan amount) at some point in the future. Such loans are called *interest-only loans.* Notice that if there is just one period, a pure discount loan and an interest-only loan are the same thing.

For example, with a three-year, 10 percent, interest-only loan of $1,000, the borrower would pay $1,000 × .10 = $100 in interest at the end of the first and second years. At the end of the third year, the borrower would return the $1,000 along with another $100 in interest for that year. Similarly, a 50-year interest-only loan would call for the borrower to pay interest every year for the next 50 years and then repay the principal. In the extreme, the borrower pays the interest every period forever and never repays any principal. As we discussed earlier in the chapter, the result is a perpetuity.

Most corporate bonds have the general form of an interest-only loan. Because we will be considering bonds in some detail in the next chapter, we will defer a further discussion of them for now.

Amortized Loans

With a pure discount or interest-only loan, the principal is repaid all at once. An alternative is an *amortized loan,* with which the lender may require the borrower to repay parts of the loan amount over time. The process of paying off a loan by making regular principal reductions is called *amortizing* the loan.

A simple way of amortizing a loan is to have the borrower pay the interest each period plus some fixed amount. This approach is common with medium-term business loans. For example, suppose a business takes out a $5,000, five-year loan at 9 percent. The loan agreement calls for the borrower to pay the interest on the loan balance each year and to reduce the loan balance each year by $1,000. Since the loan amount declines by $1,000 each year, it is fully paid in five years.

In the case we are considering, notice that the total payment will decline each year. The reason is that the loan balance goes down, resulting in a lower interest charge each year, while the $1,000 principal reduction is constant. For example, the interest in the first year will be $5,000 × .09 = $450. The total payment will be $1,000 + 450 = $1,450. In the second year, the loan balance is $4,000, so the interest is $4,000 × .09 = $360, and the total payment is $1,360. We can calculate the total payment in each of the remaining years by preparing a simple *amortization schedule* as follows:

Year	Beginning Balance	Total Payment	Interest Paid	Principal Paid	Ending Balance
1	$5,000	$1,450	$ 450	$1,000	$4,000
2	4,000	1,360	360	1,000	3,000
3	3,000	1,270	270	1,000	2,000
4	2,000	1,180	180	1,000	1,000
5	1,000	1,090	90	1,000	0
Totals		$6,350	$1,350	$5,000	

Notice that, in each year, the interest paid is just given by the beginning balance multiplied by the interest rate. Also notice that the beginning balance is given by the ending balance from the previous year.

Probably the most common way of amortizing a loan is to have the borrower make a single, fixed payment every period. Almost all consumer loans (such as car loans) and mortgages work this way. For example, suppose our five-year, 9 percent, $5,000 loan was amortized this way. How would the amortization schedule look?

We first need to determine the payment. From our discussion earlier in the chapter, we know that this loan's cash flows are in the form of an ordinary annuity. In this case, we can solve for the payment as follows:

$$\$5,000 = C \times (1 - 1/1.09^5)/.09$$
$$= C \times (1 - .6499)/.09$$

This gives us:

$$C = \$5,000/3.8897$$
$$= \$1,285.46$$

The borrower will therefore make five equal payments of $1,285.46. Will this pay off the loan? We will check by filling in an amortization schedule.

In our previous example, we knew the principal reduction each year. We then calculated the interest owed to get the total payment. In this example, we know the total payment. We will thus calculate the interest and then subtract it from the total payment to get the principal portion in each payment.

In the first year, the interest is $450, as we calculated before. Since the total payment is $1,285.46, the principal paid in the first year must be:

Principal paid = $1,285.46 − 450 = $835.46

The ending loan balance is thus:

Ending balance = $5,000 − 835.46 = $4,164.54

The interest in the second year is $4,164.54 × .09 = $374.81, and the loan balance declines by $1,285.46 − 374.81 = $910.65. We can summarize all of the relevant calculations in the following schedule:

Year	Beginning Balance	Total Payment	Interest Paid	Principal Paid	Ending Balance
1	$5,000.00	$1,285.46	$ 450.00	$ 835.46	$4,164.54
2	4,164.54	1,285.46	374.81	910.65	3,253.88
3	3,253.88	1,285.46	292.85	992.61	2,261.27
4	2,261.27	1,285.46	203.51	1,081.95	1,179.32
5	1,179.32	1,285.46	106.14	1,179.32	.00
Totals		$6,427.30	$1,427.31	$5,000.00	

Since the loan balance declines to zero, the five equal payments do pay off the loan. Notice that the interest paid declines each period. This isn't surprising since the loan balance is going down. Given that the total payment is fixed, the principal paid must be rising each period.

If you compare the two loan amortizations in this section, you will see that the total interest is greater for the equal total payment case, $1,427.31 versus $1,350. The reason for this is that the loan is repaid more slowly early on, so the interest is somewhat higher. This doesn't mean that one loan is better than the other; it simply means that one is effectively paid off faster than the other. For example, the principal reduction in the first year is $835.46 in the equal total payment case compared to $1,000 in the first case.

Loan Amortization Using a Spreadsheet

SPREADSHEET strategies

Loan amortization is a very common spreadsheet application. To illustrate, we will set up the problem that we have just examined, a five-year, $5,000, 9 percent loan with constant payments. Our spreadsheet looks like this:

	A	B	C	D	E	F	G	H
1								
2			Using a spreadsheet to amortize a loan					
3								
4			Loan amount:	$5,000				
5			Interest rate:	.09				
6			Loan term:	5				
7			Loan payment:	$1,285.46				
8				Note: payment is calculated using-PMT(rate,nper,-pv,fv).				
9			Amortization table:					
10								
11		Year	Beginning	Total	Interest	Principal	Ending	
12			Balance	Payment	Paid	Paid	Balance	
13		1	$5,000.00	$1,285.46	$450.00	$835.46	$4,164.54	
14		2	4,164.54	1,285.46	374.81	910.65	3,253.88	
15		3	3,253.88	1,285.46	292.85	992.61	2,261.27	
16		4	2,261.27	1,285.46	203.51	1,081.95	1,179.32	
17		5	1,179.32	1,285.46	106.14	1,179.32	.00	
18		Totals		$6,427.31	$1,427.31	$5,000.00		
19								
20		Formulas in the amortization table:						
21								
22		Year	Beginning	Total	Interest	Principal	Ending	
23			Balance	Payment	Paid	Paid	Balance	
24		1	=+D4	=$D$7	=+$D$5*C13	=+D13-E13	=+C13-F13	
25		2	=+G13	=$D$7	=+$D$5*C14	=+D14-E14	=+C14-F14	
26		3	=+G14	=$D$7	=+$D$5*C15	=+D15-E15	=+C15-F15	
27		4	=+G15	=$D$7	=+$D$5*C16	=+D16-E16	=+C16-F16	
28		5	=+G16	=$D$7	=+$D$5*C17	=+D17-E17	=+C17-F17	
29								
30		Note: totals in the amortization table are calculated using the SUM formula.						
31								

CONCEPT QUESTIONS

5.4a What is a pure discount loan?

5.4b What does it mean to amortize a loan?

SUMMARY AND CONCLUSIONS

This chapter rounds out your understanding of fundamental concepts related to the time value of money and discounted cash flow valuation. Several important topics were covered, including:

1. There are two ways of calculating present and future values when there are multiple cash flows. Both approaches are straightforward extensions of our earlier analysis of single cash flows.

2. A series of constant cash flows that arrive or are paid at the end of each period is called an ordinary annuity, and we described some useful shortcuts for determining the present and future values of annuities.

3. Interest rates can be quoted in a variety of ways. For financial decisions, it is important that any rates being compared be first converted to effective rates. The relationship between a quoted rate, such as an annual percentage rate, or APR, and an effective annual rate, or EAR, is given by:

    $$\text{EAR} = (1 + \text{Quoted rate}/m)^m - 1$$

    where m is the number of times during the year the money is compounded, or, equivalently, the number of payments during the year.

4. Many loans are annuities. The process of paying off a loan gradually is called amortizing the loan, and we discussed how amortization schedules are prepared and interpreted.

CHAPTER REVIEW AND SELF-TEST PROBLEMS

5.1 **Present Values with Multiple Cash Flows.**   A first-round draft choice quarterback has been signed to a three-year, $10 million contract. The details provide for an immediate cash bonus of $1 million. The player is to receive $2 million in salary at the end of the first year, $3 million the next, and $4 million at the end of the last year. Assuming a 10 percent discount rate, is this package worth $10 million? How much is it worth?

5.2 **Future Value with Multiple Cash Flows.**   You plan to make a series of deposits in an interest-bearing account. You will deposit $1,000 today, $2,000 in two years, and $8,000 in five years. If you withdraw $3,000 in three years and $5,000 in seven years, how much will you have after eight years if the interest rate is 9 percent? What is the present value of these cash flows?

5.3 **Annuity Present Value.**   You are looking into an investment that will pay you $12,000 per year for the next 10 years. If you require a 15 percent return, what is the most you would pay for this investment?

5.4 **APR versus EAR.**   The going rate on student loans is quoted as 9 percent APR. The terms of the loan call for monthly payments. What is the effective annual rate, or EAR, on such a student loan?

5.5   **It's the Principal That Matters.**   Suppose you borrow $10,000. You are going to repay the loan by making equal annual payments for five years. The interest rate on the loan is 14 percent per year. Prepare an amortization schedule for the loan. How much interest will you pay over the life of the loan?

5.6   **Just a Little Bit Each Month.**   You've recently finished your MBA at the Darnit School. Naturally, you must purchase a new BMW immediately. The car costs about $21,000. The bank quotes an interest rate of 15 percent APR for a 72-month loan with a 10 percent down payment. What will your monthly payment be? What is the effective interest rate on the loan?

▩ Answers to Chapter Review and Self-Test Problems

5.1   Obviously, the package is not worth $10 million because the payments are spread out over three years. The bonus is paid today, so it's worth $1 million. The present values for the three subsequent salary payments are:

$$\$2/1.1 + 3/1.1^2 + 4/1.1^3 \quad = \$2/1.1 + 3/1.21 + 4/1.331$$
$$= \$7.3028$$

The package is worth a total of $8.3028 million.

5.2   We will calculate the future value for each of the cash flows separately and then add the results up. Notice that we treat the withdrawals as negative cash flows:

$$
\begin{aligned}
\$1,000 \times 1.09^8 &= \quad \$1,000 \times 1.9926 = \$\ \ 1,992.60 \\
\$2,000 \times 1.09^6 &= \quad \$2,000 \times 1.6771 = \quad 3,354.20 \\
-\$3,000 \times 1.09^5 &= -\$3,000 \times 1.5386 = -4,615.87 \\
\$8,000 \times 1.09^3 &= \quad \$8,000 \times 1.2950 = \quad 10,360.23 \\
-\$5,000 \times 1.09^1 &= -\$5,000 \times 1.0900 = \underline{-5,450.00} \\
&\quad\quad \text{Total future value} = \underline{\$\ 5,641.12}
\end{aligned}
$$

This value includes a small rounding error.

   To calculate the present value, we could discount each cash flow back to the present or we could discount back a single year at a time. However, since we already know that the future value in eight years is $5,641.12, the easy way to get the PV is just to discount this amount back eight years:

$$
\begin{aligned}
\text{Present value} &= \$5,641.12/1.09^8 \\
&= \$5,641.12/1.9926 \\
&= \$2,831.03
\end{aligned}
$$

We again ignore a small rounding error. For practice, you can verify that this is what you get if you discount each cash flow back separately.

5.3   The most you would be willing to pay is the present value of $12,000 per year for 10 years at a 15 percent discount rate. The cash flows here are in ordinary annuity form, so the relevant present value factor is:

$$
\begin{aligned}
\text{Annuity present value factor} &= [1 - (1/1.15^{10})]/.15 \\
&= (1 - .2472)/.15 \\
&= 5.0188
\end{aligned}
$$

The present value of the 10 cash flows is thus:

$$\text{Present value} = \$12,000 \times 5.0188$$
$$= \$60,225$$

This is the most you would pay.

5.4   A rate of 9 percent with monthly payments is actually 9%/12 = .75% per month. The EAR is thus:

$$\text{EAR} = (1 + .09/12)^{12} - 1 = 9.38\%$$

5.5   We first need to calculate the annual payment. With a present value of $10,000, an interest rate of 14 percent, and a term of five years, the payment can be determined from:

$$\$10,000 = \text{Payment} \times (1 - 1/1.14^5)/.14$$
$$= \text{Payment} \times 3.4331$$

Therefore, the payment is $10,000/3.4331 = $2,912.84 (actually, it's $2,912.8355; this will create some small rounding errors in the schedule below). We can now prepare the amortization schedule as follows:

Year	Beginning Balance	Total Payment	Interest Paid	Principal Paid	Ending Balance
1	$10,000.00	$ 2,912.84	$1,400.00	$ 1,512.84	$8,487.16
2	8,487.16	2,912.84	1,188.20	1,724.63	6,762.53
3	6,762.53	2,912.84	946.75	1,966.08	4,796.45
4	4,796.45	2,912.84	671.50	2,241.33	2,555.12
5	2,555.12	2,912.84	357.72	2,555.12	.00
Totals		$14,564.17	$4,564.17	$10,000.00	

5.6   The cash flows on the car loan are in annuity form, so we only need to find the payment. The interest rate is 15%/12 = 1.25% per month, and there are 72 months. The first thing we need is the annuity factor for 72 periods at 1.25 percent per period:

$$\text{Annuity present value factor} = (1 - \text{Present value factor})/r$$
$$= [1 - (1/1.0125^{72})]/.0125$$
$$= [1 - (1/2.4459)]/.0125$$
$$= (1 - .4088)/.0125$$
$$= 47.2925$$

The present value is the amount we finance. With a 10 percent down payment, we will be borrowing 90 percent of $21,000, or $18,900.

So, to find the payment, we need to solve for C in the following:

$$\$18,900 = C \times \text{Annuity present value factor}$$
$$= C \times 47.2925$$

Rearranging things a bit, we have:

$$C = \$18,900 \times (1/47.2925)$$
$$= \$18,900 \times .02115$$
$$= \$399.64$$

Your payment is just under $400 per month.

The actual interest rate on this loan is 1.25 percent per month. Based on our work in the chapter, we can calculate the effective annual rate as:

$$EAR = 1.0125^{12} - 1 = 16.08\%$$

The effective rate is about one point higher than the quoted rate.

CRITICAL THINKING AND CONCEPTS REVIEW

1.   **Annuity Factors.**   There are four pieces to an annuity present value. What are they?

2.   **Annuity Period.**   As you increase the length of time involved, what happens to the present value of an annuity? What happens to the future value?

3.   **Interest Rates.**   What happens to the future value of an annuity if you increase the rate *r?* What happens to the present value?

4.   **Present Value.**   The Tri-State Megabucks lottery advertises a $500,000 prize; however, the lump-sum option is $250,000. Is this deceptive advertising?

5.   **Present Value.**   If you were an athlete negotiating a contract, would you want a big signing bonus payable immediately and smaller payments in the future, or vice versa? How about looking at it from the team's perspective?

6.   **Present Value.**   Suppose two athletes sign 10-year contracts for $80 million. In one case, we're told that the $80 million will be paid in 10 equal installments. In the other case, we're told that the $80 million will be paid in 10 installments, but the installments will increase by 5 percent per year. Who got the better deal?

7.   **APR and EAR.**   Should lending laws be changed to require lenders to report EARs instead of APRs? Why or why not?

8.   **Time Value.**   On subsidized Stafford loans, a common source of financial aid for college students, interest does not begin to accrue until repayment begins. Who receives a bigger subsidy, a freshman or a senior? Explain.

9.   **Time Value.**   In words, how would you go about valuing the subsidy on a subsidized Stafford loan?

10.   **Time Value.**   Eligibility for a subsidized Stafford loan is based on current financial need. However, both subsidized and unsubsidized Stafford loans are repaid out of future income. Given this, do you see a possible objection to having two types?

QUESTIONS AND PROBLEMS

Basic
(Questions 1–28)

1.   **Present Value and Multiple Cash Flows.**   Gepeto Shaved Ice Co. has identified an investment project with the following cash flows. If the discount rate is 10 percent, what is the present value of these cash flows? What is the present value at 18 percent? At 24 percent?

Year	Cash Flow
1	$ 800
2	500
3	1,800
4	1,300

Present Value and Multiple Cash Flows. Investment X offers to pay you $2,000 per year for 10 years, whereas Investment Y offers to pay you $4,000 per year for 4 years. Which of these cash flow streams has the higher present value if the discount rate is 5 percent? If the discount rate is 15 percent?

 Future Value and Multiple Cash Flows. Officer, Inc., has identified an investment project with the following cash flows. If the discount rate is 8 percent, what is the future value of these cash flows in Year 4? What is the future value at a discount rate of 11 percent? At 24 percent?

Year	Cash Flow
1	$ 700
2	800
3	900
4	1,000

4. **Calculating Annuity Present Value.** An investment offers $5,000 per year for 15 years, with the first payment occurring 1 year from now. If the required return is 10 percent, what is the value of the investment? What would the value be if the payments occurred for 40 years? For 75 years? Forever?

5. **Calculating Annuity Cash Flows.** If you put up $10,000 today in exchange for an 8.5 percent, 12-year annuity, what will the annual cash flow be?

6. **Calculating Annuity Values.** Your company will generate $55,000 in revenue each year for the next eight years from a new information database. The computer system needed to set up the database costs $250,000. If you can borrow the money to buy the computer system at 8.25 percent annual interest, can you afford the new system?

7. **Calculating Annuity Values.** If you deposit $2,000 at the end of each of the next 20 years into an account paying 9.5 percent interest, how much money will you have in the account in 20 years? How much will you have if you make deposits for 40 years?

8. **Calculating Annuity Values.** You want to have $50,000 in your savings account five years from now, and you're prepared to make equal annual deposits into the account at the end of each year. If the account pays 4.5 percent interest, what amount must you deposit each year?

9. **Calculating Annuity Values.** Biktimirov's Bank offers you a $25,000, seven-year term loan at 12 percent annual interest. What will your annual loan payment be?

10. **Calculating Perpetuity Values.** Kramer's Life Insurance Co. is trying to sell you an investment policy that will pay you and your heirs $10,000 per year forever. If the required return on this investment is 12 percent, how much will you pay for the policy?

11. **Calculating Perpetuity Values.** In the previous problem, suppose Kramer's told you the policy costs $95,000. At what interest rate would this be a fair deal?

12. **Calculating EAR.** Find the EAR in each of the following cases:

Stated Rate (APR)	Number of Times Compounded	Effective Rate (EAR)
9%	Quarterly	
10	Monthly	
7	Daily	
15	Semiannually	

13. **Calculating APR.** Find the APR, or stated rate, in each of the following cases:

Stated Rate (APR)	Number of Times Compounded	Effective Rate (EAR)
	Semiannually	10%
	Monthly	18
	Weekly	7
	Daily	14

14. **Calculating EAR.** First National Bank charges 10.5 percent compounded quarterly on its business loans. First United Bank charges 10.6 percent compounded semiannually. As a potential borrower, which bank would you go to for a new loan?

15. **Calculating APR.** Ervin Credit Corp. wants to earn an effective annual return on its consumer loans of 15 percent per year. The bank uses daily compounding on its loans. What interest rate is the bank required by law to report to potential borrowers? Explain why this rate is misleading to an uninformed borrower.

16. **Calculating Future Values.** What is the future value of $950 in 12 years assuming an interest rate of 11 percent compounded semiannually?

17. **Calculating Future Values.** Kingen Credit Bank is offering 5.5 percent compounded daily on its savings accounts. If you deposit $5,000 today, how much will you have in the account in five years? In 10 years? In 20 years?

18. **Calculating Present Values.** An investment will pay you $45,000 in six years. If the appropriate discount rate is 8 percent compounded daily, what is the present value?

19. **EAR versus APR.** Ricky Ripov's Pawn Shop charges an interest rate of 18 percent per month on loans to its customers. Like all lenders, Ricky must report an APR to consumers. What rate should the shop report? What is the effective annual rate?

20. **Calculating Loan Payments.** You want to buy a new sports coupe for $52,350, and the finance office at the dealership has quoted you a 12.3 percent APR loan for 60 months to buy the car. What will your monthly payments be? What is the effective annual rate on this loan?

21. **Calculating Number of Periods.** One of your customers is delinquent on his accounts payable balance. You've mutually agreed to a repayment schedule of $400 per month. You will charge 1.2 percent per month interest on the overdue balance. If the current balance is $10,054, how long will it take for the account to be paid off?

22. **Calculating EAR.** Friendly's Quick Loans, Inc., offers you "two for four or I knock on your door." This means you get $2 today and repay $4 when you get your paycheck in one week (or else). What's the effective annual return Friendly's earns on this lending business? If you were brave enough to ask, what APR would Friendly's say you were paying?

23. **Valuing Perpetuities.** Maybepay Life Insurance Co. is selling a perpetual annuity contract that pays $1,000 monthly. The contract currently sells for $50,000. What is the monthly return on this investment vehicle? What is the APR? The effective annual return?

24. **Calculating Annuity Future Values.** You are to make monthly deposits of $150 into a retirement account that pays 12 percent interest compounded monthly. If your first deposit will be made one month from now, how large will your retirement account be in 30 years?

25. **Calculating Annuity Future Values.** In the previous problem, suppose you make $1,800 annual deposits into the same retirement account. How large will your account balance be in 30 years?

26. **Calculating Annuity Present Values.**   Beginning three months from now, you want to be able to withdraw $1,000 each quarter from your bank account to cover college expenses over the next four years. If the account pays .75 percent interest per quarter, how much do you need to have in your bank account today to meet your expense needs over the next four years?

27. **Discounted Cash Flow Analysis.**   If the appropriate discount rate for the following cash flows is 9 percent compounded quarterly, what is the present value of the cash flows?

Year	Cash Flow
1	$600
2	900
3	400
4	700

28. **Discounted Cash Flow Analysis.**   If the appropriate discount rate for the following cash flows is 12.25 percent per year, what is the present value of the cash flows?

Year	Cash Flow
1	$1,500
2	3,200
3	7,200
4	9,600

Intermediate
(Questions 29–56)

29. **Simple Interest versus Compound Interest.**   First Simple Bank pays 6 percent simple interest on its investment accounts. If First Complex Bank pays interest on its accounts compounded annually, what rate should the bank set if it wants to match First Simple Bank over an investment horizon of 10 years?

30. **Calculating Annuities Due.**   You want to buy a new sports car from Muscle Motors for $65,000. The purchase contract is in the form of a 48-month annuity due at a 10.5 percent APR. What will your monthly payment be?

31. **Calculating Interest Expense.**   You receive a credit card application from Shady Banks Savings and Loan offering an introductory rate of 2.90 percent per year, compounded monthly for the first six months, increasing thereafter to 19 percent compounded monthly. Assuming you transfer the $4,000 balance from your existing credit card and make no subsequent payments, how much interest will you owe at the end of the first year?

32. **Calculating the Number of Periods.**   You are saving to buy a $100,000 house. There are two competing banks in your area, both offering certificates of deposit yielding 6 percent. How long will it take your initial $65,000 investment to reach the desired level at First Bank, which pays simple interest? How long at Second Bank, which compounds interest monthly?

33. **Calculating Future Values.**   You have an investment that will pay you 1.25 percent per month. How much will you have per dollar invested in one year? In two years?

34. **Calculating the Number of Periods.**   You have $600 today. You need $750. If you earn .75 percent per month, how many months will you wait?

35. **Comparing Cash Flow Streams.**   You've just joined the investment banking firm of Peng, Yi and Lee. They've offered you two different salary arrangements. You can have $6,250 per month for the next two years, or you can have $4,600 per month for the next two years, along with a $30,000 signing bonus today. If the interest rate is 8 percent compounded monthly, which do you prefer?

36. **Calculating Present Value of Annuities.**   Peter Lynchpin wants to sell you an investment contract that pays equal $20,000 amounts at the end of each of the next 20 years. If you require an effective annual return of 13 percent on this investment, how much will you pay for the contract today?

37. **Calculating Rates of Return.**   You're trying to choose between two different investments, both of which have up-front costs of $40,000. Investment G returns $80,000 in six years. Investment H returns $140,000 in 11 years. Which of these investments has the higher return?

38. **Present Value and Interest Rates.**   What is the relationship between the value of an annuity and the level of interest rates? Suppose you just bought a 10-year annuity of $3,000 per year at the current interest rate of 10 percent per year. What happens to the value of your investment if interest rates suddenly drop to 5 percent? What if interest rates suddenly rise to 15 percent?

39. **Calculating the Number of Payments.**   You're prepared to make monthly payments of $100, beginning at the end of this month, into an account that pays 12 percent interest compounded monthly. How many payments will you have made when your account balance reaches $25,000?

40. **Calculating Annuity Present Values.**   You want to borrow $50,000 from your local bank to buy a new sailboat. You can afford to make monthly payments of $1,050, but no more. Assuming monthly compounding, what is the highest rate you can afford on a 60-month APR loan?

41. **Calculating Present Values.**   In the 1994 NBA draft, no one was surprised when the Milwaukee Bucks took Glenn "Big Dog" Robinson with the first pick. But Robinson wanted big bucks from the Bucks: a 13-year deal worth a total of $100 million. He had to settle for about $68 million over 10 years. His contract called for $2.9 million the first year, with annual raises of $870,000. So, how big a bite did Big Dog really take? Assume a 10 percent discount rate.

42. **Calculating Present Values.**   In our previous question, we looked at the numbers for Big Dog's basketball contract. Now let's take a look at the terms for Shaquille "Shaq" O'Neal, the number one pick in 1992 who was drafted by the Orlando Magic. Shaquille signed a seven-year contract with estimated total payments of about $40 million. Although the precise terms were not disclosed, it was reported that Shaq would receive a salary of $3 million the first year, with raises of $900,000 each year thereafter. If the cash flows are discounted at the same 10 percent discount rate we used for Robinson, does the "Shaq Attack" result in the same kind of numbers? Did Robinson achieve his goal of being paid more than any other rookie in NBA history, including Shaq? Are the different contract lengths a factor? (Hint: Yes.)

43. **EAR versus APR.**   You have just purchased a new warehouse. To finance the purchase, you've arranged for a 30-year mortgage loan for 80 percent of the $850,000 purchase price. The monthly payment on this loan will be $6,300. What is the APR on this loan? The EAR?

44. **Present Value and Break-Even Interest.** Consider a firm with a contract to sell an asset for $95,000 three years from now. The asset costs $56,000 to produce today. Given a relevant discount rate on this asset of 12 percent per year, will the firm make a profit on this asset? At what rate does the firm just break even?

45. **Discount Interest Loans.** This question illustrates what is known as *discount interest*. Imagine you are discussing a loan with a somewhat unscrupulous lender. You want to borrow $12,000 for one year. The interest rate is 11 percent. You and the lender agree that the interest on the loan will be $.11 \times \$12,000 = \$1,320$. So the lender deducts this interest amount from the loan up front and gives you $10,680. In this case, we say that the discount is $1,320. What's wrong here?

46. **Calculating Annuities Due.** As discussed in the text, an ordinary annuity assumes equal payments at the end of each period over the life of the annuity. An *annuity due* is the same thing except the payments occur at the beginning of each period instead. Thus, a three-year annual annuity due would have periodic payment cash flows occurring at Years 0, 1, and 2, whereas a three-year annual ordinary annuity would have periodic payment cash flows occurring at Years 1, 2, and 3.

 a. At a 10 percent annual discount rate, find the present value of a four-year ordinary annuity contract of $550 payments.

 b. Find the present value of the same contract if it is an annuity due.

47. **Present Value and Interest Rates.** You've just won the U.S. Lottery. Lottery officials offer you the choice of two alternative payouts: either $2 million today, or $6 million 10 years from now. Which payout will you choose if the relevant discount rate is 0 percent? If it is 10 percent? If it is 20 percent?

48. **Calculating Present Values.** A 5-year annuity of 10 $4,000 semiannual payments will begin 9 years from now, with the first payment coming 9.5 years from now. If the discount rate is 14 percent compounded monthly, what is the value of this annuity five years from now? What is the value three years from now? What is the current value of the annuity?

49. **Present Value and Multiple Cash Flows.** What is the present value of $750 per year, at a discount rate of 10 percent, if the first payment is received 5 years from now and the last payment is received 20 years from now?

50. **Variable Interest Rates.** A 10-year annuity pays $1,500 per month, and payments are made at the end of each month. If the interest rate is 14 percent compounded monthly for the first four years, and 11 percent compounded monthly thereafter, what is the present value of the annuity?

51. **Comparing Cash Flow Streams.** You have your choice of two investment accounts. Investment A is a 10-year annuity that features end-of-month $1,000 payments and has an interest rate of 8 percent compounded monthly. Investment B is a 7 percent annually compounded lump-sum investment, also good for 10 years. How much money would you need to invest in B today for it to be worth as much as Investment A 10 years from now?

52. **Calculating Present Value of a Perpetuity.** Given an interest rate of 6.5 percent per year, what is the value at date $t = 9$ of a perpetual stream of $425 payments that begin at date $t = 14$?

53. **Calculating EAR.** A local finance company quotes a 14 percent interest rate on one-year loans. So, if you borrow $20,000, the interest for the year will be $2,800. Because you must repay a total of $22,800 in one year, the finance company requires you to pay $22,800/12, or $1,900, per month over the next 12 months. Is this a 14 percent loan? What rate would legally have to be quoted? What is the effective annual rate?

54. **Calculating Future Values.** If today is Year 0, what is the future value of the following cash flows five years from now? What is the future value 10 years from now? Assume a discount rate of 9.5 percent per year.

Year	Cash Flow
2	$25,000
3	50,000
5	75,000

55. **Amortization with Equal Payments.** Prepare an amortization schedule for a three-year loan of $40,000. The interest rate is 11 percent per year, and the loan calls for equal annual payments. How much interest is paid in the third year? How much total interest is paid over the life of the loan?

56. **Amortization with Equal Principal Payments.** Rework Problem 55 assuming that the loan agreement calls for a principal reduction of $13,333.33 every year instead of equal annual payments.

www.mhhe.com/rwj

Spreadsheet Templates 3, 4, 7, 31

CHAPTER 6

Interest Rates and Bond Valuation

AFTER READING THIS CHAPTER, YOU SHOULD UNDERSTAND:

■ Important bond features and types of bonds

■ Bond values and why they fluctuate

■ Bond ratings and what they mean

■ The impact of inflation on interest rates

■ The term structure of interest rates and the determinants of bond yields

WHAT DOES THE classic rock 'n' roll album *The Rise and Fall of Ziggy Stardust and the Spiders from Mars* have to do with the bond market? More than you might think. Rock star David Bowie, the artist behind the album, rakes in at least $5 million annually from the sale of his records. However, in 1997, Bowie decided that he needed lots of money immediately, so he turned to creative financiers to help him out. His investment bankers set up a trust account into which all of the royalties Bowie receives from the sale of his albums would be placed. Then they created bonds that are to be repaid from money that flows into the trust account. And investors bought $55 million worth!

This process of packaging a set of cash flows and then selling claims (such as bonds) against them is known as "securitization," and the claims are known as "asset-backed securities." The Bowie bonds are just a small part of a $150-billion-a-year-and-growing market for asset-backed securities. In recent years, asset-backed securities have become quite creative. In addition to Bowie's royalty fees, the market has seen the securitization of truck rentals, lottery winnings, health club membership fees, and encyclopedia receivables, just to name a few examples.

This chapter takes what we have learned about the time value of money and shows how it can be used to value one of the most common of all financial assets, a bond. It then discusses bond features, bond types, and the operation of the bond market.

What we will see is that bond prices depend critically on interest rates, so we will go on to discuss some very fundamental issues regarding interest rates. Clearly, interest rates are important to everybody because they underlie what businesses of all types—small and large—must pay to borrow money.

O ur goal in this chapter is to introduce you to bonds. We begin by showing how the techniques we developed in Chapters 4 and 5 can be applied to bond valuation. From there, we go on to discuss bond features and how bonds are bought and sold. One important thing we learn is that bond values depend, in large part, on interest rates. We therefore close out the chapter with an examination of interest rates and their behavior.

6.1 BONDS AND BOND VALUATION

When a corporation (or government) wishes to borrow money from the public on a long-term basis, it usually does so by issuing, or selling, debt securities that are generically called bonds. In this section, we describe the various features of corporate bonds and some of the terminology associated with bonds. We then discuss the cash flows associated with a bond and how bonds can be valued using our discounted cash flow procedure.

Bond Features and Prices

As we mentioned in our previous chapter, a bond is normally an interest-only loan, meaning that the borrower will pay the interest every period, but none of the principal will be repaid until the end of the loan. For example, suppose the Beck Corporation wants to borrow $1,000 for 30 years. The interest rate on similar debt issued by similar corporations is 12 percent. Beck will thus pay $.12 \times \$1,000 = \$120$ in interest every year for 30 years. At the end of 30 years, Beck will repay the $1,000. As this example suggests, a bond is a fairly simple financing arrangement. There is, however, a rich jargon associated with bonds, so we will use this example to define some of the more important terms.

In our example, the $120 regular interest payments that Beck promises to make are called the bond's **coupons.** Because the coupon is constant and paid every year, the type of bond we are describing is sometimes called a *level coupon bond.* The amount that will be repaid at the end of the loan is called the bond's **face value,** or **par value.** As in our example, this par value is usually $1,000 for corporate bonds, and a bond that sells for its par value is called a *par value bond.* Government bonds frequently have much larger face, or par, values. Finally, the annual coupon divided by the face value is called the **coupon rate** on the bond; in this case, because $120/1,000 = 12\%$, the bond has a 12 percent coupon rate.

The number of years until the face value is paid is called the bond's time to **maturity.** A corporate bond will frequently have a maturity of 30 years when it is originally issued, but this varies. Once the bond has been issued, the number of years to maturity declines as time goes by.

Bond Values and Yields

As time passes, interest rates change in the marketplace. The cash flows from a bond, however, stay the same. As a result, the value of the bond will fluctuate. When interest rates rise, the present value of the bond's remaining cash flows declines, and the bond is worth less. When interest rates fall, the bond is worth more.

To determine the value of a bond at a particular point in time, we need to know the number of periods remaining until maturity, the face value, the coupon, and the market interest rate for bonds with similar features. This interest rate required in the market on a bond is called the bond's **yield to maturity (YTM).** This rate is sometimes called the bond's *yield* for short. Given all this information, we can calculate the present value of the cash flows as an estimate of the bond's current market value.

For example, suppose the Xanth (pronounced "zanth") Co. were to issue a bond with 10 years to maturity. The Xanth bond has an annual coupon of $80. Similar bonds have a yield to maturity of 8 percent. Based on our preceding discussion, the Xanth bond will pay

coupon

Stated interest payment made on a bond.

face value

The principal amount of a bond that is repaid at the end of the term. Also, par value.

coupon rate

The annual coupon divided by the face value of a bond.

maturity

Date on which the principal amount of a bond is paid.

yield to maturity (YTM)

The rate required in the market on a bond.

Cash flows for Xanth Co. bond   **FIGURE 6.1**

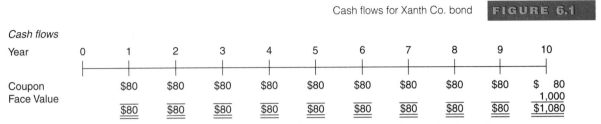

Cash flows

Year	0	1	2	3	4	5	6	7	8	9	10
Coupon		$80	$80	$80	$80	$80	$80	$80	$80	$80	$ 80
Face Value											1,000
		$80	$80	$80	$80	$80	$80	$80	$80	$80	$1,080

As shown, the Xanth bond has an annual coupon of $80 and a face, or par, value of $1,000 paid at maturity in 10 years.

$80 per year for the next 10 years in coupon interest. In 10 years, Xanth will pay $1,000 to the owner of the bond. The cash flows from the bond are shown in Figure 6.1. What would this bond sell for?

As illustrated in Figure 6.1, the Xanth bond's cash flows have an annuity component (the coupons) and a lump sum (the face value paid at maturity). We thus estimate the market value of the bond by calculating the present value of these two components separately and adding the results together. First, at the going rate of 8 percent, the present value of the $1,000 paid in 10 years is:

$$\text{Present value} = \$1,000/1.08^{10} = \$1,000/2.1589 = \$463.19$$

Second, the bond offers $80 per year for 10 years; the present value of this annuity stream is:

$$\begin{aligned}\text{Annuity present value} &= \$80 \times (1 - 1/1.08^{10})/.08 \\ &= \$80 \times (1 - 1/2.1589)/.08 \\ &= \$80 \times 6.7101 \\ &= \$536.81\end{aligned}$$

We can now add the values for the two parts together to get the bond's value:

$$\text{Total bond value} = \$463.19 + 536.81 = \$1,000$$

This bond sells for exactly its face value. This is not a coincidence. The going interest rate in the market is 8 percent. Considered as an interest-only loan, what interest rate does this bond have? With an $80 coupon, this bond pays exactly 8 percent interest only when it sells for $1,000.

To illustrate what happens as interest rates change, suppose that a year has gone by. The Xanth bond now has nine years to maturity. If the interest rate in the market has risen to 10 percent, what will the bond be worth? To find out, we repeat the present value calculations with 9 years instead of 10, and a 10 percent yield instead of an 8 percent yield. First, the present value of the $1,000 paid in nine years at 10 percent is:

$$\text{Present value} = \$1,000/1.10^{9} = \$1,000/2.3579 = \$424.10$$

Second, the bond now offers $80 per year for nine years; the present value of this annuity stream at 10 percent is:

$$\begin{aligned}\text{Annuity present value} &= \$80 \times (1 - 1/1.10^{9})/.10 \\ &= \$80 \times (1 - 1/2.3579)/.10 \\ &= \$80 \times 5.7590 \\ &= \$460.72\end{aligned}$$

We can now add the values for the two parts together to get the bond's value:

$$\text{Total bond value} = \$424.10 + 460.72 = \$884.82$$

Therefore, the bond should sell for about $885. In the vernacular, we say that this bond, with its 8 percent coupon, is priced to yield 10 percent at $885.

The Xanth Co. bond now sells for less than its $1,000 face value. Why? The market interest rate is 10 percent. Considered as an interest-only loan of $1,000, this bond only pays 8 percent, its coupon rate. Because this bond pays less than the going rate, investors are only willing to lend something less than the $1,000 promised repayment. Because the bond sells for less than face value, it is said to be a *discount bond*.

The only way to get the interest rate up to 10 percent is to lower the price to less than $1,000 so that the purchaser, in effect, has a built-in gain. For the Xanth bond, the price of $885 is $115 less than the face value, so an investor who purchased and kept the bond would get $80 per year and would have a $115 gain at maturity as well. This gain compensates the lender for the below-market coupon rate.

Another way to see why the bond is discounted by $115 is to note that the $80 coupon is $20 below the coupon on a newly issued par value bond, based on current market conditions. The bond would be worth $1,000 only if it had a coupon of $100 per year. In a sense, an investor who buys and keeps the bond gives up $20 per year for nine years. At 10 percent, this annuity stream is worth:

$$\text{Annuity present value} = \$20 \times (1 - 1/1.10^9)/.10$$
$$= \$20 \times 5.7590$$
$$= \$115.18$$

This is just the amount of the discount.

What would the Xanth bond sell for if interest rates had dropped by 2 percent instead of rising by 2 percent? As you might guess, the bond would sell for more than $1,000. Such a bond is said to sell at a *premium* and is called a *premium bond*.

This case is just the opposite of that of a discount bond. The Xanth bond now has a coupon rate of 8 percent when the market rate is only 6 percent. Investors are willing to pay a premium to get this extra coupon amount. In this case, the relevant discount rate is 6 percent, and there are nine years remaining. The present value of the $1,000 face amount is:

$$\text{Present value} = \$1,000/1.06^9 = \$1,000/1.6895 = \$591.89$$

The present value of the coupon stream is:

$$\text{Annuity present value} = \$80 \times (1 - 1/1.06^9)/.06$$
$$= \$80 \times (1 - 1/1.6895)/.06$$
$$= \$80 \times 6.8017$$
$$= \$544.14$$

We can now add the values for the two parts together to get the bond's value:

$$\text{Total bond value} = \$591.89 + 544.14 = \textbf{\$1,136.03}$$

Total bond value is therefore about $136 in excess of par value. Once again, we can verify this amount by noting that the coupon is now $20 too high, based on current market conditions. The present value of $20 per year for nine years at 6 percent is:

$$\text{Annuity present value} = \$20 \times (1 - 1/1.06^9)/.06$$
$$= \$20 \times 6.8017$$
$$= \$136.03$$

This is just as we calculated.

Based on our examples, we can now write the general expression for the value of a bond. If a bond has (1) a face value of F paid at maturity, (2) a coupon of C paid per period, (3) t periods to maturity, and (4) a yield of r per period, its value is:

$$\text{Bond value} = C \times [1 - 1/(1 + r)^t]/r + F/(1 + r)^t$$

$$\begin{aligned}\text{Bond value} = & \quad\text{Present value} \quad + \quad\text{Present value} \\ & \quad\text{of the coupons} \qquad \text{of the face amount}\end{aligned} \qquad [6.1]$$

Semiannual Coupons | EXAMPLE 6.1

In practice, bonds issued in the United States usually make coupon payments twice a year. So, if an ordinary bond has a coupon rate of 14 percent, then the owner will get a total of $140 per year, but this $140 will come in two payments of $70 each. Suppose we are examining such a bond. The yield to maturity is quoted at 16 percent.

Bond yields are quoted like APRs; the quoted rate is equal to the actual rate per period multiplied by the number of periods. In this case, with a 16 percent quoted yield and semiannual payments, the true yield is 8 percent per six months. The bond matures in seven years. What is the bond's price? What is the effective annual yield on this bond?

Based on our discussion, we know that the bond will sell at a discount because it has a coupon rate of 7 percent every six months when the market requires 8 percent every six months. So, if our answer exceeds $1,000, we know that we have made a mistake.

To get the exact price, we first calculate the present value of the bond's face value of $1,000 paid in seven years. This seven-year period has 14 periods of six months each. At 8 percent per period, the value is:

Present value = $1,000/1.08^{14} = $1,000/2.9372 = $340.46

The coupons can be viewed as a 14-period annuity of $70 per period. At an 8 percent discount rate, the present value of such an annuity is:

$$\begin{aligned}\text{Annuity present value} &= \$70 \times (1 - 1/1.08^{14})/.08 \\ &= \$70 \times (1 - .3405)/.08 \\ &= \$70 \times 8.2442 \\ &= \$577.10\end{aligned}$$

The total present value gives us what the bond should sell for:

Total present value = $340.46 + 577.10 = **$917.56**

To calculate the effective yield on this bond, note that 8 percent every six months is equivalent to:

Effective annual rate = $(1 + .08)^2 - 1$ = 16.64%

The effective yield, therefore, is 16.64 percent.

As we have illustrated in this section, bond prices and interest rates always move in opposite directions. When interest rates rise, a bond's value, like any other present value, will decline. Similarly, when interest rates fall, bond values rise. Even if we are considering a bond that is riskless in the sense that the borrower is certain to make all the payments, there is still risk in owning a bond. We discuss this next.

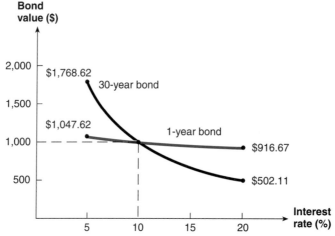

FIGURE 6.2

Interest rate risk and time to maturity

Value of a Bond with a 10 Percent Coupon Rate for Different Interest Rates and Maturities

	Time to Maturity	
Interest Rate	1 Year	30 Years
5%	$1,047.62	$1,768.62
10	1,000.00	1,000.00
15	956.52	671.70
20	916.67	502.11

Interest Rate Risk

The risk that arises for bond owners from fluctuating interest rates is called *interest rate risk*. How much interest rate risk a bond has depends on how sensitive its price is to interest rate changes. This sensitivity directly depends on two things: the time to maturity and the coupon rate. As we will see momentarily, you should keep the following in mind when looking at a bond:

1. All other things being equal, the longer the time to maturity, the greater the interest rate risk.

2. All other things being equal, the lower the coupon rate, the greater the interest rate risk.

We illustrate the first of these two points in Figure 6.2. As shown, we compute and plot prices under different interest rate scenarios for 10 percent coupon bonds with maturities of 1 year and 30 years. Notice how the slope of the line connecting the prices is much steeper for the 30-year maturity than it is for the 1-year maturity. This steepness tells us that a relatively small change in interest rates will lead to a substantial change in the bond's value. In comparison, the one-year bond's price is relatively insensitive to interest rate changes.

Intuitively, we can see that the reason that longer-term bonds have greater interest rate sensitivity is that a large portion of a bond's value comes from the $1,000 face amount. The present value of this amount isn't greatly affected by a small change in interest rates if the amount is to be received in one year. Even a small change in the interest rate, however, once it is compounded for 30 years, can have a significant effect on the present value. As a result, the present value of the face amount will be much more volatile with a longer-term bond.

The other thing to know about interest rate risk is that, like most things in finance and economics, it increases at a decreasing rate. In other words, if we compared a 10-year bond to a 1-year bond, we would see that the 10-year bond has much greater interest rate risk.

However, if you were to compare a 20-year bond to a 30-year bond, you would find that the 30-year bond has somewhat greater interest rate risk because it has a longer maturity, but the difference in the risk would be fairly small.

The reason that bonds with lower coupons have greater interest rate risk is easy to understand. As we discussed earlier, the value of a bond depends on the present value of its coupons and the present value of the face amount. If two bonds with different coupon rates have the same maturity, then the value of the one with the lower coupon is proportionately more dependent on the face amount to be received at maturity. As a result, all other things being equal, its value will fluctuate more as interest rates change. Put another way, the bond with the higher coupon has a larger cash flow early in its life, so its value is less sensitive to changes in the discount rate.

Until recently, bonds were almost never issued with maturities longer than 30 years. However, in November of 1995, BellSouth's main operating unit issued $500 million in 100-year bonds. Similarly, Walt Disney, Coca-Cola, and Dutch banking giant ABN-Amro all issued 100-year bonds in the summer and fall of 1993. The reason that these companies issued bonds with such long maturities was that interest rates had fallen to very low levels by historical standards, and the issuers wanted to lock in the low rates for a *long* time. The current record holder for corporations appears to be Safra Republic Holdings SA, an international bank holding company, which, in October of 1997, sold bonds with 1,000 years to maturity! Before these fairly recent issues, it appears that the last time 100-year bonds had been sold was in May 1954, by the Chicago and Eastern Railroad.

We can illustrate our points concerning interest rate risk using the 100-year BellSouth issue and two other BellSouth issues. The following table provides some basic information on the three issues, along with their prices at various points in time.

Maturity	Coupon Rate	Price on 12/31/95	Price on 7/31/96	Percentage Change in Price from 12/31/95 to 7/31/96	Price on 12/31/99	Percentage Change in Price from 7/31/96 to 12/31/99
2095	7.00%	$1,000.00	$800.00	−20.0%	$997.20	+24.7%
2033	6.75	976.25	886.25	−9.2	985.00	+11.1
2033	7.50	1,040.00	960.00	−7.7	996.20	+3.8

Several points emerge from this table. First, interest rates apparently rose from 12/31/95 to 7/31/96 (why?). The longer-term bond, with a maturity of 100 years, lost fully 20 percent of its value, as compared to a loss of value of less than 10 percent for the other two, thereby illustrating that bonds with greater maturities have greater interest rate risk. For the two issues maturing in 2033, notice that the one with the lower coupon had the larger loss, which illustrates our second point regarding the impact of coupon rates on interest rate risk. After 7/31/96, interest rates declined, returning all three bonds to prices near par value as of 12/31/99.

Finding the Yield to Maturity: More Trial and Error

Frequently, we will know a bond's price, coupon rate, and maturity date, but not its yield to maturity. For example, suppose we are interested in a six-year, 8 percent coupon bond. A broker quotes a price of $955.14. What is the yield on this bond?

We've seen that the price of a bond can be written as the sum of its annuity and lump-sum components. Knowing that there is an $80 coupon for six years and a $1,000 face value, we can say that the price is:

$$\$955.14 = \$80 \times [1 - 1/(1 + r)^6]/r + 1,000/(1 + r)^6$$

TABLE 6.1
Summary of bond valuation

I. Finding the value of a bond

Bond value = $C \times [1 - 1/(1 + r)^t]/r + F/(1 + r)^t$

where

C = Coupon paid each period
r = Rate per period
t = Number of periods
F = Bond's face value

II. Finding the yield on a bond

Given a bond value, coupon, time to maturity, and face value, it is possible to find the implicit discount rate, or yield to maturity, by trial and error only. To do this, try different discount rates in the formula above until the calculated bond value equals the given bond value. Remember that increasing the rate *decreases* the bond value.

where r is the unknown discount rate, or yield to maturity. We have one equation here and one unknown, but we cannot solve for r explicitly. The only way to find the answer is to use trial and error.

This problem is essentially identical to the one we examined in the last chapter when we tried to find the unknown interest rate on an annuity. However, finding the rate (or yield) on a bond is even more complicated because of the $1,000 face amount.

We can speed up the trial-and-error process by using what we know about bond prices and yields. In this case, the bond has an $80 coupon and is selling at a discount. We thus know that the yield is greater than 8 percent. If we compute the price at 10 percent:

$$\text{Bond value} = \$80 \times (1 - 1/1.10^6)/.10 + 1,000/1.10^6$$
$$= \$80 \times 4.3553 + 1,000/1.7716$$
$$= \$912.89$$

At 10 percent, the value we calculate is lower than the actual price, so 10 percent is too high. The true yield must be somewhere between 8 and 10 percent. At this point, it's "plug and chug" to find the answer. You would probably want to try 9 percent next. If you did, you would see that this is in fact the bond's yield to maturity.

Our discussion of bond valuation is summarized in Table 6.1.

EXAMPLE 6.2 | Bond Yields

You're looking at two bonds identical in every way except for their coupons and, of course, their prices. Both have 12 years to maturity. The first bond has a 10 percent coupon rate and sells for $935.08. The second has a 12 percent coupon rate. What do you think it would sell for?

Because the two bonds are very similar, they will be priced to yield about the same rate. We first need to calculate the yield on the 10 percent coupon bond. Proceeding as before, we know that the yield must be greater than 10 percent because the bond is selling at a discount. The bond has a fairly long maturity of 12 years. We've seen that long-term bond prices are relatively sensitive to interest rate changes, so the yield is probably close to 10 percent. A little trial and error reveals that the yield is actually 11 percent:

$$\text{Bond value} = \$100 \times (1 - 1/1.11^{12})/.11 + 1,000/1.11^{12}$$
$$= \$100 \times 6.4924 + 1,000/3.4985$$
$$= \$649.24 + 285.84$$
$$= \$935.08$$

With an 11 percent yield, the second bond will sell at a premium because of its $120 coupon. Its value is:

Bond value = $120 × (1 − 1/1.11^{12})/.11 + 1,000/1.11^{12}

     = $120 × 6.4924 + 1,000/3.4985

     = $779.08 + 285.84

     = $1,064.92

How to Calculate Bond Prices and Yields Using a Financial Calculator

CALCULATOR hints

Many financial calculators have fairly sophisticated built-in bond valuation routines. However, these vary quite a lot in implementation, and not all financial calculators have them. As a result, we will illustrate a simple way to handle bond problems that will work on just about any financial calculator.

To begin, of course, we first remember to clear out the calculator! Next, for Example 6.2, we have two bonds to consider, both with 12 years to maturity. The first one sells for $935.08 and has a 10 percent coupon rate. To find its yield, we can do the following:

Notice that here we have entered both a future value of $1,000, representing the bond's face value, and a payment of 10 percent of $1,000, or $100, per year, representing the bond's annual coupon. Also notice that we have a negative sign on the bond's price, which we have entered as the present value.

For the second bond, we now know that the relevant yield is 11 percent. It has a 12 percent coupon and 12 years to maturity, so what's the price? To answer, we just enter the relevant values and solve for the present value of the bond's cash flows:

There is an important detail that comes up here. Suppose we have a bond with a price of $902.29, 10 years to maturity, and a coupon rate of 6 percent. As we mentioned earlier, most bonds actually make semiannual payments. Assuming that this is the case for the bond here, what's the bond's yield? To answer, we need to enter the relevant numbers like this:

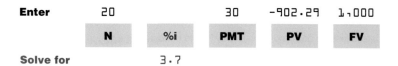

Notice that we entered $30 as the payment because the bond actually makes payments of $30 every six months. Similarly, we entered 20 for N because there are actually 20 six-month periods. When we solve for the yield, we get 3.7 percent, but the tricky thing to remember is that this is the yield *per six months,* so we have to double it to get the right answer: 2 × 3.7 = 7.4 percent, which would be the bond's reported yield.

How to Calculate Bond Prices and Yields Using a Spreadsheet

strategies

Like financial calculators, most spreadsheets have fairly elaborate routines available for calculating bond values and yields; many of these routines involve details that we have not discussed. However, setting up a simple spreadsheet to calculate prices or yields is straightforward, as our next two spreadsheets show:

	A	B	C	D	E	F	G	H
1								
2		**Using a spreadsheet to calculate bond values**						
3								
4	Suppose we have a bond with 22 years to maturity, a coupon rate of 8 percent, and a price of							
5	$960.17. If the bond makes semiannual payments, what is its yield to maturity?							
6								
7	Settlement date:	1/1/00						
8	Maturity date:	1/1/22						
9	Annual coupon rate:	.08						
10	Bond price (% of par):	96.017						
11	Face value (% of par):	100						
12	Coupons per year:	2						
13	Yield to maturity:	**.084**						
14								
15	The formula entered in cell b13 is =YIELD(b7,b8,b9,b10,b11,b12); notice that face value and bond price							
16	are entered as a percentage of face value.							
17								

	A	B	C	D	E	F	G	H
1								
2		**Using a spreadsheet to calculate bond values**						
3								
4	Suppose we have a bond with 22 years to maturity, a coupon rate of 8 percent, and a yield to							
5	maturity of 9 percent. If the bond makes semiannual payments, what is its price today?							
6								
7	Settlement date:	1/1/00						
8	Maturity date:	1/1/22						
9	Annual coupon rate:	.08						
10	Yield to maturity:	.09						
11	Face value (% of par):	100						
12	Coupons per year:	2						
13	Bond price (% of par):	**90.49**						
14								
15	The formula entered in cell b13 is =PRICE(b7,b8,b9,b10,b11,b12); notice that face value and bond price							
16	are given as a percentage of face value.							
17								

In our spreadsheets, notice that we had to enter two dates, a settlement date and a maturity date. The settlement date is just the date you actually pay for the bond, and the maturity date is the day the bond actually matures. In most of our problems, we don't explicitly have these dates, so we have to make them up. For example, since our bond has 22 years to maturity, we just picked 1/1/2000 (January 1, 2000) as the settlement date and 1/1/2022 (January 1, 2022) as the maturity date. Any two dates would do as long as they were exactly 22 years apart, but these are particularly easy to work with. Finally, notice that we had to enter the coupon rate and yield to maturity in annual terms and then explicitly provide the number of coupon payments per year.

CONCEPT QUESTIONS

6.1a What are the cash flows associated with a bond?

6.1b What is the general expression for the value of a bond?

6.1c Is it true that the only risk associated with owning a bond is that the issuer will not make all the payments? Explain.

MORE ON BOND FEATURES | 6.2

In this section, we continue our discussion of corporate debt by describing in some detail the basic terms and features that make up a typical long-term corporate bond. We discuss additional issues associated with long-term debt in subsequent sections.

Securities issued by corporations may be classified roughly as *equity securities* and *debt securities*. At the crudest level, a debt represents something that must be repaid; it is the result of borrowing money. When corporations borrow, they generally promise to make regularly scheduled interest payments and to repay the original amount borrowed (that is, the principal). The person or firm making the loan is called the *creditor*, or *lender*. The corporation borrowing the money is called the *debtor*, or *borrower*.

From a financial point of view, the main differences between debt and equity are the following:

1. Debt is not an ownership interest in the firm. Creditors generally do not have voting power.

2. The corporation's payment of interest on debt is considered a cost of doing business and is fully tax deductible. Dividends paid to stockholders are *not* tax deductible.

3. Unpaid debt is a liability of the firm. If it is not paid, the creditors can legally claim the assets of the firm. This action can result in liquidation or reorganization, two of the possible consequences of bankruptcy. Thus, one of the costs of issuing debt is the possibility of financial failure. This possibility does not arise when equity is issued.

Is It Debt or Equity?

Sometimes it is not clear if a particular security is debt or equity. For example, suppose a corporation issues a perpetual bond with interest payable solely from corporate income if and only if earned. Whether or not this is really a debt is hard to say and is primarily a legal and semantic issue. Courts and taxing authorities would have the final say.

Corporations are very adept at creating exotic, hybrid securities that have many features of equity but are treated as debt. Obviously, the distinction between debt and equity is very important for tax purposes. So one reason that corporations try to create a debt security that is really equity is to obtain the tax benefits of debt and the bankruptcy benefits of equity.

As a general rule, equity represents an ownership interest, and it is a residual claim. This means that equity holders are paid after debt holders. As a result of this, the risks and benefits associated with owning debt and equity are different. To give just one example, note that the maximum reward for owning a debt security is ultimately fixed by the amount of the loan, whereas there is no upper limit to the potential reward from owning an equity interest.

Long-Term Debt: The Basics

Ultimately, all long-term debt securities are promises made by the issuing firm to pay principal when due and to make timely interest payments on the unpaid balance. Beyond this, there are a number of features that distinguish these securities from one another. We discuss some of these features next.

The maturity of a long-term debt instrument is the length of time the debt remains outstanding with some unpaid balance. Debt securities can be short-term (with maturities of one year or less) or long-term (with maturities of more than one year).[1] Short-term debt is sometimes referred to as *unfunded debt.*[2]

Debt securities are typically called *notes, debentures,* or *bonds.* Strictly speaking, a bond is a secured debt. However, in common usage, the word *bond* refers to all kinds of secured and unsecured debt. We will therefore continue to use the term generically to refer to long-term debt.

The two major forms of long-term debt are public issue and privately placed. We concentrate on public-issue bonds. Most of what we say about them holds true for private-issue, long-term debt as well. The main difference between public-issue and privately placed debt is that the latter is directly placed with a lender and not offered to the public. Because this is a private transaction, the specific terms are up to the parties involved.

There are many other dimensions to long-term debt, including such things as security, call features, sinking funds, ratings, and protective covenants. The following table illustrates these features for a bond issued by May Department Stores on August 4, 1994. If some of these terms are unfamiliar, have no fear. We will discuss them all presently.

Features of a May Department Stores Bond		
Term		**Explanation**
Amount of issue	$200 million	The company issued $200 million worth of bonds.
Date of issue	8/4/94	The bonds were sold on 8/4/94.
Maturity	8/1/24	The principal will be paid 30 years after the issue date.
Face value	$1,000	The denomination of the bonds is $1,000.
Annual coupon	8.375	Each bondholder will receive $83.75 per bond per year (8.375% of face value).
Offer price	100	The offer price will be 100% of the $1,000 face value per bond.
Coupon payment dates	2/1, 8/1	Coupons of $83.75/2 = $41.875 will be paid on these dates.
Security	None	The bonds are debentures.
Sinking fund	Annual, beginning 8/1/05	The firm will make annual payments towards the sinking fund.
Call provision	Not callable before 8/1/04	The bonds have a deferred call feature.
Call price	104.188 initially, declining to 100	After 8/1/04, the company can buy back the bonds for $1,041.88 per bond, with this price declining to $1,000 on 8/1/14.
Rating	Moody's A2	This is one of Moody's higher ratings. The bonds have a low probability of default.

Many of these features will be detailed in the bond indenture, so we discuss this first.

The Indenture

indenture

The written agreement between the corporation and the lender detailing the terms of the debt issue.

The **indenture** is the written agreement between the corporation (the borrower) and its creditors. It is sometimes referred to as the *deed of trust.*[3] Usually, a trustee (a bank, perhaps) is appointed by the corporation to represent the bondholders. The trust company must

---

[1]There is no universally agreed-upon distinction between short-term and long-term debt. In addition, people often refer to intermediate-term debt, which has a maturity of more than 1 year and less than 3 to 5, or even 10, years.

[2]The word *funding* is part of the jargon of finance. It generally refers to the long term. Thus a firm planning to "fund" its debt requirements may be replacing short-term debt with long-term debt.

[3]The term *loan agreement* or *loan contract* is usually used for privately placed debt and term loans.

(1) make sure the terms of the indenture are obeyed, (2) manage the sinking fund (described in the following pages), and (3) represent the bondholders in default, that is, if the company defaults on its payments to them.

The bond indenture is a legal document. It can run several hundred pages and generally makes for very tedious reading. It is an important document, however, because it generally includes the following provisions:

1. The basic terms of the bonds
2. The total amount of bonds issued
3. A description of property used as security
4. The repayment arrangements
5. The call provisions
6. Details of the protective covenants

We discuss these features next.

Terms of a Bond   Corporate bonds usually have a face value (that is, a denomination) of $1,000. This is called the *principal value* and it is stated on the bond certificate. So, if a corporation wanted to borrow $1 million, 1,000 bonds would have to be sold. The par value (that is, initial accounting value) of a bond is almost always the same as the face value, and the terms are used interchangeably in practice.

Corporate bonds are usually in **registered form.** For example, the indenture might read as follows:

> Interest is payable semiannually on July 1 and January 1 of each year to the person in whose name the bond is registered at the close of business on June 15 or December 15, respectively.

registered form
The form of bond issue in which the registrar of the company records ownership of each bond; payment is made directly to the owner of record.

This means that the company has a registrar who will record the ownership of each bond and record any changes in ownership. The company will pay the interest and principal by check mailed directly to the address of the owner of record. A corporate bond may be registered and have attached "coupons." To obtain an interest payment, the owner must separate a coupon from the bond certificate and send it to the company registrar (the paying agent).

Alternatively, the bond could be in **bearer form.** This means that the certificate is the basic evidence of ownership, and the corporation will "pay the bearer." Ownership is not otherwise recorded, and, as with a registered bond with attached coupons, the holder of the bond certificate detaches the coupons and sends them to the company to receive payment.

bearer form
The form of bond issue in which the bond is issued without record of the owner's name; payment is made to whoever holds the bond.

There are two drawbacks to bearer bonds. First, they are difficult to recover if they are lost or stolen. Second, because the company does not know who owns its bonds, it cannot notify bondholders of important events. Bearer bonds were once the dominant type, but they are now much less common (in the United States) than registered bonds.

Security   Debt securities are classified according to the collateral and mortgages used to protect the bondholder.

Collateral is a general term that frequently means securities (for example, bonds and stocks) that are pledged as security for payment of debt. For example, collateral trust bonds often involve a pledge of common stock held by the corporation. However, the term *collateral* is commonly used to refer to any asset pledged on a debt.

Mortgage securities are secured by a mortgage on the real property of the borrower. The property involved is usually real estate, for example, land or buildings. The legal document that describes the mortgage is called a *mortgage trust indenture* or *trust deed.*

Sometimes mortgages are on specific property, for example, a railroad car. More often, blanket mortgages are used. A blanket mortgage pledges all the real property owned by the company.[4]

debenture

An unsecured debt, usually with a maturity of 10 years or more.

Bonds frequently represent unsecured obligations of the company. A **debenture** is an unsecured bond, for which no specific pledge of property is made. The May Department Stores bond examined in the table is an example. The term **note** is generally used for such instruments if the maturity of the unsecured bond is less than 10 or so years when the bond is originally issued. Debenture holders only have a claim on property not otherwise pledged, in other words, the property that remains after mortgages and collateral trusts are taken into account.

note

An unsecured debt, usually with a maturity under 10 years.

The terminology that we use here and elsewhere in this chapter is standard in the United States. Outside the United States, these same terms can have different meanings. For example, bonds issued by the British government ("gilts") are called treasury "stock." Also, in the United Kingdom, a debenture is a *secured* obligation.

At the current time, almost all public bonds issued in the United States by industrial and financial companies are debentures. However, most utility and railroad bonds are secured by a pledge of assets.

Seniority   In general terms, *seniority* indicates preference in position over other lenders, and debts are sometimes labeled as *senior* or *junior* to indicate seniority. Some debt is *subordinated,* as in, for example, a subordinated debenture.

In the event of default, holders of subordinated debt must give preference to other specified creditors. Usually, this means that the subordinated lenders will be paid off only after the specified creditors have been compensated. However, debt cannot be subordinated to equity.

Repayment   Bonds can be repaid at maturity, at which time the bondholder will receive the stated, or face, value of the bond, or they may be repaid in part or in entirety before maturity. Early repayment in some form is more typical and is often handled through a sinking fund.

sinking fund

An account managed by the bond trustee for early bond redemption.

A **sinking fund** is an account managed by the bond trustee for the purpose of repaying the bonds. The company makes annual payments to the trustee, who then uses the funds to retire a portion of the debt. The trustee does this by either buying up some of the bonds in the market or calling in a fraction of the outstanding bonds. This second option is discussed in the next section.

There are many different kinds of sinking fund arrangements, and the details would be spelled out in the indenture. For example:

1. Some sinking funds start about 10 years after the initial issuance.
2. Some sinking funds establish equal payments over the life of the bond.
3. Some high-quality bond issues establish payments to the sinking fund that are not sufficient to redeem the entire issue. As a consequence, there is the possibility of a large "balloon payment" at maturity.

call provision

An agreement giving the corporation the option to repurchase the bond at a specific price prior to maturity.

The Call Provision   A **call provision** allows the company to repurchase, or "call," part or all of the bond issue at stated prices over a specific period. Corporate bonds are usually callable.

call premium

The amount by which the call price exceeds the par value of the bond.

Generally, the call price is above the bond's stated value (that is, the par value). The difference between the call price and the stated value is the **call premium.** The amount of the call premium usually becomes smaller over time. One arrangement is to initially set the

---

[4]Real property includes land and things "affixed thereto." It does not include cash or inventories.

call premium equal to the annual coupon payment and then make it decline to zero as the call date moves closer to the time of maturity.

Call provisions are not usually operative during the first part of a bond's life. This makes the call provision less of a worry for bondholders in the bond's early years. For example, a company might be prohibited from calling its bonds for the first 10 years. This is a **deferred call provision.** During this period of prohibition, the bond is said to be **call protected.**

Protective Covenants   A **protective covenant** is that part of the indenture or loan agreement that limits certain actions a company might otherwise wish to take during the term of the loan. Protective covenants can be classified into two types: negative covenants and positive (or affirmative) covenants.

A *negative covenant* is a "thou shalt not" type of covenant. It limits or prohibits actions that the company might take. Here are some typical examples:

1. The firm must limit the amount of dividends it pays according to some formula.
2. The firm cannot pledge any assets to other lenders.
3. The firm cannot merge with another firm.
4. The firm cannot sell or lease any major assets without approval by the lender.
5. The firm cannot issue additional long-term debt.

A *positive covenant* is a "thou shalt" type of covenant. It specifies an action that the company agrees to take or a condition the company must abide by. Here are some examples:

1. The company must maintain its working capital at or above some specified minimum level.
2. The company must periodically furnish audited financial statements to the lender.
3. The firm must maintain any collateral or security in good condition.

This is only a partial list of covenants; a particular indenture may feature many different ones.

deferred call provision
A call provision prohibiting the company from redeeming the bond prior to a certain date.

call protected bond
A bond that currently cannot be redeemed by the issuer.

protective covenant
A part of the indenture limiting certain actions that might be taken during the term of the loan, usually to protect the lender.

CONCEPT QUESTIONS

6.2a What are the distinguishing features of debt as compared to equity?
6.2b What is the indenture? What are protective covenants? Give some examples.
6.2c What is a sinking fund?

BOND RATINGS | 6.3

Firms frequently pay to have their debt rated. The two leading bond-rating firms are Moody's and Standard and Poor's (S&P). The debt ratings are an assessment of the creditworthiness of the corporate issuer. The definitions of creditworthiness used by Moody's and S&P are based on how likely the firm is to default and the protection creditors have in the event of a default.

It is important to recognize that bond ratings are concerned *only* with the possibility of default. Earlier, we discussed interest rate risk, which we defined as the risk of a change in the value of a bond resulting from a change in interest rates. Bond ratings do not address this issue. As a result, the price of a highly rated bond can still be quite volatile.

Bond ratings are constructed from information supplied by the corporation. The rating classes and some information concerning them are shown in the following table.

| | Investment-Quality Bond Ratings | | | | Low-Quality, Speculative, and/or "Junk" Bond Ratings | | | | |
	High Grade		**Medium Grade**		**Low Grade**		**Very Low Grade**		
Standard & Poor's	AAA	AA	A	BBB	BB	B	CCC	CC	C	D
Moody's	Aaa	Aa	A	Baa	Ba	B	Caa	Ca	C	D

Moody's	S&P	
Aaa	AAA	Debt rated Aaa and AAA has the highest rating. Capacity to pay interest and principal is extremely strong.
Aa	AA	Debt rated Aa and AA has a very strong capacity to pay interest and repay principal. Together with the highest rating, this group comprises the high-grade bond class.
A	A	Debt rated A has a strong capacity to pay interest and repay principal, although it is somewhat more susceptible to the adverse effects of changes in circumstances and economic conditions than debt in high-rated categories.
Baa	BBB	Debt rated Baa and BBB is regarded as having an adequate capacity to pay interest and repay principal. Whereas it normally exhibits adequate protection parameters, adverse economic conditions or changing circumstances are more likely to lead to a weakened capacity to pay interest and repay principal for debt in this category than in higher-rated categories. These bonds are medium-grade obligations.
Ba, B Caa Ca	BB, B CCC CC	Debt rated in these categories is regarded, on balance, as predominantly speculative with respect to capacity to pay interest and repay principal in accordance with the terms of the obligation. BB and Ba indicate the lowest degree of speculation, and CC and Ca the highest degree of speculation. Although such debt is likely to have some quality and protective characteristics, these are outweighed by large uncertainties or major risk exposures to adverse conditions. Some issues may be in default.
C	C	This rating is reserved for income bonds on which no interest is being paid.
D	D	Debt rated D is in default, and payment of interest and/or repayment of principal is in arrears.

At times, both Moody's and S&P use adjustments to these ratings. S&P uses plus and minus signs: A+ is the strongest A rating and A− the weakest. Moody's uses a 1, 2, or 3 designation, with 1 being the highest.

The highest rating a firm's debt can have is AAA or Aaa, and such debt is judged to be the best quality and to have the lowest degree of default risk. For example, the 100-year BellSouth issue we discussed earlier was rated AAA. This rating is not awarded very often; AA or Aa ratings indicate very good quality debt and are much more common. The lowest rating is D, for debt that is in default.

Beginning in the 1980s, a growing part of corporate borrowing has taken the form of low-grade, or "junk," bonds. If these low-grade corporate bonds are rated at all, they are rated below investment grade by the major rating agencies. Investment-grade bonds are bonds rated at least BBB by S&P or Baa by Moody's.

Some bonds are called "crossover" or "5B" bonds. The reason is that they are rated triple-B (or Baa) by one rating agency and double-B (or Ba) by another, a "split rating." For example, in June 1996, TCI Communications sold one such issue of three-year notes rated BBB by S&P and Ba by Moody's. Thus, one agency rated the bonds as medium grade, while the other rated them as junk.

A bond's credit rating can change as the issuer's financial strength improves or deteriorates. For example, on Wednesday, September 22, 1999, Phelps Dodge Corp. announced plans to acquire two rival copper producers for $2.78 billion, of which about $1 billion would be paid in cash. Moody's immediately announced that it was reviewing Phelps Dodge's debt to see if the bond ratings needed to be downgraded in light of the planned acquisition. The credit-rating agency was concerned that such a large purchase might require so much additional borrowing by Phelps Dodge as to hinder the company's competitive position. In 1999, Moody's actually downgraded the long-term debt of drugstore giant Rite Aid Corp. to Ba2 from Baa3, pushing it from investment-grade into junk bond status.

CONCEPT QUESTIONS

6.3a What is a junk bond?

6.3b What does a bond rating say about the risk of fluctuations in a bond's value resulting from interest rate changes?

SOME DIFFERENT TYPES OF BONDS 6.4

Thus far, we have considered only "plain vanilla" corporate bonds. In this section, we briefly look at bonds issued by governments and also at bonds with unusual features.

Government Bonds

The biggest borrower in the world—by a wide margin—is everybody's favorite family member, Uncle Sam. In 2000, the total debt of the U.S. government was $5.8 *trillion.* When the government wishes to borrow money for more than one year, it sells what are known as Treasury notes and bonds to the public (in fact, it does so every month). Currently, Treasury notes and bonds have original maturities ranging from 2 to 30 years.

Most U.S. Treasury issues are just ordinary coupon bonds. Some older issues are callable, and a very few have some unusual features. There are two important things to keep in mind, however. First, U.S. Treasury issues, unlike essentially all other bonds, have no default risk because (we hope) the Treasury can always come up with the money to make the payments. Second, Treasury issues are exempt from state income taxes (though not federal income taxes). In other words, the coupons you receive on a Treasury note or bond are only taxed at the federal level.

State and local governments also borrow money by selling notes and bonds. Such issues are called *municipal* notes and bonds, or just "munis." Unlike Treasury issues, munis have varying degrees of default risk, and, in fact, they are rated much like corporate issues. Also, they are almost always callable. The most intriguing thing about munis is that their coupons are exempt from federal income taxes (though not state income taxes), which makes them very attractive to high-income, high–tax bracket investors.

Because of the enormous tax break they receive, the yields on municipal bonds are much lower than the yields on taxable bonds. For example, in early 2000, long-term, high-quality corporate bonds were yielding about 8 percent. At the same time, long-term, high-quality munis were yielding about 5.8 percent. Suppose an investor was in a 30 percent tax bracket. All else being the same, would this investor prefer a Aa corporate bond or a Aa municipal bond?

To answer, we need to compare the *aftertax* yields on the two bonds. Ignoring state and local taxes, the muni pays 5.8 percent on both a pretax and an aftertax basis. The corporate issue pays 8 percent before taxes, but it only pays $.08 \times (1 - .30) = .056$, or 5.6 percent, once we account for the 30 percent tax bite. Given this, the muni has a better yield.

Taxable versus Municipal Bonds **EXAMPLE 6.3**

Suppose taxable bonds are currently yielding 8 percent, while at the same time, munis of comparable risk and maturity are yielding 6 percent. Which is more attractive to an investor in a 40 percent bracket? What is the break-even tax rate? How do you interpret this rate?

For an investor in a 40 percent tax bracket, a taxable bond yields 8 × (1 − .40) = 4.8 percent after taxes, so the muni is much more attractive. The break-even tax rate is the tax rate at which an investor would be indifferent between a taxable and a nontaxable issue. If we let t^* stand for the break-even tax rate, then we can solve for it as follows:

$$.08 \times (1 - t^*) = .06$$
$$1 - t^* = .06/.08 = .75$$
$$t^* = .25$$

Thus, an investor in a 25 percent tax bracket would make 6 percent after taxes from either bond.

Zero Coupon Bonds

zero coupon bond

A bond that makes no coupon payments, thus is initially priced at a deep discount.

A bond that pays no coupons at all must be offered at a price that is much lower than its stated value. Such bonds are called **zero coupon bonds,** or just *zeroes*.[5]

Suppose the Eight-Inch Nails (EIN) Company issues a $1,000 face value, five-year zero coupon bond. The initial price is set at $497. It is straightforward to verify that, at this price, the bond yields 15 percent to maturity. The total interest paid over the life of the bond is $1,000 − 497 = $503.

For tax purposes, the issuer of a zero coupon bond deducts interest every year even though no interest is actually paid. Similarly, the owner must pay taxes on interest accrued every year, even though no interest is actually received.

The way in which the yearly interest on a zero coupon bond is calculated is governed by tax law. Before 1982, corporations could calculate the interest deduction on a straight-line basis. For EIN, the annual interest deduction would have been $503/5 = $100.60 per year.

Under current tax law, the implicit interest is determined by amortizing the loan. We do this by first calculating the bond's value at the beginning of each year. For example, after one year, the bond will have four years until maturity, so it will be worth $1,000/1.15^4 = $572; the value in two years will be $1,000/1.15^3 = $658; and so on. The implicit interest each year is simply the change in the bond's value for the year. The values and interest expenses for the EIN bond are listed in Table 6.2.

Notice that under the old rules, zero coupon bonds were more attractive for corporations because the deductions for interest expense were larger in the early years (compare the implicit interest expense with the straight-line expense).

TABLE 6.2	Year	Beginning Value	Ending Value	Implicit Interest Expense	Straight-line Interest Expense
Interest expense for EIN's zeroes	1	$497	$572	$ 75	$100.60
	2	572	658	86	100.60
	3	658	756	98	100.60
	4	756	870	114	100.60
	5	870	1,000	130	100.60
	Total			$503	$503.00

[5]A bond issued with a very low coupon rate (as opposed to a zero coupon rate) is an original-issue discount (OID) bond.

Under current tax law, EIN could deduct $75 in interest paid the first year and the owner of the bond would pay taxes on $75 of taxable income (even though no interest was actually received). This second tax feature makes taxable zero coupon bonds less attractive to individuals. However, they are still a very attractive investment for tax-exempt investors with long-term dollar-denominated liabilities, such as pension funds, because the future dollar value is known with relative certainty.

Some bonds are zero coupon bonds for only part of their lives. For example, General Motors has a debenture outstanding that is a combination of a zero coupon and a coupon-bearing issue. These bonds were issued March 15, 1996, and pay no coupons until September 15, 2016. At that time, they begin paying coupons at a rate of 7.75 percent per year (payable semiannually), and they do so until they mature on March 15, 2036.

Floating-Rate Bonds

The conventional bonds we have talked about in this chapter have fixed-dollar obligations because the coupon rate is set as a fixed percentage of the par value. Similarly, the principal is set equal to the par value. Under these circumstances, the coupon payment and principal are completely fixed.

With *floating-rate bonds (floaters),* the coupon payments are adjustable. The adjustments are tied to an interest rate index such as the Treasury bill interest rate or the 30-year Treasury bond rate. For example, U.S. Government EE Savings Bonds pay interest at a rate that is adjusted every six months. The rate is set equal to 90 percent of the average yield on ordinary five-year Treasury notes over the previous six months.

The value of a floating-rate bond depends on exactly how the coupon payment adjustments are defined. In most cases, the coupon adjusts with a lag to some base rate. For example, suppose a coupon rate adjustment is made on June 1. The adjustment might be based on the simple average of Treasury bond yields during the previous three months. In addition, the majority of floaters have the following features:

1. The holder has the right to redeem the note at par on the coupon payment date after some specified amount of time. This is called a *put* provision, and it is discussed in the following section.

2. The coupon rate has a floor and a ceiling, meaning that the coupon is subject to a minimum and a maximum. In this case, the coupon rate is said to be "capped," and the upper and lower rates are sometimes called the *collar.*

A particularly interesting type of floating-rate bond is an *inflation-linked* bond. Such bonds have coupons that are adjusted according to the rate of inflation (the principal amount may be adjusted as well). The U.S. Treasury began issuing such bonds in January of 1997. The issues are sometimes called "TIPS," or Treasury Inflation Protection Securities. Other countries, including Canada, Israel, and Britain, have issued similar securities.

Other Types of Bonds

Many bonds have unusual, or exotic, features. So-called disaster bonds provide an interesting example. In 1996, USAA, a big seller of car and home insurance based in San Antonio, announced plans to issue $500 million in "act of God" bonds. The way these work is that USAA will pay interest and principal in the usual way unless it has to cover more than $1 billion in hurricane claims from a single storm over any single one-year period. If this happens, investors stand to lose both principal and interest.

A similar issue was being planned by the proposed California Earthquake Authority, a public agency whose purpose would be to alleviate a growing home insurance availability crunch in the state. The issue, expected to be about $3.35 billion, would have a 10-year maturity, and investors would risk interest paid in the first 4 years in the event of a catastrophic earthquake.

As these examples illustrate, bond features are really only limited by the imaginations of the parties involved. Unfortunately, there are far too many variations for us to cover in detail here. We therefore close out this discussion by mentioning only a few of the more common types.

Income bonds are similar to conventional bonds, except that coupon payments are dependent on company income. Specifically, coupons are paid to bondholders only if the firm's income is sufficient. This would appear to be an attractive feature, but income bonds are not very common.

A *convertible bond* can be swapped for a fixed number of shares of stock anytime before maturity at the holder's option. Convertibles are relatively common, but the number has been decreasing in recent years.

A *put bond* allows the *holder* to force the issuer to buy the bond back at a stated price. The put feature is therefore just the reverse of the call provision and is a relatively new development.

A given bond may have many unusual features. To give just one example, Merrill Lynch created a very popular bond called a *liquid yield option note,* or LYON ("lion"). A LYON is the "kitchen sink" of bonds: a callable, puttable, convertible, zero coupon, subordinated note. Valuing a bond of this sort can be quite complex. The nearby *Reality Bytes* box provides some more examples of exotic bonds.

CONCEPT QUESTIONS

6.4a Why might an income bond be attractive to a corporation with volatile cash flows? Can you think of a reason why income bonds are not more popular?

6.4b What do you think would be the effect of a put feature on a bond's coupon? How about a convertibility feature? Why?

6.5 | BOND MARKETS

Bonds are bought and sold in enormous quantities every day. You may be surprised to learn that the trading volume in bonds on a typical day is many, many times larger than the trading volume in stocks (by trading volume, we simply mean the amount of money that changes hands). Here is a finance trivia question: What is the largest securities market in the world? Most people would guess the New York Stock Exchange. As if! In fact, the largest securities market in the world in terms of trading volume is the U.S. Treasury market.

How Bonds Are Bought and Sold

As we mentioned all the way back in Chapter 1, most trading in bonds takes place over the counter, or OTC. Recall that this means that there is no particular place where buying and selling occur. Instead, dealers around the country (and around the world) stand ready to buy and sell. The various dealers are connected electronically.

One reason the bond markets are so big is that the number of bond issues far exceeds the number of stock issues. There are two reasons for this. First, a corporation would typically have only one common stock issue outstanding (there are exceptions to this that we discuss in our next chapter). However, a single large corporation could easily have a dozen or more note and bond issues outstanding. Beyond this, federal, state, and local borrowing is simply enormous. For example, even a small city would usually have a wide variety of

reality BYTES

EXOTIC BONDS

The Bowie bonds discussed at the beginning of this chapter are bonds linked to the artist's future royalties and are an example of "celebrity" bonds. Similarly, the USAA bonds discussed later in the chapter were the first bonds tied to losses from natural disasters. Such bonds are called "act of God" or "catastrophe" bonds, or simply "cats." While the Bowie bonds are a relatively straightforward investment, the cats are not. As you might imagine, these innovative bonds have led to similar but equally creative successors.

For example, there have been similar issues from the wonderful world of sports. In 1998, the National Football League issued $600 million in bonds using its multibillion-dollar television contract and merchandising and ticket sales as sources of repayment for the bonds. The bonds are further backed by each team in the league, so bondholders have many sources of recourse should the bonds go flat. An issue from outside the United States comes from Newcastle United, one of Britain's soccer teams, which sold £55 million in bonds in 1999 backed by future ticket sales. Clearly, the Newcastle bonds present a different set of risks to bondholders than the NFL bonds because they are essentially tied to the fortunes of one team. As with the Bowie bonds, these sports borrowers were able to convert future cash inflows into an immediate lump sum of cash. The risk for bondholders is obviously that the royalties or revenues might not appear.

In addition to celebrity and catastrophe bonds, there are "weather bonds." Koch Industries Inc. of Kansas and Enron Corp. of Houston have both recently issued bonds tied to the weather in cities where they operate. For example, suppose the temperatures in the 19 cities served by Koch are colder than normal. Koch would be forced to buy more energy to supply to its clients, potentially at a loss. However, Koch has passed at least some of this risk along to bondholders by agreeing to pay a higher interest rate if the weather is warmer than normal. Conversely, as the temperature drops, so does the interest rate on the bonds. In extreme conditions, not only will the interest rate fall but the principal can disappear as well.

Toyota Motor Corp. recently issued bonds tied to the market values of cars coming off lease. While Toyota likes leasing cars, it bears a lot of risk when the leases end. If the used car market is strong when a car comes off lease, it is easy to resell the leased vehicle. However, if the market is poor, Toyota stands to lose when lease customers turn their cars back in. Enter creative financiers who helped Toyota create $566 million in bonds backed by leases on 260,000 Toyotas in North America. The payout on the bonds depends on the market value of the vehicles versus the residual values when they come off lease. If all goes well, the bondholders get all of their money. However, if the market for used cars is poor, the bondholders could receive reduced interest payments or even a reduction in principal.

As these examples show, bond issues are more and more frequently coming in a variety of exotic flavors. The asset-backed, or securitized, bonds, such as the celebrity bonds or the NFL and Newcastle bonds, are tied to the future revenues of the issuer. Bondholders have to be confident that the issuer will remain financially secure until the bonds are paid off. Other bonds, such as cat bonds, weather bonds, and the Toyota bonds, are a way for borrowers to shift some risk to the bondholders. As compensation for the added risk, bondholders demand a higher return than they would otherwise. However, these bonds are unusual in that the investor can lose some of the principal invested, which is possible on generic bonds only if the issuer defaults.

Sources: "Football and Finance: British Soccer Team Begins Selling Bonds," *Globe and Mail,* 21 September 1999, Metro, p. B19.

"Bond Watch: Traders Tackle $600-million NFL Issue in Uncertain Times, Where Better to Invest Than in Football?" *Globe and Mail,* 16 October 1998, p. B13.

"A Brisk Market in Insurance Risk These Days, Bondholders Are Snapping Up What Used to Be Laid Off on Reinsurers," *Business Week,* 12 July 1999, p. 116.

"Celebrity Bonds Gain Popularity," KRTBN Knight-Ridder Tribune Business News: The Arizona Republic, 16 February 1999.

notes and bonds outstanding, representing money borrowed to pay for things like roads, sewers, and schools. When you think about how many small cities there are in the United States, you begin to get the picture!

Because the bond market is almost entirely OTC, it has little or no *transparency.* A financial market is transparent if it is possible to easily observe its prices and trading volume.

On the New York Stock Exchange, for example, it is possible to see the price and quantity for every single transaction. In contrast, in the bond market, it is usually not possible to observe either. Transactions are privately negotiated between parties, and there is little or no centralized reporting of transactions.

Although the total volume of trading in bonds far exceeds that in stocks, only a very small fraction of the total bond issues that exist actually trade on a given day. This fact, combined with the lack of transparency in the bond market, means that getting up-to-date prices on individual bonds is often difficult or impossible, particularly for smaller corporate or municipal issues. Instead, a variety of sources of estimated prices exist and are very commonly used.

Bond Price Reporting

Although most bond trading is OTC, there is a corporate bond market associated with the New York Stock Exchange. If you were to look in *The Wall Street Journal* (or similar financial newspaper), you would find price and volume information from this market on a relatively small number of bonds issued by larger corporations. This particular market represents only a sliver of the total market, however. Mostly, it is a "retail" market, meaning that smaller orders from individual investors are transacted here.

Figure 6.3 reproduces a small section of the bond page from the March 31, 2000, issue of *The Wall Street Journal*. If you look down the list, you will come to an entry marked "ATT 7½06." This designation tells us that the bond was issued by AT&T, and that it will mature in 06, meaning the year 2006. The 7½ is the bond's coupon rate, so the coupon is 7.5 percent of the face value. Assuming the face value is $1,000, the annual coupon on this bond is .075 × $1,000 = $75.

The column marked "Close" gives us the last available price on the bond at close of business the day before. As with the coupon, the price is quoted as a percentage of face value; so, again assuming a face value of $1,000, this bond last sold for 101 percent of $1,000, or $1,010.00. Because this bond is selling for more than 100 percent of its par value, it is trading at a premium. The "+1/4" in the last column, marked "Net Chg," indicates that the closing price was ¼ of 1 percent higher than the previous day's closing price.

current yield
A bond's coupon payment divided by its closing price.

The bond's **current yield** (abbreviated as "Cur Yld") is given in the first column. The current yield is equal to the coupon payment divided by the bond's closing price. For this bond, assuming a face value of $1,000, this works out to be $75/$1,010.00 = 7.43%, or 7.4 percent rounded off to one decimal place. Notice that this is not equal to the bond's yield to maturity (unless the bond sells for par). Finally, the volume for the day (the number of bonds that were bought and sold) is reported in the second column ("Vol"). For this particular issue, only 45 bonds changed hands during the day (in this market).

EXAMPLE 6.4 | **Current Yields**

Following are several bond quotations for the Albanon Corporation. Assuming these are from *The Wall Street Journal,* supply the missing information for each.

Albanon 8s98	?.?	8	84.5	+½
Albanon ?s06	9.4	8	74.5	+⅛
Albanon 8s10	9.0	8	??.?	+¼

In each case, we need to recall that the current yield is equal to the *annual* coupon divided by the price (even if the bond makes semiannual payments). Also, remember that the price is expressed as a percentage of par. In the first case, the coupon rate is 8 percent and the price is 84.5, so the current yield must be 8/84.5, or 9.5 percent. In the second case, the current yield is 9.4 percent, so the coupon rate must be such that:

FIGURE 6.3

Sample *Wall Street Journal* bond quotation

NEW YORK EXCHANGE BONDS

Quotations as of 4 P.M. Eastern Time
Thursday, March 30, 2000

CORPORATION BONDS

Volume, $8,112,000

Bonds	Cur Yld	Vol	Close		Net Chg
AMR 9s16	8.9	195	100¾	−	1⅛
AON 7.4s02	7.5	20	98⅝	−	1⅜
ATT 5⅛01	5.2	20	98	−	⅛
ATT 7⅛02	7.1	70	100¾	+	¾
ATT 6¾04	6.9	21	97⅞	+	½
ATT 5⅝04	6.0	41	94⅛	+	¼
ATT 7s05	7.1	25	98⅞	−	⅛
ATT 7½06	7.4	45	101	+	¼
ATT 7¾07	7.6	70	102¼	+	¼
ATT 6s09	6.6	111	90¼	+	⅜
ATT 8⅛22	8.1	85	100		. . .
ATT 8⅛24	8.1	15	100¼	−	½
ATT 6½29	7.5	27	86⅛	+	¼
ATT 8⅝31	8.5	30	101½		. . .
Alza 5s06	cv	75	106	−	1
Alza zr14	. . .	5	50½	−	⅝
AForP 5s30	8.7	5	57½	−	2½
Amresco 10s03	14.1	20	71	−	2
ArmWld 9¾08	9.5	50	102⅞	−	2⅜
BkrHgh zr08	. . .	10	70½	−	1
BkOne 7¼04	7.3	5	99¾	−	⅛
BankAm 8½07	8.3	3	102¼	−	3⅝
BellPa 7⅛12	7.6	25	93⅞	−	1⅛
BellsoT 6¼03	6.4	10	98	+	1⅛
BellsoT 6⅜04	6.6	62	96¼	−	¼
BellsoT 7s05	7.0	9	99¼	+	¼
BellsoT 6½05	6.8	87	96⅛	+	⅝
BellsoT 5⅞09	6.6	25	89½	+	½
BellsoT 8¼32	8.2	9	100⅞	+	½
BellsoT 7⅞32	8.0	22	97⅞	+	⅜
BellsoT 7½33	8.1	5	92⅞	−	⅜
BellsoT 6¾33	8.1	113	83¾	−	1¼
BellsoT 7⅝35	8.1	145	93⅞	+	½
BethSt 8⅜01	8.3	9	100 31/32	+	⅜
BethSt 8.45s05	9.0	69	94	−	1⅜
Bevrly 9s06	10.5	10	85⅞	−	⅝
Bluegrn 8¼12	cv	25	67½	+	½
Bordn 8⅜16	12.0	13	70	+	⅛
BosCelts 6s38	11.2	14	53⅜	−	⅛
BoydGm 9½07	10.1	25	94⅜		. . .
BrnSh 9½06	10.1	25	94	−	1

Source: Reprinted by permission of *The Wall Street Journal,* March 31, 2000.

Coupon rate/74.5% = 9.4%

Therefore, the coupon rate must be about 7 percent. Finally, in the third case, the price must be such that:

8%/Price = 9%

Therefore, the price is 8/9, or 88.9 percent of par value.

As we mentioned before, the U.S. Treasury market is the largest securities market in the world. As with bond markets in general, it is an OTC market, so there is limited transparency. However, unlike the situation with bond markets in general, trading in Treasury issues, particularly recently issued ones, is very heavy. Each day, representative prices for outstanding Treasury issues are reported.

Figure 6.4 shows a portion of the daily Treasury note and bond listings from *The Wall Street Journal*. The entry that begins "9 Nov 18" is highlighted. Reading from left to right, the 9 is the bond's coupon rate, and the "Nov 18" tells us that the bond's maturity is November of 2018. Treasury bonds all make semiannual payments and have a face value of $1,000, so this bond will pay $45 per six months until it matures.

The next two pieces of information are the **bid** and **asked prices.** In general, in any OTC or dealer market, the bid price represents what a dealer is willing to pay for a security, and the asked price (or just "ask" price) is what a dealer is willing to take for it. The difference between the two prices is called the **bid-ask spread** (or just "spread"), and it represents the dealer's profit.

For historical reasons, Treasury prices are quoted in 32nds. Thus, the bid price on the 9 Nov 18 bond, 129:23, actually translates into $129\frac{23}{32}$, or 129.71875 percent of face value. With a $1,000 face value, this represents $1,297.1875. Because prices are quoted in 32nds, the smallest possible price change is $\frac{1}{32}$. This is called the "tick" size.

The next number quoted is the change in the asked price from the previous day, measured in ticks (i.e., in 32nds), so this issue's asked price rose by $\frac{40}{32}$ of 1 percent, or 1.25 percent, of face value from the previous day. Finally, the last number reported is the yield to maturity, based on the asked price. Notice that this is a premium bond because it sells for more than its face value. Not surprisingly, its yield to maturity (6.26 percent) is less than its coupon rate (9 percent).

Some of the maturity dates in Figure 6.4 have an "n" after them. This just means that these issues are notes rather than bonds. Other entries have a range of maturity dates. These issues are callable. For example, locate the issue whose maturity is given as "Nov 04-09." This bond is callable as of November 2004 and has a final maturity of November 2009. The issues with an "i" after the maturity date are the inflation-linked notes we mentioned earlier.

The very last bond listed, in this case the 6¼ May 30, is often called the "bellwether" bond. This bond's yield is the one that is usually reported in the evening news. So, for example, when you hear that long-term interest rates rose, what is really being said is that the yield on this bond went up (and its price went down). If you examine the yields on the various issues in Figure 6.4, you will clearly see that they vary by maturity. Why this occurs and what it might mean is one of the things we discuss in our next section.

---

bid price

The price a dealer is willing to pay for a security.

asked price

The price a dealer is willing to take for a security.

bid-ask spread

The difference between the bid price and the asked price.

EXAMPLE 6.5 | Treasury Quotes

Locate the Treasury note in Figure 6.4 maturing in February 2006. What is its coupon rate? What is its bid price? What was the *previous day's* asked price?

The note listed as 5⅝ Feb 06n is the one we seek. Its coupon rate is 5⅝, or 5.625 percent of face value. The bid price is 96:11, or 96.34375 percent of face value. The ask price is 96:13, which is up by 14 ticks from the previous day. This means that the ask price on the previous day was equal to $96\frac{13}{32} - \frac{14}{32} = 95\frac{31}{32} = 95{:}31$.

Sample *Wall Street Journal* U.S. Treasury note and bond prices **FIGURE 6.4**

TREASURY BONDS, NOTES & BILLS

Thursday, March 30, 2000

Representative and Indicative Over-the-Counter quotations based on $1 million

GOV'T BONDS & NOTES

Rate	Maturity Mo/Yr	Bid	Asked	Chg.	Ask Yld.
5½	Apr 00n	99:30	100:00	....	5.36
5⅝	Apr 00n	99:29	99:31	....	5.87
6¾	Apr 00n	100:00	100:02	....	5.82
6⅜	May 00n	100:00	100:02	....	5.73
8⅞	May 00n	100:11	100:13	....	5.39
5½	May 00n	99:28	99:30	....	5.77
6¼	May 00n	100:00	100:02	....	5.75
5⅜	Jun 00n	99:26	99:28	....	5.80
5⅞	Jun 00n	99:30	100:00	....	5.79
5⅜	Jul 00n	99:23	99:25	....	5.99
6⅛	Jul 00n	99:31	100:01	....	5.97
6	Aug 00n	99:29	99:31	....	6.04
8¾	Aug 00n	100:29	100:31	− 1	6.07
5⅛	Aug 00n	99:16	99:18	+ 1	6.18
6¼	Aug 00n	99:30	100:00	....	6.22
4½	Sep 00n	99:02	99:04	....	6.31
6⅛	Sep 00n	99:28	99:30	....	6.25
4	Oct 00n	98:20	98:22	....	6.32
5¾	Oct 00n	99:20	99:22	....	6.29
5¾	Nov 00n	99:19	99:21	+ 1	6.31
8½	Nov 00n	101:09	101:11	+ 1	6.25
4⅝	Nov 00n	98:27	98:29	....	6.31
5⅝	Nov 00n	99:16	99:18	+ 1	6.29
4⅝	Dec 00n	98:22	98:24	+ 1	6.35
5½	Dec 00n	99:10	99:12	+ 1	6.35
4½	Jan 01n	98:15	98:17	+ 1	6.32
5¼	Jan 01n	99:02	99:04	+ 1	6.33
5⅜	Feb 01n	99:04	99:06	+ 1	6.33
7¾	Feb 01n	101:04	101:06	+ 1	6.33
11¾	Feb 01	104:18	104:20	+ 1	6.24
5	Feb 01n	98:24	98:26	+ 1	6.35
5⅝	Feb 01n	99:10	99:12	+ 1	6.33
4⅞	Mar 01n	98:16	98:18	+ 1	6.38
6⅜	Mar 01n	99:31	100:01	+ 2	6.34
5	Apr 01n	98:17	98:19	+ 2	6.36
6¼	Apr 01n	99:26	99:28	+ 2	6.36
5⅝	May 01n	99:03	99:05	+ 2	6.41
8	May 01n	101:20	101:22	+ 1	6.41
13⅛	May 01	107:04	107:06	+ 1	6.38
5¼	May 01n	98:20	98:22	+ 2	6.43
6½	May 01n	100:00	100:02	+ 2	6.43
5¾	Jun 01n	99:03	99:05	+ 3	6.45
6⅝	Jun 01n	100:05	100:07	+ 3	6.43
5½	Jul 01n	98:23	98:25	+ 3	6.46
6⅝	Jul 01n	100:04	100:06	+ 3	6.47
7⅞	Aug 01n	101:24	101:26	+ 3	6.47
13⅜	Aug 01	108:28	108:30	+ 3	6.48
5½	Aug 01n	98:20	98:22	+ 3	6.43
6½	Aug 01n	99:31	100:01	+ 4	6.47
5⅝	Sep 01n	98:23	98:25	+ 4	6.49
6⅜	Sep 01n	99:24	99:26	+ 3	6.51
5⅞	Oct 01n	99:00	99:02	+ 4	6.50
6¼	Oct 01n	99:18	99:20	+ 4	6.50
7½	Nov 01n	101:14	101:16	+ 4	6.50
15¾	Nov 01	113:30	114:02	+ 4	6.47
5⅞	Nov 01n	98:31	99:01	+ 5	6.49
6⅛	Dec 01n	99:11	99:13	+ 5	6.48
6¼	Jan 02n	99:16	99:18	+ 5	6.50
6⅜	Jan 02n	99:24	99:26	+ 6	6.48
14¼	Feb 02	113:13	113:17	+ 6	6.47
6¼	Feb 02n	99:17	99:19	+ 6	6.47

Rate	Maturity Mo/Yr	Bid	Asked	Chg.	Ask Yld.
6½	Feb 02n	99:29	99:30	+ 3	6.53
6½	**Mar 02n**	**99:31**	**100:00**	**....**	**6.50**
6⅝	Mar 02n	100:05	100:07	+ 4	6.51
6⅝	Apr 02n	100:05	100:07	+ 5	6.51
7½	May 02n	101:28	101:30	+ 5	6.50
6½	May 02n	99:30	100:00	+ 5	6.49
6¼	Jun 02n	99:14	99:16	+ 5	6.49
3⅝	Jul 02i	99:18	99:19	+ 1	3.81
6	Jul 02n	98:29	98:31	+ 6	6.48
6⅜	Aug 02n	99:22	99:24	+ 6	6.49
6¼	Aug 02n	99:13	99:15	+ 6	6.49
5⅞	Sep 02n	98:17	98:19	+ 6	6.49
5¾	Oct 02n	98:07	98:09	+ 7	6.48
11⅝	Nov 02	111:29	112:01	+ 7	6.55
5¾	Nov 02n	98:03	98:05	+ 6	6.51
5⅝	Dec 02n	97:25	97:27	+ 6	6.49
5½	Jan 03n	97:15	97:17	+ 7	6.46
6¼	Feb 03n	99:11	99:13	+ 7	6.48
10¾	Feb 03	110:27	110:31	+ 7	6.50
5½	Feb 03n	97:13	97:15	+ 8	6.46
5½	**Mar 03n**	**97:11**	**97:13**	**+ 7**	**6.46**
5¾	Apr 03n	97:31	98:01	+ 7	6.46
10¾	May 03	111:21	111:25	+ 8	6.51
5½	May 03n	97:06	97:08	+ 8	6.47
5⅜	Jun 03n	96:27	96:29	+ 8	6.44
5¼	Aug 03n	96:12	96:14	+ 8	6.44
5¾	Aug 03n	97:27	97:29	+ 9	6.45
11⅛	Aug 03	113:22	113:26	+ 9	6.50
4¼	Nov 03n	93:03	93:05	+ 9	6.39
11⅞	Nov 03	117:00	117:04	+10	6.49
4¾	Feb 04n	94:13	94:15	+10	6.38
5⅞	Feb 04n	98:05	98:07	+10	6.40
5¼	May 04n	95:28	95:30	+11	6.38
7¼	May 04n	102:28	102:30	+11	6.42
12⅜	May 04	120:24	120:30	+11	6.50
6	Aug 04n	98:16	98:17	+10	6.39
7¼	Aug 04n	103:02	103:04	+12	6.42
13¾	Aug 04	127:01	127:07	+13	6.50
5⅞	**Nov 04n**	**98:01**	**98:02**	**+12**	**6.36**
7⅞	Nov 04n	105:21	105:23	+13	6.42
11⅝	Nov 04	120:05	120:11	+14	6.46
7½	Feb 05n	104:13	104:15	+12	6.42
6½	May 05n	100:15	100:17	+13	6.37
8¼	May 00–05	100:09	100:11	....	5.29
12	May 05	123:21	123:27	+15	6.46
6½	Aug 05n	100:13	100:15	+13	6.39
10¾	Aug 05	119:03	119:07	+15	6.46
5⅞	Nov 05n	97:19	97:21	+14	6.38
5⅝	Feb 06n	96:11	96:13	+14	6.37
9⅜	Feb 06	114:03	114:07	+15	6.43
6⅞	May 06n	102:12	102:14	+16	6.39
7	Jul 06n	103:02	103:04	+16	6.39
6½	Oct 06n	100:17	100:19	+16	6.39
3⅜	Jan 07i	95:29	95:30	+ 2	4.06
6¼	Feb 07n	99:13	99:15	+17	6.34
7⅝	Feb 02–07	101:21	101:23	+ 5	6.63
6⅝	May 07n	101:15	101:17	+18	6.35
6⅛	Aug 07n	98:22	98:24	+18	6.34
7⅞	Nov 02–07	102:31	103:01	+ 7	6.59
3⅝	Jan 08i	97:08	97:09	+11	4.03
5½	Feb 08n	94:31	95:01	+18	6.31

Rate	Maturity Mo/Yr	Bid	Asked	Chg.	Ask Yld.
5⅝	May 08n	95:23	95:25	+19	6.30
8⅜	Aug 03–08	105:07	105:09	+ 9	6.60
4¾	Nov 08n	89:29	89:31	+19	6.27
8¾	Nov 03–08	106:23	106:25	+10	6.61
3⅞	Jan 09i	98:24	98:25	+10	4.04
5½	May 09n	94:26	94:28	+21	6.24
9⅛	May 04–09	108:26	108:28	+11	6.63
6	Aug 09n	98:13	98:14	+23	6.22
10⅜	Nov 04–09	114:23	114:27	+13	6.59
4¼	Jan 10i	101:24	101:25	+13	4.03
6½	**Feb 10n**	**103:04**	**103:05**	**+23**	**6.07**
11¾	Feb 05–10	121:03	121:09	+14	6.58
10	May 05–10	114:17	114:21	+14	6.58
12¾	Nov 05–10	128:15	128:21	+16	6.57
13⅞	May 06–11	136:14	136:20	+18	6.52
14	Nov 06–11	139:17	130:23	+20	6.52
10⅜	Nov 07–12	122:25	122:31	+21	6.50
12	Aug 08–13	134:30	135:04	+24	6.50
13¼	May 09–14	145:27	146:01	+27	6.48
12½	Aug 09–14	141:15	141:21	+26	6.50
11¾	Nov 09–14	137:15	137:21	+27	6.44
11¼	Feb 15	147:03	147:09	+39	6.31
10⅝	Aug 15	142:02	142:08	+38	6.30
9⅞	Nov 15	135:05	135:11	+38	6.29
9¼	Feb 16	129:13	129:19	+37	6.28
7¼	May 16	109:29	109:31	+33	6.26
7½	Nov 16	112:21	112:25	+35	6.25
8¾	May 17	125:19	125:25	+37	6.27
8⅞	Aug 17	127:06	127:12	+38	6.27
9⅛	May 18	130:18	130:24	+40	6.25
9	Nov 18	129:23	129:29	+40	6.26
8⅞	Feb 19	128:21	128:27	+40	6.25
8⅛	Aug 19	120:28	121:02	+40	6.24
8½	Feb 20	125:13	125:19	+41	6.24
8¾	May 20	128:13	128:19	+42	6.24
8¾	Aug 20	128:20	128:26	+43	6.23
7⅞	Feb 21	119:02	119:06	+41	6.22
8⅛	May 21	122:04	122:10	+42	6.21
8⅛	Aug 21	122:08	122:14	+42	6.21
8	Nov 21	121:02	121:08	+43	6.20
7¼	Aug 22	112:20	112:24	+41	6.19
7⅝	Nov 22	117:05	117:09	+42	6.19
7⅛	Feb 23	111:08	111:12	+40	6.19
6¼	Aug 23	100:28	100:30	+38	6.17
7½	Nov 24	116:24	116:28	+43	6.16
7⅝	Feb 25	118:18	118:22	+44	6.15
6⅞	Aug 25	109:10	109:12	+42	6.14
6	Feb 26	98:11	98:13	+39	6.12
6¾	Aug 26	108:05	108:07	+43	6.12
6½	Nov 26	105:00	105:02	+42	6.11
6⅝	Feb 27	106:23	106:25	+43	6.11
6⅜	Aug 27	103:19	103:21	+42	6.10
6⅛	Nov 27	100:14	100:16	+41	6.09
3⅝	Apr 28i	94:19	94:20	+15	3.94
5½	Aug 28	92:07	92:09	+39	6.07
5¼	Nov 28	89:01	89:03	+39	6.06
5¼	Feb 29	89:05	89:07	+39	6.04
3⅞	Apr 29i	98:28	98:29	+22	3.94
6⅛	Aug 29	101:12	101:13	+39	6.02
6¼	**May 30**	**105:02**	**105:03**	**+45**	**5.89**

Source: Reprinted by permission of *The Wall Street Journal*, March 31, 2000.

6.6 INFLATION AND INTEREST RATES

So far, we haven't considered the role of inflation in our various discussions of interest rates, yields, and returns. Because this is an important consideration, we consider the impact of inflation next.

Real versus Nominal Rates

In examining interest rates, or any other financial market rates such as discount rates, bond yields, rates of return, and required returns, it is often necessary to distinguish between **real rates** and **nominal rates.** Nominal rates are called "nominal" because they have not been adjusted for inflation. Real rates are rates that have been adjusted for inflation.

real rates

Interest rates or rates of return that have been adjusted for inflation.

nominal rates

Interest rates or rates of return that have not been adjusted for inflation.

To see the effect of inflation, suppose prices are currently rising by 5 percent per year. In other words, the rate of inflation is 5 percent. An investment is available that will be worth $115.50 in one year. It costs $100 today. Notice that with a present value of $100 and a future value in one year of $115.50, this investment has a 15.5 percent rate of return. In calculating this 15.5 percent return, we did not consider the effect of inflation, however, so this is the nominal return.

What is the impact of inflation here? To answer, suppose pizzas cost $5 apiece at the beginning of the year. With $100, we can buy 20 pizzas. Because the inflation rate is 5 percent, pizzas will cost 5 percent more, or $5.25, at the end of the year. If we take the investment, how many pizzas can we buy at the end of the year? Measured in pizzas, what is the rate of return on this investment?

Our $115.50 from the investment will buy us $115.50/5.25 = 22 pizzas. This is up from 20 pizzas, so our pizza rate of return is 10 percent. What this illustrates is that even though the nominal return on our investment is 15.5 percent, our buying power goes up by only 10 percent because of inflation. Put another way, we are really only 10 percent richer. In this case, we say that the real return is 10 percent.

Alternatively, we can say that with 5 percent inflation, each of the 115.50 nominal dollars we get is worth 5 percent less in real terms, so the real dollar value of our investment in a year is:

$115.50/1.05 = $110

What we have done is to *deflate* the $115.50 by 5 percent. Because we give up $100 in current buying power to get the equivalent of $110, our real return is again 10 percent. Now that we have removed the effect of future inflation, this $110 is said to be measured in current dollars.

The difference between nominal and real rates is important and bears repeating:

The nominal rate on an investment is the percentage change in the number of dollars you have.
The real rate on an investment is the percentage change in how much you can buy with your dollars, in other words, the percentage change in your buying power.

The Fisher Effect

Our discussion of real and nominal returns illustrates a relationship often called the **Fisher effect** (after the great economist Irving Fisher). Because investors are ultimately concerned with what they can buy with their money, they require compensation for inflation. Let R stand for the nominal rate and r stand for the real rate. The Fisher effect tells us that the relationship between nominal rates, real rates, and inflation can be written as:

$$1 + R = (1 + r) \times (1 + h) \qquad [6.2]$$

Fisher effect

The relationship between nominal returns, real returns, and inflation.

where h is the inflation rate.

In the preceding example, the nominal rate was 15.50 percent and the inflation rate was 5 percent. What was the real rate? We can determine it by plugging in these numbers:

$$1 + .1550 = (1 + r) \times (1 + .05)$$
$$1 + r_{;} = 1.1550/1.05 = 1.10$$
$$r = 10\%$$

This real rate is the same as we had before. If we take another look at the Fisher effect, we can rearrange things a little as follows:

$$1 + R = (1 + r) \times (1 + h)$$
$$R = r + h + r \times h \qquad [6.3]$$

What this tells us is that the nominal rate has three components. First, there is the real rate on the investment, r. Next, there is the compensation for the decrease in the value of the money originally invested because of inflation, h. The third component represents compensation for the fact that the dollars earned on the investment are also worth less because of the inflation.

This third component is usually small, so it is often dropped. The nominal rate is then approximately equal to the real rate plus the inflation rate:

$$R \approx r + h \qquad [6.4]$$

The Fisher Effect | EXAMPLE 6.6

If investors require a 10 percent real rate of return, and the inflation rate is 8 percent, what must be the approximate nominal rate? The exact nominal rate?

First of all, the nominal rate is approximately equal to the sum of the real rate and the inflation rate: 10% + 8% = 18%. From the Fisher effect, we have:

$$1 + R = (1 + r) \times (1 + h)$$
$$= 1.10 \times 1.08$$
$$= 1.1880$$

Therefore, the nominal rate will actually be closer to 19 percent.

It is important to note that financial rates, such as interest rates, discount rates, and rates of return, are almost always quoted in nominal terms. To remind you of this, we will henceforth use the symbol R instead of r in most of our discussions about such rates.

CONCEPT QUESTIONS

6.6a What is the difference between a nominal and a real return? Which is more important to a typical investor?

6.6b What is the Fisher effect?

6.7 | DETERMINANTS OF BOND YIELDS

We are now in a position to discuss the determinants of a bond's yield. As we will see, the yield on any particular bond is a reflection of a variety of factors, some common to all bonds and some specific to the issue under consideration.

The Term Structure of Interest Rates

At any point in time, short-term and long-term interest rates will generally be different. Sometimes short-term rates are higher, sometimes lower. Figure 6.5 gives us a long-range perspective on this by showing almost two centuries of short- and long-term interest rates. As shown, through time, the difference between short- and long-term rates has ranged from essentially zero to up to several percentage points, both positive and negative.

term structure of interest rates

The relationship between nominal interest rates on default-free, pure discount securities and time to maturity; that is, the pure time value of money.

The relationship between short- and long-term interest rates is known as the **term structure of interest rates.** To be a little more precise, the term structure of interest rates tells us what *nominal* interest rates are on *default-free, pure discount* bonds of all maturities. These rates are, in essence, "pure" interest rates because they involve no risk of default and a single, lump-sum future payment. In other words, the term structure tells us the pure time value of money for different lengths of time.

When long-term rates are higher than short-term rates, we say that the term structure is upward sloping, and, when short-term rates are higher, we say it is downward sloping.

FIGURE 6.5   U.S. interest rates: 1800–1997

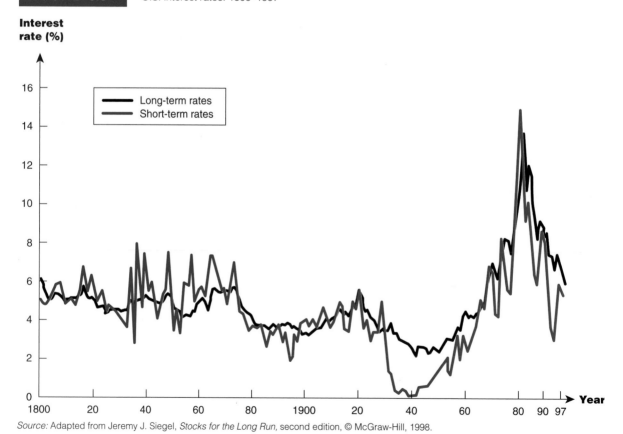

Source: Adapted from Jeremy J. Siegel, *Stocks for the Long Run,* second edition, © McGraw-Hill, 1998.

The term structure can also be "humped." When this occurs, it is usually because rates increase at first, but then begin to decline as we look at longer- and longer-term rates. The most common shape of the term structure, particularly in modern times, is upward sloping, but the degree of steepness has varied quite a bit.

What determines the shape of the term structure? There are three basic components. The first two are the ones we discussed in our previous section, the real rate of interest and the rate of inflation. The real rate of interest is the compensation investors demand for forgoing the use of their money. You can think of it as the pure time value of money after adjusting for the effects of inflation.

The real rate of interest is the basic component underlying every interest rate, regardless of the time to maturity. When the real rate is high, all interest rates will tend to be higher, and vice versa. Thus, the real rate doesn't really determine the shape of the term structure; instead, it mostly influences the overall level of interest rates.

In contrast, the prospect of future inflation very strongly influences the shape of the term structure. Investors thinking about loaning money for various lengths of time recognize that future inflation erodes the value of the dollars that will be returned. As a result, investors demand compensation for this loss in the form of higher nominal rates. This extra compensation is called the **inflation premium.**

If investors believe that the rate of inflation will be higher in the future, then long-term nominal interest rates will tend to be higher than short-term rates. Thus, an upward-sloping term structure may be a reflection of anticipated increases in inflation. Similarly, a downward-sloping term structure probably reflects the belief that inflation will be falling in the future.

The third, and last, component of the term structure has to do with interest rate risk. As we discussed earlier in the chapter, longer-term bonds have much greater risk of loss resulting from changes in interest rates than do shorter-term bonds. Investors recognize this risk, and they demand extra compensation in the form of higher rates for bearing it. This extra compensation is called the **interest rate risk premium.** The longer is the term to maturity, the greater is the interest rate risk, so the interest rate risk premium increases with maturity. However, as we discussed earlier, interest rate risk increases at a decreasing rate, so the interest rate risk premium does as well.[6]

Putting the pieces together, we see that the term structure reflects the combined effect of the real rate of interest, the inflation premium, and the interest rate risk premium. Figure 6.6 shows how these can interact to produce an upward-sloping term structure (in the top part of Figure 6.6) or a downward-sloping term structure (in the bottom part).

In the top part of Figure 6.6, notice how the rate of inflation is expected to rise gradually. At the same time, the interest rate risk premium increases at a decreasing rate, so the combined effect is to produce a pronounced upward-sloping term structure. In the bottom part of Figure 6.6, the rate of inflation is expected to fall in the future, and the expected decline is enough to offset the interest rate risk premium and produce a downward-sloping term structure. Notice that if the rate of inflation was expected to decline by only a small amount, we could still get an upward-sloping term structure because of the interest rate risk premium.

We assumed in drawing Figure 6.6 that the real rate would remain the same. Actually, expected future real rates could be larger or smaller than the current real rate. Also, for simplicity, we used straight lines to show expected future inflation rates as rising or declining,

inflation premium
The portion of a nominal interest rate that represents compensation for expected future inflation.

interest rate risk premium
The compensation investors demand for bearing interest rate risk.

---

[6]In days of old, the interest rate risk premium was called a "liquidity" premium. Today, the term *liquidity premium* has an altogether different meaning, which we explore in our next section. Also, the interest rate premium is sometimes called a maturity risk premium. Our terminology is consistent with the modern view of the term structure.

FIGURE 6.6

The term structure of
interest rates

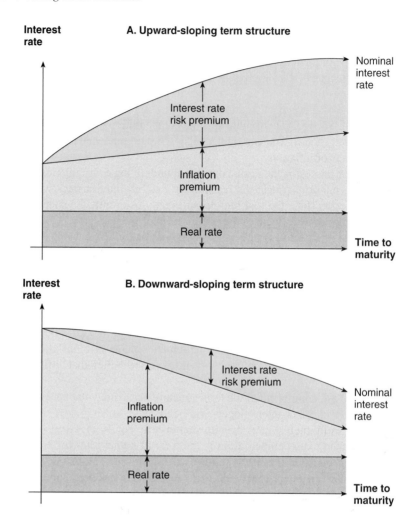

but they do not necessarily have to look like this. They could, for example, rise and then fall, leading to a humped yield curve.

Bond Yields and the Yield Curve: Putting It All Together

Going back to Figure 6.4, recall that we saw that the yields on Treasury notes and bonds of different maturities are not the same. Each day, in addition to the Treasury prices and yields shown in Figure 6.4, *The Wall Street Journal* provides a plot of Treasury yields relative to maturity. This plot is called the **Treasury yield curve** (or just the yield curve). Figure 6.7 shows the yield curve drawn from the yields in Figure 6.4.

As you probably now suspect, the shape of the yield curve is a reflection of the term structure of interest rates. In fact, the Treasury yield curve and the term structure of interest rates are almost the same thing. The only difference is that the term structure is based on pure discount bonds, whereas the yield curve is based on coupon bond yields. As a result, Treasury yields depend on the three components that underlie the term structure—the real rate, expected future inflation, and the interest rate risk premium.

Treasury yield curve

A plot of the yields on Treasury notes and bonds relative to maturity.

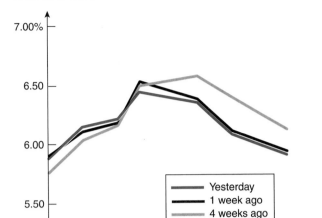

Treasury Yield Curve
Thursday, March 30, 2000
Yields as of 4:30 p.m. Eastern time

FIGURE 6.7

The Treasury yield
curve

Source: Reprinted by permission of *The Wall Street Journal,* March 31, 2000. © 2000 by Dow Jones & Company, Inc. All Rights Reserved Worldwide.

Treasury notes and bonds have three important features that we need to remind you of: they are default-free, they are taxable, and they are highly liquid. This is not true of bonds in general, so we need to examine what additional factors come into play when we look at bonds issued by corporations or municipalities.

The first thing to consider is credit risk, that is, the possibility of default. Investors recognize that issuers other than the Treasury may or may not make all the promised payments on a bond, so they demand a higher yield as compensation for this risk. This extra compensation is called the **default risk premium.** Earlier in the chapter, we saw how bonds were rated based on their credit risk. What you will find if you start looking at bonds of different ratings is that lower-rated bonds have higher yields.

An important thing to recognize about a bond's yield is that it is calculated assuming that all the promised payments will be made. As a result, it is really a promised yield, and it may or may not be what you will earn. In particular, if the issuer defaults, your actual yield will be lower, probably much lower. This fact is particularly important when it comes to junk bonds. Thanks to a clever bit of marketing, such bonds are now commonly called high-yield bonds, which has a much nicer ring to it; but now you recognize that these are really high–*promised* yield bonds.

Next, recall that we discussed earlier how municipal bonds are free from most taxes and, as a result, have much lower yields than taxable bonds. Investors demand the extra yield on a taxable bond as compensation for the unfavorable tax treatment. This extra compensation is the **taxability premium.**

Finally, bonds have varying degrees of liquidity. As we discussed earlier, there is an enormous number of bond issues, most of which do not trade on a regular basis. As a result, if you wanted to sell quickly, you would probably not get as good a price as you could otherwise. Investors prefer liquid assets to illiquid ones, so they demand a

default risk premium
The portion of a nominal interest rate or bond yield that represents compensation for the possibility of default.

taxability premium
The portion of a nominal interest rate or bond yield that represents compensation for unfavorable tax status.

liquidity premium

The portion of a nominal interest rate or bond yield that represents compensation for lack of liquidity.

liquidity premium on top of all the other premiums we have discussed. As a result, all else being the same, less liquid bonds will have higher yields than more liquid bonds.

Conclusion

If we combine all of the things we have discussed regarding bond yields, we find that bond yields represent the combined effect of no fewer than six things. The first is the real rate of interest. On top of the real rate are five premiums representing compensation for (1) expected future inflation, (2) interest rate risk, (3) default risk, (4) taxability, and (5) lack of liquidity. As a result, determining the appropriate yield on a bond requires careful analysis of each of these effects.

CONCEPT QUESTIONS

6.7a What is the term structure of interest rates? What determines its shape?

6.7b What is the Treasury yield curve?

6.7c What are the six components that make up a bond's yield?

SUMMARY AND CONCLUSIONS

This chapter has explored bonds and bond yields. We saw that:

1. Determining bond prices and yields is an application of basic discounted cash flow principles.
2. Bond values move in the direction opposite that of interest rates, leading to potential gains or losses for bond investors.
3. Bonds have a variety of features spelled out in a document called the indenture.
4. Bonds are rated based on their default risk. Some bonds, such as Treasury bonds, have no risk of default, whereas so-called junk bonds have substantial default risk.
5. A wide variety of bonds exist, many of which contain exotic, or unusual, features.
6. Almost all bond trading is OTC, with little or no market transparency. As a result, bond price and volume information can be difficult to find.
7. Bond yields reflect the effect of six different things: the real rate and five premiums that investors demand as compensation for inflation, interest rate risk, default risk, taxability, and lack of liquidity.

In closing, we note that bonds are a vital source of financing to governments and corporations of all types. Bond prices and yields are a rich subject, and our one chapter, necessarily, touches on only the most important concepts and ideas. There is a great deal more we could say, but, instead, we will move on to stocks in our next chapter.

CHAPTER REVIEW AND SELF-TEST PROBLEMS

6.1 **Bond Values.** A Microgates Industries bond has a 10 percent coupon rate and a $1,000 face value. Interest is paid semiannually, and the bond has 20 years to maturity. If investors require a 12 percent yield, what is the bond's value? What is the effective annual yield on the bond?

6.2 **Yields.** A Macrohard Corp. bond carries an 8 percent coupon, paid semiannually. The par value is $1,000, and the bond matures in six years. If the bond currently sells for $911.37, what is its yield to maturity? What is the effective annual yield?

Answers to Chapter Review and Self-Test Problems

6.1 Because the bond has a 10 percent coupon yield and investors require a 12 percent return, we know that the bond must sell at a discount. Notice that, because the bond pays interest semiannually, the coupons amount to $100/2 = $50 every six months. The required yield is 12%/2 = 6% every six months. Finally, the bond matures in 20 years, so there are a total of 40 six-month periods.

The bond's value is thus equal to the present value of $50 every six months for the next 40 six-month periods plus the present value of the $1,000 face amount:

$$\text{Bond value} = \$50 \times (1 - 1/1.06^{40})/.06 + 1{,}000/1.06^{40}$$
$$= \$50 \times 15.04630 + 1{,}000/10.2857$$
$$= \$849.54$$

Notice that we discounted the $1,000 back 40 periods at 6 percent per period, rather than 20 years at 12 percent. The reason is that the effective annual yield on the bond is $1.06^2 - 1 = 12.36\%$, not 12 percent. We thus could have used 12.36 percent per year for 20 years when we calculated the present value of the $1,000 face amount, and the answer would have been the same.

6.2 The present value of the bond's cash flows is its current price, $911.37. The coupon is $40 every six months for 12 periods. The face value is $1,000. So the bond's yield is the unknown discount rate in the following:

$$\$911.37 = \$40 \times [1 - 1/(1 + r)^{12}]/r + 1{,}000/(1 + r)^{12}$$

The bond sells at a discount. Because the coupon rate is 8 percent, the yield must be something in excess of that.

If we were to solve this by trial and error, we might try 12 percent (or 6 percent per six months):

$$\text{Bond value} = \$40 \times (1 - 1/1.06^{12})/.06 + 1{,}000/1.06^{12}$$
$$= \$832.32$$

This is less than the actual value, so our discount rate is too high. We now know that the yield is somewhere between 8 and 12 percent. With further trial and error (or a little machine assistance), the yield works out to be 10 percent, or 5 percent every six months.

By convention, the bond's yield to maturity would be quoted as $2 \times 5\% = 10\%$. The effective yield is thus $1.05^2 - 1 = 10.25\%$.

CRITICAL THINKING AND CONCEPTS REVIEW

1. **Treasury Bonds.** Is it true that a U.S. Treasury security is risk-free?

2. **Interest Rate Risk.** Which has greater interest rate risk, a 30-year Treasury bond or a 30-year BB corporate bond?

3. **Treasury Pricing.** With regard to bid and ask prices on a Treasury bond, is it possible for the bid price to be higher? Why or why not?

4. **Yield to Maturity.** Treasury bid and ask quotes are sometimes given in terms of yields, so there would be a bid yield and an ask yield. Which do you think would be larger? Explain.

5. **Call Provisions.** A company is contemplating a long-term bond issue. It is debating whether or not to include a call provision. What are the benefits to the company from including a call provision? What are the costs? How do these answers change for a put provision?

6.   **Coupon Rate.**   How does a bond issuer decide on the appropriate coupon rate to set on its bonds? Explain the difference between the coupon rate and the required return on a bond.

7.   **Real and Nominal Returns.**   Are there any circumstances under which an investor might be more concerned about the nominal return on an investment than the real return?

8.   **Bond Ratings.**   Companies pay rating agencies such as Moody's and S&P to rate their bonds, and the costs can be substantial. However, companies are not required to have their bonds rated in the first place; doing so is strictly voluntary. Why do you think they do it?

9.   **Bond Ratings.**   U.S. Treasury bonds are not rated. Why? Often, junk bonds are not rated. Why?

10.   **Term Structure.**   What is the difference between the term structure of interest rates and the yield curve?

11.   **Crossover Bonds.**   Looking back at the crossover bonds we discussed in the chapter, why do you think split ratings such as these occur?

12.   **Municipal Bonds.**   Why is it that municipal bonds are not taxed at the federal level, but are taxable across state lines? Why is it that U.S. Treasury bonds are not taxable at the state level? (You may need to dust off the history books for this one.)

13.   **Bond Market.**   What are the implications for bond investors of the lack of transparency in the bond market?

14.   **Treasury Market.**   All Treasury bonds are relatively liquid, but some are more liquid than others. Take a look back at Figure 6.4. Which issues appear to be the most liquid? The least liquid?

15.   **Rating Agencies.**   A controversy erupted regarding bond-rating agencies when some agencies began to provide unsolicited bond ratings. Why do you think this is controversial?

16.   **Bonds as Equity.**   The 100-year bonds we discussed in the chapter have something in common with junk bonds. Critics charge that, in both cases, the issuers are really selling equity in disguise. What are the issues here? Why would a company want to sell "equity in disguise"?

QUESTIONS AND PROBLEMS

Basic
(Questions 1–14)

1.   **Interpreting Bond Yields.**   Is the yield to maturity on a bond the same thing as the required return? Is YTM the same thing as the coupon rate? Suppose today a 10 percent coupon bond sells at par. Two years from now, the required return on the same bond is 8 percent. What is the coupon rate on the bond now? The YTM?

2.   **Interpreting Bond Yields.**   Suppose you buy a 7 percent coupon, 20-year bond today when it's first issued. If interest rates suddenly rise to 15 percent, what happens to the value of your bond? Why?

3.   **Bond Prices.**   ULJ, Inc., has 7 percent coupon bonds on the market that have 12 years left to maturity. The bonds make annual payments. If the YTM on these bonds is 8 percent, what is the current bond price?

4.   **Bond Yields.**   Whatever Co. has 10 percent coupon bonds on the market with eight years left to maturity. The bonds make annual payments. If the bond currently sells for $896.50, what is its YTM?

5. **Coupon Rates.** Merton Enterprises has bonds on the market making annual payments, with 13 years to maturity, and selling for $850. At this price, the bonds yield 8.2 percent. What must the coupon rate be on Merton's bonds?

6. **Bond Prices.** Mullineaux Co. issued 11-year bonds 1 year ago at a coupon rate of 8.25 percent. The bonds make semiannual payments. If the YTM on these bonds is 9.2 percent, what is the current bond price?

7. **Bond Yields.** Furst Co. issued 12-year bonds 2 years ago at a coupon rate of 8.4 percent. The bonds make semiannual payments. If these bonds currently sell for 87 percent of par value, what is the YTM?

8. **Coupon Rates.** Joe Kernan Corporation has bonds on the market with 10.5 years to maturity, a YTM of 8 percent, and a current price of $1,075. The bonds make semiannual payments. What must the coupon rate be on Kernan's bonds?

9. **Calculating Real Rates of Return.** If Treasury bills are currently paying 6 percent and the inflation rate is 3.5 percent, what is the approximate real rate of interest? The exact real rate?

10. **Inflation and Nominal Returns.** Suppose the real rate is 3.5 percent and the inflation rate is 4 percent. What rate would you expect to see on a Treasury bill?

11. **Nominal and Real Returns.** An investment offers a 13 percent total return over the coming year. Alan Wingspan thinks the total real return on this investment will be only 8 percent. What does Alan believe the inflation rate will be over the next year?

12. **Nominal versus Real Returns.** Say you own an asset that had a total return last year of 14 percent. If the inflation rate last year was 6 percent, what was your real return?

13. **Using Treasury Quotes.** Locate the Treasury issue in Figure 6.4 maturing in November 2008. Is this a note or a bond? What is its coupon rate? What is its bid price? What was the *previous day's* asked price?

14. **Using Treasury Quotes.** Locate the Treasury bond in Figure 6.4 maturing in November 2028. Is this a premium or a discount bond? What is its current yield? What is its yield to maturity? What is the bid-ask spread?

15. **Bond Price Movements.** Bond X is a premium bond making annual payments. The bond pays a 10 percent coupon, has a YTM of 8 percent, and has 13 years to maturity. Bond Y is a discount bond making annual payments. This bond pays a 6 percent coupon, has a YTM of 8 percent, and also has 13 years to maturity. What are the prices of these bonds today? If interest rates remain unchanged, what do you expect the prices of these bonds to be in one year? In three years? In eight years? In 12 years? In 13 years? What's going on here? Illustrate your answers by graphing bond prices versus time to maturity.

Intermediate
(Questions 15–30)

16. **Interest Rate Risk.** Both Bond Twain and Bond Brooks have 7 percent coupons, make semiannual payments, and are priced at par value. Bond Twain has 2 years to maturity, whereas Bond Brooks has 15 years to maturity. If interest rates suddenly rise by 2 percent, what is the percentage change in the price of Bond Twain? Of Bond Brooks? If rates were to suddenly fall by 2 percent instead, what would the percentage change in the price of Bond Twain be then? Of Bond Brooks? Illustrate your answers by graphing bond prices versus YTM. What does this problem tell you about the interest rate risk of longer-term bonds?

17.   **Interest Rate Risk.**   Bond J is a 3 percent coupon bond. Bond S is a 12 percent coupon bond. Both bonds have 8 years to maturity, make semiannual payments, and have a YTM of 7 percent. If interest rates suddenly rise by 2 percent, what is the percentage price change of these bonds? What if rates suddenly fall by 2 percent instead? What does this problem tell you about the interest rate risk of lower-coupon bonds?

18.   **Bond Yields.**   Carhart Software has 10 percent coupon bonds on the market with 9 years to maturity. The bonds make semiannual payments and currently sell for 105 percent of par. What is the current yield on Carhart's bonds? The YTM? The effective annual yield?

19.   **Bond Yields.**   BDJ Co. wants to issue new 20-year bonds for some much-needed expansion projects. The company currently has 9 percent coupon bonds on the market that sell for $1,135, make semiannual payments, and mature in 20 years. What coupon rate should the company set on its new bonds if it wants them to sell at par?

20.   **Using Bond Quotes.**   Suppose the following bond quote for IOU Corporation appears on the financial page of today's newspaper. If this bond has a face value of $1,000, what closing price appeared in *yesterday's* newspaper?

Bonds	Cur Yld	Vol	Close	Net Chg
IOU 7.35 s18	8.9	10	??	+ ¼

21.   **Bond Prices versus Yields.**

   a. What is the relationship between the price of a bond and its YTM?

   b. Explain why some bonds sell at a premium over par value while other bonds sell at a discount. What do you know about the relationship between the coupon rate and the YTM for premium bonds? What about for discount bonds? For bonds selling at par value?

   c. What is the relationship between the current yield and YTM for premium bonds? For discount bonds? For bonds selling at par value?

22.   **Interest on Zeroes.**   Sipowitz Corporation needs to raise funds to finance a plant expansion, and it has decided to issue 15-year zero coupon bonds to raise the money. The required return on the bonds will be 8 percent.

   a. What will these bonds sell for at issuance?

   b. Using the IRS amortization rule, what interest deduction can Sipowitz Corporation take on these bonds in the first year? In the last year?

   c. Repeat part (*b*) using the straight-line method for the interest deduction.

   d. Based on your answers in (*b*) and (*c*), which interest deduction method would Sipowitz Corporation prefer? Why?

23.   **Zero Coupon Bonds.**   Suppose your company needs to raise $10 million and you want to issue 20-year bonds for this purpose. Assume the required return on your bond issue will be 9 percent, and you're evaluating two issue alternatives: a 9 percent annual coupon bond and a zero coupon bond. Your company's tax rate is 35 percent.

   a. How many of the coupon bonds would you need to issue to raise the $10 million? How many of the zeroes would you need to issue?

   b. In 20 years, what will your company's repayment be if you issue the coupon bonds? What if you issue the zeroes?

c. Based on your answers in (*a*) and (*b*), why would you ever want to issue the zeroes? To answer, calculate the firm's aftertax cash outflows for the first year under the two different scenarios. Assume that the IRS amortization rules apply for the zero coupon bonds.

d. Verify that the present values of the cash flows from the two alternative bond issues are the same.

24. **Finding the Maturity.**   You've just found a 10 percent coupon bond on the market that sells for par value. What is the maturity on this bond (Warning: Possible trick question)?

Use the following bond quotes to answer Questions 25–27. To calculate the number of years until maturity, assume that it is November 2000.

Rate	Maturity Mo/Yr	Bid	Asked	Chg	Ask Yld
??	Nov 02	111:30	112:02	−6	6.62
9 ⅞	Nov 15	131:25	131:31	−23	??
5 ¼	Nov 28	??	??	−12	6.34

25. **Bond Yields.**   In the table, find the Treasury bond that matures in November 2015. What is the yield to maturity for this bond?

26. **Bond Prices.**   In the table, find the Treasury bond that matures in November 2028. What is the asked price of this bond? If the bid-ask spread for this bond is two ticks, what is the bid price?

27. **Coupon Rates.**   Find the Treasury bond that matures in November 2002. What is the coupon rate for this bond?

Use the following bond quotes to answer Questions 28–30. To calculate the number of years until maturity, assume that it is November 2000 and the bonds listed all mature in November.

Bonds	Cur Yld	Vol	Close	Net Chg
BosCelts 6s38	11.3	9	53	+ ⅛
Dole ?s03	7.7	86	90⅜	−1
Polaroid 11 1/2 06	??	36	??	+ ½

28. **Bond Yields.**   What is the yield to maturity for the bond issued by the Boston Celtics?

29. **Bond Prices.**   The yield to maturity for the bond issued by Polaroid is 10.72 percent. What price would you expect to see quoted for this bond? What is the current yield?

30. **Coupon Rates.**   The yield to maturity for the bond issued by Dole is 10.74 percent. What is the coupon rate for this bond?

www.mhhe.com/rwj

Spreadsheet Templates 3, 4, 15, 16

Equity Markets and Stock Valuation

AFTER TAKING STOCK IN THIS CHAPTER (PUN COMPLETELY INTENTIONAL), YOU SHOULD KNOW:

- How stock prices depend on future dividends and dividend growth

- The different ways corporate directors are elected to office

- How the stock markets work

- How stock prices are reported in the financial press

WHEN THE STOCK MARKET CLOSED on April 13, 2000, the common stock of Wal-Mart, the largest retailer in the U.S., was going for $60 per share. On that same day, stock in DaimlerChrysler, maker of Mercedes and Chrysler automobiles, closed at $65.75, while Ariba, a leading provider of Intranet- and Internet-based business-to-business electronic commerce solutions and relative newcomer to the stock pages, closed at $65.06. Since the stock prices of these three companies were so similar, you might expect that the three companies would be offering similar dividends to their stockholders, but you would be wrong. In fact, DaimlerChrysler's annual dividend was $2.29 per share, Wal-Mart's was $.24 per share, and Ariba was paying no dividends at all!

As we will see in this chapter, the dividends currently being paid are one of the primary factors we look at when we attempt to value common stocks. However, it is obvious from looking at Ariba that current dividends are not the end of the story, so this chapter explores dividends, stock values, and the connection between the two.

Going back to Chapter 1, we saw that the goal of financial management is to maximize stock prices, so an understanding of what determines share values is obviously a key concern. When a corporation has publicly held stock, its shares will often be bought and sold on one or more of the major stock exchanges, so we will examine how stocks are traded. We will also see that the shareholders in a corporation have certain rights, and that just how these rights are allocated can have a significant impact on corporate control and governance.

n our previous chapter, we introduced you to bonds and bond valuation. In this chapter, we turn to the other major source of financing for corporations, common and preferred stock. We first describe the cash flows associated with a share of stock and then go on to develop a very famous result, the dividend growth model. From there, we move on to examine various important features of common and preferred stock, focusing on shareholder rights. We close out the chapter with a discussion of how shares of stock are traded and how stock prices and other important information are reported in the financial press.

7.1 | COMMON STOCK VALUATION

A share of common stock is more difficult to value in practice than a bond, for at least three reasons. First, with common stock, not even the promised cash flows are known in advance. Second, the life of the investment is essentially forever, since common stock has no maturity. Third, there is no way to easily observe the rate of return that the market requires. Nonetheless, as we will see, there are cases in which we can come up with the present value of the future cash flows for a share of stock and thus determine its value.

Cash Flows

Imagine that you are considering buying a share of stock today. You plan to sell the stock in one year. You somehow know that the stock will be worth $70 at that time. You predict that the stock will also pay a $10 per share dividend at the end of the year. If you require a 25 percent return on your investment, what is the most you would pay for the stock? In other words, what is the present value of the $10 dividend along with the $70 ending value at 25 percent?

If you buy the stock today and sell it at the end of the year, you will have a total of $80 in cash. At 25 percent:

Present value = ($10 + 70)/1.25 = $64

Therefore, $64 is the value you would assign to the stock today.

More generally, let P_0 be the current price of the stock, and assign P_1 to be the price in one period. If D_1 is the cash dividend paid at the end of the period, then:

$$P_0 = (D_1 + P_1)/(1 + R) \qquad [7.1]$$

where R is the required return in the market on this investment.

Notice that we really haven't said much so far. If we wanted to determine the value of a share of stock today (P_0), we would first have to come up with the value in one year (P_1). This is even harder to do, so we've only made the problem more complicated.

What is the price in one period, P_1? We don't know in general. Instead, suppose we somehow knew the price in two periods, P_2. Given a predicted dividend in two periods, D_2, the stock price in one period would be:

$$P_1 = (D_2 + P_2)/(1 + R)$$

If we were to substitute this expression for P_1 into our expression for P_0, we would have:

$$
P_0 = \frac{D_1 + P_1}{1 + R} = \frac{D_1 + \dfrac{D_2 + P_2}{1 + R}}{1 + R}
$$

$$
= \frac{D_1}{(1 + R)^1} + \frac{D_2}{(1 + R)^2} + \frac{P_2}{(1 + R)^2}
$$

Now we need to get a price in two periods. We don't know this either, so we can procrastinate again and write:

$$P_2 = (D_3 + P_3)/(1 + R)$$

If we substitute this back in for P_2, we have:

$$P_0 = \frac{D_1}{(1 + R)^1} + \frac{D_2}{(1 + R)^2} + \frac{P_2}{(1 + R)^2}$$

$$= \frac{D_1}{(1 + R)^1} + \frac{D_2}{(1 + R)^2} + \frac{\dfrac{D_3 + P_3}{1 + R}}{(1 + R)^2}$$

$$= \frac{D_1}{(1 + R)^1} + \frac{D_2}{(1 + R)^2} + \frac{D_3}{(1 + R)^3} + \frac{P_3}{(1 + R)^3}$$

You should start to notice that we can push the problem of coming up with the stock price off into the future forever. It is important to note that no matter what the stock price is, the present value is essentially zero if we push the sale of the stock far enough away. What we are eventually left with is the result that the current price of the stock can be written as the present value of the dividends beginning in one period and extending out forever:

$$P_0 = \frac{D_1}{(1 + R)^1} + \frac{D_2}{(1 + R)^2} + \frac{D_3}{(1 + R)^3} + \frac{D_4}{(1 + R)^4} + \frac{D_5}{(1 + R)^5} + \cdots$$

We have illustrated here that the price of the stock today is equal to the present value of all of the future dividends. How many future dividends are there? In principle, there can be an infinite number. This means that we still can't compute a value for the stock because we would have to forecast an infinite number of dividends and then discount them all. In the next section, we consider some special cases in which we can get around this problem.

Growth Stocks | **EXAMPLE 7.1**

You might be wondering about shares of stock in companies such as America Online that currently pay no dividends. Small, growing companies frequently plow back everything and thus pay no dividends. Are such shares worth nothing? It depends. When we say that the value of the stock is equal to the present value of the future dividends, we don't rule out the possibility that some number of those dividends are zero. They just can't *all* be zero.

Imagine a company that has a provision in its corporate charter that prohibits the paying of dividends now or ever. The corporation never borrows any money, never pays out any money to stockholders in any form whatsoever, and never sells any assets. Such a corporation couldn't really exist because the IRS wouldn't like it; and the stockholders could always vote to amend the charter if they wanted to. If it did exist, however, what would the stock be worth?

The stock is worth absolutely nothing. Such a company is a financial "black hole." Money goes in, but nothing valuable ever comes out. Because nobody would ever get any return on this investment, the investment has no value. This example is a little absurd, but it illustrates that when we speak of companies that don't pay dividends, what we really mean is that they are not *currently* paying dividends.

Some Special Cases

There are a few very useful special circumstances under which we can come up with a value for the stock. What we have to do is make some simplifying assumptions about the pattern of future dividends. The two cases we consider are the following: (1) the dividend has a zero growth rate, and (2) the dividend grows at a constant rate. We consider each of these separately.

Zero Growth   The case of zero growth is one we've already seen. A share of common stock in a company with a constant dividend is much like a share of preferred stock. From Chapter 5 (Example 5.7), we know that the dividend on a share of preferred stock has zero growth and thus is constant through time. For a zero growth share of common stock, this implies that:

$$D_1 = D_2 = D_3 = D = \text{constant}$$

So, the value of the stock is:

$$P_0 = \frac{D}{(1 + R)^1} + \frac{D}{(1 + R)^2} + \frac{D}{(1 + R)^3} + \frac{D}{(1 + R)^4} + \frac{D}{(1 + R)^5} + \cdots$$

Because the dividend is always the same, the stock can be viewed as an ordinary perpetuity with a cash flow equal to D every period. The per-share value is thus given by:

$$P_0 = D/R \qquad\qquad [7.2]$$

where R is the required return.

For example, suppose the Paradise Prototyping Company has a policy of paying a $10 per share dividend every year. If this policy is to be continued indefinitely, what is the value of a share of stock if the required return is 20 percent? The stock in this case amounts to an ordinary perpetuity, so the stock is worth $10/.20 = $50 per share.

Constant Growth   Suppose we know that the dividend for some company always grows at a steady rate. Call this growth rate g. If we let D_0 be the dividend just paid, then the next dividend, D_1, is:

$$D_1 = D_0 \times (1 + g)$$

The dividend in two periods is:

$$
\begin{aligned}
D_2 &= D_1 \times (1 + g)\\
&= [D_0 \times (1 + g)] \times (1 + g)\\
&= D_0 \times (1 + g)^2
\end{aligned}
$$

We could repeat this process to come up with the dividend at any point in the future. In general, from our discussion of compound growth in Chapter 4, we know that the dividend t periods into the future, D_t, is given by:

$$D_t = D_0 \times (1 + g)^t$$

An asset with cash flows that grow at a constant rate forever is called a *growing perpetuity*. As we will see momentarily, there is a simple expression for determining the value of such an asset.

The assumption of steady dividend growth might strike you as peculiar. Why would the dividend grow at a constant rate? The reason is that, for many companies, steady growth in dividends is an explicit goal. This subject falls under the general heading of dividend policy, so we will defer further discussion of it to a later chapter.

Dividend Growth | **EXAMPLE 7.2**

The Hedless Corporation has just paid a dividend of $3 per share. The dividend of this company grows at a steady rate of 8 percent per year. Based on this information, what will the dividend be in five years?

Here we have a $3 current amount that grows at 8 percent per year for five years. The future amount is thus:

$3 \times 1.08^5 = \$3 \times 1.4693 = \$4.41$

The dividend will therefore increase by $1.41 over the coming five years.

If the dividend grows at a steady rate, then we have replaced the problem of forecasting an infinite number of future dividends with the problem of coming up with a single growth rate, a considerable simplification. In this case, if we take D_0 to be the dividend just paid and g to be the constant growth rate, the value of a share of stock can be written as:

$$P_0 = \frac{D_1}{(1+R)^1} + \frac{D_2}{(1+R)^2} + \frac{D_3}{(1+R)^3} + \cdots$$

$$= \frac{D_0(1+g)^1}{(1+R)^1} + \frac{D_0(1+g)^2}{(1+R)^2} + \frac{D_0(1+g)^3}{(1+R)^3} + \cdots$$

As long as the growth rate, g, is less than the discount rate, R, the present value of this series of cash flows can be written very simply as:

$$P_0 = \frac{D_0 \times (1+g)}{R-g} = \frac{D_1}{R-g} \qquad [7.3]$$

This elegant result goes by a lot of different names. We will call it the **dividend growth model**. By any name, it is very easy to use. To illustrate, suppose D_0 is $2.30, R is 13 percent, and g is 5 percent. The price per share in this case is:

$$P_0 = D_0 \times (1+g)/(R-g)$$
$$= \$2.30 \times 1.05/(.13 - .05)$$
$$= \$2.415/.08$$
$$= \$30.19$$

dividend growth model

A model that determines the current price of a stock as its dividend next period divided by the discounted rate less the dividend growth rate.

We can actually use the dividend growth model to get the stock price at any point in time, not just today. In general, the price of the stock as of time t is:

$$P_t = \frac{D_t \times (1+g)}{R-g} = \frac{D_{t+1}}{R-g} \qquad [7.4]$$

In our example, suppose we are interested in the price of the stock in five years, P_5. We first need the dividend at Time 5, D_5. Because the dividend just paid is $2.30 and the growth rate is 5 percent per year, D_5 is:

$$D_5 = \$2.30 \times 1.05^5 = \$2.30 \times 1.2763 = \$2.935$$

From the dividend growth model, we get that the price of the stock in five years is:

$$P_5 = \frac{D_5 \times (1+g)}{R-g} = \frac{\$2.935 \times 1.05}{.13 - .05} = \frac{\$3.0822}{.08} = \$38.53$$

EXAMPLE 7.3 | **Gordon Growth Company**

The next dividend for the Gordon Growth Company will be $4 per share. Investors require a 16 percent return on companies such as Gordon. Gordon's dividend increases by 6 percent every year. Based on the dividend growth model, what is the value of Gordon's stock today? What is the value in four years?

The only tricky thing here is that the next dividend, D_1, is given as $4, so we won't multiply this by $(1 + g)$. With this in mind, the price per share is given by:

$$P_0 = D_1/(R - g)$$
$$= \$4/(.16 - .06)$$
$$= \$4/.10$$
$$= \$40$$

Because we already have the dividend in one year, we know that the dividend in four years is equal to $D_1 \times (1 + g)^3 = \$4 \times 1.06^3 = \$4.764$. The price in four years is therefore:

$$P_4 = D_4 \times (1 + g)/(R - g)$$
$$= \$4.764 \times 1.06/(.16 - .06)$$
$$= \$5.05/.10$$
$$= \$50.50$$

Notice in this example that P_4 is equal to $P_0 \times (1 + g)^4$.

$$P_4 = \$50.50 = \$40 \times 1.06^4 = P_0 \times (1 + g)^4$$

To see why this is so, notice first that:

$$P_4 = D_5/(R - g)$$

However, D_5 is just equal to $D_1 \times (1 + g)^4$, so we can write P_4 as:

$$P_4 = D_1 \times (1 + g)^4/(R - g)$$
$$= [D_1/(R - g)] \times (1 + g)^4$$
$$= P_0 \times (1 + g)^4$$

This last example illustrates that the dividend growth model makes the implicit assumption that the stock price will grow at the same constant rate as the dividend. This really isn't too surprising. What it tells us is that if the cash flows on an investment grow at a constant rate through time, so does the value of that investment.

You might wonder what would happen with the dividend growth model if the growth rate, g, were greater than the discount rate, R. It looks like we would get a negative stock price because $R - g$ would be less than zero. This is not what would happen.

Instead, if the constant growth rate exceeds the discount rate, then the stock price is infinitely large. Why? If the growth rate is bigger than the discount rate, then the present value of the dividends keeps on getting bigger and bigger. Essentially, the same is true if the growth rate and the discount rate are equal. In both cases, the simplification that allows us to replace the infinite stream of dividends with the dividend growth model is "illegal," so the answers we get from the dividend growth model are nonsense unless the growth rate is less than the discount rate.

Finally, the expression we came up with for the constant growth case will work for any growing perpetuity, not just dividends on common stock. If C_1 is the next cash flow on a growing perpetuity, then the present value of the cash flows is given by:

Present value $= C_1/(R - g) = C_0(1 + g)/(R - g)$

Notice that this expression looks like the result for an ordinary perpetuity except that we have $R - g$ on the bottom instead of just R.

Components of the Required Return

Thus far, we have taken the required return, or discount rate, R, as given. We will have quite a bit to say on this subject in Chapters 10 and 11. For now, we want to examine the implications of the dividend growth model for this required return. Earlier, we calculated P_0 as:

$P_0 = D_1/(R - g)$

If we rearrange this to solve for R, we get:

$R - g = D_1/P_0$

$R = D_1/P_0 + g$ [7.5]

This tells us that the total return, R, has two components. The first of these, D_1/P_0, is called the **dividend yield**. Because this is calculated as the expected cash dividend divided by the current price, it is conceptually similar to the current yield on a bond.

    The second part of the total return is the growth rate, g. We know that the dividend growth rate is also the rate at which the stock price grows (see Example 7.3). Thus, this growth rate can be interpreted as the **capital gains yield**, that is, the rate at which the value of the investment grows.[1]

    To illustrate the components of the required return, suppose we observe a stock selling for $20 per share. The next dividend will be $1 per share. You think that the dividend will grow by 10 percent per year more or less indefinitely. What return does this stock offer you if this is correct?

    The dividend growth model calculates the total return as:

$R =$ Dividend yield $+$ Capital gains yield

$R = D_1/P_0 + g$

In this case, the total return works out to be:

$R = \$1/20 + 10\%$

$= 5\% + 10\%$

$= 15\%$

This stock, therefore, has a required return of 15 percent.

    We can verify this answer by calculating the price in one year, P_1, using 15 percent as the required return. Based on the dividend growth model, this price is:

$P_1 = D_1 \times (1 + g)/(R - g)$

$= \$1 \times 1.10/(.15 - .10)$

$= \$1.10/.05$

$= \$22$

dividend yield
A stock's expected cash dividend divided by its current price.

capital gains yield
The dividend growth rate, or the rate at which the value of an investment grows.

---

[1]Here and elsewhere, we use the term *capital gains* a little loosely. For the record, a capital gain (or loss) is, strictly speaking, something defined by the IRS. For our purposes, it would be more accurate (but less common) to use the term *price appreciation* instead of *capital gain*.

TABLE 7.1

Summary of stock
valuation

I. The general case

In general, the price today of a share of stock, P_0, is the present value of all of its future dividends, $D_1, D_2, D_3, \ldots$:

$$P_0 = \frac{D_1}{(1 + R)^1} = \frac{D_2}{(1 + R)^2} + \frac{D_3}{(1 + R)^3} + \cdots$$

where R is the required return.

II. Constant growth case

If the dividend is constant and equal to D, then the price can be written as:

$$P_0 = \frac{D}{R}$$

If the dividend grows at a steady rate, g, then the price can be written as:

$$P_0 = \frac{D_1}{R - g}$$

This result is called the *dividend growth model.*

III. The required return, R, can be written as the sum of two things:

$$R = D_1/P_0 + g$$

where D_1/P_0 is the *dividend yield* and g is the *capital gains yield* (which is the same thing as the growth rate in dividends for the steady growth case).

Notice that this $22 is $20 × 1.1, so the stock price has grown by 10 percent, as it should. If you pay $20 for the stock today, you will get a $1 dividend at the end of the year, and you will have a $22 − 20 = $2 gain. Your dividend yield is thus $1/20 = 5%. Your capital gains yield is $2/20 = 10%, so your total return would be 5% + 10% = 15%.

To get a feel for actual numbers in this context, consider that, according to the 2000 Value Line *Investment Survey,* Procter and Gamble's dividends were expected to grow by 13 percent over the next 5 or so years, compared to a historical growth rate of 12.5 percent over the preceding 5 years and 11 percent over the preceding 10 years. In 2000, the projected dividend for the coming year was given as $1.28. The stock price at that time was about $103 per share. What is the return investors require on P&G? Here, the dividend yield is 1.24 percent and the capital gains yield is 13 percent, giving a total required return of 14.24 percent on P&G stock.

Our discussion of stock valuation is summarized in Table 7.1.

CONCEPT QUESTIONS

7.1a What are the relevant cash flows for valuing a share of common stock?

7.1b Does the value of a share of stock depend on how long you expect to keep it?

7.1c What is the value of a share of stock when the dividend grows at a constant rate?

7.2 | SOME FEATURES OF COMMON AND PREFERRED STOCK

In discussing common stock features, we focus on shareholder rights and dividend payments. For preferred stock, we explain what the "preferred" means, and we also debate whether preferred stock is really debt or equity.

Common Stock Features

The term **common stock** means different things to different people, but it is usually applied to stock that has no special preference either in paying dividends or in bankruptcy.

common stock
Equity without priority for dividends or in bankruptcy.

Shareholder Rights   The conceptual structure of the corporation assumes that shareholders elect directors who, in turn, hire management to carry out their directives. Shareholders, therefore, control the corporation through the right to elect the directors. Generally, only shareholders have this right.

Directors are elected each year at an annual meeting. Although there are exceptions (discussed in a moment), the general idea is "one share, one vote" (*not* one share*holder,* one vote). Corporate democracy is thus very different from our political democracy. With corporate democracy, the "golden rule" prevails absolutely.[2]

Directors are elected at an annual shareholders' meeting by a vote of the holders of a majority of shares who are present and entitled to vote. However, the exact mechanism for electing directors differs across companies. The most important difference is whether shares must be voted cumulatively or voted straight.

To illustrate the two different voting procedures, imagine that a corporation has two shareholders: Smith with 20 shares and Jones with 80 shares. Both want to be a director. Jones does not want Smith, however. We assume that there are a total of four directors to be elected.

The effect of **cumulative voting** is to permit minority participation.[3] If cumulative voting is permitted, the total number of votes that each shareholder may cast is determined first. This is usually calculated as the number of shares (owned or controlled) multiplied by the number of directors to be elected.

cumulative voting
A procedure in which a shareholder may cast all votes for one member of the board of directors.

With cumulative voting, the directors are elected all at once. In our example, this means that the top four vote getters will be the new directors. Individual shareholders can distribute votes however they wish.

Will Smith get a seat on the board? If we ignore the possibility of a five-way tie, then the answer is yes. Smith will cast $20 \times 4 = 80$ votes, and Jones will cast $80 \times 4 = 320$ votes. If Smith gives all his votes to himself, he is assured of a directorship. The reason is that Jones can't divide 320 votes among four candidates in such a way as to give all of them more than 80 votes, so Smith will finish fourth at worst.

In general, if there are N directors up for election, then $1/(N + 1)$ percent of the stock plus one share will guarantee you a seat. In our current example, this is $1/(4 + 1) = 20\%$ (plus one). So the more seats that are up for election at one time, the easier (and cheaper) it is to win one.

With **straight voting** the directors are elected one at a time. Each time, Smith can cast 20 votes and Jones can cast 80. As a consequence, Jones will elect all of the candidates. The only way to guarantee a seat is to own 50 percent plus one share. This also guarantees that you will win every seat, so it's really all or nothing.

straight voting
A procedure in which a shareholder may cast all votes for each member of the board of directors.

Buying the Election | **EXAMPLE 7.4**

Stock in JRJ Corporation sells for $20 per share and features cumulative voting. There are 10,000 shares outstanding. If three directors are up for election, how much does it cost to ensure yourself a seat on the board?

---

[2]The golden rule: Whoever has the gold makes the rules.

[3]By minority participation, we mean participation by shareholders with relatively small amounts of stock.

The question here is how many shares of stock it will take to get a seat. The answer is 2,501, so the cost is 2,501 × $20 = $50,020. Why 2,501? Because there is no way the remaining 7,499 votes can be divided among three people to give all of them more than 2,501 votes. For example, suppose two people receive 2,502 votes and the first two seats. A third person can receive at most 10,000 − 2,502 − 2,502 − 2,501 = 2,495, so the third seat is yours. Verify that we arrived at 2,501 using the formula described earlier.

As we've illustrated, straight voting can "freeze out" minority shareholders; that is the reason many states have mandatory cumulative voting. In states where cumulative voting is mandatory, devices have been worked out to minimize its impact.

One such device is to stagger the voting for the board of directors. With staggered elections, only a fraction of the directorships are up for election at a particular time. Thus, if only two directors are up for election at any one time, it will take 1/(2 + 1) = 33.33% of the stock plus one share to guarantee a seat.

Overall, staggering has two basic effects:

1. Staggering makes it more difficult for a minority to elect a director when there is cumulative voting because there are fewer directors to be elected at one time.

2. Staggering makes takeover attempts less likely to be successful because it makes it more difficult to vote in a majority of new directors.

We should note that staggering may serve a beneficial purpose. It provides "institutional memory," that is, continuity on the board of directors. This may be important for corporations with significant long-range plans and projects.

proxy

A grant of authority by a shareholder allowing another individual to vote that shareholder's shares.

Proxy Voting　A **proxy** is the grant of authority by a shareholder to someone else to vote the shareholder's shares. For convenience, much of the voting in large public corporations is actually done by proxy.

As we have seen, with straight voting, each share of stock has one vote. The owner of 10,000 shares has 10,000 votes. Large companies have hundreds of thousands or even millions of shareholders. Shareholders can come to the annual meeting and vote in person, or they can transfer their right to vote to another party.

Obviously, management always tries to get as many proxies as possible transferred to it. However, if shareholders are not satisfied with management, an "outside" group of shareholders can try to obtain votes via proxy. They can vote by proxy in an attempt to replace management by electing enough directors. The resulting battle is called a *proxy fight*.

Classes of Stock　Some firms have more than one class of common stock. Often, the classes are created with unequal voting rights. The Ford Motor Company, for example, has Class B common stock, which is not publicly traded (it is held by Ford family interests and trusts). This class has about 40 percent of the voting power, even though it represents less than 10 percent of the total number of shares outstanding.

There are many other cases of corporations with different classes of stock. For example, at one time, General Motors had its "GM Classic" shares (the original) and two additional classes, Class E ("GME") and Class H ("GMH"). These classes were created to help pay for two large acquisitions, Electronic Data Systems and Hughes Aircraft.

In principle, the New York Stock Exchange does not allow companies to create classes of publicly traded common stock with unequal voting rights. Exceptions (e.g., Ford) appear to have been made. In addition, many non-NYSE companies have dual classes of common stock.

A primary reason for creating dual or multiple classes of stock has to do with control of the firm. If such stock exists, management of a firm can raise equity capital by issuing nonvoting or limited-voting stock while maintaining control.

The subject of unequal voting rights is controversial in the United States, and the idea of one share, one vote has a strong following and a long history. Interestingly, however, shares with unequal voting rights are quite common in the United Kingdom and elsewhere around the world.

Other Rights   The value of a share of common stock in a corporation is directly related to the general rights of shareholders. In addition to the right to vote for directors, shareholders usually have the following rights:

1. The right to share proportionally in dividends paid.
2. The right to share proportionally in assets remaining after liabilities have been paid in a liquidation.
3. The right to vote on stockholder matters of great importance, such as a merger. Voting is usually done at the annual meeting or a special meeting.

In addition, shareholders sometimes have the right to share proportionally in any new stock sold. This is called the *preemptive right.*

Essentially, a preemptive right means that a company that wishes to sell stock must first offer it to the existing stockholders before offering it to the general public. The purpose is to give stockholders the opportunity to protect their proportionate ownership in the corporation.

Dividends   A distinctive feature of corporations is that they have shares of stock on which they are authorized by law to pay dividends to their shareholders. **Dividends** paid to shareholders represent a return on the capital directly or indirectly contributed to the corporation by the shareholders. The payment of dividends is at the discretion of the board of directors.

Some important characteristics of dividends include the following:

dividends
Payments by a corporation to shareholders, made in either cash or stock.

1. Unless a dividend is declared by the board of directors of a corporation, it is not a liability of the corporation. A corporation cannot default on an undeclared dividend. As a consequence, corporations cannot become bankrupt because of nonpayment of dividends. The amount of the dividend and even whether it is paid are decisions based on the business judgment of the board of directors.
2. The payment of dividends by the corporation is not a business expense. Dividends are not deductible for corporate tax purposes. In short, dividends are paid out of the corporation's aftertax profits.
3. Dividends received by individual shareholders are for the most part considered ordinary income by the IRS and are fully taxable. However, corporations that own stock in other corporations are permitted to exclude 70 percent of the dividend amounts they receive and are taxed only on the remaining 30 percent.[4]

Conclusion   The various common stock features and rights we have discussed are the ones most commonly found. However, as the accompanying *Reality Bytes* box illustrates, some unusual corporations have unusual shareholder rights.

---

[4]For the record, the 70 percent exclusion applies when the recipient owns less than 20 percent of the outstanding stock in a corporation. If a corporation owns more than 20 percent but less than 80 percent, the exclusion is 80 percent. If more than 80 percent is owned, the corporation can file a single "consolidated" return and the exclusion is effectively 100 percent.

reality BYTES

PLAY WITH THE PROS

If you like pro sports, then you probably think that to become an owner of a pro team would be pretty cool, but maybe not exactly in your budget. Actually, however, you can become an owner by buying stock in any one of a number of publicly traded teams. For example, the National Basketball Association's Boston Celtics went public in 1986 for about $18.50 a share. Since then, the stock, like the team, hasn't done so well (it was trading in early 2000 for as low as $9.125). Plus, if you thought you could buy enough shares of stock in the Celtics to fire coach Rick Pitino, you can forget it, because the general public owns only about 40 percent of the team's stock.

If it's National Football League teams you're interested in, you're probably out of luck. The NFL has barred its teams from issuing stock to the public. Your one hope is to somehow acquire stock in the Green Bay Packers, which was publicly owned before the rule was put in place. However, while the Pack is publicly owned, its shares cannot be bought or sold. Instead, shares can be transferred only by death of the owner or by gift of the shares to another family member. Furthermore, if you are "lucky" enough to own one of these shares, you could be fined for betting on NFL games or for criticizing NFL officials or other teams. And, the team could bill you for more money if the Packers needed cash. Still, you do get your one vote per share of stock you own.

Switching sports again, there's the National Hockey League's Florida Panthers. The owner, Wayne Huizenga, took the holding company that owns the team public in 1996. However, Huizenga retained all of the Class B shares of stock, each of which carried 10,000 votes in team matters. The publicly traded Class A shares each carry a measly one vote per share. Shares in the firm were trading at $8.50 each in early 2000, significantly below even the initial public offering price of $10 per share in 1996.

Major League Baseball's Cleveland Indians was one of the more successful publicly traded sports franchises, at least in terms of returns to investors. The team went public in 1996 with team owner Richard Jacobs selling about 51 percent of the club. However, the shares sold to the public were Class A shares, which carried a normal one vote per share. Jacobs retained the Class B shares, each of which carried a supervoting power of 10,000 votes per share. Structuring things in this way, Jacobs retained about 99 percent of the voting rights for club matters. The stock went public at $15 a share, but the team was sold in early 2000 for $323 million, or about $22.66 per share for the public owners. Thus, even though the public owners of the stock had little control, their stock turned out to be the only hit of the ones discussed so far.

There are other examples of publicly traded sports teams and organizations, but, if making serious investments is your game, you might want to avoid them. Although some have done well, in most cases, the stocks are little more than novelties. The owners typically retain voting power over the franchises, which prevents the public from exercising any degree of control over their investments. Also, most of the stocks pay no dividends. Finally, for the most part, it's difficult to make a case that the franchise managers are maximizing shareholder value. Does any of this inspire you to give a share of stock such as one of these as a gift? For a hefty fee, most can be acquired at www.oneshare.com. Otherwise, most investment advisors point out that there are more "sporting" investments elsewhere.

"Baseball Cleveland Indians' Success on Field Can't Halt Their Stock Slide," *Financial Post*, 25 September 1998, p. 51.
"How to Own Your Own Sports Team," *The Wall Street Journal*, 27 September 1996, p. B17.
"Scorecard: A Piece of the Pack," *Sports Illustrated*, 87, no. 21 (24 November 1997), p. 24.
"Know the Score There's Good Reason Not to Be a Fan of a Sports Team's Stock," *Chicago Tribune*, 11 November 1998, p. 1.
"Field of Dreams: Cleveland Indians' IPO Scores Only with True Fans," *Barron's*, 4 May 1998, p. 30.
"Pro Sports IPOS: Stocks Generally Regarded as Novelties," Dow Jones News Service, 30 March 1998.

preferred stock
Stock with dividend priority over common stock, normally with a fixed dividend rate, sometimes without voting rights.

Preferred Stock Features

Preferred stock differs from common stock because it has preference over common stock in the payment of dividends and in the distribution of corporation assets in the event of liquidation. *Preference* means only that the holders of the preferred shares must receive a dividend (in the case of an ongoing firm) before holders of common shares are entitled to anything.

Preferred stock is a form of equity from a legal and tax standpoint. It is important to note, however, that holders of preferred stock sometimes have no voting privileges.

Stated Value   Preferred shares have a stated liquidating value, usually $100 per share. The cash dividend is described in terms of dollars per share. For example, General Motors "$5 preferred" easily translates into a dividend yield of 5 percent of stated value.

Cumulative and Noncumulative Dividends   A preferred dividend is *not* like interest on a bond. The board of directors may decide not to pay the dividends on preferred shares, and their decision may have nothing to do with the current net income of the corporation.

Dividends payable on preferred stock are either *cumulative* or *noncumulative;* most are cumulative. If preferred dividends are cumulative and are not paid in a particular year, they will be carried forward as an *arrearage.* Usually, both the accumulated (past) preferred dividends and the current preferred dividends must be paid before the common shareholders can receive anything.

Unpaid preferred dividends are *not* debts of the firm. Directors elected by the common shareholders can defer preferred dividends indefinitely. However, in such cases, common shareholders must also forgo dividends. In addition, holders of preferred shares are often granted voting and other rights if preferred dividends have not been paid for some time. For example, as of summer 1996, US Airways had failed to pay dividends on one of its preferred stock issues for six quarters. As a consequence, the holders of the shares were allowed to nominate two people to represent their interests on the airline's board. Because preferred stockholders receive no interest on the accumulated dividends, some have argued that firms have an incentive to delay paying preferred dividends, but, as we have seen, this may mean sharing control with preferred stockholders.

Is Preferred Stock Really Debt?   A good case can be made that preferred stock is really debt in disguise, a kind of equity bond. Preferred shareholders are only entitled to receive a stated dividend, and, if the corporation is liquidated, preferred shareholders are only entitled to the stated value of their preferred shares. Often, preferred stocks carry credit ratings much like those of bonds. Furthermore, preferred stock is sometimes convertible into common stock, and preferred stocks are often callable.

In addition, in recent years, many new issues of preferred stock have had obligatory sinking funds. The existence of such a sinking fund effectively creates a final maturity because it means that the entire issue will ultimately be retired. For these reasons, preferred stock seems to be a lot like debt. However, for tax purposes, preferred dividends are treated like common stock dividends.

CONCEPT QUESTIONS

7.2a   What rights do stockholders have?

7.2b   What is a proxy?

7.2c   Why is preferred stock called preferred?

THE STOCK MARKETS | 7.3

Back in Chapter 1, we very briefly mentioned that shares of stock are bought and sold on various stock exchanges, the two most important of which are the New York Stock Exchange and the Nasdaq. From our earlier discussion, recall that the stock market consists of a **primary market** and a **secondary market.** In the primary, or new-issue, market, shares of stock are first brought to the market and sold to investors. In the secondary market, existing shares are traded among investors.

In the primary market, companies sell securities to raise money. We will discuss this process in detail in a later chapter. We therefore focus mainly on secondary-market activity in this section. We conclude with a discussion of how stock prices are quoted in the financial press.

Dealers and Brokers

Because most securities transactions involve dealers and brokers, it is important to understand exactly what is meant by the terms *dealer* and *broker*. A **dealer** maintains an inventory and stands ready to buy and sell at any time. In contrast, a **broker** brings buyers and sellers together, but does not maintain an inventory. Thus, when we speak of used car dealers and real estate brokers, we recognize that the used car dealer maintains an inventory, whereas the real estate broker does not.

In the securities markets, a dealer stands ready to buy securities from investors wishing to sell them and sell securities to investors wishing to buy them. Recall from our previous chapter that the price the dealer is willing to pay is called the bid price. The price at which the dealer will sell is called the ask price (sometimes called the asked, offered, or offering price). The difference between the bid and ask prices is called the spread, and it is the basic source of dealer profits.

Dealers exist in all areas of the economy, not just the stock markets. For example, your local college bookstore is probably both a primary- and a secondary-market textbook dealer. If you buy a new book, this is a primary-market transaction. If you buy a used book, this is a secondary-market transaction, and you pay the store's ask price. If you sell the book back, you receive the store's bid price, often half of the ask price. The bookstore's spread is the difference between the two prices.

In contrast, a securities broker arranges transactions between investors, matching investors wishing to buy securities with investors wishing to sell securities. The distinctive characteristic of security brokers is that they do not buy or sell securities for their own accounts. Facilitating trades by others is their business.

Organization of the NYSE

The New York Stock Exchange, or NYSE, popularly known as the Big Board, recently celebrated its bicentennial. It has occupied its current location on Wall Street since the turn of the century. Measured in terms of dollar volume of activity and the total value of shares listed, it is the largest stock market in the world.

Members   The NYSE has about 1,400 exchange **members,** who are said to own "seats" on the exchange. Collectively, the members of the exchange are its owners. Exchange seat owners can buy and sell securities on the exchange floor without paying commissions. For this and other reasons, exchange seats are valuable assets and are regularly bought and sold. In recent years, seats have sold for well over $2 million. Interestingly, prior to 1986, the highest seat price paid was $625,000, just before the 1929 market crash. Since then, the lowest seat price paid has been $55,000, in 1977.

The largest number of NYSE members are registered as **commission brokers.** The business of a commission broker is to execute customer orders to buy and sell stocks. A commission broker's primary responsibility to customers is to get the best possible prices for their orders. The exact number varies, but, usually, about 500 NYSE members are com-

---

primary market
The market in which new securities are originally sold to investors.

secondary market
The market in which previously issued securities are traded among investors.

dealer
An agent who buys and sells securities from inventory.

broker
An agent who arranges security transactions among investors.

member
The owner of a seat on the NYSE.

commission brokers
NYSE members who execute customer orders to buy and sell stock transmitted to the exchange floor.

mission brokers. NYSE commission brokers typically are employees of brokerage companies such as Merrill Lynch.

Second in number of NYSE members are **specialists,** so named because each of them acts as an assigned dealer for a small set of securities. With a few exceptions, each security listed for trading on the NYSE is assigned to a single specialist. Specialists are also called "market makers" because they are obligated to maintain a fair, orderly market for the securities assigned to them.

Specialists post bid prices and ask prices for securities assigned to them. Specialists make a market by standing ready to buy at bid prices and sell at asked prices when there is a temporary disparity between the flow of buy orders and that of sell orders for a security. In this capacity, they act as dealers for their own accounts.

Third in number of exchange members are **floor brokers.** Floor brokers are used by commission brokers who are too busy to handle certain orders themselves. Such commission brokers will delegate some orders to floor brokers for execution. Floor brokers are sometimes called $2 brokers, a name earned at a time when the standard fee for their service was only $2.

In recent years, floor brokers have become less important on the exchange floor because of the efficient **SuperDOT system** (the *DOT* stands for Designated Order Turnaround), which allows orders to be transmitted electronically directly to the specialist. SuperDOT trading now accounts for a substantial percentage of all trading on the NYSE, particularly on smaller orders.

Finally, a small number of NYSE members are **floor traders** who independently trade for their own accounts. Floor traders try to anticipate temporary price fluctuations and profit from them by buying low and selling high. In recent decades, the number of floor traders has declined substantially, suggesting that it has become increasingly difficult to profit from short-term trading on the exchange floor.

Operations   Now that we have a basic idea of how the NYSE is organized and who the major players are, we turn to the question of how trading actually takes place. Fundamentally, the business of the NYSE is to attract and process **order flow.** The term *order flow* means the flow of customer orders to buy and sell stocks. The customers of the NYSE are the millions of individual investors and tens of thousands of institutional investors who place their orders to buy and sell shares in NYSE-listed companies. The NYSE has been quite successful in attracting order flow. Currently, it is not unusual for 1 billion shares to change hands in a single day.

Floor Activity   It is quite likely that you have seen footage of the NYSE trading floor on television, or you may have visited the NYSE and viewed exchange floor activity from the visitors' gallery (it's worth the trip). Either way, you would have seen a big room, about the size of a basketball gym. This big room is called, technically, "the Big Room." There are a couple of other, smaller rooms that you normally don't see, one of which is called "the Garage" because that is literally what it was before it was taken over for trading.

On the floor of the exchange are a number of stations, each with a roughly figure-eight shape. These stations have multiple counters with numerous terminal screens above and on the sides. People operate behind and in front of the counters in relatively stationary positions.

Other people move around on the exchange floor, frequently returning to the many telephones positioned along the exchange walls. In all, you may be reminded of worker ants moving around an ant colony. It is natural to wonder, What are all those people doing down there (and why are so many wearing funny-looking coats)?

specialist
An NYSE member acting as a dealer in a small number of securities on the exchange floor; often called a market maker.

floor brokers
NYSE members who execute orders for commission brokers on a fee basis; sometimes called $2 brokers.

SuperDOT system
An electronic NYSE system allowing orders to be transmitted directly to the specialist.

floor traders
NYSE members who trade for their own accounts, trying to anticipate temporary price fluctuations.

order flow
The flow of customer orders to buy and sell securities.

specialist's post
A fixed place on the exchange floor where the specialist operates.

[handwritten marginal notes:]
Specialist in front
Clerical employees behind.

As an overview of exchange floor activity, here is a quick look at what goes on. Each of the counters at a figure-eight–shaped station is a **specialist's post.** Specialists normally operate in front of their posts to monitor and manage trading in the stocks assigned to them. Clerical employees working for the specialists operate behind the counter. Moving from the many telephones lining the walls of the exchange out to the exchange floor and back again are swarms of commission brokers, receiving telephoned customer orders, walking out to specialists' posts where the orders can be executed, and returning to confirm order executions and receive new customer orders.

To better understand activity on the NYSE trading floor, imagine yourself as a commission broker. Your phone clerk has just handed you an order to sell 2,000 shares of Wal-Mart for a customer of the brokerage company that employs you. The customer wants to sell the stock at the best possible price as soon as possible. You immediately walk (running violates exchange rules) to the specialist's post where Wal-Mart stock is traded.

As you approach the specialist's post where Wal-Mart is traded, you check the terminal screen for information on the current market price. The screen reveals that the last executed trade was at 25.63, and that the specialist is bidding 25.50 per share. You could immediately sell to the specialist at 25.50, but that would be too easy.

Instead, as the customer's representative, you are obligated to get the best possible price. It is your job to "work" the order, and your job depends on providing satisfactory order execution service. So you look around for another broker who represents a customer who wants to buy Wal-Mart stock. Luckily, you quickly find another broker at the specialist's post with an order to buy 2,000 shares. Noticing that the dealer is asking 27.75 per share, you both agree to execute your orders with each other at a price of 25.63. This price is about halfway between the specialist's bid and ask prices, and it saves each of your customers $.13 \times 2,000 = \$260$ as compared to dealing at the posted prices.

For a very actively traded stock, there may be many buyers and sellers around the specialist's post, and most of the trading will be done directly between brokers. This is called trading in the "crowd." In such cases, the specialist's responsibility is to maintain order and to make sure that all buyers and sellers receive a fair price. In other words, the specialist essentially functions as a referee.

More often, however, there will be no crowd at the specialist's post. Going back to our Wal-Mart example, suppose you are unable to quickly find another broker with an order to buy 2,000 shares. Because you have an order to sell immediately, you may have no choice but to sell to the specialist at the bid price of 25.50. In this case, the need to execute an order quickly takes priority, and the specialist provides the liquidity necessary to allow immediate order execution.

Finally, note that colored coats are worn by many of the people on the floor of the exchange. The color of the coat indicates the person's job or position. Clerks, runners, visitors, exchange officials, and so on wear particular colors to identify themselves. Also, things can get a little hectic on a busy day, with the result that good clothing doesn't last long; the cheap coats offer some protection.

Nasdaq Operations

In terms of the number of companies listed and, on many days, the number of shares traded, the Nasdaq is even bigger than the NYSE. As we mentioned in Chapter 1, the somewhat odd name is derived from the all-capitals acronym *NASDAQ,* which stands for National Association of Securities Dealers Automated Quotations system; but Nasdaq is now a name in its own right.

Introduced in 1971, the Nasdaq market is a computer network of securities dealers who disseminate timely security price quotes to Nasdaq subscribers. These dealers act as market makers for securities listed on the Nasdaq. As market makers, Nasdaq dealers post bid and asked prices at which they accept sell and buy orders, respectively. With each price quote, they also post the number of stock shares that they obligate themselves to trade at their quoted prices.

Unlike the NYSE specialist system, Nasdaq requires that there be multiple market makers for actively traded stocks. Thus, there are two key differences between the NYSE and Nasdaq: (1) Nasdaq is a computer network and has no physical location where trading takes place, and (2) Nasdaq has a multiple market maker system rather than a specialist system. Notice that all trading on the Nasdaq is done through dealers; there is no direct trading in the crowd as there may be on the NYSE.

About 5,000 companies are listed on the Nasdaq system, with an average of about a dozen market makers for each security. Traditionally, shares of stock in smaller companies were listed on the Nasdaq, and there was a tendency for companies to move from the Nasdaq to the NYSE once they became large enough. Today, however, giant companies such as Microsoft, MCI, and Intel have chosen to remain on the Nasdaq.

The Nasdaq network operates with three levels of information access. Level 1 is designed to provide registered representatives with a timely, accurate source of price quotations for their clients. Bid and asked prices available on Level 1 are typical quotes from all registered market makers for a particular security, and these prices are freely available over the Internet.

Level 2 connects market makers with brokers and other dealers and allows subscribers to view price quotes from all Nasdaq market makers. In particular, this level allows access to **inside quotes.** Inside quotes are the highest bid quotes and the lowest asked quotes for a Nasdaq-listed security. Access to inside quotes is necessary to get the best prices for member firm customers. Level 3 is for the use of market makers only. This access level allows Nasdaq dealers to enter or change their price quote information.

Stock Market Reporting

If you look through the pages of *The Wall Street Journal* (or other financial newspaper), you will find information on a large number of stocks in several different markets. Figure 7.1 reproduces a small section of the stock page for the New York Stock Exchange from Thursday, August 24, 2000. Information on most Nasdaq issues is reported in the same way. In Figure 7.1, locate the line for McDonald's. With the column headings, the line reads:

| 52 Weeks | | STOCK | SYM | DIV | YLD % | PE | VOL 100S | HI | LO | CLOSE | NET CHG |
HI	LO										
49^{56}	29^{81}	McDonalds	MCD	.20	.6	21	34133	31^{75}	30^{94}	31^{19}	-0^{13}

The first two numbers, 49^{56} and 29^{81}, are the high and low price for the last 52 weeks. As you would probably guess, the high price wasn't 49 to the power of 56; instead, the 49^{56} means $49.56 (to save space, *The Wall Street Journal* uses a superscript for the "cents" part of the quote). The .20 is the annual dividend. Because McDonald's, like most companies, pays dividends quarterly, this $.20 is actually the last quarterly dividend multiplied by 4. So, the last cash dividend paid was $.20/4 = $.05.

Jumping ahead just a bit, the Hi(gh), Lo(w), and Close figures are the high, low, and closing prices during the day. The "Net Chg" of -0^{13} tells us that the closing price of 31^{19} per share is 0^{13}, or $0.13, lower than the closing price of the day before; so we say that McDonald's was down .13 for the day.

The column marked "Yld %" gives the dividend yield based on the current dividend and the closing price. For McDonald's, this is $.20/31.19 = .6%, as shown. The next column, labeled "PE" (short for price-earnings, or PE, ratio), gives the closing price of

Level 1 I

Reg. Rep → Client
∴ Internet Quot.

Level II

inside quotes
The highest bid quotes and the lowest ask quotes for a security.

FIGURE 7.1

Sample stock-quotation from *The Wall Street Journal*

NEW YORK STOCK EXCHANGE
COMPOSITE TRANSACTIONS
Quotations as of 4 P.M. Eastern Time
Thursday, August 24, 2000

HI	LO	STOCK	SYM	DIV	%	PE	100s	HI	LO	CLOSE	CHG
33^{69}	16^{81}	Masco	MAS	.48	2.5	14	21603	19^{94}	19^{19}	19^{25}	– 0^{63}
17^{69}	10^{50}	Mascotech	MSX	.32	1.9	9	345	16^{50}	16^{44}	16^{44}	...
17^{25}	9^{50}	Masisa ADS	MYS	.32e	2.5	...	46	13^{50}	13^{19}	13^{19}	– 0^{31}
23^{75}	17^{63}	MassMulnv	MCI	1.88f	8.0	...	132	23^{50}	22^{88}	23^{38}	+ 0^{38}
11	8^{50}	MassMuPrt	MPV	.96a	8.8	...	124	11	10^{81}	10^{88}	– 0^{06}
s 60^{17}	18^{33}	MasTec	MTZ		...	19	3404	28^{94}	27^{38}	28^{69}	+ 0^{44}
49^{94}	25^{81}	Matav	MTA	.15	.5	...	772	29^{63}	28^{94}	29^{06}	– 0^{81}
15^{25}	9^{38}	MaterlSci	MSC		...	10	142	10^{63}	10^{25}	10^{25}	– 0^{25}
5^{50}	1^{44}	MatlackSys	MLK		...	dd	390	2^{44}	2^{38}	2^{38}	+ 0^{06}
303	191	MatsuElec	MC	1.14e	.4	...	34	273^{75}	270^{75}	270^{75}	– 3^{31}
24^{19}	8^{94}	Mattel	MAT	.36	3.4	dd	13635	10^{75}	10^{44}	10^{50}	– 0^{13}
4^{38}	2^{31}	Mavesa ADR	MAV	.09	2.4	10	685	3^{88}	3^{75}	3^{81}	+ 0^{06}
41^{19}	23	MayDeptStrs	MAY	.93	3.8	10	10289	25^{50}	24^{38}	24^{75}	+ 0^{38}
68^{81}	25^{94}	Maytag	MYG	.72	1.9	10	5025	38^{19}	37^{13}	37^{31}	– 0^{81}
45^{13}	28^{75}	McClatchy A	MNI	.40	1.1	19	166	35^{81}	35^{63}	35^{75}	– 0^{44}
36^{56}	23^{75}	♣McCrmkCo	MKC	.76	2.6	16	376	29^{25}	28^{63}	28^{75}	– 0^{25}
25^{81}	7^{19}	McDermInt	MDR	j	...	29	3491	7^{81}	7^{63}	7^{75}	...
49^{56}	29^{81}	McDonalds	MCD	.20	.6	21	34133	31^{75}	30^{94}	31^{19}	– 0^{13}
25^{44}	21^{63}	McDonalds sbdb		1.88	7.8	...	82	24^{13}	23^{88}	24^{13}	+ 0^{13}
25^{63}	21^{75}	McDonalds 2037		1.88	7.8	...	69	24^{25}	24	24^{25}	+ 0^{25}
63^{13}	41^{88}	McGrawH	MHP	.94	1.6	25	3791	62^{13}	59^{13}	59^{75}	+ 0^{50}
34^{94}	16	McKessnHBOC	MCK	.24	1.0	10	3946	25^{50}	25	25^{13}	– 0^{38}
25	10^{38}	McMoRanExpl	MMR		...	dd	901	10^{94}	10^{63}	10^{81}	+ 0^{13}
45^{13}	24^{38}	Mead	MEA	.68	2.7	12	8998	26^{25}	25^{31}	25^{50}	– 0^{63}
13	4^{25}	♣MdwbrkInsGp	MIG	.12	2.7	dd	76	4^{38}	4^{25}	4^{38}	+ 0^{13}
9^{25}	3^{06}	MediaArts	MDA		...	3	501	4^{13}	3^{88}	4	– 0^{13}
26	24^{38}	MedOne A TOPrS		2.33	9.2	...	5925	25^{39}	25^{36}	25^{38}	...
26^{25}	24^{50}	MedOne B TOPrS		2.38	9.3	...	34	25^{69}	25^{38}	25^{63}	– 0^{06}
26^{13}	23^{63}	MedOne C TOPrS		2.26	8.9	...	85	25^{50}	25^{38}	25^{38}	...
24^{88}	21^{50}	MediaOne X TOPrS		1.99	8.6	...	14	23^{38}	23^{25}	23^{25}	– 0^{13}
25	22^{50}	MediaOne Y TOPrS		2.06	8.4	...	8	24^{63}	24^{50}	24^{50}	– 0^{25}
n 59^{50}	36^{75}	MedOne PIES II		3.04	8.1	...	2321	37^{75}	37	37^{50}	– 0^{50}
135	78^{50}	MedOne PIES I		3.63	4.4	...	1525	82^{63}	81^{75}	81^{75}	– 1^{88}
26^{19}	10	MedAssrnce	MAI	stk	...	8	1018	12^{06}	11^{88}	12^{06}	+ 0^{06}
64^{75}	22^{75}	MedicisPhrm	MRX		...	38	3781	61^{88}	57^{81}	60	+ 2
9^{25}	1^{81}	♣MeditrCp	MT		...	dd	3068	2^{13}	2	2^{06}	...
17^{63}	9^{38}	♣MeditrCp pfA		2.25	17.4	...	122	13^{19}	12^{88}	12^{94}	– 0^{19}
11^{63}	5^{50}	MedPtnr TAPS	MDX	1.44	13.4	...	501	10^{75}	10^{63}	10^{75}	+ 0^{13}
s 57^{88}	29^{94}	Medtronic	MDT	.20f	.4	54	35372	51^{31}	49^{50}	50^{88}	+ 1^{50}
▲ 44^{44}	26^{81}	MellonFnl	MEL	.88	2.0	23	17619	44^{75}	43^{38}	43^{38}	– 0^{94}
8^{06}	6^{94}	MentIncoFd	MRF	.72	9.2	...	373	7^{88}	7^{81}	7^{81}	– 0^{06}
81^{13}	52	Merck	MRK	1.36f	1.9	27	30840	73^{31}	71^{81}	72^{38}	– 0^{06}
31^{50}	20^{94}	♣MercuryGen	MCY	.96	3.6	12	542	26^{56}	26^{44}	26^{50}	...

$31.19 divided by annual earnings per share (based on the most recent four quarters). In the jargon of Wall Street, we might say that McDonald's "sells for 21 times earnings."

The remaining column, marked "Vol 100s," tells us how many shares traded during the day (in hundreds). For example, the 34133 for McDonald's tells us that 3,413,300, or about 3.4 million, shares changed hands on this day alone. If the average price during the day was $31 or so, then the dollar volume of transactions was on the order of $31 × 3.4 million = $105.4 million worth for McDonald's stock alone. This was a somewhat slow day of trading in McDonald's shares, so this amount might be a little smaller than is typical, but it serves to illustrate how active the market can be.

CONCEPT QUESTIONS

7.3a What is the difference between a securities broker and a securities dealer?

7.3b Which is bigger, the bid price or the ask price? Why?

7.3c What are the four types of members of the New York Stock Exchange, or NYSE?

7.3d How does Nasdaq differ from the NYSE?

SUMMARY AND CONCLUSIONS

This chapter has covered the basics of stocks and stock valuation. The key points include:

1. The cash flows from owning a share of stock come in the form of future dividends. We saw that in certain special cases it is possible to calculate the present value of all the future dividends and thus come up with a value for the stock.

2. As the owner of shares of common stock in a corporation, you have various rights, including the right to vote to elect corporate directors. Voting in corporate elections can be either cumulative or straight. Most voting is actually done by proxy, and a proxy battle breaks out when competing sides try to gain enough votes to have their candidates for the board elected.

3. In addition to common stock, some corporations have issued preferred stock. The name stems from the fact that preferred stockholders must be paid first, before common stockholders can receive anything. Preferred stock has a fixed dividend.

4. The two biggest stock markets in the United States are the NYSE and the Nasdaq. We discussed the organization and operation of these two markets, and we saw how stock price information is reported in the financial press.

This chapter completes Part 4 of our book. By now, you should have a good grasp of what we mean by present value. You should also be familiar with how to calculate present values, loan payments, and so on. In Part 5, we cover capital budgeting decisions. As you will see, the techniques you have learned in Chapters 4–7 form the basis for our approach to evaluating business investment decisions.

CHAPTER REVIEW AND SELF-TEST PROBLEMS

7.1 Dividend Growth and Stock Valuation. The Brigapenski Co. has just paid a cash dividend of $2 per share. Investors require a 16 percent return from investments such as this. If the dividend is expected to grow at a steady 8 percent per year, what is the current value of the stock? What will the stock be worth in five years?

7.2 Required Returns. Suppose we observe a stock selling for $40 per share. The next dividend will be $1 per share, and you think the dividend will grow at 12 percent per year forever. What is the dividend yield in this case? The capital gains yield? The total required return?

◼ Answers to Chapter Review and Self-Test Problems

7.1 The last dividend, D_0, was $2. The dividend is expected to grow steadily at 8 percent. The required return is 16 percent. Based on the dividend growth model, we can say that the current price is:

$$P_0 = D_1/(R - g) = D_0 \times (1 + g)/(R - g)$$
$$= \$2 \times 1.08/(.16 - .08)$$
$$= \$2.16/.08$$
$$= \$27$$

We could calculate the price in five years by calculating the dividend in five years and then using the growth model again. Alternatively, we could recognize that the stock price will increase by 8 percent per year and calculate the future price directly. We'll do both. First, the dividend in five years will be:

$$D_5 = D_0 \times (1 + g)^5$$
$$= \$2 \times 1.08^5$$
$$= \$2.9387$$

The price in five years would therefore be:

$$P_5 = D_5 \times (1 + g)/(R - g)$$
$$= \$2.9387 \times 1.08/.08$$
$$= \$3.1738/.08$$
$$= \$39.67$$

Once we understand the dividend model, however, it's easier to notice that:

$$P_5 = P_0 \times (1 + g)^5$$
$$= \$27 \times 1.08^5$$
$$= \$27 \times 1.4693$$
$$= \$39.67$$

Notice that both approaches yield the same price in five years.

7.2 The dividend yield is the next dividend, D_1, divided by the current price, P_0, or $\$1/40 = 2.5\%$. The capital gains yield is the same as the dividend growth rate, 12 percent. The total required return is the sum of the two, $2.5\% + 12\% = 14.5\%$.

CRITICAL THINKING AND CONCEPTS REVIEW

1. **Stock Valuation.**   Why does the value of a share of stock depend on dividends?

2. **Stock Valuation.**   A substantial percentage of the companies listed on the NYSE and the Nasdaq don't pay dividends, but investors are nonetheless willing to buy shares in them. How is this possible given your answer to the previous question?

3. **Dividend Policy.**   Referring to the previous questions, under what circumstances might a company choose not to pay dividends?

4. **Dividend Growth Model.**   Under what two assumptions can we use the dividend growth model presented in the chapter to determine the value of a share of stock? Comment on the reasonableness of these assumptions.

5. **Common versus Preferred Stock.**   Suppose a company has a preferred stock issue and a common stock issue. Both have just paid a $2 dividend. Which do you think will have a higher price, a share of the preferred or a share of the common?

6. **Dividend Growth Model.**   Based on the dividend growth model, what are the two components of the total return on a share of stock? Which do you think is typically larger?

7. **Growth Rate.**   In the context of the dividend growth model, is it true that the growth rate in dividends and the growth rate in the price of the stock are identical?

8. **Voting Rights.**   When it comes to voting in elections, what are the differences between U.S. political democracy and U.S. corporate democracy?

9. **Corporate Ethics.**   Is it unfair or unethical for corporations to create classes of stock with unequal voting rights?

10. **Voting Rights.** Some companies, such as Reader's Digest, have created classes of stock with no voting rights at all. Why would investors buy such stock?

11. **Stock Valuation.** Evaluate the following statement: Managers should not focus on the current stock value because doing so will lead to an overemphasis on short-term profits at the expense of long-term profits.

QUESTIONS AND PROBLEMS

Basic
(Questions 1–12)

1. **Stock Values.** Aikman, Inc., just paid a dividend of $3 per share on its stock. The dividends are expected to grow at a constant rate of 5 percent per year, indefinitely. If investors require a 12 percent return on Aikman stock, what is the current price? What will the price be in three years? In 15 years?

2. **Stock Values.** The next dividend payment by BJG, Inc., will be $2 per share. The dividends are anticipated to maintain a 6 percent growth rate, forever. If BJG stock currently sells for $35.00 per share, what is the required return?

3. **Stock Values.** For the company in the previous problem, what is the dividend yield? What is the expected capital gains yield?

4. **Stock Values.** Motorheadache Corporation will pay a $4.00 per share dividend next year. The company pledges to increase its dividend by 4 percent per year, indefinitely. If you require a 13 percent return on your investment, how much will you pay for the company's stock today?

5. **Stock Valuation.** Garage, Inc., is expected to maintain a constant 5 percent growth rate in its dividends, indefinitely. If the company has a dividend yield of 7.5 percent, what is the required return on the company's stock?

6. **Stock Valuation.** Suppose you know that a company's stock currently sells for $70 per share and the required return on the stock is 18 percent. You also know that the total return on the stock is evenly divided between capital gains yield and a dividend yield. If it's the company's policy to always maintain a constant growth rate in its dividends, what is the current dividend per share?

7. **Stock Valuation.** Buckcherry Corp. pays a constant $12 dividend on its stock. The company will maintain this dividend for the next seven years and will then cease paying dividends forever. If the required return on this stock is 10 percent, what is the current share price?

8. **Valuing Preferred Stock.** Fuel, Inc., has an issue of preferred stock outstanding that pays a $4.50 dividend every year, in perpetuity. If this issue currently sells for $46 per share, what is the required return?

9. **Voting Rights.** After successfully completing your corporate finance class, you feel the next challenge ahead is to serve on the board of directors of Huckaba Enterprises. Unfortunately you will be the only individual voting for you. If Huckaba has 100,000 shares outstanding and the stock currently sells for $60, how much will it cost you to buy a seat if the company uses straight voting? Assume that Huckaba uses cumulative voting and there are four seats in the current election; how much will it cost you to buy a seat now?

10. **Growth Rates.** The stock price of Sunburn Co. is $75. Investors require a 12 percent rate of return on similar stocks. If the company plans to pay a dividend of $3.65 next year, what growth rate is expected for the company's stock price?

11. **Valuing Preferred Stock.** Rebecca, Inc., has a new issue of preferred stock it calls 20/20 preferred. The stock will pay a $20 dividend per year, but the first dividend will not be paid for 20 years. If you require a 9 percent return on this stock, how much should you pay today?

12. Stock Valuation. Creed Corp. will pay a dividend of $5.00 next year. The company has stated that it will maintain a constant growth rate of 4 percent a year forever. If you want a 15 percent rate of return, how much will you pay for the stock? What if you want a 10 percent rate of return? What does this tell you about the relationship between the required return and the stock price?

Intermediate
(Questions 13–25)

13. Nonconstant Growth. Metallica Bearings, Inc., is a young start-up company. No dividends will be paid on the stock over the next six years, because the firm needs to plow back its earnings to fuel growth. The company will then pay an $8 per share dividend in year 7 and will increase the dividend by 5 percent per year thereafter. If the required return on this stock is 16 percent, what is the current share price? Hint: The stock price in six years is $P_6 = D_7/R - g$.

14. Nonconstant Dividends. Hetfield and Ulrich, Inc., has an odd dividend policy. The company has just paid a dividend of $20 per share and has announced that it will increase the dividend by $2 per share for each of the next four years, and then never pay another dividend. If you require an 11 percent return on the company's stock, how much will you pay for a share today?

15. Nonconstant Dividends. Clapper Corporation is expected to pay the following dividends over the next four years: $10, $14, $7, and $2. Afterwards, the company pledges to maintain a constant 5 percent growth rate in dividends, forever. If the required return on the stock is 14 percent, what is the current share price? Hint: Combine the approaches in the previous two questions.

16. Supernormal Growth. Rolston Co. is growing quickly. Dividends are expected to grow at a 20 percent rate for the next three years, with the growth rate falling off to a constant 6 percent thereafter. If the required return is 14 percent and the company just paid a $2.25 dividend, what is the current share price? Hint: Calculate the first four dividends.

17. Negative Growth. Antiques 'R' Us is a mature manufacturing firm. The company just paid an $8 dividend, but management expects to reduce the payout by 10 percent per year, indefinitely. If you require a 14 percent return on this stock, what will you pay for a share today?

18. Finding the Dividend. Tubby Corporation stock currently sells for $64 per share. The market requires a 14 percent return on the firm's stock. If the company maintains a constant 5 percent growth rate in dividends, what was the most recent dividend per share paid on the stock?

19. Using Stock Quotes. You have found the following stock quote for RJW Enterprises, Inc., in the financial pages of today's newspaper. What was the closing price for this stock that appeared in *yesterday's* paper? If the company currently has one million shares of stock outstanding, what was net income for the most recent four quarters?

| 52 Weeks | | | | | Yld | | Vol | | | | Net |
Hi	Lo	Stock	Sym	Div	%	PE	100s	Hi	Lo	Close	Chg
58^{75}	29	RJW	RJW	2.00	5.0	16	8342	46^{50}	37^{25}	??	-0^{25}

20. Capital Gains versus Income. Consider four different stocks, all of which have a required return of 20 percent and a most recent dividend of $3.75 per share. Stocks W, X, and Y are expected to maintain constant growth rates in dividends for the foreseeable future of 10 percent, 0 percent, and -5 percent per year, respectively. Stock

Z is a growth stock that will increase its dividend by 20 percent for the next two years and then maintain a constant 12 percent growth rate, thereafter. What is the dividend yield for each of these four stocks? What is the expected capital gains yield? Discuss the relationship among the various returns that you find for each of these stocks.

Use the following stock quotes to answer questions 21–25.

| 52 Weeks | | | | | Yld | | Vol | | | | Net |
Hi	Lo	Stock	Sym	Div	%	PE	100s	Hi	Lo	Close	Chg
26^{18}	21^{38}	AppalchPwr pf		2.06	9.2	...	51	22^{63}	22^{25}	22^{38}	+ .13
39	23^{38}	Disney	DIS	.84	.7	71	82305	35^{50}	33^{75}	35^{25}	+ 1^{38}
61^{25}	45^{75}	DukeEngy	DUK	2.20	4.3	23	12476	53	49^{63}	51^{63}	+ 2^{25}
54^{06}	15^{38}	JC Penney	JCP	1.15	7.54	13	151882	15^{63}	15	15^{38}	+ .13
64	19	Xerox	XRX	.80	3.1	13	98903	??	??	??	− .13

21. **Preferred Stock.** The stock listed for Appalachian Power is a preferred stock, designed by the "pf." What is the required return for this stock at the current market price? What is the highest required return over the past 52 weeks? The lowest?

22. **Stock Valuation.** Investors expect that Disney will have a 6 percent growth rate in dividends for the foreseeable future. What is the required return for Disney at the current market price?

23. **Stock Valuation.** The growth rate for Duke Energy dividends is 2 percent. What is the required return for investors? Does this number seem low? Why do you think this is?

24. **Negative Growth.** The growth rate in dividends for JC Penney over the last 10 years has been −1.2 percent. If investors feel that this growth rate will continue, what is the required return for JC Penney stock? What are some potential causes of this negative growth rate in dividends?

25. **Stock Valuation.** What was the closing price for Xerox on this day? What was yesterday's closing price? If the expected growth rate for dividends is 6 percent, what is the required return?

www.mhhe.com/rwj

Spreadsheet Templates 1, 12, 13

CHAPTER

8

Net Present Value and Other Investment Criteria

AFTER STUDYING THIS CHAPTER, YOU SHOULD HAVE A GOOD UNDERSTANDING OF:

- The payback rule and some of its shortcomings

- Accounting rates of return and some of the problems with them

- The internal rate of return criterion and its strengths and weaknesses

- Why the net present value criterion is the best way to evaluate proposed investments

IN FEBRUARY 2000, Corning, Inc., announced plans to spend $750 million to expand by 50 percent its manufacturing capacity of optical fiber, a crucial component of today's high-speed communications networks. Of that, $650 million would be spent to expand its facilities in North Carolina while another $100 million would be spent to double the size of a smaller plant near Melbourne, Australia. At the time, Corning was the world's leading maker of optical fiber with about 40 percent of the market. The expansion plans were made amid a worldwide shortage of optical fiber stemming from the rapid expansion of telephone and data communications networks.

Corning's announcement offers an example of a capital budgeting decision. An expansion such as this one, with a $750 million price tag, is obviously a major undertaking, and the potential risks and rewards must be carefully weighed. In this chapter, we discuss the basic tools used in making such decisions.

This chapter introduces you to the practice of capital budgeting. Back in Chapter 1, we saw that increasing the value of the stock in a company is the goal of financial management. Thus, what we need to learn is how to tell whether a particular investment will achieve that or not. This chapter considers a variety of techniques that are actually used in practice. More importantly, it shows how many of these techniques can be misleading, and it explains why the net present value approach is the right one.

n Chapter 1, we identified the three key areas of concern to the financial manager. The first of these was the following: What long-term investments should we make? We called this the *capital budgeting decision.* In this chapter, we begin to deal with the issues that arise in answering this question.

The process of allocating, or budgeting, capital is usually more involved than just deciding on whether or not to buy a particular fixed asset. We will frequently face broader issues like whether or not we should launch a new product or enter a new market. Decisions such as these will determine the nature of a firm's operations and products for years to come, primarily because fixed asset investments are generally long-lived and not easily reversed once they are made.

For these reasons, the capital budgeting question is probably the most important issue in corporate finance. How a firm chooses to finance its operations (the capital structure question) and how a firm manages its short-term operating activities (the working capital question) are certainly issues of concern, but it is the fixed assets that define the business of the firm. Airlines, for example, are airlines because they operate airplanes, regardless of how they finance them.

Any firm possesses a huge number of possible investments. Each possible investment is an option available to the firm. Some options are valuable and some are not. The essence of successful financial management, of course, is learning to identify which are which. With this in mind, our goal in this chapter is to introduce you to the techniques used to analyze potential business ventures to decide which are worth undertaking.

We present and compare several different procedures used in practice. Our primary goal is to acquaint you with the advantages and disadvantages of the various approaches. As we shall see, the most important concept in this area is the idea of net present value. We consider this next.

8.1 | NET PRESENT VALUE

In Chapter 1, we argued that the goal of financial management is to create value for the stockholders. The financial manager must therefore examine a potential investment in light of its likely effect on the price of the firm's shares. In this section, we describe a widely used procedure for doing this, the net present value approach.

The Basic Idea

An investment is worth undertaking if it creates value for its owners. In the most general sense, we create value by identifying an investment worth more in the marketplace than it costs us to acquire. How can something be worth more than it costs? It's a case of the whole being worth more than the cost of the parts.

For example, suppose you buy a run-down house for $25,000 and spend another $25,000 on painters, plumbers, and so on to get it fixed up. Your total investment is $50,000. When the work is completed, you place the house back on the market and find that it's worth $60,000. The market value ($60,000) exceeds the cost ($50,000) by $10,000. What you have done here is to act as a manager and bring together some fixed assets (a house), some labor (plumbers, carpenters, and others), and some materials (carpeting, paint, and so on). The net result is that you have created $10,000 in value. Put another way, this $10,000 is the *value added* by management.

With our house example, it turned out *after the fact* that $10,000 in value was created. Things thus worked out very nicely. The real challenge, of course, would have been to somehow identify *ahead of time* whether or not investing the necessary $50,000 was a good idea in the first place. This is what capital budgeting is all about, namely, trying to determine whether a proposed investment or project will be worth more than it costs once it is in place.

For reasons that will be obvious in a moment, the difference between an investment's market value and its cost is called the **net present value** of the investment, abbreviated **NPV**. In other words, net present value is a measure of how much value is created or added today by undertaking an investment. Given our goal of creating value for the stockholders, the capital budgeting process can be viewed as a search for investments with positive net present values.

With our run-down house, you can probably imagine how we would go about making the capital budgeting decision. We would first look at what comparable, fixed-up properties were selling for in the market. We would then get estimates of the cost of buying a particular property, fixing it up, and bringing it to market. At this point, we have an estimated total cost and an estimated market value. If the difference is positive, then this investment is worth undertaking because it has a positive estimated net present value. There is risk, of course, because there is no guarantee that our estimates will turn out to be correct.

As our example illustrates, investment decisions are greatly simplified when there is a market for assets similar to the investment we are considering. Capital budgeting becomes much more difficult when we cannot observe the market price for at least roughly comparable investments. The reason is that we are then faced with the problem of estimating the value of an investment using only indirect market information. Unfortunately, this is precisely the situation the financial manager usually encounters. We examine this issue next.

> **net present value (NPV)**
> The difference between an investment's market value and its cost.

Estimating Net Present Value

Imagine we are thinking of starting a business to produce and sell a new product, say, organic fertilizer. We can estimate the start-up costs with reasonable accuracy because we know what we will need to buy to begin production. Would this be a good investment? Based on our discussion, you know that the answer depends on whether or not the value of the new business exceeds the cost of starting it. In other words, does this investment have a positive NPV?

This problem is much more difficult than our "fixer-upper" house example, because entire fertilizer companies are not routinely bought and sold in the marketplace; so it is essentially impossible to observe the market value of a similar investment. As a result, we must somehow estimate this value by other means.

Based on our work in Chapters 4 and 5, you may be able to guess how we will go about estimating the value of our fertilizer business. We will first try to estimate the future cash flows we expect the new business to produce. We will then apply our basic discounted cash flow procedure to estimate the present value of those cash flows. Once we have this estimate, we then estimate NPV as the difference between the present value of the future cash flows and the cost of the investment. As we mentioned in Chapter 5, this procedure is often called **discounted cash flow, or DCF, valuation**.

> **discounted cash flow (DCF) valuation**
> The process of valuing an investment by discounting its future cash flows.

To see how we might go about estimating NPV, suppose we believe the cash revenues from our fertilizer business will be $20,000 per year, assuming everything goes as expected. Cash costs (including taxes) will be $14,000 per year. We will wind down the business in eight years. The plant, property, and equipment will be worth $2,000 as salvage at that time. The project costs $30,000 to launch. We use a 15 percent discount rate on new projects such as this one. Is this a good investment? If there are 1,000 shares of stock outstanding, what will be the effect on the price per share from taking it?

From a purely mechanical perspective, we need to calculate the present value of the future cash flows at 15 percent. The net cash inflow will be $20,000 cash income less $14,000

FIGURE 8.1

Project cash flows ($000)

Time (years)	0	1	2	3	4	5	6	7	8
Initial cost	−$30								
Inflows		$20	$20	$20	$20	$20	$20	$20	$20
Outflows		− 14	− 14	− 14	− 14	− 14	− 14	− 14	− 14
Net inflow		$ 6	$ 6	$ 6	$ 6	$ 6	$ 6	$ 6	$ 6
Salvage									2
Net cash flow	−$30	$ 6	$ 6	$ 6	$ 6	$ 6	$ 6	$ 6	$ 8

in costs per year for eight years. These cash flows are illustrated in Figure 8.1. As Figure 8.1 suggests, we effectively have an eight-year annuity of $20,000 − 14,000 = $6,000 per year along with a single lump-sum inflow of $2,000 in eight years. Calculating the present value of the future cash flows thus comes down to the same type of problem we considered in Chapter 5. The total present value is:

$$\text{Present value} = \$6,000 \times (1 - 1/1.15^8)/.15 + 2,000/1.15^8$$
$$= \$6,000 \times 4.4873 + 2,000/3.0590$$
$$= \$26,924 + 654$$
$$= \$27,578$$

When we compare this to the $30,000 estimated cost, the NPV is:

$$\text{NPV} = -\$30,000 + 27,578 = -\$2,422$$

Therefore, this is *not* a good investment. Based on our estimates, taking it would *decrease* the total value of the stock by $2,422. With 1,000 shares outstanding, our best estimate of the impact of taking this project is a loss of value of $2,422/1,000 = $2.422 per share.

Our fertilizer example illustrates how NPV estimates can be used to determine whether or not an investment is desirable. From our example, notice that if the NPV is negative, the effect on share value will be unfavorable. If the NPV were positive, the effect would be favorable. As a consequence, all we need to know about a particular proposal for the purpose of making an accept-reject decision is whether the NPV is positive or negative.

Given that the goal of financial management is to increase share value, our discussion in this section leads us to the *net present value rule:*

> An investment should be accepted if the net present value is positive and rejected if it is negative.

In the unlikely event that the net present value turned out to be exactly zero, we would be indifferent between taking the investment and not taking it.

Two comments about our example are in order. First and foremost, it is not the rather mechanical process of discounting the cash flows that is important. Once we have the cash flows and the appropriate discount rate, the required calculations are fairly straightforward. The task of coming up with the cash flows and the discount rate in the first place is much more challenging. We will have much more to say about this in our next chapter. For the remainder of this chapter, we take it as given that we have estimates of the cash revenues and costs and, where needed, an appropriate discount rate.

The second thing to keep in mind about our example is that the −$2,422 NPV is an estimate. Like any estimate, it can be high or low. The only way to find out the true NPV would be to place the investment up for sale and see what we could get for it. We generally won't be doing this, so it is important that our estimates be reliable. Once again, we will have more to say about this later. For the rest of this chapter, we will assume that the estimates are accurate.

Using the NPV Rule | EXAMPLE 8.1

Suppose we are asked to decide whether or not a new consumer product should be launched. Based on projected sales and costs, we expect that the cash flows over the five-year life of the project will be $2,000 in the first two years, $4,000 in the next two, and $5,000 in the last year. It will cost about $10,000 to begin production. We use a 10 percent discount rate to evaluate new products. What should we do here?

Given the cash flows and discount rate, we can calculate the total value of the product by discounting the cash flows back to the present:

Present value = $2,000/1.1 + 2,000/1.1^2 + 4,000/1.1^3 + 4,000/1.1^4 + 5,000/1.1^5

= $1,818 + 1,653 + 3,005 + 2,732 + 3,105

= $12,313

The present value of the expected cash flows is $12,313, but the cost of getting those cash flows is only $10,000, so the NPV is $12,313 − 10,000 = $2,313. This is positive; so, based on the net present value rule, we should take on the project.

As we have seen in this section, estimating NPV is one way of assessing the profitability of a proposed investment. It is certainly not the only way profitability is assessed, and we now turn to some alternatives. As we will see, when compared to NPV, each of the ways of assessing profitability that we examine is flawed in some key way; so NPV is the preferred approach in principle, if not always in practice.

Calculating NPVs with a Spreadsheet | SPREADSHEET

strategies

Spreadsheets and financial calculators are commonly used to calculate NPVs. The procedures used by various financial calculators are too different for us to illustrate here, so we will focus on using a spreadsheet (financial calculators are covered in Appendix D). Examining the use of spreadsheets in this context also allows us to issue an important warning. Let's rework Example 8.1:

	A	B	C	D	E	F	G	H
1								
2			**Using a spreadsheet to calculate net present values**					
3								
4	From Example 8.1, the project's cost is $10,000. The cash flows are $2,000 per year for the first two years,							
5	$4,000 per year for the next two, and $5,000 in the last year. The discount rate is							
6	10 percent; what's the NPV?							
7								
8		Year	Cash flow					
9		0	−$10,000	Discount rate =		10%		
10		1	2,000					
11		2	2,000		NPV =	$2,102.72 *(wrong* answer)		
12		3	4,000		NPV =	$2,312.99 *(right* answer)		
13		4	4,000					
14		5	5,000					
15								
16	The formula entered in cell F11 is =NPV(F9,C9:C14). This gives the wrong answer because the							
17	NPV function actually calculates present values, not net present values.							
18								
19	The formula entered in cell F12 is =NPV(F9,C10:C14) + C9. This gives the right answer because the							
20	NPV function is used to calculate the present value of the cash flows and then the initial cost is							
21	subtracted to calculate the answer. Notice that we added cell C9 because it is already negative.							

In our spreadsheet, notice that we have provided two answers. By comparing the answers to that found in Example 8.1, we see that the first answer is wrong even though we used the spreadsheet's NPV formula. What happened is that the "NPV" function in our spreadsheet is actually a PV function; unfortunately, one of the original spreadsheet programs many years ago got the definition wrong, and subsequent spreadsheets have copied it! Our second answer shows how to use the formula properly.

The example here illustrates the danger of blindly using calculators or computers without understanding what is going on; we shudder to think of how many capital budgeting decisions in the real world are based on incorrect use of this particular function. We will see another example of something that can go wrong with a spreadsheet later in the chapter.

CONCEPT QUESTIONS

8.1a What is the net present value rule?

8.1b If we say an investment has an NPV of $1,000, what exactly do we mean?

8.2 | THE PAYBACK RULE

It is very common in practice to talk of the payback on a proposed investment. Loosely, the *payback* is the length of time it takes to recover our initial investment, or "get our bait back." Because this idea is widely understood and used, we will examine it in some detail.

Defining the Rule

payback period

The amount of time required for an investment to generate cash flows to recover its initial cost.

We can illustrate how to calculate a payback with an example. Figure 8.2 below shows the cash flows from a proposed investment. How many years do we have to wait until the accumulated cash flows from this investment equal or exceed the cost of the investment? As Figure 8.2 indicates, the initial investment is $50,000. After the first year, the firm has recovered $30,000, leaving $20,000 outstanding. The cash flow in the second year is exactly $20,000, so this investment "pays for itself" in exactly two years. Put another way, the **payback period** (or just payback) is two years. If we require a payback of, say, three years or less, then this investment is acceptable. This illustrates the *payback period rule:*

> Based on the payback rule, an investment is acceptable if its calculated payback period is less than some prespecified number of years.

In our example, the payback works out to be exactly two years. This won't usually happen, of course. When the numbers don't work out exactly, it is customary to work with fractional years. For example, suppose the initial investment is $60,000, and the cash flows are $20,000 in the first year and $90,000 in the second. The cash flows over the first two years are $110,000, so the project obviously pays back sometime in the second year. After the first year, the project has paid back $20,000, leaving $40,000 to be recovered. To figure out the fractional year, note that this $40,000 is $40,000/90,000 = 4/9 of the second year's cash flow. Assuming that the $90,000 cash flow is paid uniformly throughout the year, the payback would thus be 1⁴⁄₉ years.

FIGURE 8.2

Net project cash flows

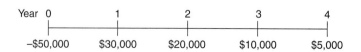

Year	0	1	2	3	4
	−$50,000	$30,000	$20,000	$10,000	$5,000

Calculating Payback | EXAMPLE 8.2

The projected cash flows from a proposed investment are:

Year	Cash Flow
1	$100
2	200
3	500

This project costs $500. What is the payback period for this investment?

The initial cost is $500. After the first two years, the cash flows total $300. After the third year, the total cash flow is $800, so the project pays back sometime between the end of Year 2 and the end of Year 3. Since the accumulated cash flows for the first two years are $300, we need to recover $200 in the third year. The third-year cash flow is $500, so we will have to wait $200/500 = .40 year to do this. The payback period is thus 2.4 years, or about two years and five months.

Now that we know how to calculate the payback period on an investment, using the payback period rule for making decisions is straightforward. A particular cutoff time is selected, say, two years, and all investment projects that have payback periods of two years or less are accepted, and all of those that pay back in more than two years are rejected.

Table 8.1 illustrates cash flows for five different projects. The figures shown as the Year 0 cash flows are the cost of the investment. We examine these to indicate some peculiarities that can, in principle, arise with payback periods.

The payback for the first project, A, is easily calculated. The sum of the cash flows for the first two years is $70, leaving us with $100 − 70 = $30 to go. Since the cash flow in the third year is $50, the payback occurs sometime in that year. When we compare the $30 we need to the $50 that will be coming in, we get $30/50 = .60; so, payback will occur 60 percent of the way into the year. The payback period is thus 2.6 years.

Project B's payback is also easy to calculate: It *never* pays back because the cash flows never total up to the original investment. Project C has a payback of exactly four years because it supplies the $130 that B is missing in Year 4. Project D is a little strange. Because of the negative cash flow in Year 3, you can easily verify that it has two different payback periods, two years and four years. Which of these is correct? Both of them; the way the payback period is calculated doesn't guarantee a single answer. Finally, Project E is obviously unrealistic, but it does pay back in six months, thereby illustrating the point that a rapid payback does not guarantee a good investment.

Year	A	B	C	D	E
0	−$100	−$200	−$200	−$200	−$ 50
1	30	40	40	100	100
2	40	20	20	100	− 50,000,000
3	50	10	10	−200	
4	60		130	200	

TABLE 8.1

Expected cash flows for Projects A through E

Year	Long	Short
0	−$250	−$250
1	100	100
2	100	200
3	100	0
4	100	0

Analyzing the Rule

When compared to the NPV rule, the payback period rule has some rather severe short-comings. First, the payback period is calculated by simply adding up the future cash flows. There is no discounting involved, so the time value of money is completely ignored. The payback rule also fails to consider risk differences. The payback would be calculated the same way for both very risky and very safe projects.

Perhaps the biggest problem with the payback period rule is coming up with the right cutoff period, because we don't really have an objective basis for choosing a particular number. Put another way, there is no economic rationale for looking at payback in the first place, so we have no guide as to how to pick the cutoff. As a result, we end up using a number that is arbitrarily chosen.

Suppose we have somehow decided on an appropriate payback period, say two years or less. As we have seen, the payback period rule ignores the time value of money for the first two years. More seriously, cash flows after the second year are ignored entirely. To see this, consider the two investments, Long and Short, in Table 8.2. Both projects cost $250. Based on our discussion, the payback on Long is $2 + \$50/100 = 2.5$ years, and the payback on Short is $1 + \$150/200 = 1.75$ years. With a cutoff of two years, Short is acceptable and Long is not.

Is the payback period rule giving us the right decisions? Maybe not. Suppose again that we require a 15 percent return on this type of investment. We can calculate the NPV for these two investments as:

$$\text{NPV(Short)} = -\$250 + 100/1.15 + 200/1.15^2 = -\$11.81$$
$$\text{NPV(Long)} = -\$250 + 100 \times (1 - 1/1.15^4)/.15 = \$35.50$$

Now we have a problem. The NPV of the shorter-term investment is actually negative, meaning that taking it diminishes the value of the shareholders' equity. The opposite is true for the longer-term investment—it increases share value.

Our example illustrates two primary shortcomings of the payback period rule. First, by ignoring time value, we may be led to take investments (like Short) that actually are worth less than they cost. Second, by ignoring cash flows beyond the cutoff, we may be led to reject profitable long-term investments (like Long). More generally, using a payback period rule will tend to bias us towards shorter-term investments.

Redeeming Qualities of the Rule

Despite its shortcomings, the payback period rule is often used by large and sophisticated companies when they are making relatively minor decisions. There are several reasons for this. The primary reason is that many decisions simply do not warrant detailed analysis because the cost of the analysis would exceed the possible loss from a mistake. As a practical matter, an investment that pays back rapidly and has benefits extending beyond the cutoff period probably has a positive NPV.

Small investment decisions are made by the hundreds every day in large organizations. Moreover, they are made at all levels. As a result, it would not be uncommon for a corporation to require, for example, a two-year payback on all investments of less than $10,000. Investments larger than this are subjected to greater scrutiny. The requirement of a two-year payback is not perfect for reasons we have seen, but it does exercise some control over expenditures and thus has the effect of limiting possible losses.

In addition to its simplicity, the payback rule has two other positive features. First, because it is biased towards short-term projects, it is biased towards liquidity. In other words, a payback rule tends to favor investments that free up cash for other uses more quickly. This could be very important for a small business; it would be less so for a large corporation. Second, the cash flows that are expected to occur later in a project's life are probably more uncertain. Arguably, a payback period rule adjusts for the extra riskiness of later cash flows, but it does so in a rather draconian fashion—by ignoring them altogether.

We should note here that some of the apparent simplicity of the payback rule is an illusion. The reason is that we still must come up with the cash flows first, and, as we discuss above, this is not at all easy to do. Thus, it would probably be more accurate to say that the *concept* of a payback period is both intuitive and easy to understand.

Summary of the Rule

To summarize, the payback period is a kind of "break-even" measure. Because time value is ignored, you can think of the payback period as the length of time it takes to break even in an accounting sense, but not in an economic sense. The biggest drawback to the payback period rule is that it doesn't ask the right question. The relevant issue is the impact an investment will have on the value of our stock, not how long it takes to recover the initial investment.

Nevertheless, because it is so simple, companies often use it as a screen for dealing with the myriad of minor investment decisions they have to make. There is certainly nothing wrong with this practice. Like any simple rule of thumb, there will be some errors in using it, but it wouldn't have survived all this time if it weren't useful. Now that you understand the rule, you can be on the alert for those circumstances under which it might lead to problems. To help you remember, the following table lists the pros and cons of the payback period rule.

Advantages and Disadvantages of the Payback Period Rule	
Advantages	**Disadvantages**
1. Easy to understand.	1. Ignores the time value of money.
2. Adjusts for uncertainty of later cash flows.	2. Requires an arbitrary cutoff point.
	3. Ignores cash flows beyond the cutoff date.
3. Biased towards liquidity.	4. Biased against long-term projects, such as research and development, and new projects.

CONCEPT QUESTIONS

8.2a In words, what is the payback period? The payback period rule?

8.2b Why do we say that the payback period is, in a sense, an accounting break-even measure?

8.3 | THE AVERAGE ACCOUNTING RETURN

average accounting return (AAR)

An investment's average net income divided by its average book value.

Another attractive, but flawed, approach to making capital budgeting decisions involves the **average accounting return (AAR)**. There are many different definitions of the AAR. However, in one form or another, the AAR is always defined as:

$$\frac{\text{Some measure of average accounting profit}}{\text{Some measure of average accounting value}}$$

The specific definition we will use is:

$$\frac{\text{Average net income}}{\text{Average book value}}$$

To see how we might calculate this number, suppose we are deciding whether or not to open a store in a new shopping mall. The required investment in improvements is $500,000. The store would have a five-year life because everything reverts to the mall owners after that time. The required investment would be 100 percent depreciated (straight-line) over five years, so the depreciation would be $500,000/5 = $100,000 per year. The tax rate is 25 percent. Table 8.3 contains the projected revenues and expenses. Based on these figures, net income in each year is also shown.

To calculate the average book value for this investment, we note that we started out with a book value of $500,000 (the initial cost) and ended up at $0. The average book value during the life of the investment is thus ($500,000 + 0)/2 = $250,000. As long as we use straight-line depreciation and a zero salvage value, the average investment will always be one-half of the initial investment.[1]

Looking at Table 8.3, we see that net income is $100,000 in the first year, $150,000 in the second year, $50,000 in the third year, $0 in Year 4, and −$50,000 in Year 5. The average net income, then, is:

$$[\$100,000 + 150,000 + 50,000 + 0 + (-50,000)]/5 = \$50,000$$

The average accounting return is:

$$\text{AAR} = \frac{\text{Average net income}}{\text{Average book value}} = \frac{\$50,000}{250,000} = 20\%$$

If the firm has a target AAR less than 20 percent, then this investment is acceptable; otherwise it is not. The *average accounting return rule* is thus:

> Based on the average accounting return rule, a project is acceptable if its average accounting return exceeds a target average accounting return.

As we will see next, this rule has a number of problems.

You should recognize the chief drawback to the AAR immediately. Above all else, the AAR is not a rate of return in any meaningful economic sense. Instead, it is the ratio of two accounting numbers, and it is not comparable to the returns offered, for example, in financial markets.[2]

---

[1]We could, of course, calculate the average of the six book values directly. In thousands, we would have ($500 + 400 + 300 + 200 + 100 + 0)/6 = $250.

[2]The AAR is closely related to the return on assets, or ROA, discussed in Chapter 3. In practice, the AAR is sometimes computed by first calculating the ROA for each year, and then averaging the results. This produces a number that is similar, but not identical, to the one we computed.

	Year 1	Year 2	Year 3	Year 4	Year 5
Revenue	$433,333	$450,000	$266,667	$200,000	$133,333
Expenses	200,000	150,000	100,000	100,000	100,000
Earnings before depreciation	$233,333	$300,000	$166,667	$100,000	$ 33,333
Depreciation	100,000	100,000	100,000	100,000	100,000
Earnings before taxes	$133,333	$200,000	$ 66,667	$ 0	−$ 66,667
Taxes (25%)	33,333	50,000	16,667	0	− 16,667
Net income	$100,000	$150,000	$ 50,000	$ 0	−$ 50,000

TABLE 8.3

Projected yearly revenue and costs for average accounting return

$$\text{Average net income} = \frac{(\$100,000 + 150,000 + 50,000 + 0 - 50,000)}{5} = \$50,000$$

$$\text{Average book value} = \frac{\$500,000 + 0}{2} = \$250,000$$

One of the reasons the AAR is not a true rate of return is that it ignores time value. When we average figures that occur at different times, we are treating the near future and the more distant future the same way. There was no discounting involved when we computed the average net income, for example.

The second problem with the AAR is similar to the problem we had with the payback period rule concerning the lack of an objective cutoff period. Since a calculated AAR is really not comparable to a market return, the target AAR must somehow be specified. There is no generally agreed-upon way to do this. One way of doing it is to calculate the AAR for the firm as a whole and use this as a benchmark, but there are lots of other ways as well.

The third, and perhaps worst, flaw in the AAR is that it doesn't even look at the right things. Instead of cash flow and market value, it uses net income and book value. These are both poor substitutes. As a result, an AAR doesn't tell us what the effect on share price will be from taking an investment, so it doesn't tell us what we really want to know.

Does the AAR have any redeeming features? About the only one is that it almost always can be computed. The reason is that accounting information will almost always be available, both for the project under consideration and for the firm as a whole. We hasten to add that once the accounting information is available, we can always convert it to cash flows, so even this is not a particularly important fact. The AAR is summarized in the table below.

Advantages and Disadvantages of the Average Accounting Return	
Advantages	**Disadvantages**
1. Easy to calculate.	1. Not a true rate of return; time value of money is ignored.
2. Needed information will usually be available.	2. Uses an arbitrary benchmark cutoff rate.
	3. Based on accounting net income and book values, not cash flows and market values.

CONCEPT QUESTIONS

8.3a What is an average accounting rate of return, or AAR?

8.3b What are the weaknesses of the AAR rule?

8.4 | THE INTERNAL RATE OF RETURN

We now come to the most important alternative to NPV, the **internal rate of return,**. universally known as the **IRR.** As we will see, the IRR is closely related to NPV. With the IRR, we try to find a single rate of return that summarizes the merits of a project. Furthermore, we want this rate to be an "internal" rate in the sense that it only depends on the cash flows of a particular investment, not on rates offered elsewhere.

To illustrate the idea behind the IRR, consider a project that costs $100 today and pays $110 in one year. Suppose you were asked, "What is the return on this investment?" What would you say? It seems both natural and obvious to say that the return is 10 percent because, for every dollar we put in, we get $1.10 back. In fact, as we will see in a moment, 10 percent is the internal rate of return, or IRR, on this investment.

Is this project with its 10 percent IRR a good investment? Once again, it would seem apparent that this is a good investment only if our required return is less than 10 percent. This intuition is also correct and illustrates the *IRR rule:*

internal rate of return (IRR)

The discount rate that makes the NPV of an investment zero.

> Based on the IRR rule, an investment is acceptable if the IRR exceeds the required return. It should be rejected otherwise.

Imagine that we wanted to calculate the NPV for our simple investment. At a discount rate of R, the NPV is:

$$NPV = -\$100 + 110/(1 + R)$$

Now, suppose we didn't know the discount rate. This presents a problem, but we could still ask how high the discount rate would have to be before this project was unacceptable. We know that we are indifferent between taking and not taking this investment when its NPV is just equal to zero. In other words, this investment is *economically* a break-even proposition when the NPV is zero because value is neither created nor destroyed. To find the break-even discount rate, we set NPV equal to zero and solve for R:

$$NPV = 0 = -\$100 + 110/(1 + R)$$
$$\$100 = \$110/(1 + R)$$
$$1 + R = \$110/100 = 1.10$$
$$R = 10\%$$

This 10 percent is what we already have called the return on this investment. What we have now illustrated is that the internal rate of return on an investment (or just "return" for short) is the discount rate that makes the NPV equal to zero. This is an important observation, so it bears repeating:

> The IRR on an investment is the required return that results in a zero NPV when it is used as the discount rate.

The fact that the IRR is simply the discount rate that makes the NPV equal to zero is important because it tells us how to calculate the returns on more complicated investments. As we have seen, finding the IRR turns out to be relatively easy for a single-period investment. However, suppose you were now looking at an investment with the cash flows shown in Figure 8.3. As illustrated, this investment costs $100 and has a cash flow of $60 per year for two years, so it's only slightly more complicated than our single-period example. However, if

Year 0   1   2

         −$100   +$60   +$60

FIGURE 8.3

Project cash flows

Discount Rate	NPV
0%	$20.00
5	11.56
10	4.13
15	− 2.46
20	− 8.33

TABLE 8.4

NPV at different
discount rates

you were asked for the return on this investment, what would you say? There doesn't seem to be any obvious answer (at least to us). However, based on what we now know, we can set the NPV equal to zero and solve for the discount rate:

$$NPV = 0 = -\$100 + 60/(1 + IRR) + 60/(1 + IRR)^2$$

Unfortunately, the only way to find the IRR in general is by trial and error, either by hand or by calculator. This is precisely the same problem that came up in Chapter 5 when we found the unknown rate for an annuity and in Chapter 6 when we found the yield to maturity on a bond. In fact, we now see that, in both of those cases, we were finding an IRR.

In this particular case, the cash flows form a two-period, $60 annuity. To find the unknown rate, we can try some different rates until we get the answer. If we were to start with a 0 percent rate, the NPV would obviously be $120 − 100 = $20. At a 10 percent discount rate, we would have:

$$NPV = -\$100 + 60/1.1 + 60/1.1^2 = \$4.13$$

Now, we're getting close. We can summarize these and some other possibilities as shown in Table 8.4. From our calculations, the NPV appears to be zero between 10 percent and 15 percent, so the IRR is somewhere in that range. With a little more effort, we can find that the IRR is about 13.1 percent. So, if our required return is less than 13.1 percent, we would take this investment. If our required return exceeds 13.1 percent, we would reject it.

By now, you have probably noticed that the IRR rule and the NPV rule appear to be quite similar. In fact, the IRR is sometimes simply called the *discounted cash flow,* or *DCF, return.* The easiest way to illustrate the relationship between NPV and IRR is to plot the numbers we calculated in Table 8.4. We put the different NPVs on the vertical axis, or y-axis, and the discount rates on the horizontal axis, or x-axis. If we had a very large number of points, the resulting picture would be a smooth curve called a **net present value profile**. Figure 8.4 illustrates the NPV profile for this project. Beginning with a 0 percent discount rate, we have $20 plotted directly on the y-axis. As the discount rate increases, the NPV declines smoothly. Where will the curve cut through the x-axis? This will occur where the NPV is just equal to zero, so it will happen right at the IRR of 13.1 percent.

In our example, the NPV rule and the IRR rule lead to identical accept-reject decisions. We will accept an investment using the IRR rule if the required return is less than 13.1 percent. As Figure 8.4 illustrates, however, the NPV is positive at any discount rate less than 13.1 percent, so we would accept the investment using the NPV rule as well. The two rules are equivalent in this case.

net present value profile
A graphical representation of the relationship between an investment's NPVs and various discount rates.

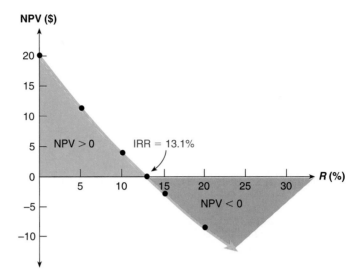

FIGURE 8.4

An NPV profile

EXAMPLE 8.3 | Calculating the IRR

A project has a total up-front cost of $435.44. The cash flows are $100 in the first year, $200 in the second year, and $300 in the third year. What's the IRR? If we require an 18 percent return, should we take this investment?

We'll describe the NPV profile and find the IRR by calculating some NPVs at different discount rates. You should check our answers for practice. Beginning with 0 percent, we have:

Discount Rate	NPV
0%	$164.56
5	100.36
10	46.15
15	.00
20	− 39.61

The NPV is zero at 15 percent, so 15 percent is the IRR. If we require an 18 percent return, then we should not take the investment. The reason is that the NPV is negative at 18 percent (verify that it is −$24.47). The IRR rule tells us the same thing in this case. We shouldn't take this investment because its 15 percent return is below our required 18 percent return.

At this point, you may be wondering whether the IRR and NPV rules always lead to identical decisions. The answer is yes as long as two very important conditions are met. First, the project's cash flows must be *conventional,* meaning that the first cash flow (the initial investment) is negative and all the rest are positive. Second, the project must be *independent,* meaning that the decision to accept or reject this project does not affect the decision to accept or reject any other. The first of these conditions is typically met, but the second often is not. In any case, when one or both of these conditions are not met, problems can arise. We discuss some of these in a moment.

Calculating IRRs with a Spreadsheet | SPREADSHEET

Because IRRs are so tedious to calculate by hand, financial calculators and, especially, spreadsheets are generally used. The procedures used by various financial calculators are too different for us to illustrate here, so we will focus on using a spreadsheet (financial calculators are covered in Appendix D). As the following example illustrates, using a spreadsheet is very easy:

	A	B	C	D	E	F	G	H
1								
2		Using a spreadsheet to calculate internal rates of return						
3								
4	Suppose we have a four-year project that costs $500. The cash flows over the four-year life will be $100,							
5	$200, $300, and $400. What is the IRR?							
6								
7		Year	Cash flow					
8		0	−$500					
9		1	100		IRR =	27.3%		
10		2	200					
11		3	300					
12		4	400					
13								
14								
15	The formula entered in cell F9 is =IRR(C8:C12). Notice that the Year 0 cash flow has a negative							
16	sign representing the initial cost of the project.							
17								

Problems with the IRR

The problems with the IRR come about when the cash flows are not conventional or when we are trying to compare two or more investments to see which is best. In the first case, surprisingly, the simple question "What's the return?" can become very difficult to answer. In the second case, the IRR can be a misleading guide.

Nonconventional Cash Flows

Suppose we have a strip-mining project that requires a $60 investment. Our cash flow in the first year will be $155. In the second year, the mine is depleted, but we have to spend $100 to restore the terrain. As Figure 8.5 illustrates, both the first and third cash flows are negative.

To find the IRR on this project, we can calculate the NPV at various rates:

Discount Rate	NPV
0%	−$5.00
10	− 1.74
20	− .28
30	.06
40	− .31

The NPV appears to be behaving in a very peculiar fashion here. First, as the discount rate increases from 0 percent to 30 percent, the NPV starts out negative and

Project cash flows

NPV profile

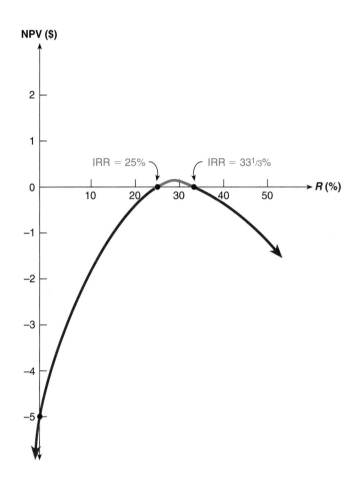

becomes positive. This seems backward because the NPV is rising as the discount rate rises. It then starts getting smaller and becomes negative again. What's the IRR? To find out, we draw the NPV profile in Figure 8.6.

In Figure 8.6, notice that the NPV is zero when the discount rate is 25 percent, so this is the IRR. Or is it? The NPV is also zero at 33⅓ percent. Which of these is correct? The answer is both or neither; more precisely, there is no unambiguously correct answer. This is the **multiple rates of return** problem. Many financial computer packages aren't aware of this problem and just report the first IRR that is found. Others report only the smallest positive IRR, even though this answer is no better than any other. For example, if you enter this problem in our spreadsheet above, it will simply report that the IRR is 25 percent.

In our current example, the IRR rule breaks down completely. Suppose our required return were 10 percent. Should we take this investment? Both IRRs are greater than 10 percent, so, by the IRR rule, maybe we should. However, as Figure 8.6 shows, the NPV is negative at any discount rate less than 25 percent, so this is not a good investment. When should we take it? Looking at Figure 8.6 one last time, we see that the NPV is positive only if our required return is between 25 percent and 33⅓ percent.

The moral of the story is that when the cash flows aren't conventional, strange things can start to happen to the IRR. This is not anything to get upset about, however, because the

multiple rates of return

The possiblity that more than one discount rate makes the NPV of an investment zero.

NPV rule, as always, works just fine. This illustrates that, oddly enough, the obvious question "What's the rate of return?" may not always have a good answer.

What's the IRR? | **EXAMPLE 8.4**

You are looking at an investment that requires you to invest $51 today. You'll get $100 in one year, but you must pay out $50 in two years. What is the IRR on this investment?

You're on the alert now to the nonconventional cash flow problem, so you probably wouldn't be surprised to see more than one IRR. However, if you start looking for an IRR by trial and error, it will take you a long time. The reason is that there is no IRR. The NPV is negative at every discount rate, so we shouldn't take this investment under any circumstances. What's the return on this investment? Your guess is as good as ours.

Mutually Exclusive Investments   Even if there is a single IRR, another problem can arise concerning **mutually exclusive investment decisions**. If two investments, X and Y, are mutually exclusive, then taking one of them means that we cannot take the other. Two projects that are not mutually exclusive are said to be independent. For example, if we own one corner lot, then we can build a gas station or an apartment building, but not both. These are mutually exclusive alternatives.

mutually exclusive investment decisions

A situation where taking one investment prevents the taking of another.

Thus far, we have asked whether or not a given investment is worth undertaking. There is a related question, however, that comes up very often: Given two or more mutually exclusive investments, which one is the best? The answer is simple enough: The best one is the one with the largest NPV. Can we also say that the best one has the highest return? As we show, the answer is no.

To illustrate the problem with the IRR rule and mutually exclusive investments, consider the cash flows from the following two mutually exclusive investments:

Year	Investment A	Investment B
0	−$100	−$100
1	50	20
2	40	40
3	40	50
4	30	60

The IRR for A is 24 percent, and the IRR for B is 21 percent. Since these investments are mutually exclusive, we can only take one of them. Simple intuition suggests that Investment A is better because of its higher return. Unfortunately, simple intuition is not always correct.

To see why Investment A is not necessarily the better of the two investments, we've calculated the NPV of these investments for different required returns:

Discount rate	NPV (A)	NPV (B)
0 %	$60.00	$70.00
5	43.13	47.88
10	29.06	29.79
15	17.18	14.82
20	7.06	2.31
25	− 1.63	− 8.22

FIGURE 8.7

NPV profiles for
mutually exclusive
investments

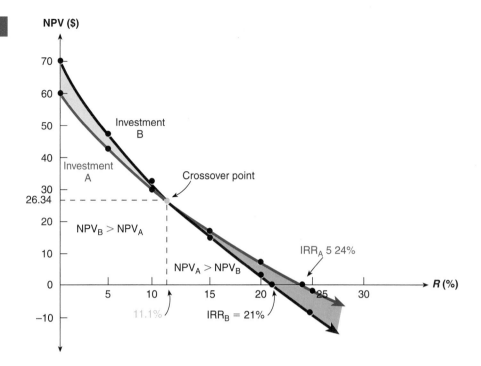

The IRR for A (24 percent) is larger than the IRR for B (21 percent). However, if you compare the NPVs, you'll see that which investment has the higher NPV depends on our required return. B has greater total cash flow, but it pays back more slowly than A. As a result, it has a higher NPV at lower discount rates.

In our example, the NPV and IRR rankings conflict for some discount rates. If our required return is 10 percent, for instance, then B has the higher NPV and is thus the better of the two even though A has the higher return. If our required return is 15 percent, then there is no ranking conflict: A is better.

The conflict between the IRR and NPV for mutually exclusive investments can be illustrated by plotting their NPV profiles as we have done in Figure 8.7. In Figure 8.7, notice that the NPV profiles cross at about 11 percent. Notice also that at any discount rate less than 11.1 percent, the NPV for B is higher. In this range, taking B benefits us more than taking A, even though A's IRR is higher. At any rate greater than 11.1 percent, Investment A has the greater NPV.

This example illustrates that whenever we have mutually exclusive projects, we shouldn't rank them based on their returns. More generally, anytime we are comparing investments to determine which is best, IRRs can be misleading. Instead, we need to look at the relative NPVs to avoid the possibility of choosing incorrectly. Remember, we're ultimately interested in creating value for the shareholders, so the option with the higher NPV is preferred, regardless of the relative returns.

If this seems counterintuitive, think of it this way. Suppose you have two investments. One has a 10 percent return and makes you $100 richer immediately. The other has a 20 percent return and makes you $50 richer immediately. Which one do you like better? We would rather have $100 than $50, regardless of the returns, so we like the first one better.

Redeeming Qualities of the IRR

Despite its flaws, the IRR is very popular in practice, more so than even the NPV. It probably survives because it fills a need that the NPV does not. In analyzing investments, people in general, and financial analysts in particular, seem to prefer talking about rates of return rather than dollar values.

In a similar vein, the IRR also appears to provide a simple way of communicating information about a proposal. One manager might say to another, "Remodeling the clerical wing has a 20 percent return." This may somehow be simpler than saying, "At a 10 percent discount rate, the net present value is $4,000."

Finally, under certain circumstances, the IRR may have a practical advantage over the NPV. We can't estimate the NPV unless we know the appropriate discount rate, but we can still estimate the IRR. Suppose we didn't know the required return on an investment, but we found, for example, that it had a 40 percent return. We would probably be inclined to take it since it is very unlikely that the required return would be that high. The advantages and disadvantages of the IRR are summarized below.

Advantages and Disadvantages of the Internal Rate of Return

Advantages	Disadvantages
1. Closely related to NPV, often leading to identical decisions.	1. May result in multiple answers with nonconventional cash flows.
2. Easy to understand and communicate.	2. May lead to incorrect decisions in comparisons of mutually exclusive investments.

CONCEPT QUESTIONS

8.4a Under what circumstances will the IRR and NPV rules lead to the same accept-reject decisions? When might they conflict?

8.4b Is it generally true that an advantage of the IRR rule over the NPV rule is that we don't need to know the required return to use the IRR rule?

THE PROFITABILITY INDEX | 8.5

Another method used to evaluate projects involves the **profitability index (PI),** or benefit-cost ratio. This index is defined as the present value of the future cash flows divided by the initial investment. So, if a project costs $200 and the present value of its future cash flows is $220, the profitability index value would be $220/200 = 1.10. Notice that the NPV for this investment is $20, so it is a desirable investment.

More generally, if a project has a positive NPV, then the present value of the future cash flows must be bigger than the initial investment. The profitability index would thus be bigger than 1.00 for a positive NPV investment and less than 1.00 for a negative NPV investment.

How do we interpret the profitability index? In our example, the PI was 1.10. This tells us that, per dollar invested, $1.10 in value or $.10 in NPV results. The profitability index thus measures "bang for the buck," that is, the value created per dollar invested. For this reason, it is often proposed as a measure of performance for government or other not-for-profit investments. Also, when capital is scarce, it may make sense to allocate it to those projects with the highest PIs.

The PI is obviously very similar to the NPV. However, consider an investment that costs $5 and has a $10 present value and an investment that costs $100 with a $150 present value. The first of these investments has an NPV of $5 and a PI of 2. The second has an NPV of $50 and a PI of 1.50. If these are mutually exclusive investments, then the second one is preferred even though it has a lower PI. This ranking problem is very similar to the

profitability index (PI)

The present value of an investment's future cash flows divided by its initial cost. Also, benefit-cost ratio.

IRR ranking problem we saw in the previous section. In all, there seems to be little reason to rely on the PI instead of the NPV. Our discussion of the PI is summarized below.

Advantages and Disadvantages of the Profitability Index

Advantages	Disadvantages
1. Closely related to NPV, generally leading to identical decisions.	1. May lead to incorrect decisions in comparisons of mutually exclusive investments.
2. Easy to understand and communicate.	
3. May be useful when available investment funds are limited.	

CONCEPT QUESTIONS

8.5a What does the profitability index measure?

8.5b How would you state the profitability index rule?

8.6 | THE PRACTICE OF CAPITAL BUDGETING

Given that NPV seems to be telling us directly what we want to know, you might be wondering why there are so many other procedures and why alternative procedures are commonly used. Recall that we are trying to make an investment decision and that we are frequently operating under considerable uncertainty about the future. We can only *estimate* the NPV of an investment in this case. The resulting estimate can be very "soft," meaning that the true NPV might be quite different.

Because the true NPV is unknown, the astute financial manager seeks clues to assess whether the estimated NPV is reliable. For this reason, firms would typically use multiple criteria for evaluating a proposal. For example, suppose we have an investment with a positive estimated NPV. Based on our experience with other projects, this one appears to have a short payback and a very high AAR. In this case, the different indicators seem to agree that it's "all systems go." Put another way, the payback and the AAR are consistent with the conclusion that the NPV is positive.

On the other hand, suppose we had a positive estimated NPV, a long payback, and a low AAR. This could still be a good investment, but it looks like we need to be much more careful in making the decision since we are getting conflicting signals. If the estimated NPV is based on projections in which we have little confidence, then further analysis is probably in order. We will consider how to go about this analysis in more detail in the next chapter.

There have been a number of surveys conducted asking firms what types of investment criteria they actually use. Table 8.5 summarizes the results of several of these. The first part of the table is a historical comparison looking at the primary capital budgeting techniques used by large firms through time. In 1959, only 19 percent of the firms surveyed used either IRR or NPV, and 68 percent used either payback periods or accounting returns. It is clear that, by the 1980s, IRR and NPV had become the dominant criteria.

Capital budgeting techniques in practice **TABLE 8.5**

A. Historical Comparison of the Primary Use of Various Capital Budgeting Techniques

	1959	1964	1970	1975	1977	1979	1981
Payback period	34%	24%	12%	15%	9%	10%	5.0%
Average accounting return (AAR)	34	30	26	10	25	14	10.7
Internal rate of return (IRR)	19	38	57	37	54	60	65.3
Net present value (NPV)	—	—	—	26	10	14	16.5
IRR or NPV	19	38	57	63	64	74	81.8

B. Percentage of CFOs Who Always or Almost Always Use a Given Technique in 1999

Capital Budgeting Technique	Percentage Always or Almost Always Use	Average Score Scale is 4 (always) to 0 (never)		
		Overall	Large Firms	Small Firms
Internal rate of return	76%	3.09	3.41	2.87
Net present value	75	3.08	3.42	2.83
Payback period	57	2.53	2.25	2.72
Discounted payback period	29	1.56	1.55	1.58
Accounting rate of return	20	1.34	1.25	1.41
Profitability index	12	0.83	0.75	0.88

Sources: J. R. Graham and C. R. Harvey, "The Theory and Practice of Corporate Finance: Evidence from the Field," *Journal of Financial Economics,* forthcoming. J. S. Moore and A. K. Reichert, "An Analysis of the Financial Management Techniques Currently Employed by Large U.S. Corporations," *Journal of Business Finance and Accounting,* Winter 1983, pp. 623–45; M. T. Stanley and S. R. Block, "A Survey of Multinational Capital Budgeting," *The Financial Review,* March 1984, pp. 36–51.

Panel B of Table 8.5 summarizes the results of a 1999 survey of chief financial officers (CFOs) at both large and small firms in the United States. A total of 392 CFOs responded. What is shown is the percentage of CFOs who always or almost always use the various capital budgeting techniques we described in this chapter. Not surprisingly, IRR and NPV are the two most widely used techniques, particularly at larger firms. However, over half of the respondents always, or almost always, use the payback criterion as well. In fact, among smaller firms, payback is used just about as much as NPV and IRR. Less commonly used are discounted payback, accounting rates of return, and the profitability index.

CONCEPT QUESTIONS

8.6a What are the most commonly used capital budgeting procedures?

8.6b Since NPV is conceptually the best tool for capital budgeting, why do you think multiple measures are used in practice?

TABLE 8.6   Summary of investment criteria

I. **Discounted cash flow criteria**

A. *Net present value (NPV).* The NPV of an investment is the difference between its market value and its cost. The NPV rule is to take a project if its NPV is positive. NPV is frequently estimated by calculating the present value of the future cash flows (to estimate market value) and then subtracting the cost. NPV has no serious flaws; it is the preferred decision criterion.

B. *Internal rate of return (IRR).* The IRR is the discount rate that makes the estimated NPV of an investment equal to zero; it is sometimes called the *discounted cash flow (DCF) return.* The IRR rule is to take a project when its IRR exceeds the required return. IRR is closely related to NPV, and it leads to exactly the same decisions as NPV for conventional, independent projects. When project cash flows are not conventional, there may be no IRR or there may be more than one. More seriously, the IRR cannot be used to rank mutually exclusive projects; the project with the highest IRR is not necessarily the preferred investment.

C. *Profitability index (PI).* The PI, also called the *benefit-cost ratio,* is the ratio of present value to cost. The PI rule is to take an investment if the index exceeds 1. The PI measures the present value of an investment per dollar invested. It is quite similar to NPV, but, like IRR, it cannot be used to rank mutually exclusive projects. However, it is sometimes used to rank projects when a firm has more positive NPV investments than it can currently finance.

II. **Payback criteria**

A. *Payback period.* The payback period is the length of time until the sum of an investment's cash flows equals its cost. The payback period rule is to take a project if its payback is *less* than some cutoff. The payback period is a flawed criterion primarily because it ignores risk, the time value of money, and cash flows beyond the cutoff point.

III. **Accounting criteria**

A. *Average accounting return (AAR).* The AAR is a measure of accounting profit relative to book value. It is *not* related to the IRR, but it is similar to the accounting return on assets (ROA) measure in Chapter 3. The AAR rule is to take an investment if its AAR exceeds a benchmark AAR. The AAR is seriously flawed for a variety of reasons, and it has little to recommend it.

SUMMARY AND CONCLUSIONS

This chapter has covered the different criteria used to evaluate proposed investments. The five criteria, in the order in which we discussed them, are:

1. Net present value (NPV)
2. Payback period
3. Average accounting return (AAR)
4. Internal rate of return (IRR)
5. Profitability index (PI)

We illustrated how to calculate each of these and discussed the interpretation of the results. We also described the advantages and disadvantages of each of them. Ultimately, a good capital budgeting criterion must tell us two things. First, is a particular project a good investment? Second, if we have more than one good project, but we can only take one of them, which one should we take? The main point of this chapter is that only the NPV criterion can always provide the correct answer to both questions.

For this reason, NPV is one of the two or three most important concepts in finance, and we will refer to it many times in the chapters ahead. When we do, keep two things in mind: (1) NPV is always just the difference between the market value of an asset or project and its cost; and (2) the financial manager acts in the shareholders' best interests by identifying and taking positive NPV projects.

Finally, we noted that NPVs can't normally be observed in the market; instead, they must be estimated. Because there is always the possibility of a poor estimate, financial managers use multiple criteria for examining projects. These other criteria provide additional information about whether a project truly has a positive NPV.

CHAPTER REVIEW AND SELF-TEST PROBLEMS

8.1 **Investment Criteria.** This problem will give you some practice calculating NPVs and paybacks. A proposed overseas expansion has the following cash flows:

Year	Cash Flow
0	−$100
1	50
2	40
3	40
4	15

Calculate the payback and NPV at a required return of 15 percent.

8.2 **Mutually Exclusive Investments.** Consider the following two mutually exclusive investments. Calculate the IRR for each. Under what circumstances will the IRR and NPV criteria rank the two projects differently?

Year	Investment A	Investment B
0	−$100	−$100
1	50	70
2	70	75
3	40	10

8.3 **Average Accounting Return.** You are looking at a three-year project with a projected net income of $1,000 in Year 1, $2,000 in Year 2, and $4,000 in Year 3. The cost is $9,000, which will be depreciated straight-line to zero over the three-year life of the project. What is the average accounting return, or AAR?

◼ Answers to Chapter Review and Self-Test Problems

8.1 In the table below, we have listed the cash flows and their discounted values (at 15 percent).

	Cash Flow	
Year	Undiscounted	Discounted (at 15%)
1	$ 50	$ 43.5
2	40	30.2
3	40	26.3
4	15	8.6
Total	$145	$108.6

Recall that the initial investment is $100. Examining the undiscounted cash flows, we see that the payback occurs between Years 2 and 3. The cash flows for the first two years are $90 total, so, going into the third year, we are short by $10. The total cash flow in Year 3 is $40, so the payback is $2 + \$10/40 = 2.25$ years.

Looking at the discounted cash flows, we see that the sum is $108.6, so the NPV is $8.6.

8.2   To calculate the IRR, we might try some guesses as in the following table:

Discount rate	NPV(A)	NPV(B)
0%	$60.00	$55.00
10	33.36	33.13
20	13.43	16.20
30	− 1.91	2.78
40	− 14.01	− 8.09

Several things are immediately apparent from our guesses. First, the IRR on A must be just a little less than 30 percent (why?). With some more effort, we find that it's 28.61 percent. For B, the IRR must be a little more than 30 percent (again, why?); it works out to be 32.37 percent. Also, notice that at 10 percent, the NPVs are very close, indicating that the NPV profiles cross in that vicinity. Verify that the NPVs are the same at 10.61 percent.

Now, the IRR for B is always higher. As we've seen, A has the larger NPV for any discount rate less than 10.61 percent, so the NPV and IRR rankings will conflict in that range. Remember, if there's a conflict, we will go with the higher NPV. Our decision rule is thus very simple: Take A if the required return is less than 10.61 percent, take B if the required return is between 10.61 percent and 32.37 percent (the IRR on B), and take neither if the required return is more than 32.37 percent.

8.3   Here we need to calculate the ratio of average net income to average book value to get the AAR. Average net income is:

$$\text{Average net income} = (\$1{,}000 + 2{,}000 + 4{,}000)/3$$
$$= \$2{,}333.33$$

Average book value is:

$$\text{Average book value} = \$9{,}000/2 = \$4{,}500$$

So the average accounting return is:

$$\text{AAR} = \$2{,}333.33/4{,}500 = 51.85\%$$

This is an impressive return. Remember, however, that it isn't really a rate of return like an interest rate or an IRR, so the size doesn't tell us a lot. In particular, our money is probably not going to grow at 51.85 percent per year, sorry to say.

CRITICAL THINKING AND CONCEPTS REVIEW

1.   **Payback Period and Net Present Value.**   If a project with conventional cash flows has a payback period less than its life, can you definitively state the algebraic sign of the NPV? Why or why not?

2.   **Net Present Value.**   Suppose a project has conventional cash flows and a positive NPV. What do you know about its payback? Its profitability index? Its IRR? Explain.

3. **Payback Period.**   Concerning payback:

    a. Describe how the payback period is calculated and describe the information this measure provides about a sequence of cash flows. What is the payback criterion decision rule?

    b. What are the problems associated with using the payback period as a means of evaluating cash flows?

    c. What are the advantages of using the payback period to evaluate cash flows? Are there any circumstances under which using payback might be appropriate? Explain.

4. **Average Accounting Return.**   Concerning AAR:

    a. Describe how the average accounting return is usually calculated and describe the information this measure provides about a sequence of cash flows. What is the AAR criterion decision rule?

    b. What are the problems associated with using the AAR as a means of evaluating a project's cash flows? What underlying feature of AAR is most troubling to you from a financial perspective? Does the AAR have any redeeming qualities?

5. **Net Present Value.**   Concerning NPV:

    a. Describe how NPV is calculated and describe the information this measure provides about a sequence of cash flows. What is the NPV criterion decision rule?

    b. Why is NPV considered to be a superior method of evaluating the cash flows from a project? Suppose the NPV for a project's cash flows is computed to be $2,500. What does this number represent with respect to the firm's shareholders?

6. **Internal Rate of Return.**   Concerning IRR:

    a. Describe how the IRR is calculated and describe the information this measure provides about a sequence of cash flows. What is the IRR criterion decision rule?

    b. What is the relationship between IRR and NPV? Are there any situations in which you might prefer one method over the other? Explain.

    c. Despite its shortcomings in some situations, why do most financial managers use IRR along with NPV when evaluating projects? Can you think of a situation in which IRR might be a more appropriate measure to use than NPV? Explain.

7. **Profitability Index.**   Concerning the profitability index:

    a. Describe how the profitability index is calculated and describe the information this measure provides about a sequence of cash flows. What is the profitability index decision rule?

    b. What is the relationship between the profitability index and the NPV? Are there any situations in which you might prefer one method over the other? Explain.

8. **Payback and Internal Rate of Return.**   A project has perpetual cash flows of C per period, a cost of I, and a required return of R. What is the relationship between the project's payback and its IRR? What implications does your answer have for long-lived projects with relatively constant cash flows?

9. **International Investment Projects.**   In 1996, Fuji Film, the Japanese manufacturer of photo film and related products, broke ground on a film plant in South Carolina. Fuji apparently felt that it would be better able to compete and create value with a U.S.-based facility. Other companies, such as BMW and Mercedes-Benz,

have reached similar conclusions and taken similar actions. What are some of the reasons that foreign manufacturers of products as diverse as photo film and luxury automobiles might arrive at this same conclusion?

10. **Capital Budgeting Problems.**   What are some of the difficulties that might come up in actual applications of the various criteria we discussed in this chapter? Which one would be the easiest to implement in actual applications? The most difficult?

11. **Capital Budgeting in Not-for-Profit Entities.**   Are the capital budgeting criteria we discussed applicable to not-for-profit corporations? How should such entities make capital budgeting decisions? What about the U.S. government? Should it evaluate spending proposals using these techniques?

QUESTIONS AND PROBLEMS

Basic
(Questions 1–23)

1. **Calculating Payback.**   What is the payback period for the following set of cash flows?

Year	Cash Flow
0	−$2,500
1	300
2	1,500
3	900
4	300

2. **Calculating Payback.**   An investment project provides cash inflows of $600 per year for eight years. What is the project payback period if the initial cost is $3,400? What if the initial cost is $3,750? What if it is $5,500?

3. **Calculating Payback.**   Offshore Drilling Products, Inc., imposes a payback cutoff of three years for its international investment projects. If the company has the following two projects available, should it accept either of them?

Year	Cash Flow (A)	Cash Flow (B)
0	−$38,000	−$ 60,000
1	25,000	10,000
2	12,000	15,000
3	18,000	20,000
4	5,000	250,000

4. **Calculating AAR.**   You're trying to determine whether or not to expand your business by building a new manufacturing plant. The plant has an installation cost of $12 million, which will be depreciated straight-line to zero over its four-year life. If the plant has projected net income of $1,627,000, $1,512,000, $1,101,000, and $1,313,000 over these four years, what is the project's average accounting return (AAR)?

5. **Calculating IRR.**   A firm evaluates all of its projects by applying the IRR rule. If the required return is 18 percent, should the firm accept the following project?

Year	Cash Flow
0	−$80,000
1	35,000
2	45,000
3	40,000

6. **Calculating NPV.** For the cash flows in the previous problem, suppose the firm uses the NPV decision rule. At a required return of 9 percent, should the firm accept this project? What if the required return was 23 percent?

7. **Calculating NPV and IRR.** A project that provides annual cash flows of $900 for eight years costs $4,000 today. Is this a good project if the required return is 8 percent? What if it's 24 percent? At what discount rate would you be indifferent between accepting the project and rejecting it?

8. **Calculating IRR.** What is the IRR of the following set of cash flows?

Year	Cash Flow
0	−$2,400
1	640
2	800
3	2,000

9. **Calculating NPV.** For the cash flows in the previous problem, what is the NPV at a discount rate of zero percent? What if the discount rate is 10 percent? If it is 20 percent? If it is 30 percent?

10. **NPV versus IRR.** Darby & Davis, LLC, has identified the following two mutually exclusive projects:

Year	Cash Flow (A)	Cash Flow (B)
0	−$17,000	−$17,000
1	8,000	2,000
2	7,000	5,000
3	5,000	9,000
4	3,000	9,500

   a. What is the IRR for each of these projects? If you apply the IRR decision rule, which project should the company accept? Is this decision necessarily correct?

   b. If the required return is 11 percent, what is the NPV for each of these projects? Which project will you choose if you apply the NPV decision rule?

   c. Over what range of discount rates would you choose Project A? Project B? At what discount rate would you be indifferent between these two projects? Explain.

11. **NPV versus IRR.** Consider the following two mutually exclusive projects:

Year	Cash Flow (X)	Cash Flow (Y)
0	−$4,000	−$4,000
1	2,500	1,500
2	1,500	2,000
3	1,800	2,600

Sketch the NPV profiles for X and Y over a range of discount rates from zero to 25 percent. What is the crossover rate for these two projects?

12.   **Problems with IRR.**   Burkeen Petroleum, Inc., is trying to evaluate a generation project with the following cash flows:

Year	Cash Flow
0	−$28,000,000
1	53,000,000
2	− 8,000,000

a.   If the company requires a 10 percent return on its investments, should it accept this project? Why?

b.   Compute the IRR for this project. How many IRRs are there? If you apply the IRR decision rule, should you accept the project or not? What's going on here?

13.   **Calculating Profitability Index.**   What is the profitability index for the following set of cash flows if the relevant discount rate is 10 percent? What if the discount rate is 15 percent? If it is 22 percent?

Year	Cash Flow
0	−$5,000
1	3,000
2	2,000
3	1,200

14.   **Problems with Profitability Index.**   The McConnel Computer Corporation is trying to choose between the following two mutually exclusive design projects:

Year	Cash Flow (I)	Cash Flow (II)
0	−$20,000	−$3,000
1	10,000	2,500
2	10,000	2,500
3	10,000	2,500

a.   If the required return is 9 percent and McConnel applies the profitability index decision rule, which project should the firm accept?

b.   If the company applies the NPV decision rule, which project should it take?

c.   Explain why your answers in (a) and (b) are different.

15.   **Comparing Investment Criteria.**   Consider the following two mutually exclusive projects:

Year	Cash Flow (A)	Cash Flow (B)
0	−$170,000	−$18,000
1	10,000	10,000
2	25,000	6,000
3	25,000	10,000
4	380,000	8,000

Whichever project you choose, if any, you require a 15 percent return on your investment.

a. If you apply the payback criterion, which investment will you choose? Why?

b. If you apply the NPV criterion, which investment will you choose? Why?

c. If you apply the IRR criterion, which investment will you choose? Why?

d. If you apply the profitability index criterion, which investment will you choose? Why?

e. Based on your answers in (a) through (d), which project will you finally choose? Why?

16. **NPV and IRR.** M. Ellis Company is presented with the following two mutually exclusive projects. The required return for both projects is 13 percent.

Year	Project M	Project N
0	−$25,000	−$550,000
1	10,000	220,000
2	21,000	250,000
3	12,000	240,000
4	10,000	195,000

a. What is the IRR for each project?

b. What is the NPV for each project?

c. Which, if either, of the projects should the company accept?

17. **NPV and Profitability Index.** Melissa Manufacturing has the following two possible projects. The required return is 12 percent.

Year	Project Y	Project Z
0	−$25,000	−$40,000
1	10,000	15,000
2	10,000	15,000
3	10,000	15,000
4	10,000	15,000

a. What is the profitability index for each project?

b. What is the NPV for each project?

c. Which, if either, of the projects should the company accept?

18. **Crossover Point.** Burk Enterprises has gathered projected cash flows for two projects. At what interest rate would Burk be indifferent between the two projects? Which project is better if the required return is above this interest rate? Why?

Year	Project I	Project J
0	−$45,000	−$45,000
1	20,000	15,000
2	18,000	17,000
3	16,000	19,000
4	14,000	21,000

19. **NPV and Profitability Index.**   B. C. Rogers, Inc., is presented with the following two mutually exclusive projects. The required return is 15 percent.

Year	Project K	Project S
0	−$35,000	−$350,000
1	18,000	120,000
2	17,000	115,000
3	16,000	110,000
4	15,000	105,000
5	14,000	100,000

   a.   What is the profitability index for each project?
   b.   What is the NPV for each project?
   c.   Which, if either, of the projects should the company choose?

20. **Payback Period and IRR.**   Suppose you have a project with a payback period exactly equal to the life of the project. What do you know about the IRR of the project? Suppose that the payback period is never. What do you know about the IRR of the project now?

21. **NPV and Discount Rates.**   An investment has an installed cost of $323,580. The cash flows over the four-year life of the investment are projected to be $91,452, $172,148, $118,473, and $88,612. If the discount rate is zero, what is the NPV? If the discount rate is infinite, what is the NPV? At what discount rate is the NPV just equal to zero? Sketch the NPV profile for this investment based on these three points.

22. **NPV and Payback Period.**   Kvernmoe Konstruction, Inc., has the following three projects available. The company has historically used a three-year cutoff for projects. The required return is 12 percent.

Year	Project F	Project G	Project H
0	−$50,000	−$75,000	−$100,000
1	30,000	45,000	30,000
2	15,000	30,000	35,000
3	15,000	25,000	30,000
4	10,000	25,000	80,000
5	10,000	20,000	50,000

   a.   Calculate the payback period for all three projects.
   b.   Calculate the NPV for all three projects.
   c.   Which project, if any, should the company accept?

23. **NPV and IRR.**   Mizell Machinery, Inc., has the following two projects available. The required return is 14 percent.

Year	Project X	Project Y
0	−$50,000	−$100,000
1	20,000	70,000
2	30,000	50,000
3	40,000	40,000
4	30,000	30,000

    a. Calculate the IRR for each project.
    b. Calculate the NPV for each project.
    c. Which project, if either, should the company accept?

24. **NPV and Payback Period.** Sowell Auto has the following two projects available. **Intermediate** (Questions 24–29)

Year	Project R	Project S
0	−$30,000	−$40,000
1	15,000	20,000
2	10,000	15,000
3	15,000	20,000
4	5,000	15,000
5	5,000	10,000

What is the crossover rate for these two projects? What is the NPV of each project at the crossover rate?

25. **NPV and IRR.** Bedknobs and Broomsticks, Inc., has the following two projects available. The required return is 14 percent.

Year	Project C	Project D
0	−$100,000	−$150,000
1	30,000	70,000
2	30,000	50,000
3	30,000	60,000
4	20,000	30,000

    a. What is the IRR for each project?
    b. What is the NPV for each project?
    c. Which, if either, of these two projects should the company choose?

26. **Calculating IRR.** A project has the following cash flows:

Year	Cash Flow
0	$25,000
1	− 10,000
2	− 21,000

What is the IRR for this project? If the required return is 12 percent, should the firm accept the project? What is the NPV of this project? What is the NPV of the project if the required return is 0 percent? 25 percent? What is going on here? Sketch the NPV profile to help you with your answer.

27. **Multiple IRRs.** This problem is useful for testing the ability of financial calculators and computer software. Consider the following cash flows. When should we take this project (hint: search for IRRs between 20 percent and 70 percent)?

Year	Cash Flow
0	−$ 252
1	1,431
2	− 3,035
3	2,850
4	− 1,000

28.   **NPV and the Profitability Index.**   If we define the NPV index as the ratio of NPV to cost, what is the relationship between this index and the profitability index?

29.   **Cash Flow Intuition.**   A project has an initial cost of I, has a required return of R, and pays C annually for N years.

   a.   Find C in terms of I and N such that the project has a payback period just equal to its life.

   b.   Find C in terms of I, N, and R such that this is a profitable project according to the NPV decision rule.

   c.   Find C in terms of I, N, and R such that the project has a benefit-cost ratio of 2.

www.mhhe.com/rwj

Spreadsheet Templates 5, 6, 11, 15

Making Capital Investment Decisions

IN LATE APRIL 2000, Unilever PLC, the Anglo-Dutch consumer products giant, announced it would make two significant additions to its menu of products at a total cost of $2.6 billion. First, in a bid to be a player in the diet sector, Unilever acquired SlimFast Foods, Inc., the Florida-based maker of diet products, in a deal valued at $2.3 billion. At the time, SlimFast commanded roughly a 45 percent share of the U.S. market for diet and nutrition products. Second, to increase its market share in a decidedly un-diet sector, Unilever acquired Ben & Jerry's Homemade, Inc., the well-known ice cream chain, for $326 million. Both moves were aimed at increasing the firm's presence in the U.S. market.

As you no doubt recognize from your study of the previous chapter, these acquisitions represent capital budgeting decisions. In this chapter, we 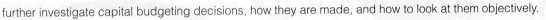 further investigate capital budgeting decisions, how they are made, and how to look at them objectively.

This chapter follows up on our previous one by delving more deeply into capital budgeting. We have two main tasks. First, recall that in the last chapter, we saw that cash flow estimates are the critical input into a net present value analysis, but we didn't say very much about where these cash flows come from; so we will now examine this question in some detail. Our second goal is to learn how to critically examine NPV estimates, and, in particular, how to evaluate the sensitivity of NPV estimates to assumptions made about the uncertain future.

So far, we've covered various parts of the capital budgeting decision. Our task in this chapter is to start bringing these pieces together. In particular, we will show you how to "spread the numbers" for a proposed investment or project and, based on those numbers, make an initial assessment about whether or not the project should be undertaken.

In the discussion that follows, we focus on the process of setting up a discounted cash flow analysis. From the last chapter, we know that the projected future cash flows are the key element in such an evaluation. Accordingly, we emphasize working with financial and accounting information to come up with these figures.

In evaluating a proposed investment, we pay special attention to deciding what information is relevant to the decision at hand and what information is not. As we shall see, it is easy to overlook important pieces of the capital budgeting puzzle. We also describe how to go about evaluating the results of our discounted cash flow analysis.

9.1 | PROJECT CASH FLOWS: A FIRST LOOK

The effect of taking a project is to change the firm's overall cash flows today and in the future. To evaluate a proposed investment, we must consider these changes in the firm's cash flows and then decide whether or not they add value to the firm. The first (and most important) step, therefore, is to decide which cash flows are relevant and which are not.

Relevant Cash Flows

incremental cash flows
The difference between a firm's future cash flows with a project and those without the project.

What is a relevant cash flow for a project? The general principle is simple enough: A relevant cash flow for a project is a change in the firm's overall future cash flow that comes about as a direct consequence of the decision to take that project. Because the relevant cash flows are defined in terms of changes in, or increments to, the firm's existing cash flow, they are called the **incremental cash flows** associated with the project.

The concept of incremental cash flow is central to our analysis, so we will state a general definition and refer back to it as needed:

> The incremental cash flows for project evaluation consist of *any and all* changes in the firm's future cash flows that are a direct consequence of taking the project.

This definition of incremental cash flows has an obvious and important corollary: Any cash flow that exists regardless of whether or *not* a project is undertaken is *not* relevant.

The Stand-Alone Principle

stand-alone principle
The assumption that evaluation of a project may be based on the project's incremental cash flows.

In practice, it would be very cumbersome to actually calculate the future total cash flows to the firm with and without a project, especially for a large firm. Fortunately, it is not really necessary to do so. Once we identify the effect of undertaking the proposed project on the firm's cash flows, we need only focus on the project's resulting incremental cash flows. This is called the **stand-alone principle**.

What the stand-alone principle says is that, once we have determined the incremental cash flows from undertaking a project, we can view that project as a kind of "minifirm" with its own future revenues and costs, its own assets, and, of course, its own cash flows. We will then be primarily interested in comparing the cash flows from this minifirm to the cost of acquiring it. An important consequence of this approach is that we will be evaluating the proposed project purely on its own merits, in isolation from any other activities or projects.

CONCEPT QUESTIONS

9.1a What are the relevant incremental cash flows for project evaluation?

9.1b What is the stand-alone principle?

INCREMENTAL CASH FLOWS | 9.2

We are concerned here only with those cash flows that are incremental and that result from a project. Looking back at our general definition, it seems easy enough to decide whether a cash flow is incremental or not. Even so, there are a few situations where mistakes are easy to make. In this section, we describe some of these common pitfalls and how to avoid them.

Sunk Costs

A **sunk cost**, by definition, is a cost we have already paid or have already incurred the liability to pay. Such a cost cannot be changed by the decision today to accept or reject a project. Put another way, the firm will have to pay this cost no matter what. Based on our general definition of incremental cash flow, such a cost is clearly not relevant to the decision at hand. So, we will always be careful to exclude sunk costs from our analysis.

That a sunk cost is not relevant seems obvious given our discussion. Nonetheless, it's easy to fall prey to the sunk cost fallacy. For example, suppose General Milk Company hires a financial consultant to help evaluate whether or not a line of chocolate milk should be launched. When the consultant turns in the report, General Milk objects to the analysis because the consultant did not include the hefty consulting fee as a cost of the chocolate milk project.

Who is correct? By now, we know that the consulting fee is a sunk cost, because the consulting fee must be paid whether or not the chocolate milk line is actually launched (this is an attractive feature of the consulting business).

> **sunk cost**
> A cost that has already been incurred and cannot be recouped and therefore should not be considered in an investment decision.

Opportunity Costs

When we think of costs, we normally think of out-of-pocket costs, namely, those that require us to actually spend some amount of cash. An **opportunity cost** is slightly different; it requires us to give up a benefit. A common situation arises where a firm already owns some of the assets a proposed project will be using. For example, we might be thinking of converting an old rustic cotton mill we bought years ago for $100,000 into "upmarket" condominiums.

If we undertake this project, there will be no direct cash outflow associated with buying the old mill since we already own it. For purposes of evaluating the condo project, should we then treat the mill as "free"? The answer is no. The mill is a valuable resource used by the project. If we didn't use it here, we could do something else with it. Like what? The obvious answer is that, at a minimum, we could sell it. Using the mill for the condo complex thus has an opportunity cost: We give up the valuable opportunity to do something else with it.[1]

There is another issue here. Once we agree that the use of the mill has an opportunity cost, how much should the condo project be charged? Given that we paid $100,000, it might seem that we should charge this amount to the condo project. Is this correct? The answer is no, and the reason is based on our discussion concerning sunk costs.

> **opportunity cost**
> The most valuable alternative that is given up if a particular investment is undertaken.

---

[1]Economists sometimes use the acronym *TANSTAAFL,* which is short for "There ain't no such thing as a free lunch," to describe the fact that only very rarely is something truly free.

The fact that we paid $100,000 some years ago is irrelevant. That cost is sunk. At a minimum, the opportunity cost that we charge the project is what the mill would sell for today (net of any selling costs), because this is the amount that we give up by using it instead of selling it.

Side Effects

Remember that the incremental cash flows for a project include all the changes in the *firm's* future cash flows. It would not be unusual for a project to have side, or spillover, effects, both good and bad. For example, if the Innovative Motors Company (IMC) introduces a new car, some of the sales might come at the expense of other IMC cars. This is called **erosion,** and the same general problem could occur for any multiline consumer product producer or seller.[2] In this case, the cash flows from the new line should be adjusted downward to reflect lost profits on other lines.

In accounting for erosion, it is important to recognize that any sales lost as a result of our launching a new product might be lost anyway because of future competition. Erosion is only relevant when the sales would not otherwise be lost.

erosion

The cash flows of a new project that come at the expense of a firm's existing projects.

Net Working Capital

Normally, a project will require that the firm invest in net working capital in addition to long-term assets. For example, a project will generally need some amount of cash on hand to pay any expenses that arise. In addition, a project will need an initial investment in inventories and accounts receivable (to cover credit sales). Some of this financing will be in the form of amounts owed to suppliers (accounts payable), but the firm will have to supply the balance. This balance represents the investment in net working capital.

It's easy to overlook an important feature of net working capital in capital budgeting. As a project winds down, inventories are sold, receivables are collected, bills are paid, and cash balances can be drawn down. These activities free up the net working capital originally invested. So, the firm's investment in project net working capital closely resembles a loan. The firm supplies working capital at the beginning and recovers it towards the end.

Financing Costs

In analyzing a proposed investment, we will not include interest paid or any other financing costs such as dividends or principal repaid, because we are interested in the cash flow generated by the assets of the project. As we mentioned in Chapter 2, interest paid, for example, is a component of cash flow to creditors, not cash flow from assets.

More generally, our goal in project evaluation is to compare the cash flow from a project to the cost of acquiring that project in order to estimate NPV. The particular mixture of debt and equity a firm actually chooses to use in financing a project is a managerial variable and primarily determines how project cash flow is divided between owners and creditors. This is not to say that financing arrangements are unimportant. They are just something to be analyzed separately. We will cover this in later chapters.

Other Issues

There are some other things to watch out for. First, we are only interested in measuring cash flow. Moreover, we are interested in measuring it when it actually occurs, not when it accrues in an accounting sense. Second, we are always interested in *aftertax* cash flow since

---

[2]More colorfully, erosion is sometimes called *piracy* or *cannibalism.*

taxes are definitely a cash outflow. In fact, whenever we write "incremental cash flows," we mean aftertax incremental cash flows. Remember, however, that aftertax cash flow and accounting profit, or net income, are entirely different things.

CONCEPT QUESTIONS

9.2a What is a sunk cost? An opportunity cost?

9.2b Explain what erosion is and why it is relevant.

9.2c Explain why interest paid is not a relevant cash flow for project evaluation.

PRO FORMA FINANCIAL STATEMENTS AND PROJECT CASH FLOWS

9.3

The first thing we need when we begin evaluating a proposed investment is a set of pro forma, or projected, financial statements. Given these, we can develop the projected cash flows from the project. Once we have the cash flows, we can estimate the value of the project using the techniques we described in the previous chapter.

Getting Started: Pro Forma Financial Statements

Pro forma financial statements are a convenient and easily understood means of summarizing much of the relevant information for a project. To prepare these statements, we will need estimates of quantities such as unit sales, the selling price per unit, the variable cost per unit, and total fixed costs. We will also need to know the total investment required, including any investment in net working capital.

To illustrate, suppose we think we can sell 50,000 cans of shark attractant per year at a price of $4.00 per can. It costs us about $2.50 per can to make the attractant, and a new product such as this one typically has only a three-year life (perhaps because the customer base dwindles rapidly). We require a 20 percent return on new products.

Fixed costs for the project, including such things as rent on the production facility, will run $12,000 per year. Further, we will need to invest a total of $90,000 in manufacturing equipment. For simplicity, we will assume that this $90,000 will be 100 percent depreciated over the three-year life of the project. Furthermore, the cost of removing the equipment will roughly equal its actual value in three years, so it will be essentially worthless on a market value basis as well. Finally, the project will require an initial $20,000 investment in net working capital. As usual, the tax rate is 34 percent.

In Table 9.1, we organize these initial projections by first preparing the pro forma income statement for each of the three years. Once again, notice that we have *not* deducted any interest expense. This will always be so. As we described earlier, interest paid is a financing expense, not a component of operating cash flow.

We can also prepare a series of abbreviated balance sheets that show the capital requirements for the project as we've done in Table 9.2. Here we have net working capital of $20,000 in each year. Fixed assets are $90,000 at the start of the project's life (Year 0), and they decline by the $30,000 in depreciation each year, ending up at zero. Notice that the total investment given here for future years is the total book, or accounting, value, not market value.

At this point, we need to start converting this accounting information into cash flows. We consider how to do this next.

pro forma financial statements
Financial statements projecting future years' operations.

Projected income
statement, shark
attractant project,
years 1–3

Sales (50,000 units at $4.00/unit)	$200,000
Variable costs ($2.50/unit)	125,000
Gross profit	$ 75,000
Fixed costs	12,000
Depreciation ($90,000/3)	30,000
EBIT	$ 33,000
Taxes (34%)	11,220
Net income	$ 21,780

Projected capital
requirements, shark
attractant project

	Year			
	0	**1**	**2**	**3**
Net working capital	$ 20,000	$20,000	$20,000	$20,000
Net fixed assets	90,000	60,000	30,000	0
Total investment	$110,000	$80,000	$50,000	$20,000

Project Cash Flows

To develop the cash flows from a project, we need to recall (from Chapter 2) that cash flow from assets has three components: operating cash flow, capital spending, and additions to net working capital. To evaluate a project, or minifirm, we need to arrive at estimates for each of these.

Once we have estimates of the components of cash flow, we will calculate cash flow for our minifirm just as we did in Chapter 2 for an entire firm:

Project cash flow = Project operating cash flow

— Project change in net working capital

— Project capital spending

We consider these components next.

Project Operating Cash Flow   To determine the operating cash flow associated with a project, we first need to recall the definition of operating cash flow:

Operating cash flow = Earnings before interest and taxes

+ Depreciation

— Taxes

To illustrate the calculation of operating cash flow, we will use the projected information from the shark attractant project. For ease of reference, Table 9.3 repeats the income statement.

Given the income statement in Table 9.3, calculating the operating cash flow is very straightforward. As we see in Table 9.4, projected operating cash flow for the shark attractant project is $51,780.

Project Net Working Capital and Capital Spending   We next need to take care of the fixed asset and net working capital requirements. Based on our balance sheets above, the firm must spend $90,000 up front for fixed assets and invest an additional $20,000 in net working capital. The immediate outflow is thus $110,000. At the end of the project's

Sales	$200,000
Variable costs	125,000
Fixed costs	12,000
Depreciation	30,000
EBIT	$ 33,000
Taxes (34%)	11,220
Net income	$ 21,780

TABLE 9.3

Projected income statement, shark attractant project

EBIT	$33,000
Depreciation	+ 30,000
Taxes	− 11,220
Operating cash flow	$51,780

TABLE 9.4

Projected operating cash flow, shark attractant project

	Year			
	0	**1**	**2**	**3**
Operating cash flow		$51,780	$51,780	$51,780
Change in NWC	−$ 20,000			+ 20,000
Capital spending	− 90,000			
Total project cash flow	−$110,000	$51,780	$51,780	$71,780

TABLE 9.5

Projected total cash flows, shark attractant project

life, the fixed assets will be worthless (the salvage value will be zero), but the firm will recover the $20,000 that was tied up in working capital. This will lead to a $20,000 cash *inflow* in the last year.

On a purely mechanical level, notice that whenever we have an investment in net working capital, that same investment has to be recovered; in other words, the same number needs to appear at some time in the future with the opposite sign.

Projected Total Cash Flow and Value

Given the information we've accumulated, we can finish the preliminary cash flow analysis as illustrated in Table 9.5.

Now that we have cash flow projections, we are ready to apply the various criteria we discussed in the last chapter. First, the NPV at the 20 percent required return is:

$$\text{NPV} = -\$110,000 + 51,780/1.2 + 51,780/1.2^2 + 71,780/1.2^3$$
$$= \$10,648$$

So, based on these projections, the project creates over $10,000 in value and should be accepted. Also, the return on this investment obviously exceeds 20 percent (since the NPV is positive at 20 percent). After some trial and error, we find that the IRR works out to be about 25.8 percent.

In addition, if required, we could go ahead and calculate the payback and the average accounting return, or AAR. Inspection of the cash flows shows that the payback on this project is just a little over two years (verify that it's about 2.1 years).

From the last chapter, we know that the AAR is average net income divided by average book value. The net income each year is $21,780. The average (in thousands) of the four book values (from Table 9.2) for total investment is ($110 + 80 + 50 + 20)/4 = $65, so the AAR is $21,780/65,000 = 33.51 percent. We've already seen that the return on this investment (the IRR) is about 26 percent. The fact that the AAR is larger illustrates again why the AAR cannot be meaningfully interpreted as the return on a project.

CONCEPT QUESTIONS

9.3a What is the definition of project operating cash flow? How does this differ from net income?

9.3b In the shark attractant project, why did we add back the firm's net working capital investment in the final year?

9.4 MORE ON PROJECT CASH FLOW

In this section, we take a closer look at some aspects of project cash flow. In particular, we discuss project net working capital in more detail. We then examine current tax laws regarding depreciation.

A Closer Look at Net Working Capital

In calculating operating cash flow, we did not explicitly consider the fact that some of our sales might be on credit. Also, we may not have actually paid some of the costs shown. In either case, the cash flow has not yet occurred. We show here that these possibilities are not a problem as long as we don't forget to include additions to net working capital in our analysis. This discussion thus emphasizes the importance and the effect of doing so.

Suppose during a particular year of a project we have the following simplified income statement:

Sales	$500
Costs	310
Net income	$190

Depreciation and taxes are zero. No fixed assets are purchased during the year. Also, to illustrate a point, we assume that the only components of net working capital are accounts receivable and payable. The beginning and ending amounts for these accounts are:

	Beginning of Year	End of Year	Change
Accounts receivable	$880	$910	+ $30
Accounts payable	550	605	+ 55
Net working capital	$330	$305	−$25

Based on this information, what is total cash flow for the year? We can first just mechanically apply what we have been discussing to come up with the answer. Operating cash flow in this particular case is the same as EBIT since there are no taxes or depreciation and thus equals $190. Also, notice that net working capital actually *declined* by $25, so the change in net working capital is negative. This just means that $25 was freed up during the year. There was no capital spending, so the total cash flow for the year is:

$$\text{Total cash flow} = \text{Operating cash flow} - \text{Change in NWC} - \text{Capital spending}$$
$$= \$190 - (-25) - 0$$
$$= \$215$$

Now, we know that this $215 total cash flow has to be "dollars in" less "dollars out" for the year. We could therefore ask a different question: What were cash revenues for the year? Also, what were cash costs?

To determine cash revenues, we need to look more closely at net working capital. During the year, we had sales of $500. However, accounts receivable rose by $30 over the same time period. What does this mean? The $30 increase tells us that sales exceeded collections by $30. In other words, we haven't yet received the cash from $30 of the $500 in sales. As a result, our cash inflow is $500 − 30 = $470. In general, cash income is sales minus the increase in accounts receivable.

Cash outflows can be similarly determined. We show costs of $310 on the income statement, but accounts payable increased by $55 during the year. This means that we have not yet paid $55 of the $310, so cash costs for the period are just $310 − 55 = $255. In other words, in this case, cash costs equal costs less the increase in accounts payable.

Putting this information together, cash inflows less cash outflows is $470 − 255 = $215, just as we had before. Notice that:

$$\text{Cash flow} = \text{Cash inflow} - \text{Cash outflow}$$
$$= (\$500 - 30) - (310 - 55)$$
$$= (\$500 - 310) - (30 - 55)$$
$$= \text{Operating cash flow} - \text{Change in NWC}$$
$$= \$190 - (-25)$$
$$= \$215$$

More generally, this example illustrates that including net working capital changes in our calculations has the effect of adjusting for the discrepancy between accounting sales and costs and actual cash receipts and payments.

Cash Collections and Costs | **EXAMPLE 9.1**

For the year just completed, the Combat Wombat Telestat Co. (CWT) reports sales of $998 and costs of $734. You have collected the following beginning and ending balance sheet information:

	Beginning	**Ending**
Accounts receivable	$100	$110
Inventory	100	80
Accounts payable	100	70
Net working capital	$100	$120

Based on these figures, what are cash inflows? Cash outflows? What happened to each account? What is net cash flow?

Sales were $998, but receivables rose by $10. So cash collections were $10 less than sales, or $988. Costs were $734, but inventories fell by $20. This means that we didn't replace $20 worth of inventory, so costs are actually overstated by this amount. Also, payables fell by $30. This means that, on a net basis, we actually paid our suppliers $30 more than we received from them, resulting in a $30 understatement of costs. Adjusting for these events, cash costs are $734 − 20 + 30 = $744. Net cash flow is $988 − 744 = $244.

Finally, notice that net working capital increased by $20 overall. We can check our answer by noting that the original accounting sales less costs of $998 − 734 is $264. In addition, CWT spent $20 on net working capital, so the net result is a cash flow of $264 − 20 = $244, as we calculated.

Depreciation

As we note elsewhere, accounting depreciation is a noncash deduction. As a result, depreciation has cash flow consequences only because it influences the tax bill. The way that depreciation is computed for tax purposes is thus the relevant method for capital investment decisions. Not surprisingly, the procedures are governed by tax law. We now discuss some specifics of the depreciation system enacted by the Tax Reform Act of 1986. This system is a modification of the **Accelerated Cost Recovery System (ACRS)** instituted in 1981.

Accelerated Cost Recovery System (ACRS)

Depreciation method under U.S. tax law allowing for the accelerated write-off of property under various classifications.

Modified ACRS (MACRS) Depreciation   Calculating depreciation is normally very mechanical. While there are a number of *if*s, *and*s, and *but*s involved, the basic idea is that every asset is assigned to a particular class. An asset's class establishes its life for tax purposes. Once an asset's tax life is determined, we compute the depreciation for each year by multiplying the cost of the asset by a fixed percentage. The expected salvage value (what we think the asset will be worth when we dispose of it) and the actual expected economic life (how long we expect the asset to be in service) are not explicitly considered in the calculation of depreciation.

Some typical depreciation classes are described in Table 9.6, and associated percentages (rounded to two decimal places) are shown in Table 9.7. Remember that land cannot be depreciated.

TABLE 9.6

Modified ACRS property classes

Class	Examples
3-year	Equipment used in research
5-year	Autos, computers
7-year	Most industrial equipment

TABLE 9.7

Modified ACRS depreciation allowances

	Property Class		
Year	3-Year	5-Year	7-Year
1	33.33%	20.00%	14.29%
2	44.44	32.00	24.49
3	14.82	19.20	17.49
4	7.41	11.52	12.49
5		11.52	8.93
6		5.76	8.93
7			8.93
8			4.45

To illustrate how depreciation is calculated, we consider an automobile costing $12,000. Autos are normally classified as five-year property. Looking at Table 9.7, we see that the relevant figure for the first year of a five-year asset is 20 percent. The depreciation in the first year is thus $12,000 × .20 = $2,400. The relevant percentage in the second year is 32 percent, so the depreciation in the second year is $12,000 × .32 = $3,840, and so on. We can summarize these calculations as follows:

Year	MACRS Percentage	Depreciation
1	20.00%	.2000 × $12,000 = $ 2,400.00
2	32.00	.3200 × 12,000 = 3,840.00
3	19.20	.1920 × 12,000 = 2,304.00
4	11.52	.1152 × 12,000 = 1,382.40
5	11.52	.1152 × 12,000 = 1,382.40
6	5.76	.0576 × 12,000 = 691.20
	100.00%	$12,000.00

Notice that the ACRS percentages sum up to 100 percent. As a result, we write off 100 percent of the cost of the asset, or $12,000 in this case.

Book Value versus Market Value In calculating depreciation under current tax law, the economic life and future market value of the asset are not an issue. As a result, the book value of an asset can differ substantially from its actual market value. For example, with our $12,000 car, book value after the first year is $12,000 less the first year's depreciation of $2,400, or $9,600. The remaining book values are summarized in Table 9.8. After six years, the book value of the car is zero.

Suppose we wanted to sell the car after five years. Based on historical averages, it will be worth, say, 25 percent of the purchase price, or .25 × $12,000 = $3,000. If we actually sold it for this, then we would have to pay taxes at the ordinary income tax rate on the difference between the sale price of $3,000 and the book value of $691.20. For a corporation in the 34 percent bracket, the tax liability is .34 × $2,308.80 = $784.99.

The reason that taxes must be paid in this case is that the difference in market value and book value is "excess" depreciation, and it must be "recaptured" when the asset is sold. What this means is that, as it turns out, we overdepreciated the asset by $3,000 − 691.20 = $2,308.80. Since we deducted $2,308.80 too much in depreciation, we paid $784.99 too little in taxes, and we simply have to make up the difference.

Notice that this is *not* a tax on a capital gain. As a general (albeit rough) rule, a capital gain only occurs if the market price exceeds the original cost. However, what is and what is not a capital gain is ultimately up to taxing authorities, and the specific rules can be very complex. We will ignore capital gains taxes for the most part.

Year	Beginning Book Value	Depreciation	Ending Book Value
1	$12,000.00	$2,400.00	$9,600.00
2	9,600.00	3,840.00	5,760.00
3	5,760.00	2,304.00	3,456.00
4	3,456.00	1,382.40	2,073.60
5	2,073.60	1,382.40	691.20
6	691.20	691.20	0.00

TABLE 9.8

MACRS book values

Finally, if the book value exceeds the market value, then the difference is treated as a loss for tax purposes. For example, if we sell the car after two years for $4,000, then the book value exceeds the market value by $1,760. In this case, a tax saving of .34 × $1,760 = $598.40 occurs.

EXAMPLE 9.2 | MACRS Depreciation

The Staple Supply Co. has just purchased a new computerized information system with an installed cost of $160,000. The computer is treated as five-year property. What are the yearly depreciation allowances? Based on historical experience, we think that the system will be worth only $10,000 when we get rid of it in four years. What are the tax consequences of the sale? What is the total aftertax cash flow from the sale?

The yearly depreciation allowances are calculated by just multiplying $160,000 by the five-year percentages in Table 9.7:

Year	MACRS Percentage	Depreciation	Ending Book Value
1	20.00%	.2000 × $160,000 = $ 32,000	$128,000
2	32.00	.3200 × 160,000 = 51,200	76,800
3	19.20	.1920 × 160,000 = 30,720	46,080
4	11.52	.1152 × 160,000 = 18,432	27,648
5	11.52	.1152 × 160,000 = 18,432	9,216
6	5.76	.0576 × 160,000 = 9,216	0
	100.00%	$160,000	

Notice that we have also computed the book value of the system as of the end of each year. The book value at the end of Year 4 is $27,648. If we sell the system for $10,000 at that time, we will have a loss of $17,648 (the difference) for tax purposes. This loss, of course, is like depreciation because it isn't a cash expense.

What really happens? Two things. First: We get $10,000 from the buyer. Second: We save .34 × $17,648 = $6,000 in taxes. So the total aftertax cash flow from the sale is a $16,000 cash inflow.

An Example: The Majestic Mulch and Compost Company (MMCC)

At this point, we want to go through a somewhat more involved capital budgeting analysis. Keep in mind as you read that the basic approach here is exactly the same as that in the shark attractant example above. We have only added some more "real-world" detail (and a lot more numbers).

MMCC is investigating the feasibility of a new line of power mulching tools aimed at the growing number of home composters. Based on exploratory conversations with buyers for large garden shops, it projects unit sales as follows:

Year	Unit Sales
1	3,000
2	5,000
3	6,000
4	6,500
5	6,000
6	5,000
7	4,000
8	3,000

Year	Unit Price	Unit Sales	Revenues
1	$120	3,000	$360,000
2	120	5,000	600,000
3	120	6,000	720,000
4	110	6,500	715,000
5	110	6,000	660,000
6	110	5,000	550,000
7	110	4,000	440,000
8	110	3,000	330,000

TABLE 9.9

Projected revenues, power mulcher project

Year	MACRS Percentage	Depreciation	Ending Book Value
1	14.29%	.1429 × $800,000 = $114,320	$685,680
2	24.49	.2449 × 800,000 = 195,920	489,760
3	17.49	.1749 × 800,000 = 139,920	349,840
4	12.49	.1249 × 800,000 = 99,920	249,920
5	8.93	.0893 × 800,000 = 71,440	178,480
6	8.93	.0893 × 800,000 = 71,440	107,040
7	8.93	.0893 × 800,000 = 71,440	35,600
8	4.45	.0445 × 800,000 = 35,600	0
	100.00%	$800,000	

TABLE 9.10

Annual depreciation, power mulcher project

The new power mulcher will be priced to sell at $120 per unit to start. When the competition catches up after three years, however, MMCC anticipates that the price will drop to $110.

The power mulcher project will require $20,000 in net working capital at the start. Subsequently, total net working capital at the end of each year will be about 15 percent of sales for that year. The variable cost per unit is $60, and total fixed costs are $25,000 per year.

It will cost about $800,000 to buy the equipment necessary to begin production. This investment is primarily in industrial equipment and thus qualifies as seven-year MACRS property. The equipment will actually be worth about 20 percent of its cost in eight years, or .20 × $800,000 = $160,000. The relevant tax rate is 34 percent, and the required return is 15 percent. Based on this information, should MMCC proceed?

Operating Cash Flows There is a lot of information here that we need to organize. The first thing we can do is calculate projected sales. Sales in the first year are projected at 3,000 units at $120 apiece, or $360,000 total. The remaining figures are shown in Table 9.9.

Next, we compute the depreciation on the $800,000 investment in Table 9.10. With this information, we can prepare the pro forma income statements, as shown in Table 9.11 (on page 254). From here, computing the operating cash flows is straightforward. The results are illustrated in the first part of Table 9.13 (on page 255).

TABLE 9.11   Pro forma income statements, power mulcher project

	Year							
	1	**2**	**3**	**4**	**5**	**6**	**7**	**8**
Unit price	$ 120	$ 120	$ 120	$ 110	$ 110	$ 110	$ 110	$ 110
Unit sales	3,000	5,000	6,000	6,500	6,000	5,000	4,000	3,000
Revenues	$360,000	$600,000	$720,000	$715,000	$660,000	$550,000	$440,000	$330,000
Variable costs	180,000	300,000	360,000	390,000	360,000	300,000	240,000	180,000
Fixed costs	25,000	25,000	25,000	25,000	25,000	25,000	25,000	25,000
Depreciation	114,320	195,920	139,920	99,920	71,440	71,440	71,440	35,600
EBIT	$ 40,680	$ 79,080	$195,080	$200,080	$203,560	$153,560	$103,560	$ 89,400
Taxes (34%)	13,831	26,887	66,327	68,027	69,210	52,210	35,210	30,396
Net income	$ 26,849	$ 52,193	$128,753	$132,053	$134,350	$101,350	$ 68,350	$ 59,004

TABLE 9.12

Changes in net working capital, power mulcher project

Year	Revenues	Net Working Capital	Cash Flow
0		$ 20,000	−$20,000
1	$360,000	54,000	− 34,000
2	600,000	90,000	− 36,000
3	720,000	108,000	− 18,000
4	715,000	107,250	750
5	660,000	99,000	8,250
6	550,000	82,500	16,500
7	440,000	66,000	16,500
8	330,000	49,500	16,500

Changes in NWC   Now that we have the operating cash flows, we need to determine the changes in NWC. By assumption, net working capital requirements change as sales change. In each year, we will generally either add to or recover some of our project net working capital. Recalling that NWC starts out at $20,000 and then rises to 15 percent of sales, we can calculate the amount of NWC for each year as illustrated in Table 9.12.

As illustrated, during the first year, net working capital grows from $20,000 to .15 × $360,000 = $54,000. The increase in net working capital for the year is thus $54,000 − 20,000 = $34,000. The remaining figures are calculated the same way.

Remember that an increase in net working capital is a cash outflow, so we use a negative sign in this table to indicate an additional investment that the firm makes in net working capital. A positive sign represents net working capital returning to the firm. Thus, for example, $16,500 in NWC flows back to the firm in Year 6. Over the project's life, net working capital builds to a peak of $108,000 and declines from there as sales begin to drop off.

We show the result for changes in net working capital in the second part of Table 9.13. Notice that at the end of the project's life there is $49,500 in net working capital still to be recovered. Therefore, in the last year, the project returns $16,500 of NWC during the year and then returns the remaining $49,500 at the end of the year for a total of $66,000.

Capital Spending   Finally, we have to account for the long-term capital invested in the project. In this case, we invest $800,000 at Year 0. By assumption, this equipment will be

TABLE 9.13 Projected cash flows, power mulcher project

					Year				
	0	1	2	3	4	5	6	7	8
I. Operating Cash Flow									
EBIT		$ 40,680	$ 79,080	$195,080	$200,080	$203,560	$153,560	$103,560	$ 89,400
Depreciation		114,320	195,920	139,920	99,920	71,440	71,440	71,440	35,600
Taxes		− 13,831	− 26,887	− 66,327	− 68,027	− 69,210	− 52,210	− 35,210	− 30,396
Operating cash flow		$141,169	$248,113	$268,673	$231,973	$205,790	$172,790	$139,790	$ 94,604
II. Net Working Capital									
Initial NWC	−$ 20,000								
Increases in NWC		−$ 34,000	−$ 36,000	−$ 18,000	$ 750	$ 8,250	$ 16,500	$ 16,500	$ 16,500
NWC recovery									49,500
Changes in NWC	−$ 20,000	−$ 34,000	−$ 36,000	−$ 18,000	$ 750	$ 8,250	$ 16,500	$ 16,500	$ 66,000
III. Capital Spending									
Initial outlay	−$800,000								
Aftertax salvage									$105,600
Capital spending	−$800,000								$105,600

255

TABLE 9.14   Projected total cash flows, power mulcher project

	0	1	2	3	4	5	6	7	8
					Year				
Operating cash flow		$ 141,169	$248,113	$268,673	$231,973	$205,790	$172,790	$139,790	$ 94,604
Changes in NWC	–$ 20,000	– 34,000	– 36,000	– 18,000	750	8,250	16,500	16,500	66,000
Capital spending	– 800,000								105,600
Total project cash flow	–$820,000	$107,169	$212,113	$250,673	$232,723	$214,040	$189,290	$156,290	$266,204
Cumulative cash flow	–$820,000	–$712,831	–$500,718	–$250,045	–$ 17,322	$196,718	$386,008	$542,298	$808,502
Discounted cash flow @ 15%	– 820,000	93,190	160,388	164,821	133,060	106,416	81,835	58,755	87,023

Net present value (15%) = $65,488
Internal rate of return   = 17.24%
Payback   = 4.08 years

worth $160,000 at the end of the project. It will have a book value of zero at that time. As we discussed above, this $160,000 excess of market value over book value is taxable, so the aftertax proceeds will be $160,000 × (1 − .34) = $105,600. These figures are shown in the third part of Table 9.13.

Total Cash Flow and Value   We now have all the cash flow pieces, and we put them together in Table 9.14. In addition to the total project cash flows, we have calculated the cumulative cash flows and the discounted cash flows. At this point, it's essentially plug-and-chug to calculate the net present value, internal rate of return, and payback.

If we sum the discounted flows and the initial investment, the net present value (at 15 percent) works out to be $65,488. This is positive, so, based on these preliminary projections, the power mulcher project is acceptable. The internal, or DCF, rate of return is greater than 15 percent since the NPV is positive. It works out to be 17.24 percent, again, indicating that the project is acceptable.

Looking at the cumulative cash flows, we see that the project has almost paid back after four years since the cumulative cash flow is almost zero at that time. As indicated, the fractional year works out to be $17,322/214,040 = .08, so the payback is 4.08 years. We can't say whether or not this is good since we don't have a benchmark for MMCC. This is the usual problem with payback periods.

Conclusion

This completes our preliminary DCF analysis. Where do we go from here? If we have a great deal of confidence in our projections, then there is no further analysis to be done. We should begin production and marketing immediately. It is unlikely that this will be the case. It is important to remember that the result of our analysis is an estimate of NPV, and we will usually have less than complete confidence in our projections. This means we have more work to do. In particular, we will almost surely want to spend some time evaluating the quality of our estimates. We will take up this subject in the next several sections.

CONCEPT QUESTIONS

9.4a Why is it important to consider changes in net working capital in developing cash flows? What is the effect of doing so?

9.4b How is depreciation calculated for fixed assets under current tax law? What effect do expected salvage value and estimated economic life have on the calculated depreciation deduction?

EVALUATING NPV ESTIMATES | 9.5

As we discussed in Chapter 8, an investment has a positive net present value if its market value exceeds its cost. Such an investment is desirable because it creates value for its owner. The primary problem in identifying such opportunities is that most of the time we can't actually observe the relevant market value. Instead, we estimate it. Having done so, it is only natural to wonder whether or not our estimates are at least close to the true values. We consider this question next.

The Basic Problem

Suppose we are working on a preliminary DCF analysis along the lines we described in previous sections. We carefully identify the relevant cash flows, avoiding such things as sunk costs, and we remember to consider working capital requirements. We add back any depreciation; we account for possible erosion; and we pay attention to opportunity costs. Finally, we double-check our calculations, and, when all is said and done, the bottom line is that the estimated NPV is positive.

Now what? Do we stop here and move on to the next proposal? Probably not. The fact that the estimated NPV is positive is definitely a good sign, but, more than anything, this tells us that we need to take a closer look.

If you think about it, there are two circumstances under which a discounted cash flow analysis could lead us to conclude that a project has a positive NPV. The first possibility is that the project really does have a positive NPV. That's the good news. The bad news is the second possibility: A project may appear to have a positive NPV because our estimate is inaccurate.

Notice that we could also err in the opposite way. If we conclude that a project has a negative NPV when the true NPV is positive, then we lose a valuable opportunity.

forecasting risk
The possibility that errors in projected cash flows will lead to incorrect decisions. Also, estimation risk.

Forecasting Risk

The key inputs into a DCF analysis are projected future cash flows. If these projections are seriously in error, then we have a classic GIGO, or garbage-in, garbage-out, system. In this case, no matter how carefully we arrange the numbers and manipulate them, the resulting answer can still be grossly misleading. This is the danger in using a relatively sophisticated technique like DCF. It is sometimes easy to get caught up in number crunching and forget the underlying nuts-and-bolts economic reality.

The possibility that we will make a bad decision because of errors in the projected cash flows is called **forecasting risk** (or *estimation risk*). Because of forecasting risk, there is the danger that we will think a project has a positive NPV when it really does not. How is this possible? It happens if we are overly optimistic about the future, and, as a result, our projected cash flows don't realistically reflect the possible future cash flows.

So far, we have not explicitly considered what to do about the possibility of errors in our forecasts, so our goal is to develop some tools that will be useful in identifying areas where potential errors exist and where they might be especially damaging. In one form or another, we will be trying to assess the economic "reasonableness" of our estimates. We will also be wondering how much damage will be done by errors in those estimates.

Sources of Value

The first line of defense against forecasting risk is simply to ask: What is it about this investment that leads to a positive NPV? We should be able to point to something specific as the source of value. For example, if the proposal under consideration involved a new product, then we might ask questions such as the following: Are we certain that our new product is significantly better than that of the competition? Can we truly manufacture at lower cost, or distribute more effectively, or identify undeveloped market niches, or gain control of a market?

These are just a few of the potential sources of value. There are many others. A key factor to keep in mind is the degree of competition in the market. It is a basic principle of economics that positive NPV investments will be rare in a highly competitive environment. Therefore, proposals that appear to show significant value in the face of stiff competition are particularly troublesome, and the likely reaction of the competition to any innovations must be closely examined.

The point to remember is that positive NPV investments are probably not all that common, and the number of positive NPV projects is almost certainly limited for any given firm. If we can't articulate some sound economic basis for thinking ahead of time that we have found something special, then the conclusion that our project has a positive NPV should be viewed with some suspicion.

CONCEPT QUESTIONS

9.5a What is forecasting risk? Why is it a concern for the financial manager?

9.5b What are some potential sources of value in a new project?

SCENARIO AND OTHER WHAT-IF ANALYSES | 9.6

Our basic approach to evaluating cash flow and NPV estimates involves asking what-if questions. Accordingly, we discuss some organized ways of going about a what-if analysis. Our goal in doing so is to assess the degree of forecasting risk and to identify those components most critical to the success or failure of an investment.

Getting Started

We are investigating a new project. Naturally, the first thing we do is estimate NPV based on our projected cash flows. We will call this the *base case*. Now, however, we recognize the possibility of error in those cash flow projections. After completing the base case, we thus wish to investigate the impact of different assumptions about the future on our estimates.

One way to organize this investigation is to put an upper and lower bound on the various components of the project. For example, suppose we forecast sales at 100 units per year. We know this estimate may be high or low, but we are relatively certain it is not off by more than 10 units in either direction. We would thus pick a lower bound of 90 and an upper bound of 110. We go on to assign such bounds to any other cash flow components we are unsure about.

When we pick these upper and lower bounds, we are not ruling out the possibility that the actual values could be outside this range. What we are saying, loosely speaking, is that it is unlikely that the true average (as opposed to our estimated average) of the possible values is outside this range.

An example is useful to illustrate the idea here. The project under consideration costs $200,000, has a five-year life, and has no salvage value. Depreciation is straight-line to zero. The required return is 12 percent, and the tax rate is 34 percent. In addition, we have compiled the following information:

	Base Case	Lower Bound	Upper Bound
Unit sales	6,000	5,500	6,500
Price per unit	$80	$75	$85
Variable costs per unit	$60	$58	$62
Fixed costs per year	$50,000	$45,000	$55,000

With this information, we can calculate the base-case NPV by first calculating net income:

Sales	$480,000
Variable costs	360,000
Fixed costs	50,000
Depreciation	40,000
EBIT	$ 30,000
Taxes (34%)	10,200
Net income	$ 19,800

Operating cash flow is thus $30,000 + 40,000 − 10,200 = $59,800 per year. At 12 percent, the five-year annuity factor is 3.6048, so the base-case NPV is:

$$\text{Base-case NPV} = -\$200,000 + 59,800 \times 3.6048$$
$$= \$15,567$$

Thus, the project looks good so far.

Scenario Analysis

scenario analysis
The determination of what happens to NPV estimates when we ask what-if questions.

The basic form of what-if analysis is called **scenario analysis.** What we do is investigate the changes in our NPV estimates that result from asking questions like, What if unit sales realistically should be projected at 5,500 units instead of 6,000?

Once we start looking at alternative scenarios, we might find that most of the plausible ones result in positive NPVs. In this case, we have some confidence in proceeding with the project. If a substantial percentage of the scenarios look bad, then the degree of forecasting risk is high and further investigation is in order.

There are a number of possible scenarios we could consider. A good place to start is with the worst-case scenario. This will tell us the minimum NPV of the project. If this is positive, we will be in good shape. While we are at it, we will go ahead and determine the other extreme, the best case. This puts an upper bound on our NPV.

To get the worst case, we assign the least favorable value to each item. This means *low* values for items like units sold and price per unit and *high* values for costs. We do the reverse for the best case. For our project, these values would be:

	Worst Case	Best Case
Unit sales	5,500	6,500
Price per unit	$75	$85
Variable costs per unit	$62	$58
Fixed costs	$55,000	$45,000

With this information, we can calculate the net income and cash flows under each scenario (check these for yourself):

Scenario	Net Income	Cash Flow	Net Present Value	IRR
Base case	$19,800	$59,800	$ 15,567	15.1%
Worst case*	− 15,510	24,490	− 111,719	−14.4
Best case	59,730	99,730	159,504	40.9

*We assume a tax credit is created in our worst-case scenario.

What we learn is that under the worst scenario, the cash flow is still positive at $24,490. That's good news. The bad news is that the return is −14.4 percent in this case, and the NPV is −$111,719. Since the project costs $200,000, we stand to lose a little more than half of the original investment under the worst possible scenario. The best case offers an attractive 41 percent return.

The terms *best case* and *worst case* are very commonly used, and we will stick with them, but we should note that they are somewhat misleading. The absolutely best thing that could happen would be something absurdly unlikely, such as launching a new diet soda and subsequently learning that our (patented) formulation also just happens to cure the common cold. Similarly, the true worst case would involve some incredibly remote possibility of total disaster. We're not claiming that these things don't happen; once in a while they do. Some products, such as personal computers, succeed beyond the wildest of expectations, and some, such as asbestos, turn out to be absolute catastrophes. Instead, our point is that in assessing the reasonableness of an NPV estimate, we need to stick to cases that are reasonably likely to occur.

Instead of *best* and *worst,* then, it is probably more accurate to say *optimistic* and *pessimistic*. In broad terms, if we were thinking about a reasonable range for, say, unit sales, then what we call the best case would correspond to something near the upper end of that range. The worst case would simply correspond to the lower end.

As we have mentioned, there is an unlimited number of different scenarios that we could examine. At a minimum, we might want to investigate two intermediate cases by going halfway between the base amounts and the extreme amounts. This would give us five scenarios in all, including the base case.

Beyond this point, it is hard to know when to stop. As we generate more and more possibilities, we run the risk of "paralysis of analysis." The difficulty is that no matter how many scenarios we run, all we can learn are possibilities, some good and some bad. Beyond that, we don't get any guidance as to what to do. Scenario analysis is thus useful in telling us what can happen and in helping us gauge the potential for disaster, but it does not tell us whether or not to take the project.

Sensitivity Analysis

Sensitivity analysis is a variation on scenario analysis that is useful in pinpointing the areas where forecasting risk is especially severe. The basic idea with a sensitivity analysis is to freeze all of the variables except one and then see how sensitive our estimate of NPV is to changes in that one variable. If our NPV estimate turns out to be very sensitive to relatively small changes in the projected value of some component of project cash flow, then the forecasting risk associated with that variable is high.

To illustrate how sensitivity analysis works, we go back to our base case for every item except unit sales. We can then calculate cash flow and NPV using the largest and smallest unit sales figures.

sensitivity analysis
Investigation of what happens to NPV when only one variable is changed.

Scenario	Unit Sales	Cash Flow	Net Present Value	IRR
Base case	6,000	$59,800	$15,567	15.1%
Worst case	5,500	53,200	− 8,226	10.3
Best case	6,500	66,400	39,357	19.7

The results of our sensitivity analysis for unit sales can be illustrated graphically as in Figure 9.1. Here we place NPV on the vertical axis and unit sales on the horizontal axis. When we plot the combinations of unit sales versus NPV, we see that all possible combinations fall

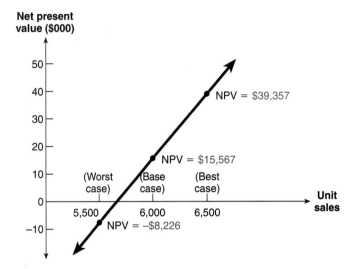

FIGURE 9.1

Sensitivity analysis for
unit sales

on a straight line. The steeper the resulting line is, the greater is the sensitivity of the estimated
NPV to the projected value of the variable being investigated.

By way of comparison, we now freeze everything except fixed costs and repeat the
analysis:

Scenario	Unit Sales	Cash Flow	Net Present Value	IRR
Base case	$50,000	$59,800	$15,567	15.1%
Worst case	55,000	56,500	3,670	12.7
Best case	45,000	63,100	27,461	17.4

What we see here is that, given our ranges, the estimated NPV of this project is more sensitive to projected unit sales than it is to projected fixed costs. In fact, under the worst case
for fixed costs, the NPV is still positive.

As we have illustrated, sensitivity analysis is useful in pinpointing those variables
that deserve the most attention. If we find that our estimated NPV is especially sensitive
to a variable that is difficult to forecast (such as unit sales), then the degree of forecasting risk is high. We might decide that further market research would be a good idea in
this case.

Because sensitivity analysis is a form of scenario analysis, it suffers from the same
drawbacks. Sensitivity analysis is useful for pointing out where forecasting errors will do
the most damage, but it does not tell us what to do about possible errors.

CONCEPT QUESTIONS

9.6a What are scenario and sensitivity analyses?

9.6b What are the drawbacks to what-if analyses?

ADDITIONAL CONSIDERATIONS IN CAPITAL BUDGETING | 9.7

Our final task for this chapter is a brief discussion of two additional considerations in capital budgeting: managerial options and capital rationing. Both of these can be very important in practice, but, as we will see, explicitly dealing with either of them is difficult.

Managerial Options and Capital Budgeting

In our capital budgeting analysis thus far, we have more or less ignored the possibility of future managerial actions. Implicitly, we have assumed that once a project is launched, its basic features cannot be changed. For this reason, we say that our analysis is *static* (as opposed to dynamic).

In reality, depending on what actually happens in the future, there will always be ways to modify a project. We will call these opportunities **managerial options.** Because they involve real (as opposed to financial) assets, such options are often called "real" options. There are a great number of these options. The way a product is priced, manufactured, advertised, and produced can all be changed, and these are just a few of the possibilities. We discuss some of the most important managerial options in the next few sections.

managerial options
Opportunities that managers can exploit if certain things happen in the future. Also known as "real" options.

Contingency Planning   The various what-if procedures in this chapter have another use. We can also view them as primitive ways of exploring the dynamics of a project and investigating managerial options. What we think about in this case are some of the possible futures that could come about and what actions we might take if they do.

For example, we might find that a project fails to break even when sales drop below 10,000 units. This is a fact that is interesting to know, but the more important thing is to then go on and ask, What actions are we going to take if this actually occurs? This is called **contingency planning,** and it amounts to an investigation of some of the managerial options implicit in a project.

contingency planning
Taking into account the managerial options implicit in a project.

There is no limit to the number of possible futures, or contingencies, that we could investigate. However, there are some broad classes, and we consider these next.

The option to expand   One particularly important option we have not explicitly addressed is the option to expand. If we truly find a positive NPV project, then there is an obvious consideration. Can we expand the project or repeat it to get an even larger NPV? Our static analysis implicitly assumes that the scale of the project is fixed.

For example, if the sales demand for a particular product were to greatly exceed expectations, we might investigate increasing production. If this were not feasible for some reason, then we could always increase cash flow by raising the price. Either way, the potential cash flow is higher than we have indicated because we have implicitly assumed that no expansion or price increase is possible. Overall, because we ignore the option to expand in our analysis, we *underestimate* NPV (all other things being equal).

The option to abandon   At the other extreme, the option to scale back or even abandon a project is also quite valuable. For example, if a project does not even cover its own expenses, we might be better off if we just abandoned it. Our DCF analysis implicitly assumes that we would keep operating even in this case.

In reality, if sales demand were significantly below expectations, we might be able to sell off some capacity or put it to another use. Maybe the product or service could be redesigned or otherwise improved. Regardless of the specifics, we once again *underestimate* NPV if we assume that the project must last for some fixed number of years, no matter what happens in the future.

The option to wait   Implicitly, we have treated proposed investments as if they were "go or no-go" decisions. Actually, there is a third possibility. The project can be postponed, perhaps in hope of more favorable conditions. We call this the option to wait.

For example, suppose an investment costs $120 and has a perpetual cash flow of $10 per year. If the discount rate is 10 percent, then the NPV is $10/.10 − 120 = −$20, so the project should not be undertaken now. However, this does not mean that we should forget about the project forever, because in the next period, the appropriate discount rate could be different. If it fell to, say, 5 percent, then the NPV would be $10/.05 − 120 = $80, and we would take the project.

More generally, as long as there is some possible future scenario under which a project has a positive NPV, then the option to wait is valuable.

strategic options
Options for future, related business products or strategies.

Strategic Options   Companies sometimes undertake new projects just to explore possibilities and evaluate potential future business strategies. This is a little like testing the water by sticking a toe in before diving. Such projects are difficult to analyze using conventional DCF methods because most of the benefits come in the form of **strategic options,** that is, options for future, related business moves. Projects that create such options may be very valuable, but that value is difficult to measure. Research and development, for example, is an important and valuable activity for many firms precisely because it creates options for new products and procedures.

To give another example, a large manufacturer might decide to open a retail outlet as a pilot study. The primary goal is to gain some market insight. Because of the high start-up costs, this one operation won't break even. However, based on the sales experience from the pilot, we can then evaluate whether or not to open more outlets, to change the product mix, to enter new markets, and so on. The information gained and the resulting options for actions are all valuable, but coming up with a reliable dollar figure is probably not feasible.

Conclusion   We have seen that incorporating options into capital budgeting analysis is not easy. What can we do about them in practice? The answer is that we can only keep them in the back of our minds as we work with the projected cash flows. We will tend to underestimate NPV by ignoring options. The damage might be small for a highly structured, very specific proposal, but it might be great for an exploratory one.

capital rationing
The situation that exists if a firm has positive NPV projects but cannot obtain the necessary financing.

Capital Rationing

Capital rationing is said to exist when we have profitable (positive NPV) investments available but we can't get the needed funds to undertake them. For example, as division managers for a large corporation, we might identify $5 million in excellent projects, but find that, for whatever reason, we can spend only $2 million. Now what? Unfortunately, for reasons we will discuss, there may be no truly satisfactory answer.

soft rationing
The situation that occurs when units in a business are allocated a certain amount of financing for capital budgeting.

Soft Rationing   The situation we have just described is **soft rationing.** This occurs when, for example, different units in a business are allocated some fixed amount of money each year for capital spending. Such an allocation is primarily a means of controlling and keeping track of overall spending. The important thing about soft rationing is that the corporation as a whole isn't short of capital; more can be raised on ordinary terms if management so desires.

If we face soft rationing, the first thing to do is try and get a larger allocation. Failing that, then one common suggestion is to generate as large a net present value as possible within the existing budget. This amounts to choosing those projects with the largest benefit-cost ratio (profitability index).

Strictly speaking, this is the correct thing to do only if the soft rationing is a one-time event; that is, it won't exist next year. If the soft rationing is a chronic problem, then something is amiss. The reason goes all the way back to Chapter 1. Ongoing soft rationing means we are constantly bypassing positive NPV investments. This contradicts our goal of the firm. If we are not trying to maximize value, then the question of which projects to take becomes ambiguous because we no longer have an objective goal in the first place.

Hard Rationing   With **hard rationing,** a business cannot raise capital for a project under any circumstances. For large, healthy corporations, this situation probably does not occur very often. This is fortunate because with hard rationing, our DCF analysis breaks down, and the best course of action is ambiguous.

The reason DCF analysis breaks down has to do with the required return. Suppose we say that our required return is 20 percent. Implicitly, we are saying that we will take a project with a return that exceeds this. However, if we face hard rationing, then we are not going to take a new project no matter what the return on that project is, so the whole concept of a required return is ambiguous. About the only interpretation we can give this situation is that the required return is so large that no project has a positive NPV in the first place.

Hard rationing can occur when a company experiences financial distress, meaning that bankruptcy is a possibility. Also, a firm may not be able to raise capital without violating a preexisting contractual agreement. We discuss these situations in greater detail in a later chapter.

hard rationing
The situation that occurs when a business cannot raise financing for a project under any circumstances.

CONCEPT QUESTIONS

9.7a   Why do we say that our standard discounted cash flow analysis is static?

9.7b   What are managerial options in capital budgeting? Give some examples.

9.7c   What is capital rationing? What types are there? What problems does capital rationing create for discounted cash flow analysis?

SUMMARY AND CONCLUSIONS

This chapter has described how to go about putting together a discounted cash flow analysis and evaluating the results. In it, we covered:

1. The identification of relevant project cash flows. We discussed project cash flows and described how to handle some issues that often come up, including sunk costs, opportunity costs, financing costs, net working capital, and erosion.

2. Preparing and using pro forma, or projected, financial statements. We showed how pro forma financial statement information is useful in coming up with projected cash flows.

3. The use of scenario and sensitivity analysis. These tools are widely used to evaluate the impact of assumptions made about future cash flows and NPV estimates.

4. Additional issues in capital budgeting. We examined the managerial options implicit in many capital budgeting situations. We also discussed the capital rationing problem.

The discounted cash flow analysis we've covered here is a standard tool in the business world. It is a very powerful tool, so care should be taken in its use. The most important thing is to get the cash flows identified in a way that makes economic sense. This chapter gives you a good start on learning to do this.

CHAPTER REVIEW AND SELF-TEST PROBLEMS

9.1   Calculating Operating Cash Flow.   Mater Pasta, Inc., has projected a sales volume of $1,432 for the second year of a proposed expansion project. Costs normally run 70 percent of sales, or about $1,002 in this case. The depreciation expense will be $80, and the tax rate is 34 percent. What is the operating cash flow?

9.2   Scenario Analysis.   A project under consideration costs $500,000, has a five-year life, and has no salvage value. Depreciation is straight-line to zero. The required return is 15 percent, and the tax rate is 34 percent. Sales are projected at 400 units per year. Price per unit is $3,000, variable cost per unit is $1,900, and fixed costs are $250,000 per year. No net working capital is required.

Suppose you think the unit sales, price, variable cost, and fixed cost projections are accurate to within 5 percent. What are the upper and lower bounds for these projections? What is the base-case NPV? What are the best- and worst-case scenario NPVs?

■ Answers to Chapter Review and Self-Test Problems

9.1   First, we can calculate the project's EBIT, its tax bill, and its net income.

$$\text{EBIT} = \$1,432 - 1,002 - 80 = \$350$$
$$\text{Taxes} = \$350 \times .34 = \$119$$
$$\text{Net income} = \$350 - 119 = \$231$$

With these numbers, operating cash flow is:

$$\text{OCF} = \text{EBIT} + \text{Depreciation} - \text{Taxes}$$
$$= \$350 + 80 - 119$$
$$= \$311$$

9.2   We can summarize the relevant information as follows:

	Base Case	**Lower Bound**	**Upper Bound**
Unit sales	400	380	420
Price per unit	$3,000	$2,850	$3,150
Variable costs per unit	$1,900	$1,805	$1,995
Fixed costs	$250,000	$237,500	$262,500

The depreciation is $100,000 per year, and the tax rate is 34 percent, so we can calculate the cash flows under each scenario. Remember that we assign high costs and low prices and volume under the worst case and just the opposite for the best case.

Scenario	Unit Sales	Price	Variable Costs	Fixed Costs	Cash Flow
Base case	400	$3,000	$1,900	$250,000	$159,400
Best case	420	3,150	1,805	237,500	250,084
Worst case	380	2,850	1,995	262,500	75,184

At 15 percent, the five-year annuity factor is 3.35216, so the NPVs are:

$$\text{Base-case NPV} = -\$500,000 + 159,400 \times 3.35216$$
$$= \$34,334$$
$$\text{Best-case NPV} = -\$500,000 + 250,084 \times 3.35216$$
$$= \$338,320$$
$$\text{Worst-case NPV} = -\$500,000 + 75,184 \times 3.35216$$
$$= -\$247,972$$

CRITICAL THINKING AND CONCEPTS REVIEW

1. **Opportunity Cost.** In the context of capital budgeting, what is an opportunity cost?

2. **Depreciation.** Given the choice, would a firm prefer to use MACRS depreciation or straight-line depreciation? Why?

3. **Net Working Capital.** In our capital budgeting examples, we assumed that a firm would recover all of the working capital it invested in a project. Is this a reasonable assumption? When might it not be valid?

4. **Stand-Alone Principle.** Suppose a financial manager is quoted as saying, "Our firm uses the stand-alone principle. Because we treat projects like minifirms in our evaluation process, we include financing costs because they are relevant at the firm level." Critically evaluate this statement.

5. **Cash Flow and Depreciation.** "When evaluating projects, we're only concerned with the relevant incremental aftertax cash flows. Therefore, because depreciation is a noncash expense, we should ignore its effects when evaluating projects." Critically evaluate this statement.

6. **Capital Budgeting Considerations.** A major college textbook publisher has an existing finance textbook. The publisher is debating whether or not to produce an "essentialized" version, meaning a shorter (and lower-priced) book. What are some of the considerations that should come into play?

To answer the next three questions, refer to the following example.
In early 1998, General Motors announced plans to launch the Cadillac Escalade, its first truck under the Cadillac brand name and its first luxury sport-utility vehicle (SUV). GM's decision was primarily a reaction to the runaway success of such new luxury SUVs as Ford's Lincoln Navigator and Mercedes-Benz's new M-class. These vehicles were exceptionally profitable; for example, each of the 18,500

Lincoln Navigators that sold in the four months after their introduction in June 1997 generated well over $10,000 in profit for Ford. GM had previously been unwilling to build a luxury SUV, but these profit margins were too large to ignore.

GM planned to introduce the truck as a revised version of the new GMC Denali, which was introduced in February 1998. However, some analysts questioned GM's decision, suggesting that GM was too late entering the market; concerns were also expressed about whether GM would just end up taking sales from its other SUV lines.

7. **Erosion.** In evaluating the Escalade, under what circumstances might GM have concluded that erosion of the Denali line was irrelevant?

8. **Capital Budgeting.** GM was not the only manufacturer looking at the big sport-utility category. Chrysler, however, initially decided *not* to go ahead with an entry (Chrysler later reversed course on this issue). Why might one company decide to proceed when another would not?

9. **Capital Budgeting.** In evaluating the Escalade, what do you think GM needs to assume regarding the enormous profit margins that exist in this market? Is it likely they will be maintained when GM and others enter this market?

10. **Sensitivity Analysis and Scenario Analysis.** What is the essential difference between sensitivity analysis and scenario analysis?

11. **Marginal Cash Flows.** A co-worker claims that looking at all this marginal this and incremental that is just a bunch of nonsense, and states, "Listen, if our average revenue doesn't exceed our average cost, then we will have a negative cash flow, and we will go broke!" How do you respond?

12. **Capital Rationing.** Going all the way back to Chapter 1, recall that we saw that partnerships and proprietorships can face difficulties when it comes to raising capital. In the context of this chapter, the implication is that small businesses will generally face what problem?

13. **Forecasting Risk.** What is forecasting risk? In general, would the degree of forecasting risk be greater for a new product or a cost-cutting proposal? Why?

14. **Options and NPV.** What is the option to abandon? The option to expand? Explain why we tend to underestimate NPV when we ignore these options.

QUESTIONS AND PROBLEMS

Basic
(Questions 1–20)

1. **Relevant Cash Flows.** Gilligan, Inc., is looking at setting up a new manufacturing plant in South Park. The company bought some land six years ago for $6 million in anticipation of using it as a warehouse and distribution site, but the company has since decided to rent facilities elsewhere. The land was appraised last week at $1.2 million. The company now wants to build its new manufacturing plant on this land; the plant will cost $9 million to build, and the site requires $350,000 worth of grading before it is suitable for construction. What is the proper cash flow amount to use as the initial investment in fixed assets when evaluating this project? Why?

2. **Relevant Cash Flows.** Speedy Racer Corp. currently sells 18,000 motor homes per year at $40,000 each, and 6,000 luxury motor coaches per year at $55,000 each. The company wants to introduce a new portable camper to fill out its product line; it hopes to sell 12,000 of these campers per year at $10,000 each. An independent consultant has determined that if Speedy Racer introduces the new campers, it should boost the sales of its existing motor homes by 5,000 units per year, and re-

duce the sales of its motor coaches by 2,000 units per year. What is the amount to use as the annual sales figure when evaluating this project? Why?

3. **Calculating Projected Net Income.** A proposed new investment has projected sales of $700,000. Variable costs are 60 percent of sales, and fixed costs are $165,000; depreciation is $75,000. Prepare a pro forma income statement assuming a tax rate of 35 percent. What is the projected net income?

4. **Calculating OCF.** Consider the following income statement:

Sales	$847,150
Costs	423,820
Depreciation	109,000
EBIT	?
Taxes (34%)	?
Net income	?

Fill in the missing numbers and then calculate the OCF. What is the depreciation tax shield?

5. **Calculating Depreciation.** A piece of newly purchased industrial equipment costs $924,000 and is classified as seven-year property under MACRS. Calculate the annual depreciation allowances and end-of-the-year book values for this equipment.

6. **Calculating Salvage Value.** Consider an asset that costs $448,000 and is depreciated straight-line to zero over its eight-year tax life. The asset is to be used in a five-year project; at the end of the project, the asset can be sold for $115,000. If the relevant tax rate is 35 percent, what is the aftertax cash flow from the sale of this asset?

7. **Calculating Salvage Value.** An asset used in a four-year project falls in the five-year MACRS class for tax purposes. The asset has an acquisition cost of $8,500,000 and will be sold for $1,800,000 at the end of the project. If the tax rate is 34 percent, what is the aftertax salvage value of the asset?

8. **Identifying Cash Flows.** Last year, Carl's Bail Bonds reported sales of $58,200 and costs of $22,700. The following information was also reported for the same period:

	Beginning	Ending
Accounts receivable	$24,880	$21,520
Inventory	4,270	6,512
Accounts payable	40,680	44,540

Based on this information, what was Carl's change in net working capital for last year? What was the net cash flow?

9. **Calculating Project OCF.** D. Ervin, Inc., is considering a new three-year expansion project that requires an initial fixed asset investment of $1.5 million. The fixed asset will be depreciated straight-line to zero over its three-year tax life, after which time it will be worthless. The project is estimated to generate $1,750,000 in annual sales, with costs of $575,000. If the tax rate is 35 percent, what is the OCF for this project?

10. **Calculating Project NPV.** In the previous problem, suppose the required return on the project is 18 percent. What is the project's NPV?

11. **Calculating Project Cash Flow from Assets.** In the previous problem, suppose the project requires an initial investment in net working capital of $275,000 and the

fixed asset will have a market value of $325,000 at the end of the project. What is the project's Year 0 net cash flow? Year 1? Year 2? Year 3? What is the new NPV?

12.   **NPV and Modified ACRS.**   In the previous problem, suppose the fixed asset actually falls into the three-year MACRS class. All the other facts are the same. What is the project's Year 1 net cash flow now? Year 2? Year 3? What is the new NPV?

13.   **Project Evaluation.**   Kaleb's Korndogs is looking at a new sausage system with an installed cost of $485,000. This cost will be depreciated straight-line to zero over the project's five-year life, at the end of which the sausage system can be scrapped for $60,000. The sausage system will save the firm $123,000 per year in pretax operating costs, and the system requires an initial investment in net working capital of $27,000. If the tax rate is 34 percent and the discount rate is 10 percent, what is the NPV of this project?

14.   **Project Evaluation.**   Your firm is contemplating the purchase of a new $650,000 computer-based order entry system. The system will be depreciated straight-line to zero over its five-year life. It will be worth $150,000 at the end of that time. You will save $300,000 before taxes per year in order processing costs, and you will be able to reduce working capital by $63,000 at the beginning of the project. Working capital will revert back to normal at end of the project. If the tax rate is 35 percent, what is the IRR for this project?

15.   **Project Evaluation.**   In the previous problem, suppose your required return on the project is 20 percent and your pretax cost savings are only $250,000 per year. Will you accept the project? What if the pretax cost savings are only $200,000 per year? At what level of pretax cost savings would you be indifferent between accepting the project and not accepting it?

16.   **Scenario Analysis.**   Covington Transmissions, Inc., has the following estimates for its new gear assembly project: price = $1,320 per unit; variable costs = $120 per unit; fixed costs = $8 million; quantity = 90,000 units. Suppose the company believes all of its estimates are accurate only to within ±15 percent. What values should the company use for the four variables given here when it performs its best-case scenario analysis? What about the worst-case scenario?

17.   **Sensitivity Analysis.**   For the company in the previous problem, suppose management is most concerned about the impact of its price estimate on the project's profitability. How could you address this concern for Covington Transmissions? Describe how you would calculate your answer. What values would you use for the other forecast variables?

18.   **Sensitivity Analysis and Break-Even.**   We are evaluating a project that costs $1,200,000, has a six-year life, and has no salvage value. Assume that depreciation is straight-line to zero over the life of the project. Sales are projected at 110,000 units per year. Price per unit is $34.00, variable cost per unit is $18, and fixed costs are $900,000 per year. The tax rate is 35 percent, and we require a 15 percent return on this project.

   a.   Calculate the base-case cash flow and NPV. What is the sensitivity of NPV to changes in the sales figure? Explain what your answer tells you about a 500-unit decrease in projected sales.

   b.   What is the sensitivity of OCF to changes in the variable cost figure? Explain what your answer tells you about a $1 decrease in estimated variable costs.

19.   **Scenario Analysis.**   In the previous problem, suppose the projections given for price, quantity, variable costs, and fixed costs are all accurate to within ±10 percent. Calculate the best-case and worst-case NPV figures.

20.   **Calculating Project Cash Flows and NPV.**   Pappy's Potato has come up with a new product, the Pet Potato (they are freeze-dried to last longer). Pappy's paid

$120,000 for a marketing survey to determine the viability of the product. It is felt that Pet Potato will generate sales of $270,000 per year. The fixed costs associated with this will be $115,000 per year, and variable costs will amount to 30 percent of sales. The equipment necessary for production of the Potato Pets will cost $200,000 and will be depreciated in a straight-line manner for the four years of the product life (as with all fads, it is felt the sales will end quickly). This is the only initial cost for the production. Pappy's is in a 40 percent tax bracket and has a required return of 9 percent. Calculate the payback period, NPV, and IRR.

21. **Cost-Cutting Proposals.** Kurt's Auto Shop is considering a four-year project to improve its production efficiency. Buying a new machine press for $450,000 is estimated to result in $195,000 in annual pretax cost savings. The press falls in the MACRS five-year class, and it will have a salvage value at the end of the project of $90,000. The press also requires an initial investment in spare parts inventory of $18,000, along with an additional $3,000 in inventory for each succeeding year of the project. If the shop's tax rate is 34 percent and its discount rate is 15 percent, should KAS buy and install the machine press?

Intermediate
(Questions 21–25)

22. **Sensitivity Analysis.** Consider a three-year project with the following information: initial fixed asset investment = $375,000; straight-line depreciation to zero over the three-year life; zero salvage value; price = $26; variable costs = $15; fixed costs = $165,000; quantity sold = 110,000 units; tax rate = 34 percent. How sensitive is OCF to changes in quantity sold?

23. **Project Analysis.** You are considering a new product launch. The project will cost $700,000, have a four-year life, and have no salvage value; depreciation is straight-line to zero. Sales are projected at 140 units per year; price per unit will be $18,000, variable cost per unit will be $13,000, and fixed costs will be $125,000 per year. The required return on the project is 15 percent, and the relevant tax rate is 35 percent.

    a. Based on your experience, you think the unit sales, variable cost, and fixed cost projections given here are probably accurate to within ±10 percent. What are the upper and lower bounds for these projections? What is the base-case NPV? What are the best-case and worst-case scenarios?

    b. Evaluate the sensitivity of your base-case NPV to changes in fixed costs.

24. **Project Analysis.** McGilla Golf has decided to sell a new line of golf clubs. The clubs will sell for $600 per set and have a variable cost of $240 per set. The company has spent $150,000 for a marketing study that determined the company will sell 50,000 sets per year for seven years. The marketing study also determined that the company will lose sales of 12,000 sets of its high-priced clubs. The high-priced clubs sell at $1,000 and have variable costs of $550. The company will also increase sales of its cheap clubs by 10,000 sets. The cheap clubs sell for $300 and have variable costs of $100 per set. The fixed costs each year will be $7,000,000. The company has also spent $1,000,000 on research and development for the new clubs. The plant and equipment required will cost $15,400,000 and will be depreciated on a straight-line basis. The new clubs will also require an increase in net working capital of $900,000 that will be returned at the end of the project. The tax rate is 40 percent, and the cost of capital is 14 percent. Calculate the payback period, the NPV, and the IRR.

25. **Scenario Analysis.** In the previous problem, you feel that the values are accurate to within only ±10 percent. What are the best-case and worst-case NPVs? (Hint: The price and variable costs for the two existing sets of clubs are known with certainty; only the sales gained or lost are uncertain.)

www.mhhe.com/rwj

Spreadsheet Templates 5, 18, 20

CHAPTER

10

Some Lessons from Capital Market History

AFTER STUDYING THIS CHAPTER, YOU SHOULD HAVE A GOOD UNDERSTANDING OF:

- How to calculate the return on an investment

- The historical returns on various important types of investments

- The historical risks on various important types of investments

NO MATTER HOW you slice it, the Nasdaq was the place to invest in 1999 and early 2000. As of the end of April 2000, the Nasdaq Composite Index was up 51.8 percent over its close just 12 months earlier. To put that in perspective, the Dow Jones Industrial Average was down .5 percent over that same period. However, these numbers mask the wild ride that Nasdaq took investors on over those 12 months. At the end of April 2000, the Nasdaq was actually down 23.5 percent from its all-time high reached just a month and a half earlier.

Perhaps the biggest mover on the Nasdaq over this period was Puma Technology, whose stock price rose from $2.72 to $30.63, for a staggering increase of 1,026 percent. Again, however, there's more to the story. Puma's stock price actually topped out at $98 on March 9, 2000. If you were unlucky enough to have bought at the peak and held to the end of April, your investment would have declined an equally staggering 69 percent in just a month and a half! These examples illustrate that there were tremendous potential returns to be made during 1999 and 2000, but there was also the risk of losing money, and lots of it. So what should you, as a stock market investor, expect when you invest your own money? In this chapter, we study over seven decades of market history to find out.

This chapter and the next take us into new territory: the relation between risk and return. As you will see, this chapter has a lot of very practical information for anyone thinking of investing in financial assets such as stocks and bonds. For example, suppose you were to start investing in stocks today. Do you think your money would grow at an average rate of 5 percent per year? Or 10 percent? Or 20 percent? This chapter gives you an idea of what to expect (the answer may surprise you). The chapter also shows how risky certain investments can be, and it gives you the tools to think about risk in an objective way.

Thus far, we haven't had much to say about what determines the required return on an investment. In one sense, the answer is very simple: The required return depends on the risk of the investment. The greater the risk, the greater is the required return.

Having said this, we are left with a somewhat more difficult problem. How can we measure the amount of risk present in an investment? Put another way, what does it mean to say that one investment is riskier than another? Obviously, we need to define what we mean by risk if we are going to answer these questions. This is our task in the next two chapters.

From these last several chapters, we know that one of the responsibilities of the financial manager is to assess the value of proposed investments. In doing this, it is important that we first look at what financial investments have to offer. At a minimum, the return we require from a proposed nonfinancial investment must be at least as large as what we can get from buying financial assets of similar risk.

Our goal in this chapter is to provide a perspective on what capital market history can tell us about risk and return. The most important thing to get out of this chapter is a feel for the numbers. What is a high return? What is a low one? More generally, what returns should we expect from financial assets and what are the risks from such investments? This perspective is essential for understanding how to analyze and value risky investment projects.

We start our discussion of risk and return by describing the historical experience of investors in the U.S. financial markets. In 1931, for example, the stock market lost 43 percent of its value. Just two years later, the stock market gained 54 percent. In more recent memory, the market lost about 25 percent of its value on October 19, 1987, alone. What lessons, if any, can financial managers learn from such shifts in the stock market? We will explore the last half century (and then some) of market history to find out.

Not everyone agrees on the value of studying history. On the one hand, there is philosopher George Santayana's famous comment "Those who do not remember the past are condemned to repeat it." On the other hand, there is industrialist Henry Ford's equally famous comment "History is more or less bunk." Nonetheless, perhaps everyone would agree with the following observation from Mark Twain: "October. This is one of the peculiarly dangerous months to speculate in stocks in. The others are July, January, September, April, November, May, March, June, December, August, and February."

There are two central lessons that emerge from our study of market history. First: There is a reward for bearing risk. Second: The greater the potential reward is, the greater is the risk. To understand these facts about market returns, we devote much of this chapter to reporting the statistics and numbers that make up the modern capital market history of the United States. In the next chapter, these facts provide the foundation for our study of how financial markets put a price on risk.

10.1 | RETURNS

We wish to discuss historical returns on different types of financial assets. The first thing we need to do, then, is to briefly discuss how to calculate the return from investing.

Dollar Returns

If you buy an asset of any sort, your gain (or loss) from that investment is called your *return on investment*. This return will usually have two components. First: You may receive some cash directly while you own the investment. This is called the income component of your return. Second: The value of the asset you purchase will often change. In this case, you have a capital gain or capital loss on your investment.[1]

---

[1]As we mentioned in an earlier chapter, strictly speaking, what is and what is not a capital gain (or loss) is determined by the IRS. We thus use the terms loosely.

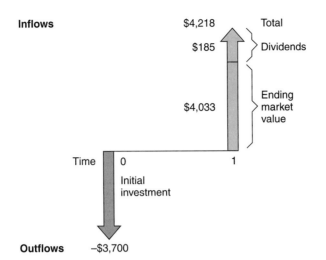

Inflows

$4,218   Total

$185   } Dividends

$4,033   } Ending market value

Time   0   1

Initial investment

Outflows   −$3,700

FIGURE 10.1

Dollar returns

To illustrate, suppose the Video Concept Company has several thousand shares of stock outstanding. You purchased some of these shares of stock in the company at the beginning of the year. It is now year-end, and you want to determine how well you have done on your investment.

First, over the year, a company may pay cash dividends to its shareholders. As a stockholder in Video Concept Company, you are a part owner of the company. If the company is profitable, it may choose to distribute some of its profits to shareholders (we discuss the details of dividend policy in a later chapter). So, as the owner of some stock, you will receive some cash. This cash is the income component from owning the stock.

In addition to the dividend, the other part of your return is the capital gain or capital loss on the stock. This part arises from changes in the value of your investment. For example, consider the cash flows illustrated in Figure 10.1. At the beginning of the year, the stock is selling for $37 per share. If you buy 100 shares, you have a total outlay of $3,700. Suppose, over the year, the stock pays a dividend of $1.85 per share. By the end of the year, then, you will have received income of:

Dividend = $1.85 × 100 = $185

Also, the value of the stock rises to $40.33 per share by the end of the year. Your 100 shares are worth $4,033, so you have a capital gain of:

Capital gain = ($40.33 − 37) × 100 = $333

On the other hand, if the price had dropped to, say, $34.78, you would have had a capital loss of:

Capital loss = ($34.78 − 37) × 100 = −$222

Notice that a capital loss is the same thing as a negative capital gain.

The total dollar return on your investment is the sum of the dividend and the capital gain:

Total dollar return = Dividend income + Capital gain (or loss)   **[10.1]**

In our first example, the total dollar return is thus given by:

Total dollar return = $185 + 333 = $518

Notice that, if you sold the stock at the end of the year, the total amount of cash you would have would be your initial investment plus the total return. In the preceding example, then:

$$\text{Total cash if stock is sold} = \text{Initial investment} + \text{Total return}$$
$$= \$3,700 + 518$$
$$= \$4,218 \qquad \qquad [10.2]$$

As a check, notice that this is the same as the proceeds from the sale of the stock plus the dividends:

$$\text{Proceeds from stock sale} + \text{Dividends} = \$40.33 \times 100 + 185$$
$$= \$4,033 + 185$$
$$= \$4,218$$

Suppose you hold on to your Video Concept stock and don't sell it at the end of the year. Should you still consider the capital gain as part of your return? Isn't this only a "paper" gain and not really a return if you don't sell the stock?

The answer to the first question is a strong yes, and the answer to the second is an equally strong no. The capital gain is every bit as much a part of your return as the dividend, and you should certainly count it as part of your return. That you actually decided to keep the stock and not sell (you don't "realize" the gain) is irrelevant because you could have converted it to cash if you had wanted to. Whether you choose to do so or not is up to you.

After all, if you insisted on converting your gain to cash, you could always sell the stock at year-end and immediately reinvest by buying the stock back. There is no net difference between doing this and just not selling (assuming, of course, that there are no tax consequences from selling the stock). Again, the point is that whether you actually cash out and buy sodas (or whatever) or reinvest by not selling doesn't affect the return you earn.

Percentage Returns

It is usually more convenient to summarize information about returns in percentage terms, rather than dollar terms, because that way your return doesn't depend on how much you actually invest. The question we want to answer is this: How much do we get for each dollar we invest?

To answer this question, let P_t be the price of the stock at the beginning of the year and let D_{t+1} be the dividend paid on the stock during the year. Consider the cash flows in Figure 10.2. These are the same as those in Figure 10.1, except that we have now expressed everything on a per-share basis.

In our example, the price at the beginning of the year was $37 per share and the dividend paid during the year on each share was $1.85. As we discussed in Chapter 7, expressing the dividend as a percentage of the beginning stock price results in the dividend yield:

$$\text{Dividend yield} = D_{t+1}/P_t$$
$$= \$1.85/37 = .05 = 5\%$$

This says that, for each dollar we invest, we get five cents in dividends.

The second component of our percentage return is the capital gains yield. Recall (from Chapter 7) that this is calculated as the change in the price during the year (the capital gain) divided by the beginning price:

$$\text{Capital gains yield} = (P_{t+1} - P_t)/P_t$$
$$= (\$40.33 - 37)/37$$
$$= \$3.33/37$$
$$= 9\%$$

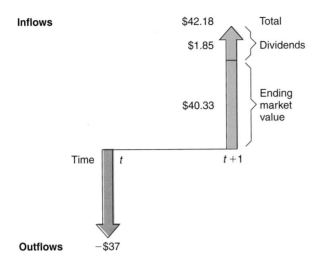

Inflows

$42.18   Total

$1.85   Dividends

$40.33   Ending market value

Time t $t+1$

Outflows   −$37

FIGURE 10.2

Dollar returns per share

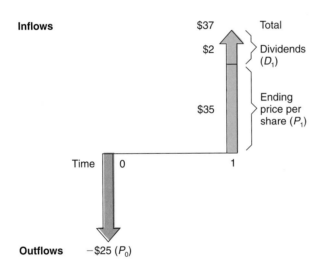

Inflows

$37   Total

$2   Dividends ($D_1$)

$35   Ending price per share (P_1)

Time   0   1

Outflows   −$25 ($P_0$)

FIGURE 10.3

Cash flow—an investment example

So, per dollar invested, we get nine cents in capital gains.

Putting it together, per dollar invested, we get 5 cents in dividends and 9 cents in capital gains; so we get a total of 14 cents. Our percentage return is 14 cents on the dollar, or 14 percent.

To check this, notice that we invested $3,700 and ended up with $4,218. By what percentage did our $3,700 increase? As we saw, we picked up $4,218 − 3,700 = $518. This is a $518/3,700 = 14% increase.

Calculating Returns | **EXAMPLE 10.1**

Suppose you buy some stock for $25 per share. At the end of the year, the price is $35 per share. During the year, you get a $2 dividend per share. This is the situation illustrated in Figure 10.3. What is the dividend yield? The capital gains yield? The percentage return? If your total investment was $1,000, how much do you have at the end of the year?

Your $2 dividend per share works out to a dividend yield of:

Dividend yield = D_{t+1}/P_t

       = $2/25 = .08 = 8%

The per-share capital gain is $10, so the capital gains yield is:

$$\text{Capital gains yield} = (P_{t+1} - P_t)/P_t$$
$$= (\$35 - 25)/25$$
$$= \$10/25$$
$$= 40\%$$

The total percentage return is thus 48 percent.

If you had invested $1,000, you would have had $1,480 at the end of the year, representing a 48 percent increase. To check this, note that your $1,000 would have bought you $1,000/25 = 40 shares. Your 40 shares would then have paid you a total of 40 × $2 = $80 in cash dividends. Your $10 per share gain would have given you a total capital gain of $10 × 40 = $400. Add these together, and you get the $480 increase.

CONCEPT QUESTIONS

10.1a What are the two parts of total return?

10.1b Why are unrealized capital gains or losses included in the calculation of returns?

10.1c What is the difference between a dollar return and a percentage return? Why are percentage returns more convenient?

10.2 | THE HISTORICAL RECORD

Roger Ibbotson and Rex Sinquefield conducted a famous set of studies dealing with rates of return in U.S. financial markets.[2] They presented year-to-year historical rates of return on five important types of financial investments. The returns can be interpreted as what you would have earned if you had held portfolios of the following:

1. Large-company stocks. The large-company stock portfolio is based on the Standard & Poor's 500 index, which contains 500 of the largest companies (in terms of total market value of outstanding stock) in the United States.

2. Small-company stocks. This is a portfolio composed of stock of smaller companies, where "small" corresponds to the smallest 20 percent of the companies listed on the New York Stock Exchange, again as measured by market value of outstanding stock.

3. Long-term corporate bonds. This is a portfolio of high-quality bonds with 20 years to maturity.

4. Long-term U.S. government bonds. This is a portfolio of U.S. government bonds with 20 years to maturity.

5. U.S. Treasury bills. This is a portfolio of Treasury bills (T-bills for short) with a three-month maturity.

These returns are not adjusted for inflation or taxes; thus, they are nominal, pretax returns.

---

[2]R. G. Ibbotson and R. A. Sinquefield, *Stocks, Bonds, Bills, and Inflation* [SBBI] (Charlottesville, Va.: Financial Analysis Research Foundation, 1982).

In addition to the year-to-year returns on these financial instruments, the year-to-year percentage change in the consumer price index (CPI) is also computed. This is a commonly used measure of inflation, so we can calculate real returns using this as the inflation rate.

A First Look

Before looking closely at the different portfolio returns, we take a look at the big picture. Figure 10.4 shows what happened to $1 invested in these different portfolios at the beginning of 1926. The growth in value for each of the different portfolios over the 74-year period ending in 1999 is given separately (the long-term corporate bonds are omitted). Notice that to get everything on a single graph, some modification in scaling is used. As is commonly done with financial series, the vertical axis is scaled such that equal distances measure equal percentage (as opposed to dollar) changes in values.

FIGURE 10.4

A $1 investment in different types of portfolios: 1926–99 (Year-end 1925 = $1)

Looking at Figure 10.4, we see that the small-company, or "small-cap" (short for small-capitalization), investment did the best overall. Every dollar invested grew to a remarkable $6,640.79 over the 74 years. The larger common stock portfolio did less well; a dollar invested in it grew to $2,845.63.

At the other end, the T-bill portfolio grew to only $15.64. This is even less impressive when we consider the inflation over this period. As illustrated, the increase in the price level was such that $9.39 is needed just to replace the original $1.

Given the historical record, why would anybody buy anything other than small-cap stocks? If you look closely at Figure 10.4, you will probably see the answer. The T-bill portfolio and the long-term government bond portfolio grew more slowly than did the stock portfolios, but they also grew much more steadily. The small stocks ended up on top, but, as you can see, they grew quite erratically at times. For example, the small stocks were the worst performers for about the first 10 years and had a smaller return than long-term government bonds for almost 15 years.

A Closer Look

To illustrate the variability of the different investments, Figures 10.5 through 10.8 plot the year-to-year percentage returns in the form of vertical bars drawn from the horizontal axis. The height of the bar tells us the return for the particular year. For example, looking at the long-term government bonds (Figure 10.7), we see that the largest historical return (40.35 percent) occurred in 1982. This was a good year for bonds. In comparing these charts, notice the differences in the vertical axis scales. With these differences in mind, you can see how predictably the Treasury bills (Figure 10.7) behaved compared to the small stocks (Figure 10.6).

The returns shown in these bar graphs are sometimes very large. Looking at the graphs, we see, for example, that the largest single-year return was a remarkable 143 percent for the small-cap stocks in 1933. In the same year, the large-company stocks "only" returned 53 percent. In contrast, the largest Treasury bill return was 15 percent, in 1981. For future reference, the actual year-to-year returns for the S&P 500, long-term government bonds, Treasury bills, and the CPI are shown in Table 10.1.

CONCEPT QUESTIONS

10.2a With 20-20 hindsight, what was the best investment for the period 1926–35?

10.2b Why doesn't everyone just buy small stocks as investments?

10.2c What was the smallest return observed over the 74 years for each of these investments? Approximately when did it occur?

10.2d About how many times did large stocks (common stocks) return more than 30 percent? How many times did they return less than −20 percent?

10.2e What was the longest "winning streak" (years without a negative return) for large stocks? For long-term government bonds?

10.2f How often did the T-bill portfolio have a negative return?

Year-to-year total returns on large-company stocks: 1926–99   **FIGURE 10.5**

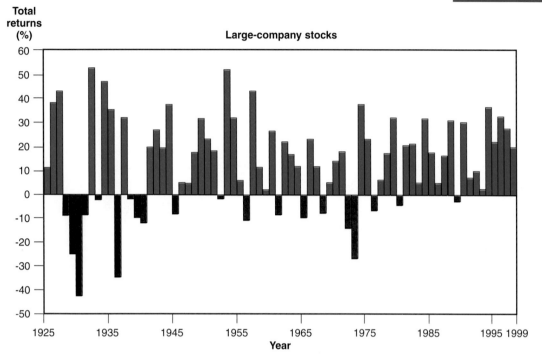

Source: Stocks, Bonds, Bills, and Inflation Yearbook™, Ibbotson Associates, Inc., Chicago (annually updates work by Roger G. Ibbotson and Rex A. Sinquefield). All rights reserved.

Year-to-year total returns on small-company stocks: 1926–99   **FIGURE 10.6**

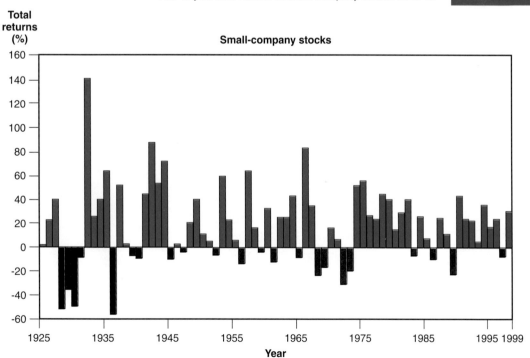

Source: Stocks, Bonds, Bills, and Inflation Yearbook™, Ibbotson Associates, Inc., Chicago (annually updates work by Roger G. Ibbotson and Rex A. Sinquefield). All rights reserved.

FIGURE 10.7   Year-to-year total returns on bonds and bills: 1926–99

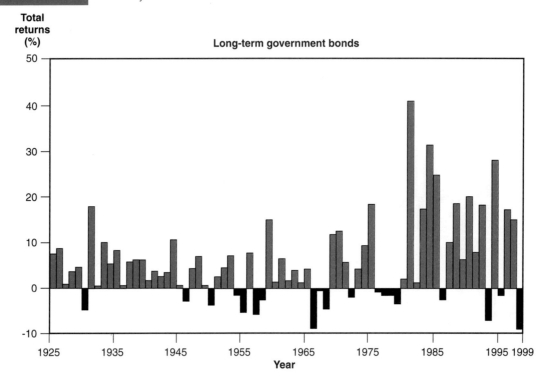

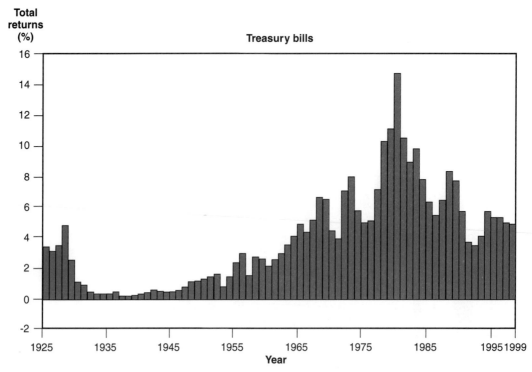

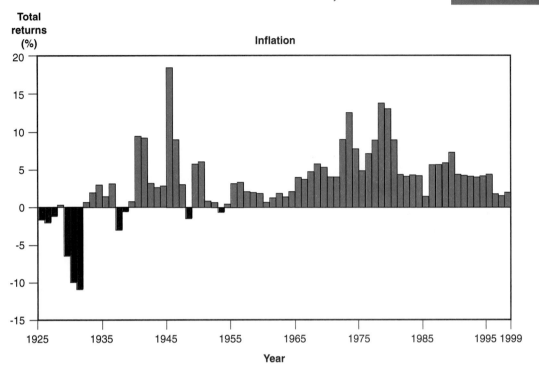

AVERAGE RETURNS: THE FIRST LESSON | 10.3

As you've probably begun to notice, the history of capital market returns is too complicated to be of much use in its undigested form. We need to begin summarizing all these numbers. Accordingly, we discuss how to go about condensing the detailed data. We start out by calculating average returns.

Calculating Average Returns

The obvious way to calculate the average returns on the different investments in Table 10.1 is simply to add up the yearly returns and divide by 74. The result is the historical average of the individual values.

For example, if you add up the returns for the common stocks for the 74 years, you will get about 9.85. The average annual return is thus 9.85/74 = 13.3%. You interpret this 13.3 percent just like any other average. If you picked a year at random from the 74-year history and you had to guess what the return in that year was, the best guess would be 13.3 percent.

Average Returns: The Historical Record

Table 10.2 shows the average returns for the investments we have discussed. As shown, in a typical year, the small stocks increased in value by 17.6 percent. Notice also how much larger the stock returns are than the bond returns.

These averages are, of course, nominal since we haven't worried about inflation. Notice that the average inflation rate was 3.2 percent per year over this 74-year span. The nominal return on U.S. Treasury bills was 3.8 percent per year. The average real return on Treasury

TABLE 10.1
Year-to-year total returns: 1926–99

Year	Large-Company Stocks	Long-Term Government Bonds	U.S. Treasury Bills	Consumer Price Index
1926	13.70%	6.40%	4.40%	− 1.10%
1927	35.80	4.51	4.21	− 2.33
1928	45.14	.18	4.87	− 1.14
1929	− 8.88	5.66	6.05	.63
1930	−25.22	4.16	3.72	− 6.45
1931	−43.75	.41	2.63	− 9.23
1932	− 8.38	5.61	2.95	−10.29
1933	53.11	5.92	1.66	.68
1934	− 2.41	5.95	1.04	1.63
1935	46.94	3.22	.29	2.94
1936	32.35	1.73	.15	1.43
1937	−35.68	4.63	.44	2.81
1938	32.29	4.74	.07	− 2.74
1939	− 1.54	2.26	.00	.00
1940	−10.54	4.25	.00	.77
1941	−12.14	1.56	.07	9.90
1942	20.98	1.82	.36	9.01
1943	25.52	2.00	.36	2.97
1944	19.46	2.28	.36	2.26
1945	36.35	5.23	.36	2.31
1946	− 8.48	.54	.43	18.09
1947	4.96	− .93	.57	8.83
1948	4.95	2.62	.99	2.98
1949	17.74	4.53	1.12	− 2.08
1950	30.04	− .92	1.25	5.99
1951	23.88	− .14	1.51	5.94
1952	18.44	2.42	1.76	.81
1953	− 1.11	2.32	1.93	.74
1954	52.44	3.07	.98	− .73
1955	31.65	− .69	1.68	.34
1956	6.90	− 1.61	2.66	3.01
1957	−10.53	6.75	3.34	2.92
1958	43.73	− 1.61	1.79	1.76
1959	12.02	− 1.89	3.35	1.67
1960	0.45	11.04	3.13	1.40
1961	26.90	2.24	2.32	.66
1962	− 8.79	6.03	2.80	1.31
1963	22.72	1.42	3.20	1.65
1964	16.43	3.89	3.56	.98

Year	Large-Company Stocks	Long-Term Government Bonds	U.S. Treasury Bills	Consumer Price Index
1965	12.37	1.05	4.02	1.95
1966	−10.10	4.81	4.90	3.43
1967	24.04	− 2.36	4.49	3.05
1968	11.03	1.66	5.42	4.70
1969	− 8.47	− 4.82	6.81	6.20
1970	4.00	18.15	6.68	5.56
1971	14.35	11.39	4.51	3.28
1972	19.00	2.51	4.04	3.40
1973	−14.85	3.50	6.98	8.72
1974	−26.58	3.82	8.09	12.32
1975	37.42	5.63	6.04	6.97
1976	23.76	15.20	5.16	4.84
1977	− 7.38	.55	5.26	6.71
1978	6.54	− .99	7.23	9.02
1979	18.59	.50	10.32	13.30
1980	32.61	− .63	12.04	12.51
1981	− 4.97	2.62	15.21	8.92
1982	21.67	43.98	11.28	3.85
1983	22.57	2.03	8.89	3.78
1984	6.19	15.96	10.04	3.96
1985	31.85	30.34	7.70	3.79
1986	18.68	22.86	6.18	1.10
1987	5.22	− 3.24	5.87	4.44
1988	16.58	6.86	6.73	4.42
1989	31.75	18.64	8.48	4.65
1990	− 3.13	7.26	7.85	6.10
1991	30.53	18.52	5.71	3.06
1992	7.62	8.52	3.57	2.89
1993	10.07	13.45	3.08	2.75
1994	1.27	− 7.31	4.15	2.68
1995	37.80	24.86	5.64	2.53
1996	22.74	1.63	5.12	3.32
1997	33.43	10.89	5.22	1.70
1998	28.13	13.44	5.06	1.61
1999	21.03	− 7.12	4.85	2.69

TABLE 10.1

(concluded)

Source: Author calculations based on data obtained from *Global Financial Data.*

Investment	Average Return
Large stocks	13.3%
Small stocks	17.6
Long-term corporate bonds	5.9
Long-term government bonds	5.5
U.S. Treasury bills	3.8
Inflation	3.2

Source: Stocks, Bonds, Bills, and Inflation Yearbook™,
Ibbotson Associates, Inc., Chicago (annually updates work
by Roger G. Ibbotson and Rex A. Sinquefield).

bills was thus approximately .6 percent per year; so the real return on T-bills has been quite low historically.

At the other extreme, small stocks had an average real return of about $17.6\% - 3.2\%$ $= 14.4\%$, which is relatively large. If you remember the Rule of 72 (Chapter 4), then you recall that a quick back-of-the-envelope calculation tells us that 14 percent real growth doubles your buying power about every five years. Notice also that the real value of the large stock portfolio increased by 10.1 percent in a typical year.

Risk Premiums

Now that we have computed some average returns, it seems logical to see how they compare with each other. Based on our discussion above, one such comparison involves government-issued securities. These are free of much of the variability we see in, for example, the stock market.

The government borrows money by issuing bonds. These bonds come in different forms. The ones we will focus on are the Treasury bills. These have the shortest time to maturity of the different government bonds. Because the government can always raise taxes to pay its bills, this debt is virtually free of any default risk over its short life. Thus, we will call the rate of return on such debt the *risk-free return,* and we will use it as a kind of benchmark.

A particularly interesting comparison involves the virtually risk-free return on T-bills and the very risky return on common stocks. The difference between these two returns can be interpreted as a measure of the *excess return* on the average risky asset (assuming the stock of a large U.S. corporation has about average risk compared to all risky assets).

risk premium

The excess return required from an investment in a risky asset over that required from a risk-free investment.

We call this the "excess" return since it is the additional return we earn by moving from a relatively risk-free investment to a risky one. Because it can be interpreted as a reward for bearing risk, we will call it a **risk premium.**

From Table 10.2, we can calculate the risk premiums for the different investments. We report only the nominal risk premium in Table 10.3 because there is only a slight difference between the historical nominal and real risk premiums.

The risk premium on T-bills is shown as zero in the table because we have assumed that they are riskless.

The First Lesson

Looking at Table 10.3, we see that the average risk premium earned by a typical large common stock is $13.3\% - 3.8\% = 9.5\%$. This is a significant reward. The fact that it exists historically is an important observation, and it is the basis for our first lesson: Risky assets, on average, earn a risk premium. Put another way: There is a reward for bearing risk.

Investment	Average Return	Risk Premium	TABLE 10.3
Large stocks	13.3%	9.5%	Average annual returns and risk premiums: 1926–99
Small stocks	17.6	13.8	
Long-term corporate bonds	5.9	2.1	
Long-term government bonds	5.5	1.7	
U.S. Treasury bills	3.8	0.0	

Source: Stocks, Bonds, Bills, and Inflation Yearbook™, Ibbotson Associates, Inc., Chicago (annually updates work by Roger G. Ibbotson and Rex A. Sinquefield). All rights reserved.

Why is this so? Why, for example, is the risk premium for small stocks so much larger than the risk premium for large stocks? More generally, what determines the relative sizes of the risk premiums for the different assets? The answers to these questions are at the heart of modern finance, and the next chapter is devoted to them. For now, part of the answer can be found by looking at the historical variability of the returns of these different investments. So, to get started, we now turn our attention to measuring variability in returns.

CONCEPT QUESTIONS

10.3a What do we mean by excess return and risk premium?

10.3b What was the real (as opposed to nominal) risk premium on the common stock portfolio?

10.3c What was the nominal risk premium on corporate bonds? The real risk premium?

10.3d What is the first lesson from capital market history?

THE VARIABILITY OF RETURNS: | 10.4
THE SECOND LESSON

We have already seen that the year-to-year returns on common stocks tend to be more volatile than the returns on, say, long-term government bonds. We now discuss measuring this variability so we can begin examining the subject of risk.

Frequency Distributions and Variability

To get started, we can draw a *frequency distribution* for the common stock returns like the one in Figure 10.9. What we have done here is to count up the number of times the annual return on the large stock portfolio falls within each 10 percent range. For example, in Figure 10.9, the height of 12 in the range 20 percent to 30 percent means that 12 of the 74 annual returns were in that range. Notice also that the most frequent returns are in the 10 to 20 percent range and the 30 to 40 percent range. In both cases, the large stock portfolio's return fell within the range 13 times in 74 years.

variance
The average squared difference between the actual return and the average return.

What we need to do now is to actually measure the spread in returns. We know, for example, that the return on small stocks in a typical year was 17.6 percent. We now want to know how far the actual return deviates from this average in a typical year. In other words, we need a measure of how volatile the return is. The **variance** and its square root, the **standard deviation,** are the most commonly used measures of volatility. We describe how to calculate them next.

standard deviation
The positive square root of the variance.

Frequency distribution of returns on common stocks: 1926–99

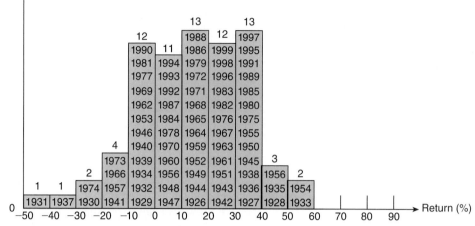

Source: Stocks, Bonds, Bills, and Inflation Yearbook™, Ibbotson Associates, Inc., Chicago (annually updates work by Roger G. Ibbotson and Rex A. Sinquefield). All rights reserved.

The Historical Variance and Standard Deviation

The variance essentially measures the average squared difference between the actual returns and the average return. The bigger this number is, the more the actual returns tend to differ from the average return. Also, the larger the variance or standard deviation is, the more spread out the returns will be.

The way we will calculate the variance and standard deviation depends on the specific situation. In this chapter, we are looking at historical returns; so the procedure we describe here is the correct one for calculating the *historical* variance and standard deviation. If we were examining projected future returns, then the procedure would be different. We describe this procedure in the next chapter.

To illustrate how we calculate the historical variance, suppose a particular investment had returns of 10 percent, 12 percent, 3 percent, and −9 percent over the last four years. The average return is (.10 + .12 + .03 − .09)/ 4 = 4%. Notice that the return is never actually equal to 4 percent. Instead, the first return deviates from the average by .10 − .04 = .06, the second return deviates from the average by .12 − .04 = .08, and so on. To compute the variance, we square each of these deviations, add up the squares, and divide the result by the number of returns less 1, or 3 in this case. This information is summarized in the following table.

Year	(1) Actual Return	(2) Average Return	(3) Deviation (1) − (2)	(4) Squared Deviation
1	.10	.04	.06	.0036
2	.12	.04	.08	.0064
3	.03	.04	−.01	.0001
4	−.09	.04	−.13	.0169
Totals	.16		.00	.0270

In the first column, we write down the four actual returns. In the third column, we calculate the difference between the actual returns and the average by subtracting out 4 percent. Finally, in the fourth column, we square the numbers in Column 3 to get the squared deviations from the average.

The variance can now be calculated by dividing .0270, the sum of the squared deviations, by the number of returns less 1. Let Var(R) or σ^2 (read this as "sigma squared") stand for the variance of the return:

$$\text{Var}(R) = \sigma^2 = .027/(4 - 1) = .009$$

The standard deviation is the square root of the variance. So, if SD(R) or σ stands for the standard deviation of the return:

$$\text{SD}(R) = \sigma = \sqrt{.009} = .09487$$

The square root of the variance is used because the variance is measured in "squared" percentages and thus is hard to interpret. The standard deviation is an ordinary percentage, so the answer here could be written as 9.487 percent.

In the table above, notice that the sum of the deviations is equal to zero. This will always be the case, and it provides a good way to check your work. In general, if we have T historical returns, where T is some number, we can write the historical variance as:

$$\text{Var}(R) = \frac{1}{T-1}[(R_1 - \overline{R})^2 + ... + (R_T - \overline{R})^2] \qquad [10.3]$$

This formula tells us to do just what we did above: Take each of the T individual returns $(R_1, R_2, ...)$ and subtract the average return, $\overline{R}$; square the results, and add up all these squares; and finally, divide this total by the number of returns less 1 $(T - 1)$. The standard deviation is always the square root of Var(R).

Calculating the Variance and Standard Deviation	**EXAMPLE 10.2**

Suppose the Supertech Company and the Hyperdrive Company have experienced the following returns in the last four years:

Year	Supertech Returns	Hyperdrive Returns
1997	−.20	.05
1998	.50	.09
1999	.30	−.12
2000	.10	.20

What are the average returns? The variances? The standard deviations? Which investment was more volatile?

To calculate the average returns, we add up the returns and divide by 4. The results are:

Supertech average return = $\overline{R}$ = .70/4 = .175

Hyperdrive average return = $\overline{R}$ = .22/4 = .055

To calculate the variance for Supertech, we can summarize the relevant calculations as follows:

Since there are four years of returns, we calculate the variances by dividing .2675 by $(4 - 1) = 3$:

Year	(1) Actual Return	(2) Average Return	(3) Deviation (1) − (2)	(4) Squared Deviation
1997	−.20	.175	−.375	.140625
1998	.50	.175	.325	.105625
1999	.30	.175	.125	.015625
2000	.10	.175	−.075	.005625
Totals	.70		.000	.267500

	Supertech	Hyperdrive
Variance (σ^2)	.2675/3 = .0892	.0529/3 = .0176
Standard deviation (σ)	$\sqrt{.0892} = .2987$	$\sqrt{.0176} = .1327$

For practice, verify that you get the same answer as we do for Hyperdrive. Notice that the standard deviation for Supertech, 29.87 percent, is a little more than twice Hyperdrive's 13.27 percent; Supertech was thus the more volatile investment.

The Historical Record

Figure 10.10 summarizes much of our discussion of capital market history so far. It displays average returns, standard deviations, and frequency distributions of annual returns on a common scale. In Figure 10.10, notice, for example, that the standard deviation for the small-stock portfolio (33.6 percent per year) is more than 10 times larger than the T-bill portfolio's standard deviation (3.2 percent per year). We will return to these figures momentarily.

Normal Distribution

normal distribution

A symmetric, bell-shaped frequency distribution that is completely defined by its average and standard deviation.

For many different random events in nature, a particular frequency distribution, the **normal distribution** (or *bell curve*), is useful for describing the probability of ending up in a given range. For example, the idea behind "grading on a curve" comes from the fact that exam scores often resemble a bell curve.

Figure 10.11 illustrates a normal distribution and its distinctive bell shape. As you can see, this distribution has a much cleaner appearance than the actual return distributions illustrated in Figure 10.10. Even so, like the normal distribution, the actual distributions do appear to be at least roughly mound shaped and symmetric. When this is true, the normal distribution is often a very good approximation.

Also, keep in mind that the distributions in Figure 10.10 are based on only 74 yearly observations, while Figure 10.11 is, in principle, based on an infinite number. So, if we had been able to observe returns for, say, 1,000 years, we might have filled in a lot of the irregularities and ended up with a much smoother picture. For our purposes, it is enough to observe that the returns are at least roughly normally distributed.

The usefulness of the normal distribution stems from the fact that it is completely described by the average and the standard deviation. If you have these two numbers, then there is nothing else to know. For example, with a normal distribution, the probability that we end up within one standard deviation of the average is about ⅔. The probability that we end up

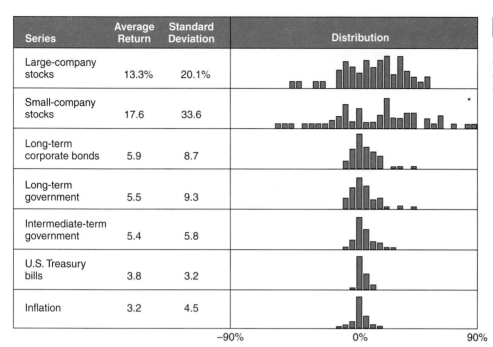

Source: Stocks, Bonds, Bills, and Inflation Yearbook™, Ibbotson Associates, Inc., Chicago (annually updates work by Roger G. Ibbotson and Rex A. Sinquefield). All rights reserved.

FIGURE 10.10

Historical returns, standard deviations, and frequency distributions: 1926–99

*The 1933 small-company stock total return was 142.9 percent.

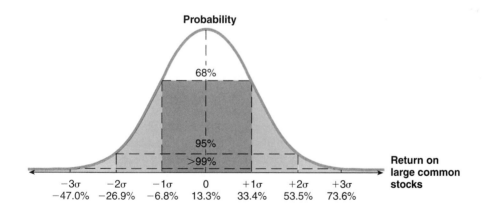

FIGURE 10.11

The normal distribution. Illustrated returns are based on the historical return and standard deviation for a portfolio of large common stocks.

within two standard deviations is about 95 percent. Finally, the probability of being more than three standard deviations away from the average is less than 1 percent. These ranges and the probabilities are illustrated in Figure 10.11.

To see why this is useful, recall from Figure 10.10 that the standard deviation of returns on the large common stocks is 20.1 percent. The average return is 13.3 percent. So, assuming that the frequency distribution is at least approximately normal, the probability that the return in a given year is in the range of −6.8 percent to 33.4 percent (13.3 percent plus or minus one standard deviation, 20.1 percent) is about ⅔. This range is illustrated in Figure 10.11. In other words, there is about one chance in three that the return will be *outside* this range. This literally tells you that, if you buy stocks in large companies, you should expect to be outside this range in one year out of every three. This reinforces our earlier observations about stock market volatility. However, there is only a 5 percent chance (approximately) that we would end up outside the range of −26.9 percent to 53.5 percent (13.3 percent plus or minus 2 × 20.1%). These points are also illustrated in Figure 10.11.

The Second Lesson

Our observations concerning the year-to-year variability in returns are the basis for our second lesson from capital market history. On average, bearing risk is handsomely rewarded, but, in a given year, there is a significant chance of a dramatic change in value. Thus, our second lesson is this: The greater the potential reward, the greater is the risk.

Thus far in this chapter, we have emphasized the year-to-year variability in returns. We should note that even day-to-day movements can exhibit considerable volatility. For example, just recently, on October 27, 1997, the Dow Jones Industrial Average (DJIA) plummeted 554.26 points. By historical standards, it was one of the worst days ever for the 30 stocks that comprise the DJIA(as well as for a majority of stocks in the market). Still, while the drop was the largest decrease in the DJIA ever in terms of points, it actually was the 12th largest one-day percentage decrease in history, as illustrated in the following table:

Top 12 One-Day Percentage Changes in the Dow Jones Industrial Average			
October 19, 1987	−22.6%	March 14, 1907	−8.3%
October 28, 1929	−12.8	October 26, 1987	−8.0
October 29, 1929	−11.7	July 21, 1933	−7.8
November 6, 1929	− 9.9	October 18, 1937	−7.7
December 18, 1899	− 8.7	February 1, 1917	−7.2
August 12, 1932	− 8.4	October 27, 1997	−7.2

Source: Dow Jones.

This discussion also highlights the importance of looking at returns in terms of percentages rather than dollar amounts or index points. For example, as we noted before, the biggest one-day loss in terms of points was on October 27, 1997, when the DJIA declined by 554 points. The second worst was the 508-point drop of October 19, 1987. By contrast, the 5.57-point drop in the DJIA on December 18, 1899, marked the fifth worst day in the history of the index, but a 5.6-point loss in the DJIA in today's market would hardly be noticed. This is precisely why we relied on percentage returns when we examined market history in this chapter.[3]

Using Capital Market History

Based on the discussion in this section, you should begin to have an idea of the risks and rewards from investing. For example, in 2000, Treasury bills were paying about 6 percent. Suppose we had an investment that we thought had about the same risk as a portfolio of large-firm common stocks. At a minimum, what return would this investment have to offer for us to be interested?

From Table 10.3, the risk premium on larger common stocks has been 9.5 percent historically, so a reasonable estimate of our required return would be this premium plus the T-bill rate, 9.5% + 6.0% = 15.5%. This may strike you as high, but, if we were thinking of starting a new business, then the risks of doing so might resemble those of investing in

---

[3]By the way, as you may have noticed, what's kind of weird is that 6 of the 12 worst days in the history of the DJIA occurred in October, including the top 3. We have no clue as to why. Furthermore, looking back at the Mark Twain quote near the beginning of the chapter, how do you suppose he knew? Sounds like a case for the X-Files.

reality | **BYTES**

JANUARY AND THE SANTA CLAUS EFFECT

A December 1999 *USA Today* headline reads, "Market Peak Might Be Now, 'January Effect' Could Be Hitting Early, on Way Out," while a December 1999 *Toronto Star* headline says, "Investors Hoping for a Santa Claus Rally." What both newspapers are talking about is the tendency for the prices of stocks to, on average, increase in January. This type of pattern is known as a "seasonality," since it tends to reappear at regular intervals each year. While there are numerous patterns of this type, the January effect tends to capture more headlines than do the others.

First, it's important to get the terminology straight. The January effect refers to the tendency of stock prices, more specifically those of small-company stocks, to increase sharply in January and change little during the rest of the year. The January effect usually is defined to include returns for the last five days in December and the first two days in January, and this pattern is more affectionately known as the Santa Claus rally, for obvious reasons. According to the *Stock Trader's Almanac,* "If Santa Claus Should Fail to Call, Bears Will Come to Broad & Wall." In fact, according to the *Almanac,* in the years spanning 1952 to 1998, the Santa Claus rally gave a false signal only in the years 1966, 1984, 1992, and 1994 (excluding 1990 because of the Gulf War).

This pattern is not to be confused with the January Barometer, which refers to the fact that stock market returns in January tend to set the tone for the rest of the year. "As January Goes, So Goes the Rest of the Year," at least according to the *Stock Trader's Almanac.* Again, according to the *Almanac,* in the 32 years from 1950 to 1982, the January Barometer failed to predict returns in the rest of the year in only 2 years, for a stunning accuracy rate. In the 20 years from 1980 to 1999, the barometer fell off some, correctly predicting future returns in only 14 years, for a still respectable 70 percent accuracy rate. Since the effect refers to the relative returns on small-company stocks as compared to those on large-company stocks, you might wonder how it works for large-company stocks. Well, statistics abound on things such as these. Since 1900, the Dow Jones Industrial Average has had a negative return in January 35 times. In those years, the index ended in a full-year decline 22 times, which is about 63 percent of the time, a percentage representing little better than chance.

The January patterns are generally viewed as resulting from tax-loss selling around the end of the calendar year. In December, investors sell stocks that have done poorly for the year to realize the capital losses for tax purposes. This money is then reinvested in the market in January. Small-company stocks are popular buys in January, and the excess buying pressure pushes up share prices. While there is some evidence to support this hypothesis, many believe it is unlikely that this is the sole cause of the January effect.

There are other so-called market regularities, and they exist in markets other than the U.S. stock market. In fact, they have been found in markets all around the world. For example, a December 1999 headline from the Dow Jones International News service said, "Singapore Shares Open Up As Santa Claus Rally Continues," while a January 2000 *Australian Financial Review* headline stated, "January Should Set the Year's Tone Again." One word of caution before you leap: History has shown that none of these regularities occur with such certainty that traders can make easy money implementing simple trading rules based on them. Still, savvy investors worldwide watch these patterns and try to use them to enhance returns.

"January Should Set the Year's Tone Again," *Australian Financial Review,* 4 January 2000, p. 39.
"Singapore Shares Open Up As Santa Claus Rally Continues," Dow Jones International News, 29 December 1999.
"Investors Hoping for a Santa Claus Rally," *The Toronto Star,* 26 December 1999, p. CT11.

---

small-company stocks. In this case, the risk premium is 13.8 percent, so we might require as much as 19.8 percent from such an investment at a minimum.

We will discuss the relationship between risk and required return in more detail in the next chapter. For now, you should notice that a projected internal rate of return, or IRR, on a risky investment in the 15 percent to 25 percent range isn't particularly outstanding. It depends on how much risk there is. This, too, is an important lesson from capital market history.

The discussion in this section shows that there is much to be learned from capital market history. As the accompanying *Reality Bytes* box describes, capital market history also provides some unsolved mysteries.

EXAMPLE 10.3 | **Investing in Growth Stocks**

The term *growth stock* is frequently a euphemism for small-company stock. Are such investments suitable for "widows and orphans"? Before answering, you should consider the historical volatility. For example, from the historical record, what is the approximate probability that you will actually lose 16 percent or more of your money in a single year if you buy a portfolio of such companies?

Looking back at Figure 10.10, we see that the average return on small stocks is 17.6 percent and the standard deviation is 33.6 percent. Assuming that the returns are approximately normal, there is about a ⅓ probability that you will experience a return outside the range of −16 percent to 51.2 percent (17.6% ± 33.6%).

Because the normal distribution is symmetric, the odds of being above or below this range are equal. There is thus a ⅙ chance (half of ⅓) that you will lose more than 16 percent. So you should expect this to happen once in every six years, on average. Such investments can thus be *very* volatile, and they are not well suited for those who cannot afford the risk.

CONCEPT QUESTIONS

10.4a In words, how do we calculate a variance? A standard deviation?

10.4b With a normal distribution, what is the probability of ending up more than one standard deviation below the average?

10.4c Assuming that long-term corporate bonds have an approximately normal distribution, what is the approximate probability of earning 14 percent or more in a given year? With T-bills, approximately what is this probability?

10.4d What is the second lesson from capital market history?

10.5 | CAPITAL MARKET EFFICIENCY

Capital market history suggests that the market values of stocks and bonds can fluctuate widely from year to year. Why does this occur? At least part of the answer is that prices change because new information arrives, and investors reassess asset values based on that information.

The behavior of market prices has been extensively studied. A question that has received particular attention is whether prices adjust quickly and correctly when new information arrives. A market is said to be *efficient* if this is the case. To be more precise, in an **efficient capital market,** current market prices fully reflect available information. By this we simply mean that, based on available information, there is no reason to believe that the current price is too low or too high.

efficient capital market
Market in which security prices reflect available information.

The concept of market efficiency is a rich one, and much has been written about it. A full discussion of the subject goes beyond the scope of our study of business finance. However, because the concept figures so prominently in studies of market history, we briefly describe the key points here.

Price Behavior in an Efficient Market

To illustrate how prices behave in an efficient market, suppose the F-Stop Camera Corporation (FCC) has, through years of secret research and development, developed a camera whose autofocusing system will double the speed of those now available. FCC's capital budgeting analysis suggests that launching the new camera is a highly profitable move; in other words, the NPV appears to be positive and substantial. The key assumption thus far is that FCC has not released any information about the new system; so, the fact of its existence is "inside" information only.

Now consider a share of stock in FCC. In an efficient market, its price reflects what is known about FCC's current operations and profitability, and it reflects market opinion about FCC's potential for future growth and profits. The value of the new autofocusing system is not reflected, however, because the market is unaware of its existence.

If the market agrees with FCC's assessment of the value of the new project, FCC's stock price will rise when the decision to launch is made public. For example, assume the announcement is made in a press release on Wednesday morning. In an efficient market, the price of shares in FCC will adjust quickly to this new information. Investors should not be able to buy the stock on Wednesday afternoon and make a profit on Thursday. This would imply that it took the stock market a full day to realize the implication of the FCC press release. If the market is efficient, the price of shares of FCC stock on Wednesday afternoon will already reflect the information contained in the Wednesday morning press release.

Figure 10.12 presents three possible stock price adjustments for FCC. In Figure 10.12, Day 0 represents the announcement day. As illustrated, before the announcement, FCC's stock sells for $140 per share. The NPV per share of the new system is, say, $40, so the new price will be $180 once the value of the new project is fully reflected.

The solid line in Figure 10.12 represents the path taken by the stock price in an efficient market. In this case, the price adjusts immediately to the new information and no further changes in the price of the stock take place. The broken line in Figure 10.12 depicts a delayed reaction. Here, it takes the market eight days or so to fully absorb the information. Finally, the dotted line illustrates an overreaction and subsequent adjustment to the correct price.

The broken line and the dotted line in Figure 10.12 illustrate paths that the stock price might take in an inefficient market. If, for example, stock prices don't adjust immediately to new information (the broken line), then buying stock immediately following the release of new information and then selling it several days later would be a positive NPV activity because the price is too low for several days after the announcement.

Reaction of stock price to new information in efficient and inefficient markets   **FIGURE 10.12**

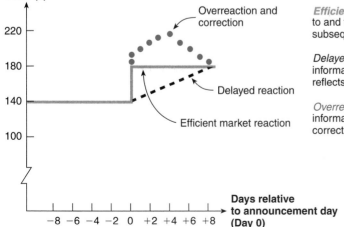

Efficient market reaction: The price instantaneously adjusts to and fully reflects new information; there is no tendency for subsequent increases and decreases.

Delayed reaction: The price partially adjusts to the new information; eight days elapse before the price completely reflects the new information.

Overreaction and correction: The price overadjusts to the new information; it overshoots the new price and subsequently corrects.

The Efficient Markets Hypothesis

The **efficient markets hypothesis (EMH)** asserts that well-organized capital markets, such as the NYSE, are efficient markets, at least as a practical matter. In other words, an advocate of the EMH might argue that while inefficiencies may exist, they are relatively small and not common.

If a market is efficient, then there is a very important implication for market participants: All investments in an efficient market are *zero* NPV investments. The reason is not complicated. If prices are neither too low nor too high, then the difference between the market value of an investment and its cost is zero; hence, the NPV is zero. As a result, in an efficient market, investors get exactly what they pay for when they buy securities, and firms receive exactly what their stocks and bonds are worth when they sell them.

What makes a market efficient is competition among investors. Many individuals spend their entire lives trying to find mispriced stocks. For any given stock, they study what has happened in the past to the stock's price and its dividends. They learn, to the extent possible, what a company's earnings have been, how much it owes to creditors, what taxes it pays, what businesses it is in, what new investments are planned, how sensitive it is to changes in the economy, and so on.

Not only is there a great deal to know about any particular company, there is a powerful incentive for knowing it, namely, the profit motive. If you know more about some company than other investors in the marketplace, you can profit from that knowledge by investing in the company's stock if you have good news and by selling it if you have bad news.

The logical consequence of all this information being gathered and analyzed is that mispriced stocks will become fewer and fewer. In other words, because of competition among investors, the market will become increasingly efficient. A kind of equilibrium comes into being where there is just enough mispricing around for those who are best at identifying it to make a living at it. For most other investors, the activity of information gathering and analysis will not pay.[4] Having said this, the accompanying *Reality Bytes* box indicates just how hard it is for *anybody* to "beat the market."

Some Common Misconceptions about the EMH

No idea in finance has attracted as much attention as that of efficient markets, and not all of the attention has been flattering. Rather than rehash the arguments here, we will be content to observe that some markets are more efficient than others. For example, financial markets on the whole are probably much more efficient than real asset markets.

Having said this, it is the case that much of the criticism of the EMH is misguided because it is based on a misunderstanding of what the hypothesis says and what it doesn't say. For example, when the notion of market efficiency was first publicized and debated in the popular financial press, it was often characterized by words to the effect that "throwing darts at the financial page will produce a portfolio that can be expected to do as well as any managed by professional security analysts."

---

[4]The idea behind the EMH can be illustrated by the following short story: A student was walking down the hall with her finance professor when they both saw a $20 bill on the ground. As the student bent down to pick it up, the professor shook his head slowly and, with a look of disappointment on his face, said patiently to the student, "Don't bother. If it were really there, someone else would have picked it up already." The moral of the story reflects the logic of the efficient markets hypothesis: If you think you have found a pattern in stock prices or a simple device for picking winners, you probably have not.

reality BYTES

CAN THE PROS BEAT THE MARKET?

Although the idea has been around for some time, there are still plenty of people who scoff at the hypothesis that the stock market is efficient. Perhaps the most skeptical group is made up of professional money managers, that is, those in charge of managing the wide array of funds competing for the investing public's money. In general, the performance of these managers is measured against the market as a whole. If a manager's fund earns a greater return than the S&P 500 index, for example, the manager beat the market. A question of significance to the efficient markets hypothesis is how professional money managers rate compared to the market. If they regularly beat the market, the hypothesis is in jeopardy.

One would expect money managers to at least be able to do better than random chance. *The Wall Street Journal* tests this in an ongoing contest between investment professionals and randomly chosen stocks. In each contest, four pros pick stocks, and their portfolio performance is compared to the performance of stocks chosen by *Journal* staffers throwing darts at a dartboard. All investments are held for six months. As of April 2000, the pros had an edge, having beaten the darts in 72 of 118 contests. However, they outperformed the Dow Jones Industrial Average only 63 to 55. The average returns make the pros look even better. The average six-month gain for the pros for the 118 contests was 12.2 percent, while the Dow increased by 6.9 percent and the darts earned 5.6 percent. Random selection with darts did only slightly worse than the Dow Jones Average, while the pros did better. This contest suggests that the pros can beat random chance and do at least as well as the market average, but it involves a small sample of pros and a small portfolio of stocks. To realistically gauge money manager performance requires a broader study.

According to Lipper, Inc., the mutual-fund tracker, 505 diversified U.S. stock funds lasted the full 10 years of the 1990s. Of those, only one-third beat the annualized return of their market benchmark. The numbers would probably have been much worse if the hundreds of funds that disappeared during the decade had been included. Generally, the funds that don't survive are those that have performed the worst. Of course, the bar was set rather high for the decade, with the Nasdaq composite index returning an average of 24.5 percent and the Dow Jones Industrial Average generating returns of 18.2 percent per year on average. The average stock mutual fund returned 15.4 percent a year, which is good by historical standards, but certainly short of the market averages. Taken together, these numbers suggest that, in 67 percent of the cases, investors would have earned a higher return by investing in a fund that mirrored the S&P 500 than by investing with this group of pros. They could have done so by investing in an index fund, which is a mutual fund structured to mirror a well-known market index, requiring no active portfolio management. When investors choose an index fund, they accept the fate of performing as the market index does, no better and no worse.

None of this evidence proves that markets are efficient. The evidence does, however, lend credence to the semistrong form version of market efficiency. Plus, it adds to a growing body of evidence that tends to support a basic premise: While it may be possible to outperform the market for relatively short periods of time, it is very difficult to do so consistently over the long haul.

"Most Diversified Stock Funds Had a Dull Decade," *The Wall Street Journal,* 21 January 2000, p. C1.

"Investment Dartboard: Pros Rack Up 92.8 Percent Advance in Stock Contest, but Readers Fare Even Better with 94 Percent Gain," *The Wall Street Journal,* 6 April 2000, p. C20.

"Your Investments: Annual Markets and Mutual Fund Review and Outlook," *Los Angeles Times,* 4 January 2000, p. S-1.

Confusion over statements of this sort has often led to a failure to understand the implications of market efficiency. For example, sometimes it is wrongly argued that market efficiency means that it doesn't matter how you invest your money because the efficiency of the market will protect you from making a mistake. However, a random dart thrower might wind up with all of the darts sticking into one or two high-risk stocks that deal in genetic engineering. Would you really want all of your money in two such stocks?

What efficiency does imply is that the price a firm will obtain when it sells a share of its stock is a "fair" price in the sense that it reflects the value of that stock given the information available about the firm. Shareholders do not have to worry that they are paying too much for a stock with a low dividend or some other sort of characteristic because the market has already incorporated that characteristic into the price. We sometimes say the information has been "priced out."

The concept of efficient markets can be explained further by replying to a frequent objection. It is sometimes argued that the market cannot be efficient because stock prices fluctuate from day to day. If the prices are right, the argument goes, then why do they change so much and so often? From our discussion above, we can see that these price movements are in no way inconsistent with efficiency. Investors are bombarded with information every day. The fact that prices fluctuate is, at least in part, a reflection of that information flow. In fact, the absence of price movements in a world that changes as rapidly as ours would suggest inefficiency.

The Forms of Market Efficiency

It is common to distinguish between three forms of market efficiency. Depending on the degree of efficiency, we say that markets are either *weak form efficient, semistrong form efficient,* or *strong form efficient.* The difference between these forms relates to what information is reflected in prices.

We start with the extreme case. If the market is strong form efficient, then *all* information of *every* kind is reflected in stock prices. In such a market, there is no such thing as inside information. Therefore, in our FCC example above, we apparently were assuming that the market was not strong form efficient.

Casual observation, particularly in recent years, suggests that inside information does exist and it can be valuable to possess. Whether it is lawful or ethical to use that information is another issue. In any event, we conclude that private information about a particular stock may exist that is not currently reflected in the price of the stock. For example, prior knowledge of a takeover attempt could be very valuable.

The second form of efficiency, semistrong efficiency, is the most controversial. If a market is semistrong form efficient, then all *public* information is reflected in the stock price. The reason this form is controversial is that it implies that security analysts who try to identify mispriced stocks using, for example, financial statement information are wasting their time because that information is already reflected in the current price.

The third form of efficiency, weak form efficiency, suggests that, at a minimum, the current price of a stock reflects its own past prices. In other words, studying past prices in an attempt to identify mispriced securities is futile if the market is weak form efficient. While this form of efficiency might seem rather mild, it implies that searching for patterns in historical prices that are useful in identifying mispriced stocks will not work (this practice is quite common).

What does capital market history say about market efficiency? Here again, there is great controversy. At the risk of going out on a limb, the evidence does seem to tell us three things. First: Prices do appear to respond very rapidly to new information, and the response is at least not grossly different from what we would expect in an efficient market. Second: The future of market prices, particularly in the short run, is very difficult to predict based on publicly available information. Third: If mispriced stocks do exist, then there is no obvious means of identifying them. Put another way: Simpleminded schemes based on public information will probably not be successful.

SUMMARY AND CONCLUSIONS

This chapter has explored the subject of capital market history. Such history is useful because it tells us what to expect in the way of returns from risky assets. We summed up our study of market history with two key lessons:

1. Risky assets, on average, earn a risk premium. There is a reward for bearing risk.
2. The greater the potential reward from a risky investment, the greater is the risk.

These lessons have significant implications for the financial manager. We will be considering these implications in the chapters ahead.

We also discussed the concept of market efficiency. In an efficient market, prices adjust quickly and correctly to new information. Consequently, asset prices in efficient markets are rarely too high or too low. How efficient capital markets (such as the NYSE) are is a matter of debate, but, at a minimum, they are probably much more efficient than most real asset markets.

CHAPTER REVIEW AND SELF-TEST PROBLEMS

10.1 **Recent Return History.**   Use Table 10.1 to calculate the average return over the years 1990–94 for common stocks, small stocks, and Treasury bills.

10.2 **More Recent Return History.**   Calculate the standard deviations using information from Problem 10.1. Which of the investments was the most volatile over this period?

Answers to Chapter Review and Self-Test Problems

10.1 We calculate the averages as follows:

	Actual Returns and Averages		
Year	Large-Company Stocks	Long-Term Government Bonds	Treasury Bills
1995	.3780	.2486	.0564
1996	.2274	.0163	.0512
1997	.3343	.1089	.0522
1998	.2813	.1344	.0506
1999	.2103	−.0712	.0485
Average:	.2863	.0874	.0518

10.2   We first need to calculate the deviations from the average returns. Using the averages from Problem 10.1, we get:

	Deviations from Average Returns		
Year	**Large-Company Stocks**	**Long-Term Government Bonds**	**Treasury Bills**
1995	.0918	.1612	.0046
1996	−.0589	−.0711	−.0005
1997	.0480	.0215	.0004
1998	−.0050	.0470	−.0012
1999	−.0759	−.1586	−.0033
Total:	.0000	.0000	.0000

We square these deviations and calculate the variances and standard deviations:

	Squared Deviations from Average Returns		
Year	**Large-Company Stocks**	**Long-Term Government Bonds**	**Treasury Bills**
1995	.008420	.025988	.000021
1996	.003468	.005057	.000000
1997	.002304	.000462	.000000
1998	.000025	.002207	.000001
1999	.005764	.025143	.000011
Variance:	.004995	.014714	.000009
Standard deviation:	.070676	.121302	.002928

To calculate the variances we added up the squared deviations and divided by 4, the number of returns less 1. Notice that the small stocks had substantially greater volatility with a larger average return. Once again, such investments are risky, particularly over short periods of time.

CRITICAL THINKING AND CONCEPTS REVIEW

1.   **Investment Selection.**   Given that Puma Technology was up by almost 4,000 percent for 1999, why didn't all investors hold Puma Technology?

2.   **Investment Selection.**   Given that Rite Aid was down by 77 percent for 1999, why did some investors hold the stock? Why didn't they sell out before the price declined so sharply?

3.   **Risk and Return.**   We have seen that, over long periods of time, stock investments have tended to substantially outperform bond investments. However, it is not at all uncommon to observe investors with long horizons holding entirely bonds. Are such investors irrational?

4.   **Market Efficiency Implications.**   Explain why a characteristic of an efficient market is that investments in that market have zero NPVs.

5.   **Efficient Markets Hypothesis.**   A stock market analyst is able to identify mispriced stocks by comparing the average price for the last 10 days to the average price for the last 60 days. If this is true, what do you know about the market?

6. **Semistrong Efficiency.** If a market is semistrong form efficient, is it also weak form efficient? Explain.

7. **Efficient Markets Hypothesis.** What are the implications of the efficient markets hypothesis for investors who buy and sell stocks in an attempt to "beat the market"?

8. **Stocks versus Gambling.** Critically evaluate the following statement: Playing the stock market is like gambling. Such speculative investing has no social value, other than the pleasure people get from this form of gambling.

9. **Efficient Markets Hypothesis.** There are several celebrated investors and stock pickers frequently mentioned in the financial press who have recorded huge returns on their investments over the past two decades. Is the success of these particular investors an invalidation of the EMH? Explain.

10. **Efficient Markets Hypothesis.** For each of the following scenarios, discuss whether profit opportunities exist from trading in the stock of the firm under the conditions that (1) the market is not weak form efficient, (2) the market is weak form but not semistrong form efficient, (3) the market is semistrong form but not strong form efficient, and (4) the market is strong form efficient.
    a. The stock price has risen steadily each day for the past 30 days.
    b. The financial statements for a company were released three days ago, and you believe you've uncovered some anomalies in the company's inventory and cost control reporting techniques that are causing the firm's true liquidity strength to be understated.
    c. You observe that the senior management of a company has been buying a lot of the company's stock on the open market over the past week.

QUESTIONS AND PROBLEMS

Basic
(Questions 1–23)

1. **Calculating Returns.** Suppose a stock had an initial price of $63 per share, paid a dividend of $1.25 per share during the year, and had an ending share price of $52. Compute the percentage total return.

2. **Calculating Yields.** In Problem 1, what was the dividend yield? The capital gains yield?

3. **Calculating Returns.** Rework Problems 1 and 2 assuming the ending share price is $75.

4. **Calculating Returns.** Suppose you bought a 12 percent coupon bond one year ago for $1,120. The bond sells for $1,085 today.
    a. Assuming a $1,000 face value, what was your total dollar return on this investment over the past year?
    b. What was your total nominal rate of return on this investment over the past year?
    c. If the inflation rate last year was 4 percent, what was your total real rate of return on this investment?

5. **Nominal versus Real Returns.** What was the average annual return on large-company stock from 1926 through 1999:
    a. In nominal terms?
    b. In real terms?

6. **Bond Returns.** What is the historical real return on long-term government bonds? On long-term corporate bonds?

7.   **Calculating Returns and Variability.**   Using the following returns, calculate the average returns, the variances, and the standard deviations for X and Y.

	Returns	
Year	**X**	**Y**
1	10%	26%
2	18	− 4
3	− 8	−10
4	12	42
5	6	21

8.   **Risk Premiums.**   Refer to Table 10.1 in the text and look at the period from 1990 through 1997.
   a. Calculate the average returns for large-company stocks and T-bills over this time period.
   b. Calculate the standard deviation of the returns for large-company stocks and T-bills over this time period.
   c. Calculate the observed risk premium in each year for the large-company stocks versus the T-bills. What was the average risk premium over this period? What was the standard deviation of the risk premium over this period?
   d. Is it possible for the risk premium to be negative before an investment is undertaken? Can the risk premium be negative after the fact? Explain.

9.   **Calculating Returns and Variability.**   You've observed the following returns on Belmont Data Corporation's stock over the past five years: 9 percent, −10 percent, 2 percent, 25 percent, and 17 percent.
   a. What was the average return on Belmont's stock over this five-year period?
   b. What was the variance of Belmont's returns over this period? The standard deviation?

10.   **Calculating Real Returns and Risk Premiums.**   For Problem 9, suppose the average inflation rate over this period was 3.5 percent and the average T-bill rate over the period was 3.8 percent.
   a. What was the average real return on Belmont's stock?
   b. What was the average nominal risk premium on Belmont's stock?

11.   **Calculating Real Rates.**   Given the information in Problem 10, what was the average real risk-free rate over this time period? What was the average real risk premium?

12.   **Effects of Inflation.**   Look at Table 10.1 and Figure 10.7 in the text. When were T-bill rates at their highest over the period from 1926 through 1999? Why do you think they were so high during this period? What relationship underlies your answer?

13.   **Calculating Returns.**   You purchased a zero coupon bond one year ago for $239.39. The market interest rate is now 12 percent. If the bond had 15 years to maturity when you originally purchased it, what was your total return for the past year?

14.   **Calculating Returns.**   You bought a share of 7 percent preferred stock for $87.50 last year. The market price for your stock is now $95.75. What is your total return for last year?

15.   **Calculating Returns.**   You purchased a bond from Melba's Bread Co. last year. When you purchased the bond it had 15 years until maturity and a YTM of 7.5 percent. The coupon rate is 10 percent paid annually. The current market rate for bonds of this type is 9 percent. What was your rate of return for the year?

16.   **Calculating Returns and Variability.**   A stock has had returns of 10 percent, −15 percent, 18 percent, 12 percent, and 15 percent for the last five years. What are the average return and standard deviation for this stock?

17. **Calculating Returns.** You bought a stock three months ago for $10.25 per share. The stock paid no dividends. The current share price is $12.00. What is the APR of your investment? The EAR?

18. **Calculating Real Returns.** Refer to Table 10.1. What was the average real return for Treasury bills from 1926 through 1932?

19. **Calculating Returns and Variability.** A stock had annual returns of −18 percent, −7 percent, 25 percent, 12 percent, and 16 percent. What are the average return and standard deviation for this stock?

20. **Calculating Returns.** A stock was priced at $105.25 at the beginning of the year and $116.75 at the end of the year. The company also paid a dividend of $1.50 per share. What was the total return for the year?

21. **Calculating Returns and Variability.** A stock had annual returns of 8 percent, −6 percent, 14 percent, 24 percent, 16 percent, and 12 percent for the past six years. What are the average return and standard deviation for this stock?

22. **Return Distributions.** Refer back to Figure 10.10. What range of returns would you expect to see 68 percent of the time for long-term corporate bonds? What about 95 percent of the time?

23. **Return Distributions.** Refer back to Figure 10.10 What range of returns would you expect to see 68 percent of the time for long-term government bonds? What about 95 percent of the time?

24. **Calculating Returns.** Refer to Table 10.1 in the text and look at the period from 1973 through 1980.
    a. Calculate the average return for Treasury bills and the average annual inflation rate (consumer price index) for this period.
    b. Calculate the standard deviation of Treasury bill returns and inflation over this time period.
    c. Calculate the real return for each year. What is the average real return for Treasury bills?
    d. Many people consider Treasury bills to be risk-free. What does this tell you about the potential risks of Treasury bills?

Intermediate
(Questions 24–28)

25. **Calculating Investment Returns.** You bought one of Tappan Manufacturing Co.'s 9 percent coupon bonds one year ago for $1,002.50. These bonds make annual payments and mature six years from now. Suppose you decide to sell your bonds today, when the required return on the bonds is 10 percent. If the inflation rate was 6.5 percent over the past year, what would be your total real return on investment?

26. **Using Return Distributions.** Suppose the returns on long-term government bonds are normally distributed. Based on the historical record, what is the approximate probability that your return on these bonds will be less than −3.8 percent in a given year? What range of returns would you expect to see 95 percent of the time? What range would you expect to see 99 percent of the time?

27. **Using Return Distributions.** Assuming that the returns from holding small-company stocks are normally distributed, what is the approximate probability that your money will double in value in a single year? What about triple in value?

28. **Distributions.** In the previous problem, what is the probability that the return is less than −100 percent (think)? What are the implications for the distribution of returns?

www.mhhe.com/rwj

Spreadsheet Templates 4, 7, 21

11

Risk and Return

**AFTER STUDYING THIS CHAPTER, YOU SHOULD HAVE
A GOOD UNDERSTANDING OF:**

■ How to calculate expected returns

■ The impact of diversification

■ The systematic risk principle

■ The security market line and the risk-return trade-off

DURING THE FIRST four months of 2000, Johnson & Johnson, Apple Computer, and Wal-Mart joined a host of other firms in announcing stellar operating results for the most recent fiscal quarter. In each case, earnings had grown significantly over the same period one year earlier, and, in each case, the numbers revealed were better than what investors had anticipated. As you might expect, news such as this tends to move stock prices.

Johnson & Johnson reported a surge in sales of 8.6 percent resulting in a growth in earnings of 16 percent over the one-year-earlier period. Investors cheered the good news by driving J&J's stock price up by 4.8 percent that day. One day later, Apple Computer announced an increase in revenues of 27 percent and an increase in net income of a whopping 73 percent. So, did investors cheer? Not exactly. Apple's stock price fell by 4.5 percent on the day of the announcement. Two months earlier, Wal-Mart had met a similar fate when it had announced a 23 percent surge in net income and watched its stock price fall 1.8 percent on the news.

These announcements would seem to be essentially the same, but two were viewed as bad news, after which the stock price fell, while the other was seen as good news, after which the stock price rose. So when is good news really good news? The answer is fundamental to understanding risk and return, and—the good news is—this chapter explores it in some detail.

This chapter continues the discussion we began in the previous chapter. We've seen pretty clearly that some investments have greater risks than others. We now begin to drill down a bit to investigate one of the most fundamental problems in finance:Just what is risk? What we will learn is that risk is not always what it seems, and the reward for bearing risk is more subtle than we have indicated so far. Understanding how risks are rewarded is important for everyone in business for the simple reason that business is risky, and only businesses that manage risk wisely will survive over the long haul.

n our last chapter, we learned some important lessons from capital market history. Most importantly, there is a reward, on average, for bearing risk. We called this reward a *risk premium.* The second lesson is that this risk premium is larger for riskier investments. This chapter explores the economic and managerial implications of this basic idea.

Thus far, we have concentrated mainly on the return behavior of a few large portfolios. We need to expand our consideration to include individual assets. Specifically, we have two tasks to accomplish. First, we have to define risk and then discuss how to measure it. We then must quantify the relationship between an asset's risk and its required return.

When we examine the risks associated with individual assets, we find there are two types of risk: systematic and unsystematic. This distinction is crucial because, as we will see, systematic risk affects almost all assets in the economy, at least to some degree, while unsystematic risk affects at most a small number of assets. We then develop the principle of diversification, which shows that highly diversified portfolios will tend to have almost no unsystematic risk.

The principle of diversification has an important implication: To a diversified investor, only systematic risk matters. It follows that in deciding whether or not to buy a particular individual asset, a diversified investor will only be concerned with that asset's systematic risk. This is a key observation, and it allows us to say a great deal about the risks and returns on individual assets. In particular, it is the basis for a famous relationship between risk and return called the *security market line,* or SML. To develop the SML, we introduce the equally famous "beta" coefficient, one of the centerpieces of modern finance. Beta and the SML are key concepts because they supply us with at least part of the answer to the question of how to go about determining the required return on an investment.

11.1 | EXPECTED RETURNS AND VARIANCES

In our previous chapter, we discussed how to calculate average returns and variances using historical data. We now begin to discuss how to analyze returns and variances when the information we have concerns future possible returns and their probabilities.

Expected Return

We start with a straightforward case. Consider a single period of time, say, a year. We have two stocks, L and U, which have the following characteristics: Stock L is expected to have a return of 25 percent in the coming year. Stock U is expected to have a return of 20 percent for the same period.

In a situation like this, if all investors agreed on the expected returns, why would anyone want to hold Stock U? After all, why invest in one stock when the expectation is that another will do better? Clearly, the answer must depend on the risk of the two investments. The return on Stock L, although it is *expected* to be 25 percent, could actually turn out to be higher or lower.

For example, suppose the economy booms. In this case, we think Stock L will have a 70 percent return. If the economy enters a recession, we think the return will be −20 percent. In this case, we say that there are two *states of the economy,* which means that these are the only two possible situations. This setup is oversimplified, of course, but it allows us to illustrate some key ideas without a lot of computation.

Suppose we think a boom and a recession are equally likely to happen, for a 50-50 chance of each. Table 11.1 illustrates the basic information we have described and some additional information about Stock U. Notice that Stock U earns 30 percent if there is a recession and 10 percent if there is a boom.

Obviously, if you buy one of these stocks, say Stock U, what you earn in any particular year depends on what the economy does during that year. However, suppose the probabilities stay the same through time. If you hold U for a number of years, you'll earn 30 per-

TABLE 11.1

States of the economy
and stock returns

| State of Economy | Security Returns If State Occurs | | |
	Probability of State of Economy	Stock L	Stock U
Recession	.5	−20%	30%
Boom	.5	70	10
	1.0		

TABLE 11.2

Calculation of
expected return

| (1) State of Economy | (2) Probability of State of Economy | Stock L | | Stock U | |
		(3) Rate of Return If State Occurs	(4) Product (2) × (3)	(5) Rate of Return If State Occurs	(6) Product (2) × (5)
Recession	.5	−.20	−.10	.30	.15
Boom	.5	.70	.35	.10	.05
	1.0		$E(R_L) = 25\%$		$E(R_U) = 20\%$

cent about half the time and 10 percent the other half. In this case, we say that your **expected return** on Stock U, $E(R_U)$, is 20 percent:

$$E(R_U) = .50 \times 30\% + .50 \times 10\% = 20\%$$

In other words, you should expect to earn 20 percent from this stock, on average.

For Stock L, the probabilities are the same, but the possible returns are different. Here we lose 20 percent half the time, and we gain 70 percent the other half. The expected return on L, $E(R_L)$, is thus 25 percent:

$$E(R_L) = .50 \times -20\% + .50 \times 70\% = 25\%$$

Table 11.2 illustrates these calculations.

In our previous chapter, we defined the risk premium as the difference between the return on a risky investment and that on a risk-free investment, and we calculated the historical risk premiums on some different investments. Using our projected returns, we can calculate the *projected,* or *expected, risk premium* as the difference between the expected return on a risky investment and the certain return on a risk-free investment.

For example, suppose risk-free investments are currently offering 8 percent. We will say that the risk-free rate, which we label as R_f, is 8 percent. Given this, what is the projected risk premium on Stock U? On Stock L? Since the expected return on Stock U, $E(R_U)$, is 20 percent, the projected risk premium is:

$$\begin{aligned} \text{Risk premium} &= \text{Expected return} - \text{Risk-free rate} \\ &= E(R_U) - R_f \\ &= 20\% - 8\% \\ &= 12\% \end{aligned} \qquad [11.1]$$

Similarly, the risk premium on Stock L is $25\% - 8\% = 17\%$.

In general, the expected return on a security or other asset is simply equal to the sum of the possible returns multiplied by their probabilities. So, if we had 100 possible returns,

expected return

Return on a risky asset expected in the future.

we would multiply each one by its probability and then add the results up. The result would be the expected return. The risk premium would then be the difference between this expected return and the risk-free rate.

EXAMPLE 11.1 | **Unequal Probabilities**

Look again at Tables 11.1 and 11.2. Suppose you thought a boom would occur only 20 percent of the time instead of 50 percent. What are the expected returns on Stocks U and L in this case? If the risk-free rate is 10 percent, what are the risk premiums?

The first thing to notice is that a recession must occur 80 percent of the time $(1 - .20 = .80)$ since there are only two possibilities. With this in mind, we see that Stock U has a 30 percent return in 80 percent of the years and a 10 percent return in 20 percent of the years. To calculate the expected return, we again just multiply the possibilities by the probabilities and add up the results:

$E(R_U) = .80 \times 30\% + .20 \times 10\% = 26\%$

Table 11.3 summarizes the calculations for both stocks. Notice that the expected return on L is −2 percent.

The risk premium for Stock U is $26\% - 10\% = 16\%$ in this case. The risk premium for Stock L is negative: $-2\% - 10\% = -12\%$. This is a little odd, but, for reasons we discuss later, it is not impossible.

Calculating the Variance

To calculate the variances of the returns on our two stocks, we first determine the squared deviations from the expected return. We then multiply each possible squared deviation by its probability. We add these up, and the result is the variance. The standard deviation, as always, is the square root of the variance.

To illustrate, Stock U above has an expected return of $E(R_U) = 20\%$. In a given year, it will actually return either 30 percent or 10 percent. The possible deviations are thus $30\% - 20\% = 10\%$ and $10\% - 20\% = -10\%$. In this case, the variance is:

$$\text{Variance} = \sigma^2_U = .50 \times (10\%)^2 + .50 \times (-10\%)^2 = .01$$

The standard deviation is the square root of this:

$$\text{Standard deviation} = \sigma_U = \sqrt{.01} = .10 = 10\%$$

TABLE 11.3			Stock L		Stock U	
Calculation of expected return	**(1)** State of Economy	**(2)** Probability of State of Economy	**(3)** Rate of Return If State Occurs	**(4)** Product **(2) × (3)**	**(5)** Rate of Return If State Occurs	**(6)** Product **(2) × (5)**
	Recession	.8	−.20	−.16	.30	.24
	Boom	.2	.70	.14	.10	.02
		1.0		$E(R_L) = -2\%$		$E(R_U) = 26\%$

	(2) Probability of State of Economy	(3) Return Deviation from Expected Return	(4) Squared Return Deviation from Expected Return	(5) Product (2) × (4)
(1) State of Economy				
Stock L				
Recession	.5	$-.20 - .25 = -.45$	$-.45^2 = .2025$	.10125
Boom	.5	$.70 - .25 = .45$	$.45^2 = .2025$	.10125
	1.0			$\sigma_L^2 = .2025$
Stock U				
Recession	.5	$.30 - .20 = .10$	$.10^2 = .01$	.005
Boom	.5	$.10 - .20 = -.10$	$-.10^2 = .01$	.005
	1.0			$\sigma_U^2 = .010$

TABLE 11.4

Calculation of variance

Table 11.4 summarizes these calculations for both stocks. Notice that Stock L has a much larger variance.

When we put the expected return and variability information for our two stocks together, we have:

	Stock L	Stock U
Expected return, $E(R)$	25%	20%
Variance, σ^2	.2025	.0100
Standard deviation, σ	45%	10%

Stock L has a higher expected return, but U has less risk. You could get a 70 percent return on your investment in L, but you could also lose 20 percent. Notice that an investment in U will always pay at least 10 percent.

Which of these two stocks should you buy? We can't really say; it depends on your personal preferences. We can be reasonably sure, however, that some investors would prefer L to U and some would prefer U to L.

You've probably noticed that the way we calculated expected returns and variances here is somewhat different from the way we did it in the last chapter. The reason is that, in Chapter 10, we were examining actual historical returns, so we estimated the average return and the variance based on some actual events. Here, we have projected *future* returns and their associated probabilities, so this is the information with which we must work.

More Unequal Probabilities | EXAMPLE 11.2

Going back to Example 11.1, what are the variances on the two stocks once we have unequal probabilities? The standard deviations?

We can summarize the needed calculations as follows:

(1) State of Economy	(2) Probability of State of Economy	(3) Return Deviation from Expected Return	(4) Squared Return Deviation from Expected Return	(5) Product (2) × (4)
Stock L				
Recession	.80	$-.20 - (-.02) = -.18$	.0324	.02592
Boom	.20	$.70 - (-.02) = .72$	.5184	.10368
				$\sigma_L^2 = .12960$
Stock U				
Recession	.80	$.30 - .26 = .04$	.0016	.00128
Boom	.20	$.10 - .26 = -.16$	.0256	.00512
				$\sigma_U^2 = .00640$

Based on these calculations, the standard deviation for L is $\sigma_L = \sqrt{.1296} = .36$, or 36%. The standard deviation for U is much smaller; $\sigma_U = \sqrt{.0064} = .08$, or 8%.

CONCEPT QUESTIONS

11.1a How do we calculate the expected return on a security?

11.1b In words, how do we calculate the variance of the expected return?

11.2 | PORTFOLIOS

portfolio

Group of assets such as stocks and bonds held by an investor.

Thus far in this chapter, we have concentrated on individual assets considered separately. However, most investors actually hold a **portfolio** of assets. All we mean by this is that investors tend to own more than just a single stock, bond, or other asset. Given that this is so, portfolio return and portfolio risk are of obvious relevance. Accordingly, we now discuss portfolio expected returns and variances.

Portfolio Weights

There are many equivalent ways of describing a portfolio. The most convenient approach is to list the percentages of the total portfolio's value that are invested in each portfolio asset. We call these percentages the **portfolio weights.**

For example, if we have $50 in one asset and $150 in another, then our total portfolio is worth $200. The percentage of our portfolio in the first asset is $50/200 = .25. The percentage of our portfolio in the second asset is $150/200, or .75. Our portfolio weights are thus .25 and .75. Notice that the weights have to add up to 1.00 since all of our money is invested somewhere.[1]

portfolio weight

Percentage of a portfolio's total value in a particular asset.

Portfolio Expected Returns

Let's go back to Stocks L and U. You put half your money in each. The portfolio weights are obviously .50 and .50. What is the pattern of returns on this portfolio? The expected return?

---

[1]Some of it could be in cash, of course, but we would then just consider the cash to be one of the portfolio assets.

(1) State of Economy	(2) Probability of State of Economy	(3) Portfolio Return If State Occurs	(4) Product (2) × (3)
Recession	.50	$.50 \times -20\% + .50 \times 30\% = 5\%$	.025
Boom	.50	$.50 \times 70\% + .50 \times 10\% = 40\%$	.200
	1.00		$E(R_P) = 22.5\%$

TABLE 11.5

Expected return on an equally weighted portfolio of Stock L and Stock U

To answer these questions, suppose the economy actually enters a recession. In this case, half your money (the half in L) loses 20 percent. The other half (the half in U) gains 30 percent. Your portfolio return, R_P, in a recession will thus be:

$$R_P = .50 \times -20\% + .50 \times 30\% = 5\%$$

Table 11.5 summarizes the remaining calculations. Notice that when a boom occurs, your portfolio will return 40 percent:

$$R_P = .50 \times 70\% + .50 \times 10\% = 40\%$$

As indicated in Table 11.5, the expected return on your portfolio, $E(R_P)$, is 22.5 percent.

We can save ourselves some work by calculating the expected return more directly. Given these portfolio weights, we could have reasoned that we expect half of our money to earn 25 percent (the half in L) and half of our money to earn 20 percent (the half in U). Our portfolio expected return is thus:

$$E(R_P) = .50 \times E(R_L) + .50 \times E(R_U)$$
$$= .50 \times 25\% + .50 \times 20\%$$
$$= 22.5\%$$

This is the same portfolio expected return we had before.

This method of calculating the expected return on a portfolio works no matter how many assets there are in the portfolio. Suppose we had n assets in our portfolio, where n is any number. If we let x_i stand for the percentage of our money in Asset i, then the expected return is:

$$E(R_P) = x_1 \times E(R_1) + x_2 \times E(R_2) + \ldots + x_n \times E(R_n) \qquad [11.2]$$

This says that the expected return on a portfolio is a straightforward combination of the expected returns on the assets in that portfolio. This seems somewhat obvious, but, as we will examine next, the obvious approach is not always the right one.

Portfolio Expected Return | EXAMPLE 11.3

Suppose we have the following projections on three stocks:

State of Economy	Probability of State	Returns Stock A	Returns Stock B	Returns Stock C
Boom	.40	10%	15%	20%
Bust	.60	8	4	0

We want to calculate portfolio expected returns in two cases. First: What would be the expected return on a portfolio with equal amounts invested in each of the three stocks? Second: What would be the expected return if half of the portfolio were in A, with the remainder equally divided between B and C?

From our earlier discussions, the expected returns on the individual stocks are (check these for practice):

$E(R_A) = 8.8\%$

$E(R_B) = 8.4\%$

$E(R_C) = 8.0\%$

If a portfolio has equal investments in each asset, the portfolio weights are all the same. Such a portfolio is said to be *equally weighted*. Since there are three stocks in this case, the weights are all equal to ⅓. The portfolio expected return is thus:

$E(R_P) = (1/3) \times 8.8\% + (1/3) \times 8.4\% + (1/3) \times 8.0\% = 8.4\%$

In the second case, verify that the portfolio expected return is 8.5 percent.

Portfolio Variance

From our discussion above, the expected return on a portfolio that contains equal investment in Stocks U and L is 22.5 percent. What is the standard deviation of return on this portfolio? Simple intuition might suggest that half of the money has a standard deviation of 45 percent and the other half has a standard deviation of 10 percent, so the portfolio's standard deviation might be calculated as:

$$\sigma_P = .50 \times 45\% + .50 \times 10\% = 27.5\%$$

Unfortunately, this approach is completely incorrect!

Let's see what the standard deviation really is. Table 11.6 summarizes the relevant calculations. As we see, the portfolio's variance is about .031, and its standard deviation is less than we thought—it's only 17.5 percent. What is illustrated here is that the variance on a portfolio is not generally a simple combination of the variances of the assets in the portfolio.

We can illustrate this point a little more dramatically by considering a slightly different set of portfolio weights. Suppose we put 2/11 (about 18 percent) in L and the other 9/11 (about 82 percent) in U. If a recession occurs, this portfolio will have a return of:

$$R_P = (2/11) \times -20\% + (9/11) \times 30\% = 20.91\%$$

If a boom occurs, this portfolio will have a return of:

$$R_P = (2/11) \times 70\% + (9/11) \times 10\% = 20.91\%$$

TABLE 11.6					
Variance on an equally weighted portfolio of Stock L and Stock U	**(1) State of Economy**	**(2) Probability of State of Economy**	**(3) Portfolio Return If State Occurs**	**(4) Squared Deviation from Expected Return**	**(5) Product (2) × (4)**
	Recession	.50	5%	$(.05 - .225)^2 = .030625$	.0153125
	Boom	.50	40	$(.40 - .225)^2 = .030625$	.0153125
		1.00		$\sigma^2_P = .030625$	
				$\sigma_P = \sqrt{.030625} = 17.5\%$	

Notice that the return is the same no matter what happens. No further calculations are needed: This portfolio has a zero variance. Apparently, combining assets into portfolios can substantially alter the risks faced by the investor. This is a crucial observation, and we will begin to explore its implications in the next section.

Portfolio Variance and Standard Deviation | EXAMPLE 11.4

In Example 11.3, what are the standard deviations on the two portfolios? To answer, we first have to calculate the portfolio returns in the two states. We will work with the second portfolio, which has 50 percent in Stock A and 25 percent in each of Stocks B and C. The relevant calculations can be summarized as follows:

State of Economy	Probability of State	Returns			
		Stock A	**Stock B**	**Stock C**	**Portfolio**
Boom	.40	10%	15%	20%	13.75%
Bust	.60	8	4	0	5.00

The portfolio return when the economy booms is calculated as:

$$.50 \times 10\% + .25 \times 15\% + .25 \times 20\% = 13.75\%$$

The return when the economy goes bust is calculated the same way. The expected return on the portfolio is 8.5 percent. The variance is thus:

$$\sigma^2 = .40 \times (.1375 - 085)^2 + .60 \times (.05 - .085)^2$$
$$= .0018375$$

The standard deviation is thus about 4.3 percent. For our equally weighted portfolio, verify that the standard deviation is about 5.4 percent.

CONCEPT QUESTIONS

11.2a What is a portfolio weight?

11.2b How do we calculate the expected return on a portfolio?

11.2c Is there a simple relationship between the standard deviation on a portfolio and the standard deviations of the assets in the portfolio?

ANNOUNCEMENTS, SURPRISES, | 11.3
AND EXPECTED RETURNS

Now that we know how to construct portfolios and evaluate their returns, we begin to describe more carefully the risks and returns associated with individual securities. Thus far, we have measured volatility by looking at the difference between the actual return on an asset or portfolio, *R*, and the expected return, E(*R*). We now look at why such deviations exist.

Expected and Unexpected Returns

To begin, for concreteness, we consider the return on the stock of a company called Flyers. What will determine this stock's return in, say, the coming year?

The return on any stock traded in a financial market is composed of two parts. First, the normal, or expected, return from the stock is the part of the return that shareholders in the market predict or expect. This return depends on the information shareholders have that bears on the stock, and it is based on the market's understanding today of the important factors that will influence the stock in the coming year.

The second part of the return on the stock is the uncertain, or risky, part. This is the portion that comes from unexpected information revealed within the year. A list of all possible sources of such information would be endless, but here are a few examples:

News about Flyers research

Government figures released on gross domestic product (GDP)

The results from the latest arms control talks

The news that Flyers's sales figures are higher than expected

A sudden, unexpected drop in interest rates

Based on this discussion, one way to express the return on Flyers stock in the coming year would be:

Total return = Expected return + Unexpected return

$$R = E(R) + U \qquad [11.3]$$

where R stands for the actual total return in the year, $E(R)$ stands for the expected part of the return, and U stands for the unexpected part of the return. What this says is that the actual return, R, differs from the expected return, $E(R)$, because of surprises that occur during the year. In any given year, the unexpected return will be positive or negative, but, through time, the average value of U will be zero. This simply means that, on average, the actual return equals the expected return.

Announcements and News

We need to be careful when we talk about the effect of news items on the return. For example, suppose Flyers's business is such that the company prospers when GDP grows at a relatively high rate and suffers when GDP is relatively stagnant. In this case, in deciding what return to expect this year from owning stock in Flyers, shareholders either implicitly or explicitly must think about what GDP is likely to be for the year.

When the government actually announces GDP figures for the year, what will happen to the value of Flyers stock? Obviously, the answer depends on what figure is released. More to the point, however, the impact depends on how much of that figure is *new* information.

At the beginning of the year, market participants will have some idea or forecast of what the yearly GDP will be. To the extent that shareholders have predicted GDP, that prediction will already be factored into the expected part of the return on the stock, $E(R)$. On the other hand, if the announced GDP is a surprise, then the effect will be part of U, the unanticipated portion of the return.

As an example, suppose shareholders in the market had forecast that the GDP increase this year would be .5 percent. If the actual announcement this year is exactly .5 percent, the same as the forecast, then the shareholders don't really learn anything, and the announcement isn't news. There will be no impact on the stock price as a result. This is like receiving confirmation of something that you suspected all along; it doesn't reveal anything new.

A common way of saying that an announcement isn't news is to say that the market has already "discounted" the announcement. The use of the word *discount* here is different from the use of the term in computing present values, but the spirit is the same. When we discount a dollar in the future, we say it is worth less to us because of the time value of money. When we say that we discount an announcement, or a news item, we mean that it has less of an impact on the market because the market already knew much of it.

For example, going back to Flyers, suppose the government announces that the actual GDP increase during the year has been 1.5 percent. Now shareholders have learned something, namely, that the increase is one percentage point higher than they had forecast. This difference between the actual result and the forecast, one percentage point in this example, is sometimes called the *innovation* or the *surprise*.

An announcement, then, can be broken into two parts, the anticipated, or expected, part and the surprise, or innovation:

Announcement = Expected part + Surprise   [11.4]

The expected part of any announcement is the part of the information that the market uses to form the expectation, $E(R)$, of the return on the stock. The surprise is the news that influences the unanticipated return on the stock, U.

To take another example, if shareholders knew in January that the president of the firm was going to resign, the official announcement in February would be fully expected and would be discounted by the market. Because the announcement was expected before February, its influence on the stock would have taken place before February. The announcement itself will contain no surprise, and the stock's price shouldn't change at all when it is actually made.

The fact that only the unexpected, or surprise, part of an announcement matters explains why two companies can make similar announcements but experience different stock price reactions. For example, to open the chapter, we compared Apple, Johnson & Johnson, and Wal-Mart. In Wal-Mart's case, the news of the surge in income was accompanied by comments from the company that raised worries of slower growth in the coming quarters. In Apple's case, the good news from the company was released on a day when investors turned sour on the future of technology stocks in general (keep this case in mind as you read the next section). Finally, in J&J's case, investors were pleasantly surprised by the news.

Our discussion of market efficiency in the previous chapter bears on this discussion. We are assuming that relevant information known today is already reflected in the expected return. This is identical to saying that the current price reflects relevant publicly available information. We are thus implicitly assuming that markets are at least reasonably efficient in the semistrong form sense.

Henceforth, when we speak of news, we will mean the surprise part of an announcement and not the portion that the market has expected and therefore already discounted.

CONCEPT QUESTIONS

11.3a What are the two basic parts of a return?

11.3b Under what conditions will an announcement have no effect on common stock prices?

RISK: SYSTEMATIC AND UNSYSTEMATIC | 11.4

The unanticipated part of the return, that portion resulting from surprises, is the true risk of any investment. After all, if we always receive exactly what we expect, then the investment is perfectly predictable and, by definition, risk-free. In other words, the risk of owning an asset comes from surprises—unanticipated events.

There are important differences, though, among various sources of risk. Look back at our previous list of news stories. Some of these stories are directed specifically at Flyers, and some are more general. Which of the news items are of specific importance to Flyers?

Announcements about interest rates or GDP are clearly important for nearly all companies, whereas the news about Flyers's president, its research, or its sales is of specific interest to Flyers. We will distinguish between these two types of events, because, as we shall see, they have very different implications.

Systematic and Unsystematic Risk

systematic risk

A risk that influences a large number of assets. Also, *market risk*.

The first type of surprise, the one that affects a large number of assets, we will label **systematic risk.** Because systematic risks have marketwide effects, they are sometimes called *market risks.*

The second type of surprise we will call **unsystematic risk.** An unsystematic risk is one that affects a single asset or a small group of assets. Because these risks are unique to individual companies or assets, they are sometimes called *unique* or *asset-specific risks.* We will use these terms interchangeably.

unsystematic risk

A risk that affects at most a small number of assets. Also, *unique* or *asset-specific* risk.

As we have seen, uncertainties about general economic conditions, such as GDP, interest rates, or inflation, are examples of systematic risks. These conditions affect nearly all companies to some degree. An unanticipated increase, or surprise, in inflation, for example, affects wages and the costs of the supplies that companies buy; it affects the value of the assets that companies own; and it affects the prices at which companies sell their products. Forces such as these, to which all companies are susceptible, are the essence of systematic risk.

In contrast, the announcement of an oil strike by a company will primarily affect that company and, perhaps, a few others (such as primary competitors and suppliers). It is unlikely to have much of an effect on the world oil market, however, or on the affairs of companies not in the oil business, so this is an unsystematic event.

Systematic and Unsystematic Components of Return

The distinction between a systematic risk and an unsystematic risk is never really as exact as we make it out to be. Even the most narrow and peculiar bit of news about a company ripples through the economy. This is true because every enterprise, no matter how tiny, is a part of the economy. It's like the tale of a kingdom that was lost because one horse lost a shoe. This is mostly hairsplitting, however. Some risks are clearly much more general than others. We'll see some evidence on this point in just a moment.

The distinction between the types of risk allows us to break down the surprise portion, *U,* of the return on Flyers's stock into two parts. From before, we had the actual return broken down into its expected and surprise components:

$$R = E(R) + U$$

We now recognize that the total surprise for Flyers, *U,* has a systematic and an unsystematic component, so:

$$R = E(R) + \text{Systematic portion} + \text{Unsystematic portion} \qquad [11.5]$$

Because it is traditional, we will use the Greek letter epsilon, ϵ, to stand for the unsystematic portion. Since systematic risks are often called market risks, we will use the letter *m* to stand for the systematic part of the surprise. With these symbols, we can rewrite the total return:

$$R = E(R) + U$$
$$ = E(R) + m + \epsilon$$

The important thing about the way we have broken down the total surprise, U, is that the unsystematic portion, ϵ, is more or less unique to Flyers. For this reason, it is unrelated to the unsystematic portion of return on most other assets. To see why this is important, we need to return to the subject of portfolio risk.

CONCEPT QUESTIONS

11.4a What are the two basic types of risk?

11.4b What is the distinction between the two types of risk?

DIVERSIFICATION AND PORTFOLIO RISK | 11.5

We've seen earlier that portfolio risks can, in principle, be quite different from the risks of the assets that make up the portfolio. We now look more closely at the riskiness of an individual asset versus the risk of a portfolio of many different assets. We will once again examine some market history to get an idea of what happens with actual investments in U.S. capital markets.

The Effect of Diversification: Another Lesson from Market History

In our previous chapter, we saw that the standard deviation of the annual return on a portfolio of 500 large common stocks has historically been about 20 percent per year (see Figure 10.10, for example). Does this mean that the standard deviation of the annual return on a typical stock in that group of 500 is about 20 percent? As you might suspect by now, the answer is *no*. This is an extremely important observation.

To examine the relationship between portfolio size and portfolio risk, Table 11.7 illustrates typical average annual standard deviations for portfolios that contain different numbers of randomly selected NYSE securities.

In Column 2 of Table 11.7, we see that the standard deviation for a "portfolio" of one security is about 49 percent. What this means is that, if you randomly selected a single NYSE stock and put all your money into it, your standard deviation of return would typically be a substantial 49 percent per year. If you were to randomly select two stocks and invest half your money in each, your standard deviation would be about 37 percent on average, and so on.

The important thing to notice in Table 11.7 is that the standard deviation declines as the number of securities is increased. By the time we have 100 randomly chosen stocks, the portfolio's standard deviation has declined by about 60 percent, from 49 percent to about 20 percent. With 500 securities, the standard deviation is 19.27 percent, similar to the 20 percent we saw in our previous chapter for the large common stock portfolio. The small difference exists because the portfolio securities and time periods examined are not identical.

TABLE 11.7

Standard deviations of
annual portfolio returns

(1) Number of Stocks in Portfolio	(2) Average Standard Deviation of Annual Portfolio Returns	(3) Ratio of Portfolio Standard Deviation to Standard Deviation of a Single Stock
1	49.24%	1.00
2	37.36	.76
4	29.69	.60
6	26.64	.54
8	24.98	.51
10	23.93	.49
20	21.68	.44
30	20.87	.42
40	20.46	.42
50	20.20	.41
100	19.69	.40
200	19.42	.39
300	19.34	.39
400	19.29	.39
500	19.27	.39
1,000	19.21	.39

These figures are from Table 1 in Meir Statman, "How Many Stocks Make a Diversified Portfolio?" *Journal of Financial and Quantitative Analysis* 22 (September 1987), pp. 353–64. They were derived from E. J. Elton and M. J. Gruber, "Risk Reduction and Portfolio Size: An Analytic Solution," *Journal of Business* 50 (October 1977), pp. 415–37.

The Principle of Diversification

Figure 11.1 illustrates the point we've been discussing. What we have plotted is the standard deviation of return versus the number of stocks in the portfolio. Notice in Figure 11.1 that the benefit in terms of risk reduction from adding securities drops off as we add more and more. By the time we have 10 securities, most of the effect is already realized, and by the time we get to 30 or so, there is very little remaining benefit.

Figure 11.1 illustrates two key points. First: Some of the riskiness associated with individual assets can be eliminated by forming portfolios. The process of spreading an investment across assets (and thereby forming a portfolio) is called *diversification*. The **principle of diversification** tells us that spreading an investment across many assets will eliminate some of the risk. The red shaded area in Figure 11.1, labeled "diversifiable risk," is the part that can be eliminated by diversification.

principle of diversification

Spreading an investment across a number of assets will eliminate some, but not all, of the risk.

The second point is equally important: There is a minimum level of risk that cannot be eliminated simply by diversifying. This minimum level is labeled "nondiversifiable risk" in Figure 11.1. Taken together, these two points are another important lesson from capital market history: Diversification reduces risk, but only up to a point. Put another way: Some risk is diversifiable and some is not.

Diversification and Unsystematic Risk

From our discussion of portfolio risk, we know that some of the risk associated with individual assets can be diversified away and some cannot. We are left with an obvious question: Why is this so? It turns out that the answer hinges on the distinction we made earlier between systematic and unsystematic risk.

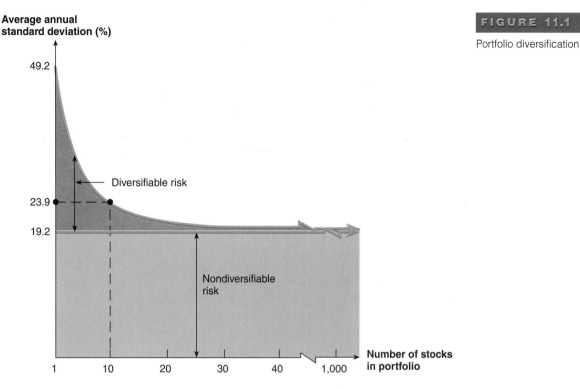

FIGURE 11.1

Portfolio diversification

By definition, an unsystematic risk is one that is particular to a single asset or, at most, a small group. For example, if the asset under consideration is stock in a single company, the discovery of positive NPV projects such as successful new products and innovative cost savings will tend to increase the value of the stock. Unanticipated lawsuits, industrial accidents, strikes, and similar events will tend to decrease future cash flows and thereby reduce share values.

Here is the important observation: If we only held a single stock, then the value of our investment would fluctuate because of company-specific events. If we hold a large portfolio, on the other hand, some of the stocks in the portfolio will go up in value because of positive company-specific events and some will go down in value because of negative events. The net effect on the overall value of the portfolio will be relatively small, however, as these effects will tend to cancel each other out.

Now we see why some of the variability associated with individual assets is eliminated by diversification. When we combine assets into portfolios, the unique, or unsystematic, events—both positive and negative—tend to "wash out" once we have more than just a few assets.

This is an important point that bears restating:

> Unsystematic risk is essentially eliminated by diversification, so a relatively large portfolio has almost no unsystematic risk.

In fact, the terms *diversifiable risk* and *unsystematic risk* are often used interchangeably.

Diversification and Systematic Risk

We've seen that unsystematic risk can be eliminated by diversifying. What about systematic risk? Can it also be eliminated by diversification? The answer is no because, by definition, a systematic risk affects almost all assets to some degree. As a result, no matter how many assets we put into a portfolio, the systematic risk doesn't go away. Thus, for obvious reasons, the terms *systematic risk* and *nondiversifiable risk* are used interchangeably.

Because we have introduced so many different terms, it is useful to summarize our discussion before moving on. What we have seen is that the total risk of an investment, as measured by the standard deviation of its return, can be written as:

$$\text{Total risk} = \text{Systematic risk} + \text{Unsystematic risk} \qquad [11.6]$$

Systematic risk is also called *nondiversifiable risk* or *market risk*. Unsystematic risk is also called *diversifiable risk, unique risk,* or *asset-specific risk.* For a well-diversified portfolio, the unsystematic risk is negligible. For such a portfolio, essentially all of the risk is systematic.

CONCEPT QUESTIONS

11.5a What happens to the standard deviation of return for a portfolio if we increase the number of securities in the portfolio?

11.5b What is the principle of diversification?

11.5c Why is some risk diversifiable?

11.5d Why can't systematic risk be diversified away?

11.6 | SYSTEMATIC RISK AND BETA

The question that we now begin to address is this: What determines the size of the risk premium on a risky asset? Put another way: Why do some assets have a larger risk premium than other assets? The answer to these questions, as we discuss next, is also based on the distinction between systematic and unsystematic risk.

The Systematic Risk Principle

Thus far, we've seen that the total risk associated with an asset can be decomposed into two components: systematic and unsystematic risk. We have also seen that unsystematic risk can be essentially eliminated by diversification. The systematic risk present in an asset, on the other hand, cannot be eliminated by diversification.

systematic risk principle

The expected return on a risky asset depends only on that asset's systematic risk.

Based on our study of capital market history, we know that there is a reward, on average, for bearing risk. However, we now need to be more precise about what we mean by risk. The **systematic risk principle** states that the reward for bearing risk depends only on the systematic risk of an investment. The underlying rationale for this principle is straightforward: Since unsystematic risk can be eliminated at virtually no cost (by diversifying), there is no reward for bearing it. Put another way: The market does not reward risks that are borne unnecessarily.

The systematic risk principle has a remarkable and very important implication:

> The expected return on an asset depends only on that asset's systematic risk.

There is an obvious corollary to this principle: No matter how much total risk an asset has, only the systematic portion is relevant in determining the expected return (and the risk premium) on that asset.

Company	Beta Coefficient (β_i)
McDonald's	.85
Gillette	.90
IBM	1.00
General Motors	1.05
Microsoft	1.10
Harley-Davidson	1.20
Dell Computer	1.35
America Online	1.75

TABLE 11.8

Beta coefficients for selected companies

Source: From *Value Line Investment Survey,* various issues, 2000.

Measuring Systematic Risk

Since systematic risk is the crucial determinant of an asset's expected return, we need some way of measuring the level of systematic risk for different investments. The specific measure we will use is called the **beta coefficient,** for which we will use the Greek symbol β. A beta coefficient, or beta for short, tells us how much systematic risk a particular asset has relative to an average asset. By definition, an average asset has a beta of 1.0 relative to itself. An asset with a beta of .50, therefore, has half as much systematic risk as an average asset; an asset with a beta of 2.0 has twice as much.

Table 11.8 contains the estimated beta coefficients for the stocks of some well-known companies. (This particular source rounds numbers to the nearest .05.) The range of betas in Table 11.8 is typical for stocks of large U.S. corporations. Betas outside this range occur, but they are less common.

The important thing to remember is that the expected return, and thus the risk premium, on an asset depends only on its systematic risk. Since assets with larger betas have greater systematic risks, they will have greater expected returns. Thus, from Table 11.8, an investor who buys stock in McDonald's, with a beta of .85, should expect to earn less, on average, than an investor who buys stock in General Motors, with a beta of about 1.05. To learn more about "real-world" betas, see the nearby *Reality Bytes* box.

beta coefficient

Amount of systematic risk present in a particular risky asset relative to that in an average risky asset.

Total Risk versus Beta | EXAMPLE 11.5

Consider the following information on two securities. Which has greater total risk? Which has greater systematic risk? Greater unsystematic risk? Which asset will have a higher risk premium?

	Standard Deviation	Beta
Security A	40%	.50
Security B	20	1.50

From our discussion in this section, Security A has greater total risk, but it has substantially less systematic risk. Since total risk is the sum of systematic and unsystematic risk, Security A must have greater unsystematic risk. Finally, from the systematic risk principle, Security B will have a higher risk premium and a greater expected return, despite the fact that it has less total risk.

reality BYTES

BETA, BETA, WHO'S GOT THE BETA?

Based on what we've studied so far, you can see that beta is a pretty important topic. You might wonder, then, are all published betas created equal? Read on for at least a partial answer to this question.

We did some checking on betas and found some interesting results. The *Value Line Investment Survey* is one of the best-known sources for information on publicly traded companies. However, with the explosion of on-line investing, there has been a corresponding increase in the amount of investment information available on line. We decided to compare the betas presented by Value Line to those reported by Yahoo (quote.yahoo.com), Excite (www.excite.com), and Wall Street Research Net (WSRN) (www.wsrn.com). What we found leads to an important note of caution.

Consider Amazon.com, the big on-line e-tailer. The betas reported for it on the Internet sites ranged from 2.48 to 2.61, a reasonably narrow range. However, these betas were much larger than Value Line's beta of 1.6. Amazon.com wasn't the only stock that showed a significant divergence in betas. In fact, for most of the technology companies we looked at, Value Line reported betas that were significantly lower than their on-line cousins. For example, the on-line betas for Lycos ranged from 2.53 to 3.12, while Value Line reported 2.25. Similarly, the betas for Yahoo ranged from 3.25 to 3.4 on line, but Value Line's was only 1.75. Interested in something less hi-tech? How about Tommy Hilfiger Corp., whose on-line beta ranged from 1.45 to 1.84, compared to Value Line's reported 1.35. By the way, don't let these examples lead you to conclude that Value Line's betas are always lower; we found many examples that went the other way.

We also found some unusual, and even hard to believe, estimates. Coca-Cola Bottling, for example, had Internet-reported betas that ranged from .01 to .05, which is obviously quite low. Value Line's reported beta was a bit higher, but still low, at .35. A more extreme case concerns on-line health company Healtheon/WebMD, which had a beta of −3.86 on Excite and −3.88 on WSRN (notice the minus signs). Yahoo reported this beta as not meaningful, while Value Line did not cover this company. How do you suppose we should interpret a beta of almost −4?

There are a few lessons to be learned from all of this. First, not all betas are created equal. Some are computed using weekly prices and some using daily prices. Some are computed using 60 months' worth of stock returns; some consider more or less. Some betas are computed by comparing the stock to the S&P 500 index, while others use alternative indexes. Finally, some reporting firms (including Value Line) make adjustments to the raw betas to reflect information other than just the fluctuation in stock prices.

The second lesson is perhaps more subtle and comes from the Healtheon/WebMD case. We are interested in knowing what the beta of a stock will be in the future, but betas have to be estimated using historical data. Anytime we use the past to predict the future, there is the danger of a poor estimate. As we will see later in this chapter (and in the next one), it is very unlikely that Healtheon/WebMD really has a beta of anything like −4. Instead, the estimate is almost certainly a poor one. The moral of the story is that, as with any financial tool, beta is not a black box that should be taken without question.

Portfolio Betas

Earlier, we saw that the riskiness of a portfolio has no simple relationship to the risks of the assets in the portfolio. A portfolio beta, however, can be calculated just like a portfolio expected return. For example, looking again at Table 11.8, suppose you put half of your money in Gillette and half in Harley-Davidson. What would the beta of this combination be? Since Gillette has a beta of .90 and Harley-Davidson has a beta of 1.20, the portfolio's beta, β_P, would be:

$$\beta_P = .50 \times \beta_{\text{Gillette}} + .50 \times \beta_{\text{Harley-Davidson}}$$
$$= .50 \times .90 + .50 \times 1.20$$
$$= 1.05$$

In general, if we had a large number of assets in a portfolio, we would multiply each asset's beta by its portfolio weight and then add the results up to get the portfolio's beta.

| | **Portfolio Betas** | **EXAMPLE 11.6** |

Suppose we had the following investments:

Security	Amount Invested	Expected Return	Beta
Stock A	$1,000	8%	.80
Stock B	2,000	12	.95
Stock C	3,000	15	1.10
Stock D	4,000	18	1.40

What is the expected return on this portfolio? What is the beta of this portfolio? Does this portfolio have more or less systematic risk than an average asset?

To answer, we first have to calculate the portfolio weights. Notice that the total amount invested is $10,000. Of this, $1,000/10,000 = 10% is invested in Stock A. Similarly, 20 percent is invested in Stock B, 30 percent is invested in Stock C, and 40 percent is invested in Stock D. The expected return, $E(R_P)$, is thus:

$$E(R_P) = .10 \times E(R_A) + .20 \times E(R_B) + .30 \times E(R_C) + .40 \times E(R_D)$$

$$= .10 \times 8\% + .20 \times 12\% + .30 \times 15\% + .40 \times 18\%$$

$$= 14.9\%$$

Similarly, the portfolio beta, β_P, is:

$$\beta_P = .10 \times \beta_A + .20 \times \beta_B + .30 \times \beta_C + .40 \times \beta_D$$

$$= .10 \times .80 + .20 \times .95 + .30 \times 1.10 + .40 \times 1.40$$

$$= 1.16$$

This portfolio thus has an expected return of 14.9 percent and a beta of 1.16. Since the beta is larger than 1.0, this portfolio has greater systematic risk than an average asset.

CONCEPT QUESTIONS

11.6a What is the systematic risk principle?

11.6b What does a beta coefficient measure?

11.6c How do you calculate a portfolio beta?

11.6d True or false: The expected return on a risky asset depends on that asset's total risk. Explain.

THE SECURITY MARKET LINE | 11.7

We're now in a position to see how risk is rewarded in the marketplace. To begin, suppose that Asset A has an expected return of $E(R_A) = 20\%$ and a beta of $\beta_A = 1.6$. Furthermore, the risk-free rate is $R_f = 8\%$. Notice that a risk-free asset, by definition, has no systematic risk (or unsystematic risk), so a risk-free asset has a beta of 0.

Beta and the Risk Premium

Consider a portfolio made up of Asset A and a risk-free asset. We can calculate some different possible portfolio expected returns and betas by varying the percentages invested in these two assets. For example, if 25 percent of the portfolio is invested in Asset A, then the expected return is:

$$E(R_P) = .25 \times E(R_A) + (1 - .25) \times R_f$$
$$= .25 \times 20\% + .75 \times 8\%$$
$$= 11.0\%$$

Similarly, the beta on the portfolio, β_P, would be:

$$\beta_P = .25 \times \beta_A + (1 - .25) \times 0$$
$$= .25 \times 1.6$$
$$= .40$$

Notice that, since the weights have to add up to 1, the percentage invested in the risk-free asset is equal to 1 minus the percentage invested in Asset A.

One thing that you might wonder about is whether it is possible for the percentage invested in Asset A to exceed 100 percent. The answer is yes. The way this can happen is for the investor to borrow at the risk-free rate. For example, suppose an investor has $100 and borrows an additional $50 at 8 percent, the risk-free rate. The total investment in Asset A would be $150, or 150 percent of the investor's wealth. The expected return in this case would be:

$$E(R_P) = 1.50 \times E(R_A) + (1 - 1.50) \times R_f$$
$$= 1.50 \times 20\% - .50 \times 8\%$$
$$= 26.0\%$$

The beta on the portfolio would be:

$$\beta_P = 1.50 \times \beta_A + (1 - 1.50) \times 0$$
$$= 1.50 \times 1.6$$
$$= 2.4$$

We can calculate some other possibilities as follows:

Percentage of Portfolio in Asset A	Portfolio Expected Return	Portfolio Beta
0%	8%	.0
25	11	.4
50	14	.8
75	17	1.2
100	20	1.6
125	23	2.0
150	26	2.4

In Figure 11.2A, these portfolio expected returns are plotted against the portfolio betas. Notice that all the combinations fall on a straight line.

The Reward-to-Risk Ratio　What is the slope of the straight line in Figure 11.2A? As always, the slope of a straight line is equal to "the rise over the run." In this case, as we move out of the risk-free asset into Asset A, the beta increases from 0 to 1.6 (a "run" of 1.6). At the same time, the expected return goes from 8 percent to 20 percent, a "rise" of 12 percent. The slope of the line is thus $12\%/1.6 = 7.50\%$.

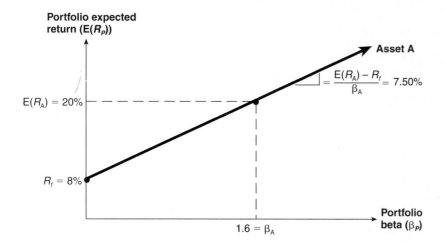

FIGURE 11.2A

Portfolio expected returns and betas for Asset A

Notice that the slope of our line is just the risk premium on Asset A, $E(R_A) - R_f$, divided by Asset A's beta, β_A:

$$\text{Slope} = \frac{E(R_A) - R_f}{\beta_A}$$

$$= \frac{20\% - 8\%}{1.6} = 7.50\%$$

What this tells us is that Asset A offers a *reward-to-risk ratio* of 7.50 percent.[2] In other words, Asset A has a risk premium of 7.50 percent per "unit" of systematic risk.

The Basic Argument   Now suppose we consider a second asset, Asset B. This asset has a beta of 1.2 and an expected return of 16 percent. Which investment is better, Asset A or Asset B? You might think that, once again, we really cannot say. Some investors might prefer A; some investors might prefer B. Actually, however, we can say: A is better because, as we shall demonstrate, B offers inadequate compensation for its level of systematic risk, at least relative to A.

To begin, we calculate different combinations of expected returns and betas for portfolios of Asset B and a risk-free asset just as we did for Asset A. For example, if we put 25 percent in Asset B and the remaining 75 percent in the risk-free asset, the portfolio's expected return would be:

$$E(R_P) = .25 \times E(R_B) + (1 - .25) \times R_f$$
$$= .25 \times 16\% + .75 \times 8\%$$
$$= 10.0\%$$

Similarly, the beta on the portfolio, β_P, would be:

$$\beta_P = .25 \times \beta_B + (1 - .25) \times 0$$
$$= .25 \times 1.2$$
$$= .30$$

Some other possibilities are as follows:

---

[2]This ratio is sometimes called the *Treynor index,* after one of its originators.

Portfolio expected
returns and betas for
Asset B

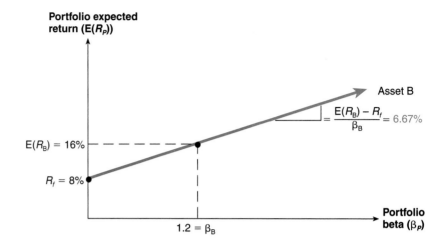

Percentage of Portfolio in Asset B	Portfolio Expected Return	Portfolio Beta
0%	8%	.0
25	10	.3
50	12	.6
75	14	.9
100	16	1.2
125	18	1.5
150	20	1.8

When we plot these combinations of portfolio expected returns and portfolio betas in Figure 11.2B, we get a straight line just as we did for Asset A.

The key thing to notice is that when we compare the results for Assets A and B, as in Figure 11.2C, the line describing the combinations of expected returns and betas for Asset A is higher than the one for Asset B. What this tells us is that for any given level of systematic risk (as measured by β), some combination of Asset A and the risk-free asset always offers a larger return. This is why we were able to state that Asset A is a better investment than Asset B.

Another way of seeing that A offers a superior return for its level of risk is to note that the slope of our line for Asset B is:

$$\text{Slope} = \frac{E(R_B) - R_f}{\beta_B}$$

$$= \frac{16\% - 8\%}{1.2} = 6.67\%$$

Thus, Asset B has a reward-to-risk ratio of 6.67 percent, which is less than the 7.5 percent offered by Asset A.

The Fundamental Result   The situation we have described for Assets A and B cannot persist in a well-organized, active market, because investors would be attracted to Asset A

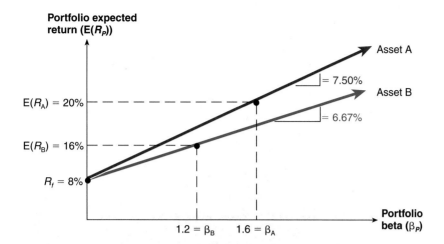

FIGURE 11.2C

Portfolio expected
returns and betas for
both assets

and away from Asset B. As a result, Asset A's price would rise and Asset B's price would fall. Since prices and returns move in opposite directions, the result would be that A's expected return would decline and B's would rise.

This buying and selling would continue until the two assets plotted on exactly the same line, which means they would offer the same reward for bearing risk. In other words, in an active, competitive market, we must have that:

$$\frac{E(R_A) - R_f}{\beta_A} = \frac{E(R_B) - R_f}{\beta_B}$$

This is the fundamental relationship between risk and return.

Our basic argument can be extended to more than just two assets. In fact, no matter how many assets we had, we would always reach the same conclusion:

> The reward-to-risk ratio must be the same for all the assets in the market.

This result is really not so surprising. What it says, for example, is that, if one asset has twice as much systematic risk as another asset, its risk premium will simply be twice as large.

Since all of the assets in the market must have the same reward-to-risk ratio, they all must plot on the same line. This argument is illustrated in Figure 11.3. As shown, Assets A and B plot directly on the line and thus have the same reward-to-risk ratio. If an asset plotted above the line, such as C in Figure 11.3, its price would rise, and its expected return would fall until it plotted exactly on the line. Similarly, if an asset plotted below the line, such as D in Figure 11.3, its expected return would rise until it too plotted directly on the line.

The arguments we have presented apply to active, competitive, well-functioning markets. The financial markets, such as the NYSE, best meet these criteria. Other markets, such as real asset markets, may or may not. For this reason, these concepts are most useful in examining financial markets. We will thus focus on such markets here. However, as we discuss in a later section, the information about risk and return gleaned from financial markets is crucial in evaluating the investments that a corporation makes in real assets.

FIGURE 11.3

Expected returns and
systematic risk

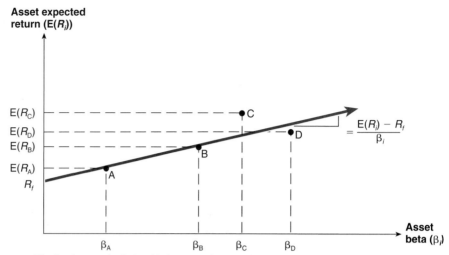

The fundamental relationship between beta and expected return is that all assets
must have the same reward-to-risk ratio, $[E(R_i) - R_f]/\beta_i$. This means that they would
all plot on the same straight line. Assets A and B are examples of this behavior.
Asset C's expected return is too high; Asset D's is too low.

EXAMPLE 11.7 | Buy Low, Sell High

An asset is said to be *overvalued* if its price is too high given its expected return and risk. Suppose you
observe the following situation:

Security	Expected Return	Beta
Mulder Co.	14%	1.3
Sculley Co.	10	.8

The risk-free rate is currently 6 percent. Is one of the two securities above overvalued relative to the
other?

To answer, we compute the reward-to-risk ratio for both. For Mulder, this ratio is $(14\% - 6\%)/1.3 =$
6.15%. For Sculley, this ratio is 5 percent. What we conclude is that Sculley offers an insufficient expected
return for its level of risk, at least relative to Mulder. Since its expected return is too low, its price is too
high. In other words, Sculley is overvalued relative to Mulder, and we would expect to see its price fall relative to Mulder's. Notice that we could also say Mulder is *undervalued* relative to Sculley.

**security market
line (SML)**

Positively sloped
straight line displaying
the relationship
between expected
return and beta.

The Security Market Line

The line that results when we plot expected returns and beta coefficients is obviously of
some importance, so it's time we gave it a name. This line, which we use to describe the relationship between systematic risk and expected return in financial markets, is usually
called the **security market line, or SML.** After NPV, the SML is arguably the most important concept in modern finance.

Market Portfolios   It will be very useful to know the equation of the SML. There are many different ways we could write it, but one way is particularly common. Suppose we consider a portfolio made up of all of the assets in the market. Such a portfolio is called a market portfolio, and we will express the expected return on this market portfolio as $E(R_M)$.

Since all the assets in the market must plot on the SML, so must a market portfolio made up of those assets. To determine where it plots on the SML, we need to know the beta of the market portfolio, β_M. Since this portfolio is representative of all of the assets in the market, it must have average systematic risk. In other words, it has a beta of 1.0. We could therefore write the slope of the SML as:

$$\text{SML slope} = \frac{E(R_M) - R_f}{\beta_M} = \frac{E(R_M) - R_f}{1} = E(R_M) - R_f$$

The term $E(R_M) - R_f$ is often called the **market risk premium** since it is the risk premium on a market portfolio.

market risk premium
Slope of the SML, the difference between the expected return on a market portfolio and the risk-free rate.

The Capital Asset Pricing Model   To finish up, if we let $E(R_i)$ and β_i stand for the expected return and beta, respectively, on any asset in the market, then we know that asset must plot on the SML. As a result, we know that its reward-to-risk ratio is the same as the overall market's:

$$\frac{E(R_i) - R_f}{\beta_i} = E(R_M) - R_f$$

If we rearrange this, then we can write the equation for the SML as:

$$E(R_i) = R_f + [E(R_M) - R_f] \times \beta_i \qquad [11.7]$$

This result is identical to the famous **capital asset pricing model (CAPM).**

What the CAPM shows is that the expected return for a particular asset depends on three things:

1. *The pure time value of money.* As measured by the risk-free rate, R_f, this is the reward for merely waiting for your money, without taking any risk.
2. *The reward for bearing systematic risk.* As measured by the market risk premium, $[E(R_M) - R_f]$, this component is the reward the market offers for bearing an average amount of systematic risk in addition to waiting.
3. *The amount of systematic risk.* As measured by β_i, this is the amount of systematic risk present in a particular asset, relative to an average asset.

capital asset pricing model (CAPM)
Equation of the SML showing the relationship between expected return and beta.

By the way, the CAPM works for portfolios of assets just as it does for individual assets. In an earlier section, we saw how to calculate a portfolio's β. To find the expected return on a portfolio, we simply use this β in the CAPM equation.

Figure 11.4 summarizes our discussion of the SML and the CAPM. As before, we plot expected return against beta. Now we recognize that, based on the CAPM, the slope of the SML is equal to the market risk premium, $[E(R_M) - R_f]$.

This concludes our presentation of concepts related to the risk-return trade-off. For future reference, Table 11.9 summarizes the various concepts in the order in which we discussed them.

FIGURE 11.4

The security market
line, or SML

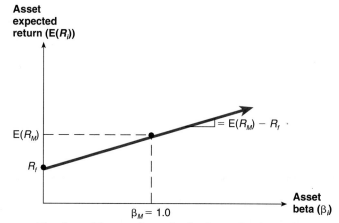

The slope of the security market line is equal to the market risk
premium, i.e., the reward for bearing an average amount of
systematic risk. The equation describing the SML can be written:

$$E(R_i) = R_f + [E(R_M) - R_f] \times \beta_i$$

which is the capital asset pricing model, or CAPM.

TABLE 11.9   Summary of risk and return concepts

I. **Total return**

The *total return* on an investment has two components: the expected return and the unexpected
return. The unexpected return comes about because
of unanticipated events. The risk from investing
stems from the possibility of an unanticipated event.

II. **Total risk**

The *total risk* of an investment is measured by the
variance or, more commonly, the standard deviation of
its return.

III. **Systematic and unsystematic risks**

Systematic risks (also called *market risks*) are unanticipated events that affect almost all assets to some
degree because the effects are economywide. *Unsystematic risks* are unanticipated events that affect single
assets or small groups of assets. Unsystematic risks
are also called *unique* or *asset-specific risks*.

IV. **The effect of diversification**

Some, but not all, of the risk associated with a risky
investment can be eliminated by diversification. The
reason is that unsystematic risks, which are unique to
individual assets, tend to wash out in a large
portfolio, but systematic risks, which affect all of the
assets in a portfolio to some extent, do not.

V. **The systematic risk principle and beta**

Because unsystematic risk can be freely eliminated
by diversification, the *systematic risk principle* states
that the reward for bearing risk depends only on the
level of systematic risk. The level of systematic risk in
a particular asset, relative to the average, is given by
the beta of that asset.

VI. **The reward-to-risk ratio and the security market
line**

The *reward-to-risk ratio* for Asset *i* is the ratio of its
risk premium, $E(R_i) - R_f$, to its beta, β_i:

$$\frac{E(R_i) - R_f}{\beta_i}$$

In a well-functioning market, this ratio is the same for
every asset. As a result, when asset expected returns
are plotted against asset betas, all assets plot on the
same straight line, called the *security market line*
(SML).

VII. **The capital asset pricing model**

From the SML, the expected return on Asset *i* can be
written:

$$E(R_i) = R_f + [E(R_M) - R_f] \times \beta_i$$

This is the *capital asset pricing model* (CAPM). The
expected return on a risky asset thus has three
components. The first is the pure time value of
money, R_f; the second is the market risk premium,
$[E(R_M) - R_f]$; and the third is the beta for that asset,
β_i.

Risk and Return | EXAMPLE 11.8

Suppose the risk-free rate is 4 percent, the market risk premium is 8.6 percent, and a particular stock has a beta of 1.3. Based on the CAPM, what is the expected return on this stock? What would the expected return be if the beta were to double?

With a beta of 1.3, the risk premium for the stock would be 1.3 × 8.6%, or 11.18 percent. The risk-free rate is 4 percent, so the expected return is 15.18 percent. If the beta doubled to 2.6, the risk premium would double to 22.36 percent, so the expected return would be 26.36 percent.

CONCEPT QUESTIONS

11.7a What is the fundamental relationship between risk and return in well-functioning markets?

11.7b What is the security market line? Why must all assets plot directly on it in a well-functioning market?

11.7c What is the capital asset pricing model, or CAPM? What does it tell us about the required return on a risky investment?

THE SML AND THE COST | 11.8
OF CAPITAL: A PREVIEW

Our goal in studying risk and return is twofold. First, risk is an extremely important consideration in almost all business decisions, so we want to discuss just what risk is and how it is rewarded in the market. Our second purpose is to learn what determines the appropriate discount rate for future cash flows. We briefly discuss this second subject now; we discuss it in more detail in Chapter 12.

The Basic Idea

The security market line tells us the reward for bearing risk in financial markets. At an absolute minimum, any new investment our firm undertakes must offer an expected return that is no worse than what the financial markets offer for the same risk. The reason for this is simply that our shareholders can always invest for themselves in the financial markets.

The only way we benefit our shareholders is by finding investments with expected returns that are superior to what the financial markets offer for the same risk. Such an investment will have a positive NPV. So, if we ask, What is the appropriate discount rate? the answer is that we should use the expected return offered in financial markets on investments with the same systematic risk.

In other words, to determine whether or not an investment has a positive NPV, we essentially compare the expected return on that new investment to what the financial market offers on an investment with the same beta. This is why the SML is so important; it tells us the "going rate" for bearing risk in the economy.

The Cost of Capital

The appropriate discount rate on a new project is the minimum expected rate of return an investment must offer to be attractive. This minimum required return is often called the **cost of capital** associated with the investment. It is called this because the required return is what

cost of capital
The minimum required return on a new investment.

the firm must earn on its capital investment in a project just to break even. It can thus be interpreted as the opportunity cost associated with the firm's capital investment.

Notice that when we say an investment is attractive if its expected return exceeds what is offered in financial markets for investments of the same risk, we are effectively using the internal rate of return, or IRR, criterion that we developed and discussed in Chapter 8. The only difference is that now we have a much better idea of what determines the required return on an investment. This understanding will be critical when we discuss cost of capital and capital structure in Part 7 of our book.

CONCEPT QUESTIONS

11.8a If an investment has a positive NPV, would it plot above or below the SML? Why?

11.8b What is meant by the term *cost of capital*?

SUMMARY AND CONCLUSIONS

This chapter has covered the essentials of risk. Along the way, we have introduced a number of definitions and concepts. The most important of these is the security market line, or SML. The SML is important because it tells us the reward offered in financial markets for bearing risk. Once we know this, we have a benchmark against which we compare the returns expected from real asset investments to determine if they are desirable.

Because we have covered quite a bit of ground, it's useful to summarize the basic economic logic underlying the SML as follows:

1. Based on capital market history, there is a reward for bearing risk. This reward is the risk premium on an asset.

2. The total risk associated with an asset has two parts: systematic risk and unsystematic risk. Unsystematic risk can be freely eliminated by diversification (this is the principle of diversification), so only systematic risk is rewarded. As a result, the risk premium on an asset is determined by its systematic risk. This is the systematic risk principle.

3. An asset's systematic risk, relative to the average, can be measured by its beta coefficient, β_i. The risk premium on an asset is then given by its beta coefficient multiplied by the market risk premium, $[E(R_M) - R_f] \times \beta_i$.

4. The expected return on an asset, $E(R_i)$, is equal to the risk-free rate, R_f, plus the risk premium:

$$E(R_i) = R_f + [E(R_M) - R_f] \times \beta_i$$

This is the equation of the SML, and it is often called the *capital asset pricing model,* or CAPM.

This chapter completes our discussion of risk and return and concludes Part 6 of our book. Now that we have a better understanding of what determines a firm's cost of capital for an investment, the next several chapters examine more closely how firms raise the long-term capital needed for investment.

CHAPTER REVIEW AND SELF-TEST PROBLEMS

11.1 Expected Return and Standard Deviation. This problem will give you some practice calculating measures of prospective portfolio performance. There are two assets and three states of the economy:

(1) State of Economy	(2) Probability of State of Economy	(3) Stock A Rate of Return If State Occurs	(4) Stock B Rate of Return If State Occurs
Recession	.10	−.20	.30
Normal	.60	.10	.20
Boom	.30	.70	.50

What are the expected returns and standard deviations for these two stocks?

11.2 Portfolio Risk and Return. In the previous problem, suppose you have $20,000 total. If you put $6,000 in Stock A and the remainder in Stock B, what will be the expected return and standard deviation on your portfolio?

11.3 Risk and Return. Suppose you observe the following situation:

Security	Beta	Expected Return
Cooley, Inc.	1.6	19%
Moyer Co.	1.2	16

If the risk-free rate is 8 percent, are these securities correctly priced? What would the risk-free rate have to be if they are correctly priced?

11.4 CAPM. Suppose the risk-free rate is 8 percent. The expected return on the market is 14 percent. If a particular stock has a beta of .60, what is its expected return based on the CAPM? If another stock has an expected return of 20 percent, what must its beta be?

Answers to Chapter Review and Self-Test Problems

11.1 The expected returns are just the possible returns multiplied by the associated probabilities:

$$E(R_A) = .10 \times -.20 + .60 \times .10 + .30 \times .70 = 25\%$$
$$E(R_B) = .10 \times .30 + .60 \times .20 + .30 \times .50 = 30\%$$

The variances are given by the sums of the squared deviations from the expected returns multiplied by their probabilities:

$$\sigma^2_A = .10 \times (-.20 - .25)^2 + .60 \times (.10 - .25)^2 + .30 \times (.70 - .25)^2$$
$$= .10 \times -.45^2 + .60 \times -.15^2 + .30 \times .45^2$$
$$= .10 \times .2025 + .60 \times .0225 + .30 \times .2025$$
$$= .0945$$
$$\sigma^2_B = .10 \times (.30 - .30)^2 + .60 \times (.20 - .30)^2 + .30 \times (.50 - .30)^2$$
$$= .10 \times .00^2 + .60 \times -.10^2 + .30 \times .20^2$$
$$= .10 \times .00 + .60 \times .01 + .30 \times .04$$
$$= .0180$$

The standard deviations are thus:

$$\sigma_A = \sqrt{.0945} = 30.74\%$$
$$\sigma_B = \sqrt{.0180} = 13.42\%$$

11.2   The portfolio weights are $6,000/20,000 = .30$ and $14,000/20,000 = .70$. The expected return is thus:

$$E(R_P) = .30 \times E(R_A) + .70 \times E(R_B)$$
$$= .30 \times 25\% + .70 \times 30\%$$
$$= 28.50\%$$

Alternatively, we could calculate the portfolio's return in each of the states:

(1) State of Economy	(2) Probability of State of Economy	(3) Portfolio Return If State Occurs
Recession	.10	$.30 \times -.20 + .70 \times .30 = .15$
Normal	.60	$.30 \times .10 + .70 \times .20 = .17$
Boom	.30	$.30 \times .70 + .70 \times .50 = .56$

The portfolio's expected return is:

$$E(R_P) = .10 \times .15 + .60 \times .17 + .30 \times .56 = 28.50\%$$

This is the same as we had before.

The portfolio's variance is:

$$\sigma^2{}_P = .10 \times (.15 - .285)^2 + .60 \times (.17 - .285)^2 + .30 \times (.56 - .285)^2$$
$$= .03245$$

So the standard deviation is $\sqrt{.03245} = 18.01\%$.

11.3   If we compute the reward-to-risk ratios, we get $(19\% - 8\%)/1.6 = 6.875\%$ for Cooley versus 6.67% for Moyer. Relative to that of Cooley, Moyer's expected return is too low, so its price is too high.

If they are correctly priced, then they must offer the same reward-to-risk ratio. The risk-free rate would have to be such that:

$$(19\% - R_f)/1.6 = (16\% - R_f)/1.2$$

With a little algebra, we find that the risk-free rate must be 7 percent:

$$(19\% - R_f) = (16\% - R_f)(1.6/1.2)$$
$$19\% - 16\% \times (4/3) = R_f - R_f \times (4/3)$$
$$R_f = 7\%$$

11.4   Since the expected return on the market is 14 percent, the market risk premium is $14\% - 8\% = 6\%$ (the risk-free rate is 8 percent). The first stock has a beta of .60, so its expected return is $8\% + .60 \times 6\% = 11.6\%$.

For the second stock, notice that the risk premium is $20\% - 8\% = 12\%$. Since this is twice as large as the market risk premium, the beta must be exactly equal to 2. We can verify this using the CAPM:

$$E(R_i) = R_f + [E(R_M) - R_f] \times \beta_i$$
$$20\% = 8\% + (14\% - 8\%) \times \beta_i$$
$$\beta_i = 12\%/6\% = 2.0$$

CRITICAL THINKING AND CONCEPTS REVIEW

1. **Diversifiable and Nondiversifiable Risks.** In broad terms, why is some risk diversifiable? Why are some risks nondiversifiable? Does it follow that an investor can control the level of unsystematic risk in a portfolio, but not the level of systematic risk?

2. **Information and Market Returns.** Suppose the government announces that, based on a just-completed survey, the growth rate in the economy is likely to be 2 percent in the coming year, as compared to 5 percent for the year just completed. Will security prices increase, decrease, or stay the same following this announcement? Does it make any difference whether or not the 2 percent figure was anticipated by the market? Explain. *Market, WAR,*   *issue spicic company*

3. **Systematic versus Unsystematic Risk.** Classify the following events as mostly systematic or mostly unsystematic. Is the distinction clear in every case?
   a. Short-term interest rates increase unexpectedly. *S*
   b. The interest rate a company pays on its short-term debt borrowing is increased by its bank. *U*
   c. Oil prices unexpectedly decline. *S*
   d. An oil tanker ruptures, creating a large oil spill. *U*
   e. A manufacturer loses a multimillion-dollar product liability suit. *U*
   f. A Supreme Court decision substantially broadens producer liability for injuries suffered by product users. *S*

4. **Systematic versus Unsystematic Risk.** Indicate whether the following events might cause stocks in general to change price, and whether they might cause Big Widget Corp.'s stock to change price.
   a. The government announces that inflation unexpectedly jumped by 2 percent last month.
   b. Big Widget's quarterly earnings report, just issued, generally fell in line with analysts' expectations.
   c. The government reports that economic growth last year was at 3 percent, which generally agreed with most economists' forecasts.
   d. The directors of Big Widget die in a plane crash.
   e. Congress approves changes to the tax code that will increase the top marginal corporate tax rate. The legislation had been debated for the previous six months.

5. **Expected Portfolio Returns.** If a portfolio has a positive investment in every asset, can the expected return on the portfolio be greater than that on every asset in the portfolio? Can it be less than that on every asset in the portfolio? If you answer yes to one or both of these questions, give an example to support your answer.

6. **Diversification.** True or false: The most important characteristic in determining the expected return of a well-diversified portfolio is the variances of the individual assets in the portfolio. Explain.

7. **Portfolio Risk.** If a portfolio has a positive investment in every asset, can the standard deviation on the portfolio be less than that on every asset in the portfolio? What about the portfolio beta?

8. **Beta and CAPM.** Is it possible that a risky asset could have a beta of zero? Explain. Based on the CAPM, what is the expected return on such an asset? Is it possible that a risky asset could have a negative beta? What does the CAPM predict about the expected return on such an asset? Can you give an explanation for your answer?

9. **Corporate Downsizing.** In recent years, it has been common for companies to experience significant stock price changes in reaction to announcements of massive

layoffs. Critics charge that such events encourage companies to fire longtime employees and that Wall Street is cheering them on. Do you agree or disagree?

10. **Earnings and Stock Returns.** As indicated by a number of examples in this chapter, earnings announcements by companies are closely followed by, and frequently result in, share price revisions. Two issues should come to mind. First: Earnings announcements concern past periods. If the market values stocks based on expectations of the future, why are numbers summarizing past performance relevant? Second: These announcements concern accounting earnings. Going back to Chapter 2, such earnings may have little to do with cash flow, so, again, why are they relevant?

QUESTIONS AND PROBLEMS

Basic
(Questions 1–31)

1. **Determining Portfolio Weights.** What are the portfolio weights for a portfolio that has 80 shares of Stock A that sell for $35 per share and 40 shares of Stock B that sell for $25 per share?

2. **Portfolio Expected Return.** You own a portfolio that has $600 invested in Stock A and $1,400 invested in Stock B. If the expected returns on these stocks are 14 percent and 22 percent, respectively, what is the expected return on the portfolio?

3. **Portfolio Expected Return.** You own a portfolio that is 60 percent invested in Stock X, 25 percent in Stock Y, and 15 percent in Stock Z. The expected returns on these three stocks are 12 percent, 16 percent, and 19 percent, respectively. What is the expected return on the portfolio?

4. **Portfolio Expected Return.** You have $10,000 to invest in a stock portfolio. Your choices are Stock X with an expected return of 18 percent and Stock Y with an expected return of 11 percent. If your goal is to create a portfolio with an expected return of 16.50 percent, how much money will you invest in Stock X? In Stock Y?

5. **Calculating Expected Return.** Based on the following information, calculate the expected return.

State of Economy	Probability of State of Economy	Rate of Return If State Occurs
Recession	.40	.02
Boom	.60	.24

6. **Calculating Expected Return.** Based on the following information, calculate the expected return.

State of Economy	Probability of State of Economy	Rate of Return If State Occurs
Recession	.30	−.08
Normal	.60	.14
Boom	.10	.30

7. **Calculating Returns and Standard Deviations.** Based on the following information, calculate the expected return and standard deviation for the two stocks.

		Rate of Return If State Occurs	
State of Economy	**Probability of State of Economy**	**Stock A**	**Stock B**
Recession	.15	.06	−.20
Normal	.65	.07	.13
Boom	.20	.11	.33

8. **Calculating Expected Returns.** A portfolio is invested 25 percent in Stock G, 55 percent in Stock J, and 20 percent in Stock K. The expected returns on these stocks are 8 percent, 17 percent, and 22 percent, respectively. What is the portfolio's expected return? How do you interpret your answer?

9. **Returns and Standard Deviations.** Consider the following information:

		Rate of Return If State Occurs		
State of Economy	**Probability of State of Economy**	**Stock A**	**Stock B**	**Stock C**
Boom	.25	.14	.15	.33
Bust	.75	.12	.03	−.06

   a. What is the expected return on an equally weighted portfolio of these three stocks?

   b. What is the variance of a portfolio invested 15 percent each in A and B, and 70 percent in C?

10. **Returns and Standard Deviations.** Consider the following information:

		Rate of Return If State Occurs		
State of Economy	**Probability of State of Economy**	**Stock A**	**Stock B**	**Stock C**
Boom	.30	.30	.45	.33
Good	.40	.12	.10	.15
Poor	.20	.01	−.15	−.05
Bust	.10	−.20	−.30	−.09

   a. Your portfolio is invested 35 percent each in A and C, and 30 percent in B. What is the expected return of the portfolio?

   b. What is the variance of this portfolio? The standard deviation?

11. **Calculating Portfolio Betas.** You own a stock portfolio invested 20 percent in Stock Q, 20 percent in Stock R, 10 percent in Stock S, and 50 percent in Stock T. The betas for these four stocks are 1.4, .6, 1.5, and 1.8, respectively. What is the portfolio beta?

12. **Calculating Portfolio Betas.** You own a portfolio equally invested in a risk-free asset and two stocks. If one of the stocks has a beta of 1.4 and the total portfolio is equally as risky as the market, what must the beta be for the other stock in your portfolio?

13. **Using CAPM.** A stock has a beta of 1.2, the expected return on the market is 12 percent, and the risk-free rate is 6 percent. What must the expected return on this stock be?

14. **Using CAPM.**   A stock has an expected return of 17 percent, the risk-free rate is 5 percent, and the market risk premium is 8 percent. What must the beta of this stock be?

15. **Using CAPM.**   A stock has an expected return of 10 percent, its beta is .9, and the risk-free rate is 5 percent. What must the expected return on the market be?

16. **Using CAPM.**   A stock has an expected return of 20 percent and a beta of 1.5, and the expected return on the market is 15 percent. What must the risk-free rate be?

17. **Using CAPM.**   A stock has a beta of 1.6 and an expected return of 16 percent. A risk-free asset currently earns 5 percent.

   a. What is the expected return on a portfolio that is equally invested in the two assets?

   b. If a portfolio of the two assets has a beta of .6, what are the portfolio weights?

   c. If a portfolio of the two assets has an expected return of 11 percent, what is its beta?

   d. If a portfolio of the two assets has a beta of 3.20, what are the portfolio weights? How do you interpret the weights for the two assets in this case? Explain.

18. **Using the SML.**   Asset W has an expected return of 16 percent and a beta of 1.2. If the risk-free rate is 5 percent, complete the following table for portfolios of Asset W and a risk-free asset. Illustrate the relationship between portfolio expected return and portfolio beta by plotting the expected returns against the betas. What is the slope of the line that results?

Percentage of Portfolio in Asset W	Portfolio Expected Return	Portfolio Beta
0%		
25		
50		
75		
100		
125		
150		

19. **Reward-to-Risk Ratios.**   Stock Y has a beta of .9 and an expected return of 12.2 percent. Stock Z has a beta of 1.4 and an expected return of 18.5 percent. If the risk-free rate is 5 percent and the market risk premium is 9 percent, are these stocks correctly priced?

20. **Reward-to-Risk Ratios.**   In the previous problem, what would the risk-free rate have to be for the two stocks to be correctly priced?

21. **Portfolio Returns.**   Using information from Table 10.2 on capital market history, determine the return on a portfolio that was equally invested in large-company stocks and long-term corporate bonds. What was the return on a portfolio that was equally invested in small stocks and Treasury bills?

22. **Portfolio Expected Return.**   You have $250,000 to invest in a stock portfolio. Your choices are Stock H with an expected return of 24 percent and Stock L with an expected return of 10 percent. If your goal is to create a portfolio with an expected return of 16 percent, how much money will you invest in Stock H? In Stock L?

23. **Calculating Expected Return.**   Based on the following information, calculate the expected return.

State of Economy	Probability of State of Economy	Rate of Return If State Occurs
Recession	.30	−.04
Boom	.70	.21

24. **Calculating Expected Return.** Based on the following information, calculate the expected return.

State of Economy	Probability of State of Economy	Rate of Return If State Occurs
Recession	.10	−.10
Normal	.70	.13
Boom	.20	.38

25. **Calculating Returns and Deviations.** Based on the following information, calculate the expected return and standard deviation for the two stocks.

State of Economy	Probability of State of Economy	Stock P Rate of Return	Stock Q Rate of Return
Recession	.15	.04	−.20
Normal	.75	.08	.20
Boom	.10	.16	.60

26. **Calculating Expected Returns.** A portfolio is invested 25 percent in Stock G, 35 percent in Stock J, and 40 percent in Stock K. The expected returns on these stocks are 11 percent, 26 percent, and 32 percent, respectively. What is the portfolio's expected return?

27. **Returns and Deviations.** Consider the following information:

State of Economy	Probability of State of Economy	Stock A Rate of Return	Stock B Rate of Return	Stock C Rate of Return
Boom	.75	.14	.18	.26
Bust	.25	.08	.02	−.02

   a. What is the expected return on an equally weighted portfolio of these three stocks?
   b. What is the variance of a portfolio invested 25 percent in A and B, and 50 percent in C?

28. **Returns and Deviations.** Consider the following information:

State of Economy	Probability of State of Economy	Stock A Rate of Return	Stock B Rate of Return	Stock C Rate of Return
Boom	.15	.11	.35	.18
Good	.50	.06	.15	.11
Poor	.30	.04	−.05	.02
Bust	.05	.00	−.40	−.06

   a. Your portfolio is invested 30 percent each in B and C, and 40 percent in A. What is the portfolio's expected return?
   b. What is the variance of this portfolio? The standard deviation?

29. **Calculating Portfolio Returns.** Stock A has an average return of 14 percent, Stock B has an average return of 18 percent, and Stock C has an average return of 26 percent. If your portfolio weights are 20 percent, 35 percent, and 45 percent, respectively, what is the expected return of your portfolio?

30. **Calculating Portfolio Weights.** Stock J has a beta of 1.2 and an expected return of 17 percent, while Stock K has a beta of .7 and an expected return of 10 percent. You want a portfolio with the same risk as the market. How much will you invest in each stock? What is the expected return of your portfolio?

31. **Calculating Portfolio Weights and Expected Return.** You have a portfolio with the following:

Stock	Number of Shares	Price	Expected Return
W	400	$34	12%
X	600	22	16
Y	300	78	14
Z	500	53	15

What is the expected return of your portfolio?

Intermediate
(Questions 32–39)

32. **Analyzing a Portfolio.** You have $100,000 to invest in either Stock D, Stock F, or a risk-free asset. You must invest all of your money. Your goal is to create a portfolio that has an expected return of .1383 percent. If D has an expected return of 19 percent, F has an expected return of 13 percent, and the risk-free rate is 6 percent, and if you invest $50,000 in Stock D, how much will you invest in Stock F?

33. **Portfolio Returns and Deviations.** Consider the following information on a portfolio of three stocks:

State of Economy	Probability of State of Economy	Stock A Rate of Return	Stock B Rate of Return	Stock C Rate of Return
Boom	.20	.06	.20	.60
Normal	.70	.10	.10	.20
Bust	.10	.12	−.12	−.40

a. If your portfolio is invested 30 percent each in A and B and 40 percent in C, what is the portfolio's expected return? The variance? The standard deviation?

b. If the expected T-bill rate is 4.25 percent, what is the expected risk premium on the portfolio?

c. If the expected inflation rate is 3 percent, what is the expected real return on the portfolio? What is the expected real risk premium on the portfolio?

34. **CAPM.** Using the CAPM, show that the ratio of the risk premiums on two assets is equal to the ratio of their betas.

35. **Portfolio Returns and Deviations.** Consider the following information on three stocks:

State of Economy	Probability of State of Economy	Rate of Return If State Occurs		
		Stock A	Stock B	Stock C
Boom	.2	.40	.02	.60
Normal	.7	.15	.10	.05
Bust	.1	−.05	.15	−.75

a. If your portfolio is invested 40 percent each in A and B and 20 percent in C, what is the portfolio expected return? The variance? The standard deviation?

b. If the expected T-bill rate is 4.80 percent, what is the expected risk premium on the portfolio?

c. If the expected inflation rate is 4.50 percent, what is the expected real return on the portfolio? What is the expected real risk premium on the portfolio?

36.   **Analyzing a Portfolio.**   You want to create a portfolio equally as risky as the market, and you have $500,000 to invest. Given this information, fill in the rest of the following table:

Asset	Investment	Beta
Stock A	$140,000	.90
Stock B	160,000	1.20
Stock C		1.60
Risk-free asset		

37.   **Analyzing a Portfolio.**   You have $100,000 to invest in a portfolio containing Stock X, Stock Y, and a risk-free asset. You must invest all of your money. Your goal is to create a portfolio that has an expected return of 20 percent and that has only 80 percent of the risk of the overall market. If X has an expected return of 30 percent and a beta of 1.60, Y has an expected return of 12 percent and a beta of 1.25, and the risk-free rate is 6 percent, how much money will you invest in Stock Y? How do you interpret your answer?

38.   **Systematic versus Unsystematic Risk.**   Consider the following information on Stocks I and II:

State of Economy	Probability of State of Economy	Rate of Return If State Occurs	
		Stock I	Stock II
Recession	.30	.08	−.25
Normal	.40	.47	.16
Irrational exuberance	.30	.23	.58

The market risk premium is 12 percent, and the risk-free rate is 4 percent. Which stock has the most systematic risk? Which one has the most unsystematic risk? Which stock is "riskier"? Explain.

39.   **SML.**   Suppose you observe the following situation:

Security	Beta	Expected Return
Spurrier Swamp Co.	1.40	.20
Mumme Pass Co.	.80	.14

Assume these securities are correctly priced. Based on the CAPM, what is the expected return on the market? What is the risk-free rate?

www.mhhe.com/rwj

Spreadsheet Templates 4, 7, 10

CHAPTER 12

Cost of Capital

AFTER STUDYING THIS CHAPTER, YOU SHOULD HAVE A GOOD UNDERSTANDING OF:

- How to determine a firm's cost of equity capital

- How to determine a firm's cost of debt

- How to determine a firm's overall cost of capital

- Some of the pitfalls associated with a firm's overall cost of capital and what to do about them

ACCORDING TO IBBOTSON ASSO-

CIATES, the well-known provider of financial information, the required return for the average firm in the agriculture, forestry, and fishing industry was 11 percent as of the beginning of 2000. At the same time, the average required return for firms in the manufacturing industry such as Ford, General Motors, and Boeing was 15.5 percent. For firms in the services industry, such as Microsoft, Electronic Data Systems, and Oracle, the required return was a whopping 17.3 percent. Obviously, required returns can vary a great deal from industry to industry. As you might expect, even greater variation can exist if we compare firms to one another.

From our chapters on capital budgeting, we know that the discount rate, or required return, on an investment is a critical input. Thus far, however, we haven't discussed how to come up with that particular number, so it's time now to do so. This chapter brings together many of our earlier discussions dealing with stocks and bonds, capital budgeting, and risk and return. Our goal is to illustrate how firms go about determining the required return on a proposed investment. Understanding required returns is important to everyone because all proposed projects, whether they relate to marketing, management, accounting, or any other area, must offer returns in excess of their required returns to be acceptable.

Suppose you have just become the president of a large company and the first decision you face is whether to go ahead with a plan to renovate the company's warehouse distribution system. The plan will cost the company $50 million, and it is expected to save $12 million per year after taxes over the next six years.

This is a familiar problem in capital budgeting. To address it, you would determine the relevant cash flows, discount them, and, if the net present value is positive, take on the project; if the NPV is negative, you would scrap it. So far, so good; but what should you use as the discount rate?

From our discussion of risk and return, you know that the correct discount rate depends on the riskiness of the warehouse distribution system. In particular, the new project will have a positive NPV only if its return exceeds what the financial markets offer on investments of similar risk. We called this minimum required return the *cost of capital* associated with the project.[1]

Thus, to make the right decision as president, you must examine what the capital markets have to offer and use this information to arrive at an estimate of the project's cost of capital. Our primary purpose in this chapter is to describe how to go about doing this. There are a variety of approaches to this task, and a number of conceptual and practical issues arise.

One of the most important concepts we develop is that of the *weighted average cost of capital* (WACC). This is the cost of capital for the firm as a whole, and it can be interpreted as the required return on the overall firm. In discussing the WACC, we will recognize the fact that a firm will normally raise capital in a variety of forms and that these different forms of capital may have different costs associated with them.

We also recognize in this chapter that taxes are an important consideration in determining the required return on an investment, because we are always interested in valuing the aftertax cash flows from a project. We will therefore discuss how to incorporate taxes explicitly into our estimates of the cost of capital.

12.1 | THE COST OF CAPITAL: SOME PRELIMINARIES

In Chapter 11, we developed the security market line, or SML, and used it to explore the relationship between the expected return on a security and its systematic risk. We concentrated on how the risky returns from buying securities looked from the viewpoint of, for example, a shareholder in the firm. This helped us understand more about the alternatives available to an investor in the capital markets.

In this chapter, we turn things around a bit and look more closely at the other side of the problem, which is how these returns and securities look from the viewpoint of the companies that issue the securities. The important fact to note is that the return an investor in a security receives is the cost of that security to the company that issued it.

Required Return versus Cost of Capital

When we say that the required return on an investment is, say, 10 percent, we usually mean that the investment will have a positive NPV only if its return exceeds 10 percent. Another way of interpreting the required return is to observe that the firm must earn 10 percent on the investment just to compensate its investors for the use of the capital needed to finance the project. This is why we could also say that 10 percent is the cost of capital associated with the investment.

---

[1]The term *cost of money* is also used.

To illustrate the point further, imagine we are evaluating a risk-free project. In this case, how to determine the required return is obvious: We look at the capital markets and observe the current rate offered by risk-free investments, and we use this rate to discount the project's cash flows. Thus, the cost of capital for a risk-free investment is the risk-free rate.

If this project is risky, then, assuming that all the other information is unchanged, the required return is obviously higher. In other words, the cost of capital for this project, if it is risky, is greater than the risk-free rate, and the appropriate discount rate would exceed the risk-free rate.

We will henceforth use the terms *required return, appropriate discount rate,* and *cost of capital* more or less interchangeably because, as the discussion in this section suggests, they all mean essentially the same thing. The key fact to grasp is that the cost of capital associated with an investment depends on the risk of that investment. In other words, it's the **use** of the money, not the source, that matters. This is one of the most important lessons in corporate finance, so it bears repeating:

> The cost of capital depends primarily on the use of the funds, not the source.

It is a common error to forget this crucial point and fall into the trap of thinking that the cost of capital for an investment depends primarily on how and where the capital is raised.

Financial Policy and Cost of Capital

We know that the particular mixture of debt and equity a firm chooses to employ—its capital structure—is a managerial variable. In this chapter, we will take the firm's financial policy as given. In particular, we will assume that the firm has a fixed debt-equity ratio that it maintains. This ratio reflects the firm's *target* capital structure. How a firm might choose that ratio is the subject of a later chapter.

From our discussion above, we know that a firm's overall cost of capital will reflect the required return on the firm's assets as a whole. Given that a firm uses both debt and equity capital, this overall cost of capital will be a mixture of the returns needed to compensate its creditors and its stockholders. In other words, a firm's cost of capital will reflect both its cost of debt capital and its cost of equity capital. We discuss these costs separately in the sections below.

CONCEPT QUESTIONS

12.1a What is the primary determinant of the cost of capital for an investment?

12.1b What is the relationship between the required return on an investment and the cost of capital associated with that investment?

THE COST OF EQUITY | 12.2

We begin with the most difficult question on the subject of cost of capital: What is the firm's overall **cost of equity?** The reason this is a difficult question is that there is no way of directly observing the return that the firm's equity investors require on their investment. Instead, we must somehow estimate it. This section discusses two approaches to determining the cost of equity: the dividend growth model approach and the security market line, or SML, approach.

cost of equity
The return that equity investors require on their investment in the firm.

The Dividend Growth Model Approach

The easiest way to estimate the cost of equity capital is to use the dividend growth model we developed in Chapter 7. Recall that, under the assumption that the firm's dividend will grow at a constant rate g, the price per share of the stock, P_0, can be written as:

$$P_0 = \frac{D_0 \times (1 + g)}{R_E - g} = \frac{D_1}{R_E - g}$$

where D_0 is the dividend just paid and D_1 is the next period's projected dividend. Notice that we have used the symbol R_E (the E stands for *equity*) for the required return on the stock.

As we discussed in Chapter 7, we can rearrange this to solve for R_E as follows:

$$R_E = D_1/P_0 + g \qquad\qquad [12.1]$$

Since R_E is the return that the shareholders require on the stock, it can be interpreted as the firm's cost of equity capital.

Implementing the Approach　To estimate R_E using the dividend growth model approach, we obviously need three pieces of information: P_0, D_0, and g. Of these, for a publicly traded, dividend-paying company, the first two can be observed directly, so they are easily obtained.[2] Only the third component, the expected growth rate in dividends, must be estimated.

To illustrate how we estimate R_E, suppose Greater States Public Service, a large public utility, paid a dividend of $4 per share last year. The stock currently sells for $60 per share. You estimate that the dividend will grow steadily at 6 percent per year into the indefinite future. What is the cost of equity capital for Greater States?

Using the dividend growth model, we calculate that the expected dividend for the coming year, D_1, is:

$$\begin{aligned} D_1 &= D_0 \times (1 + g) \\ &= \$4 \times 1.06 \\ &= \$4.24 \end{aligned}$$

Given this, the cost of equity, R_E, is:

$$\begin{aligned} R_E &= D_1/P_0 + g \\ &= \$4.24/60 + .06 \\ &= 13.07\% \end{aligned}$$

The cost of equity is thus 13.07%.

Estimating g　To use the dividend growth model, we must come up with an estimate for g, the growth rate. There are essentially two ways of doing this: (1) use historical growth rates, or (2) use analysts' forecasts of future growth rates. Analysts' forecasts are available from a variety of sources. Naturally, different sources will have different estimates, so one approach might be to obtain multiple estimates and then average them.

Alternatively, we might observe dividends for the previous, say, five years, calculate the year-to-year growth rates, and average them. For example, suppose we observe the following for some company:

---

[2]Notice that if we have D_0 and g, we can simply calculate D_1 by multiplying D_0 by $(1 + g)$.

Year	Dividend
1996	$1.10
1997	1.20
1998	1.35
1999	1.40
2000	1.55

We can calculate the percentage change in the dividend for each year as follows:

Year	Dividend	Dollar Change	Percentage Change
1996	$1.10	—	—
1997	1.20	$.10	9.09%
1998	1.35	.15	12.50
1999	1.40	.05	3.70
2000	1.55	.15	10.71

Notice that we calculated the change in the dividend on a year-to-year basis and then expressed the change as a percentage. Thus, in 1995, for example, the dividend rose from $1.10 to $1.20, for an increase of $.10. This represents a $.10/1.10 = 9.09% increase.

If we average the four growth rates, the result is $(9.09 + 12.50 + 3.70 + 10.71)/4 = 9\%$, so we could use this as an estimate for the expected growth rate, g. There are other, more sophisticated, statistical techniques that could be used, but they all amount to using past dividend growth to predict future dividend growth.

Advantages and Disadvantages of the Approach   The primary advantage of the dividend growth model approach is its simplicity. It is both easy to understand and easy to use. There are a number of associated practical problems and disadvantages.

First and foremost, the dividend growth model is obviously only applicable to companies that pay dividends. This means that the approach is useless in many cases. Furthermore, even for companies that do pay dividends, the key underlying assumption is that the dividend grows at a constant rate. As our example above illustrates, this will never be *exactly* the case. More generally, the model is really only applicable to cases in which reasonably steady growth is likely to occur.

A second problem is that the estimated cost of equity is very sensitive to the estimated growth rate. For a given stock price, an upward revision of g by just one percentage point, for example, increases the estimated cost of equity by at least a full percentage point. Since D_1 will probably be revised upward as well, the increase will actually be somewhat larger than that.

Finally, this approach really does not explicitly consider risk. Unlike the SML approach (which we consider next), this one has no direct adjustment for the riskiness of the investment. For example, there is no allowance for the degree of certainty or uncertainty surrounding the estimated growth rate in dividends. As a result, it is difficult to say whether or not the estimated return is commensurate with the level of risk.[3]

---

[3]There is an implicit adjustment for risk because the current stock price is used. All other things being equal, the higher the risk, the lower is the stock price. Further, the lower the stock price, the greater is the cost of equity, again assuming that all the other information is the same.

The SML Approach

In Chapter 11, we discussed the security market line, or SML. Our primary conclusion was that the required or expected return on a risky investment depends on three things:

1. The risk-free rate, R_f
2. The market risk premium, $E(R_M) - R_f$
3. The systematic risk of the asset relative to average, which we called its beta coefficient, β

Using the SML, we can write the expected return on the company's equity, $E(R_E)$, as:

$$E(R_E) = R_f + \beta_E \times [E(R_M) - R_f]$$

where β_E is the estimated beta for the equity. To make the SML approach consistent with the dividend growth model, we will drop the Es denoting expectations and henceforth write the required return from the SML, R_E, as:

$$R_E = R_f + \beta_E \times (R_M - R_f) \qquad [12.2]$$

Implementing the Approach   To use the SML approach, we need a risk-free rate, R_f; an estimate of the market risk premium, $R_M - R_f$; and an estimate of the relevant beta, β_E. In Chapter 10 (Table 10.3), we saw that one estimate of the market risk premium (based on large common stocks) is 9.5 percent. U.S. Treasury bills are paying about 6.2 percent as this is being written, so we will use this as our risk-free rate. Beta coefficients for publicly traded companies are widely available.[4]

To illustrate, in Chapter 11, we saw that GM had an estimated beta of 1.05 (Table 11.8). We could thus estimate GM's cost of equity as:

$$
\begin{aligned}
R_{GM} &= R_f + \beta_{GM} \times (R_M - R_f) \\
&= 6.2\% + 1.05 \times 9.5\% \\
&= 16.175\%
\end{aligned}
$$

Thus, using the SML approach, GM's cost of equity is about 16 percent.

Advantages and Disadvantages of the Approach   The SML approach has two primary advantages. First: It explicitly adjusts for risk. Second: It is applicable to companies other than just those with steady dividend growth. Thus, it may be useful in a wider variety of circumstances.

There are drawbacks, of course. The SML approach requires that two things be estimated, the market risk premium and the beta coefficient. To the extent that our estimates are poor, the resulting cost of equity will be inaccurate. For example, our estimate of the market risk premium, 9.5 percent, is based on about 75 years of returns on a particular portfolio of stocks. Using different time periods or different stocks could result in very different estimates.

Finally, as with the dividend growth model, we essentially rely on the past to predict the future when we use the SML approach. Economic conditions can change very quickly, so, as always, the past may not be a good guide to the future. In the best of all worlds, both approaches (dividend growth model and SML) are applicable and result in similar answers. If this happens, we might have some confidence in our estimates. We might also wish to compare the results to those for other, similar companies as a reality check.

---

[4]Beta coefficients can be estimated directly by using historical data. For a discussion of how to do this, see Chapters 9, 10, and 11 in S. A. Ross, R. W. Westerfield, and J. J. Jaffe, *Corporate Finance,* 5th ed. (Burr Ridge, Ill.: The McGraw-Hill Companies, 1999).

	The Cost of Equity	**EXAMPLE 12.1**

Suppose stock in Alpha Air Freight has a beta of 1.2. The market risk premium is 8 percent, and the risk-free rate is 6 percent. Alpha's last dividend was $2 per share, and the dividend is expected to grow at 8 percent indefinitely. The stock currently sells for $30. What is Alpha's cost of equity capital?

We can start off by using the SML. Doing this, we find that the expected return on the common stock of Alpha Air Freight is:

$$R_E = R_f + \beta_E \times (R_M - R_f)$$
$$= 6\% + 1.2 \times 8\%$$
$$= 15.6\%$$

This suggests that 15.6 percent is Alpha's cost of equity. We next use the dividend growth model. The projected dividend is $D_0 \times (1 + g) = \$2 \times 1.08 = \$2.16$, so the expected return using this approach is:

$$R_E = D_1/P_0 + g$$
$$= \$2.16/30 + .08$$
$$= 15.2\%$$

Our two estimates are reasonably close, so we might just average them to find that Alpha's cost of equity is approximately 15.4 percent.

CONCEPT QUESTIONS

12.2a What do we mean when we say that a corporation's cost of equity capital is 16 percent?

12.2b What are two approaches to estimating the cost of equity capital?

THE COSTS OF DEBT AND PREFERRED STOCK | 12.3

In addition to ordinary equity, firms use debt and, to a lesser extent, preferred stock to finance their investments. As we discuss next, determining the costs of capital associated with these sources of financing is much easier than determining the cost of equity.

The Cost of Debt

The **cost of debt** is the return that the firm's creditors demand on new borrowing. In principle, we could determine the beta for the firm's debt and then use the SML to estimate the required return on debt just as we estimate the required return on equity. This isn't really necessary, however.

Unlike a firm's cost of equity, its cost of debt can normally be observed either directly or indirectly, because the cost of debt is simply the interest rate the firm must pay on new borrowing, and we can observe interest rates in the financial markets. For example, if the firm already has bonds outstanding, then the yield to maturity on those bonds is the market-required rate on the firm's debt.

Alternatively, if we knew that the firm's bonds were rated, say, AA, then we could simply find out what the interest rate on newly issued AA-rated bonds was. Either way, there is no need to actually estimate a beta for the debt since we can directly observe the rate we want to know.

There is one thing to be careful about, though. The coupon rate on the firm's outstanding debt is irrelevant here. That just tells us roughly what the firm's cost of debt was back

cost of debt

The return that lenders require on the firm's debt.

when the bonds were issued, not what the cost of debt is today.[5] This is why we have to look at the yield on the debt in today's marketplace. For consistency with our other notation, we will use the symbol R_D for the cost of debt.

EXAMPLE 12.2 | **The Cost of Debt**

Suppose the General Tool Company issued a 30-year, 7 percent bond eight years ago. The bond is currently selling for 96 percent of its face value, or $960. What is General Tool's cost of debt?

Going back to Chapter 6, we need to calculate the yield to maturity on this bond. Since the bond is selling at a discount, the yield is apparently greater than 7 percent, but not much greater because the discount is fairly small. You can verify that the yield to maturity is about 7.37 percent, assuming annual coupons. General Tool's cost of debt, R_D, is thus 7.37 percent.

The Cost of Preferred Stock

Determining the *cost of preferred stock* is quite straightforward. As we discussed in Chapters 6 and 7, preferred stock has a fixed dividend paid every period forever, so a share of preferred stock is essentially a perpetuity. The cost of preferred stock, R_P, is thus:

$$R_P = D/P_0 \hspace{4cm} [12.3]$$

where D is the fixed dividend and P_0 is the current price per share of the preferred stock. Notice that the cost of preferred stock is simply equal to the dividend yield on the preferred stock. Alternatively, preferred stocks are rated in much the same way as bonds, so the cost of preferred stock can be estimated by observing the required returns on other, similarly rated shares of preferred stock.

EXAMPLE 12.3 | **Georgia Power's Cost of Preferred Stock**

In early 2000, Georgia Power had several issues of preferred stock that traded on the NYSE. One issue paid $1.90 annually per share and sold for $22.50 per share. The other paid $1.72 per share annually and sold for $20.63 per share. What was Georgia Power's cost of preferred stock?

Using the first issue, the cost of preferred stock was:

$$R_P = D/P_0$$
$$= \$1.90/22.5$$
$$= 8.44\%$$

Using the second issue, the cost was:

$$R_P = D/P_0$$
$$= \$1.72/20.625$$
$$= 8.34\%$$

So Georgia Power's cost of preferred stock appears to have been in the 8.3 to 8.4 percent range.

---

[5]The firm's cost of debt based on its historic borrowing is sometimes called the *embedded debt cost*.

THE WEIGHTED AVERAGE COST OF CAPITAL | 12.4

Now that we have the costs associated with the main sources of capital the firm employs, we need to worry about the specific mix. As we mentioned above, we will take this mix, which is the firm's capital structure, as given for now. Also, we will focus mostly on debt and ordinary equity in this discussion.

The Capital Structure Weights

We will use the symbol E (for *equity*) to stand for the *market* value of the firm's equity. We calculate this by taking the number of shares outstanding and multiplying it by the price per share. Similarly, we will use the symbol D (for *debt*) to stand for the *market* value of the firm's debt. For long-term debt, we calculate this by multiplying the market price of a single bond by the number of bonds outstanding.

If there are multiple bond issues (as there normally would be), we repeat this calculation for each and then add up the results. If there is debt that is not publicly traded (because it is held by a life insurance company, for example), we must observe the yield on similar, publicly traded debt and then estimate the market value of the privately held debt using this yield as the discount rate. For short-term debt, the book (accounting) values and market values should be somewhat similar, so we might use the book values as estimates of the market values.

Finally, we will use the symbol V (for *value*) to stand for the combined market value of the debt and equity:

$$V = E + D \qquad [12.4]$$

If we divide both sides by V, we can calculate the percentages of the total capital represented by the debt and equity:

$$100\% = E/V + D/V \qquad [12.5]$$

These percentages can be interpreted just like portfolio weights, and they are often called the *capital structure weights.*

For example, if the total market value of a company's stock were calculated as $200 million and the total market value of the company's debt were calculated as $50 million, then the combined value would be $250 million. Of this total, $E/V = \$200/250 = 80\%$, so 80 percent of the firm's financing would be equity and the remaining 20 percent would be debt.

We emphasize here that the correct way to proceed is to use the *market* values of the debt and equity. Under certain circumstances, such as when considering a privately owned company, it may not be possible to get reliable estimates of these quantities. In this case, we might go ahead and use the accounting values for debt and equity. While this would probably be better than nothing, we would have to take the answer with a grain of salt.

Taxes and the Weighted Average Cost of Capital

There is one final issue we need to discuss. Recall that we are always concerned with aftertax cash flows. If we are determining the discount rate appropriate to those cash flows, then the discount rate also needs to be expressed on an aftertax basis.

As we discussed previously in various places in this book (and as we will discuss later), the interest paid by a corporation is deductible for tax purposes. Payments to stockholders, such as dividends, are not. What this means, effectively, is that the government pays some of the interest. Thus, in determining an aftertax discount rate, we need to distinguish between the pretax and the aftertax cost of debt.

To illustrate, suppose a firm borrows $1 million at 9 percent interest. The corporate tax rate is 34 percent. What is the aftertax interest rate on this loan? The total interest bill will be $90,000 per year. This amount is tax deductible, however, so the $90,000 interest reduces our tax bill by .34 × $90,000 = $30,600. The aftertax interest bill is thus $90,000 − 30,600 = $59,400. The aftertax interest rate is thus $59,400/1 million = 5.94%.

Notice that, in general, the aftertax interest rate is simply equal to the pretax rate multiplied by 1 minus the tax rate. Thus, if we use the symbol T_C to stand for the corporate tax rate, then the aftertax rate that we use can be written as $R_D \times (1 - T_C)$. For example, using the numbers above, we find that the aftertax interest rate is 9% × (1 − .34) = 5.94%.

Collecting together the various topics we have discussed in this chapter, we now have the capital structure weights along with the cost of equity and the aftertax cost of debt. To calculate the firm's overall cost of capital, we multiply the capital structure weights by the associated costs and add up the pieces. The result of this is the **weighted average cost of capital,** or **WACC.**

weighted average cost of capital (WACC)

The weighted average of the cost of equity and the aftertax cost of debt.

$$\text{WACC} = (E/V) \times R_E + (D/V) \times R_D \times (1 - T_C) \qquad [12.6]$$

This WACC has a very straightforward interpretation. It is the overall return the firm must earn on its existing assets to maintain the value of its stock. This is an important point, so it bears repeating:

> The WACC is the overall return the firm must earn on its existing assets to maintain the value of the stock.

The WACC is also the required return on any investments by the firm that have essentially the same risks as existing operations. So, if we were evaluating the cash flows from a proposed expansion of our existing operations, this is the discount rate we would use.

The WACC is increasingly being used by corporations to evaluate financial performance. The accompanying *Reality Bytes* box provides some details on how this is being done.

EXAMPLE 12.4 | Calculating the WACC

The B. B. Lean Co. has 1.4 million shares of stock outstanding. The stock currently sells for $20 per share. The firm's debt is publicly traded and was recently quoted at 93 percent of face value. It has a total face value of $5 million, and it is currently priced to yield 11 percent. The risk-free rate is 8 percent, and the market risk premium is 7 percent. You've estimated that Lean has a beta of .74. If the corporate tax rate is 34 percent, what is the WACC of Lean Co.?

We can first determine the cost of equity and the cost of debt. From the SML, the cost of equity is 8% + .74 × 7% = 13.18%. The total value of the equity is 1.4 million × $20 = $28 million. The pretax cost of debt is the current yield to maturity on the outstanding debt, 11 percent. The debt sells for 93 percent of its face value, so its current market value is .93 × $5 million = $4.65 million. The total market value of the equity and debt together is $28 + 4.65 = $32.65 million.

From here, we can calculate the WACC easily enough. The percentage of equity used by Lean to finance its operations is $28/32.65 = 85.76%. Since the weights have to add up to 1.0, the percentage of debt is 1.0 − .8576 = 14.24%. The WACC is thus:

EVA: AN OLD IDEA MOVES INTO THE MODERN AGE

You might not think of Briggs and Stratton, Coca-Cola, and Toys 'R' Us as having much in common. However, they have all linked their fortunes to a new way of managing corporate performance. It goes by many names, but Stern Stewart and Co. of New York City calls it economic value added (EVA) and it is one of the hottest trends in corporate finance. According to Quaker CEO William Smithburg: "EVA makes managers act like shareholders. It's the true corporate faith of the 1990s." If that sounds suspiciously like maximizing shareholder wealth, there's a good reason. That is precisely the objective.

Simply stated, EVA is a method of measuring financial performance. To compute EVA, you must first identify who it is that supplies capital to your firm and measure the cost of that capital. Then, you identify how much capital is tied up in your corporate operation. Adding up balance sheet assets is a good starting point, but you should also account for other investments, such as training employees or expenditures for research and development. These are not assets in an accounting sense, but they are investments that are expected to generate benefits that will extend beyond the current year's operations. Finally, you multiply the amount of capital from Step 2 by the cost of capital from Step 1. This is the return, in dollars, you should be providing to your investors. Subtract this amount from operating cash flow and you have EVA. A positive EVA means you have generated value for your investors, while a negative EVA signals you are destroying shareholder wealth.

EVA is a useful tool for monitoring financial performance. If EVA is too low, a firm can cut costs, find ways to generate more revenue while using less capital, or revise the ways in which new investment projects are evaluated. For example, in 1996, Herman Miller, Inc., the Michigan-based maker of office furniture, began using EVA throughout its organization. By the end of 1997, the company had increased sales by 38 percent over 1995, reduced inventories by 24 percent, and reduced receivables by 22 percent. These improvements allowed the company to reallocate invested capital to more productive uses, resulting in a much higher profit margin compared to five years earlier.

EVA can also be used as an incentive plan for managers. Just ask Guidant Corp. CEO and president Ronald Dollens, whose 1999 salary of $475,000 was augmented by a $456,000 bonus tied largely to beating internal economic value added milestones. SPX Corp., AT&T, and Monsanto Corp. are just a few of the other firms that use some form of value-based incentive for managers and employees.

While the concept of EVA is sound in principle, this measure still has its shortcomings. For one thing, EVA is typically computed using asset book values instead of market values. For another, it is frequently based on accounting measures of income although basing it on cash flow would paint a more accurate picture. In addition, the early evidence on the effectiveness of EVA is spotty. According to a 1996 study, earnings per share is still a more reliable guide to stock performance than EVA and other residual income measures. A more recent study finds similar results. However, EVA and its cousin MVA (market value added) have increasingly found their way into the lexicon of business financial reporting. For example, *Fortune* magazine now provides an annual ranking of firms by EVA and MVA, and many firms now report their EVA and MVA when reporting recent fiscal year-end results. Furthermore, even with its problems, the concept of EVA focuses management attention on creating wealth for its investors. That, in itself, makes EVA a worthwhile tool.

"The 'In' Thing: Value-Based Pay Systems Are the Fad of the Moment in Compensation Circles," *The Wall Street Journal,* 10 April 1997, p. R10.
"EVA Pay Plans Aren't a Big Hit in New Study," *The Wall Street Journal,* 3 May 2000, p. C4.
"Guidant CEO Paid '99 Wage of $475,000, Bonus of $456,000," Dow Jones News Service, 29 March 2000.
"The Real Key to Creating Wealth," *Fortune,* 20 September 1993, pp. 38–50.
Information on Herman Miller is from www.sternstewart.com/action/miller.shtml.

$$\text{WACC} = (E/V) \times R_E + (D/V) \times R_D \times (1 - T_C)$$
$$= .8576 \times 13.18\% + .1424 \times 11\% \times (1 - .34)$$
$$= 12.34\%$$

B. B. Lean thus has an overall weighted average cost of capital of 12.34 percent.

Solving the Warehouse Problem and Similar Capital Budgeting Problems

Now we can use the WACC to solve the warehouse problem we posed at the beginning of the chapter. However, before we rush to discount the cash flows at the WACC to estimate NPV, we need to first make sure we are doing the right thing.

Going back to first principles, we need to find an alternative in the financial markets that is comparable to the warehouse renovation. To be comparable, an alternative must be of the same risk as the warehouse project. Projects that have the same risk are said to be in the same risk class.

The WACC for a firm reflects the risk and the target capital structure of the firm's existing assets as a whole. As a result, strictly speaking, the firm's WACC is the appropriate discount rate only if the proposed investment is a replica of the firm's existing operating activities.

In broader terms, whether or not we can use the firm's WACC to value the warehouse project depends on whether the warehouse project is in the same risk class as the firm. We will assume that this project is an integral part of the overall business of the firm. In such cases, it is natural to think that the cost savings will be as risky as the general cash flows of the firm, and the project will thus be in the same risk class as the overall firm. More generally, projects like the warehouse renovation that are intimately related to the firm's existing operations are often viewed as being in the same risk class as the overall firm.

We can now see what the president should do. Suppose the firm has a target debt-equity ratio of 1/3. From Chapter 3, we know that a debt-equity ratio of $D/E = 1/3$ implies that E/V is .75 and D/V is .25. Further suppose the cost of debt is 10 percent, and the cost of equity is 20 percent. Assuming a 34 percent tax rate, the WACC will then be:

$$
\begin{aligned}
\text{WACC} &= (E/V) \times R_E + (D/V) \times R_D \times (1 - T_C) \\
&= .75 \times 20\% + .25 \times 10\% \times (1 - .34) \\
&= 16.65\%
\end{aligned}
$$

Recall that the warehouse project had a cost of $50 million and expected aftertax cash flows (the cost savings) of $12 million per year for six years. The NPV is thus:

$$
\text{NPV} = -\$50 + \frac{12}{(1 + \text{WACC})^1} + \cdots + \frac{12}{(1 + \text{WACC})^6}
$$

Since the cash flows are in the form of an ordinary annuity, we can calculate this NPV using 16.65 percent (the WACC) as the discount rate as follows:

$$
\begin{aligned}
\text{NPV} &= -\$50 + 12 \times \frac{1 - [1/(1 + .1665)^6]}{.1665} \\
&= -\$50 + 12 \times 3.6222 \\
&= -\$6.53
\end{aligned}
$$

Should the firm take on the warehouse renovation? The project has a negative NPV using the firm's WACC. This means that the financial markets offer superior projects in the same risk class (namely, the firm itself). The answer is clear: The project should be rejected. For future reference, our discussion of the WACC is summarized in Table 12.1.

TABLE 12.1

Summary of capital
cost calculations

I. **The cost of equity, R_E**

  A. Dividend growth model approach (from Chapter 7):

$$R_E = D_1/P_0 + g$$

    where D_1 is the expected dividend in one period, g is the dividend growth rate, and P_0 is the current stock price.

  B. SML approach (from Chapter 11):

$$R_E = R_f + \beta_E \times (R_M - R_f)$$

    where R_f is the risk-free rate, R_M is the expected return on the overall market, and β_E is the systematic risk of the equity.

II. **The cost of debt, R_D**

  A. For a firm with publicly held debt, the cost of debt can be measured as the yield to maturity on the outstanding debt. The coupon rate is irrelevant. Yield to maturity is covered in Chapter 6.

  B. If the firm has no publicly traded debt, then the cost of debt can be measured as the yield to maturity on similarly rated bonds (bond ratings are discussed in Chapter 6).

III. **The weighted average cost of capital, WACC**

  A. The firm's WACC is the overall required return on the firm as a whole. It is the appropriate discount rate to use for cash flows similar in risk to the overall firm.

  B. The WACC is calculated as:

$$\text{WACC} = (E/V) \times R_E + (D/V) \times R_D \times (1 - T_C)$$

    where T_C is the corporate tax rate, E is the *market* value of the firm's equity, D is the *market* value of the firm's debt, and $V = E + D$. Note that E/V is the percentage of the firm's financing (in market value terms) that is equity, and D/V is the percentage that is debt.

CONCEPT QUESTIONS

12.4a How is the WACC calculated?

12.4b Why do we multiply the cost of debt by $(1 - T_C)$ when we compute the WACC?

12.4c Under what conditions is it correct to use the WACC to determine NPV?

DIVISIONAL AND PROJECT COSTS OF CAPITAL   12.5

As we have seen, using the WACC as the discount rate for future cash flows is only appropriate when the proposed investment is similar to the firm's existing activities. This is not as restrictive as it sounds. If we were in the pizza business, for example, and we were thinking of opening a new location, then the WACC would be the discount rate to use. The same would be true of a retailer thinking of a new store, a manufacturer thinking of expanding production, or a consumer products company thinking of expanding its markets.

Nonetheless, despite the usefulness of the WACC as a benchmark, there will clearly be situations where the cash flows under consideration have risks distinctly different from those of the overall firm. We consider how to cope with this problem next.

FIGURE 12.1

The security market
line, SML, and the
weighted average cost
of capital, WACC

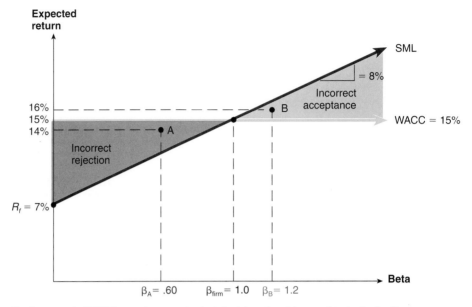

If a firm uses its WACC to make accept-reject decisions for all types of projects, it will
have a tendency towards incorrectly accepting risky projects and incorrectly rejecting
less risky projects.

The SML and the WACC

When we are evaluating investments with risks that are substantially different from those
of the overall firm, the use of the WACC will potentially lead to poor decisions. Figure 12.1
illustrates why.

In Figure 12.1, we have plotted an SML corresponding to a risk-free rate of 7 percent
and a market risk premium of 8 percent. To keep things simple, we consider an all-equity
company with a beta of 1. As we have indicated, the WACC and the cost of equity are exactly equal to 15 percent for this company since there is no debt.

Suppose our firm uses its WACC to evaluate all investments. This means that any investment with a return of greater than 15 percent will be accepted and any investment with
a return of less than 15 percent will be rejected. We know from our study of risk and return,
however, that a desirable investment is one that plots above the SML. As Figure 12.1 illustrates, using the WACC for all types of projects can result in the firm's incorrectly accepting relatively risky projects and incorrectly rejecting relatively safe ones.

For example, consider Point A. This project has a beta of $\beta_A = .60$ compared to the
firm's beta of 1.0. It has an expected return of 14 percent. Is this a desirable investment?
The answer is yes, because its required return is only:

$$\text{Required return} = R_f + \beta_A \times (R_M - R_f)$$
$$= 7\% + .60 \times 8\%$$
$$= 11.8\%$$

However, if we use the WACC as a cutoff, then this project will be rejected because its return is less than 15 percent. This example illustrates that a firm that uses its WACC as a cutoff will tend to reject profitable projects with risks less than those of the overall firm.

At the other extreme, consider Point B. This project has a beta of $\beta_B = 1.2$. It offers a
16 percent return, which exceeds the firm's cost of capital. This is not a good investment,
however, because, given its level of systematic risk, its return is inadequate. Nonetheless,

if we use the WACC to evaluate it, it will appear to be attractive. So the second error that will arise if we use the WACC as a cutoff is that we will tend to make unprofitable investments with risks greater than those of the overall firm. As a consequence, through time, a firm that uses its WACC to evaluate all projects will have a tendency to both accept unprofitable investments and become increasingly risky.

Divisional Cost of Capital

The same type of problem with the WACC can arise in a corporation with more than one line of business. Imagine, for example, a corporation that has two divisions, a regulated telephone company and an electronics manufacturing operation. The first of these (the phone operation) has relatively low risk; the second has relatively high risk.

In this case, the firm's overall cost of capital is really a mixture of two different costs of capital, one for each division. If the two divisions were competing for resources, and the firm used a single WACC as a cutoff, which division would tend to be awarded greater funds for investment?

The answer is that the riskier division would tend to have greater returns (ignoring the greater risk), so it would tend to be the "winner." The less glamorous operation might have great profit potential that would end up being ignored. Large corporations in the United States are aware of this problem, and many work to develop separate divisional costs of capital.

The Pure Play Approach

We've seen that using the firm's WACC inappropriately can lead to problems. How can we come up with the appropriate discount rates in such circumstances? Because we cannot observe the returns on these investments, there generally is no direct way of coming up with a beta, for example. Instead, what we must do is examine other investments outside the firm that are in the same risk class as the one we are considering and use the market-required returns on these investments as the discount rate. In other words, we will try to determine what the cost of capital is for such investments by trying to locate some similar investments in the marketplace.

For example, going back to our telephone division, suppose we want to come up with a discount rate to use for that division. What we can do is identify several other phone companies that have publicly traded securities. We might find that a typical phone company has a beta of .80, AA-rated debt, and a capital structure that is about 50 percent debt and 50 percent equity. Using this information, we could develop a WACC for a typical phone company and use this as our discount rate.

Alternatively, if we were thinking of entering a new line of business, we would try to develop the appropriate cost of capital by looking at the market-required returns on companies already in that business. In the language of Wall Street, a company that focuses only on a single line of business is called a *pure play*. For example, if you wanted to bet on the price of crude oil by purchasing common stocks, you would try to identify companies that dealt exclusively with this product since they would be the most affected by changes in the price of crude oil. Such companies would be called *pure plays* on the price of crude oil.

What we try to do here is to find companies that focus as exclusively as possible on the type of project in which we are interested. Our approach, therefore, is called the **pure play approach** to estimating the required return on an investment.

pure play approach
Use of a WACC that is unique to a particular project, based on companies in similar lines of business.

In Chapter 3, we discussed the subject of identifying similar companies for comparison purposes. The same problems we described there come up here. The most obvious one is that we may not be able to find any suitable companies. In this case, how to objectively determine a discount rate becomes a very difficult question. Even so, the important thing is to be aware of the issue so that we at least reduce the possibility of the kinds of mistakes that can arise when the WACC is used as a cutoff on all investments.

The Subjective Approach

Because of the difficulties that exist in objectively establishing discount rates for individual projects, firms often adopt an approach that involves making subjective adjustments to the overall WACC. To illustrate, suppose a firm has an overall WACC of 14 percent. It places all proposed projects into four categories as follows:

Category	Examples	Adjustment Factor	Discount Rate
High risk	New products	+6%	20%
Moderate risk	Cost savings, expansion of existing lines	+0	14
Low risk	Replacement of existing equipment	−4	10
Mandatory	Pollution control equipment	n/a	n/a

n/a = Not applicable.

The effect of this crude partitioning is to assume that all projects either fall into one of three risk classes or else are mandatory. In this last case, the cost of capital is irrelevant since the project must be taken. Of course, the firm's WACC may change through time as economic conditions change. As this happens, the discount rates for the different types of projects will also change.

Within each risk class, some projects will presumably have more risk than others, and the danger of incorrect decisions still exists. Figure 12.2 illustrates this point. Comparing Figures 12.1 and 12.2, we see that similar problems exist, but the magnitude of the potential error is less with the subjective approach. For example, the project labeled "A" would be accepted if the WACC were used, but it is rejected once it is classified as a high-risk investment. What this illustrates is that some risk adjustment, even if it is subjective, is probably better than no risk adjustment.

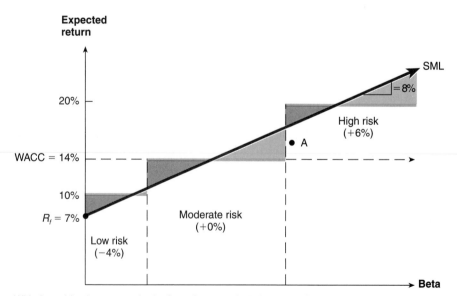

FIGURE 12.2

The security market line, SML, and the subjective approach

With the subjective approach, the firm places projects into one of several risk classes. The discount rate used to value the project is then determined by adding (for high risk) or subtracting (for low risk) an adjustment factor to or from the firm's WACC. This results in fewer incorrect decisions than if the firm simply used the WACC to make the decisions.

It would be better, in principle, to objectively determine the required return for each project separately. However, as a practical matter, it may not be possible to go much beyond subjective adjustments because either the necessary information is unavailable or else the cost and effort required are simply not worthwhile.

CONCEPT QUESTIONS

12.5a What are the likely consequences if a firm uses its WACC to evaluate all proposed investments?

12.5b What is the pure play approach to determining the appropriate discount rate? When might it be used?

SUMMARY AND CONCLUSIONS

This chapter has discussed cost of capital. The most important concept is the weighted average cost of capital, or WACC, which we interpreted as the required rate of return on the overall firm. It is also the discount rate appropriate for cash flows that are similar in risk to the overall firm. We described how the WACC can be calculated, and we illustrated how it can be used in certain types of analysis.

We also pointed out situations in which it is inappropriate to use the WACC as the discount rate. To handle such cases, we described some alternative approaches to developing discount rates, such as the pure play approach.

CHAPTER REVIEW AND SELF-TEST PROBLEMS

12.1 **Calculating the Cost of Equity.**   Suppose stock in Boone Corporation has a beta of .90. The market risk premium is 7 percent, and the risk-free rate is 8 percent. Boone's last dividend was $1.80 per share, and the dividend is expected to grow at 7 percent indefinitely. The stock currently sells for $25. What is Boone's cost of equity capital?

12.2 **Calculating the WACC.**   In addition to the information in the previous problem, suppose Boone has a target debt-equity ratio of 50 percent. Its cost of debt is 8 percent, before taxes. If the tax rate is 34 percent, what is the WACC?

■ Answers to Chapter Review and Self-Test Problems

12.1   We start off with the SML approach. Based on the information given, the expected return on Boone's common stock is:

$$R_E = R_f + \beta_E \times (R_M - R_f)$$
$$= 8\% + .9 \times 7\%$$
$$= 14.3\%$$

We now use the dividend growth model. The projected dividend is $D_0 \times (1 + g) = \$1.80 \times 1.07 = \$1.926$, so the expected return using this approach is:

$$R_E = D_1/P_0 + g$$
$$= \$1.926/25 + .07$$
$$= 14.704\%$$

Since these two estimates, 14.3 percent and 14.7 percent, are fairly close, we will average them. Boone's cost of equity is approximately 14.5 percent.

12.2   Since the target debt-equity ratio is .50, Boone uses $.50 in debt for every $1.00 in equity. In other words, Boone's target capital structure is 1/3 debt and 2/3 equity. The WACC is thus:

$$\text{WACC} = (E/V) \times R_E + (D/V) \times R_D \times (1 - T_C)$$

$$= 2/3 \times 14.5\% + 1/3 \times 8\% \times (1 - .34)$$

$$= 11.427\%$$

CRITICAL THINKING AND CONCEPTS REVIEW

1.   **WACC.**   On the most basic level, if a firm's WACC is 12 percent, what does this mean?

2.   **Book Values versus Market Values.**   In calculating the WACC, if you had to use book values for either debt or equity, which would you choose? Why?

3.   **Project Risk.**   If you can borrow all the money you need for a project at 6 percent, doesn't it follow that 6 percent is your cost of capital for the project?

4.   **WACC and Taxes.**   Why do we use an aftertax figure for cost of debt but not for cost of equity?

5.   **DCF Cost of Equity Estimation.**   What are the advantages of using the DCF model for determining the cost of equity capital? What are the disadvantages? What specific piece of information do you need to find the cost of equity using this model? What are some of the ways in which you could get an estimate of this number?

6.   **SML Cost of Equity Estimation.**   What are the advantages of using the SML approach to finding the cost of equity capital? What are the disadvantages? What are the specific pieces of information needed to use this method? Are all of these variables observable, or do they need to be estimated? What are some of the ways in which you could get these estimates?

7.   **Cost of Debt Estimation.**   How do you determine the appropriate cost of debt for a company? Does it make a difference if the company's debt is privately placed as opposed to being publicly traded? How would you estimate the cost of debt for a firm whose only debt issues are privately held by institutional investors?

8.   **Cost of Capital.**   Suppose Tom O'Bedlam, president of Bedlam Products, Inc., has hired you to determine the firm's cost of debt and cost of equity capital.

   a. The stock currently sells for $50 per share, and the dividend per share will probably be about $5. Tom argues, "It will cost us $5 per share to use the stockholders' money this year, so the cost of equity is equal to 10 percent ($5/50)." What's wrong with this conclusion?

   b. Based on the most recent financial statements, Bedlam Products's total liabilities are $8 million. Total interest expense for the coming year will be about $1 million. Tom therefore reasons, "We owe $8 million, and we will pay $1 million interest. Therefore, our cost of debt is obviously $1 million/8 million = 12.5%." What's wrong with this conclusion?

   c. Based on his own analysis, Tom is recommending that the company increase its use of equity financing, because "debt costs 12.5 percent, but equity only costs 10 percent; thus equity is cheaper." Ignoring all the other issues, what do you think about the conclusion that the cost of equity is less than the cost of debt?

9. **Company Risk versus Project Risk.** Both Dow Chemical Company, a large natural gas user, and Superior Oil, a major natural gas producer, are thinking of investing in natural gas wells near Houston. Both are all-equity–financed companies. Dow and Superior are looking at identical projects. They've analyzed their respective investments, which would involve a negative cash flow now and positive expected cash flows in the future. These cash flows would be the same for both firms. No debt would be used to finance the projects. Both companies estimate that their project would have a net present value of $1 million at an 18 percent discount rate and a $-$1.1 million NPV at a 22 percent discount rate. Dow has a beta of 1.25, whereas Superior has a beta of .75. The expected risk premium on the market is 8 percent, and risk-free bonds are yielding 12 percent. Should either company proceed? Should both? Explain.

10. **Divisional Cost of Capital.** Under what circumstances would it be appropriate for a firm to use different costs of capital for its different operating divisions? If the overall firm WACC were used as the hurdle rate for all divisions, would the riskier divisions or the more conservative divisions tend to get most of the investment projects? Why? If you were to try to estimate the appropriate cost of capital for different divisions, what problems might you encounter? What are two techniques you could use to develop a rough estimate for each division's cost of capital?

QUESTIONS AND PROBLEMS

1. **Calculating Cost of Equity.** The Bruin Co. just issued a dividend of $2.10 per share on its common stock. The company is expected to maintain a constant 6 percent growth rate in its dividends indefinitely. If the stock sells for $45 a share, what is the company's cost of equity?

Basic
(Questions 1–25)

2. **Calculating Cost of Equity.** Jet Corporation's common stock has a beta of 1.40. If the risk-free rate is 5 percent and the expected return on the market is 12 percent, what is Jet's cost of equity capital?

3. **Calculating Cost of Equity.** Stock in Sampras Industries has a beta of 1.05. The market risk premium is 8 percent, and T-bills are currently yielding 5.5 percent. Sampras's most recent dividend was $2.20 per share, and dividends are expected to grow at a 4 percent annual rate indefinitely. If the stock sells for $32 per share, what is your best estimate of Sampras's cost of equity?

4. **Estimating the DCF Growth Rate.** Suppose Massey Ltd. just issued a dividend of $.50 per share on its common stock. The company paid dividends of $.25, $.30, $.35, and $.45 per share in the last four years. If the stock currently sells for $10, what is your best estimate of the company's cost of equity capital?

5. **Calculating Cost of Preferred Stock.** Stickup Bank has an issue of preferred stock with a $6 stated dividend that just sold for $73 per share. What is the bank's cost of preferred stock?

6. **Calculating Cost of Debt.** PC, Inc., is trying to determine its cost of debt. The firm has a debt issue outstanding with seven years to maturity that is quoted at 87 percent of face value. The issue makes semiannual payments and has an embedded cost of 6.5 percent annually. What is PC's pretax cost of debt? If the tax rate is 38 percent, what is the aftertax cost of debt?

7. **Calculating Cost of Debt.** Jiminy's Cricket Farm issued a 30-year, 9 percent semiannual bond 8 years ago. The bond currently sells for 104 percent of its face value. The company's tax rate is 35 percent.
    a. What is the pretax cost of debt?
    b. What is the aftertax cost of debt?
    c. Which is more relevant, the pretax or the aftertax cost of debt? Why?

8. **Calculating Cost of Debt.**   For the firm in Problem 7, suppose the book value of the debt issue is $20 million. In addition, the company has a second debt issue, a zero coupon bond with seven years left to maturity; the book value of this issue is $70 million, and it sells for 60 percent of par. What is the total book value of debt? The total market value? What is the aftertax cost of debt now?

9. **Calculating WACC.**   Mullineaux Corporation has a target capital structure of 65 percent common stock, 10 percent preferred stock, and 25 percent debt. Its cost of equity is 14 percent, the cost of preferred stock is 7.5 percent, and the cost of debt is 9 percent. The relevant tax rate is 35 percent.

    a. What is Mullineaux's WACC? Notice that you need to include the preferred stock in your calculation, so your WACC will have three pieces instead of just two.

    b. The company president has approached you about Mullineaux's capital structure. He wants to know why the company doesn't use more preferred stock financing, since it costs less than debt. What would you tell the president?

10. **Taxes and WACC.**   Carhart Manufacturing has a target debt-equity ratio of .75. Its cost of equity is 18 percent, and its cost of debt is 11 percent. If the tax rate is 35 percent, what is Carhart's WACC?

11. **Finding the Target Capital Structure.**   Fama's Llamas has a WACC of 11.20 percent. The company's cost of equity is 14 percent, and its cost of debt is 11 percent. The tax rate is 35 percent. What is Fama's target debt-equity ratio?

12. **Book Value versus Market Value.**   Merton has 8.2 million shares of common stock outstanding. The current share price is $52, and the book value per share is $4. Merton also has two bond issues outstanding. The first bond issue has a face value of $70 million, has an 8 percent coupon, and sells for 103 percent of par. The second issue has a face value of $50 million, has a 7.5 percent coupon, and sells for 98 percent of par. The first issue matures in 10 years, the second in 6 years.

    a. What are Merton's capital structure weights on a book value basis?

    b. What are Merton's capital structure weights on a market value basis?

    c. Which are more relevant, the book or market value weights? Why?

13. **Calculating the WACC.**   In Problem 12, suppose the most recent dividend was $3.10 and the dividend growth rate is 6 percent. Assume that the overall cost of debt is the weighted average of that implied by the two outstanding debt issues. Both bonds make semiannual payments. The tax rate is 35 percent. What is the company's WACC?

14. **WACC.**   Shoven has a target debt-equity ratio of .25. Its WACC is 15.50 percent, and the tax rate is 35 percent.

    a. If Shoven's cost of equity is 18 percent, what is its pretax cost of debt?

    b. If the aftertax cost of debt is 7.5 percent, what is the cost of equity?

15. **Finding the WACC.**   Given the following information for Janicek Power Co., find the WACC. Assume the company's tax rate is 35 percent.

    Debt: 5,000 8 percent coupon bonds outstanding, $1,000 par value, 10 years to maturity, selling for 96 percent of par; the bonds make semiannual payments.

    Common stock: 60,000 shares outstanding, selling for $75 per share; beta is 1.10.

    Preferred stock: 9,000 shares of 5.5 percent preferred stock outstanding, currently selling for $60 per share.

    Market: 8 percent market risk premium and 6 percent risk-free rate.

16. **Finding the WACC.**   Filer Mining Corporation has eight million shares of common stock outstanding, one million shares of 6 percent preferred stock outstanding, and 100,000 9 percent semiannual bonds outstanding, par value $1,000 each. The

common stock currently sells for $32 per share and has a beta of 1.15, the preferred stock currently sells for $67 per share, and the bonds have 15 years to maturity and sell for 91 percent of par. The market risk premium is 10 percent, T-bills are yielding 5 percent, and Filer Mining's tax rate is 34 percent.

a. What is the firm's market value capital structure?

b. If Filer Mining is evaluating a new investment project that has the same risk as the firm's typical project, what rate should the firm use to discount the project's cash flows?

17. **SML and WACC.** An all-equity firm is considering the following projects:

Project	Beta	Expected Return
W	.70	11%
X	.95	13
Y	1.05	14
Z	1.60	16

The T-bill rate is 5 percent, and the expected return on the market is 12 percent.

a. Which projects have a higher expected return than the firm's 12 percent cost of capital?

b. Which projects should be accepted?

c. Which projects will be incorrectly accepted or rejected if the firm's overall cost of capital were used as a hurdle rate?

18. **Calculating the WACC.** Calculate the WACC for the following firm:

Debt: 3,000 bonds with an 8 percent coupon rate and a quoted price of 102.38. The bonds have 20 years to maturity.

Common stock: 90,000 shares of common stock. The dividends have a growth rate of 5 percent, the current price is $45, and the dividend next year will $4.00. The beta of the stock is 1.2.

Preferred stock: 13,000 shares of 7 percent preferred with a current price of $77.

Market: The corporate tax rate is 35 percent, the expected return on the market is 13 percent, and the risk-free rate is 5.1 percent.

19. **Calculating the WACC.** You are given the following information concerning Parrothead Enterprises:

Debt: 1,000 7 percent coupon bonds outstanding, with 20 years to maturity, and a quoted price of 90.13. These bonds pay interest semiannually.

Common stock: 50,000 shares of common stock selling for $35 per share. The stock has a beta of 1.3 and will pay a dividend of $3.25 next year. The dividend is expected to grow by 7 percent per year indefinitely.

Preferred stock: 5,000 shares of 9 percent preferred stock selling at $93 per share.

Market: A 12 percent expected return, a 4 percent risk-free rate, and a 35 percent tax rate.

Calculate the WACC for Parrothead Enterprises.

20. **Calculating the WACC.** In the previous problem, suppose that Parrothead Enterprises feels that it should have a capital structure of 20 percent debt, 10 percent preferred stock, and 70 percent equity. Assuming that the cost of each form of financing remains the same, what is Parrothead's new cost of capital?

21. **Calculating the WACC.** Calculate the cost of capital for the following firm:

Debt: 8,000 8.5 percent coupon bonds outstanding, 23 years to maturity, and a quoted price of 93. These bonds pay interest semiannually.

Common stock: 175,000 shares of common stock selling for $85 per share. The stock has a beta of .9 and will pay a dividend of $3.21 next year. The dividend is expected to grow by 7 percent per year indefinitely.

Market: A 13 percent expected return, a 5.5 percent risk-free rate, and 35 percent tax rate.

22. **Calculating Capital Structure Weights.** Kuipers Industrial Machines issued 50,000 zero coupon bonds three years ago. The bonds originally had 25 years to maturity with a 7.5 percent yield to maturity. Interest rates have recently increased, and the bonds now have a 9.25 percent yield to maturity. If Kuipers has a $20 million market value of equity, what weight should it use for debt when calculating the cost of capital?

23. **Calculating the Cost of Equity.** Over the past five years, a stock has paid dividends of $2.75, $2.84, $2.97, $3.12, and $3.29. The most recent stock price is $63. What is your best estimate of the cost of equity for this company?

24. **Calculating the WACC.** Your company has three million shares of common stock outstanding with a par value of $1 and a current market price of $18. The market risk premium is 7.5 percent, and Treasury bills are yielding 6.25 percent. There are also 32,000 bonds outstanding with an 8 percent semiannual coupon, 18 years to maturity, and a current price of 94. If the stock has a beta of 1.20, what is the WACC for your company? The tax rate is 35%.

25. **Calculating the WACC.** Gnomes R Us is considering a new project. The company has a debt-equity ratio of .67. The company's cost of equity is 13.45 percent, and the aftertax cost of debt is 7.50 percent. The firm feels that the project is riskier than the company as a whole and that it should use an adjustment factor of +3 percent. What is the WACC it should use for the project?

Intermediate
(Questions 26–30)

26. **WACC and NPV.** Sallinger, Inc., is considering a project that will result in initial aftertax cash savings of $8 million at the end of the first year, and these savings will grow at a rate of 4 percent per year indefinitely. The firm has a target debt-equity ratio of .5, a cost of equity of 16 percent, and an aftertax cost of debt of 7 percent. The cost-saving proposal is somewhat riskier than the usual project the firm undertakes; management uses the subjective approach and applies an adjustment factor of +2 percent to the cost of capital for such risky projects. Under what circumstances should Sallinger take on the project?

27. **WACC and NPV.** Cusic Cordwood Co. has a project available that will provide aftertax cash flows of $185,000 for the next six years. The project has more risk than the company, so the president has told you to use an adjustment factor of +2 percent in your calculations. The company uses 65 percent equity and 35 percent debt in its capital structure. The cost of equity is 13.5 percent, and the aftertax cost of debt is 7.8 percent. What is the most Cusic can afford to pay for the new project?

28. **Calculating the Cost of Debt.** Ying Import has several bond issues outstanding, each making semiannual interest payments. The bonds are listed in the table below. If the corporate tax rate is 34 percent, what is the aftertax cost of Ying's debt?

Bond	Coupon Rate	Price Quote	Maturity	Face Value
1	8.00%	106.38	5 years	$10,000,000
2	7.50	98	8 years	45,000,000
3	6.40	82	15½ years	35,000,000
4	9.75	101.50	25 years	45,000,000

29. **Calculating the Cost of Equity.** Goetzmann Industries stock has a beta of 1.2. The company just paid a dividend of $1.50, and the dividends are expected to grow at 5 percent. The expected return of the market is 14 percent, and Treasury bills are yielding 6 percent. The most recent stock price for Goetzmann is $45.

a. Calculate the cost of equity using the DCF method.

b. Calculate the cost of equity using the SML method.

c. Why do you think your estimates in (*a*) and (*b*) are so different?

30. **Project Evaluation.** This is a comprehensive project evaluation problem bringing together much of what you have learned in this and previous chapters. Suppose you have been hired as a financial consultant to Defense Electronics, Inc. (DEI), a large, publicly traded firm that is the market share leader in radar detection systems (RDSs). The company is looking at setting up a manufacturing plant overseas to produce a new line of RDSs. This will be a five-year project. The company bought some land three years ago for $6 million in anticipation of using it as a toxic dump site for waste chemicals, but it built a piping system to safely discard the chemicals instead. The land was appraised last week for $4.25 million. The company wants to build its new manufacturing plant on this land; the plant will cost $7.2 million to build. The following market data on DEI's securities are current:

Debt: 10,000 8 percent coupon bonds outstanding, 15 years to maturity, selling for 94 percent of par; the bonds have a $1,000 par value each and make semiannual payments.

Common stock: 250,000 shares outstanding, selling for $65 per share; the beta is 1.3.

Preferred stock: 10,000 shares of 7 percent preferred stock outstanding, selling for $81 per share.

Market: 8 percent expected market risk premium; 5.65 percent risk-free rate.

DEI's tax rate is 34 percent. The project requires $750,000 in initial net working capital investment to get operational.

a. Calculate the project's Time 0 cash flow, taking into account all side effects.

b. The new RDS project is somewhat riskier than a typical project for DEI, primarily because the plant is being located overseas. Management has told you to use an adjustment factor of +2 percent to account for this increased riskiness. Calculate the appropriate discount rate to use when evaluating DEI's project.

c. The manufacturing plant has an eight-year tax life, and DEI uses straight-line depreciation. At the end of the project (i.e., the end of Year 5), the plant can be scrapped for $2 million. What is the aftertax salvage value of this manufacturing plant?

d. The company will incur $900,000 in annual fixed costs. The plan is to manufacture 10,000 RDSs per year and sell them at $10,000 per machine; the variable production costs are $9,100 per RDS. What is the annual operating cash flow, OCF, from this project?

e. Finally, DEI's president wants you to throw all your calculations, all your assumptions, and everything else into a report for the chief financial officer; all he wants to know is what the RDS project's internal rate of return, IRR, and net present value, NPV, are. What will you report?

www.mhhe.com/rwj

Spreadsheet Templates 9, 15, 16

13

Leverage and Capital Structure

THIS CHAPTER PROVIDES YOU WITH THE BASICS ON SOME OF THE MOST IMPORTANT ISSUES IN FINANCE, INCLUDING:

■ The effect of financial leverage

■ The impact of taxes and bankruptcy on capital structure choice

■ The essentials of the bankruptcy process

WHEN HERMAN MILLER, the big office furniture manufacturer, began using EVA (or economic value added, which we discussed in our previous chapter) to evaluate operating performance, it realized that it was under-relying on debt financing. Accordingly, in 1997, Herman Miller issued $100 million in debt and returned $110 million to stockholders in the form of dividends and stock repurchases. These changes were made in an effort to meet new targets set by the board of directors calling for a debt ratio of 30 to 35 percent. The board felt that this new mixture of debt and equity would lower the firm's cost of capital.

A firm's choice of how much debt it should have relative to equity is known as a capital structure decision. Such a choice has many implications for a firm and is far from being a settled issue in either theory or practice. In this chapter, we discuss the basic ideas underlying capital structures and how firms choose them.

A firm's capital structure is really just a reflection of its borrowing policy. Should we borrow a lot of money, or just a little? At first glance, it probably seems that debt is something to be avoided. After all, the more debt a firm has, the greater is the risk of bankruptcy. What we learn is that debt is really a double-edged sword, and, properly used, debt can be enormously beneficial to the firm.

A good understanding of the effects of debt financing is important simply because the role of debt is so misunderstood, and many firms (and individuals) are far too conservative in their use of debt. Having said this, we can also say that firms sometimes err in the opposite direction, becoming much too heavily indebted, with bankruptcy as the unfortunate consequence. Striking the right balance is what the capital structure issue is all about.

Thus far, we have taken the firm's capital structure as given. Debt-equity ratios don't just drop on firms from the sky, of course, so now it's time to wonder where they do come from. Going back to Chapter 1, we call decisions about a firm's debt-equity ratio *capital structure decisions.*[1]

For the most part, a firm can choose any capital structure that it wants. If management so desired, a firm could issue some bonds and use the proceeds to buy back some stock, thereby increasing the debt-equity ratio. Alternatively, it could issue stock and use the money to pay off some debt, thereby reducing the debt-equity ratio. Activities, such as these, that alter the firm's existing capital structure are called capital *restructurings.* In general, such restructurings take place whenever the firm substitutes one capital structure for another while leaving the firm's assets unchanged.

Since the assets of a firm are not directly affected by a capital restructuring, we can examine the firm's capital structure decision separately from its other activities. This means that a firm can consider capital restructuring decisions in isolation from its investment decisions. In this chapter, then, we will ignore investment decisions and focus on the long-term financing, or capital structure, question.

What we will see in this chapter is that capital structure decisions can have important implications for the value of the firm and its cost of capital. We will also find that important elements of the capital structure decision are easy to identify, but precise measures of these elements are generally not obtainable. As a result, we are only able to give an incomplete answer to the question of what the best capital structure might be for a particular firm at a particular time.

13.1 | THE CAPITAL STRUCTURE QUESTION

How should a firm go about choosing its debt-equity ratio? Here, as always, we assume that the guiding principle is to choose the course of action that maximizes the value of a share of stock. However, when it comes to capital structure decisions, this is essentially the same thing as maximizing the value of the whole firm, and, for convenience, we will tend to frame our discussion in terms of firm value.

In Chapter 12, we discussed the concept of the firm's weighted average cost of capital, or WACC. You may recall that the WACC tells us that the firm's overall cost of capital is a weighted average of the costs of the various components of the firm's capital structure. When we described the WACC, we took the firm's capital structure as given. Thus, one important issue that we will want to explore in this chapter is what happens to the cost of capital when we vary the amount of debt financing, or the debt-equity ratio.

A primary reason for studying the WACC is that the value of the firm is maximized when the WACC is minimized. To see this, recall that the WACC is the discount rate appropriate for the firm's overall cash flows. Since values and discount rates move in opposite directions, minimizing the WACC will maximize the value of the firm's cash flows.

Thus, we will want to choose the firm's capital structure so that the WACC is minimized. For this reason, we will say that one capital structure is better than another if it results in a lower weighted average cost of capital. Further, we say that a particular debt-equity ratio represents the *optimal capital structure* if it results in the lowest possible WACC. This optimal capital structure is sometimes called the firm's *target* capital structure as well.

---

[1] It is conventional to refer to decisions regarding debt and equity as *capital structure decisions.* However, the term *financial structure* would be more accurate, and we use the terms interchangeably.

THE EFFECT OF FINANCIAL LEVERAGE | 13.2

In this section, we examine the impact of financial leverage on the payoffs to stockholders. As you may recall, financial leverage refers to the extent to which a firm relies on debt. The more debt financing a firm uses in its capital structure, the more financial leverage it employs.

As we describe, financial leverage can dramatically alter the payoffs to shareholders in the firm. Remarkably, however, financial leverage may not affect the overall cost of capital. If this is true, then a firm's capital structure is irrelevant because changes in capital structure won't affect the value of the firm. We will return to this issue a little later.

The Impact of Financial Leverage

We start by illustrating how financial leverage works. For now, we ignore the impact of taxes. Also, for ease of presentation, we describe the impact of leverage in terms of its effects on earnings per share, EPS, and return on equity, ROE. These are, of course, accounting numbers and, as such, are not our primary concern. Using cash flows instead of these accounting numbers would lead to precisely the same conclusions, but a little more work would be needed. We discuss the impact of leverage on market values in a subsequent section.

Financial Leverage, EPS, and ROE: An Example The Trans Am Corporation currently has no debt in its capital structure. The CFO, Ms. Morris, is considering a restructuring that would involve issuing debt and using the proceeds to buy back some of the outstanding equity. Table 13.1 presents both the current and proposed capital structures. As shown, the firm's assets have a market value of $8 million, and there are 400,000 shares outstanding. Because Trans Am is an all-equity firm, the price per share is $20.

The proposed debt issue would raise $4 million; the interest rate would be 10 percent. Since the stock sells for $20 per share, the $4 million in new debt would be used to purchase $4 million/20 = 200,000 shares, leaving 200,000 outstanding. After the restructuring, Trans Am would have a capital structure that was 50 percent debt, so the debt-equity ratio would be 1. Notice that, for now, we assume that the stock price will remain at $20.

To investigate the impact of the proposed restructuring, Ms. Morris has prepared Table 13.2, which compares the firm's current capital structure to the proposed capital structure under three scenarios. The scenarios reflect different assumptions about the firm's EBIT.

	Current	**Proposed**
Assets	$8,000,000	$8,000,000
Debt	$0	$4,000,000
Equity	$8,000,000	$4,000,000
Debt-equity ratio	0	1
Share price	$20	$20
Shares outstanding	400,000	200,000
Interest rate	10%	10%

TABLE 13.1

Current and proposed capital structures for the Trans Am Corporation

TABLE 13.2

Capital structure scenarios for the Trans Am Corporation

	Current Capital Structure: No Debt		
	Recession	**Expected**	**Expansion**
EBIT	$500,000	$1,000,000	$1,500,000
Interest	0	0	0
Net income	$500,000	$1,000,000	$1,500,000
ROE	6.25%	12.50%	18.75%
EPS	$1.25	$2.50	$3.75

	Proposed Capital Structure: Debt = $4 million		
	Recession	**Expected**	**Expansion**
EBIT	$500,000	$1,000,000	$1,500,000
Interest	400,000	400,000	400,000
Net income	$100,000	$ 600,000	$1,100,000
ROE	2.50%	15.00%	27.50%
EPS	$.50	$3.00	$5.50

Under the expected scenario, the EBIT is $1 million. In the recession scenario, EBIT falls to $500,000. In the expansion scenario, it rises to $1.5 million.

To illustrate some of the calculations in Table 13.2, consider the expansion case. EBIT is $1.5 million. With no debt (the current capital structure) and no taxes, net income is also $1.5 million. In this case, there are 400,000 shares worth $8 million total. EPS is therefore $1.5 million/400,000 = $3.75 per share. Also, since accounting return on equity, ROE, is net income divided by total equity, ROE is $1.5 million/8 million = 18.75%.[2]

With $4 million in debt (the proposed capital structure), things are somewhat different. Since the interest rate is 10 percent, the interest bill is $400,000. With EBIT of $1.5 million, interest of $400,000, and no taxes, net income is $1.1 million. Now there are only 200,000 shares worth $4 million total. EPS is therefore $1.1 million/200,000 = $5.5 per share versus the $3.75 per share that we calculated above. Furthermore, ROE is $1.1 million/4 million = 27.5%. This is well above the 18.75 percent we calculated for the current capital structure.

EPS versus EBIT The impact of leverage is evident in Table 13.2 when the effect of the restructuring on EPS and ROE is examined. In particular, the variability in both EPS and ROE is much larger under the proposed capital structure. This illustrates how financial leverage acts to magnify gains and losses to shareholders.

In Figure 13.1, we take a closer look at the effect of the proposed restructuring. This figure plots earnings per share, EPS, against earnings before interest and taxes, EBIT, for the current and proposed capital structures. The first line, labeled "No debt," represents the case of no leverage. This line begins at the origin, indicating that EPS would be zero if EBIT were zero. From there, every $400,000 increase in EBIT increases EPS by $1 (because there are 400,000 shares outstanding).

The second line represents the proposed capital structure. Here, EPS is negative if EBIT is zero. This follows because $400,000 of interest must be paid regardless of the firm's profits. Since there are 200,000 shares in this case, the EPS is −$2 per share as shown. Similarly, if EBIT were $400,000, EPS would be exactly zero.

The important thing to notice in Figure 13.1 is that the slope of the line in this second case is steeper. In fact, for every $400,000 increase in EBIT, EPS rises by $2, so the line is

---

[2]ROE is discussed in some detail in Chapter 3.

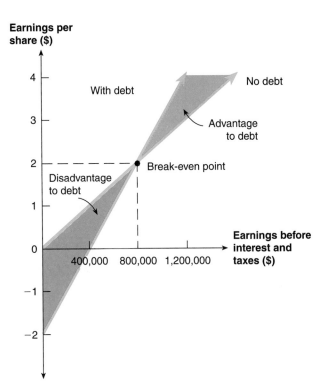

twice as steep. This tells us that EPS is twice as sensitive to changes in EBIT because of the financial leverage employed.

Another observation to make in Figure 13.1 is that the lines intersect. At that point, EPS is exactly the same for both capital structures. To find this point, note that EPS is equal to EBIT/400,000 in the no-debt case. In the with-debt case, EPS is (EBIT − $400,000)/200,000. If we set these equal to each other, EBIT is:

$$\text{EBIT}/400{,}000 = (\text{EBIT} - \$400{,}000)/200{,}000$$
$$\text{EBIT} = 2 \times (\text{EBIT} - \$400{,}000)$$
$$\text{EBIT} = \$800{,}000$$

When EBIT is $800,000, EPS is $2 per share under either capital structure. This is labeled as the break-even point in Figure 13.1; we could also call it the indifference point. If EBIT is above this level, leverage is beneficial; if it is below this point, it is not.

There is another, more intuitive, way of seeing why the break-even point is $800,000. Notice that, if the firm has no debt and its EBIT is $800,000, its net income is also $800,000. In this case, the ROE is $800,000/8,000,000 = 10%. This is precisely the same as the interest rate on the debt, so the firm earns a return that is just sufficient to pay the interest.

Break-Even EBIT | EXAMPLE 13.1

The MPD Corporation has decided in favor of a capital restructuring. Currently, MPD uses no-debt financing. Following the restructuring, however, debt will be $1 million. The interest rate on the debt will be 9 percent. MPD currently has 200,000 shares outstanding, and the price per share is $20. If the restructuring is expected to increase EPS, what is the minimum level for EBIT that MPD's management must be expecting? Ignore taxes in answering.

To answer, we calculate the break-even EBIT. At any EBIT above this the increased financial leverage will increase EPS, so this will tell us the minimum level for EBIT. Under the old capital structure, EPS is simply EBIT/200,000. Under the new capital structure, the interest expense will be $1 million × .09 = $90,000. Furthermore, with the $1 million proceeds, MPD will repurchase $1 million/20 = 50,000 shares of stock, leaving 150,000 outstanding. EPS is thus (EBIT − $90,000)/150,000.

Now that we know how to calculate EPS under both scenarios, we set the two expressions for EPS equal to each other and solve for the break-even EBIT:

$$\text{EBIT}/200{,}000 = (\text{EBIT} - \$90{,}000)/150{,}000$$
$$\text{EBIT} = (4/3) \times (\text{EBIT} - \$90{,}000)$$
$$\text{EBIT} = \$360{,}000$$

Verify that, in either case, EPS is $1.80 when EBIT is $360,000. Management at MPD is apparently of the opinion that EPS will exceed $1.80.

Corporate Borrowing and Homemade Leverage

Based on Tables 13.1 and 13.2 and Figure 13.1, Ms. Morris draws the following conclusions:

1. The effect of financial leverage depends on the company's EBIT. When EBIT is relatively high, leverage is beneficial.

2. Under the expected scenario, leverage increases the returns to shareholders, as measured by both ROE and EPS.

3. Shareholders are exposed to more risk under the proposed capital structure since the EPS and ROE are much more sensitive to changes in EBIT in this case.

4. Because of the impact that financial leverage has on both the expected return to stockholders and the riskiness of the stock, capital structure is an important consideration.

homemade leverage

The use of personal borrowing to change the overall amount of financial leverage to which the individual is exposed.

The first three of these conclusions are clearly correct. Does the last conclusion necessarily follow? Surprisingly, the answer is no. As we discuss next, the reason is that shareholders can adjust the amount of financial leverage by borrowing and lending on their own. This use of personal borrowing to alter the degree of financial leverage is called **homemade leverage.**

We will now illustrate that it actually makes no difference whether or not Trans Am adopts the proposed capital structure, because any stockholder who prefers the proposed capital structure can simply create it using homemade leverage. To begin, the first part of Table 13.3 shows what will happen to an investor who buys $2,000 worth of Trans Am stock if the proposed capital structure is adopted. This investor purchases 100 shares of stock. From Table 13.2, EPS will either be $.50, $3, or $5.50, so the total earnings for 100 shares will either be $50, $300, or $550 under the proposed capital structure.

Now, suppose Trans Am does not adopt the proposed capital structure. In this case, EPS will be $1.25, $2.50, or $3.75. The second part of Table 13.3 demonstrates how a stockholder who prefers the payoffs under the proposed structure can create them using personal borrowing. To do this, the stockholder borrows $2,000 at 10 percent on their own. Our investor uses this amount, along with their original $2,000, to buy 200 shares of stock. As shown, the net payoffs are exactly the same as those for the proposed capital structure.

How did we know to borrow $2,000 to create the right payoffs? We are trying to replicate Trans Am's proposed capital structure at the personal level. The proposed capital structure results in a debt-equity ratio of 1. To replicate this capital structure at the personal level, the stockholder must borrow enough to create this same debt-equity ratio. Since the stockholder has $2,000 in equity invested, borrowing another $2,000 will create a personal debt-equity ratio of 1.

Proposed Capital Structure			
	Recession	**Expected**	**Expansion**
EPS	$ .50	$ 3.00	$ 5.50
Earnings for 100 shares	50.00	300.00	550.00
Net cost = 100 shares at $20 = $2,000			

Original Capital Structure and Homemade Leverage			
	Recession	**Expected**	**Expansion**
EPS	$ 1.25	$ 2.50	$ 3.75
Earnings for 200 shares	250.00	500.00	750.00
Less: Interest on $2,000 at 10%	200.00	200.00	200.00
Net earnings	$ 50.00	$300.00	$550.00
Net cost = 200 shares at $20 − Amount borrowed = $4,000 − 2,000 = $2,000			

TABLE 13.3

Proposed capital structure versus original capital structure with homemade leverage

This example demonstrates that investors can always increase financial leverage themselves to create a different pattern of payoffs. It thus makes no difference whether or not Trans Am chooses the proposed capital structure.

Unlevering the Stock | EXAMPLE 13.2

In our Trans Am example, suppose management adopted the proposed capital structure. Further, suppose that an investor who owned 100 shares preferred the original capital structure. Show how this investor could "unlever" the stock to recreate the original payoffs.

To create leverage, investors borrow on their own. To undo leverage, investors must loan out money. For Trans Am, the corporation borrowed an amount equal to half its value. The investor can unlever the stock by simply loaning out money in the same proportion. In this case, the investor sells 50 shares for $1,000 total and then loans out the $1,000 at 10 percent. The payoffs are calculated in the table below.

	Recession	**Expected**	**Expansion**
EPS (proposed structure)	$ .50	$ 3.00	$ 5.50
Earnings for 50 shares	25.00	150.00	275.00
Plus: Interest on $1,000 @ 10%	100.00	100.00	100.00
Total payoff	$125.00	$250.00	$375.00

These are precisely the payoffs the investor would have experienced under the original capital structure.

CONCEPT QUESTIONS

13.2a What is the impact of financial leverage on stockholders?

13.2b What is homemade leverage?

13.2c Why is Trans Am's capital structure irrelevant?

13.3 | CAPITAL STRUCTURE AND THE COST OF EQUITY CAPITAL

We have seen that there is nothing special about corporate borrowing because investors can borrow or lend on their own. As a result, whichever capital structure Trans Am chooses, the stock price will be the same. Trans Am's capital structure is thus irrelevant, at least in the simple world we have examined.

Our Trans Am example is based on a famous argument advanced by two Nobel laureates, Franco Modigliani and Merton Miller, whom we will henceforth call M&M. What we illustrated for the Trans Am Corporation is a special case of **M&M Proposition I.** M&M Proposition I states that it is completely irrelevant how a firm chooses to arrange its finances.

M&M Proposition I

The value of the firm is independent of its capital structure.

M&M Proposition I: The Pie Model

One way to illustrate M&M Proposition I is to imagine two firms that are identical on the left-hand side of the balance sheet. Their assets and operations are exactly the same. The right-hand sides are different because the two firms finance their operations differently. In this case, we can view the capital structure question in terms of a "pie" model. Why we choose this name is apparent in Figure 13.2. Figure 13.2 gives two possible ways of cutting up this pie between the equity slice, *E,* and the debt slice, *D:* 40%-60% and 60%-40%. However, the size of the pie in Figure 13.2 is the same for both firms because the value of the assets is the same. This is precisely what M&M Proposition I states: The size of the pie doesn't depend on how it is sliced.

The Cost of Equity and Financial Leverage: M&M Proposition II

Although changing the capital structure of the firm may not change the firm's *total* value, it does cause important changes in the firm's debt and equity. We now examine what happens to a firm financed with debt and equity when the debt-equity ratio is changed. To simplify our analysis, we will continue to ignore taxes.

Based on our discussion in Chapter 12, if we ignore taxes, the weighted average cost of capital, WACC, is:

$$\text{WACC} = (E/V) \times R_E + (D/V) \times R_D$$

where $V = E + D$. We also saw that one way of interpreting the WACC is as the required return on the firm's overall assets. To remind us of this, we will use the symbol R_A to stand for the WACC and write:

$$R_A = (E/V) \times R_E + (D/V) \times R_D$$

FIGURE 13.2

Two pie models of capital structure

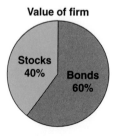

Value of firm

Stocks 40% Bonds 60%

Value of firm

Stocks 60% Bonds 40%

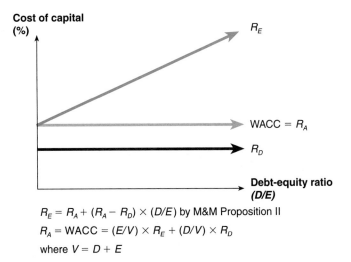

FIGURE 13.3

The cost of equity and the WACC: M&M Propositions I and II with no taxes

$R_E = R_A + (R_A - R_D) \times (D/E)$ by M&M Proposition II

$R_A = $ WACC $ = (E/V) \times R_E + (D/V) \times R_D$

where $V = D + E$

If we rearrange this to solve for the cost of equity capital, we see that:

$$R_E = R_A + (R_A - R_D) \times (D/E) \qquad [13.1]$$

This is the famous **M&M Proposition II,** which tells us that the cost of equity depends on three things: the required rate of return on the firm's assets, R_A, the firm's cost of debt, R_D, and the firm's debt-equity ratio, D/E.

Figure 13.3 summarizes our discussion thus far by plotting the cost of equity capital, R_E, against the debt-equity ratio. As shown, M&M Proposition II indicates that the cost of equity, R_E, is given by a straight line with a slope of $(R_A - R_D)$. The y-intercept corresponds to a firm with a debt-equity ratio of zero, so $R_A = R_E$ in that case. Figure 13.3 shows that, as the firm raises its debt-equity ratio, the increase in leverage raises the risk of the equity and therefore the required return, or cost of equity (R_E).

Notice in Figure 13.3 that the WACC doesn't depend on the debt-equity ratio; it's the same no matter what the debt-equity ratio is. This is another way of stating M&M Proposition I: The firm's overall cost of capital is unaffected by its capital structure. As illustrated, the fact that the cost of debt is lower than the cost of equity is exactly offset by the increase in the cost of equity from borrowing. In other words, the change in the capital structure weights $(E/V$ and $D/V)$ is exactly offset by the change in the cost of equity (R_E), so the WACC stays the same.

M&M Proposition II

A firm's cost of equity capital is a positive linear function of its capital structure.

The Cost of Equity Capital | EXAMPLE 13.3

The Ricardo Corporation has a weighted average cost of capital (ignoring taxes) of 12 percent. It can borrow at 8 percent. Assuming that Ricardo has a target capital structure of 80 percent equity and 20 percent debt, what is its cost of equity? What is the cost of equity if the target capital structure is 50 percent equity? Calculate the WACC, using your answers to verify that it is the same in both cases.

According to M&M Proposition II, the cost of equity, R_E, is:

$R_E = R_A + (R_A - R_D) \times (D/E)$

In the first case, the debt-equity ratio is .2/.8 = .25, so the cost of the equity is:

$R_E = 12\% + (12\% - 8\%) \times .25$

$\quad = 13\%$

In the second case, verify that the debt-equity ratio is 1.0, so the cost of equity is 16 percent.

We can now calculate the WACC assuming that the percentage of equity financing is 80 percent, the cost of equity is 13 percent, and the tax rate is zero:

$$WACC = (E/V) \times R_E + (D/V) \times R_D$$
$$= .80 \times 13\% + .20 \times 8\%$$
$$= 12\%$$

In the second case, the percentage of equity financing is 50 percent and the cost of equity is 16 percent. The WACC is:

$$WACC = (E/V) \times R_E + (D/V) \times R_D$$
$$= .50 \times 16\% + .50 \times 8\%$$
$$= 12\%$$

As we calculated, the WACC is 12 percent in both cases.

Business and Financial Risk

business risk

The equity risk that comes from the nature of the firm's operating activities.

financial risk

The equity risk that comes from the financial policy (i.e., capital structure) of the firm.

M&M Proposition II shows that the firm's cost of equity can be broken down into two components. The first component, R_A, is the required return on the firm's assets overall, and it depends on the nature of the firm's operating activities. The risk inherent in a firm's operations is called the **business risk** of the firm's equity. Referring back to Chapter 11, we see that this business risk depends on the systematic risk of the firm's assets. The greater a firm's business risk, the greater R_A will be, and, all other things being the same, the greater will be the firm's cost of equity.

The second component in the cost of equity, $(R_A - R_D) \times (D/E)$, is determined by the firm's financial structure. For an all-equity firm, this component is zero. As the firm begins to rely on debt financing, the required return on equity rises. This occurs because the debt financing increases the risks borne by the stockholders. This extra risk that arises from the use of debt financing is called the **financial risk** of the firm's equity.

The total systematic risk of the firm's equity thus has two parts: business risk and financial risk. The first part (the business risk) depends on the firm's assets and operations and is not affected by capital structure. Given the firm's business risk (and its cost of debt), the second part (the financial risk) is completely determined by financial policy. As we have illustrated, the firm's cost of equity rises when it increases its use of financial leverage because the financial risk of the equity increases while the business risk remains the same.

CONCEPT QUESTIONS

13.3a What does M&M Proposition I state?

13.3b What are the three determinants of a firm's cost of equity?

13.3c The total systematic risk of a firm's equity has two parts. What are they?

13.4 | CORPORATE TAXES AND CAPITAL STRUCTURE

Debt has two distinguishing features that we have not taken into proper account. First, as we have mentioned in a number of places, interest paid on debt is tax deductible. This is good for the firm, and it may be an added benefit to debt financing. Second, failure to meet debt obligations can result in bankruptcy. This is not good for the firm, and it may be an added cost of debt financing. Since we haven't explicitly considered either of these two features of debt, we may get a different answer about capital structure once we do. Accordingly, we consider taxes in this section and bankruptcy in the next one.

We can start by considering what happens when we consider the effect of corporate taxes. To do this, we will examine two firms, Firm U (unlevered) and Firm L (levered). These two firms are identical on the left-hand side of the balance sheet, so their assets and operations are the same.

We assume that EBIT is expected to be $1,000 every year forever for both firms. The difference between the two firms is that Firm L has issued $1,000 worth of perpetual bonds on which it pays 8 percent interest each year. The interest bill is thus .08 × $1,000 = $80 every year forever. Also, we assume that the corporate tax rate is 30 percent.

For our two firms, U and L, we can now calculate the following:

	Firm U	Firm L
EBIT	$1,000	$1,000
Interest	0	80
Taxable income	$1,000	$ 920
Taxes (30%)	300	276
Net income	$ 700	$ 644

The Interest Tax Shield

To simplify things, we will assume that depreciation is zero. We will also assume that capital spending is zero and that there are no additions to NWC. In this case, cash flow from assets is simply equal to EBIT − Taxes. For Firms U and L, we thus have:

Cash Flow from Assets	Firm U	Firm L
EBIT	$1,000	$1,000
−Taxes	300	276
Total	$ 700	$ 724

We immediately see that capital structure is now having some effect because the cash flows from U and L are not the same even though the two firms have identical assets.

To see what's going on, we can compute the cash flow to stockholders and bondholders.

Cash Flow	Firm U	Firm L
To stockholders	$700	$644
To bondholders	0	80
Total	$700	$724

What we are seeing is that the total cash flow to L is $24 more. This occurs because L's tax bill (which is a cash outflow) is $24 less. The fact that interest is deductible for tax purposes has generated a tax saving equal to the interest payment ($80) multiplied by the corporate tax rate (30 percent): $80 × .30 = $24. We call this tax saving the **interest tax shield.**

interest tax shield
The tax savings attained by a firm from the tax deductibility of interest expense.

Taxes and M&M Proposition I

Since the debt is perpetual, the same $24 shield will be generated every year forever. The aftertax cash flow to L will thus be the same $700 that U earns plus the $24 tax shield. Since L's cash flow is always $24 greater, Firm L is worth more than Firm U by the value of this $24 perpetuity.

Because the tax shield is generated by paying interest, it has the same risk as the debt, and 8 percent (the cost of debt) is therefore the appropriate discount rate. The value of the tax shield is thus:

$$\text{PV} = \frac{\$24}{.08} = \frac{.30 \times \$1,000 \times .08}{.08} = .30 \times \$1,000 = \$300$$

As our example illustrates, the present value of the interest tax shield can be written as:

$$\text{Present value of the interest tax shield} = (T_C \times D \times R_D)/R_D$$
$$= T_C \times D \qquad [13.2]$$

We have now come up with another famous result, M&M Proposition I with corporate taxes. We have seen that the value of Firm L, V_L, exceeds the value of Firm U, V_U, by the present value of the interest tax shield, $T_C \times D$. M&M Proposition I with taxes therefore states that:

$$V_L = V_U + T_C \times D \qquad [13.3]$$

The effect of borrowing in this case is illustrated in Figure 13.4. We have plotted the value of the levered firm, V_L, against the amount of debt, D. M&M Proposition I with corporate taxes implies that the relationship is given by a straight line with a slope of T_C.

FIGURE 13.4

M&M Proposition I with taxes

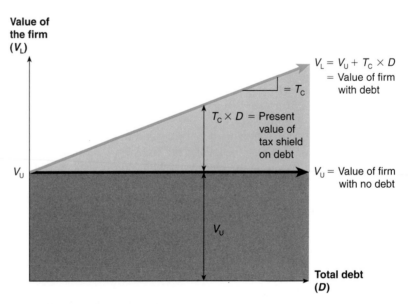

The value of the firm increases as total debt increases because of the interest tax shield. This is the basis of M&M Proposition I with taxes.

In Figure 13.4, we have also drawn a horizontal line representing V_U. As is shown, the distance between the two lines is $T_C \times D$, the present value of the tax shield.

As Figure 13.4 indicates, the value of the firm goes up by $.30 for every $1 in debt. In other words, the NPV *per dollar* of debt is $.30. It is difficult to imagine why any corporation would not borrow to the absolute maximum under these circumstances.

Conclusion

The result of our analysis in this section is that, once we include taxes, capital structure definitely matters. However, we immediately reach the illogical conclusion that the optimal capital structure is 100 percent debt. Of course, we have not yet considered the impact of bankruptcy, so our story may change. For future reference, Table 13.4 contains a summary of the various M&M calculations and conclusions.

CONCEPT QUESTIONS

13.4a What is the relationship between the value of an unlevered firm and the value of a levered firm once we consider the effect of corporate taxes?

13.4b If we only consider the effect of taxes, what is the optimum capital structure?

I. The no-tax case

   A. Proposition I: The value of the firm levered (V_L) is equal to the value of the firm unlevered (V_U):

   $$V_L = V_U$$

   B. Implications of Proposition I:

   1. A firm's capital structure is irrelevant.

   2. A firm's weighted average cost of capital, WACC, is the same no matter what mixture of debt and equity is used to finance the firm.

   C. Proposition II: The cost of equity, R_E, is:

   $$R_E = R_A + (R_A - R_D) \times D/E$$

   where R_A is the WACC, R_D is the cost of debt, and D/E is the debt-equity ratio.

   D. Implications of Proposition II:

   1. The cost of equity rises as the firm increases its use of debt financing.

   2. The risk of the equity depends on two things: the riskiness of the firm's operations (*business risk*) and the degree of financial leverage (*financial risk*). Business risk determines R_A; financial risk is determined by D/E.

II. The tax case

   A. Proposition I with taxes: The value of the firm levered (V_L) is equal to the value of the firm unlevered (V_U) plus the present value of the interest tax shield:

   $$V_L = V_U + T_C \times D$$

   where T_C is the corporate tax rate and D is the amount of debt.

   B. Implications of Proposition I with taxes:

   1. Debt financing is highly advantageous, and, in the extreme, a firm's optimal capital structure is 100 percent debt.

   2. A firm's weighted average cost of capital, WACC, decreases as the firm relies more heavily on debt financing.

TABLE 13.4

Modigliani and Miller summary

13.5 | BANKRUPTCY COSTS

One limit to the amount of debt a firm might use comes in the form of *bankruptcy costs*. As the debt-equity ratio rises, so too does the probability that the firm will be unable to pay its bondholders what was promised to them. When this happens, ownership of the firm's assets is ultimately transferred from the stockholders to the bondholders.

In principle, a firm becomes bankrupt when the value of its assets equals the value of its debt. When this occurs, the value of equity is zero and the stockholders turn over control of the firm to the bondholders. At this point, the bondholders hold assets whose value is exactly equal to what is owed on the debt. In a perfect world, there are no costs associated with this transfer of ownership, and the bondholders don't lose anything.

This idealized view of bankruptcy is not, of course, what happens in the real world. Ironically, it is expensive to go bankrupt. As we discuss, the costs associated with bankruptcy may eventually offset the tax-related gains from leverage.

Direct Bankruptcy Costs

When the value of a firm's assets equals the value of its debt, then the firm is economically bankrupt in the sense that the equity has no value. However, the formal turning over of the assets to the bondholders is a *legal* process, not an economic one. There are legal and administrative costs to bankruptcy, and it has been remarked that bankruptcies are to lawyers what blood is to sharks.

direct bankruptcy costs
The costs that are directly associated with bankruptcy, such as legal and administrative expenses.

Because of the expenses associated with bankruptcy, bondholders won't get all that they are owed. Some fraction of the firm's assets will "disappear" in the legal process of going bankrupt. These are the legal and administrative expenses associated with the bankruptcy proceeding. We call these costs **direct bankruptcy costs.**

Indirect Bankruptcy Costs

Because it is expensive to go bankrupt, a firm will spend resources to avoid doing so. When a firm is having significant problems in meeting its debt obligations, we say that it is experiencing financial distress. Some financially distressed firms ultimately file for bankruptcy, but most do not because they are able to recover or otherwise survive.

The costs of avoiding a bankruptcy filing incurred by a financially distressed firm are called **indirect bankruptcy costs.** We use the term **financial distress costs** to refer generically to the direct and indirect costs associated with going bankrupt and/or avoiding a bankruptcy filing.

indirect bankruptcy costs
The costs of avoiding a bankruptcy filing incurred by a financially distressed firm.

financial distress costs
The direct and indirect costs associated with going bankrupt or experiencing financial distress.

The problems that come up in financial distress are particularly severe, and the financial distress costs are thus larger, when the stockholders and the bondholders are different groups. Until the firm is legally bankrupt, the stockholders control it. They, of course, will take actions in their own economic interests. Since the stockholders can be wiped out in a legal bankruptcy, they have a very strong incentive to avoid a bankruptcy filing.

The bondholders, on the other hand, are primarily concerned with protecting the value of the firm's assets and will try to take control away from the stockholders. They have a strong incentive to seek bankruptcy to protect their interests and keep stockholders from further dissipating the assets of the firm. The net effect of all this fighting is that a long, drawn-out, and potentially quite expensive legal battle gets started.

Meanwhile, as the wheels of justice turn in their ponderous way, the assets of the firm lose value because management is busy trying to avoid bankruptcy instead of running the business. Normal operations are disrupted, and sales are lost. Valuable employees leave, potentially fruitful programs are dropped to preserve cash, and otherwise profitable investments are not taken.

These are all indirect bankruptcy costs, or costs of financial distress. Whether or not the firm ultimately goes bankrupt, the net effect is a loss of value because the firm chose to use debt in its capital structure. It is this possibility of loss that limits the amount of debt that a firm will choose to use.

CONCEPT QUESTIONS

13.5a What are direct bankruptcy costs?
13.5b What are indirect bankruptcy costs?

OPTIMAL CAPITAL STRUCTURE | 13.6

Our previous two sections have established the basis for an optimal capital structure. A firm will borrow because the interest tax shield is valuable. At relatively low debt levels, the probability of bankruptcy and financial distress is low, and the benefit from debt outweighs the cost. At very high debt levels, the possibility of financial distress is a chronic, ongoing problem for the firm, so the benefit from debt financing may be more than offset by the financial distress costs. Based on our discussion, it would appear that an optimal capital structure exists somewhere in between these extremes.

The Static Theory of Capital Structure

The theory of capital structure that we have outlined is called the **static theory of capital structure.** It says that firms borrow up to the point where the tax benefit from an extra dollar in debt is exactly equal to the cost that comes from the increased probability of financial distress. We call this the static theory because it assumes that the firm is fixed in terms of its assets and operations and it only considers possible changes in the debt-equity ratio.

The static theory is illustrated in Figure 13.5, which plots the value of the firm, V_L, against the amount of debt, D. In Figure 13.5, we have drawn lines corresponding to three different stories. The first is M&M Proposition I with no taxes. This is the horizontal line extending from V_U, and it indicates that the value of the firm is unaffected by its capital structure. The second case, M&M Proposition I with corporate taxes, is given by the upward-sloping straight line. These two cases are exactly the same as the ones we previously illustrated in Figure 13.4.

The third case in Figure 13.5 illustrates our current discussion: The value of the firm rises to a maximum and then declines beyond that point. This is the picture that we get from our static theory. The maximum value of the firm, V_L^*, is reached at a debt level of D^*, so this is the optimal amount of borrowing. Put another way, the firm's optimal capital structure is composed of D^*/V_L^* in debt and $(1 - D^*/V_L^*)$ in equity.

The final thing to notice in Figure 13.5 is that the difference between the value of the firm in our static theory and the M&M value of the firm with taxes is the loss in value from the possibility of financial distress. Also, the difference between the static theory value of the firm and the M&M value with no taxes is the gain from leverage, net of distress costs.

Optimal Capital Structure and the Cost of Capital

As we discussed earlier, the capital structure that maximizes the value of the firm is also the one that minimizes the cost of capital. With the help of Figure 13.6, we can illustrate this point and tie together our discussion of capital structure and cost of capital. As we have seen, there are essentially three cases. We will use the simplest of the three cases as a starting point

static theory of capital structure
Theory that a firm borrows up to the point where the tax benefit from an extra dollar in debt is exactly equal to the cost that comes from the increased probability of financial distress.

FIGURE 13.5

The static theory of capital structure: The optimal capital structure and the value of the firm

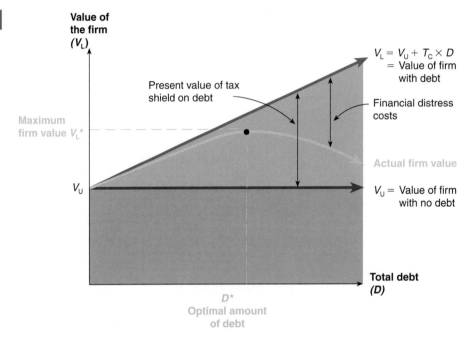

According to the static theory, the gain from the tax shield on debt is offset by financial distress costs. An optimal capital structure exists that just balances the additional gain from leverage against the added financial distress costs.

and then build up to the static theory of capital structure. Along the way, we will pay particular attention to the connection between capital structure, firm value, and cost of capital.

Figure 13.6 illustrates the original Modigliani and Miller, M&M, no-tax, no-bankruptcy argument in Case I. This is the most basic case. In the top part, we have plotted the value of the firm, V_L, against total debt, D. When there are no taxes, bankruptcy costs, or other real-world imperfections, we know that the total value of the firm is not affected by its debt policy, so V_L is simply constant. The bottom part of Figure 13.6 tells the same story in terms of the cost of capital. Here, the weighted average cost of capital, WACC, is plotted against the debt-to-equity ratio, D/E. As with total firm value, the overall cost of capital is not affected by debt policy in this basic case, so the WACC is constant.

Next, we consider what happens to the original M&M arguments once taxes are introduced. As Case II illustrates, the firm's value now critically depends on its debt policy. The more the firm borrows, the more it is worth. From our earlier discussion, we know that this happens because interest payments are tax deductible, and the gain in firm value is just equal to the present value of the interest tax shield.

In the bottom part of Figure 13.6, notice how the WACC declines as the firm uses more and more debt financing. As the firm increases its financial leverage, the cost of equity does increase, but this increase is more than offset by the tax break associated with debt financing. As a result, the firm's overall cost of capital declines.

To finish our story, we include the impact of bankruptcy, or financial distress, costs to get Case III. As is shown in the top part of Figure 13.6, the value of the firm will not be as large as we previously indicated. The reason is that the firm's value is reduced by the present value of the potential future bankruptcy costs. These costs grow as the firm borrows more and more, and they eventually overwhelm the tax advantage of debt financing. The optimal capital structure occurs at D^*, the point at which the tax saving from an additional

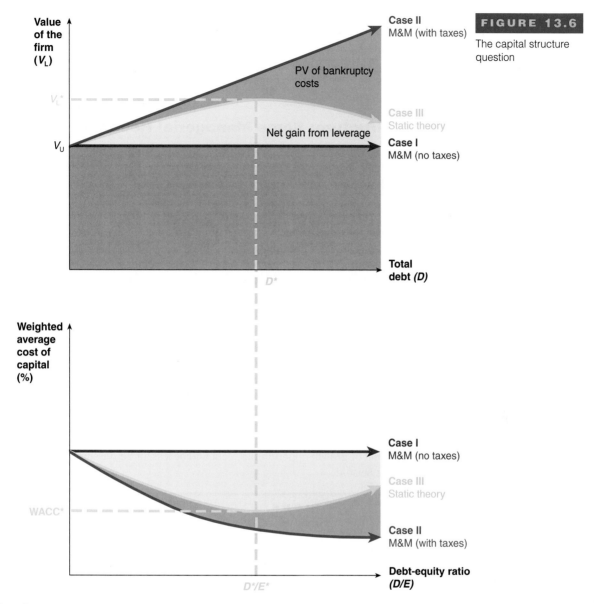

FIGURE 13.6

The capital structure question

Case I
With no taxes or bankruptcy costs, the value of the firm and its weighted average cost of capital are not affected by capital structures.

Case II
With corporate taxes and no bankruptcy costs, the value of the firm increases and the weighted average cost of capital decreases as the amount of debt goes up.

Case III
With corporate taxes and bankruptcy costs, the value of the firm, V_L, reaches a maximum at D^*, the optimal amount of borrowing. At the same time, the weighted average cost of capital, WACC, is minimized at D^*/E^*.

dollar in debt financing is exactly balanced by the increased bankruptcy costs associated with the additional borrowing. This is the essence of the static theory of capital structure.

The bottom part of Figure 13.6 presents the optimal capital structure in terms of the cost of capital. Corresponding to D^*, the optimal debt level, is the optimal debt-to-equity ratio, D^*/E^*. At this level of debt financing, the lowest possible weighted average cost of capital, WACC*, occurs.

Capital Structure: Some Managerial Recommendations

The static model that we have described is not capable of identifying a precise optimal capital structure, but it does point out two of the more relevant factors: taxes and financial distress. We can draw some limited conclusions concerning these.

Taxes First of all, the tax benefit from leverage is obviously only important to firms that are in a tax-paying position. Firms with substantial accumulated losses will get little value from the interest tax shield. Furthermore, firms that have substantial tax shields from other sources, such as depreciation, will get less benefit from leverage.

Also, not all firms have the same tax rate. The higher the tax rate, the greater the incentive to borrow.

Financial Distress Firms with a greater risk of experiencing financial distress will borrow less than firms with a lower risk of financial distress. For example, all other things being equal, the greater the volatility in EBIT, the less a firm should borrow.

In addition, financial distress is more costly for some firms than for others. The costs of financial distress depend primarily on the firm's assets. In particular, financial distress costs will be determined by how easily ownership of those assets can be transferred.

For example, a firm with mostly tangible assets that can be sold without great loss in value will have an incentive to borrow more. For firms that rely heavily on intangibles, such as employee talent or growth opportunities, debt will be less attractive since these assets effectively cannot be sold.

CONCEPT QUESTIONS

13.6a Can you describe the trade-off that defines the static theory of capital structure?

13.6b What are the important factors in making capital structure decisions?

13.7 OBSERVED CAPITAL STRUCTURES

No two firms have identical capital structures. Nonetheless, there are some regular elements that we see when we start looking at actual capital structures. We discuss a few of these next.

The most striking thing we observe about capital structures, particularly in the United States, is that most corporations seem to have relatively low debt-equity ratios. In fact, most corporations use much less debt financing than equity financing. To illustrate, Table 13.5 presents median debt ratios and debt-equity ratios for various U.S. industries classified by SIC code (we discussed such codes in Chapter 3).

In Table 13.5, what is most striking is the wide variation across industries, ranging from essentially no debt for drug, computer, and footwear companies to relatively heavy debt usage in the cable television and electric utility industries. Notice that these last two industries are the only ones for which more debt is used than equity, and most of the other industries rely far more heavily on equity than debt. This is true even though many of the companies in these industries pay substantial taxes. Table 13.5 makes it clear that corporations have not, in gen-

Capital structures for U.S. industries   **TABLE 13.5**

Industry	Ratio of Debt to Total Capital*	Ratio of Debt to Equity	Number of Companies	SIC Code	Representative Companies
Dairy products	13.18%	15.47%	8	202	Ben and Jerry's, Dreyer's
Fabric apparel	23.04	29.93	38	23	VF Corp, Jones Apparel
Paper	37.09	58.99	30	26	Kimberly-Clark, Fort James
Drugs	2.75	2.83	161	283	Pfizer, Warner-Lambert
Petroleum refining	30.32	43.55	12	29	Exxon Mobil, USX-Marathon
Rubber footwear	28.51	41.22	6	302	Nike, Reebok
Steel	55.84	126.46	28	331	Nucor, USX-US Steel
Computers	6.91	7.42	90	357	Cisco, Dell
Motor vehicles	41.59	71.21	39	371	Ford, General Motors
Aircraft	16.97	20.44	5	372	Boeing
Airlines	47.50	90.49	17	4512	Delta, Southwest
Cable television	39.77	68.66	8	484	Cablevision Sys, Cox Communications
Electric utilities	49.86	99.43	54	491	Southern Co., Enron
Department stores	50.53	110.43	8	531	Sears, Kohl's
Eating places	28.31	39.49	62	5812	McDonald's, Wendy's

*Debt is the book value of preferred stock and long-term debt, including amounts due in one year. Equity is the market value of outstanding shares. Total capital is the sum of debt and equity. Median values are shown.

Source: Cost of Capital, 2000 Yearbook (Chicago: Ibbotson Associates, Inc., 2000).

eral, issued debt up to the point that tax shelters have been completely used up, and we conclude that there must be limits to the amount of debt corporations can use.

Different industries have different operating characteristics in terms of, for example, EBIT volatility and asset types, and there does appear to be some connection between these characteristics and capital structure. Our story involving tax savings and financial distress costs undoubtedly supplies part of the reason, but, to date, there is no fully satisfactory theory that explains these regularities in capital structures.

CONCEPT QUESTIONS

13.7a Do U.S. corporations rely heavily on debt financing?

13.7b What regularities do we observe in capital structures?

A QUICK LOOK AT THE BANKRUPTCY PROCESS   **13.8**

As we have discussed, one of the consequences of using debt is the possibility of financial distress, which can be defined in several ways:

1. *Business failure.* This term is usually used to refer to a situation in which a business has terminated with a loss to creditors, but even an all-equity firm can fail.

2. *Legal bankruptcy.* Firms or creditors bring petitions to a federal court for bankruptcy. **Bankruptcy** is a legal proceeding for liquidating or reorganizing a business.

3. *Technical insolvency.* Technical insolvency occurs when a firm is unable to meet its financial obligations.

bankruptcy

A legal proceeding for liquidating or reorganizing a business.

4. *Accounting insolvency.* Firms with negative net worth are insolvent on the books. This happens when the total book liabilities exceed the book value of the total assets.

We now very briefly discuss some of the terms and more relevant issues associated with bankruptcy and financial distress.

Liquidation and Reorganization

Firms that cannot or choose not to make contractually required payments to creditors have two basic options: liquidation or reorganization. **Liquidation** means termination of the firm as a going concern, and it involves selling off the assets of the firm. The proceeds, net of selling costs, are distributed to creditors in order of established priority. **Reorganization** is the option of keeping the firm a going concern; it often involves issuing new securities to replace old securities. Liquidation or reorganization is the result of a bankruptcy proceeding. Which occurs depends on whether the firm is worth more "dead or alive."

liquidation

Termination of the firm as a going concern.

reorganization

Financial restructuring of a failing firm to attempt to continue operations as a going concern.

Bankruptcy Liquidation　Chapter 7 of the Federal Bankruptcy Reform Act of 1978 deals with "straight" liquidation. The following sequence of events is typical:

1. A petition is filed in a federal court. A corporation may file a voluntary petition, or involuntary petitions may be filed against the corporation by several of its creditors.
2. A trustee-in-bankruptcy is elected by the creditors to take over the assets of the debtor corporation. The trustee will attempt to liquidate the assets.
3. When the assets are liquidated, after payment of the bankruptcy administration costs, the proceeds are distributed among the creditors.
4. If any proceeds remain, after expenses and payments to creditors, they are distributed to the shareholders.

The distribution of the proceeds of the liquidation occurs according to the following priority list:

1. Administrative expenses associated with the bankruptcy
2. Other expenses arising after the filing of an involuntary bankruptcy petition but before the appointment of a trustee
3. Wages, salaries, and commissions
4. Contributions to employee benefit plans
5. Consumer claims
6. Government tax claims
7. Payment to unsecured creditors
8. Payment to preferred stockholders
9. Payment to common stockholders

This priority list for liquidation is a reflection of the **absolute priority rule (APR)**. The higher a claim is on this list, the more likely it is to be paid. In many of these categories, there are various limitations and qualifications that we omit for the sake of brevity.

absolute priority rule (APR)

The rule establishing priority of claims in liquidation.

Two qualifications to this list are in order. The first concerns secured creditors. Such creditors are entitled to the proceeds from the sale of the security and are outside this ordering. However, if the secured property is liquidated and provides cash insufficient to cover the amount owed, the secured creditors join with unsecured creditors in dividing the remaining liquidated value. In contrast, if the secured property is liquidated for proceeds greater than the secured claim, the net proceeds are used to pay unsecured creditors and others. The second qualification to the APR is that, in reality, what happens, and who gets what in the event of bankruptcy, is subject to much negotiation, and, as a result, the APR is frequently not followed.

Bankruptcy Reorganization   Corporate reorganization takes place under Chapter 11 of the Federal Bankruptcy Reform Act of 1978. The general objective of a proceeding under Chapter 11 is to plan to restructure the corporation with some provision for repayment of creditors. A typical sequence of events follows:

1. A voluntary petition can be filed by the corporation, or an involuntary petition can be filed by creditors.
2. A federal judge either approves or denies the petition. If the petition is approved, a time for filing proofs of claims is set.
3. In most cases, the corporation (the "debtor in possession") continues to run the business.
4. The corporation (and, in certain cases, the creditors) submits a reorganization plan.
5. Creditors and shareholders are divided into classes. A class of creditors accepts the plan if a majority of the class agrees to the plan.
6. After its acceptance by creditors, the plan is confirmed by the court.
7. Payments in cash, property, and securities are made to creditors and shareholders. The plan may provide for the issuance of new securities.
8. For some fixed length of time, the firm operates according to the provisions of the reorganization plan.

The corporation may wish to allow the old stockholders to retain some participation in the firm. Needless to say, this may involve some protest by the holders of unsecured debt.

So-called prepackaged bankruptcies are a relatively new phenomenon. What happens is that the corporation secures the necessary approval of a bankruptcy plan from a majority of its creditors first, and then it files for bankruptcy. As a result, the company enters bankruptcy and reemerges almost immediately.

For example, in October 1990, Southland Corp. (better known as 7-Eleven) filed for Chapter 11. The firm emerged from bankruptcy only four months later even though, at the time of the filing, the firm had in excess of $5 billion in liabilities including five classes of bonds plus bank loans. Southland had put together its prepackaged bankruptcy, or "prepack," by negotiating with its creditors prior to filing for bankruptcy. The accompanying *Reality Bytes* box provides more detail on prepacks.

In some cases, the bankruptcy procedure is needed to invoke the "cram-down" power of the bankruptcy court. Under certain circumstances, a class of creditors can be forced to accept a bankruptcy plan even if they vote not to approve it, hence the remarkably apt description "cram down."

Financial Management and the Bankruptcy Process

It may seem a little odd, but the right to go bankrupt is very valuable. There are several reasons why this is true. First of all, from an operational standpoint, when a firm files for bankruptcy, there is an immediate "stay" on creditors, usually meaning that payments to creditors will cease, and creditors will have to await the outcome of the bankruptcy process to find out if and how much they will be paid. This stay gives the firm time to evaluate its options, and it prevents what is usually termed a "race to the courthouse steps" by creditors and others.

Beyond this, some bankruptcy filings are actually strategic actions intended to improve a firm's competitive position, and firms have filed for bankruptcy even though they were not insolvent at the time. Probably the most famous example is Continental Airlines. In

BANKRUPTCY, "PREPACK" STYLE

On February 14, 2000, DecisionOne Corporation, a provider of computer technical support, filed for Chapter 11 reorganization under the U.S. bankruptcy code. At the time of the filing, the firm had about $932 million in debt and $370.5 million in assets. In addition to common stock, the firm's capital structure included bank loans and four different bond issues with differing levels of priority in the bankruptcy process. A firm with a financial structure such as this could reasonably expect to spend a year or longer in bankruptcy. Not so with DecisionOne, however. Its reorganization plan was confirmed by the U.S. Bankruptcy Court on March 21, 2000, not much more than six weeks after the date of filing!

Firms typically file bankruptcy to seek protection from their creditors, essentially admitting that they cannot meet their financial obligations as they are presently structured. Once in bankruptcy, the firm attempts to reorganize its financial picture so that it can survive. A key to this process is that the creditors ultimately must give their approval to the restructuring plan. The time a firm spends in Chapter 11 depends on many things, but it usually depends most on the time it takes to get creditors to agree to a plan of reorganization.

DecisionOne was able to expedite its bankruptcy by filing a presolicited, or prepackaged, bankruptcy, often called a prepack. The idea is simple. Prior to filing bankruptcy, the firm approaches its creditors with a plan for reorganization. The two sides negotiate a settlement and agree on the details of how the firm's finances will be restructured in bankruptcy. Then, the firm puts together the necessary paperwork for the bankruptcy court prior to filing for bankruptcy. A filing is a prepack if the firm essentially walks into court and, at the same time, files a reorganization plan complete with documentation of the approval of its creditors, which is exactly what DecisionOne did.

The key to the prepackaged reorganization process is that both sides have something to gain and something to lose. If bankruptcy is imminent, it may make sense for the creditors to expedite the process even though they are likely to take a financial loss in the restructuring. The faster the firm is reorganized, the faster it can concentrate on the business of making money to repay its obligations. In DecisionOne's case, some of its creditors received common stock in exchange for their debt and some received warrants to buy the firm's new stock at various prices. DecisionOne's bank lending group ended up owning about 94.5 percent of the new stock, all general and trade creditors were paid in full in cash, and the holders of the common stock before the bankruptcy ended up getting nothing. The process was probably expedited somewhat by the fact that DecisionOne's largest stockholder was also one of its creditors.

For the firm, operating in bankruptcy can be a difficult process. The bankruptcy court typically has a great deal of oversight over the firm's day-to-day operations, and putting together a reorganization plan to emerge from bankruptcy can be a tremendous drain on management time, time that would be better spent making the firm profitable again. Also, news that a firm is in bankruptcy can make skittish customers turn to competitors, endangering the future health of the firm. A prepack can't completely eliminate these problems, but, by speeding up the bankruptcy process, it can reduce the headaches involved.

Sources:"DecisionOne Reorganization Plan Is Confirmed by Court; Company Completes Restructuring," PR Newswire, 23 March 2000. "DecisionOne Reorganization Plan Gets Court Approval," Dow Jones News Service, 22 March 2000. "Frazer, Pa., Computer Technology Firm Files for Bankruptcy, Names New CEO," *The Philadelphia Inquirer,* 15 February 2000.

1983, following deregulation of the airline industry, Continental found itself competing with newly established airlines that had much lower labor costs. In response, Continental filed for reorganization under Chapter 11 even though it was not insolvent.

Continental argued that, based on pro forma data, it would become insolvent in the future, and a reorganization was therefore necessary. By filing for bankruptcy, Continental was able to terminate its existing labor agreements, lay off large numbers of workers, and slash wages for the remaining employees. In other words, at least in the eyes of critics, Continental essentially used the bankruptcy process as a vehicle for reducing labor costs. Congress has subsequently modified bankruptcy laws to make it more difficult, though not impossible, for companies to abrogate a labor contract through the bankruptcy process.

Other famous examples of strategic bankruptcies exist. For example, Manville (then known as Johns-Manville) and Dow Corning filed for bankruptcy because of expected future losses resulting from litigation associated with asbestos and silicone breast implants, respectively. Similarly, in the largest ever bankruptcy, Texaco filed in 1987 after Pennzoil was awarded a $10.3 billion judgment against it. Texaco later settled for $3.5 billion and emerged from bankruptcy. Similarly, in 1996, Sizzler International Inc. closed 136 steak houses as a restructuring move. However, Sizzler typically signs 15-year leases on the restaurant buildings it uses, and it was therefore stuck with the lease obligations for the closed stores. In response to the problem, Sizzler filed for Chapter 11 to escape the long-term leases.

Agreements to Avoid Bankruptcy

When a firm defaults on an obligation, it can avoid a bankruptcy filing. Because the legal process of bankruptcy can be lengthy and expensive, it is often in everyone's best interest to devise a "workout" that avoids a bankruptcy filing. Much of the time, creditors can work with the management of a company that has defaulted on a loan contract. Voluntary arrangements to restructure, or "reschedule," the company's debt can be and often are made. This may involve *extension,* which postpones the date of payment, or *composition,* which allows a reduced payment.

CONCEPT QUESTIONS

13.8a What is the APR (in connection with bankruptcy proceedings)?

13.8b What is the difference between liquidation and reorganization?

SUMMARY AND CONCLUSIONS

The ideal mixture of debt and equity for a firm—its optimal capital structure—is the one that maximizes the value of the firm and minimizes the overall cost of capital. If we ignore taxes, financial distress costs, and any other imperfections, we find that there is no ideal mixture. Under these circumstances, the firm's capital structure is simply irrelevant.

If we consider the effect of corporate taxes, we find that capital structure matters a great deal. This conclusion is based on the fact that interest is tax deductible and thus generates a valuable tax shield. Unfortunately, we also find that the optimal capital structure is 100 percent debt, which is not something we observe in healthy firms.

We next introduced costs associated with bankruptcy, or, more generally, financial distress. These costs reduce the attractiveness of debt financing. We concluded that an optimal capital structure exists when the net tax saving from an additional dollar in interest just equals the increase in expected financial distress costs. This is the essence of the static theory of capital structure.

When we examine actual capital structures, we find two regularities. First, firms in the United States typically do not use great amounts of debt, but they pay substantial taxes. This suggests that there is a limit to the use of debt financing to generate tax shields. Second, there is wide variation in the use of debt across industries, suggesting that the nature of a firm's assets and operations is an important determinant of its capital structure.

CHAPTER REVIEW AND SELF-TEST PROBLEMS

13.1   EBIT and EPS.   Suppose the GNR Corporation has decided in favor of a capital restructuring that involves increasing its existing $5 million in debt to $25 million. The interest rate on the debt is 12 percent and is not expected to change. The firm currently has one million shares outstanding, and the price per share is $40. If the restructuring is expected to increase the ROE, what is the minimum level for EBIT that GNR's management must be expecting? Ignore taxes in your answer.

13.2   M&M Proposition II (no taxes).   The Pro Bono Corporation has a WACC of 20 percent. Its cost of debt is 12 percent. If Pro Bono's debt-equity ratio is 2, what is its cost of equity capital? Ignore taxes in your answer.

13.3   M&M Proposition I (with corporate taxes).   Suppose TransGlobal Co. currently has no debt and its equity is worth $20,000. If the corporate tax rate is 30 percent, what will the value of the firm be if TransGlobal borrows $6,000 and uses the proceeds to buy up stock?

Answers to Chapter Review and Self-Test Problems

13.1   To answer, we can calculate the break-even EBIT. At any EBIT above this, the increased financial leverage will increase EPS. Under the old capital structure, the interest bill is $5 million $\times$ .12 = $600,000. There are one million shares of stock, so, ignoring taxes, EPS is (EBIT $-$ $600,000)/1 million.

Under the new capital structure, the interest expense will be $25 million $\times$ .12 = $3 million. Furthermore, the debt rises by $20 million. This amount is sufficient to repurchase $20 million/40 = 500,000 shares of stock, leaving 500,000 outstanding. EPS is thus (EBIT $-$ $3 million)/500,000.

Now that we know how to calculate EPS under both scenarios, we set the two expressions for EPS equal to each other and solve for the break-even EBIT:

$$\text{(EBIT} - \$600,000)/1 \text{ million} = \text{(EBIT} - \$3 \text{ million)}/500,000$$
$$\text{EBIT} - \$600,000 = 2 \times \text{(EBIT} - \$3 \text{ million)}$$
$$\text{EBIT} = \$5,400,000$$

Verify that, in either case, EPS is $4.80 when EBIT is $5.4 million.

13.2   According to M&M Proposition II (no taxes), the cost of equity is:

$$R_E = R_A + (R_A - R_D) \times (D/E)$$
$$= 20\% + (20\% - 12\%) \times 2$$
$$= 36\%$$

13.3   After the debt issue, TransGlobal will be worth the original $20,000 plus the present value of the tax shield. According to M&M Proposition I with taxes, the present value of the tax shield is $T_C \times D$, or .30 $\times$ $6,000 = $1,800, so the firm is worth $20,000 + 1,800 = $21,800.

CRITICAL THINKING AND CONCEPTS REVIEW

1.   **Business Risk versus Financial Risk.**   Explain what is meant by business and financial risk. Suppose Firm A has greater business risk than Firm B. Is it true that Firm A also has a higher cost of equity capital? Explain.

2. **M&M Propositions.**   How would you answer in the following debate?

   Q: Isn't it true that the riskiness of a firm's equity will rise if the firm increases its use of debt financing?

   A: Yes, that's the essence of M&M Proposition II.

   Q: And isn't it true that, as a firm increases its use of borrowing, the likelihood of default increases, which increases the risk of the firm's debt?

   A: Yes.

   Q: In other words, increased borrowing increases the risk of the equity *and* the debt?

   A: That's right.

   Q: Well, given that the firm uses only debt and equity financing, and given that the risk of both is increased by increased borrowing, does it not follow that increasing debt increases the overall risk of the firm and therefore decreases the value of the firm?

   A: ??

3. **Optimal Capital Structure.**   Is there an easily identifiable debt-equity ratio that will maximize the value of a firm? Why or why not?

4. **Observed Capital Structures.**   Refer to the observed capital structures given in Table 13.5 of the text. What do you notice about the types of industries with respect to their average debt-equity ratios? Are certain types of industries more likely to be highly leveraged than others? What are some possible reasons for this observed segmentation? Do the operating results and tax history of the firms play a role? How about their future earnings prospects? Explain.

5. **Financial Leverage.**   Why is the use of debt financing referred to as using financial "leverage"?

6. **Homemade Leverage.**   What is homemade leverage?

7. **Bankruptcy and Corporate Ethics.**   As mentioned in the text, some firms have filed for bankruptcy because of actual or likely litigation-related losses. Is this a proper use of the bankruptcy process?

8. **Bankruptcy and Corporate Ethics.**   Firms sometimes use the threat of a bankruptcy filing to force creditors to renegotiate terms. Critics argue that in such cases, the firm is using bankruptcy laws "as a sword rather than a shield." Is this an ethical tactic?

9. **Bankruptcy and Corporate Ethics.**   As mentioned in the text, Continental Airlines filed for bankruptcy, at least in part, as a means of reducing labor costs. Whether this move was ethical, or proper, was hotly debated. Give both sides of the argument.

10. **Capital Structure Goal.**   What is the basic goal of financial management with regard to capital structure?

QUESTIONS AND PROBLEMS

1. **EBIT and Leverage.**   Big Apple, Inc., has no debt outstanding and a total market value of $80,000. Earnings before interest and taxes, EBIT, are projected to be $10,000 if economic conditions are normal. If there is strong expansion in the economy, then EBIT will be 30 percent higher. If there is a recession, then EBIT will be 60 percent lower. Big Apple is considering a $35,000 debt issue with a 5 percent in-

Basic
(Questions 1–15)

terest rate. The proceeds will be used to repurchase shares of stock. There are currently 4,000 shares outstanding. Ignore taxes for this problem.

   a. Calculate earnings per share, EPS, under each of the three economic scenarios before any debt is issued. Also, calculate the percentage changes in EPS when the economy expands or enters a recession.

   b. Repeat part (*a*) assuming that Big Apple goes through with recapitalization. What do you observe?

2.   **EBIT, Taxes, and Leverage.**   Repeat parts (*a*) and (*b*) in Problem 1 assuming Big Apple has a tax rate of 35 percent.

3.   **ROE and Leverage.**   Suppose the company in Problem 1 has a market-to-book ratio of 1.0.

   a. Calculate return on equity, ROE, under each of the three economic scenarios before any debt is issued. Also, calculate the percentage changes in ROE for economic expansion and recession, assuming no taxes.

   b. Repeat part (*a*) assuming the firm goes through with the proposed recapitalization.

   c. Repeat parts (*a*) and (*b*) of this problem assuming the firm has a tax rate of 35 percent.

4.   **Break-Even EBIT.**   Duval Corporation is comparing two different capital structures, an all-equity plan (Plan I) and a levered plan (Plan II). Under Plan I, Duval would have 400,000 shares of stock outstanding. Under Plan II, there would be 200,000 shares of stock outstanding and $5 million in debt outstanding. The interest rate on the debt is 10 percent, and there are no taxes.

   a. If EBIT is $600,000, which plan will result in the higher EPS?

   b. If EBIT is $5.5 million, which plan will result in the higher EPS?

   c. What is the break-even EBIT?

5.   **M&M and Stock Value.**   In Problem 4, use M&M Proposition I to find the price per share of equity under each of the two proposed plans. What is the value of the firm?

6.   **Break-Even EBIT and Leverage.**   Supafuzz Co. is comparing two different capital structures. Plan I would result in 1,600 shares of stock and $28,000 in debt. Plan II would result in 1,800 shares of stock and $14,000 in debt. The interest rate on the debt is 11 percent.

   a. Ignoring taxes, compare both of these plans to an all-equity plan assuming that EBIT will be $12,000. The all-equity plan would result in 2,000 shares of stock outstanding. Which of the three plans has the highest EPS? The lowest?

   b. In part (*a*), what are the break-even levels of EBIT for each plan as compared to that for an all-equity plan? Is one higher than the other? Why?

   c. Ignoring taxes, when will EPS be identical for Plans I and II?

   d. Repeat parts (*a*), (*b*), and (*c*) assuming that the corporate tax rate is 38 percent. Are the break-even levels of EBIT different from before? Why or why not?

7.   **Leverage and Stock Value.**   Ignoring taxes in Problem 6, what is the price per share of equity under Plan I? Plan II? What principle is illustrated by your answers?

8.   **Homemade Leverage.**   Ozone Depletion, Inc., a prominent consumer products firm, is debating whether or not to convert its all-equity capital structure to one that is 40 percent debt. Currently, there are 800 shares outstanding and the price per share is $80. EBIT is expected to remain at $5,000 per year forever. The interest rate on new debt is 7 percent, and there are no taxes.

   a. Jimbo, a shareholder of the firm, owns 100 shares of stock. What is his cash flow under the current capital structure, assuming the firm has a dividend payout rate of 100 percent?

   b. What will Jimbo's cash flow be under the proposed capital structure of the firm? Assume that he keeps all 100 of his shares.

   c. Suppose Ozone does convert, but Jimbo prefers the current all-equity capital structure. Show how he could unlever his shares of stock to recreate the original capital structure.

   d. Using your answer to part (*c*), explain why Ozone's choice of capital structure is irrelevant.

9.   **Homemade Leverage.** Buffett Enterprises is considering a change from its current capital structure. Buffett currently has an all equity capital structure and is considering a capital structure with 30 percent debt. There are currently 1,000 shares outstanding at a price per share of $120. EBIT is expected to remain constant at $19,000. The interest rate on new debt is 8% and there are no taxes.

   a. Rebecca owns $12,000 worth of stock in the company. If the firm has a 100 percent payout what is her cash flow?

   b. What would her cash flow be under the new capital structure assuming that she keeps all of her shares?

   c. Suppose the company does convert to the new capital structure. Show how Rebecca can maintain her current cash flow.

   d. Under your answer to part (*c*), explain why Buffett's choice of capital structure is irrelevant.

10.   **M&M and Taxes.** Angstrom Corp. uses no debt. The weighted average cost of capital is 14 pecent. The current market value of the company is $30 million. The corporate tax rate is 40 percent. What is the value of the company if Angstrom converts to debt-equity ratio of 1? What if the debt-equity ratio is 2?

11.   **M&M and Taxes.** In the previous question, suppose the corporate tax rate was 30 percent. What is the value of the firm under each of the 3 debt-equity scenarios? What does this tell you about corporate tax rates and the value of the firm?

12.   **Calculating WACC.** Nichols Industries has a debt-equity ratio of 1.5. Its WACC is 16 percent, and its cost of debt is 11 percent. There is no corporate tax.

   a. What is Nichols's cost of equity capital?

   b. What would the cost of equity be if the debt-equity ratio were 1.0? What if it were 0.5? What if it were zero?

13.   **Calculating WACC.** Benjamin Corp. has no debt but can borrow at 9 percent. The firm's WACC is currently 15 percent, and there is no corporate tax.

   a. What is Benjamin's cost of equity?

   b. If the firm converts to 25 percent debt, what will its cost of equity be?

   c. If the firm converts to 50 percent debt, what will its cost of equity be?

   d. What is Benjamin's WACC in part (*b*)? In part (*c*)?

14.   **M&M and Taxes.** Carrey & Co. can borrow at 10 percent. Carrey currently has no debt, and the cost of equity is 22 percent. The current value of the firm is $275,000. What will the value be if Carrey borrows $75,000 and uses the proceeds to repurchase shares? The corporate tax rate is 35%.

15.   **Interest Tax Shield.** Diamond Co. has a 38 percent tax rate. Its total interest payment for the year just ended was $42 million. What is the interest tax shield? How do you interpret this amount?

16. **M&M.**   Corrado Corporation has no debt. Its current total value is $210 million. Ignoring taxes, what will Corrado's value be if it sells $70 million in debt? Suppose now that Corrado's tax rate is 40 percent. What will its overall value be if it sells $70 million in debt? Assume debt proceeds are used to repurchase equity.

17. **M&M.**   In the previous question, what is the debt-equity ratio in both cases?

18. **M&M.**   Skipper Co. has no debt. Its cost of capital is 13 percent. Suppose Skipper converts to a debt-equity ratio of 1.0. The interest rate on the debt is 9 percent. Ignoring taxes, what is Skipper's new cost of equity? What is its new WACC?

19. **Firm Value.**   Alphabet Corporation expects an EBIT of $16,500 every year forever. Alphabet currently has no debt, and its cost of equity is 18 percent. The firm can borrow at 14 percent. If the corporate tax rate is 38 percent, what is the value of the firm? What will the value be if Alphabet converts to 50 percent debt? To 100 percent debt?

www.mhhe.com/rwj

Spreadsheet Templates 1, 3, 9

14

Dividends and Dividend Policy

THIS CHAPTER WILL PAY YOU SIGNIFICANT
DIVIDENDS IF YOU STUDY IT CLOSELY. WHEN
YOU ARE FINISHED, YOU SHOULD HAVE A
GOOD UNDERSTANDING OF:

- Dividend types and how dividends are paid

- The issues surrounding dividend policy decisions

- The difference between cash and stock dividends

- Why share repurchases are an alternative to
  dividends

IN DECEMBER 1999, General Electric Corp. (better known as GE) announced a broad plan to reward shareholders for the recent success of the firm's business. Under the plan, GE would (1) boost its quarterly dividend by 17 percent from 35 cents per share to 41 cents per share, (2) expand its plans to buy back its common stock by as much as $5 billion, and (3) undertake a three-for-one stock split, meaning that each existing common share would be replaced with three new ones. Investors cheered, bidding the stock price up by 2.9 percent on the day of the announcement. Why were investors so pleased? To find out, this chapter explores all three of these actions and their implications for shareholders.

This chapter is about dividend policy. Going back to Chapter 7, we saw that the value of a share of stock depends on all the future dividends that will be paid to shareholders. In that analysis, we took the future stream of dividends as given. What we now examine is how corporations decide on the size and timing of dividend payments. What we would like to find out is how to establish an optimal dividend policy, meaning a dividend policy that maximizes the stock price. What we discover, among other things, is that it is not at all clear how to do this, or even if there is such a thing as an optimal dividend policy!

Dividend policy is an important subject in corporate finance, and dividends are a major cash outlay for many corporations. At first glance, it may seem obvious that a firm would always want to give as much as possible back to its shareholders by paying dividends. It might seem equally obvious, however, that a firm can always invest the money for its shareholders instead of paying it out. The heart of the dividend policy question is just this: Should the firm pay out money to its shareholders, or should the firm take that money and invest it for its shareholders?

It may seem surprising, but much research and economic logic suggest that dividend policy doesn't matter. In fact, it turns out that the dividend policy issue is much like the capital structure question. The important elements are not difficult to identify, but the interactions between those elements are complex and no easy answer exists.

Dividend policy is controversial. Many implausible reasons are given for why dividend policy might be important, and many of the claims made about dividend policy are economically illogical. Even so, in the real world of corporate finance, determining the most appropriate dividend policy is considered an important issue. It could be that financial managers who worry about dividend policy are wasting time, but it could also be true that we are missing something important in our discussions.

In part, all discussions of dividends are plagued by the "two-handed lawyer" problem. President Truman, while discussing the legal implications of a possible presidential decision, asked his staff to set up a meeting with a lawyer. Supposedly Mr. Truman said, "But I don't want one of those two-handed lawyers." When asked what a two-handed lawyer was, he replied, "You know, a lawyer who says, 'On the one hand I recommend you do so and so because of the following reasons, but on the other hand I recommend that you don't do it because of these other reasons.' "

Unfortunately, any sensible treatment of dividend policy will appear to have been written by a two-handed lawyer (or, in fairness, several two-handed financial economists). On the one hand, there are many good reasons for corporations to pay high dividends, but, on the other hand, there are also many good reasons to pay low dividends.

We will cover three broad topics that relate to dividends and dividend policy in this chapter. First, we describe the various kinds of dividends and how dividends are paid. Second, we consider an idealized case in which dividend policy doesn't matter. We then discuss the limitations of this case and present some real-world arguments for both high- and low-dividend payouts. Finally, we conclude the chapter by looking at some strategies that corporations might employ to implement a dividend policy, and we discuss share repurchases as an alternative to dividends.

14.1 | CASH DIVIDENDS AND DIVIDEND PAYMENT

dividend
Payment made out of a firm's earnings to its owners, in the form of either cash or stock.

distribution
Payment made by a firm to its owners from sources other than current or accumulated retained earnings.

The term **dividend** usually refers to cash paid out of earnings. If a payment is made from sources other than current or accumulated retained earnings, the term **distribution,** rather than *dividend,* is used. However, it is acceptable to refer to a distribution from earnings as a dividend and a distribution from capital as a liquidating dividend. More generally, any direct payment by the corporation to the shareholders may be considered a dividend or a part of dividend policy.

Dividends come in several different forms. The basic types of cash dividends are:

1. Regular cash dividends
2. Extra dividends
3. Special dividends
4. Liquidating dividends

Later in the chapter, we discuss dividends paid in stock instead of cash, and we also consider an alternative to cash dividends, stock repurchase.

Cash Dividends

The most common type of dividend is a cash dividend. Commonly, public companies pay **regular cash dividends** four times a year. As the name suggests, these are cash payments made directly to shareholders, and they are made in the regular course of business. In other words, management sees nothing unusual about the dividend and no reason why it won't be continued.

Sometimes firms will pay a regular cash dividend and an *extra cash dividend.* By calling part of the payment "extra," management is indicating that that part may or may not be repeated in the future. A *special dividend* is similar, but the name usually indicates that this dividend is viewed as a truly unusual or one-time event and it won't be repeated. Finally, the payment of a *liquidating dividend* usually means that some or all of the business has been liquidated, that is, sold off.

However it is labeled, a cash dividend payment reduces corporate cash and retained earnings, except in the case of a liquidating dividend (where paid-in capital may be reduced).

regular cash dividend
Cash payment made by a firm to its owners in the normal course of business, usually made four times a year.

Standard Method of Cash Dividend Payment

The decision to pay a dividend rests in the hands of the board of directors of the corporation. When a dividend has been declared, it becomes a liability of the firm and cannot be rescinded easily. Sometime after it has been declared, a dividend is distributed to all shareholders as of some specific date.

Commonly, the amount of the cash dividend is expressed in terms of dollars per share (*dividends per share*). As we have seen in other chapters, it is also expressed as a percentage of the market price (the *dividend yield*) or as a percentage of net income or earnings per share (the *dividend payout*).

Dividend Payment: A Chronology

The mechanics of a cash dividend payment can be illustrated by the example in Figure 14.1 and the following description:

1. **Declaration date.** On January 15, the board of directors passes a resolution to pay a dividend of $1 per share on February 16 to all holders of record as of January 30.

declaration date
Date on which the board of directors passes a resolution to pay a dividend.

FIGURE 14.1

Example of the procedure for dividend payment

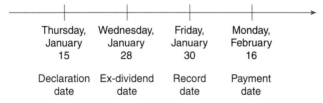

Thursday, January 15 — Declaration date
Wednesday, January 28 — Ex-dividend date
Friday, January 30 — Record date
Monday, February 16 — Payment date

1. *Declaration date:* The board of directors declares a payment of dividends.
2. *Ex-dividend date:* A share of stock goes ex dividend on the date the seller is entitled to keep the dividend; under NYSE rules, shares are traded ex dividend on and after the second business day before the record date.
3. *Record date:* The declared dividends are distributable to those who are shareholders of record as of this specific date.
4. *Payment date:* The dividend checks are mailed to shareholders of record.

ex-dividend date

Date two business days before the date of record, establishing those individuals entitled to a dividend.

2. **Ex-dividend date.** To make sure that dividend checks go to the right people, brokerage firms and stock exchanges establish an *ex-dividend date.* This date is two business days before the date of record (discussed next). If you buy the stock before this date, then you are entitled to the dividend. If you buy on this date or after, then the previous owner will get the dividend.

　　In Figure 14.1, Wednesday, January 28, is the ex-dividend date. Before this date, the stock is said to trade "with dividend," or "cum dividend." Afterwards, the stock trades "ex dividend."

　　The ex-dividend date convention removes any ambiguity about who is entitled to the dividend. Since the dividend is valuable, the stock price will be affected when the stock goes "ex." We examine this effect below.

3. **Date of record.** Based on its records, the corporation prepares a list on January 30 of all individuals believed to be stockholders. These are the *holders of record,* and January 30 is the *date of record* (or record date). The word *believed* is important here. If you bought the stock just before this date, the corporation's records might not reflect that fact because of mailing or other delays. Without some modification, some of the dividend checks would get mailed to the wrong people. This is the reason for the ex-dividend day convention.

date of record

Date by which holders must be on record to receive a dividend.

date of payment

Date that the dividend checks are mailed.

4. **Date of payment.** The dividend checks are mailed on February 16.

More on the Ex-Dividend Date

The ex-dividend date is important and is a common source of confusion. We examine what happens to the stock when it goes ex, meaning that the ex-dividend date arrives. To illustrate, suppose we have a stock that sells for $10 per share. The board of directors declares a dividend of $1 per share, and the record date is Tuesday, June 12. Based on our discussion above, we know that the ex date will be two business (not calendar) days earlier, on Friday, June 8.

　　If you buy the stock on Thursday, June 7, right as the market closes, you'll get the $1 dividend because the stock is trading cum dividend. If you wait and buy the stock right as the market opens on Friday, you won't get the $1 dividend. What will happen to the value of the stock overnight?

　　If you think about it, the stock is obviously worth about $1 less on Friday morning, so its price will drop by this amount between close of business on Thursday and the Friday opening. In general, we expect that the value of a share of stock will go down by about the dividend amount when the stock goes ex dividend. The key word here is *about.* Since dividends are taxed, the actual price drop might be closer to some measure of the aftertax value of the dividend. Determining this value is complicated because of the different tax rates and tax rules that apply for different buyers.

　　The series of events described here is illustrated in Figure 14.2.

EXAMPLE 14.1 | "Ex" Marks the Day

The board of directors of Divided Airlines has declared a dividend of $2.50 per share payable on Tuesday, May 30, to shareholders of record as of Tuesday, May 9. Cal Icon buys 100 shares of Divided on Tuesday, May 2, for $150 per share. What is the ex date? Describe the events that will occur with regard to the cash dividend and the stock price.

　　The ex date is two business days before the date of record, Tuesday, May 9, so the stock will go ex on Friday, May 5. Cal buys the stock on Tuesday, May 2, so Cal purchases the stock cum dividend. In other words, Cal will get $2.50 × 100 = $250 in dividends. The check will be mailed on Tuesday, May 30. When the stock does go ex on Friday, its value will drop overnight by about $2.50 per share.

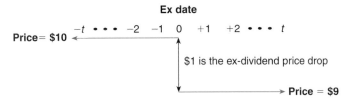

Ex date

$-t$ • • • -2 -1 0 $+1$ $+2$ • • • t

Price $= \$10$

$1 is the ex-dividend price drop

Price $= \$9$

The stock price will fall by the amount of the dividend on the ex date (Time 0). If the dividend is $1 per share, the price will be equal to $10 − 1 = $9 on the ex date.

Before ex date (Time −1) Dividend = $0 Price = $10
On ex date (Time 0) Dividend = $1 Price = $9

FIGURE 14.2

Price behavior around the ex-dividend date for a $1 cash dividend.

CONCEPT QUESTIONS

14.1a What are the different types of cash dividends?

14.1b What are the mechanics of the cash dividend payment?

14.1c How should the price of a stock change when the stock goes ex dividend?

DOES DIVIDEND POLICY MATTER? | 14.2

To decide whether or not dividend policy matters, we first have to define what we mean by dividend *policy*. All other things being the same, of course dividends matter. Dividends are paid in cash, and cash is something that everybody likes. The question we will be discussing here is whether the firm should pay out cash now or invest the cash and pay it out later. Dividend policy, therefore, is the time pattern of dividend payout. In particular, should the firm pay out a large percentage of its earnings now or a small (or even zero) percentage? This is the dividend policy question.

An Illustration of the Irrelevance of Dividend Policy

A powerful argument can be made that dividend policy does not matter. We illustrate this by considering the simple case of Wharton Corporation. Wharton is an all-equity firm that has existed for 10 years. The current financial managers plan to dissolve the firm in two years. The total cash flows the firm will generate, including the proceeds from liquidation, are $10,000 in each of the next two years.

Current Policy: Dividends Set Equal to Cash Flow At the present time, dividends at each date are set equal to the cash flow of $10,000. There are 100 shares outstanding, so the dividend per share will be $100. In Chapter 7, we showed that the value of the stock is equal to the present value of the future dividends. Assuming a 10 percent required return, the value of a share of stock today, P_0, is:

$$P_0 = \frac{D_1}{(1 + R)^1} + \frac{D_2}{(1 + R)^2}$$

$$= \frac{\$100}{1.10} + \frac{100}{1.10^2} = \$173.55$$

The firm as a whole is thus worth $100 \times \$173.55 = \$17,355$.

Several members of the board of Wharton have expressed dissatisfaction with the current dividend policy and have asked you to analyze an alternative policy.

Alternative Policy: Initial Dividend Greater Than Cash Flow   Another policy is for the firm to pay a dividend of $110 per share on the first date (Date 1), which is, of course, a total dividend of $11,000. Because the cash flow is only $10,000, an extra $1,000 must somehow be raised. One way to do this is to issue $1,000 worth of bonds or stock at Date 1. Assume that stock is issued. The new stockholders will desire enough cash flow at Date 2 so that they earn the required 10 percent return on their Date 1 investment.

What is the value of the firm with this new dividend policy? The new stockholders invest $1,000. They require a 10 percent return, so they will demand $1,000 × 1.10 = $1,100 of the Date 2 cash flow, leaving only $8,900 to the old stockholders. The dividends to the old stockholders will be:

	Date 1	Date 2
Aggregate dividends to old stockholders	$11,000	$8,900
Dividends per share	110	89

The present value of the dividends per share is therefore:

$$P_0 = \frac{\$110}{1.10} + \frac{89}{1.10^2} = \$173.55$$

This is the same value we had before.

The value of the stock is not affected by this switch in dividend policy even though we had to sell some new stock just to finance the dividend. In fact, no matter what pattern of dividend payout the firm chooses, the value of the stock will always be the same in this example. In other words, for the Wharton Corporation, dividend policy makes no difference. The reason is simple: Any increase in a dividend at some point in time is exactly offset by a decrease somewhere else, so the net effect, once we account for time value, is zero.

A Test

Our discussion to this point can be summarized by considering the following true-false test questions:

1. True or false: Dividends are irrelevant.
2. True or false: Dividend policy is irrelevant.

The first statement is surely false, and the reason follows from common sense. Clearly, investors prefer higher dividends to lower dividends at any single date if the dividend level is held constant at every other date. To be more precise regarding the first question, if the dividend per share at a given date is raised while the dividend per share at every other date is held constant, the stock price will rise. The reason is that the present value of the future dividends must go up if this occurs. This action can be accomplished by management decisions that improve productivity, increase tax savings, strengthen product marketing, or otherwise improve cash flow.

The second statement is true, at least in the simple case we have been examining. Dividend policy by itself cannot raise the dividend at one date while keeping it the same at all other dates. Rather, dividend policy merely establishes the trade-off between dividends at one date and dividends at another date. Once we allow for time value, the present value of the dividend stream is unchanged. Thus, in this simple world, dividend policy does not matter, because managers choosing either to raise or to lower the current dividend do not affect the current value of their firm. However, we have ignored several real-world factors that might lead us to change our minds; we pursue some of these in subsequent sections.

Some Real-World Factors Favoring a Low Payout

The example we used to illustrate the irrelevance of dividend policy ignored taxes and flotation costs. We will now see that these factors might lead us to prefer a low-dividend payout.

Taxes U.S. tax laws are complex, and they affect dividend policy in a number of ways. The key tax feature has to do with the taxation of dividend income and capital gains. For individual shareholders, *effective* tax rates on dividend income are higher than the tax rates on capital gains. Dividends received are taxed as ordinary income. Capital gains are taxed at somewhat lower rates, and the tax on a capital gain is deferred until the stock is sold. This second aspect of capital gains taxation makes the effective tax rate much lower because the present value of the tax is less.[1]

A firm that adopts a low-dividend payout will reinvest the money instead of paying it out. This reinvestment increases the value of the firm and of the equity. All other things being equal, the net effect is that the expected capital gains portion of the return will be higher in the future. So the fact that capital gains are taxed favorably may lead us to prefer this approach.

Flotation Costs In our example illustrating that dividend policy doesn't matter, we saw that the firm could sell some new stock if necessary to pay a dividend. As we discuss in our next chapter, selling new stock can be very expensive. If we include the costs of selling stock ("flotation" costs) in our argument, then we will find that the value of the stock decreases if we sell new stock.

More generally, imagine two firms identical in every way except that one pays out a greater percentage of its cash flow in the form of dividends. Since the other firm plows back more, its equity grows faster. If these two firms are to remain identical, then the one with the higher payout will have to periodically sell some stock to catch up. Since this is expensive, a firm might be inclined to have a low payout.

Dividend Restrictions In some cases, a corporation may face restrictions on its ability to pay dividends. For example, as we discussed in Chapter 6, a common feature of a bond indenture is a covenant prohibiting dividend payments above some level. Also, a corporation may be prohibited by state law from paying dividends if the dividend amount exceeds the firm's retained earnings.

Some Real-World Factors Favoring a High Payout

In this section, we consider reasons why a firm might pay its shareholders higher dividends even if it means the firm must issue more shares of stock to finance the dividend payments.

Desire for Current Income It has been argued that many individuals desire current income. The classic example is the group of retired people and others living on a fixed income, the proverbial "widows and orphans." It is argued that this group is willing to pay a premium to get a higher dividend yield.

It is easy to see, however, that this argument is not relevant in our simple case. An individual preferring high current cash flow but holding low-dividend securities could easily sell off shares to provide the necessary funds. Similarly, an individual desiring a low current cash flow but holding high-dividend securities could just reinvest the dividends. Thus, in a world of no transaction costs, a policy of high current dividends would be of no value to the stockholder.

---

[1]In fact, capital gains taxes can sometimes be avoided altogether. Although we do not recommend this particular tax-avoidance strategy, the capital gains tax may be avoided by dying. Your heirs are not considered to have a capital gain, so the tax liability dies when you do. In this instance, you can take it with you.

The current-income argument may have relevance in the real world. Here the sale of low-dividend stocks would involve brokerage fees and other transaction costs. Such a sale might also trigger capital gains taxes. These direct cash expenses could be avoided by an investment in high-dividend securities. In addition, the expenditure of the stockholder's own time when selling securities and the natural (though not necessarily rational) fear of consuming out of principal might further lead many investors to buy high-dividend securities.

Tax and Legal Benefits from High Dividends

Earlier we saw that dividends were taxed unfavorably for individual investors. This fact is a powerful argument for a low payout. However, there are a number of other investors who do not receive unfavorable tax treatment from holding high–dividend yield, rather than low–dividend yield, securities.

Corporate investors   A significant tax break on dividends occurs when a corporation owns stock in another corporation. A corporate stockholder receiving either common or preferred dividends is granted a 70 percent (or more) dividend exclusion. Since the 70 percent exclusion does not apply to capital gains, this group is taxed unfavorably on capital gains.

As a result of the dividend exclusion, high-dividend, low–capital gains stocks may be more appropriate for corporations to hold. In fact, this is why corporations hold a substantial percentage of the outstanding preferred stock in the economy. This tax advantage of dividends also leads some corporations to hold high-yielding stocks instead of long-term bonds because there is no similar tax exclusion of interest payments to corporate bondholders.

Tax-exempt investors   We have pointed out both the tax advantages and the tax disadvantages of a low-dividend payout. Of course, this discussion is irrelevant to those in zero tax brackets. This group includes some of the largest investors in the economy, such as pension funds, endowment funds, and trust funds.

There are some legal reasons for large institutions to favor high-dividend yields. First, institutions such as pension funds and trust funds are often set up to manage money for the benefit of others. The managers of such institutions have a *fiduciary responsibility* to invest the money prudently. It has been considered imprudent in courts of law to buy stock in companies with no established dividend record.

Second, institutions such as university endowment funds and trust funds are frequently prohibited from spending any of the principal. Such institutions might therefore prefer high–dividend yield stocks so they have some ability to spend. Like widows and orphans, this group thus prefers current income. Unlike widows and orphans, this group is very large in terms of the amount of stock owned.

Overall, individual investors (for whatever reason) may have a desire for current income and may thus be willing to pay the dividend tax. In addition, some very large investors such as corporations and tax-free institutions may have a very strong preference for high-dividend payouts.

Clientele Effects: A Resolution of Real-World Factors?

In our earlier discussion, we saw that some groups (wealthy individuals, for example) have an incentive to pursue low-payout (or zero payout) stocks. Other groups (corporations, for example) have an incentive to pursue high-payout stocks. Companies with high payouts will thus attract one group, and low-payout companies will attract another.

clientele effect
Argument that stocks attract particular groups based on dividend yield and the resulting tax effects.

These different groups are called *clienteles,* and what we have described is a **clientele effect.** The clientele effect argument states that different groups of investors desire different levels of dividends. When a firm chooses a particular dividend policy, the only effect is to attract a particular clientele. If a firm changes its dividend policy, then it just attracts a different clientele.

What we are left with is a simple supply and demand argument. Suppose 40 percent of all investors prefer high dividends, but only 20 percent of the firms pay high dividends. Here the high-dividend firms will be in short supply; thus, their stock prices will rise. Consequently, low-dividend firms will find it advantageous to switch policies until 40 percent of all firms have high payouts. At this point, the *dividend market* is in equilibrium. Further changes in dividend policy are pointless because all of the clienteles are satisfied. The dividend policy for any individual firm is now irrelevant.

To see if you understand the clientele effect, consider the following statement: In spite of the theoretical argument that dividend policy is irrelevant or that firms should not pay dividends, many investors like high dividends; because of this fact, a firm can boost its share price by having a higher dividend payout ratio. True or false?

The answer is "false" if clienteles exist. As long as enough high-dividend firms satisfy the dividend-loving investors, a firm won't be able to boost its share price by paying high dividends. An unsatisfied clientele must exist for this to happen, and there is no evidence that this is the case.

CONCEPT QUESTIONS

14.2a Are dividends irrelevant?

14.2b What are some of the reasons for a low payout?

14.2c What are the implications of dividend clienteles for payout policies?

ESTABLISHING A DIVIDEND POLICY | 14.3

In this section, we focus on a particular approach to establishing a dividend policy that reflects many of the attitudes and objectives of financial managers as well as observed corporate dividend policies.

Residual Dividend Approach

Earlier, we noted that firms with higher dividend payouts will have to sell stock more often. As we have seen, such sales are not very common and they can be very expensive. Consistent with this, we will assume that the firm wishes to minimize the need to sell new equity. We will also assume that the firm wishes to maintain its current capital structure.

If a firm wishes to avoid new equity sales, then it will have to rely on internally generated cash flow to finance new, positive NPV projects.[2] Dividends can only be paid out of what is left over. This leftover is called the *residual,* and such a dividend policy is called a **residual dividend approach.**

With a residual dividend policy, the firm's objective is to meet its investment needs and maintain its desired debt-equity ratio before paying dividends. Given this objective, we expect those firms with many investment opportunities to pay a small percentage of their earnings as dividends and other firms with fewer opportunities to pay a high percentage of their earnings as dividends. This result appears to occur in the real world. Young, fast-growing firms commonly employ a low payout ratio, whereas older, slower-growing firms in more mature industries use a higher ratio.

residual dividend approach
Policy under which a firm pays dividends only after meeting its investment needs while maintaining a desired debt-equity ratio.

---

[2] Our discussion of sustainable growth in Chapter 3 is relevant here. We assumed there that a firm has a fixed capital structure, profit margin, and capital intensity. If the firm raises no new external equity and wishes to grow at some target rate, then there is only one payout ratio consistent with these assumptions.

Dividend Stability

The key point of the residual dividend approach is that dividends are paid only after all profitable investment opportunities are exhausted. Of course, a strict residual approach might lead to a very unstable dividend payout. If investment opportunities in one period are quite high, dividends will be low or zero. Conversely, dividends might be high in the next period if investment opportunities are considered less promising.

Consider the case of Big Department Stores, Inc., a retailer whose annual earnings are forecast to be equal from year to year but whose quarterly earnings change throughout the year. They are low in each year's first quarter because of the post-Christmas business slump. Although earnings increase only slightly in the second and third quarters, they advance greatly in the fourth quarter as a result of the Christmas season. A graph of this firm's earnings is presented in Figure 14.3.

The firm can choose between at least two types of dividend policies. First, each quarter's dividend can be a fixed fraction of that quarter's earnings. Here, dividends will vary throughout the year. This is a *cyclical dividend policy.* Second, each quarter's dividend can be a fixed fraction of yearly earnings, implying that all dividend payments would be equal. This is a *stable dividend policy.* These two types of dividend policies are displayed in Figure 14.4.

FIGURE 14.3

Earnings for Big Department Stores, Inc.

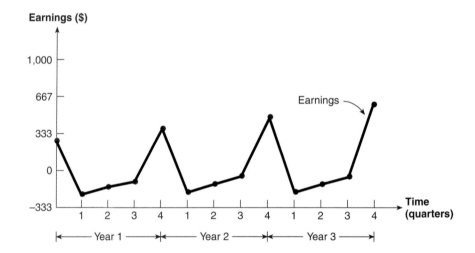

FIGURE 14.4

Alternative dividend policies for Big Department Stores, Inc.

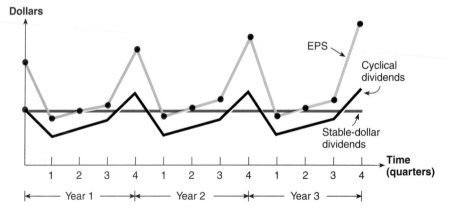

Cyclical dividend policy: Dividends are a constant proportion of earnings at each pay date.
Stable dividend policy: Dividends are a constant proportion of earnings over an earnings cycle.

Most financial managers would agree that a stable dividend policy is in the best interests of the firm and its stockholders. Dividend cuts in particular are viewed as highly undesirable because such cuts are often interpreted as a sign of financial distress. Consequently, most companies will try to maintain a steady dividend through time, increasing the dividend only when management is confident the new dividend can be sustained indefinitely.

A Compromise Dividend Policy

In practice, many firms appear to follow what amounts to a compromise dividend policy. Such a policy is based on five main goals:

1. Avoid cutting back on positive NPV projects to pay a dividend.
2. Avoid dividend cuts.
3. Avoid the need to sell equity.
4. Maintain a target debt-equity ratio.
5. Maintain a target dividend payout ratio.

These goals are ranked more or less in order of their importance. In our strict residual approach, we assume that the firm maintains a fixed debt-equity ratio. Under the compromise approach, the debt-equity ratio is viewed as a long-range goal. It is allowed to vary in the short run if necessary to avoid a dividend cut or the need to sell new equity.

In addition to showing a strong reluctance to cut dividends, financial managers tend to think of dividend payments in terms of a proportion of income, and they also tend to think investors are entitled to a "fair" share of corporate income. This share is the long-run **target payout ratio,** and it is the fraction of the earnings the firm expects to pay as dividends under ordinary circumstances. Again, this is viewed as a long-range goal, so dividends might vary in the short run if this is needed. In the long run, earnings growth is followed by dividend increases, but only with a lag.

target payout ratio
A firm's long-term desired dividend-to-earnings ratio.

One can minimize the problems of dividend instability by creating two types of dividends: regular and extra. For companies using this approach, the regular dividend would most likely be a relatively small fraction of permanent earnings, so that it could be sustained easily. Extra dividends would be granted when an increase in earnings was expected to be temporary.

Since investors look on an extra dividend as a bonus, there is relatively little disappointment when an extra dividend is not repeated. Although the extra-dividend approach appears quite sensible, few companies use it in practice. One reason is that a share repurchase, which we discuss next, does much the same thing with some extra advantages.

CONCEPT QUESTIONS

14.3a What is a residual dividend policy?

14.3b What is the chief drawback to a strict residual policy? What do many firms do in practice?

STOCK REPURCHASE: AN ALTERNATIVE TO CASH DIVIDENDS | 14.4

When a firm wants to pay cash to its shareholders, it normally pays a cash dividend. Another way is to **repurchase** its own stock. Stock repurchasing has been a major financial activity in recent years, and it appears that it will continue to be one.

repurchase
Refers to a firm's purchase of its own stock.

Cash Dividends versus Repurchase

Imagine an all-equity company with excess cash of $300,000. The firm pays no dividends, and its net income for the year just ended is $49,000. The market value balance sheet at the end of the year is represented below.

Market Value Balance Sheet
(before paying out excess cash)

Excess cash	$ 300,000	Debt	$ 0
Other assets	700,000	Equity	1,000,000
Total	$1,000,000	Total	$1,000,000

There are 100,000 shares outstanding. The total market value of the equity is $1 million, so the stock sells for $10 per share. Earnings per share, EPS, are $49,000/100,000 = $.49, and the price-earnings ratio, PE, is $10/.49 = 20.4.

One option the company is considering is a $300,000/100,000 = $3 per share extra cash dividend. Alternatively, the company is thinking of using the money to repurchase $300,000/10 = 30,000 shares of stock.

If commissions, taxes, and other imperfections are ignored in our example, the stockholders shouldn't care which option is chosen. Does this seem surprising? It shouldn't, really. What is happening here is that the firm is paying out $300,000 in cash. The new balance sheet is represented below.

Market Value Balance Sheet
(after paying out excess cash)

Excess cash	$ 0	Debt	$ 0
Other assets	700,000	Equity	700,000
Total	$700,000	Total	$700,000

If the cash is paid out as a dividend, there are still 100,000 shares outstanding, so each is worth $7.

The fact that the per-share value fell from $10 to $7 isn't a cause for concern. Consider a stockholder who owns 100 shares. At $10 per share before the dividend, the total value is $1,000.

After the $3 dividend, this same stockholder has 100 shares worth $7 each, for a total of $700, plus 100 × $3 = $300 in cash, for a combined total of $1,000. This just illustrates what we saw early on: A cash dividend doesn't affect a stockholder's wealth if there are no imperfections. In this case, the stock price simply fell by $3 when the stock went ex dividend.

Also, since total earnings and the number of shares outstanding haven't changed, EPS is still 49 cents. The price-earnings ratio, however, falls to $7/.49 = 14.3. Why we are looking at accounting earnings and PE ratios will be apparent just below.

Alternatively, if the company repurchases 30,000 shares, there will be 70,000 left outstanding. The balance sheet looks the same.

Market Value Balance Sheet
(after share purchase)

Excess cash	$ 0	Debt	$ 0
Other assets	700,000	Equity	700,000
Total	$700,000	Total	$700,000

The company is worth $700,000 again, so each remaining share is worth $700,000/70,000 = $10. Our stockholder with 100 shares is obviously unaffected. For example, if they were so inclined, they could sell 30 shares and end up with $300 in cash and $700 in stock, just as they have if the firm pays the cash dividend.

In this second case, EPS goes up since total earnings stay the same while the number of shares goes down. The new EPS will be $49,000/70,000 = $.70 per share. However, the important thing to notice is that the PE ratio is $10/.70 = 14.3, just as it was following the dividend.

This example illustrates the important point that, if there are no imperfections, a cash dividend and a share repurchase are essentially the same thing. This is just another illustration of dividend policy irrelevance when there are no taxes or other imperfections.

Real-World Considerations in a Repurchase

The example we have just described shows that a repurchase and a cash dividend are the same thing in a world without taxes and transaction costs. In the real world, there are some accounting differences between a share repurchase and a cash dividend, but the most important difference is in the tax treatment.

Under current tax law, a repurchase has a significant tax advantage over a cash dividend. A dividend is fully taxed as ordinary income, and a shareholder has no choice about whether or not to receive the dividend. In a repurchase, a shareholder pays taxes only if (1) the shareholder actually chooses to sell and (2) the shareholder has a capital gain on the sale.

If this advantage strikes you as being too good to be true, you are quite likely right. The IRS does not allow a repurchase solely for the purpose of avoiding taxes. There must be some other business-related reason for doing it. Probably the most common reason is that "the stock is a good investment." The second most common is that "investing in the stock is a good use for the money" or that "the stock is undervalued," and so on.

However it is justified, some corporations have engaged in massive repurchases in recent years. For example, despite an aggressive expansion campaign, Toys "R" Us still found itself with excess cash in 1994. It therefore announced a $1 billion share "buyback" (another term for a repurchase); at the then-current share price of $39, 12 percent of the outstanding stock would be repurchased. At about the same time, McDonald's announced plans to repurchase $1 billion worth of its common stock over the next three years. Based on the share price on the announcement date, this repurchase amounted to about 5 percent of the 350 million shares McDonald's had outstanding.

One cautionary note is in order concerning share repurchases, or buybacks. A company announcing plans to buy back some of its stock has no legal obligation to actually do it, and it turns out that many announced repurchases are never completed. Nonetheless, as the accompanying *Reality Bytes* box indicates, share buybacks are very big business, and they seem to be getting bigger and more common all the time.

reality BYTES

BUYBACKS GET BIGGER

Merck & Co., the pharmaceutical giant, made news in February 2000 when it announced plans to buy back $10 billion worth of its stock, thereby tying a record held on Wall Street for 11 years by General Electric. While the magnitude of the plan was news, share repurchase programs at Merck are not. The announced buyback was designed to augment the firm's yet to be completed $5 billion share repurchase program begun in 1998.

Merck was not alone in its plans. By the end of the third week in February 2000, Merck, along with 115 other firms, had announced a total of $34 billion in planned share repurchases, significantly more than the $25 billion in repurchases that had been announced during the same period in 1999. Firms jumping on the bandwagon included Anheuser-Busch Corp., Carnival Corp., and Hasbro, Inc. As these numbers suggest, buyback programs are both abundant and significant in terms of the dollars invested.

Firms generally institute share repurchase programs when they have an excess amount of cash on hand. Rather than increase the quarterly dividend payout, to a level they might not be able to sustain in the future, they turn to the next best alternative, a stock repurchase. When a firm repurchases shares of stock, it reduces the amount of equity outstanding. This increases earnings and cash flow per share and is viewed by many investors as a positive signal regarding the firm's future prospects. Thus, a firm's stock price often jumps when a share repurchase is announced as interest in the stock increases.

On the other hand, announced share repurchase plans are not required to be completed, and it is not uncommon for planned buybacks to fall by the wayside as conditions change. In 2000, for example, when Kimberly Clark announced plans to expand its share repurchase program by 25 million shares,

it said, "We expect to repurchase the newly authorized shares over the next few years. The actual number of shares we repurchase and the timing of the transactions will depend upon prevailing market conditions and other factors." This wording is fairly typical, leaving the door open to repurchase less stock than was initially announced.

Very often, the stated motivation for a repurchase is that the firm's management thinks its stock price is too low or that its stock is a good investment. However, if the stock price jumps before the share repurchase is completed, management may choose not to complete the repurchase at the higher price. For example, PepsiCo, Xerox Corp., and Hewlett-Packard all have share repurchase programs, but they tailor their repurchases to their cash balance, debt ratio, and PE ratio. Each of these three firms takes care to repurchase shares only if it won't unduly increase leverage and harm the firm's bond rating. A cautionary tale is that of FelCor Lodging, which specializes in hotels. When the firm expanded its share repurchase program in January 2000, Moody's Investors Services immediately lowered its bond ratings, noting that the additional repurchases would be paid for primarily with additional debt.

The total benefits of stock buybacks are difficult to pin down. For example, a 1997 study by Prudential Securities found that companies that reduced the number of shares outstanding by at least 1 percent outperformed their similar-sized peers by 3.7 percent to 5.0 percent annually. By contrast, a Credit Suisse First Boston analyst found that of the 50 companies in the S&P 500 index that undertook the most aggressive share repurchase programs in 1999, only 7 outperformed the index. However, despite the confusing evidence, one thing is clear: Investors and companies both seem to like share repurchases, and for good reason.

Share Repurchase and EPS

You may read in the popular financial press that a share repurchase is beneficial because earnings per share increases. As we have seen, this will happen. The reason is simply that a share repurchase reduces the number of outstanding shares, but it has no effect on total earnings. As a result, EPS rises.

However, the financial press may place undue emphasis on EPS figures in a repurchase agreement. In our example above, we saw that the value of the stock wasn't affected by the EPS change. In fact, the price-earnings ratio was exactly the same when we compared a cash dividend to a repurchase.

Since the increase in earnings per share is exactly tracked by the increase in the price per share, there is no net effect. Put another way, the increase in EPS is just an accounting adjustment that reflects (correctly) the change in the number of shares outstanding.

In the real world, to the extent that repurchases benefit the firm, we would argue that they do so primarily because of the tax considerations we discussed above.

CONCEPT QUESTIONS

14.4a Why might a stock repurchase make more sense than an extra cash dividend?

14.4b Why don't all firms use stock repurchases instead of cash dividends?

STOCK DIVIDENDS AND STOCK SPLITS | 14.5

Another type of dividend is paid out in shares of stock. This type of dividend is called a **stock dividend.** A stock dividend is not a true dividend because it is not paid in cash. The effect of a stock dividend is to increase the number of shares that each owner holds. Since there are more shares outstanding, each is simply worth less.

A stock dividend is commonly expressed as a percentage; for example, a 20 percent stock dividend means that a shareholder receives one new share for every five currently owned (a 20 percent increase). Since every shareholder owns 20 percent more stock, the total number of shares outstanding rises by 20 percent. As we will see in a moment, the result is that each share of stock is worth about 20 percent less.

A **stock split** is essentially the same thing as a stock dividend, except that a split is expressed as a ratio instead of a percentage. When a split is declared, each share is split up to create additional shares. For example, in a three-for-one stock split, each old share is split into three new shares.

By convention, stock dividends of less than 20 to 25 percent are called *small stock dividends*. A stock dividend greater than this 20 to 25 percent is called a *large stock dividend*. Large stock dividends are not uncommon. For example, in 1999, both Best Buy and Dell Computer declared 100 percent stock dividends, thereby doubling the number of outstanding shares. Except for some relatively minor accounting differences, this has the same effect as a two-for-one stock split.

stock dividend

Payment made by a firm to its owners in the form of stock, diluting the value of each share outstanding.

stock split

An increase in a firm's shares outstanding without any change in owners' equity.

Value of Stock Splits and Stock Dividends

The laws of logic tell us that stock splits and stock dividends can (1) leave the value of the firm unaffected, (2) increase its value, or (3) decrease its value. Unfortunately, the issues are complex enough that one cannot easily determine which of the three relationships holds.

The Benchmark Case   A strong case can be made that stock dividends and splits do not change either the wealth of any shareholder or the wealth of the firm as a whole. The reason is that they are just paper transactions and simply alter the number of shares outstanding. For example, if a firm declares a two-for-one split, all that happens is that the number of shares is doubled, with the result that each share is worth half as much. The total value is not affected.

Although this simple conclusion is relatively obvious, there are reasons that are often given to suggest that there may be some benefits to these actions. The typical financial manager is aware of many real-world complexities, and, for that reason, the stock split or stock dividend decision is not treated lightly in practice.

trading range

Price range between highest and lowest prices at which a stock is traded.

Popular Trading Range   Proponents of stock dividends and stock splits frequently argue that a security has a proper **trading range.** When the security is priced above this level, many investors do not have the funds to buy the common trading unit of 100 shares, called a *round lot.* Although securities can be purchased in *odd-lot* form (fewer than 100 shares), the commissions are greater. Thus, firms will split the stock to keep the price in this trading range.

Although this argument is a popular one, its validity is questionable for a number of reasons. Mutual funds, pension funds, and other institutions have steadily increased their trading activity since World War II and now handle a sizable percentage of total trading volume (on the order of 80 percent of NYSE trading volume, for example). Because these institutions buy and sell in huge amounts, the individual share price is of little concern.

Furthermore, we sometimes observe share prices that are quite large without appearing to cause problems. To take an extreme case, the largest company in the world (in terms of the total market value of outstanding equity) is the Japanese telecommunications giant NTT. In early 1994, NTT shares were selling for about $9,000 *each,* so a round lot would have cost a cool $900,000. This is fairly expensive, but the stock has sold for more than $20,000 per share. Closer to home, Berkshire-Hathaway, a widely respected company, sold for about $16,000 per share in 1994 (it was selling for $60,300 per share in the spring of 2000).

Finally, there is evidence that stock splits may actually decrease the liquidity of the company's shares. Following a two-for-one split, the number of shares traded should more than double if liquidity is increased by the split. This doesn't appear to happen, and the opposite is sometimes observed.

Reverse Splits

reverse split

Stock split under which a firm's number of shares outstanding is reduced.

A less frequently encountered financial maneuver is the **reverse split.** In a one-for-three reverse split, each investor exchanges three old shares for one new share. As was mentioned previously with reference to stock splits and stock dividends, a case can be made that a reverse split changes nothing substantial about the company.

Given real-world imperfections, three related reasons are cited for reverse splits. First, transaction costs to shareholders may be less after the reverse split. Second, the liquidity and marketability of a company's stock might be improved when its price is raised to the popular trading range. Third, stocks selling below a certain level are not considered respectable, meaning that investors underestimate these firms' earnings, cash flow, growth, and stability. Some financial analysts argue that a reverse split can achieve instant respectability. As was the case with stock splits, none of these reasons is particularly compelling, especially not the third one.

There are two other reasons for reverse splits. First, stock exchanges have minimum price per share requirements. A reverse split may bring the stock price up to such a minimum. Second, companies sometimes perform reverse splits and, at the same time, buy out any stockholders who end up with fewer than a certain number of shares. This second tactic can be abusive if it is used to force out minority shareholders.

CONCEPT QUESTIONS

14.5a What is the effect of a stock split on stockholder wealth?

14.5b What is a reverse split?

SUMMARY AND CONCLUSIONS

In this chapter, we first discussed the types of dividends and how they are paid. We then defined dividend policy and examined whether or not dividend policy matters. Next, we illustrated how a firm might establish a dividend policy and described an important alternative to cash dividends, a share repurchase.

In covering these subjects, we saw that:

1. Dividend policy is irrelevant when there are no taxes or other imperfections.

2. Individual shareholder income taxes and new issue flotation costs are real-world considerations that favor a low-dividend payout. With taxes and new issue costs, the firm should pay out dividends only after all positive NPV projects have been fully financed.

3. There are groups in the economy that may favor a high payout. These include many large institutions such as pension plans. Recognizing that some groups prefer a high payout and some prefer a low payout, the clientele effect supports the idea that dividend policy responds to the needs of stockholders. For example, if 40 percent of the stockholders prefer low dividends and 60 percent of the stockholders prefer high dividends, approximately 40 percent of companies will have a low-dividend payout, while 60 percent will have a high payout. This sharply reduces the impact of any individual firm's dividend policy on its market price.

4. A firm wishing to pursue a strict residual dividend payout will have an unstable dividend. Dividend stability is usually viewed as highly desirable. We therefore discussed a compromise strategy that provides for a stable dividend and appears to be quite similar to the dividend policies many firms follow in practice.

5. A stock repurchase acts much like a cash dividend, but has a significant tax advantage. Stock repurchases are therefore a very useful part of overall dividend policy.

To close out our discussion of dividends, we emphasize one last time the difference between dividends and dividend policy. Dividends are important, because the value of a share of stock is ultimately determined by the dividends that will be paid. What is less clear is whether or not the time pattern of dividends (more now versus more later) matters. This is the dividend policy question, and it is not easy to give a definitive answer to it.

CHAPTER REVIEW AND SELF-TEST PROBLEMS

14.1 Repurchase versus Cash Dividend. Trantor Corporation is deciding whether to pay out $300 in excess cash in the form of an extra dividend or a share repurchase. Current earnings are $1.50 per share, and the stock sells for $15. The market value balance sheet before paying out the $300 is as follows:

Market Value Balance Sheet
(before paying out excess cash)

Excess cash	$ 300	Debt	$ 400
Other assets	1,600	Equity	1,500
Total	$1,900	Total	$1,900

Evaluate the two alternatives in terms of the effect on the price per share of the stock, the EPS, and the PE ratio.

Answer to Chapter Review and Self-Test Problem

14.1   The market value of the equity is $1,500. The price per share is $15, so there are 100 shares outstanding. The cash dividend would amount to $300/100 = $3 per share. When the stock goes ex dividend, the price will drop by $3 per share to $12. Put another way, the total assets decrease by $300, so the equity value goes down by this amount to $1,200. With 100 shares, the new stock price is $12 per share. After the dividend, EPS will be the same, $1.50, but the PE ratio will be $12/1.50 = 8 times.

With a repurchase, $300/15 = 20 shares will be bought up, leaving 80. The equity will again be worth $1,200 total. With 80 shares, this is $1,200/80 = $15 per share, so the price doesn't change. Total earnings for Trantor must be $1.50 × 100 = $150. After the repurchase, EPS will be higher at $150/80 = $1.875. The PE ratio, however, will still be $15/1.875 = 8 times.

CRITICAL THINKING AND CONCEPTS REVIEW

1.   **Dividend Policy Irrelevance.**   How is it possible that dividends are so important, but, at the same time, dividend policy is irrelevant?

2.   **Stock Repurchases.**   What is the impact of a stock repurchase on a company's debt ratio? Does this suggest another use for excess cash?

3.   **Dividend Policy.**   What is the chief drawback to a strict residual dividend policy? Why is this a problem? How does a compromise policy work? How does it differ from a strict residual policy?

4.   **Dividend Chronology.**   On Tuesday, December 8, Hometown Power Co.'s board of directors declares a dividend of 75 cents per share payable on Wednesday, January 17, to shareholders of record as of Wednesday, January 3. When is the ex-dividend date? If a shareholder buys stock before that date, who gets the dividends on those shares, the buyer or the seller?

5.   **Alternative Dividends.**   Some corporations, like one British company that offers its large shareholders free crematorium use, pay dividends in kind (that is, offer their services to shareholders at below-market cost). Should mutual funds invest in stocks that pay these dividends in kind? (The fundholders do not receive these services.)

6.   **Dividends and Stock Price.**   If increases in dividends tend to be followed by (immediate) increases in share prices, how can it be said that dividend policy is irrelevant?

7.   **Dividends and Stock Price.**   Last month, Central Virginia Power Company, which had been having trouble with cost overruns on a nuclear power plant that it had been building, announced that it was "temporarily suspending payments due to the cash flow crunch associated with its investment program." The company's stock price dropped from $28.50 to $25 when this announcement was made. How would you interpret this change in the stock price (that is, what would you say caused it)?

8.   **Dividend Reinvestment Plans.**   The DRK Corporation has recently developed a dividend reinvestment plan (DRIP). The plan allows investors to reinvest cash dividends automatically in DRK in exchange for new shares of stock. Over time, investors in DRK will be able to build their holdings by reinvesting dividends to purchase additional shares of the company.

Over 1,000 companies offer dividend reinvestment plans. Most companies with DRIPs charge no brokerage or service fees. In fact, the shares of DRK will be purchased at a 10 percent discount from the market price.

A consultant for DRK estimates that about 75 percent of DRK's shareholders will take part in this plan. This is somewhat higher than the average.

Evaluate DRK's dividend reinvestment plan. Will it increase shareholder wealth? Discuss the advantages and disadvantages involved here.

9. **Dividend Policy.** For initial public offerings of common stock, 1999 was a very big year, with over $90 billion raised by the process. Relatively few of the almost 500 firms involved paid cash dividends. Why do you think that most chose not to pay cash dividends?

10. **Investment and Dividends.** The Phew Charitable Trust pays no taxes on its capital gains or on its dividend income or interest income. Would it be irrational for it to have low-dividend, high-growth stocks in its portfolio? Would it be irrational for it to have municipal bonds in its portfolio? Explain.

QUESTIONS AND PROBLEMS

1. **Dividends and Stock Prices.** Your portfolio is 200 shares of JCS, Inc. The stock currently sells for $75 per share. The company has announced a dividend of $1.25 per share with an ex-dividend date of April 19. Assuming no taxes, how much will your stock be worth on April 19?

Basic
(Questions 1–15)

2. **Dividends and Stock Prices.** It is April 19. Using the information in the previous problem, what is your total portfolio value?

3. **Dividends and Taxes.** What If, Inc., has declared a $3.00 per share dividend. Suppose capital gains are not taxed, but dividends are taxed at 34 percent. New IRS regulations require that taxes be withheld at the time the dividend is paid. What If sells for $70 per share, and the stock is about to go ex dividend. What do you think the ex-dividend price will be?

4. **Stock Dividends.** The owners' equity accounts for Pentagon International are shown here:

Common stock ($1 par value)	$ 8,000
Capital surplus	60,000
Retained earnings	221,000
Total owners' equity	$289,000

   a. If Pentagon stock currently sells for $30 per share and a 10 percent stock dividend is declared, how many new shares will be distributed? Show how the equity accounts would change.

   b. If Pentagon declared a 25 percent stock dividend, how would the accounts change?

5. **Stock Splits.** For the company in Problem 4, show how the equity accounts will change if:

   a. Pentagon declares a four-for-one stock split. How many shares are outstanding now? What is the new par value per share?

   b. Pentagon declares a one-for-five reverse stock split. How many shares are outstanding now? What is the new par value per share?

6. **Stock Splits and Stock Dividends.** Bermuda Triangle Corporation (BTC) currently has 300,000 shares of stock outstanding that sell for $80 per share. Assuming no market imperfections or tax effects exist, what will the share price be after:

    a. BTC has a five-for-three stock split?

    b. BTC has a 15 percent stock dividend?

    c. BTC has a 42.5 percent stock dividend?

    d. BTC has a four-for-seven reverse stock split?

    e. Determine the new number of shares outstanding in parts (*a*) through (*d*).

7.   **Regular Dividends.** The balance sheet for Penguins Pucks is shown here in market value terms. There are 15,000 shares of stock outstanding.

Market Value Balance Sheet

Cash	$ 25,000	Equity	$150,000
Fixed assets	125,000		
Total	$150,000	Total	$150,000

The company has declared a dividend of $1.25 per share. The stock goes ex dividend tomorrow. Ignoring any tax effects, what is the stock selling for today? What will it sell for tomorrow? What will the balance sheet look like after the dividends are paid?

8.   **Share Repurchase.** In the previous problem, suppose Penguins Pucks has announced it is going to repurchase $2,000 worth of stock instead of paying a dividend. What effect will this transaction have on the equity of the firm? How many shares will be outstanding? What will the price per share be after the repurchase? Ignoring tax effects, show how the share repurchase is effectively the same as a cash dividend.

9.   **Stock Dividends.** The market value balance sheet for Galloway Manufacturing is shown here. Galloway has declared a 20 percent stock dividend. The stock goes ex dividend tomorrow (the chronology for a stock dividend is similar to that for a cash dividend). There are 5,000 shares of stock outstanding. What will the ex-dividend price be?

Market Value Balance Sheet

Cash	$180,000	Debt	$200,000
Fixed assets	320,000	Equity	300,000
Total	$500,000	Total	$500,000

10.   **Stock Dividends.** The company with the common equity accounts shown here has declared a 6 percent stock dividend at a time when the market value of its stock is $10 per share. What effects on the equity accounts will the distribution of the stock dividend have?

Common stock ($1 par value)	$ 450,000
Capital surplus	1,550,000
Retained earnings	3,000,000
Total owners' equity	$5,000,000

11.   **Stock Splits.** In the previous problem, suppose the company instead decides on a five-for-one stock split. The firm's 55-cent per share cash dividend on the new (postsplit) shares represents an increase of 10 percent over last year's dividend on the presplit stock. What effect does this have on the equity accounts? What was last year's dividend per share?

12. **Residual Dividend Policy.** Pete and Repete, a litter recycling company, uses a residual dividend policy. A debt-equity ratio of .80 is considered optimal. Earnings for the period just ended were $1,800, and a dividend of $780 was declared. How much in new debt was borrowed? What were total capital outlays?

13. **Residual Dividend Policy.** Key West Corporation has declared an annual dividend of $2.00 per share. For the year just ended, earnings were $9 per share.
    a. What is Key West's payout ratio?
    b. Suppose Key West has seven million shares outstanding. Borrowing for the coming year is planned at $13 million. What are planned investment outlays assuming a residual dividend policy? What target capital structure is implicit in these calculations?

14. **Residual Dividend Policy.** Nearside Corporation follows a strict residual dividend policy. Its debt-equity ratio is 2.
    a. If earnings for the year are $800,000, what is the maximum amount of capital spending possible with no new equity?
    b. If planned investment outlays for the coming year are $3 million, will Nearside pay a dividend? If so, how much?
    c. Does Nearside maintain a constant dividend payout? Why or why not?

15. **Residual Dividend Policy.** Wildcat, Inc., predicts that earnings in the coming year will be $30 million. There are eight million shares, and Wildcat maintains a debt-equity ratio of 1.5.
    a. Calculate the maximum investment funds available without issuing new equity and the increase in borrowing that goes along with it.
    b. Suppose the firm uses a residual dividend policy. Planned capital expenditures total $40 million. Based on this information, what will the dividend per share be?
    c. In part (b), how much borrowing will take place? What is the addition to retained earnings?
    d. Suppose Wildcat plans no capital outlays for the coming year. What will the dividend be under a residual policy? What will new borrowing be?

16. **Homemade Dividends.** You own 1,000 shares of stock in Edsel Communications. You will receive a $1 per share dividend in one year. In two years, Edsel will pay a liquidating dividend of $40 per share. The required return on Edsel stock is 15 percent. What is the current share price of your stock (ignoring taxes)? If you would rather have equal dividends in each of the next two years, show how you can accomplish this by creating homemade dividends. (Hint: Dividends will be in the form of an annuity.)

17. **Homemade Dividends.** In the previous problem, suppose you want only $400 total in dividends the first year. What will your homemade dividend be in two years?

18. **Stock Repurchase.** Jagr Corporation is evaluating an extra dividend versus a share repurchase. In either case, $4,800 would be spent. Current earnings are $1.20 per share, and the stock currently sells for $40 per share. There are 300 shares outstanding. Ignore taxes and other imperfections in answering the first two questions.
    a. Evaluate the two alternatives in terms of the effect on the price per share of the stock and shareholder wealth.
    b. What will be the effect on Jagr's EPS and PE ratio under the two different scenarios?
    c. In the real world, which of these actions would you recommend? Why?

Intermediate
(Questions 16–18)

www.mhhe.com/rwj

Spreadsheet Templates 1, 6, 12

Raising Capital

**AFTER VENTURING THROUGH THIS CHAPTER,
YOU SHOULD UNDERSTAND:**

■ The venture capital market and its role in the
financing of new, high-risk ventures

■ How securities are sold to the public and the role of
investment banks in the process

■ Initial public offerings and some of the costs of
going public

ON JULY 21, 1999, MP3.com was born as a publicly traded company. On that day the firm completed its initial public offering, or IPO, by selling stock to the public for the first time. The investment turned out to be a smart one for the lucky buyers. MP3.com's stock price closed at $63.3125 per share that first day, which amounted to a one-day gain of 126 percent! The offering gave MP3.com the financing it needed to grow its business, and, as you might imagine, MP3.com was not alone. In fact, 1999 was a big year for IPOs. Even after excluding issues with low offering prices and those with unusual features, MP3.com's IPO was just 1 of about 450 offerings for the year. In addition, for the year, 117 of the IPOs doubled in value (or did better) during their first day of trading. By comparison, in the 25 years from 1974 to 1998, only 39 IPOs doubled in value on their first day of trading. What is more, 1999 sported the then-biggest one-day price gain of 698 percent, for VA Linux shares, and the then-biggest IPO ever, by United Parcel Service (UPS). In this chapter, we will examine the process by which companies like MP3.com, VA Linux, and UPS sell stock to the public, the costs of doing so, and the role of investment banks in the process.

Businesses large and small have one thing in common: They need long-term capital. This chapter describes how they get it. We pay particular attention to what is probably the most important stage in a company's financial life cycle, the initial public offering. Such offerings are the process by which companies convert from being privately owned to being publicly owned. For many, starting a company, growing it, and taking it public is the ultimate entrepreneurial dream.

All firms must, at varying times, obtain capital. To do so, a firm must either borrow the money (debt financing), sell a portion of the firm (equity financing), or both. How a firm raises capital depends a great deal on the size of the firm, its life cycle stage, and its growth prospects.

In this chapter, we examine some of the ways in which firms actually raise capital. We begin by looking at companies in the early stages of their lives and the importance of venture capital for such firms. We then look at the process of going public and the role of investment banks. Along the way, we discuss many of the issues associated with selling securities to the public and their implications for all types of firms. We close the chapter with a discussion of sources of debt capital.[1]

15.1 | THE FINANCING LIFE CYCLE OF A FIRM: EARLY-STAGE FINANCING AND VENTURE CAPITAL

One day, you and a friend have a great idea for a new computer software product that helps users communicate using the Internet. Filled with entrepreneurial zeal, you christen the product InterComm and set about bringing it to market.[2]

Working nights and weekends, you are able to create a prototype of your product. It doesn't actually work, but at least you can show it around to illustrate your idea. To actually develop the product, you need to hire programmers, buy computers, rent office space, and so on. Unfortunately, because you are both college students, your combined assets are not sufficient to fund a pizza party, much less a start-up company. You need what is often referred to as OPM—other people's money.

Your first thought might be to approach a bank for a loan. You would probably discover, however, that banks are generally not interested in making loans to start-up companies with no assets (other than an idea) run by fledgling entrepreneurs with no track record. Instead, your search for capital would very likely lead you to the **venture capital (VC)** market.

venture capital (VC)

Financing for new, often high-risk ventures.

Venture Capital

The term *venture capital* does not have a precise meaning, but it generally refers to financing for new, often high-risk ventures. For example, before it went public, Internet auctioneer eBay was VC financed. Individual venture capitalists invest their own money, whereas venture capital firms specialize in pooling funds from various sources and investing them. The underlying sources of funds for such firms include individuals, pension funds, insurance companies, large corporations, and even university endowment funds.[3]

Venture capitalists and venture capital firms recognize that many or even most new ventures will not fly, but the occasional one will. The potential profits are enormous in such cases. To limit their risk, venture capitalists generally provide financing in stages. At each stage, enough money is invested to reach the next milestone or planning stage. For example, the *first-stage* (or first "round") *financing* might be enough to get a prototype built and a manufacturing plan completed. Based on the results, the *second-stage financing* might be a major investment needed to actually begin manufacturing, marketing, and distribution. There

---

[1]We are indebted to Jay R. Ritter of the University of Florida for helpful comments and suggestions on this chapter.

[2]Neat name, don't you think?

[3]So-called vulture capitalists specialize in high-risk investments in established, but financially distressed, firms.

might be many such stages, each of which represents a key step in the process of growing the company.

Venture capital firms often specialize in different stages. Some specialize in very early "seed money," or ground floor, financing. In contrast, financing in the later stages might come from venture capitalists specializing in so-called mezzanine level financing, where *mezzanine level* refers to the level just above the ground floor.

The fact that financing is available in stages and is contingent on specified goals being met is a powerful motivating force for the firm's founders. Often, the founders receive relatively little in the way of salary and have substantial portions of their personal assets tied up in the business. At each stage of financing, the value of the founder's stake grows and the probability of success rises.

In addition to providing financing, venture capitalists often actively participate in running the firm, providing the benefit of experience with previous start-ups as well as general business expertise. This is especially true when the firm's founders have little or no hands-on experience in running a company.

Some Venture Capital Realities

Although there is a large venture capital market, the truth is that access to venture capital is really very limited. Venture capital companies receive huge numbers of unsolicited proposals, the vast majority of which end up in the circular file unread. Venture capitalists rely heavily on informal networks of lawyers, accountants, bankers, and other venture capitalists to help identify potential investments. As a result, personal contacts are important in gaining access to the venture capital market; it is very much an "introduction" market.

Another simple fact about venture capital is that it is incredibly expensive. In a typical deal, the venture capitalist will demand (and get) 40 percent or more of the equity in the company. The venture capitalist will frequently hold voting preferred stock, which gives various priorities in the event that the company is sold or liquidated. The venture capitalist will typically demand (and get) several seats on the company's board of directors and may even appoint one or more members of senior management.

Choosing a Venture Capitalist

Some start-up companies, particularly those headed by experienced, previously successful entrepreneurs, will be in such demand that they will have the luxury of looking beyond the money in choosing a venture capitalist. There are some key considerations in such a case, some of which can be summarized as follows:

1. Financial strength is important. The venture capitalist needs to have the resources and financial reserves for additional financing stages should they become necessary. This doesn't mean that bigger is necessarily better, however, because of our next consideration.

2. Style is important. Some venture capitalists will wish to be very much involved in day-to-day operations and decision making, whereas others will be content with monthly reports. Which is better depends on the firm and also on the venture capitalists' business skills. In addition, a large venture capital firm may be less flexible and more bureaucratic than a smaller "boutique" firm.

3. References are important. Has the venture capitalist been successful with similar firms? Of equal importance, how has the venture capitalist dealt with situations that didn't work out?

4. Contacts are important. A venture capitalist may be able to help the business in ways other than helping with financing and management by providing introductions to potentially important customers, suppliers, and other industry contacts. Venture capital-

ist firms frequently specialize in a few particular industries, and such specialization could prove quite valuable.

5. Exit strategy is important. Venture capitalists are generally not long-term investors. How and under what circumstances the venture capitalist will "cash out" of the business should be carefully evaluated.

Conclusion

If a start-up succeeds, the big payoff frequently comes when the company is sold to another company or goes public. Either way, investment bankers are often involved in the process.

CONCEPT QUESTIONS

15.1a What is venture capital?

15.1b Why is venture capital often provided in stages?

15.2 | SELLING SECURITIES TO THE PUBLIC: THE BASIC PROCEDURE

We discuss the process of selling securities to the public in the next several sections, paying particular attention to the process of going public.

There are many rules and regulations surrounding the process of selling securities. The Securities Act of 1933 is the origin of federal regulations for all new interstate securities issues. The Securities Exchange Act of 1934 is the basis for regulating securities already outstanding. The Securities and Exchange Commission, or SEC, administers both acts.

There is a series of steps involved in issuing securities to the public. In general terms, the basic procedure is as follows:

1. Management's first step in issuing any securities to the public is to obtain approval from the board of directors. In some cases, the number of authorized shares of common stock must be increased. This requires a vote of the shareholders.

registration statement
A statement filed with the SEC that discloses all material information concerning the corporation making a public offering.

2. The firm must prepare a **registration statement** and file it with the SEC. The registration statement is required for all public, interstate issues of securities, with two exceptions:

   a. Loans that mature within nine months
   b. Issues that involve less than $5 million

The second exception is known as the *small-issues exemption.* In such a case, simplified procedures are used. Under the basic small-issues exemption, issues of less than $5 million are governed by **Regulation A,** for which only a brief offering statement is needed. Normally, however, a registration statement contains many pages (50 or more) of financial information, including a financial history, details of the existing business, proposed financing, and plans for the future.

Regulation A
An SEC regulation that exempts public issues of less than $5 million from most registration requirements.

prospectus
A legal document describing details of the issuing corporation and the proposed offering to potential investors.

3. The SEC examines the registration statement during a waiting period. During this time, the firm may distribute copies of a preliminary **prospectus.** The prospectus contains much of the information put into the registration statement, and it is given to potential investors by the firm. The preliminary prospectus is sometimes called a **red herring,** in part because bold red letters are printed on the cover.

A registration statement becomes effective on the 20th day after its filing unless the SEC sends a *letter of comment* suggesting changes. In that case, after the changes are made, the 20-day waiting period starts again. It is important to note that the SEC does not consider the economic merits of the proposed sale; it merely makes sure that various rules and regulations are followed. Also, the SEC generally does not check the accuracy or truthfulness of information in the prospectus.

The registration statement does not initially contain the price of the new issue. Usually, a price amendment is filed at or near the end of the waiting period, and the registration becomes effective.

red herring

A preliminary prospectus distributed to prospective investors in a new issue of securities.

4. The company cannot sell these securities during the waiting period. However, oral offers can be made.

5. On the effective date of the registration statement, a price is determined and a full-fledged selling effort gets under way. A final prospectus must accompany the delivery of securities or confirmation of sale, whichever comes first.

Tombstone advertisements (or, simply, tombstones) are used by underwriters during and after the waiting period. An example is reproduced in Figure 15.1. The tombstone contains the name of the issuer (the World Wrestling Federation, or WWF, in this case). It provides some information about the issue, and it lists the investment banks (the underwriters) that are involved with selling the issue. The role of the investment banks in selling securities is discussed more fully in the following pages.

tombstone

An advertisement announcing a public offering.

The investment banks are divided into groups called *brackets* on the tombstone, based on their participation in the issue, and the names of the banks are listed alphabetically within each bracket. The brackets are often viewed as a kind of pecking order. In general, the higher the bracket, the greater is the underwriter's prestige.

CONCEPT QUESTIONS

15.2a What are the basic procedures in selling a new issue?

15.2b What is a registration statement?

ALTERNATIVE ISSUE METHODS | 15.3

When a company decides to issue a new security, it can sell it as a public issue or a private issue. In the case of a public issue, the firm is required to register the issue with the SEC. However, if the issue is to be sold to fewer than 35 investors, the sale can be carried out privately. In this case, a registration statement is not required.[4]

general cash offer

An issue of securities offered for sale to the general public on a cash basis.

For equity sales, there are two kinds of public issues: a **general cash offer** and a **rights offer** (or *rights offering*). With a cash offer, securities are offered to the general public on a "first come, first served" basis. With a rights offer, securities are initially offered only to existing owners. Rights offers are fairly common in other countries, but they are relatively rare in the United States, particularly in recent years. We therefore focus on cash offers in this chapter.

rights offer

A public issue of securities in which securities are first offered to existing shareholders. Also called a rights offering.

The first public equity issue that is made by a company is referred to as an **initial public offering,** IPO, or an *unseasoned new issue.* This issue occurs when a company decides to go public. Obviously, all initial public offerings are cash offers. If the firm's existing

initial public offering

A company's first equity issue made available to the public. Also called an unseasoned new issue or an IPO.

---

[4]A variety of different arrangements can be made for private equity issues. Selling unregistered securities avoids the costs of complying with the Securities Exchange Act of 1934. Regulation significantly restricts the resale of unregistered equity securities. For example, the purchaser may be required to hold the securities for at least two years. Many of the restrictions were significantly eased in 1990 for very large institutional investors, however. The private placement of bonds is discussed in a later section.

An example of a tombstone advertisement

This announcement is neither an offer to sell nor a solicitation of an offer to buy any of these securities. The offering is made only by the Prospectus.

New Issue

11,500,000 Shares

World Wrestling Federation Entertainment, Inc.

Class A Common Stock

Price $17.00 Per Share

Copies of the Prospectus may be obtained in any State in which this announcement is circulated from only such of the Underwriters, including the undersigned, as may lawfully offer these securities in such State.

U.S. Offering

9,200,000 Shares

This portion of the underwriting is being offered in the United States and Canada.

Bear, Stearns & Co. Inc.

Credit Suisse First Boston

Merrill Lynch & Co.

Wit Capital Corporation

Allen & Company Incorporated	Banc of America Securities LLC	Deutsche Banc Alex. Brown
Donaldson, Lufkin & Jenrette	A.G. Edwards & Sons, Inc.	Hambrecht & Quist ING Barings
Prudential Securities SG Cowen	Wassertein Perella Securities, Inc.	Advest, Inc.
Axiom Capital Management, Inc.	Blackford Securities Corp.	J.C. Bradford & Co.
Joseph Charles & Assoc., Inc.	Chatsworth Securities LLC	Gabelli & Company, Inc.
Gaines, Berland Inc. Jefferies & Company, Inc.	Josephthal & Co. Inc.	Neuberger Berman, LLC
Raymond James & Associates, Inc.		Sanders Morris Mundy
Tucker Anthony Cleary Gull		Wachovia Securities, Inc.

International Offering

2,300,000 Shares

This portion of the underwriting is being offered outside of the United States and Canada.

Bear, Stearns International Limited

Credit Suisse First Boston

Merrill Lynch International

Method	Type	Definition	
Public			**TABLE 15.1**
Traditional negotiated cash offer	Firm commitment cash offer	Company negotiates an agreement with an investment banker to underwrite and distribute the new stocks. A specified number of shares are bought by underwriters and sold at a higher price.	The methods of issuing new securities
	Best efforts cash offer	Company has investment bankers sell as many of the new shares as possible at the agreed-upon price. There is no guarantee concerning how much cash will be raised.	
Privileged subscription	Direct rights offer	Company offers the new stock directly to its existing shareholders.	
	Standby rights offer	Like the direct rights offer, this contains a privileged subscription arrangement with existing shareholders. The net proceeds are guaranteed by the underwriters.	
Nontraditional cash offer	Shelf cash offer	Qualifying companies can authorize all the shares they expect to sell over a two-year period and sell them when needed.	
	Competitive firm cash offer	Company can elect to award the underwriting contract through a public auction instead of negotiation.	
Private	Direct placement	Securities are sold directly to the purchaser, who, at least until recently, generally could not resell securities for at least two years.	

shareholders wanted to buy the shares, the firm wouldn't have to sell them publicly in the first place.

A **seasoned equity offering (SEO)** is a new issue for a company with securities that have been previously issued.[5] A seasoned equity offering of common stock can be made by using a cash offer or a rights offer.

These methods of issuing new securities are shown in Table 15.1. They are discussed in sections 15.4 through 15.9.

seasoned equity offering (SEO)
A new equity issue of securities by a company that has previously issued securities to the public.

CONCEPT QUESTIONS

15.3a Why is an initial public offering necessarily a cash offer?

15.3b What is the difference between a rights offer and a cash offer?

UNDERWRITERS | 15.4

If the public issue of securities is a cash offer, **underwriters** are usually involved. Underwriting is an important line of business for large investment firms such as Merrill Lynch. Underwriters perform services such as the following for corporate issuers:

1. Formulating the method used to issue the securities
2. Pricing the new securities
3. Selling the new securities

underwriters
Investment firms that act as intermediaries between a company selling securities and the investing public.

---

[5]The terms *secondary* and *follow-on offering* are also commonly used.

Typically, the underwriter buys the securities for less than the offering price and accepts the risk of not being able to sell them. Because underwriting involves risk, underwriters combine to form an underwriting group called a **syndicate** to share the risk and to help sell the issue.

syndicate

A group of underwriters formed to share the risk and to help sell an issue.

In a syndicate, one or more managers arrange, or co-manage, the offering. This manager is designated as the lead manager, or principal manager. The lead manager typically has the responsibility of pricing the securities. The other underwriters in the syndicate serve primarily to distribute the issue.

spread

Compensation to the underwriter, determined by the difference between the underwriter's buying price and offering price.

The difference between the underwriter's buying price and the offering price is called the **spread,** or discount. It is the basic compensation received by the underwriter. Sometimes the underwriter will get noncash compensation in the form of warrants and stock in addition to the spread.[6]

Choosing an Underwriter

A firm can offer its securities to the highest bidding underwriter on a *competitive offer* basis, or it can negotiate directly with an underwriter. Except for a few large firms, companies usually do new issues of debt and equity on a *negotiated offer* basis. The exception is public utility holding companies, which are essentially required to use competitive underwriting.

There is evidence that competitive underwriting is cheaper to use than negotiated underwriting, and the underlying reasons for the dominance of negotiated underwriting in the United States are the subject of ongoing debate.

Types of Underwriting

Two basic types of underwriting are involved in a cash offer: firm commitment and best efforts.

firm commitment underwriting

The type of underwriting in which the underwriter buys the entire issue, assuming full financial responsibility for any unsold shares.

Firm Commitment Underwriting   In **firm commitment underwriting,** the issuer sells the entire issue to the underwriters, who then attempt to resell it. This is the most prevalent type of underwriting in the United States. This is really just a purchase-resale arrangement, and the underwriter's fee is the spread. For a new issue of seasoned equity, the underwriters can look at the market price to determine what the issue should sell for, and 95 percent of all such new issues are firm commitments.

If the underwriter cannot sell all of the issue at the agreed-upon offering price, it may have to lower the price on the unsold shares. Nonetheless, with firm commitment underwriting, the issuer receives the agreed-upon amount, and all the risk associated with selling the issue is transferred to the underwriter.

Because the offering price usually isn't set until the underwriters have investigated how receptive the market is to the issue, this risk is usually minimal. Also, because the offering price usually is not set until just before selling commences, the issuer doesn't know precisely what its net proceeds will be until that time.

best efforts underwriting

The type of underwriting in which the underwriter sells as much of the issue as possible, but can return any unsold shares to the issuer without financial responsibility.

Best Efforts Underwriting   In **best efforts underwriting,** the underwriter is legally bound to use "best efforts" to sell the securities at the agreed-upon offering price. Beyond this, the underwriter does not guarantee any particular amount of money to the issuer. This form of underwriting has become rather uncommon in recent years; firm commitments are now the dominant form.

---

[6]Warrants are essentially options to buy stock at a fixed price for some fixed period of time.

The Aftermarket

The period after a new issue is initially sold to the public is referred to as the *aftermarket*. During this time, the members of the underwriting syndicate generally do not sell securities for less than the offering price.

The principal underwriter is permitted to buy shares if the market price falls below the offering price. The purpose of this would be to support the market and stabilize the price against temporary downward pressure. If the issue remains unsold after a time (for example, 30 days), members can leave the group and sell their shares at whatever price the market will allow.[7]

The Green Shoe Provision

Many underwriting contracts contain a **Green Shoe provision** (sometimes called the *overallotment option*), which gives the members of the underwriting group the option to purchase additional shares from the issuer at the offering price.[8] Essentially all IPOs and SEOs include this provision, but ordinary debt offerings generally do not. The stated reason for the Green Shoe option is to cover excess demand and oversubscriptions. Green Shoe options usually last for about 30 days and involve no more than 15 percent of the newly issued shares.

The Green Shoe option is a benefit to the underwriting syndicate and a cost to the issuer. If the market price of the new issue goes above the offering price within 30 days, the Green Shoe option allows the underwriters to buy shares from the issuer and immediately resell the shares to the public.

Green Shoe provision
A contract provision giving the underwriter the option to purchase additional shares from the issuer at the offering price. Also called the overallotment option.

Lockup Agreements

Although they are not required by law, almost all underwriting contracts contain so-called **lockup agreements.** Such agreements specify how long insiders must wait after an IPO before they can sell some or all of their stock. Lockup periods have become fairly standardized in recent years at 180 days. Thus, following an IPO, insiders can't cash out until six months have gone by, which ensures that they maintain a significant economic interest in the company going public.

Lockup periods are also important because it is not unusual for the number of locked-up shares to exceed the number of shares held by the public, sometimes by a substantial multiple. On the day the lockup period expires, there is the possibility that a large number of shares will hit the market on the same day and thereby depress values. The evidence suggests that, on average, venture capital–backed companies are particularly likely to experience a loss in value on the lockup expiration day.

lockup agreement
The part of the underwriting contract that specifies how long insiders must wait after an IPO before they can sell stock.

CONCEPT QUESTIONS

15.4a What do underwriters do?

15.4b What is the Green Shoe provision?

---

[7]Occasionally, the price of a security falls dramatically when the underwriter ceases to stabilize the price. In such cases, Wall Street humorists (the ones who didn't buy any of the stock) have referred to the period following the aftermarket as the aftermath.

[8]The term *Green Shoe provision* sounds quite exotic, but the origin is relatively mundane. The term comes from the name of the Green Shoe Company, which, in 1963, was the first issuer to grant such an option.

15.5 | IPOS AND UNDERPRICING

Determining the correct offering price is the most difficult thing an underwriter must do for an initial public offering. The issuing firm faces a potential cost if the offering price is set too high or too low. If the issue is priced too high, it may be unsuccessful and have to be withdrawn. If the issue is priced below the true market value, the issuer's existing shareholders will experience an opportunity loss when they sell their shares for less than they are worth.

Underpricing is fairly common. It obviously helps new shareholders earn a higher return on the shares they buy. However, the existing owners of the issuing firm are not helped by underpricing. To them, it is an indirect cost of issuing new securities. For example, eToys, a two-year-old on-line retailer, went public in May of 1999. Assisted by the investment bank of Goldman Sachs, eToys sold 8.2 million shares to the public at $20 per share, raising a total of $164 million. The stock was eagerly received by investors. At the end of the first day, the stock was trading for $77 per share, down from a high of $85 reached in frenzied trading. Based on the end-of-day numbers, eToys's shares were apparently underpriced by about $57 each, meaning that the company missed out on an additional $467.4 million, or almost half a billion dollars! In fact, at the high of $85, eToys was worth about 50 percent more than its "brick and mortar" competitor Toys "R" Us, even though Toys "R" Us's revenues were several hundred times larger.

Evidence on Underpricing

Figure 15.2 provides a more general illustration of the underpricing phenomenon. What is shown is the month-by-month history of underpricing for SEC-registered IPOs.[9] The period covered is 1960 through 1999. Figure 15.3 presents the number of offerings in each month for the same period.

Figure 15.2 shows that underpricing can be quite dramatic, exceeding 100 percent in some months. In such months, the average IPO more than doubled in value, sometimes in a matter of hours. Also, the degree of underpricing varies through time, and periods of severe underpricing ("hot issue" markets) are followed by periods of little underpricing ("cold issue" markets). For example, in the 1960s, the average IPO was underpriced by 21.25 percent. In the 1970s, the average underpricing was much smaller (8.95 percent), and the amount of underpricing was actually very small or even negative for much of that time. Finally, for 1990–99, IPOs were underpriced by 20.6 percent on average.

From Figure 15.3, it is apparent that the number of IPOs is also highly variable through time. Further, there are pronounced cycles in both the degree of underpricing and the number of IPOs. Comparing Figures 15.2 and 15.3, we see that increases in the number of new offerings tend to follow periods of significant underpricing by roughly 6 to 12 months. This probably occurs because companies decide to go public when they perceive that the market is highly receptive to new issues.

Table 15.2 contains a year-by-year summary of underpricing for the years 1975 to 1999. As is indicated, a grand total of 6,584 companies were included in this analysis. The degree of underpricing averaged 15.6 percent overall for the 25 years examined. Securities were overpriced on average in only 1 of the 25 years; in 1975 the average decrease in value was −1.5 percent. At the other extreme, in 1999, the 485 issues were underpriced, on average, by a remarkable 69.5 percent. The nearby *Reality Bytes* box shows that IPO underpricing is not just confined to the U.S.; instead, it seems to be a global phenomenon.

---

[9]The discussion in this section draws on Roger G. Ibbotson, Jody L. Sindelar, and Jay R. Ritter, "The Market's Problems with the Pricing of Initial Public Offerings," *Journal of Applied Corporate Finance 7* (Spring 1994).

Average first-day returns by month for SEC-registered initial public offerings: 1960–99   **FIGURE 15.2**

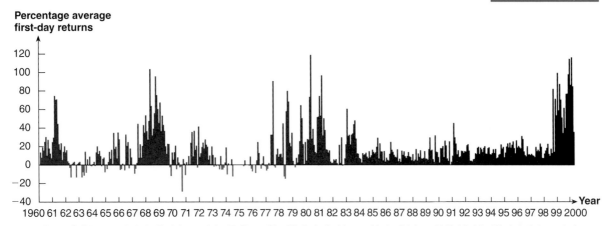

Source: Roger G. Ibbotson, Jody L. Sindelar, and Jay R. Ritter, "The Market's Problems with the Pricing of Initial Public Offerings," *Journal of Applied Corporate Finance* 7 (Spring 1994), as updated by the authors.

Number of offerings by month for SEC-registered initial public offerings: 1960–99   **FIGURE 15.3**

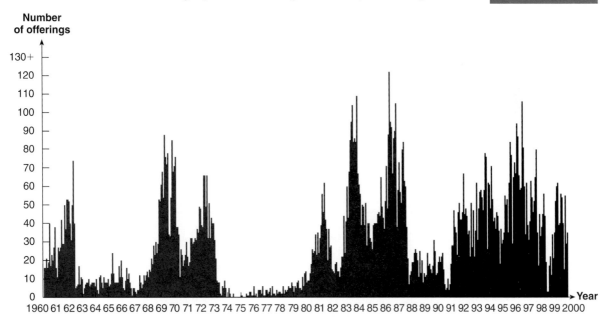

Source: Roger G. Ibbotson, Jody L. Sindelar, and Jay R. Ritter, "The Market's Problems with the Pricing of Initial Public Offerings," *Journal of Applied Corporate Finance* 7 (Spring 1994), as updated by the authors.

Underpricing: The 1999 Experience

Table 15.2, along with Figures 15.2 and 15.3, shows that 1999 was an extraordinary year in the IPO market. Almost 500 companies went public, which is a large number, but not a record. What is much more striking is that, as Table 15.2 shows, the average first-day return was 69.5 percent, by far the largest over the 25 years covered in the table.

In fact, all but one of the top 25 first-day gains occurred in 1999, the lone exception being theglobe.com's 1998 IPO. During the year, 117 IPOs doubled, or more than doubled, in value on the first day. In contrast, only 39 did so in the preceding 24 years combined. Finally,

TABLE 15.2

Number of offerings, average first-day returns, and gross proceeds of initial public offerings: 1975–99

Year	Number of Offerings*	Average First-Day Return (%)†	Gross Proceeds ($ in millions)‡
1975	12	−1.5	262
1976	26	1.9	214
1977	15	3.6	127
1978	20	11.2	209
1979	39	8.5	312
1980	78	15.2	962
1981	202	6.4	2,386
1982	83	10.6	1,081
1983	523	8.8	12,047
1984	227	2.6	3,012
1985	215	6.2	5,488
1986	464	6.0	16,195
1987	322	5.5	12,160
1988	121	5.6	4,053
1989	113	7.8	5,212
1990	111	10.5	4,453
1991	287	11.7	15,765
1992	396	10.0	22,198
1993	503	12.6	29,232
1994	412	9.7	18,103
1995	464	21.1	28,866
1996	664	16.7	41,916
1997	483	13.7	33,216
1998	319	20.0	34,856
1999	485	69.5	64,752
1975–79	112	5.7	1,124
1980–89	2,348	6.9	62,596
1990–99	4,124	20.9	293,357
Total	6,584	15.6	357,077

*The number of offerings excludes IPOs with an offer price of less than $5.00, American Depository Receipts (ADRs), best efforts offers, unit offers, Regulation A offerings (small issues, raising less than $1.5 million during the 1980s), real estate investment trusts (REITs), partnerships, and closed-end funds.

†First-day returns are computed as the percentage return from the offering price to the first closing market price.

‡Gross proceeds data are from Securities Data Co. and exclude overallotment options but include the international tranche, if any. No adjustments for inflation have been made. These data differ from those used in Figures 15.1 and 15.2 because of the exclusion of unit offerings and best efforts in all years and the exclusion of IPOs with an offer price of less than $5.00. The proceeds exclude ADRs but include the international tranche of domestic offerings. In some years, the net effect is to substantially lower the aggregate proceeds.

Source: Professor Jay R. Ritter, University of Florida.

the biggest one-day return ever was recorded by VA Linux, whose shares skyrocketed 700 percent (!), and the $4.38 billion IPO of United Parcel Service (UPS) was the biggest to date.

The dollar amount raised in 1999 by newly public companies, almost $70 billion, was also a record (the previous high was $50 billion in 1996). However, because the underpricing was so severe, companies left another $36 billion "on the table," which was substantially more than in 1990 through 1998 combined. In other words, in the aggregate, companies going public in 1999 missed out on $36 billion because of underpricing.

October 19 was one of the more memorable days in 1999. The World Wrestling Federation (WWF) and Martha Stewart Living Omnimedia both went public, so it was Martha

IPO UNDERPRICING AROUND THE WORLD

The United States is not the only country in which initial public offerings of common stock, IPOs, are underpriced. The phenomenon exists in every country with a stock market, although the amount of underpricing varies from country to country.

The 1980s and 1990s saw thousands of companies go public. Outside of the United States, certain industries, such as airlines and telephone companies, were almost entirely owned by governments 20 years ago. In the last two decades, however, firms in these industries have been "privatized" in many countries.

In many emerging markets, many of the firms going public have been old family businesses or government-owned enterprises, and their IPOs haven't always gone smoothly. The extreme example is China, where "A" shares, which can only be owned by Chinese citizens, have frequently seen first-day price jumps (initial returns) of several hundred percent.

The table below gives a summary of the average initial returns on IPOs in a number of countries around the world, with the figures collected from a number of studies by various authors.

Source: Jay R. Ritter is Cordell Professor of Finance at the University of Florida.

Country	Sample Size	Time Period	Average Initial Return	Country	Sample Size	Time Period	Average Initial Return
Australia	381	1976–95	12.1%	Malaysia	401	1980–98	104.1
Austria	76	1984–99	6.5	Mexico	37	1987–90	33.0
Belgium	28	1984–90	10.1	Netherlands	143	1982–99	10.2
Brazil	62	1979–90	78.5	New Zealand	201	1979–99	23.0
Canada	258	1971–92	5.4	Nigeria	63	1989–93	19.1
Chile	55	1982–97	8.8	Norway	68	1984–96	12.5
China	226	1990–96	388.0	Philippines	104	1987–97	22.7
Denmark	117	1984–98	5.4	Poland	149	1991–98	35.6
Finland	85	1984–92	9.6	Portugal	62	1986–87	54.4
France	187	1983–92	4.2	Singapore	128	1973–92	31.4
Germany	407	1978–99	27.7	Spain	71	1985–90	35.0
Greece	79	1987–91	48.5	Sweden	251	1980–94	34.1
Hong Kong	334	1980–96	15.9	Switzerland	42	1983–89	35.8
India	98	1992–93	35.3	Taiwan	241	1986–95	34.6
Israel	28	1993–94	4.5	Thailand	32	1988–89	58.1
Italy	135	1985–98	20.3	Turkey	138	1990–96	13.6
Japan	975	1970–96	24.0	United Kingdom	2,557	1959–99	12.5
Korea	347	1980–90	78.1	United States	14,376	1960–99	17.4

Stewart versus "Stone Cold" Steve Austin in a Wall Street version of MTV's *Celebrity Deathmatch.* Proving that good taste (usually) triumphs, it was a clear smack-down as Martha Stewart gained 98 percent on the first day compared to 48 percent for the WWF.

Why Does Underpricing Exist?

Based on the evidence we've examined, an obvious question is, Why does underpricing continue to exist? As we discuss, there are various explanations, but, to date, there is a lack of complete agreement among researchers as to which is correct.

431

Average first-day
returns, categorized by
sales, for IPOs:
1983–99*

Annual Sales of Issuing Firms	Number of Firms	1983–89 First-Day Average Return	Number of Firms	1990–98 First-Day Average Return	Number of Firms	1999 First-Day Average Return
$0<Sales<$10m	154	6.8%	587	17.9%	168	75.8%
$10m≤Sales<$20m	135	8.7	392	18.9	80	88.5
$20m≤Sales<$50m	301	8.4	763	17.2	99	80.6
$50m≤Sales<$100m	213	5.8	535	13.4	48	59.8
$100m≤Sales<$200m	160	3.4	399	11.2	31	27.8
$200m≤Sales	195	3.3	555	9.0	38	19.8

*Data are from Securities Data Co., with corrections by the author. All sales have been converted into dollars of January 1999 purchasing power, using the Consumer Price Index. Sales are for the last 12 months prior to going public. There are 4,853 IPOs, after excluding IPOs with an offer price of less than $5.00 per share, unit offerings, REITs, ADRs, closed-end funds, and those with zero or missing sales. The average first-day return is 18.0 percent. Sales are measured in millions.
Source: Professor Jay R. Ritter, University of Florida.

We present some pieces of the underpricing puzzle by stressing two important caveats to our preceding discussion. First, the average figures we have examined tend to obscure the fact that much of the apparent underpricing is attributable to the smaller, more highly speculative issues. This point is illustrated in Table 15.3, which shows the extent of underpricing for 4,853 firms over the period from 1983 through 1999. Here, the firms are grouped based on their total sales in the 12 months prior to the IPO.

As illustrated in Table 15.3, there is a tendency for underpricing to be more pronounced for firms with relatively small pre-IPO sales. These firms tend to be young firms, and such young firms can be very risky investments. Arguably, they must be significantly underpriced, on average, just to attract investors, and this is one explanation for the underpricing phenomenon.

The second caveat is that relatively few IPO buyers will actually get the initial high average returns observed in IPOs, and many will actually lose money. Although it is true that, on average, IPOs have positive initial returns, a significant fraction of them have price drops. Furthermore, when the price is too low, the issue is often "oversubscribed." This means investors will not be able to buy all of the shares they want, and the underwriters will allocate the shares among investors.

The average investor will find it difficult to get shares in a "successful" offering (one in which the price increases) because there will not be enough shares to go around. On the other hand, an investor blindly submitting orders for IPOs tends to get more shares in issues that go down in price.

To illustrate, consider this tale of two investors. Smith knows very accurately what the Bonanza Corporation is worth when its shares are offered. She is confident that the shares are underpriced. Jones knows only that prices usually rise one month after an IPO. Armed with this information, Jones decides to buy 1,000 shares of every IPO. Does he actually earn an abnormally high return on the initial offering?

The answer is no, and at least one reason is Smith. Knowing about the Bonanza Corporation, Smith invests all her money in its IPO. When the issue is oversubscribed, the underwriters have to somehow allocate the shares between Smith and Jones. The net result is that when an issue is underpriced, Jones doesn't get to buy as much of it as he wanted.

Smith also knows that the Blue Sky Corporation IPO is overpriced. In this case, she avoids its IPO altogether, and Jones ends up with a full 1,000 shares. To summarize this tale,

Jones gets fewer shares when more knowledgeable investors swarm to buy an underpriced issue and gets all he wants when the smart money avoids the issue.

This is an example of a "winner's curse," and it is thought to be another reason why IPOs have such a large average return. When the average investor "wins" and gets the entire allocation, it may be because those who knew better avoided the issue. The only way underwriters can counteract the winner's curse and attract the average investor is to underprice new issues (on average) so that the average investor still makes a profit.

A final reason for underpricing is that the underpricing is a kind of insurance for the investment banks. Conceivably, an investment bank could be sued successfully by angry customers if it consistently overpriced securities. Underpricing guarantees that, at least on average, customers will come out ahead.

CONCEPT QUESTIONS

15.5a Why is underpricing a cost to the issuing firm?

15.5b Suppose a stockbroker calls you up out of the blue and offers to sell you "all the shares you want" of a new issue. Do you think the issue will be more or less underpriced than average?

NEW EQUITY SALES AND THE VALUE OF THE FIRM | 15.6

We now turn to a consideration of seasoned offerings, which, as we discussed earlier, are offerings by firms that already have outstanding securities. It seems reasonable to believe that new long-term financing is arranged by firms after positive net present value projects are put together. As a consequence, when the announcement of external financing is made, the firm's market value should go up. Interestingly, this is not what happens. Stock prices tend to decline following the announcement of a new equity issue, although they tend to not change much following a debt announcement. A number of researchers have studied this issue. Plausible reasons for this strange result include the following:

1. **Managerial information.** If management has superior information about the market value of the firm, it may know when the firm is overvalued. If it does, it will attempt to issue new shares of stock when the market value exceeds the correct value. This will benefit existing shareholders. However, the potential new shareholders are not stupid, and they will anticipate this superior information and discount it in lower market prices at the new issue date.

2. **Debt usage.** A company's issuing new equity may reveal that the company has too much debt or too little liquidity. One version of this argument says that the equity issue is a bad signal to the market. After all, if the new projects are favorable ones, why should the firm let new shareholders in on them? It could just issue debt and let the existing shareholders have all the gain.

3. **Issue costs.** As we discuss next, there are substantial costs associated with selling securities.

The drop in value of the existing stock following the announcement of a new issue is an example of an indirect cost of selling securities. This drop might typically be on the order of 3 percent for an industrial corporation (and somewhat smaller for a public utility), so, for a large company, it can represent a substantial amount of money. We label this drop the *abnormal return* in our discussion of the costs of new issues that follows.

CONCEPT QUESTIONS

15.6a What are some possible reasons why the price of stock drops on the announcement of a new equity issue?

15.6b Explain why we might expect a firm with a positive NPV investment to finance it with debt instead of equity.

15.7 THE COST OF ISSUING SECURITIES

Issuing securities to the public isn't free, and the costs of different methods are important determinants of which is used. These costs associated with *floating* a new issue are generically called *flotation costs*. In this section, we take a closer look at the flotation costs associated with equity sales to the public.

The costs of selling stock are classified in the following table and fall into six categories: (1) the spread, (2) other direct expenses, (3) indirect expenses, (4) abnormal returns (discussed previously), (5) underpricing, and (6) the Green Shoe option.

The Costs of Issuing Securities	
1. Spread	The spread consists of direct fees paid by the issuer to the underwriting syndicate—the difference between the price the issuer receives and the offer price.
2. Other direct expenses	These are direct costs incurred by the issuer that are not part of the compensation to underwriters. These costs include filing fees, legal fees, and taxes—all reported on the prospectus.
3. Indirect expenses	These costs are not reported on the prospectus and include the cost of management time spent working on the new issue.
4. Abnormal returns	In a seasoned issue of stock, the price of the existing stock drops on average by 3 percent upon the announcement of the issue. This drop is called the abnormal return.
5. Underpricing	For initial public offerings, losses arise from selling the stock below the true value.
6. Green Shoe option	The Green Shoe option gives the underwriters the right to buy additional shares at the offer price to cover overallotments.

Table 15.4 reports direct costs as a percentage of the gross amount raised for IPOs, SEOs, straight (ordinary) bonds, and convertible bonds sold by U.S. companies over the five-year period from 1990 through 1994. These are direct costs only. Not included are indirect expenses, the cost of the Green Shoe provision, underpricing (for IPOs), and abnormal returns (for SEOs).

As Table 15.4 shows, the direct costs alone can be very large, particularly for smaller issues (less than $10 million). On a smaller IPO, for example, the total direct costs amount to 16.96 percent of the amount raised. This means that if a company sells $10 million in stock, it will only net about $8.3 million; the other $1.7 million goes to cover the underwriter spread and other direct expenses. Typical underwriter spreads on an IPO range from about 5 percent up to 10 percent or so, but, for about half of the IPOs in Table 15.4, the

Direct costs as a percentage of gross proceeds for equity (IPOs and SEOs) and straight and convertible bonds offered by domestic operating companies: 1990–94

TABLE 15.4

	Equity							
	IPOs				SEOs			
Proceeds ($ in millions)	Number of Issues	Gross Spread	Other Direct Expense	Total Direct Cost	Number of Issues	Gross Spread	Other Direct Expense	Total Direct Cost
2–9.99	337	9.05%	7.91%	16.96%	167	7.72%	5.56%	13.28%
10–19.99	389	7.24	4.39	11.63	310	6.23	2.49	8.72
20–39.99	533	7.01	2.69	9.70	425	5.60	1.33	6.93
40–59.99	215	6.96	1.76	8.72	261	5.05	.82	5.87
60–79.99	79	6.74	1.46	8.20	143	4.57	.61	5.18
80–99.99	51	6.47	1.44	7.91	71	4.25	.48	4.73
100–199.99	106	6.03	1.03	7.06	152	3.85	.37	4.22
200–499.99	47	5.67	.86	6.53	55	3.26	.21	3.47
500 and up	10	5.21	.51	5.72	9	3.03	.12	3.15
Total	1,767	7.31%	3.69%	11.00%	1,593	5.44%	1.67%	7.11%

	Bonds							
	Convertible Bonds				Straight Bonds			
Proceeds ($ in millions)	Number of Issues	Gross Spread	Other Direct Expense	Total Direct Cost	Number of Issues	Gross Spread	Other Direct Expense	Total Direct Cost
2–9.99	4	6.07%	2.68%	8.75%	32	2.07%	2.32%	4.39%
10–19.99	14	5.48	3.18	8.66	78	1.36	1.40	2.76
20–39.99	18	4.16	1.95	6.11	89	1.54	.88	2.42
40–59.99	28	3.26	1.04	4.30	90	.72	.60	1.32
60–79.99	47	2.64	.59	3.23	92	1.76	.58	2.34
80–99.99	13	2.43	.61	3.04	112	1.55	.61	2.16
100–199.99	57	2.34	.42	2.76	409	1.77	.54	2.31
200–499.99	27	1.99	.19	2.18	170	1.79	.40	2.19
500 and up	3	2.00	.09	2.09	20	1.39	.25	1.64
Total	211	2.92%	.87%	3.79%	1,092	1.62%	.62%	2.24%

Source: Inmoo Lee, Scott Lochhead, Jay Ritter, and Quanshui Zhao, "The Costs of Raising Capital," *Journal of Financial Research* 1 (Spring 1996).

spread is exactly 7 percent, so this is, by far, the most common spread. The nearby *Reality Bytes* box provides a detailed example for a particular company.

Overall, four clear patterns emerge from Table 15.4. First of all, with the possible exception of straight debt offerings (about which we will have more to say later), there are substantial economies of scale. The underwriter spreads are smaller on larger issues, and the other direct costs fall sharply as a percentage of the amount raised, a reflection of the mostly fixed nature of such costs. Second, the costs associated with selling debt are substantially less than the costs of selling equity. Third, IPOs have higher expenses than SEOs, but the difference is not as great as might originally be guessed. Finally, straight bonds are cheaper to float than convertible bonds.

As we have discussed, the underpricing of IPOs is an additional cost to the issuer. To give a better idea of the total cost of going public, Table 15.5 combines the information in

ANATOMY OF AN IPO

In June 1996, Multicom Publishing Inc., a CD-ROM publisher based in Seattle, went public via an IPO. Multicom issued 1.1 million shares of stock at a price of $6.50 each, 345,000 of which were sold by Multicom's lead underwriter, Laidlaw Equities of New York City, and 755,000 of which were sold by a syndicate made up of 25 other investment banking firms. Multicom's shares were listed on the Nasdaq Small-Cap Market following the IPO.

Even though the IPO raised a gross sum of $7.15 million, Multicom actually got to keep less than $6 million after expenses. The largest cost was the underwriter spread. Multicom sold each of the 1.1 million shares to the underwriters for $5.98, and the underwriters in turn sold these shares to the public for $6.50 each. Thus, of the $7.15 million investors paid for the shares, Multicom received only about $6.6 million. In addition, Multicom paid $145,000 to the underwriters to defray expenses incurred.

But wait, there's more. Multicom also spent $57,590 on fees to the Securities and Exchange Commission, along with exchange and listing fees. In addition, as a direct result of the public offering, Multicom spent $100,000 for insurance for directors and officers, $150,000 on accounting to obtain the necessary audits, $10,000 for a transfer agent to physically transfer the shares and maintain a list of shareholders, $75,000 for printing and engraving expenses, $200,000 for legal fees and expenses, and, finally, $12,049 for miscellaneous expenses.

As Multicom's outlays show, an IPO can be a costly undertaking! In the end, Multicom's expenses totaled $1,321,639, of which $717,000 went to the underwriters and $604,639 went to other parties. The total cost to Multicom was 18.5 percent of the issue proceeds. Still, the company may have gotten off cheap at that price. As of December 31, 1996, Multicom's stock price closed at $1.625, never having traded for higher than $7.25 a share for the year. This was clearly one IPO that investors would have been better off avoiding.

Source: *Follow the Money, Inc.* 19, no. 8 (June 1997), pp. 80–81.

Table 15.4 for IPOs with data on the underpricing experienced by these firms. Comparing the total direct costs (in the fifth column) to the underpricing (in the sixth column), we see that they are roughly the same size, so the direct costs are only about half of the total. Overall, across all size groups, the total direct costs amount to 11 percent of the amount raised and the underpricing amounts to 12 percent.

Finally, with regard to debt offerings, there is a general pattern in issue costs that is somewhat obscured in Table 15.4. Recall from Chapter 6 that bonds carry different credit ratings. Higher-rated bonds are said to be investment grade, whereas lower-rated bonds are noninvestment grade. Table 15.6 contains a breakdown of direct costs for bond issues after the investment and noninvestment grades have been separated.

Table 15.6 clarifies three things regarding debt issues. First, there are substantial economies of scale here as well. Second, investment-grade issues have much lower direct costs, particularly for straight bonds. Finally, there are relatively few noninvestment-grade issues in the smaller size categories, reflecting the fact that such issues are more commonly handled as private placements, which we discuss in our next section.

CONCEPT QUESTIONS

15.7a What are the different costs associated with security offerings?

15.7b What lessons do we learn from studying issue costs?

Proceeds ($ in millions)	Number of Issues	Gross Spread	Other Direct Expense	Total Direct Cost	Underpricing
2–9.99	337	9.05%	7.91%	16.96%	16.36%
10–19.99	389	7.24	4.39	11.63	9.65
20–39.99	533	7.01	2.69	9.70	12.48
40–59.99	215	6.96	1.76	8.72	13.65
60–79.99	79	6.74	1.46	8.20	11.31
80–99.99	51	6.47	1.44	7.91	8.91
100–199.99	106	6.03	1.03	7.06	7.16
200–499.99	47	5.67	.86	6.53	5.70
500 and up	10	5.21	.51	5.72	7.53
Total	1,767	7.31%	3.69%	11.00%	12.05%

TABLE 15.5

Direct and indirect costs, in percentages, of equity IPOs: 1990–94

Source: Inmoo Lee, Scott Lochhead, Jay Ritter, and Quanshui Zhao, "The Costs of Raising Capital," *Journal of Financial Research* 1 (Spring 1996).

TABLE 15.6

Average gross spreads and total direct costs for domestic debt issues: 1990–94

	Convertible Bonds					
	Investment Grade			Noninvestment Grade		
Proceeds ($ in millions)	Number of Issues	Gross Spread	Total Direct Cost	Number of Issues	Gross Spread	Total Direct Cost
2–9.99	0	—	—	0	—	—
10–19.99	0	—	—	1	4.00%	5.67%
20–39.99	1	1.75%	2.75%	9	3.29	4.92
40–59.99	3	1.92	2.43	19	3.37	4.58
60–79.99	4	1.31	1.76	41	2.76	3.37
80–99.99	2	1.07	1.34	10	2.83	3.48
100–199.99	20	2.03	2.33	37	2.51	3.00
200–499.99	17	1.71	1.87	10	2.46	2.70
500 and up	3	2.00	2.09	0	—	—
Total	50	1.81%	2.09%	127	2.81%	3.53%

	Straight Bonds					
	Investment Grade			Noninvestment Grade		
Proceeds ($ in millions)	Number of Issues	Gross Spread	Total Direct Cost	Number of Issues	Gross Spread	Total Direct Cost
2–9.99	14	.58%	2.19%	0	—	—
10–19.99	56	.50	1.19	2	5.13%	7.41%
20–39.99	64	.86	1.48	9	3.11	4.42
40–59.99	78	.47	.94	9	2.48	3.35
60–79.99	49	.61	.98	43	3.07	3.84
80–99.99	65	.66	.94	47	2.78	3.75
100–199.99	181	.57	.81	222	2.75	3.44
200–499.99	60	.50	.93	105	2.56	2.96
500 and up	11	.39	.57	9	2.60	2.90
Total	578	.58%	.94%	446	2.75%	3.42%

Source: Inmoo Lee, Scott Lochhead, Jay Ritter, and Quanshui Zhao, "The Costs of Raising Capital," *Journal of Financial Research* 1 (Spring 1996).

15.8 | ISSUING LONG-TERM DEBT

The general procedures followed in a public issue of bonds are the same as those for stocks. The issue must be registered with the SEC, there must be a prospectus, and so on. The registration statement for a public issue of bonds, however, is different from the one for common stock. For bonds, the registration statement must indicate an indenture.

Another important difference is that more than 50 percent of all debt is issued privately. There are two basic forms of direct private long-term financing: term loans and private placement.

term loans

Direct business loans of, typically, one to five years.

Term loans are direct business loans. These loans have maturities of between one year and five years. Most term loans are repayable during the life of the loan. The lenders include commercial banks, insurance companies, and other lenders that specialize in corporate finance. **Private placements** are very similar to term loans except that the maturity is longer.

private placements

Loans, usually long-term in nature, provided directly by a limited number of investors.

The important differences between direct private long-term financing and public issues of debt are:

1. A direct long-term loan avoids the cost of Securities and Exchange Commission registration.

2. Direct placement is likely to have more restrictive covenants.

3. It is easier to renegotiate a term loan or a private placement in the event of a default. It is harder to renegotiate a public issue because hundreds of holders are usually involved.

4. Life insurance companies and pension funds dominate the private-placement segment of the bond market. Commercial banks are significant participants in the term-loan market.

5. The costs of distributing bonds are lower in the private market.

The interest rates on term loans and private placements are often higher than those on an equivalent public issue. This difference may reflect the trade-off between a higher interest rate and more flexible arrangements in the event of financial distress, as well as the lower costs associated with private placements.

An additional, and very important, consideration is that the flotation costs associated with selling debt are much less than the comparable costs associated with selling equity.

CONCEPT QUESTIONS

15.8a What is the difference between private and public bond issues?

15.8b A private placement is likely to have a higher interest rate than a public issue. Why?

15.9 | SHELF REGISTRATION

To simplify the procedures for issuing securities, in March 1982, the SEC adopted Rule 415 on a temporary basis, and it was made permanent in November 1983. Rule 415 allows shelf registration. Both debt and equity securities can be shelf registered.

Shelf registration permits a corporation to register an offering that it reasonably expects to sell within the next two years and then sell the issue whenever it wants during that two-year period. For example, on February 18, 2000, computing product giant Hewlett-Packard (HP) announced a shelf registration to sell up to $3 billion in bonds, preferred and common stock, and other securities. According to HP, the shelf registration allowed it to "register securities in advance and sell them from time to time as financing needs arise or as favorable market conditions arise."

Not all companies can use Rule 415. The primary qualifications are:

1. The company must be rated investment grade.
2. The firm cannot have defaulted on its debt in the past three years.
3. The aggregate market value of the firm's outstanding stock must be more than $150 million.
4. The firm must not have had a violation of the Securities Act of 1934 in the past three years.

The rule has been controversial. Arguments have been constructed against shelf registration:

1. The costs of new issues might go up because underwriters might not be able to provide as much current information to potential investors as they would otherwise, so investors would pay less. The expense of selling the issue piece by piece might therefore be higher than that of selling it all at once.
2. Some investment bankers have argued that shelf registration will cause a "market overhang" that will depress market prices. In other words, the possibility that the company could increase the supply of stock at any time will have a negative impact on the current stock price. There is little evidence to support this position, however.

shelf registration
Registration permitted by SEC Rule 415, which allows a company to register all issues it expects to sell within two years at one time, with subsequent sales at any time within those two years.

CONCEPT QUESTIONS

15.9a What is shelf registration?

15.9b What are the arguments against shelf registration?

SUMMARY AND CONCLUSIONS

This chapter has looked at how corporate securities are issued. The following are the main points:

1. The venture capital market is a primary source of financing for new high-risk companies.
2. The costs of issuing securities can be quite large. They are much lower (as a percentage) for larger issues.
3. Firm commitment underwriting is far more prevalent for large issues than best efforts underwriting. This is probably connected to the uncertainty of smaller issues. For a given size offering, the direct expenses of best efforts underwriting and firm commitment underwriting are of the same magnitude.
4. The direct and indirect costs of going public can be substantial. However, once a firm is public it can raise additional capital with much greater ease.

CHAPTER REVIEW AND SELF-TEST PROBLEM

15.1 Flotation Costs.　The L5 Corporation is considering an equity issue to finance a new space station. A total of $10 million in new equity is needed. If the direct costs are estimated at 6 percent of the amount raised, how large does the issue need to be? What is the dollar amount of the flotation cost?

Answer to Chapter Review and Self-Test Problem

15.1 The firm needs to net $10 million after paying the 6 percent flotation costs. So the amount raised is given by:

Amount raised $\times$ (1 – .06) = $10 million

Amount raised = $10/.94 = $10.638 million

The total flotation cost is thus $638,000.

CRITICAL THINKING AND CONCEPTS REVIEW

1. **Debt versus Equity Offering Size.** In the aggregate, debt offerings are much more common than equity offerings and typically much larger as well. Why?

2. **Debt versus Equity Flotation Costs.** Why are the costs of selling equity so much larger than the costs of selling debt?

3. **Bond Ratings and Flotation Costs.** Why do noninvestment-grade bonds have much higher direct costs than investment-grade issues?

4. **Underpricing in Debt Offerings.** Why is underpricing not a great concern with bond offerings?

   Use the following information in answering the next three questions: Netscape Communications, maker of Internet and World Wide Web software, went public in August of 1995. Assisted by the investment bank of Morgan Stanley, Netscape sold five million shares at $28 each, thereby raising a total of $140 million. At the end of the first day of trading, the stock sold for $58.25 per share, down from a high of $71 reached earlier in the day in frenzied trading. Based on the end-of-day numbers, Netscape's shares were apparently underpriced by about $30 each, meaning that the company missed out on an additional $150 million.

5. **IPO Pricing.** The Netscape IPO was severely underpriced. This occurred even though the offering price of $28 had already been doubled from a planned $14 just weeks earlier. Should Netscape be upset with Morgan Stanley over the remaining underpricing?

6. **IPO Pricing.** In the previous question, would it affect your thinking to know that, at the time of the IPO, Netscape was only 16 months old, had only $16.6 million in revenues for the first half of the year, had never earned a profit, and was giving away its primary product over the Internet for free?

7. **IPO Pricing.** In the previous two questions, would it affect your thinking to know that, of 38 million shares total in Netscape, only 5 million were actually offered to the public? The remaining 33 million were retained by various founders of the company. For example, 24-year-old Marc Andreessen held a million shares, so he picked up $58.3 million for his 16-month effort (and that didn't include options he held to buy more shares).

8. **IPO Underpricing.** In 1980, a certain assistant professor of finance bought 12 initial public offerings of common stock. He held each of these for approximately one month and then sold. The investment rule he followed was to submit a purchase order for every firm commitment initial public offering of oil and gas exploration companies. There were 22 of these offerings, and he submitted a purchase order for approximately $1,000 in stock for each of the companies. With 10 of these, no shares were allocated to this assistant professor. With 5 of the 12 offerings that were purchased, fewer than the requested number of shares were allocated.

The year 1980 was very good for oil and gas exploration company owners: on average, for the 22 companies that went public, the stocks were selling for 80 percent above the offering price a month after the initial offering date. The assistant professor looked at his performance record and found that the $8,400 invested in the 12 companies had grown to $10,000, representing a return of only about 20 percent (commissions were negligible). Did he have bad luck, or should he have expected to do worse than the average initial public offering investor? Explain.

9.   **IPO Pricing.**   The following material represents the cover page and summary of the prospectus for the initial public offering of the Pest Investigation Control Corporation (PICC), which is going public tomorrow with a firm commitment initial public offering managed by the investment banking firm of Erlanger and Ritter. Answer the following questions:

 a. Assume that you know nothing about PICC other than the information contained in the prospectus. Based on your knowledge of finance, what is your prediction for the price of PICC tomorrow? Provide a short explanation of why you think this will occur.

 b. Assume that you have several thousand dollars to invest. When you get home from class tonight, you find that your stockbroker, whom you have not talked to for weeks, has called. She has left a message that PICC is going public tomorrow and that she can get you several hundred shares at the offering price if you call her back first thing in the morning. Discuss the merits of this opportunity.

PROSPECTUS   PICC

200,000 shares
PEST INVESTIGATION CONTROL CORPORATION

Of the shares being offered hereby, all 200,000 are being sold by the Pest Investigation Control Corporation, Inc. ("the Company"). Before the offering there has been no public market for the shares of PICC, and no guarantee can be given that any such market will develop.

These securities have not been approved or disapproved by the SEC nor has the commission passed upon the accuracy or adequacy of this prospectus. Any representation to the contrary is a criminal offense.

	Price to Public	Underwriting Discount	Proceeds to Company*
Per share	$11.00	$1.10	$9.90
Total	$2,200,000	$220,000	$1,980,000

*Before deducting expenses estimated at $27,000 and payable by the Company.

This is an initial public offering. The common shares are being offered, subject to prior sale, when, as, and if delivered to and accepted by the Underwriters and subject to approval of certain legal matters by their Counsel and by Counsel for the Company. The Underwriters reserve the right to withdraw, cancel, or modify such offer and to reject offers in whole or in part.

Erlanger and Ritter, Investment Bankers
July 12, 2000

Prospectus Summary

The Company	The Pest Investigation Control Corporation (PICC) breeds and markets toads and tree frogs as ecologically safe insect-control mechanisms.
The Offering	200,000 shares of common stock, no par value.
Listing	The Company will seek listing on Nasdaq and will trade over the counter.
Shares Outstanding	As of June 30, 2000, 400,000 shares of common stock were outstanding. After the offering, 600,000 shares of common stock will be outstanding.
Use of Proceeds	To finance expansion of inventory and receivables and general working capital, and to pay for country club memberships for certain finance professors.

Selected Financial Information
(amounts in thousands except per-share data)

	Fiscal Year Ended June 30		
	1998	**1999**	**2000**
Revenues	$60.00	$120.00	$240.00
Net earnings	3.80	15.90	36.10
Earnings per share	.01	.04	.09

	As of June 30, 2000	
	Actual	**As Adjusted for This Offering**
Working capital	$ 8	$1,961
Total assets	511	2,464
Stockholders' equity	423	2,376

QUESTIONS AND PROBLEMS

Basic
(Questions 1–7)

1. **IPO Underpricing.** The Wren Co. and the Stumpy Co. have both announced IPOs at $30 per share. One of these is undervalued by $4, and the other is overvalued by $4, but you have no way of knowing which is which. You plan on buying 1,000 shares of each issue. If an issue is underpriced, it will be rationed, and only half your order will be filled. If you *could* get 1,000 shares in Wren and 1,000 shares in Stumpy, what would your profit be? What profit do you actually expect? What principle have you illustrated?

2. **Calculating Flotation Costs.** The Lambert Corporation needs to raise $42 million to finance its expansion into new markets. The company will sell new shares of equity via a general cash offering to raise the needed funds. If the offer price is $75 per share and the company's underwriters charge an 8 percent spread, how many shares need to be sold?

3. **Calculating Flotation Costs.** In the previous problem, if the SEC filing fee and associated administrative expenses of the offering are $500,000, how many shares need to be sold now?

4. **Calculating Flotation Costs.** The Taylor Co. has just gone public. Under a firm commitment agreement, Taylor received $22 for each of the 2.5 million shares sold. The initial offering price was $24 per share, and the stock rose to $29 per share in the first few minutes of trading. Taylor paid $300,000 in legal and other direct costs, and $150,000 in indirect costs. What was the flotation cost as a percentage of funds raised?

5. **Calculating Flotation Costs.** The Fenton Corporation needs to raise $26 million to finance its expansion into new markets. The company will sell new shares of equity via a general cash offering to raise the needed funds. If the offer price is $42 per share and the company's underwriters charge a 6 percent spread, how many shares need to be sold?

6. **Calculating Flotation Costs.** In the previous problem, if the SEC filing fee and associated administrative expenses of the offering are $400,000, how many shares need to be sold now?

7. **Calculating Flotation Costs.** The Kinzer Co. has just gone public. Under a firm commitment agreement, Kinzer received $12 for each of the 3.5 million shares sold. The initial offering price was $13 per share, and the stock rose to $23 per share in the first few minutes of trading. Kinzer paid $400,000 in legal and other direct costs, and $275,000 in indirect costs. What was the flotation cost as a percentage of funds raised?

www.mhhe.com/rwj

Spreadsheet Templates 2, 3, 4

CHAPTER

16

Short-Term
Financial Planning

**AFTER MORE THAN A SHORT-TERM STUDYING
EFFORT, YOU SHOULD UNDERSTAND:**

■ The operating and cash cycles and why they are
important

■ The different types of short-term financial policy

■ The essentials of short-term financial planning

IN THE INTRODUCTION to Chapter 13, we discussed how office furniture manufacturer Herman Miller used economic value added, or EVA, to lower its cost of capital. But Herman Miller didn't stop there in its efforts to operate more efficiently. Between 1995 and 1997, the company was also able to slash inventories by $17.2 million, or 24 percent, and it reduced its accounts receivable period by 22 percent from 55 days in 1995 to 43 days in 1997. Herman Miller managed all of this despite a growth in sales of 38 percent over that same period. By reducing the investment in receivables and inventory, the firm was able to redeploy this

capital into more productive and profitable areas. Thus, as the example of Herman Miller illustrates, short-term financial management is an important component of a firm's overall operating strategy, and we devote this chapter (and the next) to the study of the activities it entails.

Short-term financial planning is one activity that concerns everyone in business. As this chapter illustrates, such planning requires, among other things, sales projections from marketing, cost numbers from accounting, and inventory requirements from operations. Perhaps a particularly good reason to study this chapter for many is that short-term planning and management are frequently where new hires start out in a corporation, especially in finance and accounting. Also, such planning is especially important for small businesses, and a lack of adequate short-term financial resources is a frequently cited reason for small business failure.

To this point, we have described many of the decisions of long-term finance, for example, capital budgeting, dividend policy, and financial structure. In this chapter, we begin to discuss short-term finance. Short-term finance is primarily concerned with the analysis of decisions that affect current assets and current liabilities.

Frequently, the term *net working capital* is associated with short-term financial decision making. As we describe in Chapter 2 and elsewhere, net working capital is the difference between current assets and current liabilities. Often, short-term financial management is called *working capital management*. These mean the same thing.

There is no universally accepted definition of short-term finance. The most important difference between short-term and long-term finance is the timing of cash flows. Short-term financial decisions typically involve cash inflows and outflows that occur within a year or less. For example, short-term financial decisions are involved when a firm orders raw materials, pays in cash, and anticipates selling finished goods in one year for cash. In contrast, long-term financial decisions are involved when a firm purchases a special machine that will reduce operating costs over, say, the next five years.

What types of questions fall under the general heading of short-term finance? To name just a very few:

1. What is a reasonable level of cash to keep on hand (in a bank) to pay bills?
2. How much should the firm borrow in the short term?
3. How much credit should be extended to customers?

This chapter introduces the basic elements of short-term financial decisions. First, we discuss the short-term operating activities of the firm. We then identify some alternative short-term financial policies. Finally, we outline the basic elements in a short-term financial plan and describe short-term financing instruments.

16.1 | TRACING CASH AND NET WORKING CAPITAL

In this section, we examine the components of cash and net working capital as they change from one year to the next. We have already discussed various aspects of this subject in Chapters 2 and 3. We briefly review some of that discussion as it relates to short-term financing decisions. Our goal is to describe the short-term operating activities of the firm and their impact on cash and working capital.

To begin, recall that *current assets* are cash and other assets that are expected to convert to cash within the year. Current assets are presented on the balance sheet in order of their liquidity—the ease with which they can be converted to cash and the time it takes to convert them. Four of the most important items found in the current asset section of a balance sheet are cash and cash equivalents, marketable securities, accounts receivable, and inventories.

Analogous to their investment in current assets, firms use several kinds of short-term debt, called *current liabilities*. Current liabilities are obligations that are expected to require cash payment within one year. Three major items found as current liabilities are accounts payable, expenses payable, including accrued wages and taxes, and notes payable.

Because we want to focus on changes in cash, we start off by defining cash in terms of the other elements of the balance sheet. This lets us isolate the cash account and explore the impact on cash from the firm's operating and financing decisions. The basic balance sheet identity can be written as:

Net working capital + Fixed assets = Long-term debt + Equity   [16.1]

Net working capital is cash plus other current assets, less current liabilities; that is,

$$\text{Net working capital} = (\text{Cash} + \text{Other current assets})$$
$$- \text{Current liabilities} \qquad [16.2]$$

If we substitute this for net working capital in the basic balance sheet identity and rearrange things a bit, we see that cash is:

$$\text{Cash} = \text{Long-term debt} + \text{Equity} + \text{Current liabilities}$$
$$- \text{Current assets other than cash} - \text{Fixed assets} \qquad [16.3]$$

This tells us in general terms that some activities naturally increase cash and some activities decrease it. We can list these along with an example of each as follows:

Activities that increase cash

Increasing long-term debt (borrowing over the long term)

Increasing equity (selling some stock)

Increasing current liabilities (getting a 90-day loan)

Decreasing current assets other than cash (selling some inventory for cash)

Decreasing fixed assets (selling some property)

Activities that decrease cash

Decreasing long-term debt (paying off a long-term debt)

Decreasing equity (repurchasing some stock)

Decreasing current liabilities (paying off a 90-day loan)

Increasing current assets other than cash (buying some inventory for cash)

Increasing fixed assets (buying some property)

Notice that our two lists are exact opposites. For example, floating a long-term bond issue increases cash (at least until the money is spent). Paying off a long-term bond issue decreases cash.

Activities that increase cash are called *sources of cash*. Those activities that decrease cash are called *uses of cash*. Looking back at our list, we see that sources of cash always involve increasing a liability (or equity) account or decreasing an asset account. This makes sense because increasing a liability means we have raised money by borrowing it or by selling an ownership interest in the firm. A decrease in an asset means that we have sold or otherwise liquidated an asset. In either case, there is a cash inflow.

Uses of cash are just the reverse. A use of cash involves decreasing a liability by paying it off, perhaps, or increasing assets by purchasing something. Both of these activities require that the firm spend some cash.

Sources and Uses | **EXAMPLE 16.1**

Here is a quick check of your understanding of sources and uses: If accounts payable go up by $100, is this a source or a use? If accounts receivable go up by $100, is this a source or a use?

Accounts payable are what we owe our suppliers. This is a short-term debt. If it rises by $100, we have effectively borrowed the money, so this is a *source* of cash. Receivables are what our customers owe to us, so an increase of $100 in accounts receivable means that we have loaned the money; this is a *use* of cash.

16.2 | THE OPERATING CYCLE AND THE CASH CYCLE

The primary concerns in short-term finance are the firm's short-run operating and financing activities. For a typical manufacturing firm, these short-run activities might consist of the following sequence of events and decisions:

Events	Decisions
1. Buying raw materials	1. How much inventory to order
2. Paying cash	2. Whether to borrow or draw down cash balances
3. Manufacturing the product	3. What choice of production technology to use
4. Selling the product	4. Whether credit should be extended to a particular customer
5. Collecting cash	5. How to collect

These activities create patterns of cash inflows and cash outflows. These cash flows are both unsynchronized and uncertain. They are unsynchronized because, for example, the payment of cash for raw materials does not happen at the same time as the receipt of cash from selling the product. They are uncertain because future sales and costs cannot be precisely predicted.

Defining the Operating and Cash Cycles

We can start with a simple case. One day, call it Day 0, you purchase $1,000 worth of inventory on credit. You pay the bill 30 days later, and, after 30 more days, someone buys the $1,000 in inventory for $1,400. Your buyer does not actually pay for another 45 days. We can summarize these events chronologically as follows:

Day	Activity	Cash Effect
0	Acquire inventory on credit	None
30	Pay for inventory	−$1,000
60	Sell inventory on credit	None
105	Collect on sale	+$1,400

operating cycle

The time period between the acquisition of inventory and the collection of cash from receivables.

The Operating Cycle   There are several things to notice in our example. First, the entire cycle, from the time we acquire some inventory to the time we collect the cash, takes 105 days. This is called the **operating cycle.**

As we illustrate, the operating cycle is the length of time it takes to acquire inventory, sell it, and collect for it. This cycle has two distinct components. The first part is the time it takes to acquire and sell the inventory. This period, a 60-day span in our example, is called the **inventory period.** The second part is the time it takes to collect on the sale, 45 days in our example. This is called the **accounts receivable period,** or, simply, the receivables period.

Based on our definitions, the operating cycle is obviously just the sum of the inventory and receivables periods:

$$\text{Operating cycle} = \text{Inventory period} \\ + \text{Accounts receivable period} \qquad [16.4] \\ 105 \text{ days} = 60 \text{ days} + 45 \text{ days}$$

inventory period
The time it takes to acquire and sell inventory.

accounts receivable period
The time between sale of inventory and collection of the receivable.

What the operating cycle describes is how a product moves through the current asset accounts. It begins life as inventory, it is converted to a receivable when it is sold, and it is finally converted to cash when we collect from the sale. Notice that, at each step, the asset is moving closer to cash.

The Cash Cycle   The second thing to notice is that the cash flows and other events that occur are not synchronized. For example, we don't actually pay for the inventory until 30 days after we acquire it. The intervening 30-day period is called the **accounts payable period.** Next, we spend cash on Day 30, but we don't collect until Day 105. Somehow, we have to arrange to finance the $1,000 for 105 − 30 = 75 days. This period is called the **cash cycle.**

The cash cycle, therefore, is the number of days that pass until we collect the cash from a sale, measured from when we actually pay for the inventory. Notice that, based on our definitions, the cash cycle is the difference between the operating cycle and the accounts payable period:

$$\text{Cash cycle} = \text{Operating cycle} - \text{Accounts payable period} \qquad [16.5] \\ 75 \text{ days} = 105 \text{ days} - 30 \text{ days}$$

accounts payable period
The time between receipt of inventory and payment for it.

cash cycle
The time between cash disbursement and cash collection.

Figure 16.1 depicts the short-term operating activities and cash flows for a typical manufacturing firm by looking at the cash flow time line. As is shown, the **cash flow time line** is made up of the operating cycle and the cash cycle. In Figure 16.1, the need for short-term financial management is suggested by the gap between the cash inflows and the cash outflows. This is related to the length of the operating cycle and the accounts payable period.

cash flow time line
Graphical representation of the operating cycle and the cash cycle.

FIGURE 16.1

Cash flow time line and the short-term operating activities of a typical manufacturing firm

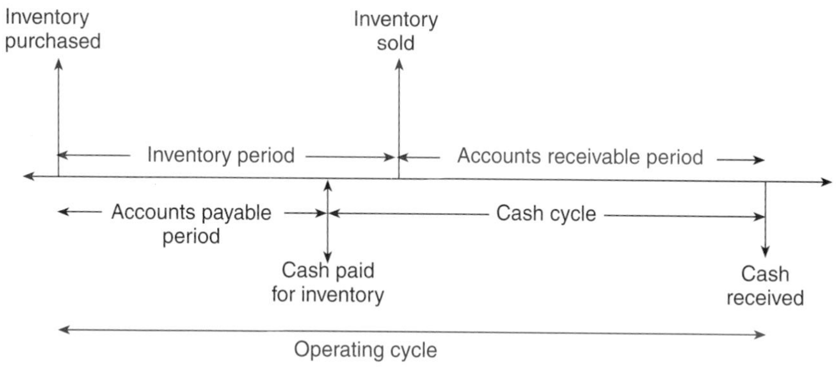

The operating cycle is the time period from inventory purchase until the receipt of cash. The cash cycle is the time period from when cash is paid out to when cash is received.

The gap between short-term inflows and outflows can be filled either by borrowing or by holding a liquidity reserve in the form of cash or marketable securities. Alternatively, the gap can be shortened by changing the inventory, receivable, and payable periods. These are all managerial options that we discuss below and in subsequent chapters.

The Operating Cycle and the Firm's Organizational Chart

Before we examine the operating and cash cycles in greater detail, it is useful to take a look at the people involved in managing a firm's current assets and liabilities. As Table 16.1 illustrates, short-term financial management in a large corporation involves a number of different financial and nonfinancial managers.[1] Examining Table 16.1, we see that selling on credit involves at least three different individuals: the credit manager, the marketing manager, and the controller. Of these three, only two are responsible to the vice president of finance (the marketing function is usually associated with the vice president of marketing). Thus, there is the potential for conflict, particularly if different managers only concentrate on part of the picture. For example, if marketing is trying to land a new account, it may seek more liberal credit terms as an inducement. However, this may increase the firm's investment in receivables or its exposure to bad-debt risk, and conflict can result.

Calculating the Operating and Cash Cycles

In our example, the lengths of time that made up the different periods were obvious. If all we have is financial statement information, we will have to do a little more work. We illustrate these calculations next.

TABLE 16.1	Managers who deal with short-term financial problems	
Title of Manager	**Duties Related to Short-Term Financial Management**	**Assets/Liabilities Influenced**
Cash manager	Collection, concentration, disbursement; short-term investments; short-term borrowing; banking relations	Cash, marketable securities, short-term loans
Credit manager	Monitoring and control of accounts receivable; credit policy decisions	Accounts receivable
Marketing manager	Credit policy decisions	Accounts receivable
Purchasing manager	Decisions on purchases, suppliers; may negotiate payment terms	Inventory, accounts payable
Production manager	Setting of production schedules and materials requirements	Inventory, accounts payable
Payables manager	Decisions on payment policies and on whether to take discounts	Accounts payable
Controller	Accounting information on cash flows; reconciliation of accounts payable; application of payments to accounts receivable	Accounts receivable, accounts payable

Source: Ned C. Hill and William L. Sartoris, *Short-Term Financial Management*, 2nd ed. (New York: Macmillan, 1992), p. 15.

---

[1]Our discussion draws on N. C. Hill and W. L. Sartoris, *Short-Term Financial Management*, 2nd ed. (New York: Macmillan, 1992), Chapter 1.

To begin, we need to determine various things such as how long it takes, on average, to sell inventory and how long it takes, on average, to collect. We start by gathering some balance sheet information such as the following (in thousands):

Item	Beginning	Ending	Average
Inventory	$2,000	$3,000	$2,500
Accounts receivable	1,600	2,000	1,800
Accounts payable	750	1,000	875

Also, from the most recent income statement, we might have the following figures (in thousands):

Net sales	$11,500
Cost of goods sold	8,200

We now need to calculate some financial ratios. We discussed these in some detail in Chapter 3; here we just define them and use them as needed.

The Operating Cycle First of all, we need the inventory period. We spent $8.2 million on inventory (our cost of goods sold). Our average inventory was $2.5 million. We thus turned our inventory over $8.2/2.5 times during the year:[2]

$$\text{Inventory turnover} = \frac{\text{Cost of goods sold}}{\text{Average inventory}}$$

$$= \frac{\$8.2 \text{ million}}{2.5 \text{ million}} = 3.28 \text{ times}$$

Loosely speaking, this tells us that we bought and sold off our inventory 3.28 times during the year. This means that, on average, we held our inventory for:

$$\text{Inventory period} = \frac{365 \text{ days}}{\text{Inventory turnover}}$$

$$= \frac{365}{3.28} = 111.3 \text{ days}$$

So the inventory period is about 111 days. On average, in other words, inventory sat for about 111 days before it was sold.[3]

Similarly, receivables averaged $1.8 million, and sales were $11.5 million. Assuming that all sales were credit sales, the receivables turnover is:[4]

$$\text{Receivables turnover} = \frac{\text{Credit sales}}{\text{Average accounts receivable}}$$

$$= \frac{\$11.5 \text{ million}}{1.8 \text{ million}} = 6.4 \text{ times}$$

---

[2]Notice that in calculating inventory turnover here, we used the *average* inventory instead of using the ending inventory as we did in Chapter 3. Both approaches are used in the real world. To gain some practice using average figures, we will stick with this approach in calculating various ratios throughout this chapter.

[3]This measure is conceptually identical to the days' sales in inventory we discussed in Chapter 3.

[4]If less than 100 percent of our sales are credit sales, then we just need a little more information, namely, credit sales for the year. See Chapter 3 for more discussion of this measure.

If we turn over our receivables 6.4 times, then the receivables period is:

$$\text{Receivables period} = \frac{365 \text{ days}}{\text{Receivables turnover}}$$

$$= \frac{365}{6.4} = 57 \text{ days}$$

The receivables period is also called the *days' sales in receivables* or the *average collection period*. Whatever it is called, it tells us that our customers took an average of 57 days to pay.

The operating cycle is the sum of the inventory and receivables periods:

$$\text{Operating cycle} = \text{Inventory period} + \text{Accounts receivable period}$$

$$= 111 \text{ days} + 57 \text{ days} = 168 \text{ days}$$

This tells us that, on average, 168 days elapse between the time we acquire inventory and, having sold it, collect for the sale.

The Cash Cycle We now need the payables period. From the information given above, average payables were $875,000, and cost of goods sold was again $8.2 million. Our payables turnover is:

$$\text{Payables turnover} = \frac{\text{Cost of goods sold}}{\text{Average payables}}$$

$$= \frac{\$8.2 \text{ million}}{.875 \text{ million}} = 9.4 \text{ times}$$

The payables period is:

$$\text{Payables period} = \frac{365 \text{ days}}{\text{Payables turnover}}$$

$$= \frac{365}{9.4} = 39 \text{ days}$$

Thus, we took an average of 39 days to pay our bills.

Finally, the cash cycle is the difference between the operating cycle and the payables period:

$$\text{Cash cycle} = \text{Operating cycle} - \text{Accounts payable period}$$

$$= 168 \text{ days} - 39 \text{ days} = 129 \text{ days}$$

So, on average, there is a 129-day delay from the time we pay for merchandise to the time we collect on the sale.

EXAMPLE 16.2 | **The Operating and Cash Cycles**

You have collected the following information for the Slowpay Company.

Item	Beginning	Ending
Inventory	$5,000	$7,000
Accounts receivable	1,600	2,400
Accounts payable	2,700	4,800

Credit sales for the year just ended were $50,000, and cost of goods sold was $30,000. How long does it take Slowpay to collect on its receivables? How long does merchandise stay around before it is sold? How long does Slowpay take to pay its bills?

We can first calculate the three turnover ratios:

Inventory turnover = $30,000/6,000 = 5 times

Receivables turnover = $50,000/2,000 = 25 times

Payables turnover = $30,000/3,750 = 8 times

We use these to get the various periods:

Inventory period = 365/5 = 73 days

Receivables period = 365/25 = 14.6 days

Payables period = 365/8 = 45.6 days

All told, Slowpay collects on a sale in 14.6 days, inventory sits around for 73 days, and bills get paid after about 46 days. The operating cycle here is the sum of the inventory and receivables periods: 73 + 14.6 = 87.6 days. The cash cycle is the difference between the operating cycle and the payables period: 87.6 − 45.6 = 42 days.

Interpreting the Cash Cycle

Our examples show that the cash cycle depends on the inventory, receivables, and payables periods. The cash cycle increases as the inventory and receivables periods get longer. It decreases if the company is able to defer payment of payables and thereby lengthen the payables period.

Most firms have a positive cash cycle, and they thus require financing for inventories and receivables. The longer the cash cycle, the more financing is required. Also, changes in the firm's cash cycle are often monitored as an early-warning measure. A lengthening cycle can indicate that the firm is having trouble moving inventory or collecting on its receivables. Such problems can be masked, at least partially, by an increased payables cycle, so both should be monitored.

We can easily see the link between the firm's cash cycle and its profitability by recalling that one of the basic determinants of profitability and growth for a firm is its total asset turnover, which is defined as Sales/Total assets. In Chapter 3, we saw that the higher this ratio is, the greater are the firm's accounting return on assets, ROA, and return on equity, ROE. Thus, all other things being the same, the shorter the cash cycle is, the lower is the firm's investment in inventories and receivables. As a result, the firm's total assets are lower, and total turnover is higher. The accompanying *Reality Bytes* box shows how some very well known firms have aggressively shortened their cash cycles.

CONCEPT QUESTIONS

16.2a What does it mean to say that a firm has an inventory turnover ratio of 4?

16.2b Describe the operating cycle and cash cycle. What are the differences?

16.2c Explain the connection between a firm's accounting-based profitability and its cash cycle.

CASH CYCLE COMPETITION

In 1997, Gateway, the South Dakota–based maker of personal computers, had a problem. Inventories had ballooned in preparation for sales that didn't happen. As a result, Gateway was stuck with about $160 million in excess inventory. At the same time, some of Gateway's competitors were fighting their own demons. Apple had yet to achieve its long-promised resurgence, and Compaq was struggling because its method of selling its products through dealers was becoming obsolete by industry standards. So, who were all of these firms chasing? Dell Computer. To see why, consider the operating and cash cycles for these four firms at the fiscal year-end nearest 1998:

	Receivables period (days)	Inventory period (days)	Operating cycle (days)	Payables period (days)	Cash cycle (days)
Gateway	30	14	44	34	10
Apple	53	23	76	44	32
Compaq	43	23	66	58	8
Dell	44	7	51	62	−11

Gateway's inventory problems might not be evident in these numbers with only 14 days in inventory, but that's still twice the inventory period maintained by Dell, which turned over its inventories three times faster than both Compaq and Apple. Furthermore, while Gateway had the shortest operating cycle, it couldn't match Dell's cash cycle, of a *negative* 11 days. Apple, with a 32-day cash cycle, was the worst in this area.

Dell's operating efficiencies spurred its competitors on, of course. Since 1997, Apple has enjoyed renewed success, while Compaq has cut its number of dealers and attempted to become more of a build-to-order seller. By the fiscal year-end nearest 2000, these four firms looked like this:

	Receivables period (days)	Inventory period (days)	Operating cycle (days)	Payables period (days)	Cash cycle (days)
Gateway	27	8	35	49	−14
Apple	41	1	42	67	−25
Compaq	63	19	82	54	28
Dell	38	6	44	64	−20

The change in these numbers is remarkable. With the exception of Compaq, all of the firms accelerated the collection of receivables and took more time to pay suppliers. All of them increased their inventory turnover, and all but Compaq were able to cut their operating and cash cycles. Perhaps the most stunning change is at Apple, where inventory lasts on average only 1 day, and the cash cycle has shortened to a negative 25 days. Given these numbers, it's not a surprise that Apple has enjoyed a surge in profitability since 1997. Also, even though Dell and Gateway have significantly improved, both have stated goals of shortening their inventory periods to about half what they were at the beginning of 2000.

Ratios such as these can vary quite a bit by industry. For example, at the end of 1999, Wal-Mart had 43 days' worth of inventory and a cash cycle of 9 days, while Caterpillar had 48 days in inventory, but a much longer cash cycle of 135 days. However, few companies in any industry can match the stats of on-line "e-tailer" Amazon.com. At the beginning of 2000, Amazon had about 49 days in inventory, but took, on average, about 125 days to pay its suppliers. Also, Amazon collects on virtually all of its sales more or less immediately from its credit card processors, so the firm had no receivables. As a result, Amazon's operating cycle is the same as its inventory period, and its cash cycle was a negative 76 days!

SOME ASPECTS OF SHORT-TERM FINANCIAL POLICY $\boxed{\textbf{16.3}}$

The short-term financial policy that a firm adopts will be reflected in at least two ways:

1. *The size of the firm's investment in current assets.* This is usually measured relative to the firm's level of total operating revenues. A *flexible,* or accommodative, short-term financial policy would maintain a relatively high ratio of current assets to sales. A *restrictive* short-term financial policy would entail a low ratio of current assets to sales.[5]

2. *The financing of current assets.* This is measured as the proportion of short-term debt (that is, current liabilities) and long-term debt used to finance current assets. A restrictive short-term financial policy means a high proportion of short-term debt relative to long-term financing, and a flexible policy means less short-term debt and more long-term debt.

If we take these two areas together, we see that a firm with a flexible policy would have a relatively large investment in current assets. It would finance this investment with relatively less in short-term debt. The net effect of a flexible policy is thus a relatively high level of net working capital. Put another way, with a flexible policy, the firm maintains a larger overall level of liquidity.

The Size of the Firm's Investment in Current Assets

Flexible short-term financial policies with regard to current assets include such actions as:

1. Keeping large balances of cash and marketable securities.
2. Making large investments in inventory.
3. Granting liberal credit terms, which results in a high level of accounts receivable.

Restrictive short-term financial policies would be just the opposite of the ones above:

1. Keeping low cash balances and little investment in marketable securities.
2. Making small investments in inventory.
3. Allowing few or no credit sales, thereby minimizing accounts receivable.

Determining the optimal level of investment in short-term assets requires an identification of the different costs of alternative short-term financing policies. The objective is to trade off the cost of a restrictive policy against the cost of a flexible one to arrive at the best compromise.

Current asset holdings are highest with a flexible short-term financial policy and lowest with a restrictive policy. So flexible short-term financial policies are costly in that they require a greater investment in cash and marketable securities, inventory, and accounts receivable. However, we expect that future cash inflows will be higher with a flexible policy. For example, sales are stimulated by the use of a credit policy that provides liberal financing to customers. A large amount of finished inventory on hand ("on the shelf") provides a quick delivery service to customers and may increase sales. Similarly, a large inventory of raw materials may result in fewer production stoppages because of inventory shortages.

A more restrictive short-term financial policy probably reduces future sales levels below those that would be achieved under flexible policies. It is also possible that higher

---

[5]Some people use the term *conservative* in place of *flexible* and the term *aggressive* in place of *restrictive.*

prices can be charged to customers under flexible working capital policies. Customers may be willing to pay higher prices for the quick delivery service and more liberal credit terms implicit in flexible policies.

Managing current assets can be thought of as involving a trade-off between costs that rise and costs that fall with the level of investment. Costs that rise with increases in the level of investment in current assets are called **carrying costs.** The larger the investment a firm makes in its current assets, the higher its carrying costs will be. Costs that fall with increases in the level of investment in current assets are called **shortage costs.**

In a general sense, carrying costs are the opportunity costs associated with current assets. The rate of return on current assets is very low when compared to that on other assets. For example, the rate of return on U.S. Treasury bills is usually well below 10 percent. This is very low compared to the rate of return firms would like to achieve overall. (U.S. Treasury bills are an important component of cash and marketable securities.)

Shortage costs are incurred when the investment in current assets is low. If a firm runs out of cash, it will be forced to sell marketable securities. Of course, if a firm runs out of cash and cannot readily sell marketable securities, it may have to borrow or default on an obligation. This situation is called a *cash-out.* A firm may lose customers if it runs out of inventory (a *stock-out*) or if it cannot extend credit to customers.

More generally, there are two kinds of shortage costs:

1. *Trading, or order, costs.* Order costs are the costs of placing an order for more cash (brokerage costs, for example) or more inventory (production setup costs, for example).
2. *Costs related to lack of safety reserves.* These are costs of lost sales, lost customer goodwill, and disruption of production schedules.

The top part of Figure 16.2 illustrates the basic trade-off between carrying costs and shortage costs. On the vertical axis, we have costs measured in dollars, and, on the horizontal axis, we have the amount of current assets. Carrying costs start out at zero when current assets are zero and then climb steadily as current assets grow. Shortage costs start out very high and then decline as we add current assets. The total cost of holding current assets is the sum of the two. Notice how the combined costs reach a minimum at CA*. This is the optimal level of current assets.

Optimal current asset holdings are highest under a flexible policy. This policy is one in which the carrying costs are perceived to be low relative to shortage costs. This is Case A in Figure 16.2. In comparison, under restrictive current asset policies, carrying costs are perceived to be high relative to shortage costs, resulting in lower current asset holdings. This is Case B in Figure 16.2.

Alternative Financing Policies for Current Assets

In previous sections, we looked at the basic determinants of the level of investment in current assets, and we thus focused on the asset side of the balance sheet. Now we turn to the financing side of the question. Here we are concerned with the relative amounts of short-term and long-term debt, assuming the investment in current assets is constant.

A growing firm can be thought of as having a total asset requirement consisting of the current assets and long-term assets needed to run the business efficiently. The total asset requirement may exhibit change over time for many reasons, including (1) a general growth trend, (2) seasonal variation around the trend, and (3) unpredictable day-to-day and month-to-month fluctuations. This situation is depicted in Figure 16.3. (We have not tried to show the unpredictable day-to-day and month-to-month variations in the total asset requirement.)

carrying costs

Costs that rise with increases in the level of investment in current assets.

shortage costs

Costs that fall with increases in the level of investment in current assets.

Carrying costs and shortage costs **FIGURE 16.2**

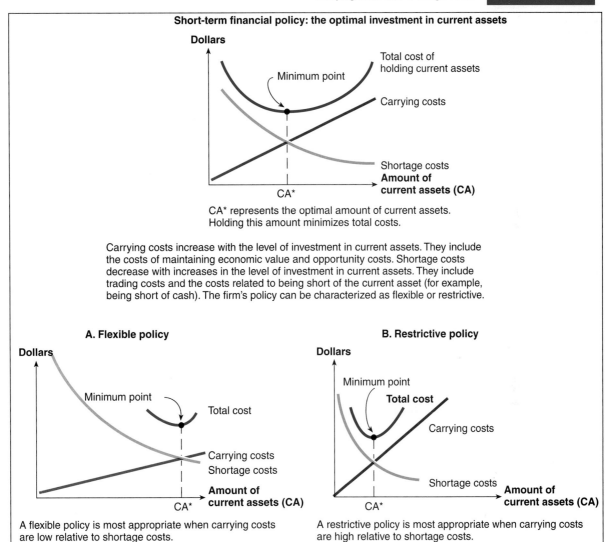

Short-term financial policy: the optimal investment in current assets

CA* represents the optimal amount of current assets.
Holding this amount minimizes total costs.

Carrying costs increase with the level of investment in current assets. They include
the costs of maintaining economic value and opportunity costs. Shortage costs
decrease with increases in the level of investment in current assets. They include
trading costs and the costs related to being short of the current asset (for example,
being short of cash). The firm's policy can be characterized as flexible or restrictive.

A. Flexible policy

A flexible policy is most appropriate when carrying costs
are low relative to shortage costs.

B. Restrictive policy

A restrictive policy is most appropriate when carrying costs
are high relative to shortage costs.

The peaks and valleys in Figure 16.3 represent the firm's total asset needs through time. For example, for a lawn and garden supply firm, the peaks might represent inventory buildups prior to the spring selling season. The valleys come about because of lower off-season inventories. There are two strategies such a firm might consider to meet its cyclical needs. First, the firm could keep a relatively large pool of marketable securities. As the need for inventory and other current assets begins to rise, the firm sells off marketable securities and uses the cash to purchase whatever is needed. Once the inventory is sold and inventory holdings begin to decline, the firm reinvests in marketable securities. This approach is the flexible policy illustrated in Figure 16.4 as Policy F. Notice that the firm essentially uses a pool of marketable securities as a buffer against changing current asset needs.

At the other extreme, the firm could keep relatively little in marketable securities. As the need for inventory and other assets begins to rise, the firm simply borrows the needed

FIGURE 16.3

The total asset
requirement over time

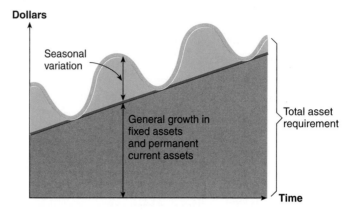

FIGURE 16.4

Alternative asset
financing policies

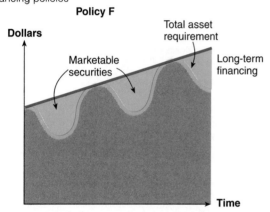

Policy F always implies a short-term cash surplus
and a large investment in cash and marketable
securities.

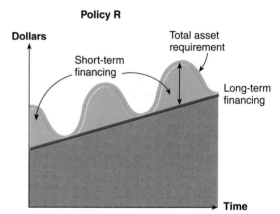

Policy R uses long-term financing for permanent
asset requirements only and short-term borrowing
for seasonal variations.

cash on a short-term basis. The firm repays the loans as the need for assets cycles back down. This approach is the restrictive policy illustrated in Figure 16.4 as Policy R.

In comparing the two strategies illustrated in Figure 16.4, notice that the chief difference is the way in which the seasonal variation in asset needs is financed. In the flexible case, the firm finances internally, using its own cash and marketable securities. In the restrictive case, the firm finances externally, borrowing the needed funds on a short-term basis. As we discussed above, all else being the same, a firm with a flexible policy will have a greater investment in net working capital.

Which Financing Policy Is Best?

What is the most appropriate amount of short-term borrowing? There is no definitive answer. Several considerations must be included in a proper analysis:

1. *Cash reserves.* The flexible financing policy implies surplus cash and little short-term borrowing. This policy reduces the probability that a firm will experience financial distress. Firms may not have to worry as much about meeting recurring short-run obligations. However, investments in cash and marketable securities are zero net present value investments at best.

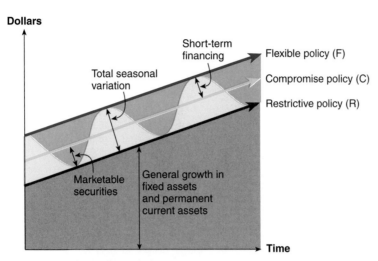

FIGURE 16.5

A compromise
financing policy

With a compromise policy, the firm keeps a reserve of liquidity that
it uses to initially finance seasonal variations in current asset needs.
Short-term borrowing is used when the reserve is exhausted.

2. *Maturity hedging.* Most firms attempt to match the maturities of assets and liabilities. They finance inventories with short-term bank loans and fixed assets with long-term financing. Firms tend to avoid financing long-lived assets with short-term borrowing. This type of maturity mismatching would necessitate frequent refinancing and is inherently risky because short-term interest rates are more volatile than longer-term rates.

3. *Relative interest rates.* Short-term interest rates are usually lower than long-term rates. This implies that it is, on the average, more costly to rely on long-term borrowing as compared to short-term borrowing.

The two policies, F and R, that we discuss above are, of course, extreme cases. With F, the firm never does any short-term borrowing, and, with R, the firm never has a cash reserve (an investment in marketable securities). Figure 16.5 illustrates these two policies along with a compromise, Policy C.

With this compromise approach, the firm borrows in the short term to cover peak financing needs, but it maintains a cash reserve in the form of marketable securities during slow periods. As current assets build up, the firm draws down this reserve before doing any short-term borrowing. This allows for some run-up in current assets before the firm has to resort to short-term borrowing.

Current Assets and Liabilities in Practice

Short-term assets represent a significant portion of a typical firm's overall assets.[6] For U.S. manufacturing, mining, and trade corporations, current assets were about 50 percent of total assets in the 1960s. Today, this figure is closer to 40 percent. Most of the decline is due to more efficient cash and inventory management. Over this same period, current liabilities rose from about 20 percent of total liabilities and equity to almost 30 percent. The result is that liquidity (as measured by the ratio of net working capital to total assets) has declined, signaling a move to more restrictive short-term policies.

---

[6]This discussion draws on Chapter 1 of N. C. Hill and W. L. Sartoris, *Short-Term Financial Management,* 2nd ed. (New York: Macmillan, 1992).

TABLE 16.2	Current assets and current liabilities as a percentage of total assets for selected industries: 1990			
	Printing and Publishing	**Industrial Chemicals**	**Iron and Steel**	**Aircraft and Missiles**
Current assets				
Cash	3.2%	1.2%	3.7%	1.2%
Marketable securities	2.2	.8	5.6	2.7
Accounts receivable	13.8	14.4	15.8	15.4
Inventory	7.1	11.2	18.9	40.2
Other current assets	4.5	3.5	1.6	1.5
Total current assets	30.8%	31.1%	45.6%	61.0%
Current liabilities				
Notes payable	3.7%	6.9%	3.7%	3.9%
Accounts payable	5.7	6.6	10.2	8.8
Accruals and other current liabilities	8.7	9.7	12.2	38.3
Total current liabilities	18.1%	23.2%	26.1%	51.0%

Source: Ned C. Hill and William L. Sartoris, *Short-Term Financial Management,* 2nd ed. (New York: Macmillan, 1992), p. 12.

The cash cycle is longer in some industries than in others because of different products and industry practices. Table 16.2 illustrates this point by comparing the current asset and liability percentages for four different industries. Of the four, the aircraft and missiles industry has more than twice the investment in inventories. Does this mean that aircraft and missile producers are less efficient? Probably not; instead, it is likely that the relatively high inventory levels consist largely of aircraft under construction. Because these are expensive products that take a long time to manufacture, inventories are naturally higher.

CONCEPT QUESTIONS

16.3a What considerations determine the optimal size of the firm's investment in current assets?

16.3b What considerations determine the optimal compromise between flexible and restrictive net working capital policies?

16.4 | THE CASH BUDGET

cash budget
A forecast of cash receipts and disbursements for the next planning period.

The **cash budget** is a primary tool in short-run financial planning. It allows the financial manager to identify short-term financial needs and opportunities. Importantly, the cash budget will help the manager explore the need for short-term borrowing. The idea of the cash budget is simple: It records estimates of cash receipts (cash in) and disbursements (cash out). The result is an estimate of the cash surplus or deficit.

Sales and Cash Collections

We start with an example for the Fun Toys Corporation. We will prepare a quarterly cash budget. We could just as well use a monthly, weekly, or even daily basis. We choose quarters for convenience and also because a quarter is a common short-term business planning period.

All of Fun Toys's cash inflows come from the sale of toys. Cash budgeting for Fun Toys must therefore start with a sales forecast for the coming year, by quarter:

	Q1	Q2	Q3	Q4
Sales (in millions)	$200	$300	$250	$400

Note that these are predicted sales, so there is forecasting risk here; actual sales could be more or less. Also, Fun Toys started the year with accounts receivable equal to $120.

Fun Toys has a 45-day receivables, or average collection, period. This means that half of the sales in a given quarter will be collected the following quarter. This happens because sales made during the first 45 days of a quarter will be collected in that quarter. Sales made in the second 45 days will be collected in the next quarter. Note that we are assuming that each quarter has 90 days, so the 45-day collection period is the same as a half-quarter collection period.

Based on the sales forecasts, we now need to estimate Fun Toys's projected cash collections. First, any receivables that we have at the beginning of a quarter will be collected within 45 days, so all of them will be collected sometime during the quarter. Second, as we discussed, any sales made in the first half of the quarter will be collected, so total cash collections are:

$$\text{Cash collections} = \text{Beginning accounts receivable} + 1/2 \times \text{Sales} \qquad [16.6]$$

For example, in the first quarter, cash collections would be the beginning receivables of $120 plus half of sales, $1/2 \times \$200 = \$100$, for a total of $220.

Since beginning receivables are all collected along with half of sales, ending receivables for a particular quarter would be the other half of sales. First-quarter sales are projected at $200, so ending receivables will be $100. This will be the beginning receivables in the second quarter. Cash collections in the second quarter will thus be $100 plus half of the projected $300 in sales, or $250 total.

Continuing this process, we can summarize Fun Toys's projected cash collections as shown in Table 16.3.

In Table 16.3, collections are shown as the only source of cash. Of course, this need not be the case. Other sources of cash could include asset sales, investment income, and receipts from planned long-term financing.

Cash Outflows

Next, we consider the cash disbursements, or payments. These come in four basic categories:

1. *Payments of accounts payable*. These are payments for goods or services rendered by suppliers, such as raw materials. Generally, these payments will be made sometime after purchases.

2. *Wages, taxes, and other expenses*. This category includes all other regular costs of doing business that require actual expenditures. Depreciation, for example, is often thought of as a regular cost of business, but it requires no cash outflow and is not included.

3. *Capital expenditures*. These are payments of cash for long-lived assets.

4. *Long-term financing expenses*. This category, for example, includes interest payments on long-term debt outstanding and dividend payments to shareholders.

TABLE 16.3

Cash collections for Fun Toys (in millions)

	Q1	Q2	Q3	Q4
Beginning receivables	$120	$100	$150	$125
Sales	200	300	250	400
Cash collections	220	250	275	325
Ending receivables	100	150	125	200

Collections = Beginning receivables + 1/2 × Sales
Ending receivables = Beginning receivables + Sales − Collections
= 1/2 × Sales

TABLE 16.4

Cash disbursements for Fun Toys (in millions)

	Q1	Q2	Q3	Q4
Payment of accounts (60% of sales)	$120	$180	$150	$240
Wages, taxes, other expenses	40	60	50	80
Capital expenditures	0	100	0	0
Long-term financing expenses (interest and dividends)	20	20	20	20
Total cash disbursements	$180	$360	$220	$340

TABLE 16.5

Net cash inflow for Fun Toys (in millions)

	Q1	Q2	Q3	Q4
Total cash collections	$220	$250	$275	$325
Total cash disbursements	180	360	220	340
Net cash inflow	$ 40	−$110	$ 55	−$ 15

Fun Toys's purchases from suppliers (in dollars) in a quarter are equal to 60 percent of the next quarter's predicted sales. Fun Toys's payments to suppliers are equal to the previous quarter's purchases, so the accounts payable period is 90 days. For example, in the quarter just ended, Fun Toys ordered .60 × $200 = $120 in supplies. This will actually be paid in the first quarter (Q1) of the coming year.

Wages, taxes, and other expenses are routinely 20 percent of sales; interest and dividends are currently $20 per quarter. In addition, Fun Toys plans a major plant expansion (a capital expenditure) of $100 in the second quarter. If we put all this information together, the cash outflows are as shown in Table 16.4.

The Cash Balance

The predicted *net cash inflow* is the difference between cash collections and cash disbursements. The net cash inflow for Fun Toys is shown in Table 16.5. What we see immediately is that there is a net cash inflow in the first and third quarters and a net outflow in the second and fourth.

We will assume that Fun Toys starts the year with a $20 cash balance. Furthermore, Fun Toys maintains a $10 minimum cash balance to guard against unforeseen contingencies and forecasting errors. So we start the first quarter with $20 in cash. This rises by $40 during the quarter, and the ending balance is $60. Of this, $10 is reserved as a minimum, so we subtract it out and find that the first-quarter surplus is $60 − 10 = $50.

Fun Toys starts the second quarter with $60 in cash (the ending balance from the previous quarter). There is a net cash inflow of −$110, so the ending balance is $60 − 110 = −$50. We need another $10 as a buffer, so the total deficit is −$60. These calculations and those for the last two quarters are summarized in Table 16.6.

	Q1	Q2	Q3	Q4	
					TABLE 16.6
Beginning cash balance	$20 →	$ 60 →	−$50 →	$ 5	Cash balance for Fun Toys (in millions)
Net cash inflow	40	− 110	55	− 15	
Ending cash balance	$60 ──	−$ 50 ──	$ 5 ──	−$10	
Minimum cash balance	− 10	− 10	− 10	− 10	
Cumulative surplus (deficit)	$50	−$ 60	−$ 5	−$20	

Beginning in the second quarter, Fun Toys has a cash shortfall of $60. This occurs because of the seasonal pattern of sales (higher towards the end of the second quarter), the delay in collections, and the planned capital expenditure.

The cash situation at Fun Toys is projected to improve to a $5 deficit in the third quarter, but, by year's end, Fun Toys is showing a $20 deficit. Without some sort of financing, this deficit will carry over into the next year. We explore this subject in the next section.

For now, we can make the following general comments on Fun Toys's cash needs:

1. Fun Toys's large outflow in the second quarter is not necessarily a sign of trouble. It results from delayed collections on sales and a planned capital expenditure (presumably a worthwhile one).

2. The figures in our example are based on a forecast. Sales could be much worse (or better) than the forecast figures.

CONCEPT QUESTIONS

16.4a How would you do a sensitivity analysis (discussed in Chapter 9) for Fun Toys's net cash balance?

16.4b What could you learn from such an analysis?

SHORT-TERM BORROWING | 16.5

Fun Toys has a short-term financing problem. It cannot meet the forecast cash outflows in the second quarter from internal sources. How it will finance the shortfall depends on its financial policy. With a very flexible policy, Fun Toys might seek up to $60 million in long-term debt financing.

In addition, note that much of the cash deficit comes from the large capital expenditure. Arguably, this is a candidate for long-term financing. Nonetheless, because we have discussed long-term financing elsewhere, we will concentrate here on two short-term borrowing options: (1) unsecured borrowing and (2) secured borrowing.

Unsecured Loans

The most common way to finance a temporary cash deficit is to arrange a short-term, unsecured bank loan. Firms that use short-term bank loans often arrange a line of credit. A **line of credit** is an agreement under which a firm is authorized to borrow up to a specified amount. To ensure that the line is used for short-term purposes, the borrower will sometimes be required to pay the line down to zero and keep it there for some period during the year, typically 60 days (called a *cleanup period*).

Short-term lines of credit are classified as either *committed* or *noncommitted*. The latter is an informal arrangement that allows firms to borrow up to a previously specified limit without going through the normal paperwork (much as you would with a credit card). A

line of credit
A formal (committed) or informal (noncommitted) prearranged, short-term bank loan.

revolving credit arrangement (or just *revolver*) is similar to a line of credit, but it is usually open for two or more years, whereas a line of credit would usually be evaluated on an annual basis.

Committed lines of credit are more formal legal arrangements and often involve a commitment fee paid by the firm to the bank. The interest rate on the line of credit will usually float. A firm that pays a commitment fee for a committed line of credit is essentially buying insurance to guarantee that the bank can't back out of the agreement (absent some material change in the borrower's status).

Secured Loans

Banks and other finance companies often require security for a short-term loan just as they do for a long-term loan. Security for short-term loans usually consists of accounts receivable, inventories, or both.

accounts receivable financing

A secured short-term loan that involves either the assignment or factoring of receivables.

Accounts Receivable Financing   **Accounts receivable financing** involves either *assigning* receivables or *factoring* receivables. Under assignment, the lender has the receivables as security, but the borrower is still responsible if a receivable can't be collected. With *conventional factoring*, the receivable is discounted and sold to the lender (the factor). Once it is sold, collection is the factor's problem, and the factor assumes the full risk of default on bad accounts. With *maturity factoring*, the factor forwards the money on an agreed-upon future date.

EXAMPLE 16.3 | **Cost of Factoring**

For the year just ended, LuLu's Pies had an average of $50,000 in accounts receivable. Credit sales were $500,000. LuLu's factors its receivables by discounting them 3 percent, in other words, by selling them for 97 cents on the dollar. What is the effective interest rate on this source of short-term financing?

To determine the interest rate, we first have to know the accounts receivable, or average collection, period. During the year, LuLu's turned over its receivables $500,000/ 50,000 = 10 times. The average collection period is therefore 365/10 = 36.5 days.

The interest paid here is a form of "discount interest." In this case, LuLu's is paying 3 cents in interest on every 97 cents of financing. The interest rate per 36.5 days is thus .03/.97 = 3.09%. The APR is 10 × 3.09% = 30.9%, but the effective annual rate is:

$$\text{EAR} = 1.0309^{10} - 1 = 35.6\%$$

The factoring is a relatively expensive source of money in this case.

We should note that if the factor takes on the risk of default by a buyer, then the factor is providing insurance as well as immediate cash. More generally, the factor essentially takes over the firm's credit operations. This can result in a significant saving. The interest rate we calculated is therefore overstated, particularly if default is a significant possibility.

---

inventory loan

A secured short-term loan to purchase inventory.

Inventory Loans   **Inventory loans,** short-term loans to purchase inventory, come in three basic forms: blanket inventory liens, trust receipts, and field warehouse financing:

1. *Blanket inventory lien.* A blanket lien gives the lender a lien against all the borrower's inventories (the blanket "covers" everything).

2. *Trust receipt.* A trust receipt is a device by which the borrower holds specific inventory in "trust" for the lender. Automobile dealer financing, for example, is done by

use of trust receipts. This type of secured financing is also called *floor planning*, in reference to inventory on the showroom floor. However, it is somewhat cumbersome to use trust receipts for, say, wheat grain.

3. *Field warehouse financing.* In field warehouse financing, a public warehouse company (an independent company that specializes in inventory management) acts as a control agent to supervise the inventory for the lender.

Other Sources

There are a variety of other sources of short-term funds employed by corporations. Two of the most important are *commercial paper* and *trade credit*.

Commercial paper consists of short-term notes issued by large and highly rated firms. Typically, these notes are of short maturity, ranging up to 270 days (beyond that limit, the firm must file a registration statement with the SEC). Because the firm issues these directly, the interest rate the borrowing firm obtains can be significantly below the rate a bank would charge for a direct loan.

Another option available to a firm is to increase the accounts payable period; in other words, it may take longer to pay its bills. This amounts to borrowing from suppliers in the form of trade credit. This is an extremely important form of financing for smaller businesses in particular. As we discuss in Chapter 17, a firm using trade credit may end up paying a much higher price for what it purchases, so this can be a very expensive source of financing.

CONCEPT QUESTIONS

16.5a What are the two basic forms of short-term financing?

16.5b Describe two types of secured loans.

A SHORT-TERM FINANCIAL PLAN | 16.6

To illustrate a completed short-term financial plan, we will assume that Fun Toys arranges to borrow any needed funds on a short-term basis. The interest rate is a 20 percent APR, and it is calculated on a quarterly basis. From Chapter 5, we know that the rate is 20%/4 = 5% per quarter. We will assume that Fun Toys starts the year with no short-term debt.

From Table 16.6, Fun Toys has a second-quarter deficit of $60 million. We will have to borrow this amount. Net cash inflow in the following quarter is $55 million. We now have to pay $60 × .05 = $3 million in interest out of that, leaving $52 million to reduce the borrowing.

We still owe $60 − 52 = $8 million at the end of the third quarter. Interest in the last quarter will thus be $8 × .05 = $.4 million. In addition, net inflows in the last quarter are −$15 million, so we have to borrow a total of $15.4 million, bringing our total borrowing up to $15.4 + 8 = $23.4 million. Table 16.7 extends Table 16.6 to include these calculations.

Notice that the ending short-term debt is just equal to the cumulative deficit for the entire year, $20, plus the interest paid during the year, $3 + .4 = $3.4, for a total of $23.4.

Our plan is very simple. For example, we ignored the fact that the interest paid on the short-term debt is tax deductible. We also ignored the fact that the cash surplus in the first quarter would earn some interest (which would be taxable). We could add on a number of refinements. Even so, our plan highlights the fact that in about 90 days Fun Toys will need to borrow $60 million or so on a short-term basis. It's time to start lining up the source of the funds.

TABLE 16.7

Short-term financial plan for Fun Toys (in millions)

	Q1	Q2	Q3	Q4
Beginning cash balance	$20	$60	$10	$10.0
Net cash inflow	40	−110	55	− 15.0
New short-term borrowing	—	60	—	15.4
Interest on short-term borrowing	—	—	− 3	− .4
Short-term borrowing repaid	—	—	− 52	—
Ending cash balance	$60	$10	$10	$10.0
Minimum cash balance	− 10	− 10	− 10	− 10.0
Cumulative surplus (deficit)	$50	$ 0	$ 0	$ .0
Beginning short-term borrowing	0	0	60	8.0
Change in short-term debt	0	60	− 52	15.4
Ending short-term debt	$0	$60	$ 8	$23.4

Our plan also illustrates that financing the firm's short-term needs will cost about $3.4 million in interest (before taxes) for the year. This is a starting point for Fun Toys to begin evaluating alternatives to reduce this expense. For example, can the $100 million planned expenditure be postponed or spread out? At 5 percent per quarter, short-term credit is expensive.

Also, if Fun Toys's sales are expected to keep growing, then the $20 million plus deficit will probably also keep growing, and the need for additional financing is permanent. Fun Toys may wish to think about raising money on a long-term basis to cover this need.

CONCEPT QUESTIONS

16.6a In Table 16.7, does Fun Toys have a projected deficit or surplus?

16.6b In Table 16.7, what would happen to Fun Toys's deficit or surplus if the minimum cash balance was reduced to $5?

SUMMARY AND CONCLUSIONS

1. This chapter has introduced the management of short-term finance. Short-term finance involves short-lived assets and liabilities. We traced and examined the short-term sources and uses of cash as they appear on the firm's financial statements. We saw how current assets and current liabilities arise in the short-term operating activities and the cash cycle of the firm.

2. Managing short-term cash flows involves the minimizing of costs. The two major costs are carrying costs, the returns foregone by keeping too much invested in short-term assets such as cash, and shortage costs, the costs of running out of short-term assets. The objective of managing short-term finance and doing short-term financial planning is to find the optimal trade-off between these two costs.

3. In an "ideal" economy, the firm could perfectly predict its short-term uses and sources of cash, and net working capital could be kept at zero. In the real world we live in, cash and net working capital provide a buffer that lets the firm meet its ongoing obligations. The financial manager seeks the optimal level of each of the current assets.

4. The financial manager can use the cash budget to identify short-term financial needs. The cash budget tells the manager what borrowing is required or what lending will be possible in the short run. The firm has available to it a number of possible ways of acquiring funds to meet short-term shortfalls, including the use of unsecured and secured loans.

CHAPTER REVIEW AND SELF-TEST PROBLEMS

16.1 The Operating and Cash Cycles. Consider the following financial statement information for the Glory Road Company:

Item	Beginning	Ending
Inventory	$1,543	$1,669
Accounts receivable	4,418	3,952
Accounts payable	2,551	2,673
Net sales	$11,500	
Cost of goods sold	8,200	

Calculate the operating and cash cycles.

16.2 Cash Balance for Masson Corporation. The Masson Corporation has a 60-day average collection period and wishes to maintain a $5 million minimum cash balance. Based on this and the information below, complete the following cash budget. What conclusions do you draw?

MASSON CORPORATION
Cash Budget
(in millions)

	Q1	Q2	Q3	Q4
Beginning receivables	$120			
Sales	90	$120	$150	$120
Cash collections				
Ending receivables				
Total cash collections				
Total cash disbursements	80	160	180	160
Net cash inflow				
Beginning cash balance	$ 5			
Net cash inflow				
Ending cash balance				
Minimum cash balance				
Cumulative surplus (deficit)				

Answers to Chapter Review and Self-Test Problems

16.1 We first need the turnover ratios. Note that we use the average values for all balance sheet items and that we base the inventory and payables turnover measures on cost of goods sold.

$$\text{Inventory turnover} = \$8,200/[(1,543 + 1,669)/2]$$
$$= 5.11 \text{ times}$$
$$\text{Receivables turnover} = \$11,500/[(4,418 + 3,952)/2]$$
$$= 2.75 \text{ times}$$
$$\text{Payables turnover} = \$8,200/[(2,551 + 2,673)/2]$$
$$= 3.14 \text{ times}$$

We can now calculate the various periods:

$$\text{Inventory period} = 365 \text{ days}/5.11 \text{ times} = 71.43 \text{ days}$$
$$\text{Receivables period} = 365 \text{ days}/2.75 \text{ times} = 132.73 \text{ days}$$
$$\text{Payables period} = 365 \text{ days}/3.14 \text{ times} = 116.24 \text{ days}$$

So the time it takes to acquire inventory and sell it is about 71 days. Collection takes another 133 days, and the operating cycle is thus $71 + 133 = 204$ days. The cash cycle is this 204 days less the payables period, $204 - 116 = 88$ days.

16.2   Since Masson has a 60-day collection period, only those sales made in the first 30 days of the quarter will be collected in the same quarter. Total cash collections in the first quarter will thus equal $30/90 = \frac{1}{3}$ of sales plus beginning receivables, or $120 + \frac{1}{3} \times 90 = \$150$. Ending receivables for the first quarter (and the second-quarter beginning receivables) are the other $\frac{2}{3}$ of sales, or $\frac{2}{3} \times \$90 = \$60$. The remaining calculations are straightforward, and the completed budget follows.

MASSON CORPORATION
Cash Budget
(in millions)

	Q1	Q2	Q3	Q4
Beginning receivables	$120	$ 60	$ 80	$100
Sales	90	120	150	120
Cash collections	150	100	130	140
Ending receivables	$ 60	$ 80	$100	$ 80
Total cash collections	$150	$100	$130	$140
Total cash disbursements	80	160	180	160
Net cash inflow	$ 70	−$ 60	−$ 50	−$ 20
Beginning cash balance	$ 5	$ 75	$ 15	−$ 35
Net cash inflow	70	− 60	− 50	− 20
Ending cash balance	$ 75	$ 15	−$ 35	−$ 55
Minimum cash balance	−$ 5	− $5	− $5	−$ 5
Cumulative surplus (deficit)	$ 70	$ 10	−$ 40	−$ 60

The primary conclusion from this schedule is that, beginning in the third quarter, Masson's cash surplus becomes a cash deficit. By the end of the year, Masson will need to arrange for $60 million in cash beyond what will be available.

CRITICAL THINKING AND CONCEPTS REVIEW

1.   **Operating Cycle.**   What are some of the characteristics of a firm with a long operating cycle?

2.   **Cash Cycle.**   What are some of the characteristics of a firm with a long cash cycle?

3. **Sources and Uses.** For the year just ended, you have gathered the following information on the Holly Corporation:

   a. A $200 dividend was paid.

   b. Accounts payable increased by $500.

   c. Fixed asset purchases were $900.

   d. Inventories increased by $625.

   e. Long-term debt decreased by $1,200.

   Label each item as a source or use of cash and describe its effect on the firm's cash balance.

4. **Cost of Current Assets.** Loftis Manufacturing, Inc., has recently installed a just-in-time (JIT) inventory system. Describe the effect this is likely to have on the company's carrying costs, shortage costs, and operating cycle.

5. **Cycles.** Is it possible for a firm's cash cycle to be longer than its operating cycle? Explain why or why not.

   Use the following information to answer Questions 6–10: In April 1994, Ameritech Corporation, one of the "Baby Bell" phone companies, told its 70,000 suppliers that it would stretch out its bill payments to 45 days from 30 days beginning on May 1. The reason given was "to control costs and optimize cash flow."

6. **Operating and Cash Cycles.** What impact did this change in payables policy have on Ameritech's operating cycle? Its cash cycle?

7. **Operating and Cash Cycles.** What impact did the announcement have on Ameritech's suppliers?

8. **Corporate Ethics.** Is it ethical for large firms to unilaterally lengthen their payables periods, particularly when dealing with smaller suppliers?

9. **Payables Period.** Why don't all firms simply increase their payables periods to shorten their cash cycles?

10. **Payables Period.** Ameritech lengthened its payables period to "control costs and optimize cash flow." Exactly what is the cash benefit to Ameritech from this change?

QUESTIONS AND PROBLEMS

1. **Changes in the Cash Account.** Indicate the impact of the following corporate actions on cash, using the letter *I* for an increase, *D* for a decrease, or *N* when no change occurs.

   Basic
   (Questions 1–6)

   a. A dividend is paid with funds received from a sale of debt.

   b. Real estate is purchased and paid for with short-term debt.

   c. Inventory is bought on credit.

   d. A short-term bank loan is repaid.

   e. Next year's taxes are prepaid.

   f. Preferred stock is issued.

   g. Sales are made on credit.

   h. Interest on long-term debt is paid.

   i. Payments for previous sales are collected.

   j. The accounts payable balance is reduced.

   k. A dividend is paid.

   l. Production supplies are purchased and paid for with a short-term note.

   m. Utility bills are paid.

   n. Cash is paid for raw materials purchased for inventory.

   o. Marketable securities are purchased.

2. **Cash Equation.** Sandy Cooks Company has a book net worth of $10,500. Long-term debt is $2,500. Net working capital, other than cash, is $4,250. Fixed assets are $4,000. How much cash does the company have? If current liabilities are $2,000, what are current assets?

3. **Changes in the Operating Cycle.** Indicate the effect that the following will have on the operating cycle. Use the letter I to indicate an increase, the letter D for a decrease, and the letter N for no change.
   a. Average receivables goes up.
   b. Credit payment times for customers are increased.
   c. Inventory turnover goes from 3 times to 7 times.
   d. Payables turnover goes from 6 times to 11 times.
   e. Receivables turnover goes from 7 times to 9 times.
   f. Payments to suppliers are accelerated.

4. **Changes in Cycles.** Indicate the impact of the following on the cash and operating cycles, respectively. Use the letter I to indicate an increase, the letter D for a decrease, and the letter N for no change.
   a. The terms of cash discounts offered to customers are made more favorable.
   b. The cash discounts offered by suppliers are increased; thus, payments are made earlier.
   c. An increased number of customers begin to pay in cash instead of with credit.
   d. Fewer raw materials than usual are purchased.
   e. A greater percentage of raw material purchases are paid for with credit.
   f. More finished goods are produced for inventory instead of for order.

5. **Calculating Cash Collections.** The Belle Meade Company has projected the following quarterly sales amounts for the coming year:

	Q1	**Q2**	**Q3**	**Q4**
Sales	$450	$600	$750	$900

   a. Accounts receivable at the beginning of the year are $500. Belle Meade has a 45-day collection period. Calculate cash collections in each of the four quarters by completing the following:

	Q1	**Q2**	**Q3**	**Q4**
Beginning receivables				
Sales				
Cash collections				
Ending receivables				

   b. Rework (a) assuming a collection period of 60 days.
   c. Rework (a) assuming a collection period of 30 days.

6. **Calculating Cycles.** Consider the following financial statement information for the Zamboni Icers Corporation:

Item	Beginning	Ending
Inventory	$8,257	$10,432
Accounts receivable	5,275	5,963
Accounts payable	7,685	7,900
Net sales		$65,327
Cost of goods sold		51,284

Calculate the operating and cash cycles. How do you interpret your answer?

7. **Factoring Receivables.** Your firm has an average collection period of 42 days. Current practice is to factor all receivables immediately at a 2 percent discount. What is the effective cost of borrowing in this case? Assume that default is extremely unlikely.

8. **Calculating Payments.** Jags Products has projected the following sales for the coming year:

	Q1	Q2	Q3	Q4
Sales	$750	$825	$950	$600

Sales in the year following this one are projected to be 15 percent greater in each quarter.

a. Calculate payments to suppliers assuming that Jags places orders during each quarter equal to 30 percent of projected sales for the next quarter. Assume that Jags pays immediately. What is the payables period in this case?

	Q1	Q2	Q3	Q4
Payment of accounts				

b. Rework (a) assuming a 90-day payables period.
c. Rework (a) assuming a 60-day payables period.

9. **Calculating Payments.** The Thunder Dan Corporation's purchases from suppliers in a quarter are equal to 75 percent of the next quarter's forecast sales. The payables period is 60 days. Wages, taxes, and other expenses are 30 percent of sales, and interest and dividends are $70 per quarter. No capital expenditures are planned.

Projected quarterly sales are:

	Q1	Q2	Q3	Q4
Sales	$900	$700	$950	$600

Sales for the first quarter of the following year are projected at $1,040. Calculate Thunder's cash outlays by completing the following:

	Q1	Q2	Q3	Q4
Payment of accounts				
Wages, taxes, other expenses				
Long-term financing expenses (interest and dividends)				
Total				

10.   **Calculating Cash Collections.**   The following is the sales budget for Golden Parachute, Inc., for the first quarter of 2000:

	January	February	March
Sales budget	$140,000	$175,000	$145,000

Credit sales are collected as follows:

65 percent in the month of the sale

20 percent in the month after the sale

15 percent in the second month after the sale

The accounts receivable balance at the end of the previous quarter was $60,000 ($32,000 of which was uncollected December sales).

a. Compute the sales for November.

b. Compute the sales for December.

c. Compute the cash collections from sales for each month from January through March.

11.   **Calculating the Cash Budget.**   Here are some important figures from the budget of Big Blast, Inc., for the second quarter of 2000:

	April	May	June
Credit sales	$295,000	$340,000	$310,000
Credit purchases	140,000	150,000	130,000
Cash disbursements			
Wages, taxes, and expenses	25,000	27,500	32,000
Interest	8,000	8,000	8,000
Equipment purchases	50,000	70,000	254,000

The company predicts that 5 percent of its credit sales will never be collected, 35 percent of its sales will be collected in the month of the sale, and the remaining 60 percent will be collected in the following month. Credit purchases will be paid in the month following the purchase.

In March 2000, credit sales were $275,000. Using this information, complete the following cash budget:

	April	May	June
Beginning cash balance	$275,000		
Cash receipts			
Cash collections from credit sales			
Total cash available			
Cash disbursements			
Purchases	115,000		
Wages, taxes, and expenses			
Interest			
Equipment purchases			
Total cash disbursements			
Ending cash balance			

12.   **Calculating Cash Collections.**   The Deuce Turbine Company has projected the
following quarterly sales amounts for the coming year:

	Q1	Q2	Q3	Q4
Sales	$1,800	$1,650	$1,200	$2,800

a. Accounts receivable at the beginning of the year are $900. Deuce Turbine has a
45-day collection period. Calculate cash collections in each of the four quarters
by completing the following:

	Q1	Q2	Q3	Q4
Beginning receivables				
Sales				
Cash collections				
Ending receivables				

b. Rework (*a*) assuming a collection period of 60 days.
c. Rework (*a*) assuming a collection period of 30 days.

13.   **Calculating Cycles.**   Consider the following financial statement information for
the Hot Air Balloon Corporation:

Item	Beginning	Ending
Inventory	$10,512	$10,300
Accounts receivable	8,128	9,147
Accounts payable	10,128	10,573
Net sales		$126,542
Cost of goods sold		53,826

Calculate the operating and cash cycles. How do you interpret your answer?

14.   **Factoring Receivables.**   Your firm has an average collection period of 35 days.
Current practice is to factor all receivables immediately at a 1.5 percent discount.
What is the effective cost of borrowing in this case? Assume that default is ex-
tremely unlikely.

15.   **Calculating Payments.**   Van Morrison Products has projected the following sales
for the coming year:

	Q1	Q2	Q3	Q4
Projected sales	$820	$750	$550	$900

Sales in the year following this one are projected to be 25 percent greater in each
quarter.

a. Calculate payments to suppliers assuming that Van Morrison places orders during each quarter equal to 50 percent of projected sales in the next quarter. Assume that Van Morrison pays immediately. What is the payables period in this
case?

	Q1	Q2	Q3	Q4
Payment of accounts				

b. Rework (*a*) assuming a 90-day payables period.

c. Rework (*a*) assuming a 60-day payables period.

16. **Calculating Payments.**　The General Tso Corporation's purchases from suppliers in a quarter are equal to 40 percent of the next quarter's forecast sales. The payables deferral period is 60 days. Wages, taxes, and other expenses are 25 percent of sales, while interest and dividends are $90 per quarter. No capital expenditures are planned.

Projected quarterly sales are:

	Q1	Q2	Q3	Q4
Projected sales	$700	$900	$860	$940

Sales in the first quarter of the following year are projected at $850. Calculate General Tso's cash outlays by completing the following:

	Q1	Q2	Q3	Q4
Payment of accounts				
Wages, taxes, other expenses				
Long-term financing expenses (interest and dividends)				
Total				

Intermediate
(Questions 17–18)

17. **Costs of Borrowing.**　You've worked out a line of credit arrangement that allows you to borrow up to $50 million at any time. The interest rate is .650 percent per month. In addition, 4 percent of the amount that you borrow must be deposited in a noninterest-bearing account. Assume that your bank uses compound interest on its line of credit loans.

    a. What is the effective annual interest rate on this lending arrangement?

    b. Suppose you need $5 million today and you repay it in six months. How much interest will you pay?

18. **Costs of Borrowing.**　A bank offers your firm a revolving credit arrangement for up to $60 million at an interest rate of 2.05 percent per quarter. The bank also requires you to maintain a compensating balance of 8 percent against the *unused* portion of the credit line, to be deposited in a noninterest-bearing account. Assume you have a short-term investment account at the bank that pays 1.25 percent per quarter, and assume that the bank uses compound interest on its revolving credit loans.

    a. What is your effective annual interest rate (an opportunity cost) on the revolving credit arrangement if your firm does not use it during the year?

    b. What is your effective annual interest rate on the lending arrangement if you borrow $40 million immediately and repay it in one year?

    c. What is your effective annual interest rate if you borrow $60 million immediately and repay it in one year?

www.mhhe.com/rwj

Spreadsheet Templates 5, 8, 11

Working Capital Management

ONCE YOU HAVE MADE YOUR WAY THROUGH THIS CHAPTER, YOU SHOULD HAVE A WORKING KNOWLEDGE OF:

- How firms manage their cash and some of the collection, concentration, and disbursement techniques used

- How firms manage their receivables and the basic components of a firm's credit policies

- The types of inventory and inventory management systems used by firms and what determines the optimal inventory level

IN EARLY 2000, Gillette Co., the Boston-based maker of shaving products, announced plans to reduce its investment in working capital by between $500 million and $1 billion, a significant chunk given that the firm's total assets were only $10.1 billion at the time. The plan, which was targeted to be completed by the end of the year 2000, was designed to reduce inventories to cut down on storage and financing costs. In addition, the firm admitted it was overdue to clean up its accounts receivable and to shorten payment terms it allowed its customers. If Gillette manages to make the changes, it will reap significant benefits. Of course, the changes won't be easy to make in the face of competition and demands by its customers for credit. In any event, what Gillette is planning to do fits naturally with what is addressed in this chapter, namely, how to shave working capital costs without cutting too closely.

This chapter considers various aspects of working capital management. Commonly, responsibility for working capital is spread across several different disciplines. Accounting is frequently responsible for payables and receivables; operations is in charge of inventory; and finance handles cash management. Marketing also plays a key role because sales forecasts are a key determinant of working capital needs. So, an understanding of working capital management is important for just about everyone in the firm.

This chapter examines working capital management. Recall from Chapter 1 that working capital management deals with a firm's short-term, or current, assets and liabilities. A firm's current liabilities consist largely of short-term borrowing. We discussed short-term borrowing in our previous chapter, so this chapter mainly focuses on current assets, in particular, cash, accounts receivable, and inventory.

17.1 | FLOAT AND CASH MANAGEMENT

We begin our analysis of working capital management by looking at how firms manage cash.[1] The basic objective in cash management is to keep the investment in cash as low as possible while still operating the firm's activities efficiently and effectively. This goal usually reduces to the dictum "Collect early and pay late." Accordingly, we discuss ways of accelerating collections and managing disbursements.

In addition, firms must invest temporarily idle cash in short-term marketable securities. As we discuss in various places, these securities can be bought and sold in the financial markets. As a group, they have very little default risk, and most are highly liquid. There are different types of these so-called money market securities, and we discuss a few of the most important ones a bit later.

Reasons for Holding Cash

John Maynard Keynes, in his great work *The General Theory of Employment, Interest, and Money,* identified three reasons why liquidity is important: the speculative motive, the precautionary motive, and the transaction motive. We discuss these next.

speculative motive
The need to hold cash to take advantage of additional investment opportunities, such as bargain purchases.

The Speculative and Precautionary Motives   The **speculative motive** is the need to hold cash in order to be able to take advantage of, for example, bargain purchase opportunities that might arise, attractive interest rates, and (in the case of international firms) favorable exchange rate fluctuations.

For most firms, reserve borrowing ability and marketable securities can be used to satisfy speculative motives. Thus, for a modern firm, there might be a speculative motive for liquidity, but not necessarily for cash per se. Think of it this way: If you have a credit card with a very large credit limit, then you can probably take advantage of any unusual bargains that come along without carrying any cash.

precautionary motive
The need to hold cash as a safety margin to act as a financial reserve.

This is also true, to a lesser extent, for precautionary motives. The **precautionary motive** is the need for a safety supply to act as a financial reserve. Once again, there probably is a precautionary motive for liquidity. However, given that the value of money market instruments is relatively certain and that instruments such as T-bills are extremely liquid, there is no real need to hold substantial amounts of cash for precautionary purposes.

transaction motive
The need to hold cash to satisfy normal disbursement and collection activities associated with a firm's ongoing operations.

The Transaction Motive   Cash is needed to satisfy the **transaction motive,** the need to have cash on hand to pay bills. Transaction-related needs come from the normal disbursement and collection activities of the firm. The disbursement of cash includes the payment of wages and salaries, trade debts, taxes, and dividends.

Cash is collected from sales, the selling of assets, and new financing. The cash inflows (collections) and outflows (disbursements) are not perfectly synchronized, and some level of cash holdings is necessary to serve as a buffer. Perfect liquidity is the characteristic of cash that allows it to satisfy the transaction motive.

---

[1]We are indebted to Jarl Kallberg and David Wright for helpful comments and suggestions on this section.

As electronic funds transfers and other high-speed, "paperless" payment mechanisms continue to develop, even the transaction demand for cash may all but disappear. Even if it does, however, there will still be a demand for liquidity and a need to manage it efficiently.

Benefits of Holding Cash   When a firm holds cash in excess of some necessary minimum, it incurs an opportunity cost. The opportunity cost of excess cash (held in currency or bank deposits) is the interest income that could be earned in the next best use, such as investment in marketable securities.

Given the opportunity cost of holding cash, why would a firm hold excess cash? The answer is that a cash balance must be maintained to provide the liquidity necessary for transaction needs—paying bills. If the firm maintains too small a cash balance, it may run out of cash. If this happens, the firm may have to raise cash on a short-term basis. This could involve, for example, selling marketable securities or borrowing.

Activities such as selling marketable securities and borrowing involve various costs. As we've discussed, holding cash has an opportunity cost. To determine the appropriate cash balance, the firm must weigh the benefits of holding cash against these costs. We discuss this subject in more detail in the sections that follow.

Understanding Float

As you no doubt know, the amount of money you have according to your checkbook can be very different from the amount of money that your bank thinks you have. The reason is that some of the checks you have written haven't yet been presented to the bank for payment. The same thing is true for a business. The cash balance that a firm shows on its books is called the firm's *book,* or *ledger, balance.* The balance shown in its bank account as available to spend is called its *available,* or *collected, balance.* The difference between the available balance and the ledger balance is called the **float,** and it represents the net effect of checks in the process of *clearing* (moving through the banking system).

float
The difference between book cash and bank cash, representing the net effect of checks in the process of clearing.

Disbursement Float   Checks written by a firm generate *disbursement float,* causing a decrease in the firm's book balance but no change in its available balance. For example, suppose General Mechanics, Inc., (GMI) currently has $100,000 on deposit with its bank. On June 8, it buys some raw materials and pays with a check for $100,000. The company's book balance is immediately reduced by $100,000 as a result.

GMI's bank, however, will not find out about this check until it is presented to GMI's bank for payment on, say, June 14. Until the check is presented, the firm's available balance is greater than its book balance by $100,000. In other words, before June 8, GMI has a zero float:

Float = Firm's available balance − Firm's book balance

      = $100,000   − 100,000

      = $0

GMI's position from June 8 to June 14 is:

Disbursement float = Firm's available balance − Firm's book balance

                  = $100,000   − 0

                  = $100,000

During this period of time while the check is clearing, GMI has a balance with the bank of $100,000. It can obtain the benefit of this cash while the check is clearing. For example, the available balance could be temporarily invested in marketable securities and thus earn some interest. We will return to this subject a little later.

Collection Float and Net Float   Checks received by the firm create *collection float.* Collection float increases book balances but does not immediately change available balances. For example, suppose GMI receives a check from a customer for $100,000 on October 8. Assume, as before, that the company has $100,000 deposited at its bank and a zero float. It deposits the check and increases its book balance by $100,000, to $200,000. However, the additional cash is not available to GMI until its bank has presented the check to the customer's bank and received $100,000. This will occur on, say, October 14. In the meantime, the cash position at GMI will reflect a collection float of $100,000. We can summarize these events. Before October 8, GMI's position is:

$$\text{Float} = \text{Firm's available balance} - \text{Firm's book balance}$$
$$= \$100,000 \qquad\qquad - 100,000$$
$$= \$0$$

GMI's position from October 8 to October 14 is:

$$\text{Collection float} = \text{Firm's available balance} - \text{Firm's book balance}$$
$$= \$100,000 \qquad\qquad - 200,000$$
$$= -\$100,000$$

In general, a firm's payment (disbursement) activities generate disbursement float, and its collection activities generate collection float. The net effect, that is, the sum of the total collection and disbursement floats, is the *net float.* The net float at any point in time is simply the overall difference between the firm's available balance and its book balance. If the net float is positive, then the firm's disbursement float exceeds its collection float and its available balance exceeds its book balance. If the available balance is less than the book balance, then the firm has a net collection float.

A firm should be concerned with its net float and available balance more than its book balance. If a financial manager knows that a check written by the company will not clear for several days, that manager will be able to keep a lower cash balance at the bank than might be true otherwise. This can generate a great deal of money.

For example, take the case of petroleum giant Exxon Mobil in early 2000. The average daily sales for Exxon Mobil were about $551 million in early 2000. If Exxon Mobil's collections could have been speeded up by a single day, then Exxon Mobil could have freed up $551 million for investing. At a relatively modest .015 percent daily rate, the interest earned would have been on the order of $83,000 *per day.*

EXAMPLE 17.1 | **Staying Afloat**

Suppose you have $5,000 on deposit. One day you write a check for $1,000 to pay for books, and you deposit $2,000. What are your disbursement, collection, and net floats?

After you write the $1,000 check, you show a balance of $4,000 on your books, but the bank shows $5,000 while the check is clearing. This means you have a disbursement float of $1,000.

After you deposit the $2,000 check, you show a balance of $6,000. Your available balance doesn't rise until the check clears. This means you have a collection float of −$2,000. Your net float is the sum of the collection and disbursement floats, or −$1,000.

Overall, you show $6,000 on your books. The bank shows a $7,000 balance, but only $5,000 is available because your deposit has not cleared. The discrepancy between your available balance and your book balance is the net float (−$1,000), and it is bad for you. If you write another check for $5,500, there may not be sufficient available funds to cover it, and it might bounce. This is the reason that the financial manager has to be more concerned with available balances than book balances.

Float Management   Float management involves controlling the collection and disbursement of cash. The objective in cash collection is to speed up collections and reduce the lag between the time customers pay their bills and the time the cash becomes available. The objective in cash disbursement is to control payments and minimize the firm's costs associated with making payments.

Total collection or disbursement times can be broken down into three parts: mailing time, processing delay, and availability delay:

1. *Mailing time* is the part of the collection and disbursement process during which checks are trapped in the postal system.
2. *Processing delay* is the time it takes the receiver of a check to process the payment and deposit it in a bank for collection.
3. Availability delay refers to the time required to clear a check through the banking system.

Speeding up collections involves reducing one or more of these components. Slowing up disbursements involves increasing one or more of them. We will describe some procedures for managing collection and disbursement times below.

Ethical and Legal Questions   The cash manager must work with collected bank cash balances and not the firm's book balance (which reflects checks that have been deposited but not collected). If this is not done, a cash manager could be drawing on uncollected cash as a source of funds for short-term investing. Most banks charge a penalty rate for the use of uncollected funds. However, banks may not have good enough accounting and control procedures to be fully aware of the use of uncollected funds. This raises some ethical and legal questions for the firm.

For example, in May 1985, Robert Fomon, chairman of E. F. Hutton (a large investment bank), pleaded guilty to 2,000 charges of mail and wire fraud in connection with a scheme the firm had operated from 1980 to 1982. E. F. Hutton employees wrote checks totaling hundreds of millions of dollars against uncollected cash. The proceeds were then invested in short-term money market assets. This type of systematic overdrafting of accounts (or check *kiting,* as it is sometimes called) is neither legal nor ethical and is apparently not a widespread practice among corporations. Also, the particular inefficiencies in the banking system that Hutton was exploiting have been largely eliminated.

For its part, E. F. Hutton paid a $2 million fine, reimbursed the government (the U.S. Department of Justice) $750,000, and reserved an additional $8 million for restitution to defrauded banks. We should note that the key issue in the case against Hutton was not its float management per se, but, rather, its practice of writing checks for no economic reason other than to exploit float.

Electronic Data Interchange: The End of Float?   *Electronic data interchange* (EDI) is a general term that refers to the growing practice of direct, electronic information exchange between all types of businesses. One important use of EDI, often called financial EDI, or FEDI, is to electronically transfer financial information and funds between parties, thereby eliminating paper invoices, paper checks, mailing, and handling. For example, it is now possible to arrange to have your checking account directly debited each month to pay many types of bills, and corporations now routinely directly deposit paychecks into employee accounts. More generally, EDI allows a seller to send a bill electronically to a buyer, thereby avoiding the mail. The buyer can then authorize payment, which also occurs electronically. Its bank then transfers the funds to the seller's account at a different bank. The net effect is that the length of time required to initiate and complete a business transaction is shortened considerably, and much of what we normally think of as float is sharply reduced or eliminated. As the use of FEDI increases (which it will), float management will evolve to focus much more on issues surrounding computerized information exchange and funds transfers.

17.2 | CASH MANAGEMENT: COLLECTION, DISBURSEMENT, AND INVESTMENT

As a part of managing its cash, a firm must make arrangements to collect from its customers, pay its suppliers, and invest any excess cash on hand. We begin by examining how firms collect and concentrate cash.

Cash Collection and Concentration

From our previous discussion, we know that collection delays work against the firm. All other things being the same, then, a firm will adopt procedures to speed up collections and thereby decrease collection times. In addition, even after cash is collected, firms need procedures to funnel, or concentrate, that cash where it can be best used. We discuss some common collection and concentration procedures next.

Components of Collection Time   Based on our discussion above, we can depict the basic parts of the cash collection process as follows: The total time in this process is made up of mailing time, check-processing delay, and the bank's availability delay.

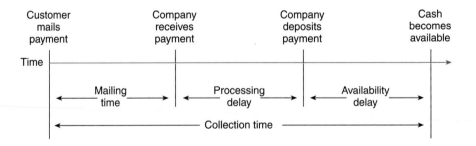

The amount of time that cash spends in each part of the cash collection process depends on where the firm's customers and banks are located and how efficient the firm is at collecting cash.

Cash Collection   How a firm collects from its customers depends in large part on the nature of the business. The simplest case would be a business such as a restaurant chain. Most of its customers will pay with cash, check, or credit card at the point of sale (this is called *over-the-counter collection*), so there is no problem with mailing delay. Normally, the funds would be deposited in a local bank, and the firm would have some means (discussed next) of gaining access to the funds.

When some or all of the payments a company receives are checks that arrive through the mail, all three components of collection time become relevant. The firm may choose to have all the checks mailed to one location, or, more commonly, the firm might have a number of different mail collection points to reduce mailing times. Also, the firm may run its collection operation itself or might hire an outside firm that specializes in cash collection. We discuss these issues in more detail below.

Other approaches to cash collection exist. One that is becoming more common is the preauthorized payment system. With this arrangement, the payment amounts and payment dates are fixed in advance. When the agreed-upon date arrives, the amount is automatically transferred from the customer's bank account to the firm's bank account, sharply reducing or even eliminating collection delays. The same approach is used by firms that have on-line terminals, meaning that when a sale is rung up, the money is immediately transferred to the firm's accounts.

Lockboxes When a firm receives its payments by mail, it must decide where the checks will be mailed and how the checks will be picked up and deposited. Careful selection of the number and locations of collection points can greatly reduce collection times. Many firms use special post office boxes called **lockboxes** to intercept payments and speed cash collection.

Figure 17.1 illustrates a lockbox system. The collection process is started by customers mailing their checks to a post office box instead of sending them to the firm. The lockbox is maintained by a local bank. A large corporation may actually have more than 20 lockboxes around the country.

lockboxes
Special post office boxes set up to intercept and speed up accounts receivable collections.

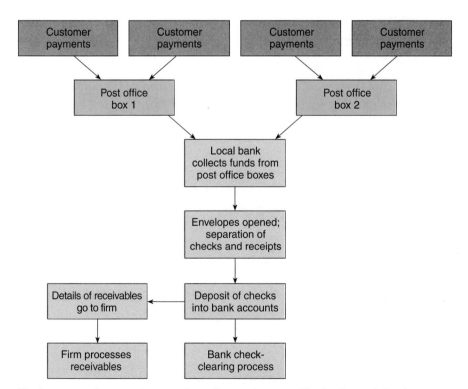

FIGURE 17.1

Overview of lockbox processing

The flow starts when a customer mails remittances to a post office box instead of to the corporation. Several times a day the bank collects the lockbox receipts from the post office. The checks are then put into the company bank accounts.

In the typical lockbox system, the local bank collects the lockbox checks from the post office several times a day. The bank deposits the checks directly to the firm's account. Details of the operation are recorded (in some computer-usable form) and sent to the firm.

A lockbox system reduces mailing time because checks are received at a nearby post office instead of at corporate headquarters. Lockboxes also reduce the processing time because the corporation doesn't have to open the envelopes and deposit checks for collection. In all, a bank lockbox should enable a firm to get its receipts processed, deposited, and cleared faster than if it were to receive checks at its headquarters and deliver them itself to the bank for deposit and clearing.

Cash Concentration   As we discussed earlier, a firm will typically have a number of cash collection points, and, as a result, cash collections may end up in many different banks and bank accounts. From here, the firm needs procedures to move the cash into its main accounts. This is called **cash concentration.** By routinely pooling its cash, the firm greatly simplifies its cash management by reducing the number of accounts that must be tracked. Also, by having a larger pool of funds available, a firm may be able to negotiate a better rate on any short-term investments.

In setting up a concentration system, firms will typically use one or more *concentration banks.* A concentration bank pools the funds obtained from local banks contained within some geographic region. Concentration systems are often used in conjunction with lockbox systems. Figure 17.2 illustrates how an integrated cash collection and cash concentration system might look.

cash concentration

The practice of and procedures for moving cash from multiple banks into the firm's main accounts.

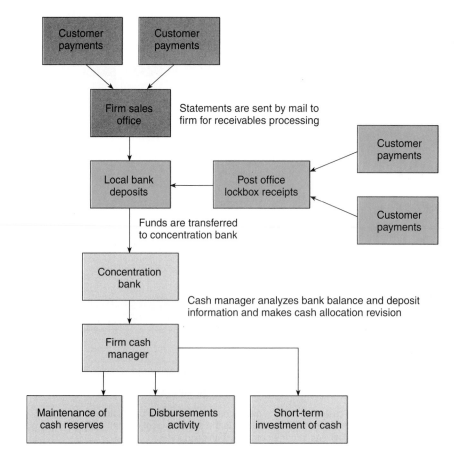

FIGURE 17.2

Lockboxes and concentration banks in a cash management system

Managing Cash Disbursements

From the firm's point of view, disbursement float is desirable, so the goal in managing disbursement float is to slow down disbursements as much as possible. To do this, the firm may develop strategies to *increase* mail float, processing float, and availability float on the checks it writes. Beyond this, firms have developed procedures for minimizing cash held for payment purposes. We discuss the most common of these below.

Increasing Disbursement Float As we have seen, float in terms of slowing down payments comes from the time involved in mail delivery, check processing, and collection of funds. Disbursement float can be increased by writing a check on a geographically distant bank. For example, a New York supplier might be paid with checks drawn on a Los Angeles bank. This will increase the time required for the checks to clear through the banking system. Mailing checks from remote post offices is another way firms slow down disbursement.

Tactics for maximizing disbursement float are debatable on both ethical and economic grounds. First, as we discuss later, payment terms very frequently offer a substantial discount for early payment. The discount is usually much larger than any possible savings from "playing the float game." In such cases, increasing mailing time will be of no benefit if the recipient dates payments based on the date received (as is common) as opposed to the postmark date.

Beyond this, suppliers are not likely to be fooled by attempts to slow down disbursement. The negative consequences from poor relations with suppliers can be costly. In broader terms, intentionally delaying payments by taking advantage of mailing times or unsophisticated suppliers may amount to avoiding paying bills when they are due, an unethical business procedure.

Controlling Disbursements We have seen that maximizing disbursement float is probably poor business practice. However, a firm will still wish to tie up as little cash as possible in disbursements. Firms have therefore developed systems for efficiently managing the disbursement process. The general idea in such systems is to have no more than the minimum amount necessary to pay bills on deposit in the bank. We discuss some approaches to accomplishing this goal next.

Zero-balance accounts With a **zero-balance account,** the firm, in cooperation with its bank, maintains a master account and a set of subaccounts. When a check written on one of the subaccounts must be paid, the necessary funds are transferred in from the master account. Figure 17.3 illustrates how such a system might work. In this case, the firm maintains two disbursement accounts, one for suppliers and one for payroll. As is shown, if the firm does not use zero-balance accounts, then each of these accounts must have a safety stock of cash to meet unanticipated demands. If the firm does use zero-balance accounts, then it can keep one safety stock in a master account and transfer the funds to the two subsidiary accounts as needed. The key is that the total amount of cash held as a buffer is smaller under the zero-balance arrangement, which frees up cash to be used elsewhere.

Controlled disbursement accounts Almost all payments that must be made in a given day are known in the morning. With a **controlled disbursement account,** the bank informs the firm of the day's total, and the firm transfers (usually by wire) the amount needed.

zero-balance account

A disbursement account in which the firm maintains a zero balance, transferring funds in from a master account only as needed to cover checks presented for payment.

controlled disbursement account

A disbursement account to which the firm transfers an amount that is sufficient to cover demands for payment.

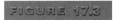

FIGURE 17.3   Zero-balance accounts

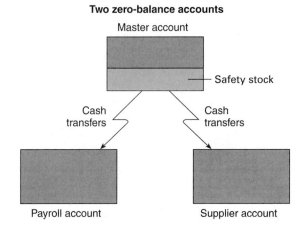

No zero-balance account

Payroll account

Supplier account

Safety stocks

Two zero-balance accounts

Master account

Safety stock

Cash transfers

Cash transfers

Payroll account

Supplier account

With no zero-balance accounts, separate safety stocks must be maintained, which ties up cash unnecessarily. With zero-balance accounts, the firm keeps a single safety stock of cash in a master account. Funds are transferred into disbursement accounts as needed.

Investing Idle Cash

If a firm has a temporary cash surplus, it can invest in short-term securities. As we have mentioned at various times, the market for short-term financial assets is called the *money market*. The maturity of short-term financial assets that trade in the money market is one year or less.

Most large firms manage their own short-term financial assets, transacting through banks and dealers. Some large firms and many small firms use money market mutual funds. These are funds that invest in short-term financial assets for a management fee. The management fee is compensation for the professional expertise and diversification provided by the fund manager.

Among the many money market mutual funds, some specialize in corporate customers. In addition, banks offer arrangements in which the bank takes all excess available funds at the close of each business day and invests them for the firm.

Temporary Cash Surpluses   Firms have temporary cash surpluses for various reasons. Two of the most important are the financing of seasonal or cyclical activities of the firm and the financing of planned or possible expenditures.

Seasonal or cyclical activities   Some firms have a predictable cash flow pattern. They have surplus cash flows during part of the year and deficit cash flows the rest of the year. For example, Toys " Я " Us, a retail toy firm, has a seasonal cash flow pattern influenced by Christmas.

A firm such as Toys " Я " Us may buy marketable securities when surplus cash flows occur and sell marketable securities when deficits occur. Of course, bank loans are another short-term financing device. The use of bank loans and marketable securities to meet temporary financing needs is illustrated in Figure 17.4. In this case, the firm is following a compromise working capital policy in the sense we discussed in the previous chapter.

Planned or possible expenditures   Firms frequently accumulate temporary investments in marketable securities to provide the cash for a plant construction program, dividend payment, or other large expenditure. Thus, firms may issue bonds and stocks before the cash is needed, investing the proceeds in short-term marketable securities and then selling the securities to finance the expenditures. Also, firms may face the possibility of hav-

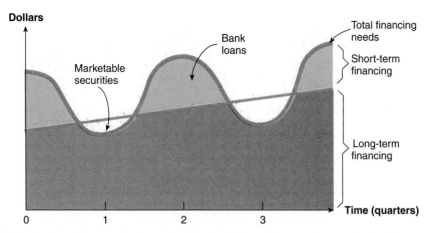

FIGURE 17.4

Seasonal cash demands

Time 1: A surplus cash position exists. Seasonal demand for current assets is low. The surplus is invested in short-term marketable securities.

Time 2: A deficit cash position exists. Seasonal demand for current assets is high. The financial deficit is financed by selling marketable securities and by bank borrowing.

ing to make a large cash outlay. An obvious example would be the possibility of losing a large lawsuit. Firms may build up cash surpluses against such a contingency.

Characteristics of Short-Term Securities   Given that a firm has some temporarily idle cash, there are a variety of short-term securities available for investing. The most important characteristics of these short-term marketable securities are their maturity, default risk, marketability, and taxability.

Maturity   Maturity refers to the time period over which interest and principal payments are made. From Chapter 6, we know that for a given change in the level of interest rates, the prices of longer-maturity securities will change more than those of shorter-maturity securities. As a consequence, firms often limit their investments in marketable securities to those maturing in less than 90 days to avoid the risk of losses in value from changing interest rates.

Default risk   Default risk refers to the probability that interest and principal will not be paid in the promised amounts on the due dates (or not paid at all). Of course, some securities have negligible default risk, such as U.S. Treasury bills. Given the purposes of investing idle corporate cash, firms typically avoid investing in marketable securities with significant default risk.

Marketability   Marketability refers to how easy it is to convert an asset to cash; so marketability and liquidity mean much the same thing. Some money market instruments are much more marketable than others. At the top of the list are U.S. Treasury bills, which can be bought and sold very cheaply and very quickly.

Taxability   Interest earned on money market securities that are not some kind of government obligation (either federal or state) is taxable at the local, state, and federal levels. U.S. Treasury obligations such as T-bills are exempt from state taxation, but other government-backed debt is not. Municipal securities are exempt from federal taxes, but they may be taxed at the state level.

Some Different Types of Money Market Securities   Money market securities are generally highly marketable and short term. They usually have low risk of default. They are issued by the U.S. government (for example, U.S. Treasury bills), domestic and foreign banks (for example, certificates of deposit), and business corporations (for example, commercial paper). There are many types in all, and we only illustrate a few of the most common here.

U.S. Treasury bills are obligations of the U.S. government that mature in 90, 180, or 360 days. The 90-day and 180-day bills are sold by auction every week, and 360-day bills are sold quarterly.

Short-term tax-exempts are short-term securities issued by states, municipalities, and certain other agencies. Since these are all considered municipal securities, they are exempt from federal taxes. Short-term tax-exempts have more default risk than U.S. Treasury issues and are less marketable. Since the interest is exempt from federal income tax, the pre-tax yield on tax-exempts is lower than that on comparable securities such as U.S. Treasury bills. Also, corporations face some restrictions on holding tax-exempts as investments.

Commercial paper refers to short-term securities issued by finance companies, banks, and corporations. Typically, commercial paper is unsecured. Maturities range from a few weeks to 270 days.

There is no especially active secondary market in commercial paper. As a consequence, the marketability can be low; however, firms that issue commercial paper will often repurchase it directly before maturity. The default risk of commercial paper depends on the financial strength of the issuer.

Certificates of deposit (CDs) are short-term loans to commercial banks. These are normally jumbo CDs—those in excess of $100,000. There are active markets in CDs of 3-month, 6-month, 9-month, and 12-month maturities.

Because 70 to 80 percent of the dividends received by one corporation from another are exempt from taxation, the relatively high dividend yields on preferred stock provide a strong incentive for investment. The only problem is that the dividend is fixed with ordinary preferred stock, so the price can fluctuate more than is desirable in a short-term investment. So-called money market preferred stock is a recent innovation featuring a floating dividend. The dividend is reset fairly often (usually every 49 days), so this type of preferred has much less price volatility than ordinary preferred, and it has become a popular short-term investment.

CONCEPT QUESTIONS

17.2a What is a lockbox? What purpose does it serve?

17.2b What is a concentration bank? What purpose does it serve?

17.2c Is maximizing disbursement float a sound business practice?

17.2d What are some types of money market securities?

17.3 | CREDIT AND RECEIVABLES

When a firm sells goods and services, it can demand cash on or before the delivery date or it can extend credit to customers and allow some delay in payment.

Why would firms grant credit? The obvious reason is that offering credit is a way of stimulating sales. The costs associated with granting credit are not trivial. First, there is the chance that the customer will not pay. Second, the firm has to bear the costs of carrying the receivables. The credit policy decision thus involves a trade-off between the benefits of increased sales and the costs of granting credit.

From an accounting perspective, when credit is granted, an account receivable is created. These receivables include credit to other firms, called *trade credit,* and credit granted consumers, called *consumer credit,* and they represent a major investment of financial resources by U.S. businesses. Furthermore, trade credit is a very important source of financing for corporations. However we look at it, receivables and receivables management are very important aspects of a firm's short-term financial policy.

Components of Credit Policy

If a firm decides to grant credit to its customers, then it must establish procedures for extending credit and collecting. In particular, the firm will have to deal with the following components of credit policy:

1. **Terms of sale.** The terms of sale establish how the firm proposes to sell its goods and services. If the firm grants credit to a customer, the terms of sale will specify (perhaps implicitly) the credit period, the cash discount and discount period, and the type of credit instrument.

2. **Credit analysis.** In granting credit, a firm determines how much effort to expend trying to distinguish between customers who will pay and customers who will not pay. Firms use a number of devices and procedures to determine the probability that customers will not pay, and, put together, these are called credit analysis.

3. **Collection policy.** After credit has been granted, the firm has the potential problem of collecting the cash when it becomes due, for which it must establish a collection policy.

In the next several sections, we will discuss these components of credit policy that collectively make up the decision to grant credit.

terms of sale
Conditions under which a firm sells its goods and services for cash or credit.

credit analysis
The process of determining the probability that customers will not pay.

collection policy
Procedures followed by a firm in collecting accounts receivable.

Terms of the Sale

As we described above, the terms of a sale are made up of three distinct elements:

1. The period for which credit is granted (the credit period)
2. The cash discount and the discount period
3. The type of credit instrument

Within a given industry, the terms of sale are usually fairly standard, but these terms vary quite a bit across industries. In many cases, the terms of sale are remarkably archaic and literally date to previous centuries. Organized systems of trade credit that resemble current practice can be easily traced to the great fairs of medieval Europe, and they almost surely existed long before then.

The Basic Form   The easiest way to understand the terms of sale is to consider an example. For bulk candy, terms of 2/10, net 60 might be quoted.[2] This means that customers have 60 days from the invoice date (discussed next) to pay the full amount. However, if payment is made within 10 days, a 2 percent cash discount can be taken.

Consider a buyer who places an order for $1,000, and assume that the terms of the sale are 2/10, net 60. The buyer has the option of paying $1,000 × (1 − .02) = $980 in 10 days, or paying the full $1,000 in 60 days. If the terms were stated as just net 30, then the customer would have 30 days from the invoice date to pay the entire $1,000, and no discount would be offered for early payment.

---

[2]The terms of sale cited from specific industries in this section and elsewhere are drawn from Theodore N. Beckman, *Credits and Collections: Management and Theory* (New York: McGraw-Hill, 1962).

In general, credit terms are interpreted in the following way:

(**take this discount off the invoice price**)/(if you pay in this many days),
(else pay the full invoice amount in this many days)

Thus, 5/10, net 45 means take a 5 percent discount from the full price if you pay within 10 days, or else pay the full amount in 45 days.

credit period

The length of time for which credit is granted.

The Credit Period   The **credit period** is the basic length of time for which credit is granted. The credit period varies widely from industry to industry, but it is almost always between 30 and 120 days. If a cash discount is offered, then the credit period has two components: the net credit period and the cash discount period.

The net credit period is the length of time the customer has to pay. The cash discount period, as the name suggests, is the time during which the discount is available. With 2/10, net 30, for example, the net credit period is 30 days and the cash discount period is 10 days.

invoice

Bill for goods or services provided by the seller to the purchaser.

The invoice date   The invoice date is the beginning of the credit period. An **invoice** is a written account of merchandise shipped to the buyer. For individual items, by convention, the invoice date is usually the shipping date or the billing date, *not* the date that the buyer receives the goods or the bill.

Length of the credit period   A number of factors influence the length of the credit period. Two of the most important are the *buyer's* inventory period and operating cycle. All other things being equal, the shorter these are, the shorter the credit period will normally be.

Based on our discussion in Chapter 16, the operating cycle has two components: the inventory period and the receivables period. The inventory period is the time it takes the buyer to acquire inventory (from us), process it, and sell it. The receivables period is the time it then takes the buyer to collect on the sale. Note that the credit period that we offer is effectively the buyer's payables period.

By extending credit, we finance a portion of our buyer's operating cycle and thereby shorten the buyer's cash cycle. If our credit period exceeds the buyer's inventory period, then we are not only financing the buyer's inventory purchases, but part of the buyer's receivables as well.

Furthermore, if our credit period exceeds our buyer's operating cycle, then we are effectively providing financing for aspects of our customer's business beyond the immediate purchase and sale of our merchandise. The reason is that the buyer effectively has a loan from us even after the merchandise is resold, and the buyer can use that credit for other purposes. For this reason, the length of the buyer's operating cycle is often cited as an appropriate upper limit to the credit period.

There are a number of other factors that influence the credit period. Many of these also influence our customers' operating cycles; so, once again, these are related subjects. Among the most important are:

1. *Perishability and collateral value.* Perishable items have relatively rapid turnover and relatively low collateral value. Credit periods are thus shorter for such goods.

2. *Consumer demand.* Products that are well established generally have more rapid turnover. Newer or slow-moving products will often have longer credit periods associated with them to entice buyers.

3. *Cost, profitability, and standardization.* Relatively inexpensive goods tend to have shorter credit periods. The same is true for relatively standardized goods and raw ma-

terials. These all tend to have lower markups and higher turnover rates, both of which lead to shorter credit periods.

4. *Credit risk.* The greater the credit risk of the buyer, the shorter the credit period is likely to be (assuming that credit is granted at all).

5. *The size of the account.* If the account is small, the credit period may be shorter, because small accounts are more costly to manage, and the customers are less important.

6. *Competition.* When the seller is in a highly competitive market, longer credit periods may be offered as a way of attracting customers.

7. *Customer type.* A single seller might offer different credit terms to different buyers. A food wholesaler, for example, might supply groceries, bakeries, and restaurants. Each group would probably have different credit terms. More generally, sellers often have both wholesale and retail customers, and they frequently quote different terms to the two types.

Cash Discounts As we have seen, **cash discounts** are often part of the terms of sale. The practice of granting discounts for cash purchases in the United States dates to the Civil War and is widespread today. One reason discounts are offered is to speed up the collection of receivables. This will have the effect of reducing the amount of credit being offered, and the firm must trade this off against the cost of the discount.

cash discount
A discount given to induce prompt payment. Also, sales discount.

Notice that when a cash discount is offered, the credit is essentially free during the discount period. The buyer only pays for the credit after the discount expires. With 2/10, net 30, a rational buyer either pays in 10 days to make the greatest possible use of the free credit or pays in 30 days to get the longest possible use of the money in exchange for giving up the discount. So, by giving up the discount, the buyer effectively gets $30 - 10 = 20$ days' credit.

Another reason for cash discounts is that they are a way of charging higher prices to customers that have had credit extended to them. In this sense, cash discounts are a convenient way of charging for the credit granted to customers.

In our examples, it might seem that the discounts are rather small. With 2/10, net 30, for example, early payment only gets the buyer a 2 percent discount. Does this provide a significant incentive for early payment? The answer is yes because the implicit interest rate is extremely high.

To see why the discount is important, we will calculate the cost to the buyer of not paying early. To do this, we will find the interest rate that the buyer is effectively paying for the trade credit. Suppose the order is for $1,000. The buyer can pay $980 in 10 days or wait another 20 days and pay $1,000. It's obvious that the buyer is effectively borrowing $980 for 20 days and that the buyer pays $20 in interest on the "loan." What's the interest rate?

With $20 in interest on $980 borrowed, the rate is $20/980 = 2.0408\%$. This is relatively low, but remember that this is the rate per 20-day period. There are $365/20 = 18.25$ such periods in a year, so, by not taking the discount, the buyer is paying an effective annual rate of:

$$\text{EAR} = 1.020408^{18.25} - 1 = 44.6\%$$

From the buyer's point of view, this is an expensive source of financing!

Given that the interest rate is so high here, it is unlikely that the seller benefits from early payment. Ignoring the possibility of default by the buyer, the decision by a customer to forgo the discount almost surely works to the seller's advantage.

EXAMPLE 17.2 | **What's the Rate?**

Ordinary tiles are often sold with terms of 3/30, net 60. What effective annual rate does a buyer pay by not taking the discount? What would the APR be if one were quoted?

Here we have 3 percent discount interest on $60 - 30 = 30$ days' credit. The rate per 30 days is $.03/.97 = 3.093\%$. There are $365/30 = 12.17$ such periods in a year, so the effective annual rate is:

$$EAR = 1.03093^{12.17} - 1 = 44.9\%$$

The APR, as always, would be calculated by multiplying the rate per period by the number of periods:

$$APR = .03093 \times 12.17 = 37.6\%$$

An interest rate calculated like this APR is often quoted as the cost of the trade credit, and, as this example illustrates, this can seriously understate the true cost.

---

credit instrument

The evidence of indebtedness.

Credit Instruments   The **credit instrument** is the basic evidence of indebtedness. Most trade credit is offered on *open account*. This means that the only formal instrument of credit is the invoice, which is sent with the shipment of goods and which the customer signs as evidence that the goods have been received. Afterwards, the firm and its customers record the exchange on their books of account.

At times, the firm may require that the customer sign a *promissory note*. This is a basic IOU and might be used when the order is large or when the firm anticipates a problem in collections. Promissory notes are not common, but they can eliminate possible controversies later about the existence of debt.

One problem with promissory notes is that they are signed after delivery of the goods. One way to obtain a credit commitment from a customer before the goods are delivered is to arrange a *commercial draft*. Typically, the firm draws up a commercial draft calling for the customer to pay a specific amount by a specified date. The draft is then sent to the customer's bank with the shipping invoices.

If immediate payment on the draft is required, it is called a *sight draft*. If immediate payment is not required, then the draft is a *time draft*. When the draft is presented and the buyer "accepts" it, meaning that the buyer promises to pay it in the future, then it is called a *trade acceptance* and is sent back to the selling firm. The seller can then keep the acceptance or sell it to someone else. If a bank accepts the draft, meaning that the bank is guaranteeing payment, then the draft becomes a *banker's acceptance*. This arrangement is common in international trade.

Optimal Credit Policy

In principle, the optimal amount of credit is determined by the point at which the incremental cash flows from increased sales are exactly equal to the incremental costs of carrying the increased investment in accounts receivable.

The Total Credit Cost Curve   The trade-off between granting credit and not granting credit isn't hard to identify, but it is difficult to quantify precisely. As a result, we can only describe an optimal credit policy.

To begin, the carrying costs associated with granting credit come in three forms:

1. The required return on receivables
2. The losses from bad debts
3. The cost of managing credit and credit collections

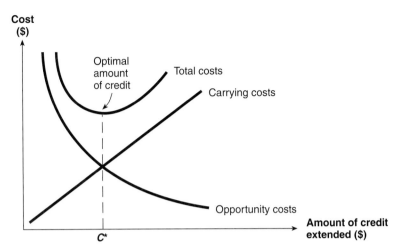

FIGURE 17.5

The costs of granting credit

Carrying costs are the cash flows that must be incurred when credit is granted. They are positively related to the amount of credit extended.

Opportunity costs are the lost sales from refusing credit. These costs go down when credit is granted.

We have already discussed the first and second of these. The third cost, the cost of managing credit, is the expense associated with running the credit department. Firms that don't grant credit have no such department and no such expense. These three costs will all increase as credit policy is relaxed.

If a firm has a very restrictive credit policy, then all of the above costs will be low. In this case, the firm will have a "shortage" of credit, so there will be an opportunity cost. This opportunity cost is the extra potential profit from credit sales that is lost because credit is refused. This forgone benefit comes from two sources, the increase in quantity sold, and, potentially, a higher price. These costs go down as credit policy is relaxed.

The sum of the carrying costs and the opportunity costs of a particular credit policy is called the total **credit cost curve.** We have drawn such a curve in Figure 17.5. As Figure 17.5 illustrates, there is a point, C^*, where the total credit cost is minimized. This point corresponds to the optimal amount of credit, or, equivalently, the optimal investment in receivables.

If the firm extends more credit than this amount, the additional net cash flow from new customers will not cover the carrying costs of the investment in receivables. If the level of receivables is below this amount, then the firm is forgoing valuable profit opportunities.

In general, the costs and benefits from extending credit will depend on characteristics of particular firms and industries. All other things being equal, for example, it is likely that firms with (1) excess capacity, (2) low variable operating costs, and (3) repeat customers will extend credit more liberally than other firms. See if you can explain why each of these contributes to a more liberal credit policy.

credit cost curve

Graphical representation of the sum of the carrying costs and the opportunity costs of a credit policy.

Organizing the Credit Function Firms that grant credit have the expense of running a credit department. In practice, firms often choose to contract out all or part of the credit function to a factor, an insurance company, or a captive finance company. Chapter 16 discussed factoring, an arrangement in which the firm sells its receivables. Depending on the specific arrangement, the factor may have full responsibility for credit checking, authorization, and collection. Smaller firms may find such an arrangement cheaper than running a credit department.

Firms that manage internal credit operations are self-insured against default, meaning that they bear all the risk of nonpayment. An alternative is to buy credit insurance through an insurance company. The insurance company offers coverage up to a preset dollar limit for accounts. As you would expect, accounts with a higher credit rating merit higher insurance limits. This type of insurance is particularly important for exporters, and government insurance is available for certain types of exports.

captive finance company

A wholly owned subsidiary that handles the credit function for the parent company.

Large firms often extend credit through a **captive finance company,** which is simply a wholly owned subsidiary that handles the credit function for the parent company. General Motors Acceptance Corporation, or GMAC, is a well-known example. General Motors sells to car dealers who in turn sell to customers. GMAC finances the dealer's inventory of cars and also finances customers who buy the cars.

Credit Analysis

Thus far, we have focused on establishing credit terms. Once a firm decides to grant credit to its customers, it must then establish guidelines for determining who will and who will not be allowed to buy on credit. *Credit analysis* refers to the process of deciding whether or not to extend credit to a particular customer. It usually involves two steps: gathering relevant information and determining creditworthiness.

Credit Information   If a firm does want credit information on customers, there are a number of sources. Information sources commonly used to assess creditworthiness include the following:

1. *Financial statements.* A firm can ask a customer to supply financial statements such as balance sheets and income statements. Minimum standards and rules of thumb based on financial ratios like the ones we discussed in Chapter 3 can then be used as a basis for extending or refusing credit.

2. *Credit reports on the customer's payment history with other firms.* Quite a few organizations sell information on the credit strength and credit history of business firms. The best-known and largest firm of this type is Dun & Bradstreet, which provides subscribers with a credit reference book and credit reports on individual firms. Experian (formerly TRW) is another well-known credit-reporting firm. Ratings and information are available for a huge number of firms, including very small ones. Equifax, Trans Union, and Experian are the major suppliers of consumer credit information.

3. *Banks.* Banks will generally provide some assistance to their business customers in acquiring information on the creditworthiness of other firms.

4. *The customer's payment history with the firm.* The most obvious way to obtain information about the likelihood of a customer's not paying is to examine whether they have settled past obligations and how quickly they have met these obligations.

five Cs of credit

The five basic credit factors to be evaluated: character, capacity, capital, collateral, and conditions.

Credit Evaluation and Scoring   There are no magical formulas for assessing the probability that a customer will not pay. In very general terms, the classic **five Cs of credit** are the basic factors to be evaluated:

1. *Character.* The customer's willingness to meet credit obligations.

2. *Capacity.* The customer's ability to meet credit obligations out of operating cash flows.

3. *Capital.* The customer's financial reserves.

4. *Collateral.* Assets pledged by the customer for security in case of default.

5. *Conditions.* General economic conditions in the customer's line of business.

Credit scoring refers to the process of calculating a numerical rating for a customer based on information collected; credit is then granted or refused based on the result. For example, a firm might rate a customer on a scale of 1 (very poor) to 10 (very good) on each of the five *C*s of credit using all the information available about the customer. A credit score could then be calculated based on the total. From experience, a firm might choose to grant credit only to customers with a score above, say, 30.

credit scoring
The process of quantifying the probability of default when granting consumer credit.

Firms such as credit card issuers have developed elaborate statistical models for credit scoring. Usually, all of the legally relevant and observable characteristics of a large pool of customers are studied to find their historic relation to default rates. Based on the results, it is possible to determine the variables that best predict whether or not a customer will pay and then calculate a credit score based on those variables.

Because credit-scoring models and procedures determine who is and who is not creditworthy, it is not surprising that they have been the subject of government regulation. In particular, the kinds of background and demographic information that can be used in the credit decision are limited.

Collection Policy

Collection policy is the final element in credit policy. Collection policy involves monitoring receivables to spot trouble and obtaining payment on past-due accounts.

Monitoring Receivables   To keep track of payments by customers, most firms will monitor outstanding accounts. First, a firm will normally keep track of its average collection period, ACP, through time. If a firm is in a seasonal business, the ACP will fluctuate during the year, but unexpected increases in the ACP are a cause for concern. Either customers in general are taking longer to pay, or some percentage of accounts receivable is seriously overdue.

The **aging schedule** is a second basic tool for monitoring receivables. To prepare one, the credit department classifies accounts by age.[3] Suppose a firm has $100,000 in receivables. Some of these accounts are only a few days old, but others have been outstanding for quite some time. The following is an example of an aging schedule.

aging schedule
A compilation of accounts receivable by the age of each account.

Aging Schedule		
Age of Account	**Amount**	**Percentage of Total Value of Accounts Receivable**
0–10 days	$ 50,000	50%
11–60 days	25,000	25
61–80 days	20,000	20
Over 80 days	5,000	5
	$100,000	100%

If this firm has a credit period of 60 days, then 25 percent of its accounts are late. Whether or not this is serious depends on the nature of the firm's collections and customers. It is often the case that accounts beyond a certain age are almost never collected. Monitoring the age of accounts is very important in such cases.

---

[3]Aging schedules are used elsewhere in business. For example, aging schedules are often prepared for inventory items.

Firms with seasonal sales will find the percentages on the aging schedule changing during the year. For example, if sales in the current month are very high, then total receivables will also increase sharply. This means that the older accounts, as a percentage of total receivables, become smaller and might appear less important. Some firms have refined the aging schedule so that they have an idea of how it should change with peaks and valleys in their sales.

Collection Effort   A firm usually goes through the following sequence of procedures for customers whose payments are overdue:

1. It sends out a delinquency letter informing the customer of the past-due status of the account.
2. It makes a telephone call to the customer.
3. It employs a collection agency.
4. It takes legal action against the customer.

At times, a firm may refuse to grant additional credit to customers until arrearages are cleared up. This may antagonize a normally good customer, and it points to a potential conflict of interest between the collections department and the sales department.

CONCEPT QUESTIONS

17.3a What are the basic components of credit policy?

17.3b Explain what terms of "3/45, net 90" mean. What is the effective interest rate?

17.3c What are the five *C*s of credit?

17.4 | INVENTORY MANAGEMENT

Like receivables, inventories represent a significant investment for many firms. For a typical manufacturing operation, inventories will often exceed 15 percent of assets. For a retailer, inventories could represent more than 25 percent of assets. From our discussion in Chapter 16, we know that a firm's operating cycle is made up of its inventory period and its receivables period. This is one reason for considering credit and inventory policy in the same chapter. Beyond this, both credit policy and inventory policy are used to drive sales, and the two must be coordinated to ensure that the process of acquiring inventory, selling it, and collecting on the sale proceeds smoothly. For example, changes in credit policy designed to stimulate sales must be simultaneously accompanied by planning for adequate inventory.

The Financial Manager and Inventory Policy

Despite the size of a typical firm's investment in inventories, the financial manager of a firm will not normally have primary control over inventory management. Instead, other functional areas such as purchasing, production, and marketing will usually share decision-making authority. Inventory management has become an increasingly important specialty in its own right, and financial management will often only have input into the decision. However, as the accompanying *Reality Bytes* box describes, inventory policy can have dramatic financial effects. We will therefore survey some basics of inventory and inventory policy in the sections ahead.

reality | BYTES

YOU SAY YOU WANT AN E-REVOLUTION?

In the e-world, business-to-consumer, or B2C in e-speak, transactions via the Internet have probably created the biggest stir and gotten most of the press. However, in early 2000, the new e-commerce buzzwords were B2B (business to business), e-procurement, and Intranets. As with most things Internet-related, the changes have put the world of B2B transactions on the verge of a revolution.

In November 1999, Ford Motor Co. announced it was launching a joint venture with database giant Oracle Corp. to create a massive on-line marketplace for its suppliers. The idea is simple. Ford spends about $80 billion annually on purchases of goods from suppliers. If Ford could find a way to speed up the ordering process, save money on each order placed, and trim inventories, the company would stand to benefit in a big way. The answer? An Intranet link between all of its suppliers. Once the link is completed, Ford estimates it will save about 20 percent of the cost of acquiring raw materials annually. The benefits don't stop there. Once linked, the suppliers will be able to transact with one another as well. Ford estimates that its 30,000 suppliers spend about $300 billion annually on their own purchases, providing fertile ground for potential savings. Not to be outdone, just hours after Ford's announcement, General Motors revealed that it was partnering with procurement software designer Commerce One to form a similar site of its own. In GM's case, it spends about $87 billion annually and estimates that its 30,000 suppliers spend more than $500 billion annually on their purchases. The benefits to GM stand to be huge.

You might guess that GM's and Ford's suppliers would be happy about the new on-line exchanges since their purchasing costs would decrease and their access to information would increase. However, many suppliers serve both companies, and it would be difficult for them to participate in two different on-line exchanges, especially for big customers like GM and Ford. As a result, the suppliers put pressure on GM and Ford

to standardize their exchanges, and, in February 2000, the automotive giants announced plans to merge their on-line exchanges into one. To make the exchange (later named Covisint) truly global, DaimlerChrysler, Nissan, Renault, and Toyota all agreed to join. Predictions of the ultimate benefits to be reaped vary quite a bit, but, by some estimates, the North American automakers could save about $1,200 per vehicle, while European automakers might save about $639 per vehicle, and Japanese automakers could save about $540 per vehicle. Most of the benefits will come from savings in the cost of acquisition of raw materials. Furthermore, it is expected that, once linked, the 30,000-plus suppliers will realize lower costs in both selling products and acquiring goods.

The auto industry is a huge network of interrelated businesses and was ripe for an on-line exchange of this type. But of course, there are other industries for which this concept will work as well. For example, a B2B exchange was launched in early 2000 by aerospace and defense industry firms Boeing, Lockheed Martin, BAE, and Raytheon. Sears launched the first global on-line exchange for the retail industry, and IBM and Wal-Mart already have their own on-line systems for use by their suppliers. By the time you read this, many more B2B exchanges will have been created. Just as the Internet has been revolutionizing business-to-consumer transactions, e-procurement will revolutionize B2B transactions, bringing with it lower costs, greater speed, and better access to information.

Sources: "Auto Giants Electrify the E-Commerce World," *Treasury and Risk Management,* November/December 1999, p. 15.
"Big Blue's E-Procurement Plans," *Treasury and Risk Management,* January/February 2000, p. 21.
"Toyota Plans to Join Buying Exchange," *The New York Times,* 23 May 2000, p. 2, col. 4.
"Study Sees B2B Saving N. American Auto Industries $1,200/Vehicle," Dow Jones News Service, 24 May, 2000.
"Big Three Car Makers Plan Net Exchange," *The Wall Street Journal,* 28 February 2000, p. A3.

Inventory Types

For a manufacturer, inventory is normally classified into one of three categories. The first category is *raw material*. This is whatever the firm uses as a starting point in its production process. Raw materials might be something as basic as iron ore for a steel manufacturer or something as sophisticated as disk drives for a computer manufacturer.

The second type of inventory is *work-in-progress,* which is just what the name suggests—unfinished product. How big this portion of inventory is depends in large part on the length of the production process. For an airframe manufacturer, for example, work-in-progress can be substantial. The third and final type of inventory is *finished goods,* that is, products ready to ship or sell.

There are three things to keep in mind concerning inventory types. First, the names for the different types can be a little misleading because one company's raw materials could be another's finished goods. For example, going back to our steel manufacturer, iron ore would be a raw material, and steel would be the final product. An auto body panel stamping operation will have steel as its raw material and auto body panels as its finished goods, and an automobile assembler will have body panels as raw materials and automobiles as finished products.

The second thing to keep in mind is that the various types of inventory can be quite different in terms of their liquidity. Raw materials that are commoditylike or relatively standardized can be easy to convert to cash. Work-in-progress, on the other hand, can be quite illiquid and have little more than scrap value. As always, the liquidity of finished goods depends on the nature of the product.

Finally, a very important distinction between finished goods and other types of inventories is that the demand for an inventory item that becomes a part of another item is usually termed *derived* or *dependent demand* because the firm's need for these inventory types depends on its need for finished items. In contrast, the firm's demand for finished goods is not derived from demand for other inventory items, so it is sometimes said to be *independent.*

Inventory Costs

As we discussed in Chapter 16, there are two basic types of costs associated with current assets in general and with inventory in particular. The first of these are *carrying costs.* Here, carrying costs represent all of the direct and opportunity costs of keeping inventory on hand. These include:

1. Storage and tracking costs
2. Insurance and taxes
3. Losses due to obsolescence, deterioration, or theft
4. The opportunity cost of capital for the invested amount

The sum of these costs can be substantial, roughly ranging from 20 to 40 percent of inventory value per year.

The other types of costs associated with inventory are *shortage costs.* These are costs associated with having inadequate inventory on hand. The two components of shortage costs are restocking costs and costs related to safety reserves. Depending on the firm's business, order or restocking costs are either the costs of placing an order with suppliers or the cost of setting up a production run. The costs related to safety reserves are opportunity losses such as lost sales and loss of customer goodwill that result from having inadequate inventory.

A basic trade-off in inventory management exists because carrying costs increase with inventory levels while shortage or restocking costs decline with inventory levels. The basic goal of inventory management is thus to minimize the sum of these two costs. We consider ways to reach this goal in the next section.

CONCEPT QUESTIONS

17.4a What are the different types of inventory?

17.4b What are three things to remember when examining inventory types?

17.4c What is the basic goal of inventory management?

INVENTORY MANAGEMENT TECHNIQUES   17.5

As we described earlier, the goal of inventory management is usually framed as cost minimization. Three techniques are discussed in this section, ranging from the relatively simple to the very complex.

The ABC Approach

The ABC approach is a simple approach to inventory management where the basic idea is to divide inventory into three (or more) groups. The underlying rationale is that a small portion of inventory in terms of quantity might represent a large portion in terms of inventory value. For example, this situation would exist for a manufacturer that uses some relatively expensive, high-tech components and some relatively inexpensive basic materials in producing its products.[4]

Figure 17.6 illustrates an ABC comparison of items in terms of the percentage of inventory value represented by each group versus the percentage of items represented. As Figure 17.6 shows, the A Group constitutes only 10 percent of inventory by item count, but it represents over half of the value of inventory. The A Group items are thus monitored closely, and inventory levels are kept relatively low. At the other end, basic inventory items, such as nuts and bolts, will also exist, but because these are crucial and inexpensive, large quantities are ordered and kept on hand. These would be C Group items. The B Group is made up of in-between items.

The Economic Order Quantity Model

The economic order quantity (EOQ) model is the best-known approach to explicitly establishing an optimal inventory level. The basic idea is illustrated in Figure 17.7, which plots the various costs associated with holding inventory (on the vertical axis) against inventory levels (on the horizontal axis). As is shown, inventory carrying costs rise and restocking costs decrease as inventory levels increase. From our discussion of the total credit cost curve in this chapter, the general shape of the total inventory cost curve is familiar. With the EOQ model, we will attempt to specifically locate the minimum total cost point, Q^*.

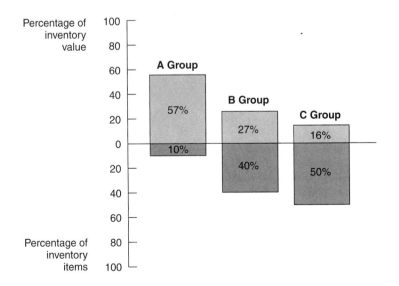

FIGURE 17.6

ABC inventory analysis

---

[4]The ABC approach to inventory should not be confused with activity-based costing, a common topic in managerial accounting.

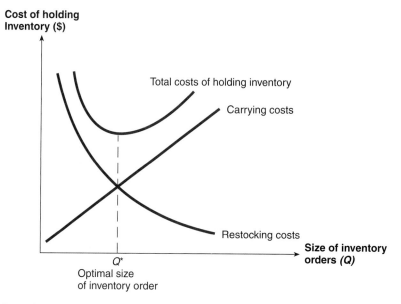

Restocking costs are greatest when the firm holds a small quantity of inventory.
Carrying costs are greatest when there is a large quantity of inventory on hand.
Total costs are the sum of the carrying and restocking costs.

In our discussion below, an important point to keep in mind is that the actual cost of the inventory itself is not included. The reason is that the *total* amount of inventory the firm needs in a given year is dictated by sales. What we are analyzing here is how much the firm should have on hand at any particular time. More precisely, we are trying to determine what order size the firm should use when it restocks its inventory.

Inventory Depletion   To develop the EOQ, we will assume that the firm's inventory is sold off at a steady rate until it hits zero. At that point, the firm restocks its inventory back to some optimal level. For example, suppose the Eyssell Corporation starts out today with 3,600 units of a particular item in inventory. Annual sales of this item are 46,800 units, which is about 900 per week. If Eyssell sells off 900 units in inventory each week, then, after four weeks, all the available inventory will be sold, and Eyssell will restock by ordering (or manufacturing) another 3,600 and start over. This selling and restocking process produces a sawtooth pattern for inventory holdings; this pattern is illustrated in Figure 17.8. As the figure shows, Eyssell always starts with 3,600 units in inventory and ends up at zero. On average, then, inventory is half of 3,600, or 1,800 units.

The Carrying Costs   As Figure 17.7 illustrates, carrying costs are normally assumed to be directly proportional to inventory levels. Suppose we let Q be the quantity of inventory that Eyssell orders each time (3,600 units); we will call this the restocking quantity. Average inventory would then just be $Q/2$, or 1,800 units. If we let CC be the carrying cost per unit per year, Eyssell's total carrying costs will be:

Total carrying costs = Average inventory $\times$ Carrying costs per unit

$$= (Q/2) \times CC \qquad \text{[17.1]}$$

FIGURE 17.8

Inventory holdings for
the Eyssell Corporation

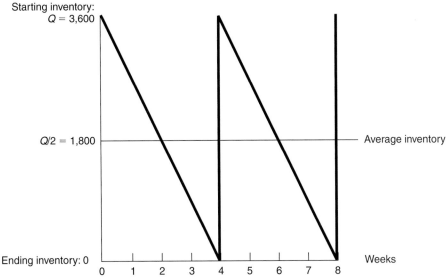

The Eyssell Corporation starts with inventory of 3,600 units. The quantity drops to zero by
the end of the fourth week. The average inventory is $Q/2 = 3,600/2 = 1,800$ over the period.

In Eyssell's case, if carrying costs were \$.75 per unit per year, then total carrying costs
would be the average inventory of 1,800 multiplied by \$.75, or \$1,350 per year.

The Shortage Costs   For now, we will focus only on the restocking costs. In essence,
we will assume that the firm never actually runs short on inventory, so that costs relating to
safety reserves are not important. We will return to this issue below.

Restocking costs are normally assumed to be fixed. In other words, every time we place
an order, there are fixed costs associated with that order (remember that the cost of the inventory itself is not considered here). Suppose we let T be the firm's total unit sales per year.
If the firm orders Q units each time, then it will need to place a total of T/Q orders. For
Eyssell, annual sales were 46,800, and the order size was 3,600. Eyssell thus places a total
of $46,800/3,600 = 13$ orders per year. If the fixed cost per order is F, the total restocking
cost for the year would be:

$$\text{Total restocking cost} = \text{Fixed cost per order} \times \text{Number of orders}$$
$$= F \times (T/Q) \qquad [17.2]$$

For Eyssell, order costs might be \$50 per order, so the total restocking cost for 13 orders
would be $\$50 \times 13 = \$650$ per year.

The Total Costs   The total costs associated with holding inventory are the sum of the
carrying costs and the restocking costs:

$$\text{Total costs} = \text{Carrying costs} + \text{Restocking costs}$$
$$= (Q/2) \times \text{CC} + F \times (T/Q) \qquad [17.3]$$

Our goal is to find the value of Q, the restocking quantity, that minimizes this cost. To see
how we might go about this, we can calculate total costs for some different values of Q. For

the Eyssell Corporation, we had carrying costs (CC) of $.75 per unit per year, fixed costs (*F*) of $50 per order, and total unit sales (*T*) of 46,800 units. With these numbers, some possible total costs are (check some of these for practice):

Restocking Quantity (Q)	Total Carrying Costs (Q/2 × CC)	+	Restocking Costs (F × T/Q)	=	Total Costs
500	$ 187.5		$4,680.0		$4,867.5
1,000	375.0		2,340.0		2,715.0
1,500	562.5		1,560.0		2,122.5
2,000	750.0		1,170.0		1,920.0
2,500	**937.5**		**936.0**		**1,873.5**
3,000	1,125.0		780.0		1,905.0
3,500	1,312.5		668.6		1,981.1

Inspecting the numbers, we see that total costs start out at almost $5,000, and they decline to just under **$1,900**. The cost-minimizing quantity appears to be approximately **2,500**.

To find the precise cost-minimizing quantity, we can take a look back at Figure 17.7. What we notice is that the minimum point occurs right where the two lines cross. At this point, carrying costs and restocking costs are the same. For the particular types of costs we have assumed here this will always be true, so we can find the minimum point just by setting these costs equal to each other and solving for Q^*:

Carrying costs = Restocking costs

$$(Q^*/2) \times CC = F \times (T/Q^*) \qquad \text{[17.4]}$$

With a little algebra, we get:

$$(Q^*)^2 = \frac{2T \times F}{CC} \qquad \text{[17.5]}$$

To solve for Q^*, we take the square root of both sides to find:

$$Q^* = \sqrt{\frac{2T \times F}{CC}} \qquad \text{[17.6]}$$

economic order quantity (EOQ)

The restocking quantity that minimizes the total inventory costs.

This reorder quantity, which minimizes the total inventory cost, is called the **economic order quantity**, or **EOQ**. For the Eyssell Corporation, the EOQ is:

$$Q^* = \sqrt{\frac{2T \times F}{CC}}$$

$$= \sqrt{\frac{(2 \times 46,800) \times \$50}{.75}}$$

$$= \sqrt{6,240,000}$$

$$= 2,498 \text{ units} \qquad \text{[17.7]}$$

Thus, for Eyssell, the economic order quantity is actually 2,498 units. At this level, verify that the restocking costs and carrying costs are identical (they're both $936.75).

Carrying Costs | EXAMPLE 17.3

Thiewes Shoes begins each period with 100 pairs of hiking boots in stock. This stock is depleted each period and reordered. If the carrying cost per pair of boots per year is $3, what are the total carrying costs for the hiking boots?

Inventories always start at 100 items and end up at 0, so average inventory is 50 items. At an annual cost of $3 per item, total carrying costs are $150.

Restocking Costs | EXAMPLE 17.4

In our previous example (Example 17.3), suppose Thiewes sells a total of 600 pairs of boots in a year. How many times per year does Thiewes restock? Suppose the restocking cost is $20 per order. What are total restocking costs?

Thiewes orders 100 items each time. Total sales are 600 items per year, so Thiewes restocks six times per year, or about every two months. The restocking costs would be 6 orders × $20 per order = $120.

The EOQ | EXAMPLE 17.5

Based on our previous two examples, what size orders should Thiewes place to minimize costs? How often will Thiewes restock? What are the total carrying and restocking costs? The total costs?

We have that the total number of pairs of boots ordered for the year (T) is 600. The restocking cost (F) is $20 per order, and the carrying cost (CC) is $3. We can calculate the EOQ for Thiewes as follows:

$$\text{EOQ} = \sqrt{\frac{2T \times F}{CC}}$$
$$= \sqrt{\frac{(2 \times 600) \times \$20}{3}}$$
$$= \sqrt{8{,}000}$$
$$= 89.44 \text{ units}$$

Since Thiewes sells 600 pairs per year, it will restock 600/89.44 = 6.71 times. The total restocking costs will be $20 × 6.71 = $134.16. Average inventory will be 89.44/2 = 44.72. The carrying costs will be $3 × 44.72 = $134.16, the same as the restocking costs. The total costs are thus $268.33.

Extensions to the EOQ Model

Thus far, we have assumed that a company will let its inventory run down to zero and then reorder. In reality, a company will wish to reorder before its inventory goes to zero for two reasons. First, by always having at least some inventory on hand, the firm minimizes the risk of a stock-out and the resulting losses of sales and customers. Second, when a firm does reorder, there will be some time lag before the inventory arrives. Thus, to finish our discussion of the EOQ, we consider two extensions, safety stocks and reordering points.

Safety Stocks A *safety stock* is the minimum level of inventory that a firm keeps on hand. Inventories are reordered whenever the level of inventory falls to the safety stock level. Part A of Figure 17.9 illustrates how a safety stock can be incorporated into an EOQ

FIGURE 17.9   Safety stocks and reorder points

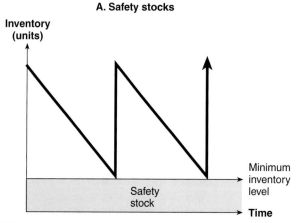

A. Safety stocks

With a safety stock, the firm reorders when inventory reaches a minimum level.

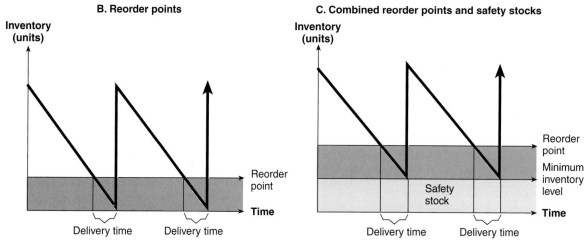

B. Reorder points

When there are lags in delivery or production times, the firm reorders when inventory reaches the reorder point.

C. Combined reorder points and safety stocks

By combining safety stocks and reorder points, the firm maintains a buffer against unforeseen events.

model. Notice that adding a safety stock simply means that the firm does not run its inventory all the way down to zero. Other than this, the situation here is identical to that considered in our earlier discussion of the EOQ.

Reorder Points   To allow for delivery time, a firm will place orders before inventories reach a critical level. The *reorder points* are the times at which the firm will actually place its inventory orders. These points are illustrated in Part B of Figure 17.9. As is shown, the reorder points simply occur some fixed number of days (or weeks or months) before inventories are projected to reach zero.

One of the reasons that a firm will keep a safety stock is to allow for uncertain delivery times. We can therefore combine our reorder point and safety stock discussions in Part C of Figure 17.9. The result is a generalized EOQ model in which the firm orders in advance of anticipated needs and also keeps a safety stock of inventory to guard against unforeseen fluctuations in demand and delivery times.

Managing Derived-Demand Inventories

The third type of inventory management technique is used to manage derived-demand inventories. As we described previously, demand for some inventory types is derived from, or dependent on, other inventory needs. A good example is given by the auto manufacturing industry, where the demand for finished products derives from consumer demand, marketing programs, and other factors related to projected unit sales. The demand for inventory items such as tires, batteries, headlights, and other components is then completely determined by the number of autos planned. Materials requirements planning and just-in-time inventory management are two methods for managing demand-dependent inventories.

Materials Requirements Planning   Production and inventory specialists have developed computer-based systems for ordering and/or scheduling production of demand-dependent types of inventories. These systems fall under the general heading of **materials requirements planning (MRP).** The basic idea behind MRP is that, once finished goods inventory levels are set, it is possible to determine what levels of work-in-progress inventories must exist to meet the need for finished goods. From there, it is possible to calculate the quantity of raw materials that must be on hand. This ability to schedule backwards from finished goods inventories stems from the dependent nature of work-in-progress and raw materials inventories. MRP is particularly important for complicated products for which a variety of components are needed to create the finished product.

materials requirements planning (MRP)
A set of procedures used to determine inventory levels for demand-dependent inventory types such as work-in-progress and raw materials.

Just-in-Time Inventory   **Just-in-time,** or **JIT, inventory** is a modern approach to managing dependent inventories. The goal of JIT is essentially to minimize such inventories, thereby maximizing turnover. The approach began in Japan, and it is a fundamental part of much of Japanese manufacturing philosophy. As the name suggests, the basic goal of JIT is to have only enough inventory on hand to meet immediate production needs.

The result of the JIT system is that inventories are reordered and restocked frequently. Making such a system work and avoiding shortages requires a high degree of cooperation among suppliers. Japanese manufacturers often have a relatively small, tightly integrated group of suppliers with whom they work closely to achieve the needed coordination. These suppliers are a part of a large manufacturer's (such as Toyota's) industrial group, or *keiretsu.* Each large manufacturer tends to have its own *keiretsu.* It also helps to have suppliers located nearby, a situation that is common in Japan.

The *kanban* is an integral part of a JIT inventory system, and JIT systems are sometimes called *kanban systems.* The literal meaning of *kanban* is "card" or "sign," but, broadly speaking, a kanban is a signal to a supplier to send more inventory. For example, a kanban could literally be a card attached to a bin of parts. When a worker pulls that bin, the card is detached and routed back to the supplier, who then supplies a replacement bin.

A JIT inventory system is an important part of a larger production planning process. A full discussion of it would necessarily shift our focus away from finance to production and operations management, so we will leave it here.

just-in-time (JIT) inventory
A system for managing demand-dependent inventories that minimizes inventory holdings.

CONCEPT QUESTIONS

17.5a What does the EOQ model determine for the firm?

17.5b Which cost component of the EOQ model does JIT inventory minimize?

SUMMARY AND CONCLUSIONS

This chapter has covered cash, receivables, and inventory management. Along the way, we have touched on a large number of subjects. Some of the more important issues we examined are:

1. Firms seek to manage their cash by keeping no more than is needed on hand. The reason is that holding cash has an opportunity cost, namely, the returns that could be earned by investing the money.

2. Float is an important consideration in cash management, and firms seek to manage collections and disbursements in ways designed to minimize the firm's net float.

3. A firm's credit policy includes the terms of sale, credit analysis, and collection policy. The terms of sale cover three related subjects: the credit period, cash discount, and credit instrument.

4. The optimal credit policy for a firm depends on many specific factors, but generally involves trading off the costs of granting credit, such as the carrying costs of receivables and the possibility of nonpayment, against the benefits in terms of increased sales.

5. There are different types of inventories that differ greatly in their liquidity and management. The basic trade-off in inventory management is the cost of carrying inventory versus the cost of restocking. We developed the famous EOQ model, which explicitly balances these costs.

6. Firms use different inventory management techniques; we described a few of the better known, including the ABC approach and just-in-time, or JIT, inventory management.

CHAPTER REVIEW AND SELF-TEST PROBLEMS

17.1 Calculating Float.   You have $10,000 on deposit with no outstanding checks or uncleared deposits. One day you write a check for $4,000 and then deposit a check for $3,000. What are your disbursement, collection, and net floats?

17.2 The EOQ.   Heusen Computer Manufacturing starts each period with 4,000 central processing units (CPUs) in stock. This stock is depleted each month and reordered. If the carrying cost per CPU is $1, and the fixed order cost is $10, is Heusen following an economically advisable strategy?

■ Answers to Chapter Review and Self-Test Problems

17.1 First, after you write the check for $4,000, you show a balance of $6,000. However, while the check is clearing, your bank shows a balance of $10,000. This is a $4,000 disbursement float, and it is good for you. Next, when you deposit the $3,000, you show a balance of $9,000, but your account will not be credited for the $3,000 until it clears. This is a −$3,000 collection float, and it is bad for you.

The sum of the disbursement float and the collection float is your net float of $1,000. In other words, on a net basis, you show a balance of $9,000, but your bank shows a $10,000 balance, so, in net terms, you are benefiting from the float.

17.2 We can answer by first calculating Heusen's carrying and restocking costs. The average inventory is 2,000 CPUs, and, since the carrying costs are $1 per CPU, total carrying costs are $2,000. Heusen restocks every month at a fixed order cost of $10, so the total restocking costs are $120. What we see is that carrying costs are large relative to reorder costs, so Heusen is carrying too much inventory.

To determine the optimal inventory policy, we can use the EOQ model. Because Heusen orders 4,000 CPUs 12 times per year, total needs (T) are 48,000 CPUs. The fixed order cost is $10, and the carrying cost per unit (CC) is $1. The EOQ is therefore:

$$EOQ = \sqrt{\frac{2T \times F}{CC}}$$

$$= \sqrt{\frac{(2 \times 48{,}000) \times \$10}{1}}$$

$$= \sqrt{960{,}000}$$

$$= \textbf{979.80 units}$$

We can check this by noting that the average inventory is about 490 CPUs, so the carrying cost is $490. Heusen will have to reorder 48,000/979.8 = 49 times. The fixed order cost is $10, so the total restocking cost is also $490.

CRITICAL THINKING AND CONCEPTS REVIEW

1. **Cash Management.**   Is it possible for a firm to have too much cash? Why would shareholders care if a firm accumulates large amounts of cash?

2. **Cash Management.**   What options are available to a firm if it believes it has too much cash? How about too little?

3. **Agency Issues.**   Are stockholders and creditors likely to agree on how much cash a firm should keep on hand?

4. **Motivations for Holding Cash.**   Most often, when news breaks about a firm's cash position, it's because the firm is running low, but that wasn't the case for Ford, Chrysler, and General Motors at the end of 1997. At that time, Ford held $20.8 billion in cash and marketable securities, GM had $14.5 billion, and Chrysler had $7.1 billion. Similarly, by the end of 1998, Nissan, the Japanese auto manufacturer, had piled up about 400 billion yen, which amounted to several billion dollars. Thus, each company had substantial cash reserves; in fact, particularly in Ford's case, *enormous* might be more descriptive. Why would firms such as these hold such large quantities of cash?

5. **Short-Term Investments.**   Why is a preferred stock with a dividend tied to short-term interest rates an attractive short-term investment for corporations with excess cash?

6. **Collection and Disbursement Floats.**   Which would a firm prefer: a net collection float or a net disbursement float? Why?

7. **Float.**   Suppose a firm has a book balance of $2 million. At the automatic teller machine (ATM), the cash manager finds out that the bank balance is $2.5 million. What is the situation here? If this is an ongoing situation, what ethical dilemma arises?

8. **Short-Term Investments.**   For each of the short-term marketable securities given here, provide an example of the potential disadvantages the investment has for meeting a corporation's cash management goals.
   a. U.S. Treasury bills
   b. Ordinary preferred stock

    c. Negotiable certificates of deposit (NCDs)

    d. Commercial paper

9.   **Agency Issues.**   It is sometimes argued that excess cash held by a firm can aggravate agency problems (discussed in Chapter 1) and, more generally, reduce incentives for shareholder wealth maximization. How would you frame the issue here?

10.   **Use of Excess Cash.**   One option a firm usually has with any excess cash is to pay its suppliers more quickly. What are the advantages and disadvantages of this use of excess cash?

11.   **Use of Excess Cash.**   Another option usually available is to reduce the firm's outstanding debt. What are the advantages and disadvantages of this use of excess cash?

12.   **Float.**   An unfortunately common practice goes like this (warning: don't try this at home): Suppose you are out of money in your checking account; however, your local grocery store will, as a convenience to you as a customer, cash a check for you. So you cash a check for $200. Of course, this check will bounce unless you do something. To prevent this, you go to the grocery the next day and cash another check for $200. You take this $200 and deposit it. You repeat this process every day, and, in doing so, you make sure that no checks bounce. Eventually, manna from heaven arrives (perhaps in the form of money from home) and you are able to cover your outstanding checks.

    To make it interesting, suppose you are absolutely certain that no checks will bounce along the way. Assuming this is true, and ignoring any question of legality (what we have described is probably illegal check kiting), is there anything unethical about this? If you say yes, then why? In particular, who is harmed?

13.   **Credit Instruments.**   Describe each of the following:

    a. Sight draft

    b. Time draft

    c. Banker's acceptance

    d. Promissory note

    e. Trade acceptance

14.   **Trade Credit Forms.**   In what form is trade credit most commonly offered? What is the credit instrument in this case?

15.   **Receivables Costs.**   What are the costs associated with carrying receivables? What are the costs associated with not granting credit? What do we call the sum of the costs for different levels of receivables?

16.   **Five *C*s of Credit. What are the five *C*s of credit? Explain why each is important.**

17.   **Credit Period Length.**   What are some of the factors that determine the length of the credit period? Why is the length of the buyer's operating cycle often considered an upper bound on the length of the credit period?

18.   **Credit Period Length.**   In each of the following pairings, indicate which firm would probably have a longer credit period and explain your reasoning.

    a. Firm A sells a miracle cure for baldness; Firm B sells toupees.

    b. Firm A specializes in products for landlords; Firm B specializes in products for renters.

    c. Firm A sells to customers with an inventory turnover of 10 times; Firm B sells to customers with an inventory turnover of 20 times.

    d. Firm A sells fresh fruit; Firm B sells canned fruit.

    e. Firm A sells and installs carpeting; Firm B sells rugs.

19. **Inventory Types.** What are the different inventory types? How do the types differ? Why are some types said to have dependent demand whereas other types are said to have independent demand?

20. **Just-in-Time Inventory.** If a company moves to a JIT inventory management system, what will happen to inventory turnover? What will happen to total asset turnover? What will happen to return on equity, ROE? (Hint: Remember the Du Pont equation from Chapter 3.)

21. **Inventory Costs.** If a company's inventory carrying costs are $5 million per year and its fixed order costs are $8 million per year, do you think the firm keeps too much inventory on hand or too little? Why?

QUESTIONS AND PROBLEMS

1. **Calculating Float.** You have $300,000 on deposit with no outstanding checks or uncleared deposits. One day you write a check for $185,000. Does this create a disbursement float or a collection float? What is your available balance? Book balance?

   Basic
   (Questions 1–16)

2. **Calculating Float.** You have $125,000 on deposit with no outstanding checks or uncleared deposits. If you deposit a check for $110,000, does this create a disbursement float or a collection float? What is your available balance? Book balance?

3. **Calculating Float.** You have $50,000 on deposit with no outstanding checks or uncleared deposits. One day you write a check for $8,000 and then deposit a check for $25,000. What are your disbursement, collection, and net floats?

4. **Cash Discounts.** You place an order for 800 units of Good X at a unit price of $90. The supplier offers terms of 2/30, net 70.
   a. How long do you have to pay before the account is overdue? If you take the full period, how much should you remit?
   b. What is the discount being offered? How quickly must you pay to get the discount? If you do take the discount, how much should you remit?
   c. If you don't take the discount, how much interest are you paying implicitly? How many days' credit are you receiving?

5. **Calculating Float.** In a typical month, the Simpson Corporation receives 100 checks totaling $90,000. These are delayed six days on average. What is the average daily float?

6. **Calculating Net Float.** Each business day, on average, a company writes checks totaling $21,000 to pay its suppliers. The usual clearing time for the checks is five days. Meanwhile, the company is receiving payments from its customers each day, in the form of checks, totaling $38,000. The cash from the payments is available to the firm after two days.
   a. Calculate the company's disbursement float, collection float, and net float.
   b. How would your answer to part (a) change if the collected funds were available in one day instead of two?

7. **Cash Discounts.** You place an order for 400 units of inventory at a unit price of $50. The supplier offers terms of 2/10, net 40.
   a. How long do you have to pay before the account is overdue? If you take the full period, how much should you remit?
   b. What is the discount being offered? How quickly must you pay to get the discount? If you do take the discount, how much should you remit?
   c. If you don't take the discount, how much interest are you paying implicitly? How many days' credit are you receiving?

8. **Size of Accounts Receivable.**   The No Mo Corporation has annual sales of $80 million. The average collection period is 65 days. What is No Mo's average investment in accounts receivable as shown on the balance sheet?

9. **ACP and Accounts Receivable.**   Nomura Data, Inc., sells earnings forecasts for Japanese securities. Its credit terms are 4/10, net 50. Based on experience, 70 percent of all customers will take the discount.

    a. What is the average collection period for Nomura?

    b. If Nomura sells 1,100 forecasts every month at a price of $2,000 each, what is its average balance sheet amount in accounts receivable?

10. **Size of Accounts Receivable.**   Three Doors Down, Inc., has weekly credit sales of $65,000, and the average collection period is 42 days. The cost of production is 80 percent of the selling price. What is TDD's average accounts receivable figure?

11. **Terms of Sale.**   A firm offers terms of 1/10, net 45. What effective annual interest rate does the firm earn when a customer does not take the discount? Without doing any calculations, explain what will happen to this effective rate if:

    a. The discount is changed to 2 percent.

    b. The credit period is increased to 60 days.

    c. The discount period is increased to 15 days.

    d. What is the EAR for each scenario?

12. **ACP and Receivables Turnover.**   Hoo-Ya, Inc., has an average collection period of 53 days. Its average daily investment in receivables is $56,000. What are annual credit sales? What is the receivables turnover?

13. **EOQ.**   Clap Off Manufacturing uses 1,900 switch assemblies per week and then reorders another 1,900. If the relevant carrying cost per switch assembly is $20, and the fixed order cost is $700, is Clap Off's inventory policy optimal? Why or why not?

14. **EOQ.**   The Trektronics store begins each week with 190 phasers in stock. This stock is depleted each week and reordered. If the carrying cost per phaser is $24 per year and the fixed order cost is $80, what is the total carrying cost? What is the restocking cost? Should Trektronics increase or decrease its order size? Describe an optimal inventory policy for Trektronics in terms of order size and order frequency.

15. **EOQ.**   Ramsey Manufacturing uses 4,000 subframes per week and then reorders another 4,000. If the relevant carrying cost per subframe is $35, and the fixed order cost is $2,600, is Ramsey's inventory policy optimal? Why or why not?

16. **EOQ.**   The Wheeling Pottery Store begins each month with 1,200 pots in stock. This stock is depleted each month and reordered. If the carrying cost per pot is $8 per year and the fixed order cost is $90, what is the total carrying cost? What is the restocking cost? Should Wheeling increase or decrease its order size? Describe an optimal inventory policy for Wheeling in terms of order size and order frequency.

www.mhhe.com/rwj

Spreadsheet Templates 1, 6, 9

CHAPTER 18

International Aspects of Financial Management

**AFTER READING THIS CHAPTER, YOU SHOULD
HAVE A GOOD UNDERSTANDING OF:**

■ How exchange rates are quoted, what they mean, and the difference between spot and forward exchange rates

■ Purchasing power parity and interest rate parity and their implications for exchange rate changes

■ The different types of exchange rate risk and ways firms manage exchange rate risk

■ The impact of political risk on international business investing

ON JANUARY 1, 1999, a new currency was born: the euro. The euro became the common currency for the 11 European nations that make up the European Economic and Monetary Union (EMU). In an extraordinary turn of events, these 11 countries effectively turned their sovereign currencies, and control of their monetary policies, over to the new European Central Bank. Some of the major proponents of the new system were businesses in the 11 countries, many of which felt the union was necessary to enhance competitiveness with countries like the United States. Ultimately, currencies such as the German mark and the French franc will become footnotes in history, which will make it easier for consumers to compare the prices of goods of all types across national borders. In this chapter, we explore the role played by currencies and exchange rates, along with a number of other key topics in international finance.

As businesses of all types have increased their reliance on international operations, all areas of business have been strongly affected. Human resources, production, marketing, accounting, and strategy, for example, all become much more complex when nondomestic considerations come into play. This chapter discusses one of the most important aspects of international business, the impact of shifting exchange rates and what companies (and individuals) can do to protect themselves against adverse exchange rate movements.

Companies with significant foreign operations are often called *international corporations* or *multinationals*. Such companies must consider many financial factors that do not directly affect purely domestic firms. These include foreign exchange rates, differing interest rates from country to country, complex accounting methods for foreign operations, foreign tax rates, and foreign government intervention.

The basic principles of corporate finance still apply to international corporations; like domestic companies, they seek to invest in projects that create more value for the shareholders (or owners) than they cost and to arrange financing that raises cash at the lowest possible cost. In other words, the net present value principle holds for both foreign and domestic operations, but it is usually more complicated to apply the NPV rule to foreign investments.

We won't have much to say here about the role of cultural and social differences in international business. We also will not be discussing the implications of differing political and economic systems. These factors are of great importance to international businesses, but it would take another book to do them justice. Consequently, we will focus only on some purely financial considerations in international finance and some key aspects of foreign exchange markets.

18.1 | TERMINOLOGY

American Depository Receipt (ADR)

Security issued in the U.S. representing shares of a foreign stock, allowing that stock to be traded in the U.S.

cross-rate

The implicit exchange rate between two currencies (usually non-U.S.) quoted in some third currency (usually the U.S. dollar).

Eurobonds

International bonds issued in multiple countries but denominated in a single currency (usually the issuer's currency).

Eurocurrency

Money deposited in a financial center outside of the country whose currency is involved.

A common buzzword for the student of business finance is *globalization.* The first step in learning about the globalization of financial markets is to conquer the new vocabulary. As with any specialty, international finance is rich in jargon. Accordingly, we get started on the subject with a highly eclectic vocabulary exercise.

The terms that follow are presented alphabetically, and they are not all of equal importance. We choose these particular ones because they appear frequently in the financial press or because they illustrate some of the colorful language of international finance.

1. An **American Depository Receipt,** or **ADR,** is a security issued in the United States that represents shares of a foreign stock, allowing that stock to be traded in the United States. Foreign companies use ADRs, which are issued in U.S. dollars, to expand the pool of potential U.S. investors. ADRs are available in two forms: company sponsored, which are listed on an exchange, and unsponsored, which usually are held by the investment bank that deals in the ADR. Both forms are available to individual investors, but only company-sponsored issues are quoted daily in newspapers.

2. The **cross-rate** is the implicit exchange rate between two currencies (usually non-U.S.) when both are quoted in some third currency, usually the U.S. dollar.

3. A **Eurobond** is a bond issued in multiple countries, but denominated in a single currency, usually the issuer's home currency. Such bonds have become an important way to raise capital for many international companies and governments. Eurobonds are issued outside the restrictions that apply to domestic offerings and are syndicated and traded mostly from London. Trading can and does take place anywhere there is a buyer and a seller.

4. **Eurocurrency** is money deposited in a financial center outside of the country whose currency is involved. For instance, Eurodollars—the most widely used Eurocurrency—are U.S. dollars deposited in banks outside the U.S. banking system.

5. **Foreign bonds,** unlike Eurobonds, are issued in a single country and are usually denominated in that country's currency. Often, the country in which these bonds are issued will draw distinctions between them and bonds issued by domestic issuers, including different tax laws, restrictions on the amount issued, and tougher disclosure rules.

   Foreign bonds often are nicknamed for the country where they are issued: Yankee bonds (United States), Samurai bonds (Japan), Rembrandt bonds (the Netherlands), and Bulldog bonds (Britain). Partly because of tougher regulations and disclosure requirements, the foreign-bond market hasn't grown in past years with the vigor of the Eurobond market. A substantial portion of all foreign bonds are issued in Switzerland.

6. **Gilts,** technically, are British and Irish government securities, although the term also includes issues of local British authorities and some overseas public-sector offerings.

7. The **London Interbank Offer Rate (LIBOR)** is the rate that most international banks charge one another for loans of Eurodollars overnight in the London market. LIBOR is a cornerstone in the pricing of money market issues and other debt issues by both government and corporate borrowers. Interest rates are frequently quoted as some spread over LIBOR, and they then float with the LIBOR rate.

8. There are two basic kinds of **swaps:** interest rate and currency. An interest rate swap occurs when two parties exchange a floating-rate payment for a fixed-rate payment or vice versa. Currency swaps are agreements to deliver one currency in exchange for another. Often both types of swaps are used in the same transaction when debt denominated in different currencies is swapped.

foreign bonds
International bonds issued in a single country, usually denominated in that country's currency.

gilts
British and Irish government securities.

London Interbank Offer Rate (LIBOR)
The rate most international banks charge one another for overnight Eurodollar loans.

swaps
Agreements to exchange two securities or currencies.

CONCEPT QUESTIONS

18.1a What are the differences between a Eurobond and a foreign bond?

18.1b What are Eurodollars?

FOREIGN EXCHANGE MARKETS AND EXCHANGE RATES | 18.2

The **foreign exchange market** is undoubtedly the world's largest financial market. It is the market where one country's currency is traded for another's. Most of the trading takes place in a few currencies such as the U.S. dollar ($), the British pound sterling (£), and the Japanese yen (¥). Table 18.1 lists some of the more common currencies and their symbols.

The foreign exchange market is an over-the-counter market, so there is no single location where traders get together. Instead, market participants are located in the major commercial and investment banks around the world. They communicate using computer terminals, telephones, and other telecommunications devices. For example, one communications network for foreign transactions is the Society for Worldwide Interbank Financial Telecommunications (SWIFT), a Belgian not-for-profit cooperative. Using data transmission lines, a bank in New York can send messages to a bank in London via SWIFT regional processing centers.

foreign exchange market
The market in which one country's currency is traded for another's.

TABLE 18.1

International currency
symbols

Country	Currency	Symbol
Australia	Dollar	A$
Austria	Schilling	Sch
Belgium	Franc	BF
Canada	Dollar	Can$
Denmark	Krone	DKr
EMU	Euro	€
Finland	Markka	FM
France	Franc	FF
Germany	Deutsche mark	DM
Greece	Drachma	Dr
India	Rupee	Rs
Iran	Rial	RI
Italy	Lira	Lit
Japan	Yen	¥
Kuwait	Dinar	KD
Mexico	Peso	Ps
Netherlands	Guilder	FL
Norway	Krone	NKr
Saudi Arabia	Riyal	SR
Singapore	Dollar	S$
South Africa	Rand	R
Spain	Peseta	Pta
Sweden	Krona	Skr
Switzerland	Franc	SF
United Kingdom	Pound	£
United States	Dollar	$

The many different types of participants in the foreign exchange market include the following:

1. Importers who pay for goods in foreign currencies.
2. Exporters who receive foreign currency and may want to convert to their domestic currency.
3. Portfolio managers who buy or sell foreign stocks and bonds.
4. Foreign exchange brokers who match buy and sell orders.
5. Traders who "make a market" in foreign currencies.
6. Speculators who try to profit from changes in exchange rates.

Exchange Rates

exchange rate
The price of one country's currency expressed in terms of another country's currency.

An **exchange rate** is simply the price of one country's currency expressed in terms of another country's currency. In practice, almost all trading of currencies takes place in terms of the U.S. dollar. For example, both the French franc and the German mark are traded with their prices quoted in U.S. dollars.

Exchange Rate Quotations   Figure 18.1 reproduces exchange rate quotations as they appear in *The Wall Street Journal*. The first column (labeled "U.S. $ equiv.") gives the

Exchange rate quotations **FIGURE 18.1**

CURRENCY TRADING

Wednesday, June 14, 2000
EXCHANGE RATES

The New York foreign exchange mid-range rates below apply to trading among banks in amounts of $1 million and more, as quoted at 4 p.m. Eastern time by Reuters and other sources. Retail transactions provide fewer units of foreign currency per dollar. Rates for the 11 Euro currency countries are derived from the latest dollar-euro rate using the exchange ratios set 1/1/99.

Country	U.S. $ equiv. Wed	Currency per U.S. $ Wed
Argentina (Peso)	1.0002	.9998
Australia (Dollar)	.5997	1.6674
Austria (Schilling)	.06961	14.365
Bahrain (Dinar)	2.6525	.3770
Belgium (Franc)	.0237	42.1129
Brazil (Real)	.5525	1.8100
Britain (Pound)	1.4995	.6669
1-month forward	1.5003	.6665
3-months forward	1.5021	.6657
6-months forward	1.5049	.6645
Canada (Dollar)	.6812	1.4680
1-month forward	.6817	1.4669
3-months forward	.6827	1.4648
6-months forward	.6842	1.4615
Chile (Peso)	.001885	530.55
China (Renminbi)	.1208	8.2768
Colombia (Peso)	.0004734	2112.25
Czech. Rep. (Koruna)		
Commercial rate	.02659	37.604
Denmark (Krone)	.1284	7.7852
Ecuador (Sucre)		
Floating rate	.00004000	25000.00
Finland (Markka)	.1611	6.2070
France (Franc)	.1460	6.8479
1-month forward	.1463	6.8347
3-months forward	.1469	6.8076
6-months forward	.1477	6.7711
Germany (Mark)	.4898	2.0418
1-month forward	.4907	2.0378
3-months forward	.4927	2.0297
6-months forward	.4953	2.0188
Greece (Drachma)	.002850	350.91
Hong Kong (Dollar)	.1283	7.7927
Hungary (Forint)	.003688	271.12
India (Rupee)	.02237	44.700
Indonesia (Rupiah)	.0001176	8505.00
Ireland (Punt)	1.2162	.8222
Israel (Shekel)	.2436	4.1043
Italy (Lira)	.0004947	2021.37

Country	U.S. $ equiv. Wed	Currency per U.S. $ Wed
Japan (Yen)	.009374	106.68
1-month forward	.009428	106.07
3-months forward	.009537	104.85
6-months forward	.009698	103.11
Jordan (Dinar)	1.4065	.7110
Kuwait (Dinar)	3.2637	.3064
Lebanon (Pound)	.0006605	1514.03
Malaysia (Ringgit)	.2632	3.8000
Malta (Lira)	2.3294	.4293
Mexico (Peso)		
Floating rate	.1021	9.7900
Netherland (Guilder)	.4347	2.3006
New Zealand (Dollar)	.4746	2.1070
Norway (Krone)	.1163	8.6009
Pakistan (Rupee)	.01922	52.035
Peru (new Sol)	.2873	3.4805
Philippines (Peso)	.02358	42.400
Poland (Zloty) (d)	.2264	4.4160
Portugal (Escudo)	.004778	209.29
Russia (Ruble) (a)	.03527	28.355
Saudi Arabia (Riyal)	.2666	3.7506
Singapore (Dollar)	.5807	1.7220
Slovak Rep. (Koruna)	.02287	43.721
South Africa (Rand)	.1442	6.9350
South Korea (Won)	.0008975	1114.25
Spain (Peseta)	.005757	173.70
Sweden (Krona)	.1175	8.5135
Switzerland (Franc)	.6128	1.6319
1-month forward	.6147	1.6269
3-months forward	.6182	1.6176
6-months forward	.6231	1.6048
Taiwan (Dollar)	.03255	30.725
Thailand (Baht)	.02562	39.025
Turkey (Lira)	.00000163	612440.00
United Arab (Dirham)	.2723	3.6729
Uruguay (New Peso)		
Financial	.08304	12.043
Venezuela (Bolivar)	.001470	680.50
SDR	1.3337	.7498
Euro	.9579	1.0440

Special Drawing Rights (SDR) are based on exchange rates for the U.S., German, British, French, and Japanese currencies. Source: International Monetary Fund.

a-Russian Central Bank rate. Trading band lowered on 8/17/98. b-Government rate. d-Floating rate; trading band suspended on 4/11/00. Foreign exchange rates are available from Reader's Reference Service (413)592-3600.

number of dollars it takes to buy one unit of foreign currency. For example, the Australian dollar is quoted at .5997, which means that you can buy one Australian dollar with .5997 U.S. dollars.

The second column shows the amount of foreign currency per U.S. dollar. The Australian dollar is quoted here at 1.6674, so you can get 1.6674 Australian dollars for one U.S. dollar. Naturally, this second exchange rate is just the reciprocal of the first one; 1/.5997 = 1.6674, allowing for a rounding error.

EXAMPLE 18.1 | On the Mark

Suppose you have $1,000. Based on the rates in Figure 18.1, how many Japanese yen can you get? Alternatively, if a Porsche costs DM 200,000 (DM is the abbreviation for deutsche marks), how many dollars will you need to buy it?

The exchange rate in terms of yen per dollar (second column) is 106.68. Your $1,000 will thus get you:

$$\$1,000 \times 106.68 \text{ yen per } \$1 = 106,680 \text{ yen}$$

Since the exchange rate in terms of dollars per DM (first column) is .4898, you will need:

$$\text{DM } 200,000 \times .4898 \text{ } \$ \text{ per DM} = \$97,960$$

Cross-Rates and Triangle Arbitrage   Using the U.S. dollar as the common denominator in quoting exchange rates greatly reduces the number of necessary cross-currency quotes. For example, with five major currencies, there would potentially be 10 exchange rates instead of just 4. Also, the fact that the dollar is used throughout cuts down on inconsistencies in the exchange rate quotations.

Earlier, we defined the cross-rate as the exchange rate for a non-U.S. currency expressed in terms of another non-U.S. currency. For example, suppose we observed the following:

$$\text{FF per } \$1 = 10.00$$
$$\text{DM per } \$1 = 2.00$$

Suppose the cross-rate is quoted as:

$$\text{FF per DM} = 4.00$$

What do you think?

The cross-rate here is inconsistent with the exchange rates. To see this, suppose you have $100. If you convert this to deutsche marks, you will receive:

$$\$100 \times \text{DM 2 per } \$1 = \text{DM 200}$$

If you convert this to francs at the cross-rate, you will have:

$$\text{DM 200} \times \text{FF 4 per DM 1} = \text{FF 800}$$

However, if you just convert your dollars to francs without going through deutsche marks, you will have:

$$\$100 \times \text{FF 10 per } \$1 = \text{FF 1,000}$$

What we see is that the franc has two prices, FF 10 per $1 and FF 8 per $1, depending on how we get the francs.

To make money, we want to buy low, sell high. The important thing to note is that francs are cheaper if you buy them with dollars because you get 10 francs instead of just 8. You should proceed as follows:

1. Buy 1,000 francs for $100.
2. Use the 1,000 francs to buy deutsche marks at the cross-rate. Since it takes four francs to buy a deutsche mark, you will receive FF 1,000/4 = DM 250.
3. Use the DM 250 to buy dollars. Since the exchange rate is DM 2 per dollar, you receive DM 250/2 = $125, for a round-trip profit of $25.
4. Repeat Steps 1 through 3.

This particular activity is called *triangle arbitrage* because the arbitrage involves moving through three different exchange rates:

To prevent such opportunities, it is not difficult to see that since a dollar will buy you either 10 francs or two deutsche marks, the cross-rate must be:

(FF 10/$1)/(DM 2/$1) = FF 5/DM 1

That is, five francs per deutsche mark. If it were anything else, there would be a triangle arbitrage opportunity.

Shedding Some Pounds | **EXAMPLE 18.2**

Suppose the exchange rates for the British pound and German mark are:

Pounds per $1 = .60

DM per $1 = 2.00

The cross-rate is three marks per pound. Is this consistent? Explain how to go about making some money.

The cross-rate should be DM 2.00/£.60 = DM 3.33 per pound. You can buy a pound for DM 3 in one market, and you can sell a pound for DM 3.33 in another. So we want to first get some marks, then use the marks to buy some pounds, and then sell the pounds. Assuming you had $100, you could:

1. Exchange dollars for marks: $100 × 2 = DM 200.
2. Exchange marks for pounds: DM 200/3 = £66.67.
3. Exchange pounds for dollars: £66.67/.60 = $111.12.

This would result in an $11.12 round-trip profit.

Types of Transactions

There are two basic types of trades in the foreign exchange market: spot trades and forward trades. A **spot trade** is an agreement to exchange currency "on the spot," which actually means that the transaction will be completed, or settled, within two business days. The exchange rate on a spot trade is called the **spot exchange rate.** Implicitly, all of the exchange rates and transactions we have discussed so far have referred to the spot market.

spot trade
An agreement to trade currencies based on the exchange rate today for settlement within two business days.

spot exchange rate
The exchange rate on a spot trade.

forward trade

Agreement to exchange currency at some time in the future.

forward exchange rate

The agreed-upon exchange rate to be used in a forward trade.

A **forward trade** is an agreement to exchange currency at some time in the future. The exchange rate that will be used is agreed upon today and is called the **forward exchange rate.** A forward trade will normally be settled sometime in the next 12 months.

If you look back at Figure 18.1, you will see forward exchange rates quoted for some of the major currencies. For example, the spot exchange rate for the Swiss franc is SF 1 = $.6128. The six-month forward exchange rate is SF 1 = $.6231. This means that you can buy a Swiss franc today for $.6128, or you can agree to take delivery of a Swiss franc in six months and pay $.6231 at that time.

Notice that the Swiss franc is more expensive in the forward market ($.6231 versus $.6128). Since the Swiss franc is more expensive in the future than it is today, it is said to be selling at a *premium* relative to the dollar. For the same reason, the dollar is said to be selling at a *discount* relative to the Swiss franc.

Why does the forward market exist? One answer is that it allows businesses and individuals to lock in a future exchange rate today, thereby eliminating any risk from unfavorable shifts in the exchange rate.

EXAMPLE 18.3 | Looking Forward

Suppose you are expecting to receive a million British pounds in six months, and you agree to a forward trade to exchange your pounds for dollars. Based on Figure 18.1, how many dollars will you get in six months? Is the pound selling at a discount or a premium relative to the dollar?

In Figure 18.1, the spot exchange rate and the six-month forward rate in terms of dollars per pound are $1.4995 = £1 and $1.5049 = £1, respectively. If you expect £1 million in six months, then you will get £1 million × $1.5049 per £ = $1.5049 million. Since it is more expensive to buy a pound in the forward market than in the spot market ($1.5049 versus $1.4995), the pound is selling at a premium relative to the dollar.

As we mentioned earlier, it is standard practice around the world (with a few exceptions) to quote exchange rates in terms of the U.S. dollar. This means that rates are quoted as the amount of currency per U.S. dollar. For the remainder of this chapter, we will stick with this form. Things get extremely confusing if you forget this. Thus, when we say things like "the exchange rate is expected to rise," it is important to remember that we are talking about the exchange rate quoted as units of foreign currency per U.S. dollar.

CONCEPT QUESTIONS

18.2a What is triangle arbitrage?

18.2b What do we mean by the three-month forward exchange rate?

18.2c If we say that the exchange rate is DM 1.90, what do we mean?

18.3 | PURCHASING POWER PARITY

purchasing power parity (PPP)

The idea that the exchange rate adjusts to keep purchasing power constant among currencies.

Now that we have discussed what exchange rate quotations mean, we can address an obvious question: What determines the level of the spot exchange rate? In addition, we know that exchange rates change through time. A related question is thus, What determines the rate of change in exchange rates? At least part of the answer in both cases goes by the name of **purchasing power parity (PPP),** and it is the idea that the exchange rate adjusts to keep purchasing power constant among currencies. As we discuss next, there are two forms of PPP, *absolute* and *relative*.

Absolute Purchasing Power Parity

The basic idea behind *absolute purchasing power parity* is that a commodity costs the same regardless of what currency is used to purchase it or where it is selling. This is a very straightforward concept. If a beer costs £2 in London, and the exchange rate is £.60 per dollar, then a beer costs £2/.60 = $3.33 in New York. In other words, absolute PPP says that $1 will buy you the same number of, say, cheeseburgers, anywhere in the world.

More formally, let S_0 be the spot exchange rate between the British pound and the U.S. dollar today (Time 0), and remember that we are quoting exchange rates as the amount of foreign currency per dollar. Let P_{US} and P_{UK} be the current U.S. and British prices, respectively, on a particular commodity, say, apples. Absolute PPP simply says that:

$$P_{UK} = S_0 \times P_{US}$$

This tells us that the British price for something is equal to the U.S. price for that same something, multiplied by the exchange rate.

The rationale behind PPP is similar to that behind triangle arbitrage. If PPP did not hold, arbitrage would be possible (in principle) if apples were moved from one country to another. For example, suppose apples in New York are selling for $4 per bushel, while in London the price is £2.40 per bushel. Absolute PPP implies that:

$$P_{UK} = S_0 \times P_{US}$$
$$£2.40 = S_0 \times \$4$$
$$S_0 = £2.40/\$4 = £.60$$

That is, the implied spot exchange rate is £.60 per dollar. Equivalently, a pound is worth $1/£.60 = $1.67.

Suppose, instead, that the actual exchange rate is £.50. Starting with $4, a trader could buy a bushel of apples in New York, ship it to London, and sell it there for £2.40. Our trader could then convert the £2.40 into dollars at the prevailing exchange rate, $S_0 = £.50$, yielding a total of £2.40/.50 = $4.80. The round-trip gain is 80 cents.

Because of this profit potential, forces are set in motion to change the exchange rate and/or the price of apples. In our example, apples would begin moving from New York to London. The reduced supply of apples in New York would raise the price of apples there, and the increased supply in Britain would lower the price of apples in London.

In addition to moving apples around, apple traders would be busily converting pounds back into dollars to buy more apples. This activity increases the supply of pounds and simultaneously increases the demand for dollars. We would expect the value of a pound to fall. This means that the dollar is getting more valuable, so it will take more pounds to buy one dollar. Since the exchange rate is quoted as pounds per dollar, we would expect the exchange rate to rise from £.50.

For absolute PPP to hold absolutely, several things must be true:

1. The transactions costs of trading apples—shipping, insurance, spoilage, and so on— must be zero.

2. There must be no barriers to trading apples, such as tariffs, taxes, or other political barriers such as VRAs (voluntary restraint agreements).

3. Finally, an apple in New York must be identical to an apple in London. It won't do for you to send red apples to London if the English eat only green apples.

Given the fact that the transactions costs are not zero and that the other conditions are rarely exactly met, it is not surprising that absolute PPP is really applicable only to traded goods, and then only to very uniform ones.

For this reason, absolute PPP does not imply that a Mercedes costs the same as a Ford or that a nuclear power plant in France costs the same as one in New York. In the case of the cars, they are not identical. In the case of the power plants, even if they were identical, they are expensive and very difficult to ship. On the other hand, we would be very surprised to see a significant violation of absolute PPP for gold.

Relative Purchasing Power Parity

As a practical matter, a relative version of purchasing power parity has evolved. *Relative purchasing power parity* does not tell us what determines the absolute level of the exchange rate. Instead, it tells what determines the *change* in the exchange rate over time.

The Basic Idea   Suppose the British pound–U.S. dollar exchange rate is currently S_0 = £.50. Further suppose that the inflation rate in Britain is predicted to be 10 percent over the coming year and (for the moment) the inflation rate in the United States is predicted to be zero. What do you think the exchange rate will be in a year?

If you think about it, a dollar currently costs .50 pounds in Britain. With 10 percent inflation, we expect prices in Britain to generally rise by 10 percent. So we expect that the price of a dollar will go up by 10 percent, and the exchange rate should rise to £.50 × 1.1 = £.55.

If the inflation rate in the United States is not zero, then we need to worry about the *relative* inflation rates in the two countries. For example, suppose the U.S. inflation rate is predicted to be 4 percent. Relative to prices in the United States, prices in Britain are rising at a rate of 10% − 4% = 6% per year. So we expect the price of the dollar to rise by 6 percent, and the predicted exchange rate is £.50 × 1.06 = £.53.

The Result   In general, relative PPP says that the change in the exchange rate is determined by the difference in the inflation rates of the two countries. To be more specific, we will use the following notation:

S_0 = Current (Time 0) spot exchange rate (foreign currency per dollar)

$E(S_t)$ = Expected exchange rate in t periods

h_{US} = Inflation rate in the United States

h_{FC} = Foreign country inflation rate

Based on our discussion just above, relative PPP says that the expected percentage change in the exchange rate over the next year, $[E(S_1) - S_0]/S_0$, is:

$$[E(S_1) - S_0]/S_0 = h_{FC} - h_{US} \qquad [18.1]$$

In words, relative PPP simply says that the expected percentage change in the exchange rate is equal to the difference in inflation rates. If we rearrange this slightly, we get:

$$E(S_1) = S_0[1 + (h_{FC} - h_{US})] \qquad [18.2]$$

This result makes a certain amount of sense, but care must be used in quoting the exchange rate.

In our example involving Britain and the United States, relative PPP tells us that the exchange rate will rise by $h_{FC} - h_{US}$ = 10% − 4% = 6% per year. Assuming that the difference in inflation rates doesn't change, the expected exchange rate in two years, $E(S_2)$, will therefore be:

$$E(S_2) = E(S_1) \times (1 + .06)$$
$$= .53 \times 1.06$$
$$= .562$$

Notice that we could have written this as:

$$E(S_2) = .53 \times 1.06$$
$$= (.50 \times 1.06) \times 1.06$$
$$= .50 \times 1.06^2$$

In general, relative PPP says that the expected exchange rate at some time in the future, $E(S_t)$, is:

$$E(S_t) = S_0 \times [1 + (h_{FC} - h_{US})]^t \qquad [18.3]$$

Because we don't really expect absolute PPP to hold for most goods, we will focus on relative PPP in any future discussion. Henceforth, when we refer to PPP without further qualification, we mean relative PPP.

It's All Relative | EXAMPLE 18.4

Suppose the Japanese exchange rate is currently 105 yen per dollar. The inflation rate in Japan over the next three years will run, say, 2 percent per year, while the U.S. inflation rate will be 6 percent. Based on relative PPP, what will the exchange rate be in three years?

Since the U.S. inflation rate is higher, we expect that a dollar will become less valuable. The exchange rate change will be 2% − 6% = −4% per year. Over three years, the exchange rate will fall to:

$$E(S_3) = S_0 \times [1 + (h_{FC} - h_{US})]^3$$
$$= 105 \times [1 + (-.04)]^3$$
$$= 92.90 \text{ yen per dollar}$$

Currency Appreciation and Depreciation We frequently hear things like "the dollar strengthened (or weakened) in financial markets today" or "the dollar is expected to appreciate (or depreciate) relative to the pound." When we say that the dollar strengthens, or appreciates, we mean that the value of a dollar rises, so it takes more foreign currency to buy a dollar.

What happens to the exchange rates as currencies fluctuate in value depends on how exchange rates are quoted. Since we are quoting them as units of foreign currency per dollar, the exchange rate moves in the same direction as the value of the dollar: It rises as the dollar strengthens, and it falls as the dollar weakens.

Relative PPP tells us that the exchange rate will rise if the U.S. inflation rate is lower than the foreign country's. This happens because the foreign currency depreciates in value and therefore weakens relative to the dollar.

CONCEPT QUESTIONS

18.3a What does absolute PPP say? Why might it not hold for many types of goods?

18.3b According to relative PPP, what determines the change in exchange rates?

18.4 | EXCHANGE RATES AND INTEREST RATES

The next issue we need to address is the relationship between spot exchange rates, forward exchange rates, and nominal interest rates. To get started, we need some additional notation:

F_t = Forward exchange rate for settlement at time t

R_{US} = U.S. nominal risk-free interest rate

R_{FC} = Foreign country nominal risk-free interest rate

As before, we will use S_0 to stand for the spot exchange rate. You can take the U.S. nominal risk-free rate, R_{US}, to be the T-bill rate.

Covered Interest Arbitrage

Suppose we observe the following information about U.S. and German currency in the market:

$$S_0 = \text{DM } 2.00 \qquad R_{US} = 10\%$$
$$F_1 = \text{DM } 1.90 \qquad R_G = 5\%$$

where R_G is the nominal risk-free rate in Germany. The period is one year, so F_1 is the 360-day forward rate.

Do you see an arbitrage opportunity here? There is one. Suppose you have $1 to invest, and you want a riskless investment. One option you have is to invest the $1 in a riskless U.S. investment such as a 360-day T-bill. We will call this Strategy 1. If you do this, then, in one period, your $1 will be worth:

$$\begin{aligned}\$ \text{ value in 1 period} &= \$1(1 + R_{US}) \\ &= \$1.10\end{aligned}$$

Alternatively, you can invest in the German risk-free investment. To do this, you need to convert your $1 to deutsche marks and simultaneously execute a forward trade to convert marks back to dollars in one year. We will call this Strategy 2. The necessary steps would be as follows:

1. Convert your $1 to $1 × S_0 = DM 2.00.
2. At the same time, enter into a forward agreement to convert marks back to dollars in one year. Since the forward rate is DM 1.90, you get $1 for every DM 1.90 that you have in one year.
3. Invest your DM 2.00 in Germany at R_G. In one year, you will have:

$$\begin{aligned}\text{DM value in 1 year} &= \text{DM } 2.00 \times (1 + R_G) \\ &= \text{DM } 2.00 \times 1.05 \\ &= \text{DM } 2.10\end{aligned}$$

4. Convert your DM 2.10 back to dollars at the agreed-upon rate of DM 1.90 = $1. You end up with:

$$\begin{aligned}\$ \text{ value in 1 year} &= \text{DM } 2.10/1.90 \\ &= \$1.1053\end{aligned}$$

Notice that the value in one year from this strategy can be written as:

$$\begin{aligned}\$ \text{ value in 1 year} &= \$1 \times S_0 \times (1 + R_G)/F_1 \\ &= \$1 \times 2.00 \times 1.05/1.90 \\ &= \$1.1053\end{aligned}$$

The return on this investment is apparently 10.53 percent. This is higher than the 10 percent we get from investing in the United States. Since both investments are risk-free, there is an arbitrage opportunity.

To exploit the difference in interest rates, you need to borrow, say, $5 million at the lower U.S. rate and invest it at the higher German rate. What is the round-trip profit from doing this? To find out, we can work through the steps above:

1. Convert the $5 million at DM 2.00 = $1 to get DM 10 million.

2. Agree to exchange marks for dollars in one year at DM 1.90 to the dollar.

3. Invest the DM 10 million for one year at $R_G = 5\%$. You end up with DM 10.5 million.

4. Convert the DM 10.5 million back to dollars to fulfill the forward contract. You receive DM 10.5 million/1.90 = $5,526,316.

5. Repay the loan with interest. You owe $5 million plus 10 percent interest, for a total of $5.5 million. You have $5,526,316, so your round-trip profit is a risk-free $26,316.

The activity that we have illustrated here goes by the name of *covered interest arbitrage.* The term *covered* refers to the fact that we are covered in the event of a change in the exchange rate since we lock in the forward exchange rate today.

Interest Rate Parity

If we assume that significant covered interest arbitrage opportunities do not exist, then there must be some relationship between spot exchange rates, forward exchange rates, and relative interest rates. To see what this relationship is, note that, in general, Strategy 1 above, investing in a riskless U.S. investment, gives us $(1 + R_{US})$ for every dollar we invest. Strategy 2, investing in a foreign risk-free investment, gives us $S_0 \times (1 + R_{FC})/F_1$ for every dollar we invest. Since these have to be equal to prevent arbitrage, it must be the case that:

$$1 + R_{US} = S_0 \times (1 + R_{FC})/F_1$$

Rearranging this a bit gets us the famous **interest rate parity (IRP)** condition:

$$F_1/S_0 = (1 + R_{FC})/(1 + R_{US}) \qquad [18.4]$$

There is a very useful approximation for IRP that illustrates very clearly what is going on and is not difficult to remember. If we define the percentage forward premium or discount as $(F_1 - S_0)/S_0$, then IRP says that this percentage premium or discount is *approximately* equal to the difference in interest rates:

$$(F_1 - S_0)/S_0 = R_{FC} - R_{US} \qquad [18.5]$$

Very loosely, what IRP says is that any difference in interest rates between two countries for some period is just offset by the change in the relative value of the currencies, thereby eliminating any arbitrage possibilities. Notice that we could also write:

$$F_1 = S_0 \times [1 + (R_{FC} - R_{US})] \qquad [18.6]$$

In general, if we have t periods instead of just one, the IRP approximation will be written as:

$$F_t = S_0 \times [1 + (R_{FC} - R_{US})]^t \qquad [18.7]$$

interest rate parity (IRP)
The condition stating that the interest rate differential between two countries is equal to the percentage difference between the forward exchange rate and the spot exchange rate.

Parity Check | **EXAMPLE 18.5**

Suppose the exchange rate for Japanese yen, S_0, is currently ¥120 = $1. If the interest rate in the United States is $R_{US} = 10\%$ and the interest rate in Japan is $R_J = 5\%$, then what must the one-year forward rate be to prevent covered interest arbitrage?

From IRP, we have:

$$F_1 = S_0 \times [1 + (R_J - R_{US})]$$
$$= ¥120 \times [1 + (.05 - .10)]$$
$$= ¥120 \times .95$$
$$= ¥114$$

Notice that the yen will sell at a premium relative to the dollar (why?).

CONCEPT QUESTIONS

18.4a What is interest rate parity?

18.4b Do you expect that interest rate parity will hold more closely than purchasing power parity? Why?

18.5   EXCHANGE RATE RISK

exchange rate risk
The risk related to having international operations in a world where relative currency values vary.

Exchange rate risk is the natural consequence of international operations in a world where relative currency values move up and down. As the accompanying *Reality Bytes* box describes, managing exchange rate risk is an important part of international finance. As we discuss next, there are three different types of exchange rate risk, or exposure: short-run exposure, long-run exposure, and translation exposure.

Short-Run Exposure

The day-to-day fluctuations in exchange rates create short-run risks for international firms. Most such firms have contractual agreements to buy and sell goods in the near future at set prices. When different currencies are involved, such transactions have an extra element of risk.

For example, imagine that you are importing imitation pasta from Italy and reselling it in the United States under the Impasta brand name. Your largest customer has ordered 10,000 cases of Impasta. You place the order with your supplier today, but you won't pay until the goods arrive in 60 days. Your selling price is $6 per case. Your cost is 8,400 Italian lira per case, and the exchange rate is currently Lit 1,500, so it takes 1,500 lira to buy $1.

At the current exchange rate, your cost in dollars from filling the order is Lit 8,400/1,500 = $5.6 per case, so your pretax profit on the order is 10,000 × ($6 − 5.6) = $4,000. However, the exchange rate in 60 days will probably be different, so your profit will depend on what the future exchange rate turns out to be.

For example, if the rate goes to Lit 1,600, your cost is Lit 8,400/1,600 = $5.25 per case. Your profit goes to $7,500. If the exchange rate goes to, say, Lit 1,400, then your cost is Lit 8,400/1,400 = $6, and your profit is zero.

The short-run exposure in our example can be reduced or eliminated in several ways. The most obvious way is to enter into a forward exchange agreement to lock in an exchange rate. For example, suppose the 60-day forward rate is Lit 1,580. What will be your profit if you hedge?

If you hedge, you lock in an exchange rate of Lit 1,580. Your cost in dollars will thus be Lit 8,400/1,580 = $5.32 per case, so your profit will be 10,000 × ($6 − 5.32) = $6,800.

WHO WINS AND WHO LOSES WHEN THE EURO SLIPS?

When the euro was introduced in 1999, it could be exchanged for $1.18 U.S. By the middle of May 2000, the euro was worth about $.92. As you have already learned, this means the euro weakened against the dollar, but, what does this mean for the companies doing business in euros and dollars? The experiences of soft-drink bottler Coca-Cola Enterprises, fast food giant McDonald's Corp., and photography film producer Eastman Kodak Co. have been bad. However, there are other firms such as Waterford Crystal, the Irish maker of crystal and china, for which the decline of the euro has been good news. Not surprisingly, while the final tally has a lot to do with which side of the ocean you are on, it's actually a little more complicated than that.

When a company from the U.S. makes a sale in one of the 11 European countries that make up what is known as "euroland," it must then convert the sale (transacted in euros) back into dollars. As the value of the euro declines against the dollar, the same sale becomes less and less valuable in terms of dollars. So, for a company like Kodak, which derives about 30 percent of its sales from Europe, the results are lower profits on the same number of units sold as the euro declines. In early 2000, the photography giant was expecting sales growth for the year to be two to three percentage points lower than previously forecasted just because of the tumbling euro. At the same time, as the euro slides, companies that export from euroland to the U.S. pay their production costs in euros but make their sales in the appreciating U.S. dollar. Waterford Crystal, for example, saw its exports to the U.S. grow in value as the euro dipped. And, since the company sells about 70 percent of its products in the U.S., the slide in the euro has proven to be quite beneficial.

As these examples suggest, the decline in the value of the euro compared to the dollar hurts U.S. firms in at least two ways. First, it decreases the value of goods shipped from the U.S. into euroland, making sales there less profitable than before. Second, it makes goods imported into the U.S. from euroland cheaper and therefore more competitive with domestically produced U.S. goods. Thus, U.S. competitors of Waterford Crystal suffer declines in the value of goods sold in Europe. At the same time, Waterford can reap extra profits on its sales in the U.S., or it can lower prices of those goods. Either way, Waterford is in a position superior to that of its U.S.-based counterparts competitively.

You might be wondering, however, if you can have your cake and eat it, too. DaimlerChrysler AG's experience provides at least a partial answer in the affirmative. As the euro has declined, the maker of Mercedes-Benz cars and Airbus aircraft has realized a boost in its profit margin on dollar-denominated sales of its European-made products. At the same time, the company sells Chrysler minivans and Jeeps in Europe, so you might expect it to be earning reduced profits on those sales. Quite to the contrary, because the company actually manufactures most of those goods in Europe. So while the value of sales has declined with the euro, so has the cost of the inputs into the production process. As a result, those sales have been largely unaffected by the change in exchange rates.

Sources: "USA: Analysis—U.S. Firms Impotent in Face of Euro Slide," Reuters English News Service, 17 May 2000.
"Xerox Profit, Excluding Charges, Dropped 36% in First Quarter," *The Wall Street Journal,* 26 April 2000, p. B6.
"Currency Woes Lift Euroland Firms," *The Wall Street Journal Europe,* 1 March 2000, p. 1.
"For Some, Euro's Fall Spells Profit, Not Angst," *The Wall Street Journal Europe,* 14 June 1999, p. 4.

Long-Run Exposure

In the long run, the value of a foreign operation can fluctuate because of unanticipated changes in relative economic conditions. For example, imagine that we own a labor-intensive assembly operation located in another country to take advantage of lower wages. Through time, unexpected changes in economic conditions can raise the foreign wage levels to the point where the cost advantage is eliminated or even becomes negative.

Hedging long-run exposure is more difficult than hedging short-term risks. For one thing, organized forward markets don't exist for such long-term needs. Instead, the primary option that firms have is to try to match up foreign currency inflows and outflows. The same thing goes for matching foreign currency–denominated assets and liabilities. For example, a firm that sells in a foreign country might try to concentrate its raw material purchases and labor expense in that country. That way, the dollar values of its revenues and costs will move up and down together.

Similarly, a firm can reduce its long-run exchange risk by borrowing in the foreign country. Fluctuations in the value of the foreign subsidiary's assets will then be at least partially offset by changes in the value of the liabilities.

Translation Exposure

When a U.S. company calculates its accounting net income and EPS for some period, it must "translate" everything into dollars. This can create some problems for the accountants when there are significant foreign operations. In particular, two issues arise:

1. What is the appropriate exchange rate to use for translating each balance sheet account?

2. How should balance sheet accounting gains and losses from foreign currency translation be handled?

To illustrate the accounting problem, suppose that we started a small foreign subsidiary in Lilliputia a year ago. The local currency is the gulliver, abbreviated GL. At the beginning of the year, the exchange rate was GL 2 = $1, and the balance sheet in gullivers looked like this:

Assets	GL 1,000	Liabilities	GL 500
		Equity	500

At two gullivers to the dollar, the beginning balance sheet in dollars was:

Assets	$500	Liabilities	$250
		Equity	250

Lilliputia is a quiet place, and nothing at all actually happened during the year. As a result, net income was zero (before consideration of exchange rate changes). However, the exchange rate did change to 4 gullivers = $1, perhaps because the Lilliputian inflation rate is much higher than the U.S. inflation rate.

Since nothing happened, the accounting ending balance sheet in gullivers is the same as the beginning one. However, if we convert it to dollars at the new exchange rate, we get:

Assets	$250	Liabilities	$125
		Equity	125

Notice that the value of the equity has gone down by $125, even though net income was exactly zero. Despite the fact that absolutely nothing really happened, there is a $125 accounting loss. How to handle this $125 loss has been a controversial accounting question.

One obvious and consistent way to handle this loss is simply to report the loss on the parent's income statement. During periods of volatile exchange rates, this kind of treatment can dramatically impact an international company's reported EPS. This is purely an accounting phenomenon, but, even so, such fluctuations are disliked by some financial managers.

The current approach to translation gains and losses is based on rules set out in Financial Accounting Standards Board (FASB) Statement Number 52, issued in December 1981. For the most part, FASB 52 requires that all assets and liabilities be translated from the subsidiary's currency into the parent's currency using the exchange rate that currently prevails.

Any translation gains and losses that occur are accumulated in a special account within the shareholders' equity section of the balance sheet. This account might be labeled something like "unrealized foreign exchange gains (losses)." These gains and losses are not reported on the income statement. As a result, the impact of translation gains and losses will not be recognized explicitly in net income until the underlying assets and liabilities are sold or otherwise liquidated.

Managing Exchange Rate Risk

For a large multinational firm, the management of exchange rate risk is complicated by the fact that there can be many different currencies involved for many different subsidiaries. It is very likely that a change in some exchange rate will benefit some subsidiaries and hurt others. The net effect on the overall firm depends on its net exposure.

For example, suppose a firm has two divisions. Division A buys goods in the United States for dollars and sells them in Britain for pounds. Division B buys goods in Britain for pounds and sells them in the United States for dollars. If these two divisions are of roughly equal size in terms of their inflows and outflows, then the overall firm obviously has little exchange rate risk.

In our example, the firm's net position in pounds (the amount coming in less the amount going out) is small, so the exchange rate risk is small. However, if one division, acting on its own, were to start hedging its exchange rate risk, then the overall firm's exchange rate risk would go up. The moral of the story is that multinational firms have to be conscious of the overall position that the firm has in a foreign currency. For this reason, management of exchange rate risk is probably best handled on a centralized basis.

CONCEPT QUESTIONS

18.5a What are the different types of exchange rate risk?

18.5b How can a firm hedge short-run exchange rate risk? Long-run exchange rate risk?

POLITICAL RISK | 18.6

One final element of risk in international investing is **political risk.** Political risk is related to changes in value that arise as a consequence of political actions. This is not a problem faced only by international firms. For example, changes in U.S. tax laws and regulations may benefit some U.S. firms and hurt others, so political risk exists nationally as well as internationally.

Some countries do have more political risk than others, however. When firms have operations in these riskier countries, the extra political risk may lead them to require higher returns on overseas investments to compensate for the risk that funds will be blocked, critical operations interrupted, and contracts abrogated. In the most extreme case, the possibility of outright confiscation may be a concern in countries with relatively unstable political environments.

political risk

Risk related to changes in value that arise because of political actions.

Political risk also depends on the nature of the business; some businesses are less likely to be confiscated because they are not particularly valuable in the hands of a different owner. An assembly operation supplying subcomponents that only the parent company uses would not be an attractive "takeover" target, for example. Similarly, a manufacturing operation that requires the use of specialized components from the parent is of little value without the parent company's cooperation.

Natural resource developments, such as copper mining or oil drilling, are just the opposite. Once the operation is in place, much of the value is in the commodity. The political risk for such investments is much higher for this reason. Also, the issue of exploitation is more pronounced with such investments, again increasing the political risk.

Political risk can be hedged in several ways, particularly when confiscation or nationalization is a concern. The use of local financing, perhaps from the government of the foreign country in question, reduces the possible loss because the company can refuse to pay on the debt in the event of unfavorable political activities. Based on our discussion above, structuring the operation in such a way that it requires significant parent company involvement to function is another way to reduce political risk.

CONCEPT QUESTIONS

18.6a What is political risk?

18.6b What are some ways of hedging political risk?

SUMMARY AND CONCLUSIONS

The international firm has a more complicated life than the purely domestic firm. Management must understand the connection between interest rates, foreign currency exchange rates, and inflation, and it must become aware of a large number of different financial market regulations and tax systems. This chapter was intended to be a concise introduction to some of the financial issues that come up in international investing.

Our coverage was necessarily brief. The main topics we discussed included:

1. Some basic vocabulary. We briefly defined some exotic terms such as *LIBOR* and *Eurocurrency*.

2. The basic mechanics of exchange rate quotations. We discussed the spot and forward markets and how exchange rates are interpreted.

3. The fundamental relationships between international financial variables:

    a. Absolute and relative purchasing power parity, or PPP

    b. Interest rate parity, or IRP

    Absolute purchasing power parity states that $1 should have the same purchasing power in each country. This means that an orange costs the same whether you buy it in New York or in Tokyo.

    Relative purchasing power parity means that the expected percentage change in exchange rates between the currencies of two countries is equal to the difference in their inflation rates.

    Interest rate parity implies that the percentage difference between the forward exchange rate and the spot exchange rate is equal to the interest rate differential. We showed how covered interest arbitrage forces this relationship to hold.

4. Exchange rate and political risk. We described the various types of exchange rate risk and discussed some commonly used approaches to managing the effect of fluctuating exchange rates on the cash flows and value of the international firm. We also discussed political risk and some ways of managing exposure to it.

CHAPTER REVIEW AND SELF-TEST PROBLEMS

18.1 **Relative Purchasing Power Parity.** The inflation rate in the United States is projected at 6 percent per year for the next several years. The German inflation rate is projected to be 2 percent during that time. The exchange rate is currently DM 2.2. Based on relative PPP, what is the expected exchange rate in two years?

18.2 **Covered Interest Arbitrage.** The spot and 360-day forward rates on the Swiss franc are SF 1.8 and SF 1.7, respectively. The risk-free interest rate in the United States is 8 percent, and the risk-free rate in Switzerland is 5 percent. Is there an arbitrage opportunity here? How would you exploit it?

Answers to Chapter Review and Self-Test Problems

18.1 From relative PPP, the expected exchange rate in two years, $E(S_2)$, is:

$$E(S_2) = S_0 \times [1 + (h_G - h_{US})]^2$$

where h_G is the German inflation rate. The current exchange rate is DM 2.2, so the expected exchange rate is:

$$E(S_2) = \text{DM } 2.2 \times [1 + (.02 - .06)]^2$$
$$= \text{DM } 2.2 \times .96^2$$
$$= \text{DM } 2.03$$

18.2 From interest rate parity, the forward rate should be (approximately):

$$F_1 = S_0 \times [1 + (R_S - R_{US})]$$
$$= 1.8 \times [1 + .05 - .08]$$
$$= 1.75$$

Since the forward rate is actually SF 1.7, there is an arbitrage opportunity.

To exploit the arbitrage opportunity, we first note that dollars are selling for SF 1.7 each in the forward market. From IRP, this is too cheap because they should be selling for SF 1.75. So we want to arrange to buy dollars with Swiss francs in the forward market. To do this, we can:

1. Today: Borrow, say, $10 million for 360 days. Convert it to SF 18 million in the spot market, and forward contract at SF 1.7 to convert it back to dollars in 360 days. Invest the SF 18 million at 5 percent.

2. In one year: Your investment has grown to SF 18 × 1.05 = SF 18.9 million. Convert this to dollars at the rate of SF 1.7 = $1. You will have SF 18.9 million/1.7 = $11,117,647. Pay off your loan with 8 percent interest at a cost of $10 million × 1.08 = $10,800,000 and pocket the difference of $317,647.

CRITICAL THINKING AND CONCEPTS REVIEW

1. **Spot and Forward Rates.** Suppose the exchange rate for the Swiss franc is quoted as SF 1.50 in the spot market and SF 1.53 in the 90-day forward market.
    a. Is the dollar selling at a premium or a discount relative to the franc?
    b. Does the financial market expect the franc to strengthen relative to the dollar? Explain.
    c. What do you suspect is true about relative economic conditions in the United States and Switzerland?

2. **Purchasing Power Parity.** Suppose the rate of inflation in Germany will run about 3 percent higher than the U.S. inflation rate over the next several years. All other things being the same, what will happen to the deutsche mark versus dollar exchange rate? What relationship are you relying on in answering?

3. **Exchange Rates.** The exchange rate for the Australian dollar is currently A$1.40. This exchange rate is expected to rise by 10 percent over the next year.
    a. Is the Australian dollar expected to get stronger or weaker?
    b. What do you think about the relative inflation rates in the United States and Australia?
    c. What do you think about the relative nominal interest rates in the United States and Australia? Relative real rates?

4. **Yankee Bonds.** Which of the following most accurately describes a Yankee bond?
    a. A bond issued by General Motors in Japan with the interest payable in U.S. dollars
    b. A bond issued by General Motors in Japan with the interest payable in yen
    c. A bond issued by Toyota in the United States with the interest payable in yen
    d. A bond issued by Toyota in the United States with the interest payable in dollars
    e. A bond issued by Toyota worldwide with the interest payable in dollars

5. **Exchange Rates.** Are exchange rate changes necessarily good or bad for a particular company?

6. **International Risks.** Duracell International confirmed in October 1995 that it was planning to open battery-manufacturing plants in China and India. Manufacturing in these countries allows Duracell to avoid import duties of between 30 and 35 percent that have made alkaline batteries prohibitively expensive for some consumers. What additional advantages might Duracell see in this proposal? What are some of the risks to Duracell?

7. **Multinational Corporations.** Given that many multinationals based in many countries have much greater sales outside their domestic markets than within them, what is the particular relevance of their domestic currency?

8. **Exchange Rate Movements.** Are the following statements true or false? Explain why.
    a. If the general price index in Great Britain rises faster than that in the United States, we would expect the pound to appreciate relative to the dollar.
    b. Suppose you are a German machine tool exporter and you invoice all of your sales in foreign currency. Further suppose that the German monetary authorities begin to undertake an expansionary monetary policy. If it is certain that the easy money policy will result in higher inflation rates in Germany relative to those in other countries, then you should use the forward markets to protect yourself against future losses resulting from the deterioration in the value of the deutsche mark.

c. If you could accurately estimate differences in the relative inflation rates of two countries over a long period of time, while other market participants were unable to do so, you could successfully speculate in spot currency markets.

9. **Exchange Rate Movements.** Some countries encourage movements in their exchange rate relative to those of some other country as a short-term means of addressing foreign trade imbalances. For each of the following scenarios, evaluate the impact the announcement would have on an American importer and an American exporter doing business with the foreign country.
   a. Officials in the administration of the United States government announce that they are comfortable with a rising deutsche mark relative to the dollar.
   b. British monetary authorities announce that they feel the pound has been driven too low by currency speculators relative to the dollar.
   c. The Brazilian government announces that it will print billions of new cruzeiros and inject them into the economy in an effort to reduce the country's 40 percent unemployment rate.

QUESTIONS AND PROBLEMS

Basic
(Questions 1–10)

1. **Using Exchange Rates.** Take a look back at Figure 18.1 to answer the following questions:
   a. If you have $100, how many Italian lira can you get?
   b. How much is one euro worth?
   c. If you have five million euros, how many dollars do you have?
   d. Which is worth more, a New Zealand dollar or a Singapore dollar?
   e. Which is worth more, a Mexican peso or a Chilean peso?
   f. How many Swiss francs can you get for a euro? What do you call this rate?
   g. Per unit, what is the most valuable currency of those listed? The least valuable?

2. **Using the Cross-Rate.** Use the information in Figure 18.1 to answer the following questions:
   a. Which would you rather have, $100 or £100? Why?
   b. Which would you rather have, FF 100 or £100? Why?
   c. What is the cross-rate for French francs in terms of British pounds? For British pounds in terms of French francs?

3. **Forward Exchange Rates.** Use the information in Figure 18.1 to answer the following questions:
   a. What is the six-month forward rate for the Japanese yen in yen per U.S. dollar? Is the yen selling at a premium or a discount? Explain.
   b. What is the three-month forward rate for German deutsche marks in U.S. dollars per deutsche mark? Is the dollar selling at a premium or a discount? Explain.
   c. What do you think will happen to the value of the dollar relative to the yen and the deutsche mark, based on the information in the figure? Explain.

4. **Using Spot and Forward Exchange Rates.** Suppose the spot exchange rate for the Canadian dollar is Can$1.32 and the six-month forward rate is Can$1.34.
   a. Which is worth more, a U.S. dollar or a Canadian dollar?
   b. Assuming absolute PPP holds, what is the cost in the United States of an Elkhead beer if the price in Canada is Can$2.19? Why might the beer actually sell at a different price in the United States?
   c. Is the U.S. dollar selling at a premium or a discount relative to the Canadian dollar?

d. Which currency is expected to appreciate in value?

e. Which country do you think has higher interest rates—the United States or Canada? Explain.

5.   **Cross-Rates and Arbitrage.**   Suppose the Japanese yen exchange rate is ¥120 = $1, and the British pound exchange rate is £1 = $1.75.

a. What is the cross-rate in terms of yen per pound?

b. Suppose the cross-rate is ¥180 = £1. Is there an arbitrage opportunity here? If there is, explain how to take advantage of the mispricing.

6.   **Interest Rate Parity.**   Use Figure 18.1 to answer the following questions. Suppose interest rate parity holds, and the current risk-free rate in the United States is 5 percent per six months. What must the six-month risk-free rate be in France? In Japan? In Switzerland?

7.   **Interest Rates and Arbitrage.**   The treasurer of a major U.S. firm has $30 million to invest for three months. The annual interest rate in the United States is .40 percent per month. The interest rate in Great Britain is .70 percent per month. The spot exchange rate is £.59, and the three-month forward rate is £.61. Ignoring transactions costs, in which country would the treasurer want to invest the company's funds? Why?

8.   **Inflation and Exchange Rates.**   Suppose the current exchange rate for the French franc is FF 6.25. The expected exchange rate in three years is FF 7.1. What is the difference in the annual inflation rates for the United States and France over this period? Assume that the anticipated rate is constant for both countries. What relationship are you relying on in answering?

9.   **Exchange Rate Risk.**   Suppose your company imports computer motherboards from Singapore. The exchange rate is given in Figure 18.1. You have just placed an order for 30,000 motherboards at a cost to you of 167.904 Singapore dollars each. You will pay for the shipment when it arrives in 90 days. You can sell the motherboards for $150 each. Calculate your profit if the exchange rate goes up or down by 10 percent over the next 90 days. What is the break-even exchange rate? What percentage rise or fall does this represent in terms of the Singapore dollar versus the U.S. dollar?

10.   **Exchange Rates and Arbitrage.**   Suppose the spot and six-month forward rates on the deutsche mark are DM 1.42 and DM 1.49, respectively. The annual risk-free rate in the United States is 6 percent, and the annual risk-free rate in Germany is 9 percent.

a. Is there an arbitrage opportunity here? If so, how would you exploit it?

b. What must the six-month forward rate be to prevent arbitrage?

Intermediate
(Questions 11–16)

11.   **Spot versus Forward Rates.**   Suppose the spot and three-month forward rates for the yen are ¥119 and ¥115, respectively.

a. Is the yen expected to get stronger or weaker?

b. What would you estimate is the difference between the inflation rates of the United States and Japan?

12.   **Expected Spot Rates.**   Suppose the spot exchange rate for the Hungarian forint is HUF 155. Interest rates in the United States are 5 percent per year. They are triple that in Hungary. What do you predict the exchange rate will be in one year? In two years? In five years? What relationship are you using?

13.   **Calculating Cross-Rates.**   Calculate the ¥/DM cross-rate given ¥104.40 = $1 and DM1.5285 = $1.

14. **Cross-Rates and Arbitrage.**   The £ trades at $1.5020 in London and $1.4300 in New York. How much profit could you earn on each trade with $10,000?

15. **Purchasing Power Parity and Exchange Rates.**   According to purchasing power parity, if a Big Mac sells for $1.99 in the U.S. and DM2.84 in Germany, what is the DM/$ exchange rate?

16. **Inflation and Exchange Rates.**   Suppose the spot and three-month forward rates for the yen are ¥135 and ¥130, respectively. What would you estimate the difference in inflation rates to be between Japan and the U.S.?

www.mhhe.com/rwj

Spreadsheet Templates 4, 6, 7

Mathematical Tables

TABLE A.1   Future value of $1 at the end of t periods $= (1 + r)^t$

Number of Periods	Interest Rate								
	1%	2%	3%	4%	5%	6%	7%	8%	9%
1	1.0100	1.0200	1.0300	1.0400	1.0500	1.0600	1.0700	1.0800	1.0900
2	1.0201	1.0404	1.0609	1.0816	1.1025	1.1236	1.1449	1.1664	1.1881
3	1.0303	1.0612	1.0927	1.1249	1.1576	1.1910	1.2250	1.2597	1.2950
4	1.0406	1.0824	1.1255	1.1699	1.2155	1.2625	1.3108	1.3605	1.4116
5	1.0510	1.1041	1.1593	1.2167	1.2763	1.3382	1.4026	1.4693	1.5386
6	1.0615	1.1262	1.1941	1.2653	1.3401	1.4185	1.5007	1.5869	1.6771
7	1.0721	1.1487	1.2299	1.3159	1.4071	1.5036	1.6058	1.7138	1.8280
8	1.0829	1.1717	1.2668	1.3686	1.4775	1.5938	1.7182	1.8509	1.9926
9	1.0937	1.1951	1.3048	1.4233	1.5513	1.6895	1.8385	1.9990	2.1719
10	1.1046	1.2190	1.3439	1.4802	1.6289	1.7908	1.9672	2.1589	2.3674
11	1.1157	1.2434	1.3842	1.5395	1.7103	1.8983	2.1049	2.3316	2.5804
12	1.1268	1.2682	1.4258	1.6010	1.7959	2.0122	2.2522	2.5182	2.8127
13	1.1381	1.2936	1.4685	1.6651	1.8856	2.1329	2.4098	2.7196	3.0658
14	1.1495	1.3195	1.5126	1.7317	1.9799	2.2609	2.5785	2.9372	3.3417
15	1.1610	1.3459	1.5580	1.8009	2.0789	2.3966	2.7590	3.1722	3.6425
16	1.1726	1.3728	1.6047	1.8730	2.1829	2.5404	2.9522	3.4259	3.9703
17	1.1843	1.4002	1.6528	1.9479	2.2920	2.6928	3.1588	3.7000	4.3276
18	1.1961	1.4282	1.7024	2.0258	2.4066	2.8543	3.3799	3.9960	4.7171
19	1.2081	1.4568	1.7535	2.1068	2.5270	3.0256	3.6165	4.3157	5.1417
20	1.2202	1.4859	1.8061	2.1911	2.6533	3.2071	3.8697	4.6610	5.6044
21	1.2324	1.5157	1.8603	2.2788	2.7860	3.3996	4.1406	5.0338	6.1088
22	1.2447	1.5460	1.9161	2.3699	2.9253	3.6035	4.4304	5.4365	6.6586
23	1.2572	1.5769	1.9736	2.4647	3.0715	3.8197	4.7405	5.8715	7.2579
24	1.2697	1.6084	2.0328	2.5633	3.2251	4.0489	5.0724	6.3412	7.9111
25	1.2824	1.6406	2.0938	2.6658	3.3864	4.2919	5.4274	6.8485	8.6231
30	1.3478	1.8114	2.4273	3.2434	4.3219	5.7435	7.6123	10.063	13.268
40	1.4889	2.2080	3.2620	4.8010	7.0400	10.286	14.974	21.725	31.409
50	1.6446	2.6916	4.3839	7.1067	11.467	18.420	29.457	46.902	74.358
60	1.8167	3.2810	5.8916	10.520	18.679	32.988	57.946	101.26	176.03

10%	12%	14%	15%	16%	18%	20%	24%	28%	32%	36%
1.1000	1.1200	1.1400	1.1500	1.1600	1.1800	1.2000	1.2400	1.2800	1.3200	1.3600
1.2100	1.2544	1.2996	1.3225	1.3456	1.3924	1.4400	1.5376	1.6384	1.7424	1.8496
1.3310	1.4049	1.4815	1.5209	1.5609	1.6430	1.7280	1.9066	2.0972	2.3000	2.5155
1.4641	1.5735	1.6890	1.7490	1.8106	1.9388	2.0736	2.3642	2.6844	3.0360	3.4210
1.6105	1.7623	1.9254	2.0114	2.1003	2.2878	2.4883	2.9316	3.4360	4.0075	4.6526
1.7716	1.9738	2.1950	2.3131	2.4364	2.6996	2.9860	3.6352	4.3980	5.2899	6.3275
1.9487	2.2107	2.5023	2.6600	2.8262	3.1855	3.5832	4.5077	5.6295	6.9826	8.6054
2.1436	2.4760	2.8526	3.0590	3.2784	3.7589	4.2998	5.5895	7.2058	9.2170	11.703
2.3579	2.7731	3.2519	3.5179	3.8030	4.4355	5.1598	6.9310	9.2234	12.166	15.917
2.5937	3.1058	3.7072	4.0456	4.4114	5.2338	6.1917	8.5944	11.806	16.060	21.647
2.8531	3.4785	4.2262	4.6524	5.1173	6.1759	7.4301	10.657	15.112	21.199	29.439
3.1384	3.8960	4.8179	5.3503	5.9360	7.2876	8.9161	13.215	19.343	27.983	40.037
3.4523	4.3635	5.4924	6.1528	6.8858	8.5994	10.699	16.386	24.759	36.937	54.451
3.7975	4.8871	6.2613	7.0757	7.9875	10.147	12.839	20.319	31.691	48.757	74.053
4.1772	5.4736	7.1379	8.1371	9.2655	11.974	15.407	25.196	40.565	64.359	100.71
4.5950	6.1304	8.1372	9.3576	10.748	14.129	18.488	31.243	51.923	84.954	136.97
5.0545	6.8660	9.2765	10.761	12.468	16.672	22.186	38.741	66.461	112.14	186.28
5.5599	7.6900	10.575	12.375	14.463	19.673	26.623	48.039	85.071	148.02	253.34
6.1159	8.6128	12.056	14.232	16.777	23.214	31.948	59.568	108.89	195.39	344.54
6.7275	9.6463	13.743	16.367	19.461	27.393	38.338	73.864	139.38	257.92	468.57
7.4002	10.804	15.668	18.822	22.574	32.324	46.005	91.592	178.41	340.45	637.26
8.1403	12.100	17.861	21.645	26.186	38.142	55.206	113.57	228.36	449.39	866.67
8.9543	13.552	20.362	24.891	30.376	45.008	66.247	140.83	292.30	593.20	1178.7
9.8497	15.179	23.212	28.625	35.236	53.109	79.497	174.63	374.14	783.02	1603.0
10.835	17.000	26.462	32.919	40.874	62.669	95.396	216.54	478.90	1033.6	2180.1
17.449	29.960	50.950	66.212	85.850	143.37	237.38	634.82	1645.5	4142.1	10143.
45.259	93.051	188.88	267.86	378.72	750.38	1469.8	5455.9	19427.	66521.	*
117.39	289.00	700.23	1083.7	1670.7	3927.4	9100.4	46890.	*	*	*
304.48	897.60	2595.9	4384.0	7370.2	20555.	56348.	*	*	*	*

*The factor is greater than 99,999.

TABLE A.2   Present value of $1 to be received after t periods $= 1/(1 + r)^t$

Number of Periods	Interest Rates								
	1%	2%	3%	4%	5%	6%	7%	8%	9%
1	0.9901	0.9804	0.9709	0.9615	0.9524	0.9434	0.9346	0.9259	0.9174
2	0.9803	0.9612	0.9426	0.9246	0.9070	0.8900	0.8734	0.8573	0.8417
3	0.9706	0.9423	0.9151	0.8890	0.8638	0.8396	0.8163	0.7938	0.7722
4	0.9610	0.9238	0.8885	0.8548	0.8227	0.7921	0.7629	0.7350	0.7084
5	0.9515	0.9057	0.8626	0.8219	0.7835	0.7473	0.7130	0.6806	0.6499
6	0.9420	0.8880	0.8375	0.7903	0.7462	0.7050	0.6663	0.6302	0.5963
7	0.9327	0.8706	0.8131	0.7599	0.7107	0.6651	0.6227	0.5835	0.5470
8	0.9235	0.8535	0.7894	0.7307	0.6768	0.6274	0.5820	0.5403	0.5019
9	0.9143	0.8368	0.7664	0.7026	0.6446	0.5919	0.5439	0.5002	0.4604
10	0.9053	0.8203	0.7441	0.6756	0.6139	0.5584	0.5083	0.4632	0.4224
11	0.8963	0.8043	0.7224	0.6496	0.5847	0.5268	0.4751	0.4289	0.3875
12	0.8874	0.7885	0.7014	0.6246	0.5568	0.4970	0.4440	0.3971	0.3555
13	0.8787	0.7730	0.6810	0.6006	0.5303	0.4688	0.4150	0.3677	0.3262
14	0.8700	0.7579	0.6611	0.5775	0.5051	0.4423	0.3878	0.3405	0.2992
15	0.8613	0.7430	0.6419	0.5553	0.4810	0.4173	0.3624	0.3152	0.2745
16	0.8528	0.7284	0.6232	0.5339	0.4581	0.3936	0.3387	0.2919	0.2519
17	0.8444	0.7142	0.6050	0.5134	0.4363	0.3714	0.3166	0.2703	0.2311
18	0.8360	0.7002	0.5874	0.4936	0.4155	0.3503	0.2959	0.2502	0.2120
19	0.8277	0.6864	0.5703	0.4746	0.3957	0.3305	0.2765	0.2317	0.1945
20	0.8195	0.6730	0.5537	0.4564	0.3769	0.3118	0.2584	0.2145	0.1784
21	0.8114	0.6598	0.5375	0.4388	0.3589	0.2942	0.2415	0.1987	0.1637
22	0.8034	0.6468	0.5219	0.4220	0.3418	0.2775	0.2257	0.1839	0.1502
23	0.7954	0.6342	0.5067	0.4057	0.3256	0.2618	0.2109	0.1703	0.1378
24	0.7876	0.6217	0.4919	0.3901	0.3101	0.2470	0.1971	0.1577	0.1264
25	0.7798	0.6095	0.4776	0.3751	0.2953	0.2330	0.1842	0.1460	0.1160
30	0.7419	0.5521	0.4120	0.3083	0.2314	0.1741	0.1314	0.0994	0.0754
40	0.6717	0.4529	0.3066	0.2083	0.1420	0.0972	0.0668	0.0460	0.0318
50	0.6080	0.3715	0.2281	0.1407	0.0872	0.0543	0.0339	0.0213	0.0134

10%	12%	14%	15%	16%	18%	20%	24%	28%	32%	36%
0.9091	0.8929	0.8772	0.8696	0.8621	0.8475	0.8333	0.8065	0.7813	0.7576	0.7353
0.8264	0.7972	0.7695	0.7561	0.7432	0.7182	0.6944	0.6504	0.6104	0.5739	0.5407
0.7513	0.7118	0.6750	0.6575	0.6407	0.6086	0.5787	0.5245	0.4768	0.4348	0.3975
0.6830	0.6355	0.5921	0.5718	0.5523	0.5158	0.4823	0.4230	0.3725	0.3294	0.2923
0.6209	0.5674	0.5194	0.4972	0.4761	0.4371	0.4019	0.3411	0.2910	0.2495	0.2149
0.5645	0.5066	0.4556	0.4323	0.4104	0.3704	0.3349	0.2751	0.2274	0.1890	0.1580
0.5132	0.4523	0.3996	0.3759	0.3538	0.3139	0.2791	0.2218	0.1776	0.1432	0.1162
0.4665	0.4039	0.3506	0.3269	0.3050	0.2660	0.2326	0.1789	0.1388	0.1085	0.0854
0.4241	0.3606	0.3075	0.2843	0.2630	0.2255	0.1938	0.1443	0.1084	0.0822	0.0628
0.3855	0.3220	0.2697	0.2472	0.2267	0.1911	0.1615	0.1164	0.0847	0.0623	0.0462
0.3505	0.2875	0.2366	0.2149	0.1954	0.1619	0.1346	0.0938	0.0662	0.0472	0.0340
0.3186	0.2567	0.2076	0.1869	0.1685	0.1372	0.1122	0.0757	0.0517	0.0357	0.0250
0.2897	0.2292	0.1821	0.1625	0.1452	0.1163	0.0935	0.0610	0.0404	0.0271	0.0184
0.2633	0.2046	0.1597	0.1413	0.1252	0.0985	0.0779	0.0492	0.0316	0.0205	0.0135
0.2394	0.1827	0.1401	0.1229	0.1079	0.0835	0.0649	0.0397	0.0247	0.0155	0.0099
0.2176	0.1631	0.1229	0.1069	0.0930	0.0708	0.0541	0.0320	0.0193	0.0118	0.0073
0.1978	0.1456	0.1078	0.0929	0.0802	0.0600	0.0451	0.0258	0.0150	0.0089	0.0054
0.1799	0.1300	0.0946	0.0808	0.0691	0.0508	0.0376	0.0208	0.0118	0.0068	0.0039
0.1635	0.1161	0.0829	0.0703	0.0596	0.0431	0.0313	0.0168	0.0092	0.0051	0.0029
0.1486	0.1037	0.0728	0.0611	0.0514	0.0365	0.0261	0.0135	0.0072	0.0039	0.0021
0.1351	0.0926	0.0638	0.0531	0.0443	0.0309	0.0217	0.0109	0.0056	0.0029	0.0016
0.1228	0.0826	0.0560	0.0462	0.0382	0.0262	0.0181	0.0088	0.0044	0.0022	0.0012
0.1117	0.0738	0.0491	0.0402	0.0329	0.0222	0.0151	0.0071	0.0034	0.0017	0.0008
0.1015	0.0659	0.0431	0.0349	0.0284	0.0188	0.0126	0.0057	0.0027	0.0013	0.0006
0.0923	0.0588	0.0378	0.0304	0.0245	0.0160	0.0105	0.0046	0.0021	0.0010	0.0005
0.0573	0.0334	0.0196	0.0151	0.0116	0.0070	0.0042	0.0016	0.0006	0.0002	0.0001
0.0221	0.0107	0.0053	0.0037	0.0026	0.0013	0.0007	0.0002	0.0001	*	*
0.0085	0.0035	0.0014	0.0009	0.0006	0.0003	0.0001	*	*	*	*

*The factor is zero to four decimal places.

TABLE A.3 Present value of an annuity of $1 per period for t periods $= [1 - 1/(1 + r)^t]/r$

Number of Periods	Interest Rate								
	1%	2%	3%	4%	5%	6%	7%	8%	9%
1	0.9901	0.9804	0.9709	0.9615	0.9524	0.9434	0.9346	0.9259	0.9174
2	1.9704	1.9416	1.9135	1.8861	1.8594	1.8334	1.8080	1.7833	1.7591
3	2.9410	2.8839	2.8286	2.7751	2.7232	2.6730	2.6243	2.5771	2.5313
4	3.9020	3.8077	3.7171	3.6299	3.5460	3.4651	3.3872	3.3121	3.2397
5	4.8534	4.7135	4.5797	4.4518	4.3295	4.2124	4.1002	3.9927	3.8897
6	5.7955	5.6014	5.4172	5.2421	5.0757	4.9173	4.7665	4.6229	4.4859
7	6.7282	6.4720	6.2303	6.0021	5.7864	5.5824	5.3893	5.2064	5.0330
8	7.6517	7.3255	7.0197	6.7327	6.4632	6.2098	5.9713	5.7466	5.5348
9	8.5660	8.1622	7.7861	7.4353	7.1078	6.8017	6.5152	6.2469	5.9952
10	9.4713	8.9826	8.5302	8.1109	7.7217	7.3601	7.0236	6.7101	6.4177
11	10.3676	9.7868	9.2526	8.7605	8.3064	7.8869	7.4987	7.1390	6.8052
12	11.2551	10.5753	9.9540	9.3851	8.8633	8.3838	7.9427	7.5361	7.1607
13	12.1337	11.3484	10.6350	9.9856	9.3936	8.8527	8.3577	7.9038	7.4869
14	13.0037	12.1062	11.2961	10.5631	9.8986	9.2950	8.7455	8.2442	7.7862
15	13.8651	12.8493	11.9379	11.1184	10.3797	9.7122	9.1079	8.5595	8.0607
16	14.7179	13.5777	12.5611	11.6523	10.8378	10.1059	9.4466	8.8514	8.3126
17	15.5623	14.2919	13.1661	12.1657	11.2741	10.4773	9.7632	9.1216	8.5436
18	16.3983	14.9920	13.7535	12.6593	11.6896	10.8276	10.0591	9.3719	8.7556
19	17.2260	15.6785	14.3238	13.1339	12.0853	11.1581	10.3356	9.6036	8.9501
20	18.0456	16.3514	14.8775	13.5903	12.4622	11.4699	10.5940	9.8181	9.1285
21	18.8570	17.0112	15.4150	14.0292	12.8212	11.7641	10.8355	10.0168	9.2922
22	19.6604	17.6580	15.9369	14.4511	13.1630	12.0416	11.0612	10.2007	9.4424
23	20.4558	18.2922	16.4436	14.8568	13.4886	12.3034	11.2722	10.3741	9.5802
24	21.2434	18.9139	16.9355	15.2470	13.7986	12.5504	11.4693	10.5288	9.7066
25	22.0232	19.5235	17.4131	15.6221	14.0939	12.7834	11.6536	10.6748	9.8226
30	25.8077	22.3965	19.6004	17.2920	15.3725	13.7648	12.4090	11.2578	10.2737
40	32.8347	27.3555	23.1148	19.7928	17.1591	15.0463	13.3317	11.9246	10.7574
50	39.1961	31.4236	25.7298	21.4822	18.2559	15.7619	13.8007	12.2335	10.9617

10%	12%	14%	15%	16%	18%	20%	24%	28%	32%
0.9091	0.8929	0.8772	0.8696	0.8621	0.8475	0.8333	0.8065	0.7813	0.7576
1.7355	1.6901	1.6467	1.6257	1.6052	1.5656	1.5278	1.4568	1.3916	1.3315
2.4869	2.4018	2.3216	2.2832	2.2459	2.1743	2.1065	1.9813	1.8684	1.7663
3.1699	3.0373	2.9137	2.8550	2.7982	2.6901	2.5887	2.4043	2.2410	2.0957
3.7908	3.6048	3.4331	3.3522	3.2743	3.1272	2.9906	2.7454	2.5320	2.3452
4.3553	4.1114	3.8887	3.7845	3.6847	3.4976	3.3255	3.0205	2.7594	2.5342
4.8684	4.5638	4.2883	4.1604	4.0386	3.8115	3.6046	3.2423	2.9370	2.6775
5.3349	4.9676	4.6389	4.4873	4.3436	4.0776	3.8372	3.4212	3.0758	2.7860
5.7590	5.3282	4.9464	4.7716	4.6065	4.3030	4.0310	3.5655	3.1842	2.8681
6.1446	5.6502	5.2161	5.0188	4.8332	4.4941	4.1925	3.6819	3.2689	2.9304
6.4951	5.9377	5.4527	5.2337	5.0286	4.6560	4.3271	3.7757	3.3351	2.9776
6.8137	6.1944	5.6603	5.4206	5.1971	4.7932	4.4392	3.8514	3.3868	3.0133
7.1034	6.4235	5.8424	5.5831	5.3423	4.9095	4.5327	3.9124	3.4272	3.0404
7.3667	6.6282	6.0021	5.7245	5.4675	5.0081	4.6106	3.9616	3.4587	3.0609
7.6061	6.8109	6.1422	5.8474	5.5755	5.0916	4.6755	4.0013	3.4834	3.0764
7.8237	6.9740	6.2651	5.9542	5.6685	5.1624	4.7296	4.0333	3.5026	3.0882
8.0216	7.1196	6.3729	6.0472	5.7487	5.2223	4.7746	4.0591	3.5177	3.0971
8.2014	7.2497	6.4674	6.1280	5.8178	5.2732	4.8122	4.0799	3.5294	3.1039
8.3649	7.3658	6.5504	6.1982	5.8775	5.3162	4.8435	4.0967	3.5386	3.1090
8.5136	7.4694	6.6231	6.2593	5.9288	5.3527	4.8696	4.1103	3.5458	3.1129
8.6487	7.5620	6.6870	6.3125	5.9731	5.3837	4.8913	4.1212	3.5514	3.1158
8.7715	7.6446	6.7429	6.3587	6.0113	5.4099	4.9094	4.1300	3.5558	3.1180
8.8832	7.7184	6.7921	6.3988	6.0442	5.4321	4.9245	4.1371	3.5592	3.1197
8.9847	7.7843	6.8351	6.4338	6.0726	5.4509	4.9371	4.1428	3.5619	3.1210
9.0770	7.8431	6.8729	6.4641	6.0971	5.4669	4.9476	4.1474	3.5640	3.1220
9.4269	8.0552	7.0027	6.5660	6.1772	5.5168	4.9789	4.1601	3.5693	3.1242
9.7791	8.2438	7.1050	6.6418	6.2335	5.5482	4.9966	4.1659	3.5712	3.1250
9.9148	8.3045	7.1327	6.6605	6.2463	5.5541	4.9995	4.1666	3.5714	3.1250

TABLE A.4   Future value of an annuity of $1 per period for t periods $= [(1 + r)^t - 1]/r$

Number of Periods	Interest Rate								
	1%	2%	3%	4%	5%	6%	7%	8%	9%
1	1.0000	1.0000	1.0000	1.0000	1.0000	1.0000	1.0000	1.0000	1.0000
2	2.0100	2.0200	2.0300	2.0400	2.0500	2.0600	2.0700	2.0800	2.0900
3	3.0301	3.0604	3.0909	3.1216	3.1525	3.1836	3.2149	3.2464	3.2781
4	4.0604	4.1216	4.1836	4.2465	4.3101	4.3746	4.4399	4.5061	4.5731
5	5.1010	5.2040	5.3091	5.4163	5.5256	5.6371	5.7507	5.8666	5.9847
6	6.1520	6.3081	6.4684	6.6330	6.8019	6.9753	7.1533	7.3359	7.5233
7	7.2135	7.4343	7.6625	7.8983	8.1420	8.3938	8.6540	8.9228	9.2004
8	8.2857	8.5830	8.8932	9.2142	9.5491	9.8975	10.260	10.637	11.028
9	9.3685	9.7546	10.159	10.583	11.027	11.491	11.978	12.488	13.021
10	10.462	10.950	11.464	12.006	12.578	13.181	13.816	14.487	15.193
11	11.567	12.169	12.808	13.486	14.207	14.972	15.784	16.645	17.560
12	12.683	13.412	14.192	15.026	15.917	16.870	17.888	18.977	20.141
13	13.809	14.680	15.618	16.627	17.713	18.882	20.141	21.495	22.953
14	14.947	15.974	17.086	18.292	19.599	21.015	22.550	24.215	26.019
15	16.097	17.293	18.599	20.024	21.579	23.276	25.129	27.152	29.361
16	17.258	18.639	20.157	21.825	23.657	25.673	27.888	30.324	33.003
17	18.430	20.012	21.762	23.698	25.840	28.213	30.840	33.750	36.974
18	19.615	21.412	23.414	25.645	28.132	30.906	33.999	37.450	41.301
19	20.811	22.841	25.117	27.671	30.539	33.760	37.379	41.446	46.018
20	22.019	24.297	26.870	29.778	33.066	36.786	40.995	45.762	51.160
21	23.239	25.783	28.676	31.969	35.719	39.993	44.865	50.423	56.765
22	24.472	27.299	30.537	34.248	38.505	43.392	49.006	55.457	62.873
23	25.716	28.845	32.453	36.618	41.430	46.996	53.436	60.893	69.532
24	26.973	30.422	34.426	39.083	44.502	50.816	58.177	66.765	76.790
25	28.243	32.030	36.459	41.646	47.727	54.865	63.249	73.106	84.701
30	34.785	40.568	47.575	56.085	66.439	79.058	94.461	113.28	136.31
40	48.886	60.402	75.401	95.026	120.80	154.76	199.64	259.06	337.88
50	64.463	84.579	112.80	152.67	209.35	290.34	406.53	573.77	815.08
60	81.670	114.05	163.05	237.99	353.58	533.13	813.52	1253.2	1944.8

10%	12%	14%	15%	16%	18%	20%	24%	28%	32%	36%
1.0000	1.0000	1.0000	1.0000	1.0000	1.0000	1.0000	1.0000	1.0000	1.0000	1.0000
2.1000	2.1200	2.1400	2.1500	2.1600	2.1800	2.2000	2.2400	2.2800	2.3200	2.3600
3.3100	3.3744	3.4396	3.4725	3.5056	3.5724	3.6400	3.7776	3.9184	4.0624	4.2096
4.6410	4.7793	4.9211	4.9934	5.0665	5.2154	5.3680	5.6842	6.0156	6.3624	6.7251
6.1051	6.3528	6.6101	6.7424	6.8771	7.1542	7.4416	8.0484	8.6999	9.3983	10.146
7.7156	8.1152	8.5355	8.7537	8.9775	9.4420	9.9299	10.980	12.136	13.406	14.799
9.4872	10.089	10.730	11.067	11.414	12.142	12.916	14.615	16.534	18.696	21.126
11.436	12.300	13.233	13.727	14.240	15.327	16.499	19.123	22.163	25.678	29.732
13.579	14.776	16.085	16.786	17.519	19.086	20.799	24.712	29.369	34.895	41.435
15.937	17.549	19.337	20.304	21.321	23.521	25.959	31.643	38.593	47.062	57.352
18.531	20.655	23.045	24.349	25.733	28.755	32.150	40.238	50.398	63.122	78.998
21.384	24.133	27.271	29.002	30.850	34.931	39.581	50.895	65.510	84.320	108.44
24.523	28.029	32.089	34.352	36.786	42.219	48.497	64.110	84.853	112.30	148.47
27.975	32.393	37.581	40.505	43.672	50.818	59.196	80.496	109.61	149.24	202.93
31.772	37.280	43.842	47.580	51.660	60.965	72.035	100.82	141.30	198.00	276.98
35.950	42.753	50.980	55.717	60.925	72.939	87.442	126.01	181.87	262.36	377.69
40.545	48.884	59.118	65.075	71.673	87.068	105.93	157.25	233.79	347.31	514.66
45.599	55.750	68.394	75.836	84.141	103.74	128.12	195.99	300.25	459.45	700.94
51.159	63.440	78.969	88.212	98.603	123.41	154.74	244.03	385.32	607.47	954.28
57.275	72.052	91.025	102.44	115.38	146.63	186.69	303.60	494.21	802.86	1298.8
64.002	81.699	104.77	118.81	134.84	174.02	225.03	377.46	633.59	1060.8	1767.4
71.403	92.503	120.44	137.63	157.41	206.34	271.03	469.06	812.00	1401.2	2404.7
79.543	104.60	138.30	159.28	183.60	244.49	326.24	582.63	1040.4	1850.6	3271.3
88.497	118.16	158.66	184.17	213.98	289.49	392.48	723.46	1332.7	2443.8	4450.0
98.347	133.33	181.87	212.79	249.21	342.60	471.98	898.09	1706.8	3226.8	6053.0
164.49	241.33	356.79	434.75	530.31	790.95	1181.9	2640.9	5873.2	12941.	28172.3
442.59	767.09	1342.0	1779.1	2360.8	4163.2	7343.9	22729.	69377.	*	*
1163.9	2400.0	4994.5	7217.7	10436.	21813.	45497.	*	*	*	*
3034.8	7471.6	18535.	29220.	46058.	*	*	*	*	*	*

*The factor is greater than 99,999.

Key Equations

CHAPTER 2

1. The balance sheet identity, or equation:

   Assets = Liabilities
   + Shareholders' equity [2.1]

2. The income statement equation:

   Revenues − Expenses = Income [2.2]

3. The cash flow identity:

   Cash flow from assets =
   Cash flow to creditors
   + Cash flow to stockholders [2.3]

   where

   a. Cash flow from assets = Operating cash flow (OCF) − Net capital spending − Change in net working capital (NWC)

   (1) Operating cash flow = Earnings before interest and taxes (EBIT) + Depreciation − Taxes

   (2) Net capital spending = Ending net fixed assets − Beginning net fixed assets + Depreciation

   (3) Change in net working capital = Ending NWC − Beginning NWC

   b. Cash flow to creditors = Interest paid − Net new borrowing

   c. Cash flow to stockholders = Dividend paid − Net new equity raised

CHAPTER 3

1. The current ratio:

$$\text{Current ratio} = \frac{\text{Current assets}}{\text{Current liabilities}} \quad [3.1]$$

2. The quick, or acid-test, ratio:

$$\text{Quick ratio} = \frac{\text{Current assets} - \text{Inventory}}{\text{Current liabilities}} \quad [3.2]$$

3. The cash ratio:

$$\text{Cash ratio} = \frac{\text{Cash}}{\text{Current liabilities}} \quad [3.3]$$

4. The total debt ratio:

   Total debt ratio

$$= \frac{\text{Total assets} - \text{Total equity}}{\text{Total assets}} \quad [3.4]$$

5. The debt-equity ratio:

   Debt-equity ratio = Total debt/Total equity [3.5]

6. The equity multiplier:

   Equity multiplier = Total assets/Total equity [3.6]

7. The times interest earned (TIE) ratio:

$$\text{Times interest earned ratio} = \frac{\text{EBIT}}{\text{Interest}} \quad [3.7]$$

8. The cash coverage ratio:

   Cash coverage ratio

$$= \frac{\text{EBIT} + \text{Depreciation}}{\text{Interest}} \quad [3.8]$$

9. The inventory turnover ratio:

   Inventory turnover

$$= \frac{\text{Cost of goods sold}}{\text{Inventory}} \quad [3.9]$$

10. The average days' sales in inventory:

    Days' sales in inventory

$$= \frac{365 \text{ days}}{\text{Inventory turnover}} \quad [3.10]$$

11. The receivables turnover ratio:

    Receivables turnover

$$= \frac{\text{Sales}}{\text{Accounts receivable}} \quad [3.11]$$

12. The days' sales in receivables:

    Days' sales in receivables

$$= \frac{365 \text{ days}}{\text{Receivables turnover}} \quad [3.12]$$

13. The total asset turnover ratio:

$$\text{Total asset turnover} = \frac{\text{Sales}}{\text{Total assets}}$$ [3.13]

14. Profit margin:

$$\text{Profit margin} = \frac{\text{Net income}}{\text{Sales}}$$ [3.14]

15. Return on assets (ROA):

$$\text{Return on assets} = \frac{\text{Net income}}{\text{Total assets}}$$ [3.15]

16. Return on equity (ROE):

$$\text{Return on equity} = \frac{\text{Net income}}{\text{Total equity}}$$ [3.16]

17. The price-earnings (PE) ratio:

$$\text{PE ratio} = \frac{\text{Price per share}}{\text{Earnings per share}}$$ [3.17]

18. The market-to-book ratio:
Market-to-book ratio

$$= \frac{\text{Market value per share}}{\text{Book value per share}}$$ [3.18]

19. The Du Pont identity:

$$\text{ROE} = \underbrace{\frac{\text{Net income}}{\text{Sales}} \times \frac{\text{Sales}}{\text{Assets}}}_{\text{Return on assets (ROA)}} \times \frac{\text{Assets}}{\text{Total equity}}$$ [3.19]

ROE = Profit margin
 $\times$ Total asset turnover
 $\times$ Equity multiplier

20. The dividend payout ratio:

$$\text{Dividend payout ratio} = \frac{\text{Cash dividend}}{\text{Net income}}$$ [3.20]

21. The retention ratio:

$$\text{Retention ratio} = \frac{\text{Addition to retained earnings}}{\text{Net income}}$$ [3.21]

22. The internal growth rate:

$$\text{Internal growth rate} = \frac{\text{ROA} \times b}{1 - \text{ROA} \times b}$$ [3.22]

23. The sustainable growth rate:

$$\text{Sustainable growth rate} = \frac{\text{ROE} \times b}{1 - \text{ROE} \times b}$$ [3.23]

CHAPTER 4

1. The future value of $1 invested for t periods at a rate of r per period:
Future value = $1 \times (1 + r)^t$ [4.1]

2. The present value of $1 to be received t periods in the future at a discount rate of r:
$PV = \$1 \times [1/(1 + r)^t] = \$1/(1 + r)^t$ [4.2]

3. The relationship between future value and present value (the basic present value equation):
$PV \times (1 + r)^t = FV_t$
$PV = FV_t /(1 + r)^t = FV_t \times [1/(1 + r)^t]$ [4.3]

CHAPTER 5

1. The present value of an annuity of C dollars per period for t periods when the rate of return, or interest rate, is r:
Annuity present value

$$= C \times \left(\frac{1 - \text{Present value factor}}{r} \right)$$

$$= C \times \left\{ \frac{1 - [1/(1 + r)^t]}{r} \right\}$$ [5.1]

2. The future value factor for an annuity:
Annuity FV factor
= (Future value factor − 1)/r
= $[(1 + r)^t - 1]/r$ [5.2]

3. Annuity due value
= Ordinary annuity value $\times (1 + r)$ [5.3]

4. Present value for a perpetuity:
PV for a perpetuity = $C/r = C \times (1/r)$ [5.4]

5. Effective annual rate (EAR), where m is the number of times the interest is compounded during the year:
EAR = $(1 + \text{Quoted rate}/m)^m - 1$ [5.5]

CHAPTER 6

1. Bond value if bond has (1) a face value of F paid at maturity, (2) a coupon of C paid per period, (3) t periods to maturity, and (4) a yield of r per period:
Bond value
= $C \times [1 - 1/(1 + r)^t]/r + F/(1 + r)^t$
Bond value

$$= \begin{matrix} \text{Present value} \\ \text{of the coupons} \end{matrix} + \begin{matrix} \text{Present value} \\ \text{of the face amount} \end{matrix}$$ [6.1]

2. The Fisher effect:
$1 + R = (1 + r) \times (1 + h)$
where h is the inflation rate [6.2]

3. $1 + R = (1 + r) \times (1 + h)$
$R = r + h + r \times h$ [6.3]

4. $R \approx r + h$ [6.4]

CHAPTER 7

1. $P_0 = (D_1 + P_1)/(1 + r)$ [7.1]

2. $P_0 = D/r$ [7.2]

3. $P_0 = \dfrac{D_0 \times (1 + g)}{r - g} = \dfrac{D_1}{r - g}$ [7.3]

4. $P_t = \dfrac{D_t \times (1 + g)}{r - g} = \dfrac{D_{t+1}}{r - g}$ [7.4]

5. $r - g = D_1/P_0$
$r = D_1/P_0 + g$ [7.5]

CHAPTER 8

1. Net present value (NPV):
NPV = Present value of future cash flows
       − Investment cost

2. Payback period:
Payback period = Number of years that pass before the sum of an investment's cash flows equals the cost of the investment

3. The average accounting return (AAR):

$$AAR = \frac{\text{Average net income}}{\text{Average book value}}$$

4. Internal rate of return (IRR):

IRR = Discount rate of required return such that the net present value of an investment is zero

5. Profitability index:

$$\text{Profitability index} = \frac{\text{PV of cash flows}}{\text{Cost of investment}}$$

CHAPTER 9

1. Project cash flow = Project operating cash flow
　− Project change in net working capital
　− Project capital spending

2. Operating cash flow = EBIT + Depreciation
　− Taxes

CHAPTER 10

1. Total dollar return = Dividend income
　　　　+ Capital gain (or loss)　　**[10.1]**

2. Total cash if stock is sold = Initial investment
　　　　+ Total return　　**[10.2]**

3. Variance of returns, Var(R), or σ^2:

$$Var(R) = \frac{1}{T-1}[(R_1 - \bar{R})^2 + \dots$$
$$+ (R_T - \bar{R})^2]　\textbf{[10.3]}$$

CHAPTER 11

1. Risk premium:
Risk premium = Expected return
　　　　− Risk-free rate
　　　　= E(R) − R_f　　**[11.1]**

2. Expected return on a portfolio:
$$E(R_P) = x_1 \times E(R_1) + x_2 \times E(R_2) + \dots$$
$$+ x_n \times E(R_n)　\textbf{[11.2]}$$

3. Total return = Expected return
　　　　+ Unexpected return
　　　　$R = E(R) + U$　　**[11.3]**

4. Announcement = Expected part + Surprise　**[11.4]**

5. $R = E(R)$ + Systematic portion
　　　　+ Unsystematic portion　**[11.5]**

6. Total risk = Systematic risk
　　　　+ Unsystematic risk　**[11.6]**

7. The capital asset pricing model (CAPM):
$$E(R_i) = R_f + [E(R_M) - R_f] \times \beta_i　\textbf{[11.7]}$$

CHAPTER 12

1. $R_E = D_1/P_0 + g$　　**[12.1]**

2. $R_E = R_f + \beta_E \times (R_M - R_f)$　　**[12.2]**

3. $R_P = D/P_0$　　**[12.3]**

4. $V = E + D$　　**[12.4]**

5. $100\% = E/V + D/V$　　**[12.5]**

6. Weighted average cost of capital (WACC)
$$= (E/V) \times R_E + (D/V) \times R_D$$
$$\times (1 - T_C)　\textbf{[12.6]}$$

CHAPTER 13

1. Modigliani-Miller Proposition II, no taxes:
$$R_E = R_A + (R_A - R_D) \times (D/E)　\textbf{[13.1]}$$

2. Modigliani-Miller propositions, with taxes:
　a. Present value of the interest tax shield:
　　Present value of the interest tax shield
　　$= (T_C \times D \times R_D)/R_D$
　　$= T_C \times D$　　**[13.2]**
　b. Proposition I:
　　$V_L = V_U + T_C \times D$　　**[13.3]**

CHAPTER 16

1. Net working capital + Fixed assets
　　= Long-term debt + Equity　　**[16.1]**

2. Net working capital = (Cash + Other current assets)
　　− Current liabilities　　**[16.2]**

3. Cash = Long-term debt + Equity + Current liabilities −
　　Current assets other than cash − Fixed assets　**[16.3]**

4. The operating cycle:
　　Operating cycle = Inventory period
　　　　+ Accounts receivable period　**[16.4]**

5. The cash cycle:
　　Cash cycle = Operating cycle
　　　　− Accounts payable period　**[16.5]**

CHAPTER 17

The economic order quantity (EOQ) model:

1. Total carrying costs:
　　Total carrying costs = Average inventory
　　　　× Carrying costs per unit
　　　　$= (Q/2) \times CC$　　**[17.1]**

2. Total restocking cost:
　　Total restocking cost = Fixed cost per order
　　　　× Number of orders
　　　　$= F \times (T/Q)$　　**[17.2]**

3. Total costs:
　　Total costs = Carrying costs
　　　　+ Restocking costs
　　　　$= (Q/2) \times CC + F \times (T/Q)$　**[17.3]**

4. Carrying costs = Restocking costs
　　$(Q^*/2) \times CC = F \times (T/Q^*)$　**[17.4]**

5. $(Q^*)^2 = \dfrac{2T \times F}{CC}$　　**[17.5]**

6. The optimal order size Q^*:
$$Q^* = \sqrt{\frac{2T \times F}{CC}}　\textbf{[17.6]}$$

CHAPTER 18

1. $[E(S_1) - S_0]/S_0 = h_{FC} - h_{US}$　**[18.1]**

2. $E(S_1) = S_0 \times [1 + (h_{FC} - h_{US})]$　**[18.2]**

3. Purchasing power parity (PPP):
　　$E(S_t) = S_0 \times [1 + (h_{FC} - h_{US})]^t$　**[18.3]**

4. Interest rate parity (IRP), exact, single period:
　　$F_1/S_0 = (1 + R_{FC})/(1 + R_{US})$　**[18.4]**

5. $(F_1 - S_0)/S_0 = R_{FC} - R_{US}$　**[18.5]**

6. $F_1 = S_0 \times [1 + (R_{FC} - R_{US})]$　**[18.6]**

7. IRP, approximate, multiperiod:
　　$F_t = S_0 \times [1 + (R_{FC} - R_{US})]^t$　**[18.7]**

Answers to Selected End-of-Chapter Problems

CHAPTER 2

2.1	Equity = $4,700
	NWC = $1,700
2.3	$55,350
2.5	Book value assets = $2.2 million
	Market value assets = $4.25 million
2.7	Average tax rate = 32.16%
	Marginal tax rate = 39%
2.9	$850,000
2.11	−$90,000
2.13	$175,000
2.15	$1,642
2.16	$445,000
2.19	Net income = −$50,000
	OCF = $500,000
2.21	a. $924
	b. $2,724
	c. −$76,000

CHAPTER 3

3.1	Current ratio = 1.31
	Quick ratio = .82
3.3	Receivables turnover = 7.33
	Days' sales in receivables = 49.80
3.5	Debt-equity ratio = .39
	Equity multiplier = 1.39
3.7	34.58%
3.9	Payables turnover = 5.30
	Days' sales in payables = 68.86

3.11	19.76%
3.13	21.67%
3.17	34.17%
3.19	13.33%
3.21	30.25%
3.23	40%
3.25	3.13%
3.27	$2,551.57
3.29	Profit margin = 5.87%
	Total asset turnover = 2.94
	ROE = 31.96%
3.31	2.19
3.33	Profit margin = −5.35%
	Net income = −$17,333.39
3.35	35.93%
3.37	15.79%
3.39	1.36

CHAPTER 4

4.1	$644.47
4.3	$12,211; $20,823
	$36,789; $5,767
4.5	41.72 years; 9.34 years; 14.19 years; 5.72 years
4.7	7.27 years; 14.55 years
4.9	35.35 years
4.11	$56.06
4.13	9.51%; $1,428,571.43
4.15	−9.37%
4.17	$44,213.86

4.19 $34,044.46
4.21 $33,003.87; $31,058.48
4.23 183.86 months
4.25 $1908.19; $17,257.32

CHAPTER 5
5.1 $3,380.78; $2,803.12; $2,464.29
5.3 $3,786.92; $3,942.02; 4,680.72
5.5 $1,361.53
5.7 $108,244.47; $773,039.98
5.9 $5,477.94
5.11 10.53%
5.13 9.76%; 16.67%
6.77%; 13.11%
5.15 13.98%
5.17 $6,582.52; $8,665.91; $15,019.59
5.19 APR = 216.00%
EAR = 628.76%
5.21 30.10 months
5.23 Monthly return = 2.00%
APR = 24.00%
EAR = 26.82%
5.25 $496,032.64
5.27 $2,098.74
5.29 4.81%
5.31 $459.48
5.33 $1.16; $1.35
5.35 $138,190.90; $131,708.50
5.37 G: 12.25%; H: 12.06%
5.39 125.90 payments
5.41 $37,734, 712.25
5.43 APR = 10.66%
EAR = 11.19%
5.45 12.36%
5.47 $6 million; $2.313 million
$.969 million
5.49 $3,542.08
5.51 $93,000.49
5.53 APR = 24.91%
EAR = 27.96%
5.55 $1,622.10; $9,105.56

CHAPTER 6
6.3 $924.64
6.5 6.28%
6.7 10.53%
6.9 2.5%; 2.42%
6.11 4.63%
6.12 7.55%
6.18 Current yield = 9.52%
YTM = 9.17%
Effective yield = 9.38%
6.19 7.67%
6.25 6.51%
6.26 $858.02 or 85:26
6.27 13 1/8
6.28 11.47%

CHAPTER 7
7.1 $45.00; $52.09; $93.55
7.3 Dividend yield = 5.71%
Capital gains yield = 6.00%
7.5 12.50%
7.7 $58.42
7.9 $3,000,060; $600,000
7.11 $43.22
7.13 $29.85
7.15 $39.27
7.17 $30.00
7.21 9.21%; 9.64%; 7.88%
7.23 6.35%

CHAPTER 8
8.1 2.78 years
8.3 A: 2.06 years; B: 3.06 years
8.5 22.75%
8.7 $1,171.98; −$920.90; 15.29%
8.9 $1,040; $345.60
−$153.70; −$523.99
8.11 Crossover rate = 17.87%
8.13 1.056; .982; .893
8.17 a. 1.215; 1.139
b. $5,373.49; $5,560.24
8.19 a. 1.559; 1.067
b. $19,563.65; $23,382.90
8.21 $147,105; $323,580; 17.25%
8.23 a. 42.39%; 38.36%
b. $35,389.15; $44,638.15
8.25 a. 4.16%; 16.93%
b. −$18,509.43; $8,137.58
8.27 25%; 33.33%; 42.86%; 66.67%

CHAPTER 9
9.1 $10.55 million
9.3 $26,000
9.5 $41,118
9.7 $1,687,392
9.9 $938,750
9.10 $541,098.72
9.13 −$37,890.42
9.15 $48,912; −$48,283
Break-even savings = $224,838
9.19 Best-case NPV = $3,382,554
Worst-case NPV = −$740,261
9.21 $50,123.94
9.23 Best-case NPV = $1,066,532
Worst-case NPV = $84,848
9.25 Best-case NPV = $24,215,360
Worst-case NPV = −$10,674,288

CHAPTER 10
10.1 −15.48%
10.2 −17.46%
10.3 19.05%
10.5 a. 13.3%
b. 9.79%

10.7 X: 7.60%; .00948; 9.74%
     Y: 15%; .04680; 21.63%

10.9 a. 8.6%
     b. .01823; 13.50%

10.11 .29%; 4.64%

10.13 −14.52%

10.15 −3.51%

10.17 68.29%; 87.86%

10.19 5.60%; 17.62%

10.21 11.33%; 10.01%

CHAPTER 11

11.1 A: .7368; B: .2632

11.3 14.05%

11.5 15.2%

11.7 A: 7.65%; 1.71%
     B: 12.05%; 15.57%

11.9 a. 7.40%
     b. .01621

11.11 1.45

11.13 13.20%

11.15 10.56%

11.17 a. 10.50%
     b. .625
     c. .87
     d. −100.00%

11.19 Y: .0800
     Z: .0964
     SML: .0900

11.21 9.6.%; 10.7%

11.23 13.5%

11.27 a. 15.17%
     b. .00713

11.29 20.80%

11.31 14.34%

11.33 a. 14.56%; .015305; .1237
     b. .1031
     c. .1122; .1001

11.35 a. 12.36%; .01099; 10.48%
     b. 7.56%
     c. 7.52%; 7.23%

11.37 $15,686

11.39 16.00%; 6.00%

CHAPTER 12

12.1 10.95%

12.3 12.53%

12.5 8.22%

12.7 a. 8.592%
     b. 5.585%

12.9 11.31%

12.11 .69

12.13 10.71%

12.15 10.00%

12.17 a. X, Y, and Z
     b. W, X, and Y

12.19 11.57%

12.21 9.68%

12.23 10.05%

12.25 14.07%

12.27 $729,162

12.29 a. 8.50%
     b. 15.60%

CHAPTER 13

13.1 a. $1; $2.50; $3.25
     b. $1; $3.67; $5.00

13.3 a. 5%; 12.5%; 16.25%
     b. 5%; 18.3%; 25%

13.5 Price = $25 per share
     I = II = $10 million

13.7 $70 per share

13.9 a. $1,900
     b. $2,303
     c. Sell 30 shares

13.11 $30 million; $34.5 million; $36 million

13.13 a. 15%
     b. 17%
     c. 21%
     d. 15%; 15%

13.15 15.96 million

13.17 .50; .42

13.19 $56,833.33; $70,164.60; $91,666.66

CHAPTER 14

14.1 $14,750

14.3 $68.02

14.5 a. 32,000; $.25
     b. 1,600; $5

14.7 $10; $8.75

14.9 $60; $50

14.11 $.20; $2.50

14.13 a. .222
     b. .265

14.17 $40,690

CHAPTER 15

15.1 $0; −$2,000

15.3 615,942

15.5 658,561

15.7 86.10%

CHAPTER 16

16.2 Cash = $4,750; CA = $11,000

16.6 Operating cycle = 98.39 days
     Cash cycle = 42.93 days

16.7 19.19%

16.9 $965; $867.50; $980; $810

16.11 $345,250; $395,750; $264,250

16.13 Operating cycle = 95.47 days
     Cash cycle = 25.28 days

16.14 17.07%

16.17 a. 8.43%
     b. $206,454.53

CHAPTER 17

17.1 $300,000; $115,000

17.3 $8,000; −$25,000; −$17,000

17.5	$18,000
17.7	a. 40 days; $20,000
	b. 2%; 10 days; $19,600
	c. $400; 30 days
17.10	$388,932
17.13	Carrying costs = $19,000
	Order cost = $36,400
	EOQ = 2,630
17.15	Carrying costs = $4,800
	Order cost = $1,080
	EOQ = 569
	25.30 orders per year

CHAPTER 18

18.1	a. $202,137
	b. $.9579
	c. $4,789,500 million
18.5	a. ¥210/£1
	b. .167 per dollar
18.7	U.S.: $30,361,442
	Britain: $29,630,013
18.9	1.11936 S$/$
18.11	b. −12.78%
18.13	¥68.3002/DM
18.15	DM1.427/$

D

Using the HP-10B and TI BA II Plus Financial Calculators

This appendix is intended to help you use your Hewlett-Packard HP-10B or Texas Instruments BA II Plus financial calculator to solve problems encountered in the introductory finance course. It describes the various calculator settings and provides keystroke solutions for nine selected problems from this book. Please see your owner's manual for more complete instructions. For more examples and problem-solving techniques, please see *Financial Analysis with an Electronic Calculator,* Fourth Edition, by Mark A. White (New York: The McGraw-Hill Companies, 2000).

CALCULATOR SETTINGS

Most calculator errors in the introductory finance course are the result of inappropriate settings. Before beginning a calculation, you should ask yourself the following questions:

1. Did I clear the financial registers?
2. Is the compounding frequency set to once per period?
3. Is the calculator in END mode?
4. Did I enter negative numbers using the +/− key?

Clearing the Registers

All calculators have areas of memory, called registers, where variables and intermediate results are stored. There are two sets of financial registers, the time value of money (TVM) registers and the cash flow (CF) registers. These must be cleared before beginning a new calculation. On the Hewlett-Packard HP-10B, pressing ▮ {CLEAR ALL} clears

both the TVM and the CF registers.[1] To clear the TVM registers on the BA II Plus, press **2nd** {CLR TVM}. Press **2nd** {CLR Work} from within the cash flow worksheet to clear the CF registers.

Compounding Frequency

Both the HP-10B and the BA II Plus are hardwired to assume monthly compounding, that is, compounding 12 times per period. Because very few problems in the introductory finance course make this assumption, you should change this default setting to once per period. On the HP-10B, press 1 ▮ {P/YR}. To verify that the default has been changed, press the ▮ key, then press and briefly hold the **INPUT** key.[2] The display should read "1 P_Yr".

On the BA II Plus, you can specify both payment frequency and compounding frequency, although they should normally be set to the same number. To set both to once per period, press the key sequence **2nd** {P/Y} 1 **ENTER**, then press ↓ 1 **ENTER**. Pressing **2nd** {QUIT} returns you to standard calculator mode.

END Mode and Annuities Due

In most problems, payment is made at the end of a period, and this is the default setting (end mode) for both the HP-10B and the BA II Plus.

---

[1]The ▮ key is colored orange and serves as a Shift key for the functions in curly brackets.

[2]This is the same keystroke used to clear all registers; pretty handy, eh?

Annuities due assumes payments are made at the *beginning* of each period (begin mode). On the HP-10B, pressing ▢ {BEG/END} toggles between begin and end mode. Press the key sequence **2nd** {BGN} **2nd** {SET} **2nd** {QUIT} to accomplish the same task on the BA II Plus. Both calculators will indicate on the display that your calculator is set for begin mode.

Sign Changes

Sign changes are used to identify the direction of cash inflows and outflows. Generally, cash inflows are entered as positive numbers and cash outflows are entered as negative numbers. To enter a negative number on either the HP-10B or the BA II Plus, first press the appropriate digit keys and then press the change sign key, +/− . Do *not* use the minus sign key, − , as its effects are quite unpredictable.

SAMPLE PROBLEMS

This section provides keystroke solutions for selected problems from the text illustrating the nine basic financial calculator skills.

1. Future Value or Present Value of a Single Sum

Compute the future value of $2,250 at a 17 percent annual rate for 30 years.

HP-10B		BA II PLUS	
−2,250.00	**PV**	−2,250.00	**PV**
30.00	**N**	30.00	**N**
17.00	**I/YR**	17.00	**I/Y**
FV	249,895.46	**CPT FV**	249,895.46

The future value is $249,895.46.

2. Present Value or Future Value of an Ordinary Annuity

Betty's Bank offers you a $20,000, seven-year term loan at 11 percent annual interest. What will your annual loan payment be?

HP-10B		BA II PLUS	
−20,000.00	**PV**	−20,000.00	**PV**
7.00	**N**	7.00	**N**
11.00	**I/YR**	11.00	**I/Y**
PMT	4,244.31	**CPT PMT**	4,244.31

Your annual loan payment will be $4,244.31.

3. Finding an Unknown Interest Rate

Assume that the total cost of a college education will be $75,000 when your child enters college in 18 years. You presently have $7,000 to invest. What rate of interest must you earn on your investment to cover the cost of your child's college education?

HP-10B		BA II PLUS	
−7,000.00	**PV**	−7,000.00	**PV**
18.00	**N**	18.00	**N**
75,000.00	**FV**	75,000.00	**FV**
I/YR	14.08	**CPT I/Y**	14.08

You must earn an annual interest rate of at least 14.08 percent to cover the expected future cost of your child's education.

4. Finding an Unknown Number of Periods

One of your customers is delinquent on his accounts payable balance. You've mutually agreed to a repayment schedule of $374 per month. You will charge 1.4 percent per month interest on the overdue balance. If the current balance is $12,000, how long will it take for the account to be paid off?

HP-10B		BA II PLUS	
−12,000.00	**PV**	−12,000.00	**PV**
1.40	**I/YR**	1.40	**I/Y**
374.00	**PMT**	374.00	**PMT**
N	42.90	**CPT N**	42.90

The loan will be paid off in 42.90 months.

5. Simple Bond Pricing

Mullineaux Co. issued 11-year bonds 1 year ago at a coupon rate of 8.25 percent. The bonds make semiannual payments. If the YTM on these bonds is 7.10 percent, what is the current bond price?

HP-10B		BA II PLUS	
41.25	**PMT**	41.25	**PMT**
1,000.00	**FV**	1,000.00	**FV**
20.00	**N**	20.00	**N**
3.55	**I/YR**	3.55	**I/Y**
PV	−1,081.35	**CPT PV**	−1,081.35

Because the bonds make semiannual payments, we must halve the coupon payment (8.25 ÷ 2 = 4.125 ==> $41.25) and double the number of periods (10 years remaining × 2 = 20 periods). Then, the current bond price is $1,081.35.

6. Simple Bond Yields to Maturity

Vasicek Co. has 12.5 percent coupon bonds on the market with eight years left to maturity. The bonds make annual payments. If one of these bonds currently sells for $1,145.68, what is its YTM?

HP-10B		BA II PLUS	
−1,145.68	**PV**	−1,145.68	**PV**
125.00	**PMT**	125.00	**PMT**
1,000.00	**FV**	1,000.00	**FV**
8.00	**N**	8.00	**N**
I/YR	9.79	**CPT I/Y**	9.79

The bond has a yield to maturity of 9.79 percent.

7. Cash Flow Analysis

What are the IRR and NPV of the following set of cash flows? Assume a discount rate of 10 percent.

Year	Cash Flow
0	−$1,300
1	400
2	300
3	1,200

HP-10B		BA II PLUS	
−1,300.00	**CFj**		**CF**
400.00	**CFj**		**2nd** {CLR Work}
1.00	{Nj}	−1,300.00	**ENTER** ↓
300.00	**CFj**	400.00	**ENTER** ↓
1.00	{Nj}	1.00	**ENTER** ↓
1,200.00	**CFj**	300.00	**ENTER** ↓
1.00	{Nj}	1.00	**ENTER** ↓
{IRR/YR}	17.40	1,200.00	**ENTER** ↓
10.00	**I/YR**	1.00	**ENTER** ↓
{NPV}	213.15	**IRR CPT**	17.40
		NPV	
		10.00	**ENTER**
		↓ **CPT**	213.15

The project has an IRR of 17.40 percent and an NPV of $213.15.

8. Loan Amortization

Prepare an amortization schedule for a three-year loan of $24,000. The interest rate is 16 percent per year, and the loan calls for equal annual payments. How much interest is paid in the third year? How much total interest is paid over the life of the loan?

To prepare a complete amortization schedule, you must amortize each payment one at a time:

HP-10B		BA II PLUS	
−24,000.00	**PV**	−24,000.00	**PV**
16.00	**I/YR**	16.00	**I/Y**
3.00	**N**	3.00	**N**
PMT	10,686.19	**CPT PMT**	10,686.19
1.00 **INPUT** {AMORT} =	3,840.00 <== Interest	**2nd** {AMORT} **2nd** {CLR Work}	
=	6,846.19 <== Principal	1.00 **ENTER** ↓	
=	−17,153.81 <== Balance	1.00 **ENTER** ↓	−17,153.81 <== Balance
2.00 **INPUT** {AMORT} =	2,744.61 <== Interest	↓	6,846.19 <== Principal
=	7,941.58 <== Principal	↓	3,840.00 <== Interest
=	−9,212.23 <== Balance	↓	
3.00 **INPUT** {AMORT} =	1,473.96 <== Interest	2.00 **ENTER** ↓	
=	9,212.23 <== Principal	2.00 **ENTER** ↓	−9,212.23 <== Balance
=	0.00 <== Balance	↓	7,941.58 <== Principal
		↓	2,744.61 <== Interest
		↓	
		3.00 **ENTER** ↓	
		3.00 **ENTER** ↓	0.00 <== Balance
		↓	9,212.23 <== Principal
		↓	1,473.96 <== Interest

Interest of $1,473.96 is paid in the third year.

Enter both a beginning and an ending period to compute the total amount of interest or principal paid over a particular period of time.

HP-10B	**BA II PLUS**
−24,000.00 **PV**	−24,000.00 **PV**
16.00 **I/YR**	16.00 **I/Y**
3.00 **N**	3.00 **N**
PMT 10,686.19	**CPT PMT** 10,686.19
1.00 **INPUT**	**2nd** {AMORT} **2nd** {CLR Work}
3.00 {AMORT} = 8,058.57 <== Interest	1.00 **ENTER** ↓
= 24,000.00 <== Principal	3.00 **ENTER** ↓ 0.00 <== Balance
= 0.00 <== Balance	↓ 24,000.00 <== Principal
	↓ 8,058.57 <== Interest

Total interest of $8,058.57 is paid over the life of the loan.

9. Interest Rate Conversions

Find the effective annual rate, EAR, corresponding to a 7 percent annual percentage rate, APR, compounded quarterly.

HP-10B	**BA II PLUS**
4.00 {P/YR}	**2nd** {IConv}
7.00 {NOM%}	7.00 **ENTER**
{EFF%} 7.19	↓ ↓
	4.00 **ENTER**
	↑ **CPT** 7.19

The effective annual rate equals 7.19 percent.

Absolute priority rule (APR) Rule establishing priority of claims in liquidation.

Accelerated Cost Recovery System (ACRS) Depreciation method under U.S. tax law allowing for the accelerated write-off of property under various classifications.

Accounts payable period The time between receipt of inventory and payment for it.

Accounts receivable financing A secured short-term loan that involves either the assignment or factoring of receivables.

Accounts receivable period The time between sale of inventory and collection of the receivable.

Agency problem The possibility of conflict of interest between the owners and management of a firm.

Aging schedule A compilation of accounts receivable by the age of each account.

American Depository Receipt (ADR) A security issued in the United States representing shares of a foreign stock and allowing that stock to be traded in the United States.

Annual percentage rate (APR) The interest rate charged per period multiplied by the number of periods per year.

Annuity A level stream of cash flows for a fixed period of time.

Annuity due An annuity for which the cash flows occur at the beginning of the period.

Applications of cash A firm's activities in which cash is spent. Also *uses of cash*.

Asset-specific risk A risk that affects at most a small number of assets. Also *unique* or *unsystematic risk*.

Average accounting return (AAR) An investment's average net income divided by its average book value.

Average tax rate Total taxes paid divided by total taxable income.

Balance sheet Financial statement showing a firm's accounting value on a particular date.

Bankruptcy A legal proceeding for liquidating or reorganizing a business. Also, the transfer of some or all of a firm's assets to its creditors.

Benefit-cost ratio The present value of an investment's future cash flows divided by its initial cost. Also *profitability index*.

Best efforts underwriting Underwriter sells as much of the issue as possible, but can return any unsold shares to the issuer without financial responsibility.

Beta coefficient Amount of systematic risk present in a particular risky asset relative to an average risky asset.

Business risk The equity risk that comes from the nature of the firm's operating activities.

Call premium Amount by which the call price exceeds the par value of the bond.

Call protected Bond during period in which it cannot be redeemed by the issuer.

Call provision Agreement giving the corporation the option to repurchase a bond at a specified price prior to maturity.

Capital asset pricing model (CAPM) Equation of the security market line showing the relationship between expected return and beta.

Capital budgeting The process of planning and managing a firm's long-term investments.

Capital gains yield The dividend growth rate, or the rate at which the value of an investment grows.

Capital intensity ratio A firm's total assets divided by its sales, or the amount of assets needed to generate $1 in sales.

Capital rationing The situation that exists if a firm has positive net present value projects but cannot find the necessary financing.

Capital structure The mixture of debt and equity maintained by a firm.

Captive finance company A wholly owned subsidiary that handles the credit function for the parent company.

Carrying costs Costs that rise with increases in the level of investment in current assets.

Cash budget A forecast of cash receipts and disbursements for the next planning period.

Cash concentration The practice of and procedures for moving cash from multiple banks into the firm's main accounts.

Cash cycle The time between cash disbursement and cash collection.

Cash discount A discount given to induce prompt payment. Also *sales discount*.

Cash flow from assets The total of cash flow to creditors and cash flow to stockholders, consisting of the following: operating cash flow, capital spending, and additions to net working capital.

Cash flow time line Graphical representation of the operating cycle and the cash cycle.

Cash flow to creditors A firm's interest payments to creditors less net new borrowings.

Cash flow to stockholders   Dividends paid out by a firm less net new equity raised.

Clientele effect   Argument that stocks attract particular groups based on dividend yield tax brackets.

Collection policy   Procedures followed by a firm in collecting accounts receivable.

Common-size statement   A standardized financial statement presenting all items in percentage terms. Balance sheet items are shown as a percentage of assets and income statement items as a percentage of sales.

Common stock   Equity without priority for dividends or in bankruptcy.

Compounding   The process of accumulating interest in an investment over time in order to earn more interest.

Compound interest   Interest earned on both the initial principal and the interest reinvested from prior periods.

Compound value   The amount an investment is worth after one or more periods. Also *future value*.

Consol   A type of perpetuity.

Contingency planning   Taking into account the managerial options implicit in a project.

Controlled disbursement account   A disbursement practice under which the firm transfers an amount to a disbursing account that is sufficient to cover demands for payment.

Corporation   A business created as a distinct legal entity composed of one or more individuals or entities.

Cost of capital   The minimum required return on a new investment.

Cost of debt   The return that lenders require on the firm's debt.

Cost of equity   The return that equity investors require on their investment in the firm.

Coupon   The stated interest payments made on a bond.

Coupon rate   The annual coupon divided by the face value of a bond.

Credit analysis   The process of determining the probability that customers will or will not pay.

Credit cost curve   Graphical representation of the sum of the carrying costs and the opportunity costs of a credit policy.

Credit instrument   The evidence of indebtedness.

Credit period   The length of time that credit is granted.

Credit scoring   The process of quantifying the probability of default when granting consumer credit.

Cross-rate   The implicit exchange rate between two currencies (usually non-U.S.) quoted in some third currency (usually the U.S. dollar).

Cumulative voting   Procedure where a shareholder may cast all votes for one member of the board of directors.

Current yield   A bond's coupon payment divided by its closing price.

Date of payment   Date that dividend checks are mailed.

Date of record   Date on which holders of record are designated to receive a dividend.

Debenture   Unsecured debt, usually with a maturity of 10 years or more.

Declaration date   Date on which the board of directors passes a resolution to pay a dividend.

Deferred call   Bond call provision prohibiting the company from redeeming the bond prior to a certain date.

Direct bankruptcy costs   The costs that are directly associated with bankruptcy, such as legal and administrative expenses.

Discount   To calculate the present value of some future amount.

Discounted cash flow (DCF) valuation   The process of valuing an investment by discounting its future cash flows.

Discount rate   The rate used to calculate the present value of future cash flows.

Distribution   Payment made by a firm to its owners from sources other than current or accumulated retained earnings.

Dividend   Payment made out of a firm's earnings to its owners, in the form of either cash or stock.

Dividend growth model   Model that determines the current price of a stock as its dividend next period divided by the discount rate less the dividend growth rate.

Dividend payout ratio   Amount of cash paid out to shareholders divided by net income.

Dividends   Payment by corporation to shareholders, made in either cash or stock.

Dividend yield   A stock's expected cash dividend divided by its current price.

Du Pont identity   Popular expression breaking ROE into three parts: operating efficiency, asset use efficiency, and financial leverage.

Economic order quantity (EOQ)   The restocking quantity that minimizes the total inventory costs.

Effective annual rate (EAR)   The interest rate expressed as if it were compounded once per year.

Efficient capital market   Market in which security prices reflect available information.

Efficient markets hypothesis (EMH)   The hypothesis that actual capital markets, such as the New York Stock Exchange, are efficient.

Erosion   The cash flows of a new project that come at the expense of a firm's existing projects.

Estimation risk   The possibility that errors in projected cash flows lead to incorrect decisions. Also *forecasting risk*.

Eurobonds   International bonds issued in multiple countries but denominated in a single currency (usually the issuer's currency).

Eurocurrency Money deposited in a financial center outside of the country whose currency is involved.

European Currency Unit (ECU) An index of European currencies intended to serve as a monetary unit for the European Monetary System (EMS).

Exchange rate The price of one country's currency expressed in terms of another country's currency.

Exchange rate risk The risk related to having international operations in a world where relative currency values vary.

Ex-dividend date Date two business days before the date of record, establishing those individuals entitled to a dividend.

Expected return Return on a risky asset expected in the future.

Face value The principal amount of a bond that is repaid at the end of the term. Also *par value*.

Financial distress costs The direct and indirect costs associated with going bankrupt or experiencing financial distress.

Financial ratios Relationships determined from a firm's financial information and used for comparison purposes.

Financial risk The equity risk that comes from the financial policy (i.e., capital structure) of the firm.

Firm commitment underwriting Underwriter buys the entire issue, assuming full financial responsibility for any unsold shares.

Fisher effect Relationship between nominal returns, real returns, and inflation.

Five *C*s of credit The five basic factors to be evaluated: character, capacity, capital, collateral, and conditions.

Float The difference between book cash and bank cash, representing the net effect of checks in the process of clearing.

Forecasting risk The possibility that errors in projected cash flows lead to incorrect decisions. Also *estimation risk*.

Foreign bonds International bonds issued in a single country, usually denominated in that country's currency.

Foreign exchange market The market in which one country's currency is traded for another's.

Forward exchange rate The agreed-upon exchange rate to be used in a forward trade.

Forward trade Agreement to exchange currency at some time in the future.

Future value (FV) The amount an investment is worth after one or more periods. Also *compound value*.

General cash offer An issue of securities offered for sale to the general public on a cash basis.

Generally Accepted Accounting Principles (GAAP) The common set of standards and procedures by which audited financial statements are prepared.

Gilts British and Irish government securities.

Green Shoe provision Contract provision giving the underwriter the option to purchase additional shares from the issuer at the offering price. Also *overallotment option*.

Hard rationing The situation that occurs when a business cannot raise financing for a project under any circumstances.

Homemade leverage The use of personal borrowing to change the overall amount of financial leverage to which an individual is exposed.

Income statement Financial statement summarizing a firm's performance over a period of time.

Incremental cash flows The difference between a firm's future cash flows with a project or without the project.

Indenture Written agreement between the corporation and the lender detailing the terms of the debt issue.

Indirect bankruptcy costs The costs of avoiding a bankruptcy filing incurred by a financially distressed firm.

Initial public offering (IPO) A company's first equity issue made available to the public. Also *unseasoned new issue*.

Interest on interest Interest earned on the reinvestment of previous interest payments.

Interest rate parity (IRP) The condition stating that the interest rate differential between two countries is equal to the percentage difference between the forward exchange rate and the spot exchange rate.

Interest tax shield The tax saving attained by a firm from interest expense.

Internal growth rate The maximum growth rate a firm can achieve without external financing of any kind.

Internal rate of return (IRR) The discount rate that makes the net present value of an investment zero.

Inventory loan A secured short-term loan to purchase inventory.

Inventory period The time it takes to acquire and sell inventory.

Invoice Bill for goods or services provided by the seller to the purchaser.

Just-in-time (JIT) inventory A system for managing demand-dependent inventories that minimizes inventory holdings.

Line of credit A formal (committed) or informal (noncommitted) prearranged, short-term bank loan.

Liquidation Termination of the firm as a going concern.

Lockboxes Special post office boxes set up to intercept and speed up accounts receivable payments.

London Interbank Offer Rate (LIBOR) The rate most international banks charge one another for overnight Eurodollar loans.

M&M Proposition I   The value of the firm is independent of its capital structure.

M&M Proposition II   A firm's cost of equity capital is a positive linear function of its capital structure.

Managerial options   Opportunities that managers can exploit if certain things happen in the future.

Marginal tax rate   Amount of tax payable on the next dollar earned.

Market risk   A risk that influences a large number of assets. Also *systematic risk.*

Market risk premium   Slope of the security market line, the difference between the expected return on a market portfolio and the risk-free rate.

Materials requirements planning (MRP)   A set of procedures used to determine inventory levels for demand-dependent inventory types, such as work-in-progress and raw materials.

Maturity   Specified date at which the principal amount of a bond is paid.

Multiple rates of return   The possibility that more than one discount rate will make the net present value of an investment zero.

Mutually exclusive investment decisions   A situation where taking one investment prevents the taking of another.

Net present value (NPV)   The difference between an investment's market value and its cost.

Net present value profile   A graphical representation of the relationship between an investment's net present values and various discount rates.

Net working capital   Current assets less current liabilities.

Nominal return   Return on an investment not adjusted for inflation.

Noncash items   Expenses charged against revenues that do not directly affect cash flow.

Normal distribution   A symmetric, bell-shaped frequency distribution that is completely defined by its mean and standard deviation.

Note   Unsecured debt, usually with a maturity of under 10 years.

Operating cash flow   Cash generated from a firm's normal business activities.

Operating cycle   The time period between the acquisition of inventory and the collection of cash from receivables.

Opportunity cost   The most valuable alternative that is given up if a particular investment is undertaken.

Overallotment option   Contract provision giving the underwriter the option to purchase additional shares from the issuer at the offering price. Also *Green Shoe provision.*

Partnership   A business formed by two or more individuals or entities.

Par value   The principal amount of a bond that is repaid at the end of the term. Also *face value.*

Payback period   The amount of time required for an investment to generate cash flows sufficient to recover its initial cost.

Percentage of sales approach   Financial planning method in which accounts are varied depending on a firm's predicted sales level.

Perpetuity   An annuity in which the cash flows continue forever.

Plowback ratio   Addition to retained earnings divided by net income. Also *retention ratio.*

Political risk   Risk related to changes in value that arise because of political actions.

Portfolio   Group of assets, such as stocks and bonds, held by an investor.

Portfolio weight   Percentage of a portfolio's total value in a particular asset.

Precautionary motive   The need to hold cash as a safety margin to act as a financial reserve.

Preferred stock   Stock with dividend priority over common stock, normally with a fixed dividend rate, sometimes without voting rights.

Present value (PV)   The current value of future cash flows discounted at the appropriate discount rate.

Principle of diversification   Spreading an investment across a number of assets will eliminate some, but not all, of the risk.

Private placements   Loans, usually long-term in nature, provided directly by a limited number of investors.

Pro forma financial statements   Financial statements projecting future years' operations.

Profitability index (PI)   The present value of an investment's future cash flows divided by its initial cost. Also *benefit-cost ratio.*

Prospectus   Legal document describing details of the issuing corporation and the proposed offering to potential investors.

Protective covenant   Part of the indenture limiting certain actions that can be taken during the term of the loan, usually to protect the lender's interest.

Proxy   Grant of authority by shareholder allowing for another individual to vote his or her shares.

Purchasing power parity (PPP)   The idea that the exchange rate adjusts to keep purchasing power constant among currencies.

Pure play approach   Use of a weighted average cost of capital that is unique to a particular project, based on companies in similar lines of business.

Quoted interest rate   The interest rate expressed in terms of the interest payment made each period. Also *stated interest rate*.

Real return   Return adjusted for the effects of inflation.

Red herring   Preliminary prospectus distributed to prospective investors in a new issue of securities.

Registered form   The registrar of a company records who owns each bond, and bond payments are made directly to the owner of record.

Registration statement   Statement filed with SEC that discloses all material information concerning the corporation making a public offering.

Regular cash dividend   Cash payment made by a firm to its owners in the normal course of business, usually four times a year.

Regulation A   SEC regulation that exempts public issues less than $1.5 million from most registration requirements.

Reorganization   Financial restructuring of a failing firm to attempt to continue operations as a going concern.

Repurchase   Refers to a firm's purchases of its own stock, an alternative to a cash dividend.

Residual dividend approach   Policy under which a firm pays dividends only after meeting its investment needs while maintaining a desired debt-equity ratio.

Retention ratio   Addition to retained earnings divided by net income. Also *plowback ratio*.

Reverse split   Stock split under which a firm's number of shares outstanding is reduced.

Rights offer   A public issue of securities in which securities are first offered to existing shareholders. Also *rights offering*.

Risk premium   The excess return required from an investment in a risky asset over a risk-free investment.

Sales discount   A discount given to induce prompt payment. Also *cash discount*.

Scenario analysis   The determination of what happens to net present value estimates when we ask "what-if" questions.

Seasoned new issue   A new equity issue of securities by a company that has previously issued securities to the public.

Security market line (SML)   Positively sloped straight line displaying the relationship between expected return and beta.

Sensitivity analysis   Investigation of what happens to net present value when only one variable is changed.

Shelf registration   SEC Rule 415 allowing a company to register all issues it expects to sell within two years at one time, with subsequent sales at any time within those two years.

Shortage costs   Costs that fall with increases in the level of investment in current assets.

Simple interest   Interest earned only on the original principal amount invested.

Sinking fund   Account managed by the bond trustee for early bond redemption.

Soft rationing   The situation that occurs when units in a business are allocated a certain amount of financing for capital budgeting.

Sole proprietorship   A business owned by a single individual.

Sources of cash   A firm's activities that generate cash.

Speculative motive   The need to hold cash to take advantage of additional investment opportunities, such as bargain purchases.

Spot exchange rate   The exchange rate on a spot trade.

Spot trade   An agreement to trade currencies based on the exchange rate today for settlement within two business days.

Spread   Compensation to the underwriter, determined by the difference between the underwriter's buying price and offering price.

Stakeholder   Someone other than a stockholder or creditor who potentially has a claim on the cash flows of the firm.

Stand-alone principle   Evaluation of a project based on the project's incremental cash flows.

Standard deviation   The positive square root of the variance.

Standard Industrial Classification (SIC) code   U.S. government code used to classify a firm by its type of business operations.

Stated interest rate   The interest rate expressed in terms of the interest payment made each period. Also *quoted interest rate*.

Statement of cash flows   A firm's financial statement that summarizes its sources and uses of cash over a specified period.

Static theory of capital structure   Theory that a firm borrows up to the point where the tax benefit from an extra dollar in debt is exactly equal to the cost that comes from the increased probability of financial distress.

Stock dividend   Payment made by a firm to its owners in the form of stock, diluting the value of each share outstanding.

Stock split   An increase in a firm's shares outstanding without any change in owners' equity.

Straight voting   Procedure in which a shareholder may cast all votes for each member of the board of directors.

Strategic options   Options for future, related business products or strategies.

Sunk cost   A cost that has already been incurred and cannot be removed and therefore should not be considered in an investment decision.

Sustainable growth rate   The maximum growth rate a firm can achieve without external equity financing while maintaining a constant debt-equity ratio.

Swaps   Agreements to exchange two securities or currencies.

Syndicate   A group of underwriters formed to share the risk and to help sell an issue.

Systematic risk   A risk that influences a large number of assets. Also *market risk*.

Systematic risk principle   The expected return on a risky asset depends only on that asset's systematic risk.

Target payout ratio   A firm's long-term desired dividend-to-earnings ratio.

Term loans   Direct business loans of, typically, one to five years.

Terms of sale   Conditions under which a firm sells its goods and services for cash or credit.

Tombstone   An advertisement announcing a public offering.

Trading range   Price range between highest and lowest prices at which a stock is traded.

Transaction motive   The need to hold cash to satisfy normal disbursement and collection activities associated with a firm's ongoing operations.

Underwriters   Investment firms that act as intermediaries between a company selling securities and the investing public.

Unique risk   A risk that affects at most a small number of assets. Also *unsystematic* or *asset-specific risk*.

Unseasoned new issue   A company's first equity issue made available to the public. Also *initial public offering*.

Unsystematic risk   A risk that affects at most a small number of assets. Also *unique* or *asset-specific risk*.

Uses of cash   A firm's activities in which cash is spent. Also *applications of cash*.

Variance   The average squared difference between the actual return and the average return.

Venture capital   Financing for new, often high-risk ventures.

Weighted average cost of capital (WACC)   The weighted average of the cost of equity and the aftertax cost of debt.

Working capital   A firm's short-term assets and liabilities.

Yield to maturity (YTM)   The rate required in the market on a bond.

Zero-balance account   A disbursement account in which the firm maintains a zero balance, transferring funds in from a master account only as needed to cover checks presented for payment.

NAME INDEX

EQUATION INDEX

SUBJECT INDEX